CONSUMER
HEALTH
CARE

CONSUMER HEALTH CARE

WITHDRAWN

VOLUME

2

M–Z
GLOSSARY
ORGANIZATIONS
STATE HEALTH INSURANCE EXCHANGES
STATE HEALTH AGENCIES
TOP HEALTH INSURANCE COMPANIES
FEDERAL HEALTH INFORMATION CENTERS
AND CLEARINGHOUSES
TOLL-FREE NUMBERS FOR HEALTH INFORMATION
GENERAL INDEX

BRIGHAM NARINS, EDITOR

GALE
CENGAGE Learning·

Farmington Hills, Mich • San Francisco • New York • Waterville, Maine
Meriden, Conn • Mason, Ohio • Chicago

Consumer Health Care

Project Editor: Brigham Narins

Editorial: Donna Batten, Laurie Fundukian, Jacqueline Longe, Kristin Key, Kristin Mallegg

Product Manager: Christine Slovey

Editorial Support Services: Andrea Lopeman

Indexing Services: Andriot Indexing, LLC.

Rights Acquisition and Management: Robyn Young

Composition: Evi Abou-El-Seoud

Manufacturing: Wendy Blurton

Imaging: John Watkins

Product Design: Kristine Julien

For product information and technology assistance, contact us at **Gale Customer Support, 1-800-877-4253.** For permission to use material from this text or product, submit all requests online at **www.cengage.com/permissions.** Further permissions questions can be emailed to **permissionrequest@cengage.com**

Library of Congress Cataloging-in-Publication Data

Consumer health care / Brigham Narins, editor.
    p. ; cm.
    Includes bibliographical references and index.
    Summary: "Consumer Health Care focuses on the U.S. healthcare system and the individual's experience with it. Entries cover topics related to the current state of health insurance, the various kinds (including government programs like Medicare and Medicaid) and methods of its delivery, as well as the history of insurance and the evolution of our current for-profit system. Healthcare legislation and reform is also discussed. The Patient Protection and Affordable Care Act is discussed in detail"–Provided by publisher.
    ISBN-13: 978-1-57302-722-9 (hardcover : set) – ISBN-13: 978-1-57302-723-6 (hardcover : volume 1) – ISBN-10: 1-57302-723-5 (hardcover : vol. 1) – ISBN-13: 978-1-57302-724-3 (hardcover : volume 2) – [etc.]
I. Narins, Brigham, 1962- editor of compilation. II. Title.
    1. United States. Patient Protection and Affordable Care Act. 2. Delivery of Health Care–United States. 3. Insurance, Health–United States. 4. Medical Assistance–United States. W 84 AA1]
    RA412.2
    368.38'200973–dc23   2013043475

Gale
27500 Drake Rd.
Farmington Hills, MI, 48331-3535

ISBN-13: 978-1-5730-2722-9 (set)
ISBN-13: 978-1-5730-2723-6 (vol. 1)
ISBN-13: 978-1-5730-2724-3 (vol. 2)

This title is also available as an e-book.
ISBN-13: 978-1-5730-2725-0
Contact your Gale, a part of Cengage Learning sales representative for ordering information.

Printed in China
1 2 3 4 5 6 7 18 17 16 15 14

CONTENTS

LIST OF ENTRIES

N

National Health Insurance Program (Canada)
National Health Service (United Kingdom)
National Health Service Corps
National Institutes of Health
National Library of Medicine
National Quality Forum (NQF)
Naturopathy
Nurse practitioner
Nursing home
Nutritional labeling
Nutritionist

O

Occupational medicine
Occupational Safety and Health Act
Osteopathy

P

Palliative care
Patient confidentiality
Patient education
Patient navigator
Patient Protection and Affordable Care Act
Patient satisfaction surveys and scores
Patient's rights
Patient-centered care
Patient-centered medical home (PCMH)
Patients Beyond Borders
Personal health record (PHR)
Personal trainer
Pharmaceutical advertising, impact on consumers
Pharmacist
Pharmacologist
Pharmacology

Physician's assistant
Preferred Provider Organization (PPO)
Preventable readmissions
Prevention and Public Health Fund
Preventive service coverage
Primary care physician
Private insurance plans
Professional-patient relationship
Psychiatrist
Psychologist
Public education campaigns
Public health

Q

Quality improvement initiatives in health care
Quality Improvement Organizations (QIOs)
Quality measures in health care

R

Red Cross
Rehabilitation hospital
Rural healthcare outreach programs

S

School-based health care
School-based health centers
Shortage of nurses
Shortage of primary care physicians
Small Business Health Options Program (SHOP)
Social Media and Health Care
Social worker
Special Supplemental Nutrition Program for Women, Infants, and Children (WIC)
Stark Law

State Health Insurance Assistance Program (SHIP)
Storefront clinic
Substance abuse and addiction treatment plans
Substance abuse clinic
Summary of Benefits and Coverage (SBC)
Supplemental insurance
Supplemental Nutrition Assistance Program (SNAP)
Surgeon general
Surgical Risk Assessment

T

Telehealth
Traditional Chinese medicine
Travel Insurance Plans
TRICARE

U

United States Public Health Service
Universal bed concept

V

Veterans Administration (VA) System
Veterans Integrated Service Networks (VISN)
Vital records registration systems
Vulnerable populations and the U.S. health care system

W

Walk-in ambulatory clinic
Workplace safety
World Health Organization (WHO)

PLEASE READ—IMPORTANT INFORMATION

Consumer Health Care is a reference product designed to inform and educate readers about a wide variety of subjects associated with the U.S. health care system. Gale, Cengage Learning believes the product to be comprehensive, but not necessarily definitive. It is intended to supplement, not replace, consultation with physicians or other health care practitioners. While Gale, Cengage Learning has made substantial efforts to provide information that is accurate, comprehensive, and up-to-date, Gale, Cengage Learning makes no representations or warranties of any kind, including without limitation, warranties of merchantability or fitness for a particular purpose, nor does it guarantee the accuracy, comprehensiveness, or timeliness of the information contained in this product. Readers should be aware that the field of medical and health care knowledge is constantly growing and changing, and that differences of opinion exist among authorities. Readers are also advised to seek professional guidance before making decisions about their own health care circumstances, and to discuss information obtained from this book with their health care provider.

INTRODUCTION

Unlike most "Gale Encyclopedia Of" medical and health titles, *Consumer Health Care* does not discuss diseases or conditions or treatments or therapies or drugs. *Consumer Health Care* is about the healthcare system in the United States, and it discusses the agencies, programs, legislation, facilities, movements, professionals, and concepts that provide, influence, and inform the health care that individual U.S. consumers require. In these two volumes, readers will find entries that explain various types of insurance, government health agencies and programs, technologies, methods of healthcare delivery, forms of healthcare improvement, healthcare-related jobs, contemporary issues facing the U.S. healthcare system, non-government healthcare organizations, non-standard medical practices, and, for comparison, the healthcare systems in other major countries. The topics are wide-ranging, but they all bear on the individual's experience with the U.S. healthcare system.

SCOPE

In *Consumer Health Care,* the entries follow a standardized format that provides information at a glance. The three standard sections, or rubrics, include:

• Definition

• Description

• Why this is important to the consumer

The Definition presents a brief answer to the implicit question, "what is this entry about?" The Description offers a full explanation of the topic. The "Why this is important to the consumer" section explains why and how the topic in question relates to an individual's practical healthcare experience.

INCLUSION CRITERIA

A preliminary list of topics was compiled from a wide variety of sources. The advisory board, composed of health educators and medical doctors, evaluated the topics and made suggestions for inclusion. Final selection of topics to include was made by the advisory board in conjunction with the Gale editor.

ABOUT THE CONTRIBUTORS

The essays were compiled by experienced medical writers, including physicians, pharmacists, nurses, and allied health care professionals. The advisers reviewed the completed essays to ensure that they are appropriate, up-to-date, and accurate.

HOW TO USE THIS BOOK

Consumer Health Care has been designed with ready reference in mind.

• Straight **alphabetical arrangement** of topics allows users to locate information quickly.

• **Bold-faced terms** within entries direct the reader to related articles.

• **Cross-references** placed throughout the encyclopedia direct readers from alternate names and related topics to entries.

• A list of **Key Terms** is provided where appropriate to define terms or concepts that may be unfamiliar to the reader.

• The **Resources section** directs readers to additional sources of information on a topic.

• Valuable **contact information** for health organizations is included with each entry. An **appendix of organizations** in the back matter contains an extensive list of health associations, agencies, and academies.

- The second volume also includes **several additional appendices** that provide a wealth of information on State Health Insurance Exchanges, State Health Agencies, Top Health Insurance Companies, Federal Health Information Centers and Clearinghouses, and Toll-Free Numbers for Health Information.
- A comprehensive general index guides readers to significant topics mentioned in the text.

GRAPHICS

Consumer Health Care is enhanced by more than 125 color photos, illustrations, and tables.

ACKNOWLEDGMENTS

The editor would like to express appreciation to all of the professionals who wrote, reviewed, and copyedited entries for *Consumer Health Care*.

ADVISORY BOARD

Experts in the fields of medicine, public health, and nursing provided invaluable assistance in the formulation of this encyclopedia. The advisory board performed a myriad of duties, from defining the scope of coverage to reviewing individual entries for accuracy and accessibility. The editor would like to express appreciation to them for their time and their expert contributions.

CONTRIBUTORS

Margaret Alic, PhD
Eastsound, Washington

Eric McLean Blyth
Falls Church, Virginia

Ray F. Brogan, PhD
Falls Church, Virginia

Peggy Elaine Browning
Olney, Texas

Rosalyn Carson-DeWitt, MD
Durham, North Carolina

Laura Jean Cataldo, RN, EdD
Myersville, Maryland

Rhonda Cloos, RN
Austin, Texas

Tish Davidson, AM
Fremont, California

Stephanie Dionne
Ann Arbor, Michigan

L. Fleming Fallon, Jr., MD, DrPH
Bowling Green, Ohio

Karl Finley
Shelby Township, Michigan

Janie F. Franz
Grand Forks, North Dakota

Rebecca J. Frey, PhD
New Haven, Connecticut

Meghan M. Gourley
Germantown, Maryland

Katherine L. Hauswirth, APRN
Deep River, Connecticut

Kevin Hillstrom
Brighton, Michigan

Laurie Collier Hillstrom
Brighton, Michigan

Fran Hodgkins
Rockport, Maine

Joel C. Kahane, PhD
Memphis, Tennessee

Renee Laux, MS
Manlius, New York

Norra M. MacReady, MD, PhD
Sherman Oaks, California

Jacqueline N. Martin, MS
Albrightsville, Pennsylvania

Cara Mia Massey
Laurel, Maryland

Susan M. Mockus, PhD
Seattle, Washington

David E. Newton, EdD
Ashland, Oregon

Deborah L. Nurmi, MS
Dacula, Georgia

Teresa G. Odle
Ruidoso Downs, New Mexico

Michael Polgar, PhD
Hazleton, Pennsylvania

Esther Csapo Rastegari, RN, BSN, EdM
Holbrook, Massachusetts

Judith L Sims, MS
Logan, Utah

Heidi Splete
Chevy Chase, Maryland

Liz Swain
San Diego, California

Samuel D. Uretsky, PharmD
Wantagh, New York

Ken R. Wells
Laguna Hills, California

Barbara Wexler
Portland, Oregon

Emily Jane Willingham, PhD
Austin, Texas

Magnet hospital

Definition

The Magnet Hospital designation is an award granted by the American Nurse Credentialing Center, a subsidiary of the American Nurses Association. Hospitals so designated are considered to be centers of nursing excellence.

Description

The designation "Magnet Hospital" is the highest acknowledgment of nursing excellence in the hospital industry. The credentialing agency, an offshoot of the American Nurses Association, based its credentialing program on fourteen principles that were delineated in a research paper outlining the characteristics of healthcare systems that showed excellence in their ability to recruit and retain nursing staff.

The original fourteen principles included:

- Quality of nursing leadership
- Organizational structure
- Management style
- Personnel policies and programs
- Professional models of care
- Quality of care
- Quality improvement
- Consultation and resources
- Autonomy
- Community and Health Care Organization
- Nurses as teachers
- Image of nursing
- Interdisciplinary relationships
- Professional development

Magnet designation requires a lengthy process of paperwork, interviews, and onsite visits. The process can take over an entire year to complete. Furthermore, the process must be repeated every four years in order for the hospital to retain the designation, and there are no guarantees that the designation will be awarded again upon re-evaluation.

According to the American Nurses Association, the advantages of a Magnet designation include

- The ability to recruit and retain the highest quality nursing staff
- Higher ratings in the areas of quality of patient care, safety, and patient satisfaction
- A more collaborative nursing culture
- Higher standards of nursing care and validated practice
- Positive business and financial ramifications

Why this is important to the consumer

Nursing care is an important determinant of outcome for inpatient hospitalizations. Quality of nursing care has been shown to impact important areas such as falls and injuries, medication error rates, death rates, inpatient hospital days, infection rate (especially pneumonia and post-surgical infections), and timeliness of rescue following complications. On the economic side, excellent nursing care is associated with reduced costs, higher revenue, improved patient satisfaction ratings, and enhanced hospital marketability. Every year, about 8% of the U.S. population ends up spending time in a hospital. Hospitalization in a Magnet Hospital improves a patient's odds of avoiding complications, being rescued from complications, and avoiding death.

The American Nurses Credentialing Center cites the following goals for the Magnet designation:

- To promote excellence in a setting that is supportive of professional nursing practice
- To recognize excellence in the delivery of nursing care to patients
- To assist in the dissemination of best practices in nursing

Resources

BOOKS

Kovner Anthony R. et al. *Health Care Delivery in the United States* 10th ed. New York: Springer Publishing Company, 2011.

Schulte, Margaret F.*Health Care Delivery in the U.S.A.: An Introduction* 2nd ed. New York: Productivity Press, 2012.

Sultz, Harry A. et al. *Health Care USA: Understanding Its Organization and Delivery* 7th ed. Sudbury, MA: Jones & Bartlett Learning, 2010.

WEBSITES

Association of American Teaching Hospitals. Teaching Hospitals [accessed September 22, 2013]. https://www.aamc.org/about/teachinghospitals/.

Duke University. What Is a Teaching Hospital? 2007 [accessed September 22, 2013]. http://www.dukehealth.org/health_library/health_articles/teachinghospital.

National Caregivers Library. Types of Care Facilities [accessed September 22, 2013]. http://www.caregiverslibrary.org/caregivers-resources/grp-care-facilities/types-of-care-facilities-article.aspx.

USA.gov. Choosing a Health Care Facility. 2013 [accessed September 22, 2013]. http://www.usa.gov/topics/health/caregivers/health-care-facility.shtml/.

ORGANIZATIONS

American Hospital Association, 155 N. Wacker Dr., Chicago, IL 60606, (312) 422-3000, http://www.aha.org/.

American Nurses Credentialing Center, 8515 Georgia Ave, Suite 400, Silver Spring, MD 20910, (800) 284-2378, http://www.nursecredentialing.org/default.aspx/.

Healthcare Facilities Accreditation Program, 142 E. Ontario Street, Chicago, IL 60611, (312) 202-8258, http://www.hfap.org/.

The Joint Commission, One Renaissance Blvd., Oakbrook Terrace, IL 60181, (630) 792-5800, http://www.jointcommission.org/.

United States Department of Labor, 200 Constitution Ave. NW, Washington, DC 20210, (800) 321-6742, https://www.osha.gov/.

Rosalyn Carson-DeWitt, MD

Managed care organization

Definition

Managed care is the sector of the health insurance industry in which health care providers are not independent businesses run by, for example, physicians in private practice, but are instead administrative firms that manage the allocation of health care benefits. Managed care organizations (MCOs) were once considered alternative delivery systems for health care services, but since the 1990s they have become the predominant form of health insurance coverage in the United States. In contrast to conventional indemnity insurers that do not govern the provision of medical care services and simply pay for them, MCOs have a significant voice in how services are administered and delivered, which enables them to exert better control over health care costs. (Indemnity insurance is traditional fee-for-service coverage in which health care providers are paid according to the service performed.)

Types of Managed Care Organizations

The term *managed care organization* covers several types of health care delivery systems, such as **health maintenance organizations (HMOs),preferred provider organizations (PPOs)**, and point-of-service (POS) plans as well as utilization review groups that oversee diagnoses, recommend treatments, and manage costs for their beneficiaries. The different types of MCOs have their own restrictions. In general, the least restrictive and more flexible plans cost more. The most common types of MCOs are:

- Health Maintenance Organizations—HMOs are health insurance programs organized to provide complete coverage for their members' health needs for negotiated, prepaid prices. The members (and/or their employers) pay a fixed amount each month (called "per member per month payments"). In return, the HMO group provides, at no extra charge or at a minimal charge, preventive care, such as routine checkups, screening, and immunizations, and care for any illness or accident. The monthly fee also covers inpatient hospitalization and referral services. HMO members generally select a primary care doctor who coordinates their care. They benefit from reduced out-of-pocket costs (they do not pay deductibles), they do not have to file claims or fill out insurance forms, and they generally pay only nominal co-payments for each office visit. Members are usually locked into the plan for a specified period—usually one year. If the necessary service is available within the HMO, patients must normally use an HMO doctor.

- Preferred Provider Organizations—PPOs are managed care organizations that offer integrated delivery systems (networks of providers) available through a wide array of health plans. PPOs are readily accountable to purchasers for access, cost, quality, and services of their networks. They use provider-selection standards, utilization management, and quality-assessment programs to complement negotiated fee reductions (discounted rates from participating physicians, hospitals, and other health care providers) as effective strategies for long-term cost control. Under a PPO benefit plan, members retain the freedom of choice of health care providers but are offered financial incentives such as lower out-of-pocket costs to use the preferred provider network. PPO members may use other physicians and hospitals, but they usually have to pay a higher proportion of the costs. PPOs are marketed directly to employers and to third-party administrators, who then market PPOs to their employer clients.

- Point of Service—point-of-service (POS) plans permit members to choose their own physicians and hospitals, either within or outside the network. However, a member who chooses an outside provider will generally have to pay a larger portion of the expenses. Physicians who do not contract with the network, but do see POS plan patients, are paid according to the services performed. POS members are given an incentive to seek care from contracted network physicians and other health care providers through comprehensive coverage offerings.

Purpose

Managed care, which has a primary purpose of controlling service utilization and costs while delivering quality health care services, represents a rapidly growing segment of the health care industry. The beneficiaries of employer-funded health plans (people who receive health benefits from their employers), as well as **Medicare** and **Medicaid** recipients, often are enrolled in this type of health care program.

Managed care organizations achieve their objectives by overseeing the care delivered to members and executing favorable contracts with physicians and other providers. MCOs use a variety of clinical performance measures to assess providers' performance and conduct regular member satisfaction surveys to ensure that members receive quality health care services.

Enrollment in MCOs

In the United States in 2012, an estimated 439 million people were enrolled in MCOs. More than 70 million were HMO members, about 246 million belonged to PPOs, and approximately 40 million were enrolled in POS plans. Another 83 million were enrolled in **high-deductible health plans** (**HDHPs**), which are insurance plans that have lower premiums and higher deductibles than conventional plans.

According to the National Conference of State Legislatures, enrollment in HMOs peaked in 2001 and has declined since then with more health care consumers opting for **PPO** and POS plans.

Enrollment in MCOs varies by employer size and geography. Employees in companies with 200 or more workers are more likely to enroll in PPOs, while workers in smaller companies favor POS plans. HMO enrollment is highest in the West and Northeast, and lowest in the South and Midwest. PPO enrollment is higher in the South and lower in the West.

People may enroll in MCOs through their employers or as individuals responsible for paying their own premiums. Persons covered by Medicare and Medicaid also may enroll in MCOs. Monthly premiums for Medicaid MCO members are paid by the state. In 2012, about 27% of Medicare beneficiaries and 66% of persons covered by Medicaid were enrolled in MCOs.

Large Managed Care Organizations

Among the nation's largest MCOs are:

- UnitedHealth Group enrolls nearly 37 million members, including 3.9 million Medicaid enrollees in 24 states.
- WellPoint, Inc. serves nearly 36 million members—one in nine Americans is covered by one of Wellpoint's affiliated plans.
- Aetna, Inc. covers 22 million people in all 50 states.

- Health Care Service Corporation is the largest customer-owned health insurance company in the United States and serves more than 13 million people.
- CIGNA is the fourth largest health insurer in the United States. Its fastest growing market is older adults—Medicare beneficiaries.
- Humana, Inc. covers about 9 million people, including Medicare and Medicaid beneficiaries.
- Kaiser Permanente is a nonprofit MCO that serves about 9 million members in nine states. Approximately three-quarters of its members are in California, where it owns the hospitals members use, enabling better cost containment.
- Health Net, Inc. provides and administers health benefits to approximately 5.4 million people through group, individual, Medicare Medicaid, U.S. Department of Defense, TRICARE and Veterans Affairs programs.
- Highmark, Inc. operates health insurance plans in Pennsylvania, Delaware, and West Virginia that serve 5.3 million members.

Resources

BOOKS

Barr, D.A. *Introduction to U.S. Health Policy: The Organization, Financing, and Delivery of Health Care in America.* Baltimore, MD: Johns Hopkins University Press, 2011.

Kongstvedt, P.R. *Managed Care: What It Is and How It Works (Managed Health Care Handbook* Boston. MA: Jones & Bartlett Publishers, 2008.

Sultz, H.A. and Young, K.M. *Health Care USA: Understanding Its Organization and Delivery, Seventh Edition.* Boston, MA: Jones & Bartlett Publishers, 2010.

PERIODICALS

Ayanian, J.Z., et al. "Medicare Beneficiaries More Likely To Receive Appropriate Ambulatory Services In HMOs Than In Traditional Medicare." *Health Affairs* 32 (July 2013): 1228–1235.

Duggan, M., T. Hayford. "Has the Shift to Managed Care Reduced Medicaid Expenditures? Evidence from State and Local Level Mandates." *Journal of Policy Analysis and Management* 32 (Summer 2013): 505–535.

Jan, SA. "Patient perspective, complexities, and challenges in managed care." *Journal of Managed Care Pharmacy* 16 (February 2010).

Knopf, A. "Medicaid expansion means more managed care." *Behavioral Healthcare* 33 (April 2, 2013): 28–29.

Markova, A. et al. "Models of care and organization of services." *Dermatologic Clinics* 30 (January 2012): 244–249.

Marmor, T., Oberlander J., "From HMOs to ACOs: The Quest for the Holy Grail in U.S. Health Policy." *Journal of General Internal Medicine* 27 (September 2012).

Silow-Carroll, S., Rodin D. "Forging community partnerships to improve health care: the experience of four

Medicaid managed care organizations." *Issue Brief Commonwealth Fund* 19 (April 2013): 1–17.

WEBSITES

AARP Health. Managed Care Plans. http://www.aarp healthcare.com/insurance/managed-care-plans.html (accessed August 28, 2013).

Accreditation Association for Ambulatory Health Care. Health Plans/Managed Care Organizations. http://www.aaahc. org/accreditation/Managed-Care-Organizations/ (accessed August 28, 2013).

Centers for Medicare & Medicaid Services. Managed Care. http://www.medicaid.gov/Medicaid-CHIP-Program-Information/By-Topics/Delivery-Systems/Managed-Care/Managed-Care.html (accessed August 28, 2013).

National Conference of State Legislatures. Managed Care, Market Reports and the States. http://www.ncsl.org/ issues-research/health/managed-care-and-the-states. aspx (accessed August 28, 2013).

ORGANIZATIONS

The Henry J. Kaiser Family Foundation, 2400 Sand Hill Road, Menlo Park, CA 94025, (650) 854-9400, kff.org.

Barbara Wexler, MPH.

Medicaid

Definition

Medicaid is the largest government-financed health insurance program in the United States and the primary program for low-income Americans who lack access to private health insurance. The federal government establishes Medicaid guidelines and provides states with matching funds; however, each state sets its own Medicaid rules and requirements. Beginning in 2014, the Medicaid program is being significantly expanded to cover uninsured Americans under the **Patient Protection and Affordable Care Act** (ACA).

Purpose

Medicaid provides millions of low-income individuals and families with access to health care. It also covers many people with disabilities and complex healthcare needs and is the predominant source of funding for **nursing home** and community-based long-term services. Medicaid is a major source of financial support for medical centers and hospitals that serve low-income and uninsured patients and for essential services such as trauma care and neonatal

Medicaid coverage among persons under age 65, by selected characteristics: United States, selected years 1984–2011

Characteristic	1984	1989	1995	1997	2000	2004 (1)	2004 (2)	2009	2010	2011
					Number in millions					
Total	**14.0**	**15.4**	**26.6**	**22.9**	**23.2**	**31.1**	**31.6**	**42.4**	**44.8**	**47.4**
					Percent of population					
Total	**6.8**	**7.2**	**11.5**	**9.7**	**9.5**	**12.3**	**12.5**	**16.1**	**16.9**	**17.8**
Age										
Under 19 years	11.7	12.2	21.1	18.0	19.2	25.4	25.8	33.9	35.7	37.5
Under 6 years	15.5	15.7	29.3	24.7	24.7	31.8	32.4	41.4	43.7	46.1
6–18 years	9.8	10.5	17.0	14.9	16.8	22.5	22.9	30.3	31.8	33.4
18–64 years	4.5	4.9	7.1	5.9	5.2	6.7	6.8	8.9	9.2	9.9
18–44 years	5.1	5.2	7.8	6.6	5.6	7.5	7.7	10.3	10.9	11.6
18–24 years	6.4	6.8	10.4	8.8	8.1	10.3	10.4	14.0	14.5	15.2
19–25 years	6.3	6.6	10.2	8.5	7.3	9.0	9.1	12.2	12.6	13.4
25–34 years	5.3	5.2	8.2	6.8	5.5	7.6	7.8	10.1	11.1	11.5
35–44 years	3.5	4.0	5.9	5.2	4.3	5.7	5.8	7.7	8.1	9.0
45–64 years	3.4	4.3	5.6	4.6	4.5	5.4	5.5	6.9	6.8	7.5
45–54 years	3.2	3.8	5.1	4.0	4.2	5.4	5.5	7.0	7.0	8.0
55–64 years	3.6	4.9	6.4	5.6	4.9	5.4	5.5	6.8	6.6	6.9
Sex										
Male	5.4	5.7	9.6	8.4	8.2	10.8	11.0	14.4	15.2	16.3
Female	8.1	8.6	13.4	11.1	10.8	13.7	13.9	17.8	18.5	19.3
Sex and marital status										
Male:										
Married	1.9	1.8	2.9	2.5	2.2	2.9	3.0	4.1	4.0	4.9
Divorced, separated, widowed	4.9	5.4	7.7	5.7	6.1	6.7	6.8	8.3	9.3	9.8
Never married	4.8	5.6	8.1	7.0	7.2	10.2	10.4	13.1	13.5	14.5
Female:										
Married	2.6	3.0	5.2	3.5	3.1	4.2	4.3	5.3	5.7	6.4
Divorced, separated, widowed	16.0	16.1	19.0	14.7	12.7	14.9	15.2	18.7	17.6	18.0
Never married	10.7	11.9	16.5	14.2	13.2	16.9	17.1	20.9	22.2	21.9
Race										
White only	4.6	5.1	8.9	7.4	7.1	10.2	10.4	13.7	14.5	15.4
Black or African American only	20.5	19.0	28.5	22.4	21.2	24.5	24.9	29.5	30.4	30.9
American Indian or Alaska Native only	28.2	29.7	19.0	19.6	15.1	18.0	18.4	29.7	21.6	29.0
Asian only	8.7	8.8	10.5	9.6	7.5	9.6	9.8	9.9	12.0	14.7
2 or more races	—	—	—	—	19.1	19.0	19.3	30.1	27.4	27.2
Hispanic origin										
Hispanic or Latino	13.3	13.5	21.9	17.6	15.5	21.9	22.5	27.6	28.6	30.1
Mexican	12.2	12.4	21.6	17.2	14.0	21.9	22.4	28.4	29.5	31.0
Puerto Rican	31.5	27.3	33.4	31.0	29.4	28.5	29.1	32.1	35.7	33.0
Cuban	4.8	7.7	13.4	7.3	9.2	17.9	17.9	16.7	17.3	20.0
Other Hispanic or Latino	7.9	11.1	18.2	15.3	14.5	19.9	20.8	24.6	24.5	27.7
Age and percent of poverty level										
Under 65 years:										
Below 100%	33.0	37.6	48.4	40.5	38.4	44.2	45.0	51.2	50.8	51.4
100%–199%	5.3	7.5	14.4	13.0	16.2	21.6	22.0	29.0	28.5	30.6
100%–133%	8.7	11.9	23.1	20.1	22.4	28.5	29.1	39.3	36.3	38.8
134%–199%	3.7	5.6	9.7	9.5	13.1	18.2	18.6	23.6	24.4	26.1
200%–399%	0.8	1.3	2.3	2.7	4.0	6.1	6.1	8.0	8.4	8.9
400% or more	0.2	0.5	0.4	0.8	0.9	1.5	1.5	1.7	2.0	1.7
Under 18 years:										
Below 100%	43.3	47.8	66.0	58.0	58.5	69.2	70.7	78.3	79.8	81.4
100%–199%	6.6	8.7	21.6	20.8	28.4	39.5	40.2	53.5	54.3	57.6
100%–133%	10.4	13.5	32.9	32.0	36.9	48.9	49.8	66.9	64.6	70.1
134%–199%	4.8	6.4	14.4	15.1	23.8	34.7	35.4	45.9	48.2	50.6
200%–399%	1.0	1.7	3.5	4.5	7.6	12.2	12.3	16.8	18.0	18.6
400% or more	—	1.1	—	1.3	2.2	3.3	3.3	3.7	4.3	3.6

(Table by PreMediaGlobal. Copyright © 2014 Cengage Learning®.)

intensive care. Thus, Medicaid is at the center of healthcare financing in the United States and an important focus for improvement and innovation in both healthcare financing and delivery.

Medicaid coverage among persons under age 65, by selected characteristics: United States, selected years 1984–2011
[CONTINUED]

Characteristic	1984	1989	1995	1997	2000	2004 (1)	2004 (2)	2009	2010	2011
18–64 years:					Percent of population					
Below 100%	25.3	29.1	34.8	28.0	24.9	28.6	28.9	33.6	32.4	33.0
100%–199%	4.5	6.8	10.2	8.6	9.1	11.9	12.2	16.2	15.7	17.1
100%–133%	7.6	10.8	16.3	13.0	13.2	17.0	17.4	23.7	21.0	22.7
134%–199%	3.1	5.1	7.2	6.5	7.2	9.5	9.7	12.4	13.0	14.1
200%–399%	0.7	1.1	1.7	1.9	2.4	3.4	3.4	4.6	4.8	5.2
400% or more	0.2	0.4	0.4	0.7	0.6	1.0	1.0	1.2	1.3	1.2
Geographic region										
Northeast	8.6	6.6	11.7	11.3	10.6	12.8	13.0	17.3	17.9	19.6
Midwest	7.4	7.6	10.5	8.4	8.0	10.2	10.4	16.4	17.3	16.7
South	5.1	6.5	11.3	8.7	9.4	12.2	12.4	14.8	16.0	17.3
West	7.0	8.5	12.9	11.7	10.4	14.2	14.4	16.8	17.1	18.4

(Table by PreMediaGlobal. Copyright © 2014 Cengage Learning®.)

Demographics

By federal law, Medicaid must cover all children, pregnant women, adults with dependent children, seniors, and people with disabilities whose incomes are below the federal poverty level (FPL), defined as $29,295 for a family of three in 2013. As of 2013, Medicaid covered more than 62 million people—one in five people in the United States. Approximately half of all Medicaid recipients in 2013 were children, and almost 25% were working parents. Most of the remaining recipients were seniors or disabled individuals. Many state programs have expanded Medicaid to cover children from families with somewhat higher incomes: in 2012, 19 states covered children with family incomes up to 150% of the FPL, including 11 states that covered children with family incomes of 200%–300% of the FPL. By January of 2013, more than one in three U.S. children—more than 31 million—were covered by Medicaid or the similar but smaller **Children's Health Insurance Program (CHIP)**. Medicaid also covered 11 million parents and caretaker relatives of eligible children, pregnant women, and other non-disabled, non-elderly adults. The program paid for more than 40% of all births in the United States. It insured more than 8.8 million non-elderly adults with disabilities and provided supplemental medical coverage to more than 4.6 million elderly and 3.7 million disabled **Medicare** recipients. More than 60% of nursing home residents were covered by Medicaid.

Beginning January 1, 2014, the ACA expands Medicaid to cover most adults under age 65 with incomes at or below 138% of the FPL. However, the U.S. Supreme Court ruled in June 2012 that individual states could decide whether to expand their Medicaid coverage.

Description

Origins

The Medicaid program was established by the 1965 Social Security Act, which also established Medicare. Its original purpose was to provide medical assistance to the poorest of families, seniors, and the disabled. Over the years, however, as access to private health insurance has diminished, the U.S. Congress and individual states have expanded Medicaid coverage. Although state participation in the program is voluntary, since 1982, all 50 states have had Medicaid programs, and Medicaid is now the largest provider of health insurance in the United States. More Americans are covered by Medicaid than by Medicare or by any single private insurer.

Medicaid benefits

Most Medicaid enrollees receive health care from private providers, primarily through managed care organizations, who are reimbursed by their state. Medicaid benefits cover basic health care and long-term care; however, because states are allowed to design their own benefits packages—as long as they meet the minimum federal requirements—Medicaid benefits vary considerably from state to state. Coverage for children is comprehensive, but services covered for adults vary greatly and are often quite limited, although Medicaid does cover many healthcare services that are excluded or severely limited by Medicare and most private insurers. States are required to offer the following basic services:

• early and periodic screening, diagnosis, and treatment (EPSDT) for children under age 21, including medically necessary services that may not be covered for adults

• childhood immunizations

• physician, physician assistant, midwife, and nurse practitioner services

• birth center services

• family planning services and supplies

• inpatient and outpatient hospital care

• laboratory and diagnostic x-ray services

• nursing home care and home health care for adults

• federally qualified health center and rural health clinic services

• transportation for medical care

• tobacco cessation

Optional services that may be provided by states include:

• clinic services

• prescription medications

• physical and occupational therapy

• services for speech, hearing, and language disorders

• respiratory care

• inpatient psychiatric care for children

• institutional care for the mentally disabled

• home or community-based care and case management for the elderly

• personal care services for the disabled

• dental and vision care

• podiatry services

• chiropractic services

• tuberculosis-related services

• prosthetics

• durable medical equipment

• hospice

• other preventive, screening, diagnostic, and rehabilitation services

In general, each state must provide all of its Medicaid enrollees with the same benefits. However, states have some flexibility in providing different or more limited benefits for some recipients. Most people who become Medicaid-eligible under the ACA expansion will receive Alternative Benefit Plans. These must include "**essential health benefits**" as defined by the ACA.

Medicaid eligibility

Federal law requires state Medicaid programs to cover specific populations:

• pregnant women and children under age six with family incomes below 133% of the FPL

• children ages 6 through 18 with family incomes below 100% of the FPL

• parents with incomes below their state's July 1996 welfare-eligibility level, which is often less than 50% of the current FPL

• low-income elderly and people with disabilities who receive Supplemental Security Income (SSI), a program with an individual income eligibility of 75% of the FPL

States have the option of covering additional populations, including:

• pregnant women, children, and parents with higher incomes

• the elderly and disabled with incomes up to 199% of the FPL

• working disabled with incomes up to 250% of the FPL

• nursing-home residents with incomes up to 300% of the SSI standard

• people who are eligible for institutionalization but are receiving care under home or community-based service waivers

• medically needy individuals who have high medical expenses and are categorically eligible but do not meet the income criteria

Although Medicaid and CHIP eligibility for children has expanded in recent decades, Medicaid eligibility for adults is very limited. In 33 states, working parents must have incomes below 100% of the FPL to be eligible for Medicaid, and in 16 of these states, incomes must be below 50% of the FPL. States often receive no federal Medicaid funds for coverage of nondisabled adults without dependent children. Legal immigrants to the United States may or may not be eligible for full Medicaid coverage, depending on the year in which they entered the country. Medicaid does cover emergency care for most legal and illegal immigrants who meet the other eligibility requirements.

Under the ACA, Medicaid eligibility for everyone will be determined solely on income, with eligibility expanded to include most non-elderly individuals with incomes up to 138% of the FPL and eliminating the categorically needy criteria. Thus, millions of previously excluded uninsured adults will become Medicaid eligible. It is projected that an additional 16 million Americans will be covered by Medicaid or CHIP by 2019.

Medicaid costs

Medicaid accounts for about 17% of total U.S. spending on personal health care. In fiscal year 2011, total Medicaid spending was $414 billion plus 5% administrative costs. Two-thirds of this money went for acute care, one-third was for long-term care, and 4% was for supplemental payments to hospitals with a disproportionate number of Medicaid and uninsured patients. Approximately two-thirds of Medicaid spending was for seniors and the disabled, even though the elderly disabled account for only 25% of Medicaid enrollees. Children account for more than half of all Medicaid beneficiaries, but for only about 18% of Medicaid spending. Medicaid spending per person increased at a slower rate than healthcare inflation and private health insurance premiums, despite expansions in eligibility, particularly among the elderly; covered services; increased costs for medical and long-term care; and increased utilization of expensive medical technologies.

The federal share of Medicaid spending depends on the per-capita income of a state. Overall, the federal government pays approximately 57% of Medicaid costs, ranging from 50% for some states to over 73% for Mississippi, the poorest state. Depending on the state, Medicaid recipients may have to pay a portion of their covered medical expenses.

Under the ACA, the federal government will initially pay 100% of the Medicaid coverage for newly eligible adults for the first three years and at least 90% thereafter. The Congressional Budget Office estimates that the federal government will pay for approximately 96% of the coverage increases due to the ACA between 2010 and 2019—$434 billion—and that states will have to pay for 4% or $4 billion.

Complications

Participation in Medicaid is optional for physicians and nursing homes, and many refuse to accept Medicaid patients because the reimbursement rates are low. Many low-income people who are dependent on Medicaid must utilize overcrowded facilities, resulting in substandard

KEY TERMS

Affordable Care Act (ACA)—The Patient Protection and Affordable Care Act (PPACA); signed into law by President Barack Obama in March of 2010, the ACA overhauled the U.S. healthcare system and included major expansion of Medicaid.

Categorically needy—Groups of people who qualify for the basic mandatory Medicaid benefits and that state Medicaid programs are either required to cover or have the option of covering.

Children's Health Insurance Program (CHIP)—Children's Medicaid; a federal program administered by the states that provides low-cost or free health insurance to children from families with incomes that are too high to qualify for Medicaid.

Early and periodic screening, diagnosis, and treatment (EPSDT)—Children's services that Medicaid programs are required to cover.

Federal poverty level (FPL)—The U.S. government's definition of poverty for families of a given size, adjusted annually for inflation, and used as the reference point for determining Medicaid eligibility.

Medically needy—Defined as people with high medical expenses whose incomes are above the eligibility limits for Medicaid, but whom states have the option of covering.

Medicare—The U.S. government health insurance system for those aged 65 and over.

Supplemental Security Income (SSI)—A federal program that provides cash assistance to low-income blind, disabled, and elderly people; in most states, people receiving SSI benefits are eligible for Medicaid.

healthcare. Geographic disparities in the healthcare workforce, medically underserved communities, and lack of access to transportation are other factors that reduce access to healthcare for Medicaid recipients.

Results

Despite ongoing criticism from politicians and numerous problems with the state systems, Medicaid has led to better access to healthcare for children and pregnant women and has improved birth outcomes and childhood health throughout the United States. Children on Medicaid score as well as children with private health insurance on core measures of preventive and primary care. Adults with Medicaid have increased access to preventive and primary care. They have lower out-of-pocket costs compared to uninsured adults and are less likely to go without needed care due to cost. The Oregon Health Study, the first-ever randomized controlled study of the impact of insuring the uninsured in the United States, has found that low-income, uninsured adults who have gained access to Medicaid report better physical and mental health, less medical debt, and better access to health care and prescription drugs, compared with uninsured adults. However, there is a growing shortage of Medicaid providers, particularly specialists and dentists, and expanded coverage under the ACA is expected to exacerbate this problem.

Resources

BOOKS

Barr, Donald A. *Introduction to U.S. Health Policy: The Organization, Financing, and Delivery of Health Care in America.* 3rd ed. Baltimore: Johns Hopkins University Press, 2011.

Brasfield, James M. *Health Policy: The Decade Ahead.* Boulder, CO: Lynne Rienner, 2011.

Duncan, R. Paul, et al. "Medicaid Program Flexibility." In *Debates on U.S. Health Care*, edited by Jennie J. Kronenfeld, Wendy E. Parmet, and Mark A. Zezza. Thousand Oaks, CA: SAGE, 2012.

Goodman, John C. *Priceless: Curing the Healthcare Crisis.* Oakland, CA: Independent Institute, 2012.

Gusmano, Michael K., and Frank J. Thompson. "The Safety-Net Hospitals at the Crossroads: Whither Medicaid DSH?" In *The Health Care "Safety Net" in a Post-Reform World*, edited by Mark A. Hall and Sara Rosenbaum. New Brunswick, NJ: Rutgers University Press, 2012.

McDonough, John E. *Inside National Health Reform.* Berkeley: University of California Press, 2011.

Miles, Toni. P. *Health Care Reform and Disparities: History, Hype, and Hope.* Santa Barbara, CA: Praeger, 2012.

Thompson, Frank J. *Medicaid Politics: Federalism, Policy Durability, and Health Reform.* Washington, DC: Georgetown University Press, 2012.

PERIODICALS

Brandon, William P. "Medicaid Transformed: Why ACA Opponents Should Keep Expanded Medicaid." *Journal of Health Care for the Poor and Underserved* 23, no. 4 (Nov. 2012): 1360–82.

Decker, Sandra L. "In 2011 Nearly One-Third of Physicians Said They Would Not Accept New Medicaid Patients, but Rising Fees May Help." *Health Affairs* 31, no. 8 (Aug. 2012): 1673–79.

Graves, John A. "Medicaid Expansion Opt-Outs and Uncompensated Care." *New England Journal of Medicine* 367, no. 25 (Dec. 2012): 2365–67.

WEBSITES

Centers for Medicare & Medicaid Services. "Affordable Care Act." Medicaid.gov. http://www.medicaid.gov/AffordableCareAct/Affordable-Care-Act.html (accessed July 26, 2013).

Centers for Medicare & Medicaid Services. "Medicaid and CHIP Program Information." Medicaid.gov. http://medicaid.gov/Medicaid-CHIP-Program-Information/Medicaid-and-CHIP-Program-Information.html (accessed July 4, 2013).

Centers for Medicare & Medicaid Services. "Medicaid Benefits." Medicaid.gov. http://www.medicaid.gov/Medicaid-CHIP-Program-Information/By-Topics/Benefits/Medicaid-Benefits.html (accessed July 4, 2013).

Kaiser Commission on Medicaid and the Uninsured. "Medicaid: A Primer." Kaiser Family Foundation. http://kff.org/medicaid/issue-brief/medicaid-a-primer (accessed July 4, 2013).

Kaiser Commission on Medicaid and the Uninsured. "The Medicaid Program at a Glance." Kaiser Family Foundation. http://kff.org/medicaid/fact-sheet/the-medicaid-program-at-a-glance-update (accessed July 4, 2013).

MedlinePlus. "Medicaid." U.S. National Library of Medicine, National Institutes of Health. http://www.nlm.nih.gov/medlineplus/medicaid.html (accessed July 4, 2013).

Rural Assistance Center. "Medicaid Frequently Asked Questions." http://www.raconline.org/topics/medicaid/faqs (accessed July 4, 2013).

U.S. Department of Health and Human Services. "Medicaid." HealthCare.gov. http://www.healthcare.gov/using-insurance/low-cost-care/medicaid (accessed July 4, 2013).

ORGANIZATIONS

Centers for Medicare & Medicaid Services, 7500 Security Blvd., Baltimore, MD 21244, (410) 786-3000, (877) 267-2323, TTY: (866) 226-1819, http://www.cms.gov.

Kaiser Family Foundation, 2400 Sand Hill Rd., Menlo Park, CA 94025, (650) 854-9400, Fax: (650) 854-4800, http://www.kff.org.

Oregon Health Study, 5211 NE Glisan St., Portland, OR 97213, (877) 215-0686, info@oregonhealthstudy.org, http://oregonhealthstudy.org.

Rural Assistance Center, 501 N. Columbia Rd., Stop 9037, Grand Forks, ND 58202-9037, (800) 270-1898, Fax: (800) 270-1913, info@raconline.org, http://www.raconline.org.

U.S. Department of Health and Human Services, 200 Independence Ave. SW, Washington, DC 20201, (877) 696-6775, http://www.hhs.gov.

L. Fleming Fallon, Jr, MD, DrPH
Margaret Alic, PhD

Medicaid Drug Rebate Program

Definition

The **Medicaid** Drug Rebate Program is a national program that helps to offset the cost of many prescription drugs for eligible low-income individuals and families. As of 2013, approximately 600 drug manufacturers and all fifty U.S. states participated in the program.

Description

Medicaid is the largest source of healthcare-related funding for people with low income and/or disabilities in the United States. In an effort to help offset the overall cost of prescription drugs under the Medicaid program, the Omnibus Budget Reconciliation Act of 1990 established the Medicaid Drug Rebate Program, under partnership with the **Centers for Medicare and Medicaid Services**, state Medicaid agencies, and participating drug manufacturers. The program was designed to increase Medicaid beneficiaries' access to safe, affordable drugs.

The Medicaid Drug Rebate Program requires drug manufacturers wishing to receive state Medicaid coverage to enter into rebate agreements with the Secretary of the **Department of Health and Human Services (HHS)**. Manufacturers are then responsible for paying quarterly rebates on all eligible drugs that have been dispensed to Medicaid patients during that time. These funds are then used at the federal and state level to help offset the cost of prescription drugs under the Medicaid program.

Under the original provisions of the Medicaid Drug Rebate Program, only traditional Medicaid "fee-for-service" programs were eligible for the rebate program; **managed care organizations** (MCOs) were excluded from participating. At the time the rebate program was established in 1990, only 2.8 million individuals were enrolled in managed care plans under Medicaid, so the full impact in terms of lost savings was minimal. As of 2011, that number had increased to 21 million, due in large part to increased MCO participation at the state level.

As a direct result of this expansion, the **Patient Protection and Affordable Care Act** of 2010 (also known as the Affordable Care Act or "Obamacare") included a specific provision to equalize the treatment of prescription drug discounts between Medicaid managed care and Medicaid fee-for-service. In addition to offering incentives to providers for higher quality care for Medicaid patients, the ACA rebate legislation was

KEY TERMS

Fee-for-service—A healthcare payment model in which individual services such as office visits, tests, or medical procedures are paid for separately and typically at time of service.

Generic drug—A generically branded drug that is comparable to a name brand version in formulation, strength, quality, and intended use, but is often considerably less expensive.

Managed care organization (MCO)—A healthcare provider that offers health plans designed to control the cost and quality of care by coordinating medical and other health-related services.

Patient Protection and Affordable Care Act (ACA)—Legislation signed into law in 2010 as part of a large-scale initiative to increase the availability, value, and affordability of health insurance in the United States.

designed to save the federal government upwards of $11 billion over ten years, according to the Congressional Budget Office.

In support of the ACA provision enabling drug rebate equalization, the director of the National Association of State Medicaid Directors, Ann Clemency Kohler, wrote the following in a 2009 letter to the Senate Finance Committee: "Allowing Medicaid MCOs to receive Medicaid rebates would allow states (and the federal government) to benefit from both the reduced cost of drugs and the MCOs' superior management of utilization, the best of both worlds."

Why this is important to the consumer

While the Medicaid Drug Rebate Program provides a significant measure of cost savings for federal and state governments, the primary benefit from a consumer standpoint is the improved quality of healthcare that results from better coordination of patient care and lower prescription costs. In contrast to traditional fee-for-service insurance programs, MCOs have been shown to charge lower dispensing fees to pharmacies and to promote the use of lower-cost generic drugs. By providing more proactive and better coordinated patient care, MCOs are also able to improve health outcomes of patients, tailor educational resources to patients' needs, and implement drug safety policies.

Resources

BOOKS

Tarach-Ritchey, Angil. *Quick Guide to Understanding Medicare, Medicaid and Other Payer Sources.* Amazon Digital Services, 2011.

PERIODICALS

Morden, Nancy E., et al. "Medicaid Prior Authorization and Controlled-Release Oxycodone." *Medical Care* 46, no. 6 (June 2008): 573–80.

WEBSITES

Health Management Associates. "The Impact of Drug Rebate Equalization on State Pharmacy Expenditures." Healthmanagement.com. http://www.healthmanagement.com/files/Weekly_Roundup/HMA_Roundup_031611.pdf (accessed October 20, 2013).

Medicaid.gov. "Medicaid Drug Rebate Program." Medicaid.gov. http://www.medicaid.gov/Medicaid-CHIP-Program-Information/By-Topics/Benefits/Prescription-Drugs/Medicaid-Drug-Rebate-Program.html (accessed October 20, 2013).

Social Security Administration. "Compilation of the Social Security Laws: Payment for Outpatient Drugs." SSA.gov. http://www.ssa.gov/OP_Home/ssact/title19/1927.htm (accessed October 20, 2013).

ORGANIZATIONS

Centers for Medicare and Medicaid Services, 7500 Security Blvd., Baltimore, MD 21244, (410) 786-0727, (877) 267-2323, http://www.cms.gov.

Health Resources and Services Administration, 5600 Fishers Ln., Rockville, MD 20857, (888) 275-4772, ask@hrsa.gov, http://www.hrsa.gov.

Stephanie Dionne

Medicaid/Medicare fraud and abuse

Definition

Medicaid/Medicare fraud and abuse refers to the illegal practice of collecting federal funds through the **Medicaid** or **Medicare** program. Two sources of this fraud and abuse are charging the programs for services and products that were never provided, and charging the programs for services and products that were not necessary. Services may include tests, operations, or follow-up checkups. Products may include medication, orthopedic equipment, or ease-of-access support.

Description

Fraud and abuse in the Medicaid and Medicare system interferes with the effective administration of these programs and costs the taxpayers $3 billion to $100 billion a year. Congress has passed several laws to identify and reduce the amount of fraud and abuse. The Office of the Inspector General (OIG) of Health and Human Services Department makes efforts to ensure that new physicians are aware of these laws, and established physicians adhere to them in their practice. The five key areas of fraud and abuse according to the Office of the Inspector General are: false claims, various types of kickback, physician self-referral, charging Medicaid and Medicare during an exclusion period, and misrepresentation on the bills to Medicaid and Medicare. Charges and fines can be filed against a physician whether the fraud is based on intentional misrepresentation or based on deficient management, practices, or controls.

False claims occur when a physician submits the charge to Medicaid or Medicare for services that were not actually provided. For example, the physician may claim to have conducted tests to better determine a patient's condition but in reality never conducted those tests. Another situation that would be considered a false claim is charging for the tests if the tests were conducted but already covered from another source. The charge to Medicaid or Medicare would be redundant, and so the charge would constitute fraud.

Any misuse of federal funds such as Medicaid or Medicare can be considered fraud or abuse. Therefore, if such tests were conducted but were not really needed, this also can be considered a false claim. The purpose of Medicaid and Medicare are to provide funds for necessary services that might otherwise be ignored because of the inability of the patient to pay. This physician should not be charging Medicaid or Medicare for any services that he or she would not recommend if Medicaid or Medicare were not available.

Some practices that are acceptable in business are not acceptable in the healthcare industry, where a person's long-term health or life is in the balance. Providing rewards for endorsements is a well-accepted practice in business. In business, if a customer does not appreciate products or services that the business person recommends, the customer is free to go elsewhere. However, such practices in the medical field can be seen as an example of the various types of kickback prohibited by Medicaid and Medicare. If a physician is recommending a drug or equipment based on rewards for endorsing it, the physician may be placing the patient's life or welfare in jeopardy. Some common cases of kickback occur when the physician recommends a particular brand-name medication instead of a generic version because of promotional rewards. Another practice that may be considered a kickback is when a physician makes referrals to other physicians in the same medical building because of promised reduced rent. Equipment such as that used for

KEY TERMS

Exclusion—The practice of not allowing a physician to participate in the Medicaid or Medicare programs.

Health and Human Services—A cabinet-level department responsible for administrating and overseeing health and welfare programs funded by the federal government.

Kickback—An unethical practice of accepting money or other reward paid by a business for referrals.

Medicaid—The federal program designed to provide funds for healthcare based on financial need.

Medicare—The federal program designed to provide funds for healthcare based on age.

Office of Inspector General—The branch of the Department of Health and Human Services responsible for detecting and preventing fraud and abuse.

Self-referral—An unethical practice of a professional (such as a physician) deceptively referring customers to a business owned in some way by the professional.

joint replacements or increased mobility might be recommended because of a reward from the supplier to the physician; if so, this would be a violation of the kickback law.

\Physician self-referral happens when a physician has an interest in a related business and refers patients to that particular business. These businesses may be medical supply stores or medical services such as physical therapy or home healthcare. This prohibition also applies to businesses in which close relatives of the physician have investments of any level. While Medicare and Medicaid authorities expect that the physician will use best professional decision, the physician having a financial interest in the companies that he or she recommends can interfere with his or her best judgment. The OIG presents a recent violation where a physician owned an oxygen supply company. He routinely charged Medicare for oxygen prescribed to patients with conditions for which oxygen would not ordinarily be prescribed.

The OIG of Health and Human Services is allowed to exclude physicians from participating in Medicaid and Medicare for various reasons. This exclusion may be temporary or permanent. During this exclusion, the physician may not charge Medicaid and Medicare for services that would otherwise fall under their provision. As the system monitoring is not perfect, there are easy-to-find ways around this exclusion. A physician who, during the exclusion period, still charges Medicaid or Medicare can face steep penalties.

The Civil Monetary Penalties Law is designed to collect money paid out under Medicaid and Medicare through misrepresentation on the bills from participating physicians. Any violation of the false claims could result in additional penalties under this law. For example, a physician who charges for the more expensive surgery-related blood test could face charges if in reality the less expensive routine blood test was administered.

Why this is important to the consumer

Fraud and abuse can harm the consumer by increasing the use of unnecessary services or products, offering inferior equipment or medication, and deteriorating the doctor-patient trust. Furthermore, it reduces the amount of funds available to help those who truly need it. Healthcare consumers who rely on Medicaid or Medicare need to be aware of the possibility of fraud and abuse. When a physician makes false claims, the false representation may end up on the patient's health record. Tests or services that were claimed but not delivered will appear on the patient's health record as evidence of good health or as a health problem solved. In reality, neither is true. When a physician takes a kickback, there is a good chance that a lesser medication will be prescribed instead of a more effective one. The physician prescribing products or services only because he or she has a vested interest in the company that provides them is interfering with the patient's recovery. Unnecessary services or products may also be harmful.

The worst effect of fraud and abuse is the deterioration of the trust that the patient has in the physician. Ultimately, the physician's stock in trade is his or her trustworthy advice and guidance. When the trust is gone, the patient has to question every recommendation from the physician; thus, the healthcare becomes polluted. The physician can encourage speedy recovery and a smooth transition back to full health, but without trust from the patient, the encouragement can be lost.

Resources

BOOKS

Bozic, Kevin J., and Benedict U. Nwachukwu. "Medicare and Its Evolution to 2011." *An Introduction to Health Policy.* Springer New York, 2013. 15-25.

Gosfield, Alice. *Medicare and Medicaid Fraud and Abuse,* 2013 edition. Thomson West: 2013.

PERIODICALS

DiSantostefano, Jan. "Medicare Fraud and Abuse Issues." *Journal for Nurse Practitioners* 9.1 (2013): 61.

Hoppel, Ann M. "Career code red: unintentional Medicare billing fraud." *Clinician Reviews* (October 2012): 1.

Lovette, Madeleine. "Medicare fraud and abuse 101: an introduction to the False Claims, Anti-Kickback, Stark, Exclusion, and Civil Monetary Penalty laws." *AAOS* (Nowember 2011): 28.

Lundqvist, Hanna, et al. "Health care fraud." *American Criminal Law Review* (Spring 2012): 863.

Merrill Matthews, Medicare and Medicaid Fraud Is Costing Taxpayers Billions, *Forbes* (May 31, 2012).

WEBSITES

Centers for Medicare & Medicaid Services. "Join the Fight Against Medicare Fraud." March 5, 2013. The Medicare Blog: The official blog for the U.S. Medicare program. http://blog.medicare.gov/2013/03/05/join-the-fight-against-medicare-fraud-3/ (accessed September 19, 2013).

U.S. Department of Health & Human Services, Office of Inspector General. *A Roadmap for New Physicians: Avoiding Medicare and Medicaid Fraud and Abuse.* https://oig.hhs.gov/compliance/physician-education/roadmap_web_version.pdf (accessed September 19, 2013).

ORGANIZATIONS

Office of Inspector General, U.S. Department of Health and Human Services, 330 Independence Avenue, SW, Washington, DC, USA 20201, 202- 619-0335 , 1-800-447-8477, Public.Affairs@oig.hhs.gov, https://oig.hhs.gov.

Ray F Brogan, Ph.D.

Medical billing

Definition

Medical billing is the process of collecting fees for medical services. A medical bill is called a claim.

Description

The purpose of medical billing is to ensure that the provider receives fair payment for services rendered. Payment should reflect the services performed and should be received in a timely manner. Medical billing may be handled directly by the physician and his or her staff, or it may be administered by a third party. The third party is an independent contractor or company that specializes in handling medical billing.

Laws regarding medical billing procedures include:

- The Fair Debt Collection Act. This federal law dictates how and when to collect a debt. It protects patients and consumers from unlawful threats.

- The **Health Insurance Portability and Accountability Act (HIPAA)** of 1996 contains an administrative portion that increases the efficiency of data exchange for healthcare financial transactions and protects the privacy of electronic data transmission. This protection is especially important for confidential patient records. Violators are subject to financial penalties.

Physician fees

A physician sets fees for his or her services. There are some important concepts in fee setting. One is usual, reasonable, and customary (UCR). Usual fees represent the fair value of a service. Customary rates are rates similar to those of other physicians. Reasonable rates meet the criteria for the other two factors.

Another method used in setting fees is the Resource-Based Relative Value Scale (RBRVS), which examines the relative value of a service and relates it to geographic peculiarities. This method considers the time and skills needed to perform a service, intensity of the service, office (overhead) expenses, and the malpractice insurance premiums that the physician pays. The geographic differences allow for consideration of health care cost variations around the nation.

Fees should be discussed with the patient in advance of treatment. Often, the medical office personnel are called upon to do this. If any co-payments are due, they usually are collected at the time of service.

Not all patients pay the same fee for the same service. Adjustments may be made for certain payors, such as managed care companies (**Health Maintenance Organizations, Preferred Provider Organizations,** etc.) and **Medicare** and **Medicaid** patients. In these cases, physicians and managed care companies or the federal government negotiate fees for various services. Sometimes certain patients receive discounts. This practice may be enforced when the patient works in the health care field.

Basic bookkeeping

Before computers were widely used in medical offices, a day sheet was compiled that recorded all transactions that occurred in one day. This information is placed into a board called a pegboard. Each patient's card, called a ledger card, is also inserted into the pegboard. It contains a record of his or her charges, credits, and payments. This legal document

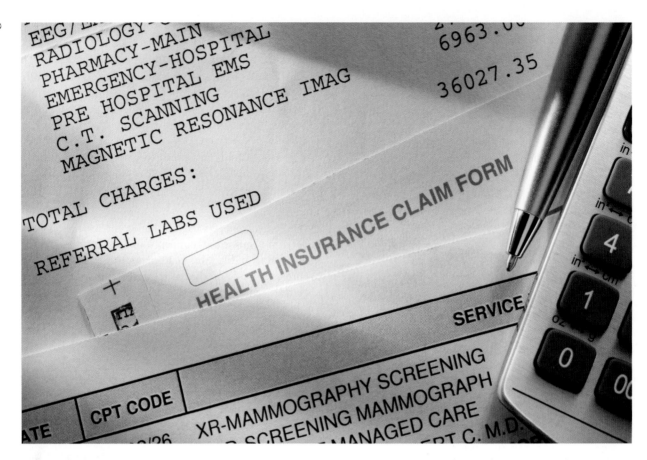

Medical bills may be paid by the patient or by a third party, such as a private insurance company or a managed care company. *(DNY59/Getty Images)*

was to be held as long as the patient's medical record. The information, including patient's name, diagnosis, treatments, charges, payments, and credits, were entered into a pre-printed bill called a superbill. In the 2010s, much of this information is recorded on computers, allowing automation of many parts of the billing process.

The medical claim

When a service such as an office visit is complete, the staff begins preparing the claim or sends the patient information to a third party for billing. A physician's office sends out a claim if that physician accepts assignment of benefits. To accept assignment of benefits, the physician must receive the patient's signature allowing his or her office to receive payment directly from the insurance company.

Claim preparation begins with proper coding. Medical procedures and diagnoses have codes. The Current Procedural Terminology (CPT), developed in 1966 by the American Medical Association, lists medical procedures and corresponding codes. Each

medical procedure has a code that is listed in a CPT manual. The book is divided into sections so that similar procedures appear in the same area.

The major sections of the CPT book are:

• evaluation/management

• anesthesia

• surgery

• radiology

• pathology and laboratory

• medicine

In addition to procedure codes, there are codes for diagnoses, called ICD-9 codes. This practice was established in 1983 when Medicare began using diagnosis-related groups (DRGs). An ICD-9 book lists each diagnosis within the DRGs. Each DRG corresponds to a fee. Coding must be accurate because it determines reimbursement.

Health plans issue identification numbers to providers. This number is placed on claim forms so that payors can quickly and accurately identify providers.

The medical claim also contains important information, such as:

- provider name, address, telephone number, and ID number
- name of insurance plan and group number
- ID number of insurance holder
- patient's name, date of birth
- insured person's name, date of birth
- patient's address and telephone number
- insured person's address and telephone number
- relationship between patient and insured person
- other health insurance the patient may have
- patient's medical condition, and whether it was related to a job automobile accident, or other type of accident
- other information, such as the patient's history of related illness, may need to appear on the claim

The use of computer software allows medical offices to submit claims electronically. This method shortens the time between filing the claim and reimbursement.

Payment

Medical bills may be paid by the patient or by a third party, such as private insurance company, managed care company, or government insurance program such as Medicare. Often, the patient pays for a portion of the care (co-payment or deductible), and an insurance or managed care company is billed for the remaining fees. In some cases, patients may ask to pay their portion over time, and credit may be extended to them. The medical office may charge interest as long as the patient has been informed. This practice is called truth-in-lending. Credit laws vary by state.

Payment received from an insurance or managed care company contains a document called the **explanation of benefits (EOB)**. This statement explains what was paid and what services were not covered and is sent to the provider and the patient. A service may not be covered if a patient has not met his or her yearly deductible. Some services (e.g., cosmetic surgery) are considered elective and are not covered. In this case, the provider bills the patient for his or her fee. It is common to bill patients once a month.

When a payment arrives, it is endorsed with a rubber stamp that contains the name of the provider and the bank account number. Endorsing is a form of protection because only the provider who endorsed it can cash the check in the event it is lost or stolen. The provider should have a deposit procedure.

The team involved in billing includes the physician, office manager, nurse, receptionist, medical assistant, and insurance clerk, with these billing-related duties:

- Performs billable service: physician, nurse, medical assistant.
- Explains fees/billing: physician, receptionist, nurse, medical assistant, insurance clerk.
- Prepares day sheet, ledger, superbill: nurse, medical assistant, insurance clerk.
- Files (sends out) claim: insurance clerk.
- Reminds patient of overdue payment: receptionist, nurse, medical assistant, insurance clerk.
- Communicates with insurance companies: receptionist, medical assistant, nurse, insurance clerk.

Billing complications

Complications impact bill collection. Accurate coding, standard office procedures, and good communication within a provider group minimize complications.

OVERDUE PAYMENTS. In some cases, a patient may not pay his or her bill within a month or by the claim's due date. A document called an aging schedule lists overdue accounts. The information includes the patient's name, amount due, payments received, and comments. An account is aged beginning with the billing date rather than the date the procedure was performed. Providers attempt to collect 80% of fees within a month of billing. If this number falls to 50% or less, collection procedures should be examined.

A patient must be reminded of an overdue bill. This can be done with a written notice, phone call, or during the next office visit.

DENIED CLAIMS. If the insurance or managed care company's EOB indicates that the claim is denied, it is important to determine why this happened. The claim should be double-checked to determine if an error has occurred. If the patient is not entitled to coverage, he or she is billed when the monthly billings are sent out.

FRAUD. Medicare and Medicaid have the right to audit a physician's office and examine its billing practices. Errors in claims are checked to determine the presence of fraudulent practices. A medical office must not bill for services that were not performed and must not inaccurately code a service to receive a higher level of payment. These practices are examples of fraud.

Health care professionals who report fraud are called whistle-blowers. The Federal Claims Act protects and rewards these individuals when they report

KEY TERMS

Adjustment—Changes to a standard fee. Changes may be made because of managed care agreements or other discounts.

Aging schedule—A list of overdue medical accounts calculated from date of original bill to current date.

Claim—Medical bill.

Diagnostic related groups (DRGs)—Diagnosis categories that are used when doing physician or hospital billing. Each diagnosis is placed into the appropriate category.

Managed care—A type of health plan with a network of providers and pre-arranged fee schedule. Examples include a health maintenance organization (HMO) or preferred provider organization (PPO).

Payor—One who pays a medical claim. A third party payor is an entity other than the patient, such as the insurance company.

Provider—Health team professional or entity (hospital) that offers care.

Medicare or Medicaid fraud. States also have anti-fraud regulations.

COLLECTING FEES AFTER A PATIENT'S DEATH. If a patient has died, the physician may collect fees from his or her estate.

Why this is important to the consumer

The purpose of medical billing is to ensure that the provider receives fair payment for services rendered. Payment should reflect the services performed and should be received in a timely manner.

There are laws regarding medical billing procedures. Staff members involved in collecting fees must be aware of these regulations.

These laws are designed to protect both the provider and the patient. Inaccurate billing, whether accidental or intentional fraud, increases the cost of medical insurance for everyone and, in the case of government healthcare programs, wastes taxpayer money. Consumers should review their medical bills and EOBs to make sure they and their insurer are bring charged only for services that were provided. It is in the interest of consumers to report errors and

fraud to their insurers to keep down the cost of insurance.

Clear communication within a provider group helps ensure that claims are properly coded, patients are informed of fees, and fair reimbursement is billed and received. The physician must be questioned if there is any doubt that a service was performed or if the diagnosis is not clear.

Resources

BOOKS

Brown, Sharon, and Lori Tyler. *Guide to Medical Billing*, 3rd edition. Prentice Hall, 2012.

Green, Michelle A. *Understanding Health Insurance: A Guide to Billing and Reimbursement*, 11th edition. Delmar Cengage Learning, 2012.

WEBSITES

AARP. "How to Read Your Medical Bill." http://www.aarp.org/health/health-care-reform/info-03-2011/how_to_read_your_medical_bill_cpt_codes.html (accessed November 29, 2013).

American Academy of Family Physicians. "Understanding Your Medical Bills." http://familydoctor.org/familydoctor/en/healthcare-management/insurance-bills/understanding-your-medical-bills.html (accessed November 29, 2013).

. "Medical Bills 101: Understanding Your Medical Bills." Mint.com http://www.mint.com/blog/consumer-iq/medical-bills-101-understanding-your-medical-bills-122011 (accessed November 29, 2013).

ORGANIZATIONS

American Medical Association, 515 N. State Street, Chicago, IL 60610, (800) 621-8335, http://www.ama-assn.org.

Rhonda Cloos, R.N.
Tish Davidson, AM

Medical charts

Definition

The medical chart is a confidential document that contains detailed and comprehensive information on individual patients and their care.

Description

The purpose of the medical chart is to serve as both a medical and legal record of patient clinical status, care, history, and caregiver involvement. The detailed information contained in the chart is intended

More health care institutions are adopting computerized charting systems that aid in clear documentation, enhanced access, and efficient storage of patient records. *(© Barry Slaven, MD, PhD / Phototake)*

to provide a record of the patient's clinical condition by detailing diagnoses, treatments, tests and response to treatment, as well as any other factors that may affect the clinical state of the patient.

The term medical chart or medical record is a general description of a collection of information on a patient. However, different clinical settings and systems use different forms of documentation to achieve this purpose. As technology progresses, more institutions are adopting computerized systems and **electronic health records (EHRs)** that aid in clear documentation, enhanced access, and efficient storage of patient records.

New uses of technology have also raised concerns about **patient confidentiality.** Confidentiality, or patient privacy, is an important principle related to the chart. Whatever system may be in place, it is essential that the health care provider protect the patient's privacy by limiting access to authorized

individuals only. Generally, physicians and nurses write most frequently in the chart. The documentation by the clinician who is leading treatment decisions (usually the physician) often focuses on diagnosis and prognosis, while the documentation by the nursing team generally focuses on patient responses to treatment and details of day-to-day progress. In many institutions, the medical and nursing staff may complete separate forms or areas of the chart specific to their disciplines.

Other on-staff health care professionals that have access to the chart include **physician assistants; social workers; psychologists; nutritionists;** physical, occupational, speech, or respiratory therapists; and consultants. It is important that the various disciplines view the notes written by other specialties in order to form a complete picture of the patient and provide continuity of care. Quality assurance and regulatory organizations, legal bodies, and insurance companies may also have access to the chart for specific purposes such as documentation, institutional audits, legal proceedings, or verification of information for care reimbursement. It is important to know the institution's policies regarding chart access in order to ensure the privacy of the patient.

The medical record should be stored in a predesignated, secure area and discussed only in appropriate and private clinical areas. The patient has a right to view and obtain copies of his or her own record. Special state statutes may cover especially sensitive information such as psychiatric, communicable disease (e.g., HIV), or substance abuse records. Institutional and government policies govern what is contained in the chart, how it is documented, who has access, and policies for regulating access to the chart and protecting its integrity and confidentiality.

In cases where chart contents need to be accessed by individuals outside of the immediate care system, the patient (the patient's representative or a **patient navigator**) is asked for written permission to release records. Patients often are asked to sign these releases so that caregivers in new clinical settings may review their charts. The **Health Insurance Portability and Accountability Act (HIPAA)** of 1996 contains an administrative portion that protects the privacy of paper records and electronic data transmission. This protection is especially important for confidential patient records. Violators are subject to financial penalties.

All members of the health care team require thorough understanding of the medical chart and documentation guidelines in order to provide thorough care and maintain a clear, concise, and pertinent record. Health care systems often employ methods to guarantee thorough and continuous use and review of charts across disciplines. For example, nursing staff may be required to sign below every new physician order to indicate that this information has been communicated, or internal quality assurance teams may study groups of charts to determine trends in missing or unclear documentation. In legal settings, health care team members may be called upon to interpret or explain chart notations as they relate to the individual legal case.

Operation

Documentation in the medical record begins when the patient enters the care system, which may be a specific place such as a hospital or a program such as a home health care service. Frequently the facility will request permission to obtain copies of previous

records so that they have complete information on the patient. Although chart systems vary from institution to institution, there are many aspects of the chart that are universal. Frequently used chart sections include:

- Admission paperwork: includes legal paperwork such as living will or health care proxy, consents for admission to the facility or program, demographics, and contact information.
- History and physical: contains comprehensive review of patient's medical history and physical exam.
- Orders: contains medication and treatment orders by the doctor, nurse practitioner, physician assistant, or other qualified health care team members.
- Medication record: notes all medications administered.
- Treatment record: documents all treatments received, such as dressing changes or respiratory therapy.
- Procedures: summarizes diagnostic or therapeutic procedures, including colonoscopy or open-heart surgery, for example.
- Tests: provides reports and results of diagnostic evaluations, such as laboratory tests and electrocardiography or radiography images or summaries.
- Progress notes: includes regular notes on the patient's status by the interdisciplinary care team.
- Consultations: contains notes from specialized diagnosticians or care providers.
- Consents: includes permissions signed by patient for procedures, tests, or access to chart. May also contain releases, such as the release signed by the patient when leaving the facility against medical advice (AMA).
- Flow records: tracks specific aspects of patient care that occur on a routine basis, using tables or chart format.
- Care plans: documents treatment goals and plans for future care within the facility or following discharge.
- Discharge: contains final instructions for the patient and reports by the care team before the chart is closed and stored following patient discharge.
- Insurance information: lists health care benefit coverage and insurance provider contact information.

These general categories may be further divided for the individual facility's purposes. For example, a psychiatric facility may use a special section for psychometric testing, or a hospital may provide sections specifically for operations, x-ray reports, or electrocardiograms. In addition, certain details such as allergies or do-not-resuscitate orders may be displayed prominently (for instance, on large colored stickers or special chart sections) on the chart in order to communicate uniquely important information.

Certain practices that protect the integrity of the chart and provide essential information are recommended for adding information and maintaining the chart:

- Include date and time on all records.
- Include full patient name and other identifiers (e.g., medical record number, date of birth) on all records.
- Mark continued records clearly (e.g., if note continued on reverse of page).
- Sign each page of documentation.
- Use blue or black non-erasable ink on handwritten records.
- Keep records in chronological order.
- Prevent disposal or obliteration of any records.
- Note documentation errors and correct clearly (e.g., by drawing one line through the error and noting presence of error, initialing the area).
- Avoid excess empty space on the page.
- Avoid abbreviations or use only universally accepted abbreviations.
- Avoid other unclear documentation, such as illegible penmanship.
- Avoid including contradictory information. For example, if a nurse documents that a patient has complained of abdominal pain throughout the shift, while the physician documents that the patient is free of pain, these discrepancies should be discussed and clarified.
- Describe all events involving the patient as objectively as possible.
- Document any occurrence that might affect the patient. Only documented information is considered credible in court. Undocumented information is considered questionable since there is no written record of its occurrence.
- Always use current date and time with documentation. For example, if adding a note after the fact, it can be labeled "addendum" and inserted in correct chronological order, rather than trying to insert the information on the date of the actual occurrence.
- Record actual statements of patients or other individuals in quotes.
- Never leave the chart in an unprotected environment where unauthorized individuals may read or alter the contents.

Several methods of documentation have arisen in response to the need to accurately summarize the patient experience. In the critical care setting, flow records are often used to track the frequent patient evaluations, checks of equipment, and changes of equipment settings that are required. Flow records also offer the advantages of displaying a large amount of information in a relatively small space and allowing for quick comparison. Flow records can also save time for the busy clinician by allowing completion of checklists versus narrative notes.

Narrative progress notes, while more time consuming, are often the best way to capture specific information about the patient. Some institutions require only charting by exception (CBE), which requires notes for significant or unusual findings only. While this method may decrease repetition and lower required documentation time, most institutions that use CBE notes also require a separate flow record that documents regular contact with the patient. Many facilities or programs require notes at regular intervals (e.g., every nursing shift) even when there are no significant occurrences. Frequently used formats in patient notes include SOAP (Subjective, Objective, Assessment, and Plan) notes. SOAP notes use a subjective patient statement to capture an important aspect of care, then follow with a key objective statement regarding the patient's status, a description of the patient assessment, and a plan for how to address patient problems or concerns. Focus charting and PIE (problem-intervention-evaluation) charting use similar systems of notes that begin with a particular focus such as a patient concern or a nursing diagnosis. Nursing diagnoses are often used as guides to nursing care by focusing on individual patient needs and responses to treatment. An example of a nursing diagnosis would be "fluid volume deficit" for a patient that is dehydrated. The notes would then focus on assessment for dehydration, interventions to address the problem, and a plan for continued care, such as measurement of input and output and intravenous therapy.

Maintenance

Current medical charts are maintained by the health care team and usually require clerical assistance, such as the unit clerk in the hospital setting. No alterations should be made to the record unless they are required to clarify or correct information and are clearly marked as such. After patient discharge, the medical records department of a facility checks for completeness and retains the record. Sometimes the record will be made available in another format (e.g., recording paper charts on microfilm or computer imaging). Institutional and state laws govern storage

KEY TERMS

Consultation—Evaluation by an expert or specialist.

Continuity—Consistency or coordination of details.

Discipline—In health care, a specific area of preparation or training, for example, social work, nursing, or nutrition.

Documentation—The process of recording information in the medical chart, or the materials in a medical chart.

Interdisciplinary—Consisting of several interacting disciplines that work together to care for the patient.

Objective—Not biased by personal opinion

Prognosis—Expected outcome of an illness or injury.

Regulatory organization—Organization designed to maintain or control quality in health care, such as The Joint Commission (TJC) formerly the Joint Commission on Accreditation of Healthcare Organizations (JCAHO), Department of Health (DOH), or the Food and Drug Administration (FDA).

Subjective—Influenced by personal opinion or experience.

of charts on- and off-site and length of storage time required.

Why this is important to the consumer

The information in the chart should be clear and concise, so that those consulting the record can easily access accurate information. The medical chart can aid in clinical problem solving by tracking the patient's baseline, or status, on admission; orders and treatments provided in response to specific problems; and patient responses. An accurate medical chart also allows the transfer of vital information from one healthcare professional to another as the patient moves through the medical care system. It helps reduce the need for duplicate medical tests and alerts the care team to unique patient information such as allergies and patient directives such as do-not-resuscitate orders.

Another reason for the standard of clear documentation is the possibility of the legal use of the record, when documentation serves as evidence in exploring and evaluating the patient's care experience. When medical care is being referred to or questioned by the legal system, the chart contents are frequently cited in court.

Resources

BOOKS

Keogh, James. *Schaum's Outline of Medical Charting*. Chicago: McGraw-Hill, 2012.

Richards, Joan and James Keogh. *Medical Charting Demystified*. New York: McGraw-Hill, 2008.

PERIODICALS

Apfeld, Jordan C., A. Alex Jahangir, and Manish K. Sethi. "The lowdown on EMRs: will they really lower costs and increase the quality of health care?" *AAOS Now* (2013): 20.

Grantham, Dennis. "Confidentiality alternatives for exchanging electronic medical records take shape: progress is accelerating, though large-scale solutions appear years away." *Behavioral Healthcare* 33.3 (2013): 37.

Hickner, John. "End EMR tyranny!" *Journal of Family Practice* (April 2013): 173.

Huang, Yi Chao. "Mining association rules between abnormal health examination results and outpatient medical records." *Health Information Management Journal* 42.2 (2013): 23.

Motara, F., et al. "Audit of medical records: use of a structured form in emergency departments." *South African Medical Journal* 103.7 (2013): 438.

WEBSITES

American Academy of Orthopaedic Surgeons. "Charting a Path to Safety." http://www.aaos.org/news/aaosnow/apr09/managing7.asp (accessed November 28, 3013).

Stimpfel, Nancy. "Quality Medical Charts: The Importance of Proper Medical Documentation." TransforMed. http://www.transformed.com/workingpapers/quality medicalcharts.pdf (accessed November 28, 2013).

ORGANIZATIONS

American Health Information Management Association (AHIMA), 233 N. Michigan Avenue, 21st Floor, Chicago, IL 60601-5809, (312) 233-1100, (800) 335-5535, Fax: (312) 233-1500, http://www.ahima.org.

Katherine L. Hauswirth, APRN
Tish Davidson, AM

Medical ethics

Definition

Medical ethics refers to the discussion and application of moral values and responsibilities in the areas of medical practice and research.

Description

While questions of medical ethics have been debated since the beginnings of Western medicine in the fifth century B.C., medical ethics as a distinctive field came into prominence only since World War II. This change has come about largely as a result of advances in medical technology, scientific research, and telecommunications. These developments have affected nearly every aspect of clinical practice, from the confidentiality of patient records to end-of-life issues. Moreover, the increased involvement of government in medical research as well as the allocation of health care resources brings with it an additional set of ethical questions.

The Hippocratic tradition

Medical ethics generally traces its origins to the ancient Greek physician Hippocrates (460–377 B.C.), who is credited with defining the first ethical standard in medicine: "Do no harm." The oath attributed to Hippocrates was traditionally recited by medical students as part of their medical school graduation ceremonies. A modern version of the Hippocratic Oath that has been approved by the American Medical Association (AMA) reads as follows:

You do solemnly swear, each by whatever he or she holds most sacred

That you will be loyal to the Profession of Medicine and just and generous to its members

That you will lead your lives and practice your art in uprightness and honor

That into whatsoever house you shall enter, it shall be for the good of the sick to the utmost of your power, your holding yourselves far aloof from wrong, from corruption, from the tempting of others to vice

That you will exercise your art solely for the cure of your patients, and will give no drug, perform no operation, for a criminal purpose, even if solicited, far less suggest it

That whatsoever you shall see or hear of the lives of men or women which is not fitting to be spoken, you will keep inviolably secret

These things do you swear. Let each bow the head in sign of acquiescence

And now, if you will be true to this your oath, may prosperity and good repute be ever yours; the opposite, if you shall prove yourselves forsworn.

Religious traditions and medical ethics

Ancient Greece was not the only pre-modern culture that set ethical standards for physicians. Both Indian and Chinese medical texts from the third century B.C. list certain moral virtues that practitioners were to exemplify, among them humility, compassion, and concern for the patient's well-being. In the West, both Judaism and Christianity gave extensive consideration to the importance of the physician's moral character as well as his duties to patients. In Judaism, medical ethics is rooted in the study of specific case histories interpreted in the light of Jewish law. This case-based approach is known as casuistry. In Christianity, ethical reflection on medical questions has taken the form of an emphasis on duty, moral obligation, and right action. In both faiths, the relationship between the medical professional and the patient is still regarded as a covenant or sacred bond of trust rather than a business contract. In contemporary Buddhism, discussions of medical ethics reflect specifically Buddhist understandings of suffering, the meaning of human personhood, and the significance of death.

The Enlightenment and the nineteenth century

The eighteenth century in Europe witnessed a number of medical as well as general scientific advances, and the application of scientific principles to medical education led to a new interest in medical ethics. The first book on medical ethics in English was published by a British physician, Thomas Percival, in 1803. In the newly independent United States, Benjamin Rush—a signer of the Declaration of Independence as well as a physician—lectured to the medical students at the University of Pennsylvania on the importance of high ethical standards in their profession. Rush recommended service to the poor as well as the older Hippocratic virtues of honesty and justice.

In the middle of the nineteenth century, physicians in the United States and Canada began to form medical societies with stated codes of ethics. These codes were drawn up partly because there was no government licensing of physicians or regulation of medical practice at that time. The medical profession felt a need to regulate itself as well as set itself apart from quacks, **faith healers,** homeopaths, and other practitioners of what would now be called **alternative medicine.** The American Medical Association, which was formed in 1847, has revised its Code of Ethics from time to time as new ethical issues have arisen. The present version consists of seven principles. The Canadian Medical Association (CMA) was formed in 1867 and has a Code of Ethics with 40 guidelines for the ethical practice of medicine.

Professional training

There is increasing emphasis in the medical field on the importance of studying ethical issues during one's professional education. Many medical, dental, and nursing schools now include courses in their curricula that deal with such topics as moral decision-making, definitions of life and death, the ethical complexities of **professional-patient relationships,** and the moral safeguards of medical research. More than 25 universities in the United States and Canada offer graduate degrees in medical ethics.

Not all training and insight in medical ethics comes from the medical field itself. The necessity of interdisciplinary conversation and cooperation is becoming increasingly recognized. Physicians can benefit from the insights of scholars in the social sciences, philosophy, theology, law, and history. At the same time, they have much to offer professionals in other fields on the basis of their clinical experience.

Viewpoints

PHILOSOPHICAL FRAMEWORKS. Since the early Middle Ages, questions of medical ethics have sometimes been discussed within the framework of specific philosophical positions or concepts. A follower of Immanuel Kant (1724–1804), for example, would test an ethical decision by the so-called categorical imperative, which states that one should act as if one's actions would serve as the basis of universal law. Another philosophical position that sometimes appears in discussions of medical ethics is utilitarianism, or the belief that moral virtue is based on usefulness. From a utilitarian perspective, the best decision is that which serves the greatest good of the greatest number of people. An American contribution to philosophical approaches to medical ethics is pragmatism, which is the notion that practical results, rather than theories or principles, provide the most secure basis for evaluating ethical decisions.

CASUISTRY. Casuistry can be defined as a case-based approach to medical ethics. An ethicist in this tradition, if confronted with a complicated ethical decision, would study a similar but simpler case in order to work out an answer to the specific case under discussion. As has already been mentioned, casuistry has been used as a method of analysis for centuries in Jewish medical ethics.

THE "FOUR PRINCIPLES" APPROACH. Another approach to medical ethics was developed in the 1970s by philosopher Tom Beauchamp and theologian James Childress. Beauchamp and Childress drew up a list of four principles that they thought could be weighed against one another in ethical decision-making in medicine. The four principles are:

- the principle of autonomy, or respecting each person's right to make his or her own decisions
- the principle of beneficence, or doing good as the primary goal of medicine
- the principle of nonmaleficence, or refraining from harming people
- the principle of justice, or distributing the benefits and burdens of a specific decision fairly

One limitation of the "Four Principles" approach is that different individuals involved in an ethical decision might well disagree about the relative weight to be given to each principle. For example, a patient who wants to be taken off a life-support system could argue that the principle of autonomy should be paramount, while the clinical staff could maintain that the principles of beneficence and nonmaleficence are more important. The principles themselves do not define or imply a hierarchical ranking or ordering.

Current issues in medical ethics

PHYSICIAN-ASSISTED SUICIDE. Throughout North America, committing suicide or attempting to commit suicide is no longer a criminal offense. In most states, however, assisting someone to commit suicide is a criminal act. This includes physician-assisted suicide, when a physician supplies information and/or the means of committing suicide (e.g., prescribing a lethal dose of sleeping pills or supplying carbon monoxide gas) to a person, so that that person can terminate his or her own life.

This issue was pushed to the forefront of the medical ethics debate when Jack Kevorkian (1928–2011), a Michigan pathologist, assisted with the deaths of hundreds of patients. Originally, he hooked his patients up to a machine that delivered measured doses of medications, but only after the patient pushed a button to initiate the sequence. Later, he provided carbon monoxide and a facemask so that his patient could initiate the flow of gas. On November 22, 1998, the *60 Minutes* news program aired a videotape showing Kevorkian giving a lethal injection to Thomas Youk, 52, who suffered from Lou Gehrig's disease. The broadcast triggered an intense debate within medical, legal, and media circles. In 1999, Kevorkian was convicted of second-degree murder and illegal delivery of a controlled substance in the death of Youk. A Michigan judge sentenced Kevorkian to 10–25 years in prison. (He was released in 2007 after promising not to assist any more suicides.)

As of 2013, three states—Oregon, Washington, and Vermont—have laws making it legal for people who are terminally ill and in intractable pain to get a lethal prescription from their physician. The state of Montana does not have a specific assisted-suicide law on the books, but the State Supreme Court ruled in 2009 in *Baxter et al v. Montana* that assisted suicide was allowable under state law. In 1997, the United States Supreme Court heard two cases, *Glucksberg v. Washington* and *Vacco v. Quill* on the issue of physician-assisted suicide. The court ruled that there was no right to assisted-suicide under the United States Constitution, but encouraged each state to consider the issue for themselves. It is not expected that the Supreme Court will consider the issue again in the near future.

OTHER TOPICS OF MEDICAL ETHICS. One well-known writer in the field of medical ethics has written an article listing what he considers cutting-edge topics in medical ethics. While space does not permit discussion of these subjects here, they serve as a useful summary of the impact of technology and globalization on medical ethics in the new millennium:

- End-of-life care. Medical advances that have led to a dramatic lengthening of the life span for adults in the developed countries and a corresponding increase in the elderly population have made end-of-life care a pressing issue.

- Medical error. The proliferation of new medications, new surgical techniques, and other innovations means that the consequences of medical errors are often very serious. All persons involved in health care have an ethical responsibility to help improve the quality of care.

- Setting priorities. The fair allocation of health care resources is one example of setting priorities.

- Biotechnology. Medical ethicists are still divided over the legitimacy of stem cell research, cloning, and other procedures that advances in biotechnology have made possible.

- eHealth. The expansion of the Internet and other rapid changes in information technology have raised many questions about the confidentiality of electronic medical records as well as the impact of online education on medical training.

- Global bioethics. Global bioethics represents an attempt to consider the ethical problems confronting the poorer countries of the world, rather than concentrating on medical issues from the perspective of the wealthy countries. Of the 54 million deaths that occur each year around the world, 46 million occur in low- and middle-income countries.

KEY TERMS

Casuistry—A case-based approach to medical ethics.

Categorical imperative—The principle that one should act in such a way that one's deeds could become universal rules of conduct.

Ethics—A system or set of moral principles; also, the study of values relating to human conduct.

Hippocratic Oath—The ethical oath attributed to Hippocrates that is used as a standard for care by physicians worldwide.

Pragmatism—A philosophical position that regards practical results, rather than abstract principles or theories, as the essential criterion of moral value.

Utilitarianism—An ethical position based on the premise that usefulness is the best measure of moral worth, and that ethical decisions should promote the good of the largest number of persons.

Why this is important to the consumer

A consumer's relationship with his or her doctor is one that must rely very heavily on trust. Many medical procedures are complex, and consumers often rely on their doctors for advice and guidance as to which procedures are appropriate. It is therefore of highest importance that consumers are able to trust that the advice they are receiving is based on a genuine desire to help heal and care for them, and not other motives such as profiting from expensive and unnecessary treatment.

A medical profession filled with individuals with the highest level of integrity means that consumers can trust their medical professionals with their care at every level, from a nurse administering a vaccination to a surgeon recommending removal of an organ. It is also of fundamental importance that consumers who are concerned that a medical professional is acting unethically have somewhere trustworthy to turn. State and national boards of medical professionals often provide hotlines for consumers to report concerns and have channels with which to launch investigations into improper behavior. These oversights, combined with intensive training in medical ethics during schooling and continuing education, help to ensure that the medical profession remains committed first and foremost to the health and well being of patients.

Resources

BOOKS

DeGrazia, David, and Brand-Ballard, Jeffrey, Eds. *Biomedical Ethics*, 7th edition. New York: McGraw-Hill Higher Education, 2011.

Merino, Noel, Ed. *Medical Ethics*. Detroit: Greenhaven Press, 2011.

Stauch, Marc, Wheat, Kay, and Tingle, John. *Text, Cases and Materials on Medical Law and Ethics*. New York: Routledge 2011.

PERIODICALS

Chang, E. "The Paradox of Professionalism." *Academic Medicine* (August, 2013): 1128.

Smith, Martin. "Thinking Ethically About Medical Mistakes." *Journal of Child Neurology* (June 2013): 809–811.

Vertrees, S. M., Shuman, A. G., and Fins, J. J. "Learning By Doing: Effectively Incorporating Ethics Education into Residency Training." *Journal of General Internal Medicine* (April 2013): 578–582.

ORGANIZATIONS

American Medical Association, Council on Ethical and Judicial Affairs. 515 North State St., Chicago, IL 60610. (800) 621-8335. www.ama-assn.org

American Nurses Association. 8515 Georgia Ave., Ste. 400, Silver Spring, MD 20910. (800) 274-4262. www.nursingworld.org.

American Society for Bioethics and Humanities. 4700 W. Lake, Glenview, IL 60025. (847) 375-4745. www.asbh.org.

Canadian Medical Association. 1867 Alta Vista Drive, Ottawa, ON K1G 3Y6. (800) 457-4205. www.cma.ca.

Ken R. Wells
Tish Davidson, AM

Medical law

Definition

Medical law refers to the complex system of state and federal laws that regulate the practice of medicine in the United States.

Description

Medical law includes educational and licensing requirements, civil litigation involving physicians or their employees (such as lawsuits for malpractice or negligence), criminal cases in which physicians are called as expert witnesses, duties involving birth or death certificates, and duties to report diseases and suspected abuse. Laws related to these aspects of medical practice are usually administered at the state level. Federal laws affecting medical practice include such matters as regulation of controlled substances (narcotics); laws related to fair hiring and employment practices, **occupational safety and health,** and workers' compensation; laws concerning credit reporting and debt collection practices; and similar matters.

History

The practice of medicine in the United States was not always as highly regulated as it is in the early twenty-first century. Prior to the early twentieth century, medical education was not even standardized. People could enter the profession in one of three ways: by serving an apprenticeship with a practicing physician; by completing a course of study at a proprietary school (a medical college owned by a group of local physicians); or by graduating from a medical school affiliated with a university and a teaching hospital. There was no standard curriculum. The various schools taught osteopathy, homeopathy, chiropractic, and naturopathy as well as scientific medicine. Of the 155 medical schools in the United States in 1900, three were open only to women and eight only to African Americans.

In 1904, the American Medical Association (AMA) formed a Council on Medical Education (CME) in order to standardize requirements for entry into the profession. The CME pressed for two reforms: the standardization of undergraduate premedical course requirements, and the institution of an "ideal" curriculum for the MD degree—two years of laboratory work in science followed by two years of clinical rotation in an **academic teaching hospital.** In 1908, Abraham Flexner was hired by the Carnegie Foundation for the Advancement of Teaching to survey all 155 medical schools in the United States. He issued a report in 1910 that emphasized the importance of raising admission standards and educational requirements for medical practice. The Flexner Report became the basis for a gradual elimination of proprietary medical colleges and other schools that were academically weak. One of the unfortunate side effects of the Flexner Report was the closing of all but two of the African American medical schools, resulting in a large underserved rural and minority population, particularly in the South.

Medical practice acts and licensure regulations

In addition to curricular reform, Abraham Flexner was also responsible for proposing that medical licensure should be regulated by the government of each state. State licensing boards were formed in quick succession after 1910. In 1912, a group of these new boards formed the Federation of State Medical Boards (FSMB), currently based in Dallas, Texas.

Three years later, the National Board of Medical Examiners (NBME) was established in Philadelphia to provide a nationwide voluntary examination that the various state boards could accept as a standard for a medical license. Prior to 1992, the NBME administered a three-part certifying examination, while the FSMB offered a Federation Licensing Examination, or FLEX. The NBME and FSMB then jointly sponsored a successor examination called the United States Medical Licensing Examination, or USMLE. The USMLE is a three-step examination administered all year round by computer at various test centers:

• Step 1 assesses the candidate's knowledge of basic science and ability to apply it to the practice of medicine.

• Step 2 assesses the candidate's clinical skills. These portions of the USMLE can be taken at test centers outside as well as inside the United States.

• Step 3, which must be taken at a test center within the United States, measures whether the candidate is competent to practice medicine without supervision.

The next phase in obtaining licensure is the submission of a resume or curriculum vitae (CV) to the state licensing board. This document allows the board to evaluate potential problem areas as well as verify the candidate's credentials. The AMA advises candidates "never [to] try to hide derogatory information from the licensing board," as false statements on an application for licensure are usually grounds for denial. It may take 60 days or longer for a state board to grant a license after all the documentation has been submitted. A valid license is an absolute necessity for practicing medicine in the United States, in that anyone who practices without one is liable to lawsuits.

SPECIALTY CERTIFICATION. In addition to general state licensure, the majority of practicing physicians in the United States are certified by one or more specialty boards. Board certification is one form of professional self-regulation for physicians. The first specialty board, the American Board for Ophthalmic Examinations, was formed in 1917, and others soon followed. Today, the American Board of Medical Specialties (ABMS) has twenty-four member specialty boards in fields ranging from allergy and immunology to thoracic surgery and urology. The boards issue 37 general and 92 subspecialty certificates.

Important changes in specialty board certification were implemented in 2005 in response to concerns about quality of care and standards set by such entities as the **Joint Commission** on Accreditation of Healthcare Organizations. The first change was that board

certification was no longer lifelong. Some specialty boards began issuing time-limited certificates as early as 1970, but most did not. Beginning in 2006, all member boards of the ABMS issue time-limited certification for periods of ten years or less.

The second change in the board certification process was that each specialty board would submit a plan for eventually moving from recertification through examinations every six to ten years, to an ongoing "maintenance of certification" assessment of physicians' competence.

MONITORING SYSTEMS. In addition to state and specialty board regulations of medical licensure, the United States **Department of Health and Human Services** maintains a National Practitioner Data Bank (NPDB), which serves as a flagging system to alert state licensing boards, hospitals, insurance companies, and other entities to records of malpractice payments or other adverse events on a physician's or dentist's record. The NPDB was set up in 1990 following several high-profile cases involving incompetent or mentally disturbed physicians who moved from state to state to conceal negative histories, including criminal records. The data bank is prohibited by law from revealing information about a specific practitioner to the general public.

Professional liability

The concept of professional liability has been expanded in recent years to include all healthcare professionals associated with a specific case. As a result, physicians must assume legal responsibility for actions performed by their employees as well as their own acts. Most lawsuits against physicians are brought for either malpractice or negligence.

MALPRACTICE AND NEGLIGENCE. Malpractice refers to "any professional misconduct, unreasonable lack of skill or fidelity in professional or fiduciary duties, evil practices, or immoral or illegal conduct." Negligence refers to carelessness or failure to take reasonable and prudent measures to ensure that others are not harmed by one's actions It may include performing an action incorrectly (commission) as well as failing to take appropriate action (omission). Incorrect performance of an otherwise proper or lawful act is known as misfeasance, while failure to perform a necessary action is called nonfeasance. Malpractice and negligence are classified as torts, which are civil cases involving wrongful acts that result in harm to another person or to property.

Malpractice litigation is generally considered a contributing factor in the shortage of physicians in many parts of the United States and in the rising cost of healthcare. Some physicians are leaving the practice of medicine altogether, relocating to other states, or no longer performing certain procedures because of the risk of litigation. One study found that 48% of medical students mentioned liability as a factor in their choice of specialties, as some specialties, including emergency medicine, obstetrics/gynecology, neurosurgery, orthopedic surgery, and radiology, are at considerably higher risk of malpractice lawsuits than others. Another group of researchers reported that 93% of the physicians they surveyed practiced so-called defensive medicine; that is, they ordered imaging tests and diagnostic procedures that were not always clinically necessary. Another 42% of survey respondents reported that they had restricted their practice in the preceding three years by eliminating complex procedures or by avoiding patients perceived as likely to sue.

RESPONDEAT SUPERIOR. *Respondeat superior* is a Latin phrase that means "let the master (employer) answer," and it refers to the legal principle that an employer is legally responsible for the actions of an employee carried out "in the course of employment." Since most physicians have an office staff of two or more employees, anything that a staff member does that injures a patient may lead to a lawsuit against the physician as well as the medical assistant or other staff member. The doctrine of *respondeat superior* is one reason why the type of medical practice known as sole proprietorship, in which one doctor hires other doctors and pays them salaries, is rapidly disappearing in the United States. In this type of practice, the doctor who owns the practice is legally responsible for the actions of all the other doctors he or she employs.

REDUCING THE RISK OF LITIGATION. Legal professionals advise physicians to take the following steps to protect themselves against lawsuits for malpractice or negligence:

- Keep a copy of all signed applications for licensing or specialty board credentials in a safe place so that the documents can be consulted for consistency when later applications are made or if questions are raised by the certifying board.

- Make sure that all members of the practice are properly licensed and qualified to perform their tasks, and that they are not carrying out tasks for which they are not licensed or certified.

- Make sure that all members of the practice carry their own malpractice insurance.

- Be sure that hospital staff privileges and federal drug registrations for members of the practice who write prescriptions are maintained in good standing. A

violation of the Controlled Substances Act of 1970 is a criminal offense that can result in the loss of licensure as well as a fine and a prison sentence.

- Verify that all offices, surgery centers, and laboratories are properly licensed.

- Insist that office staff handle patient complaints promptly and properly.

- Make sure that all patient files, billing records, and computer documents are handled with strict confidentiality.

- Maintain prompt and appropriate compliance with all third-party payor rules and requirements.

One innovation that appears to be effective in reducing the number of malpractice suits is the "Sorry Works!" program for review and compensation of medical errors. Many patients reported feeling frustrated that doctors and hospitals did not apologize when errors were made, staying silent in an attempt to reduce admissions of error or guilt that could be used against them in court. Research found that the bad feelings this caused may be a significant factor in many patient decisions to sue. To address this, many states and hospitals began implementing programs to change the way patients were communicated with after an adverse event. Illinois became the first state to institute a pilot program for dealing with these incidents. The Illinois program outlines four steps for dealing with medical errors:

- The hospital(s) and physician(s) involved investigate the incident thoroughly without regard to the outcome.

- The hospital contacts the patient and/or family and schedules a meeting with the family's attorney present.

- If a mistake was made, the hospital and physician apologize and (if appropriate) offer compensation. They then draw up a plan to prevent recurrence of the error.

- If no mistake was made, the hospital and physician offer their sympathy together with full disclosure of the patient's file and investigation findings.

Public duties

Physicians are required by law to carry out certain public duties. These include signing certificates of live births and natural deaths. Most states require death certificates to be signed within 24–72 hours after death. In cases of violent death, suicide, suspected murder, no physician present at the time of death, death of an unknown or unidentifiable person, death in prison, or other types of suspicious death, the certificate usually requires the signature of a medical examiner or coroner.

Physicians are required by law to report any of the following:

• Cases of communicable diseases that are considered a public health threat. These include tuberculosis, rubella, tetanus, cholera, polio, rheumatic fever, diphtheria, AIDS and other sexually transmitted diseases, and meningococcal meningitis. Case reports of influenza or West Nile virus may be required during epidemics. Some states add Lyme disease and other communicable diseases to the list.

• Adverse reactions to any childhood vaccines.

• Suspected child abuse, elder abuse, or spouse abuse.

• Abuse of prescription medications.

• Many states require the filing of reports for such noncommunicable diseases as cancer or epilepsy in order to maintain accurate public health statistics.

Most states also require physicians to report instances of malpractice or inappropriate treatment on the part of colleagues.

Ethical violations

Ethical violations refer to breaking rules that reflect the values or goals of the medical profession. The AMA has a formal Code of Ethics that enjoins physicians to exemplify the values of integrity, honesty, respect for all humans, fairness, and responsibility to the community. A physician who is accused of unethical behavior such as fee splitting, falsifying data for a drug research study, performing medical procedures while impaired by the use of drugs or alcohol, sexual relationships with patients, violating **patient confidentiality,** or other types of professional misconduct, may be censured by the AMA. The AMA's Board of Examiners may also recommend expulsion or suspension of membership in the physician's state or local medical association. Although expulsion is a professional rather than a legal penalty, it severely limits a physician's ability to practice medicine. The AMA recommends that patients who wish to report a physician for ethical violations contact the state medical society first before reporting the incident(s) to the AMA itself.

Forensic medicine

Forensic medicine refers to the practice of medicine in courtroom settings or otherwise related to legal matters. It includes such matters as investigating the causes of violent or suspicious deaths and providing advanced training for physicians or dentists to serve as expert witnesses in criminal or civil trials. An expert witness is a person called by a judge to explain specialized information in a case. Physicians or dentists may be called as expert witnesses to explain the causes of death in a murder case, or to testify to generally accepted standards of care in a medical malpractice case.

Expert witnesses are paid a fee for their service to the court. The fee, however, should not depend on the outcome of the trial, as the law considers physicians who appear as expert witnesses to be engaged in the practice of medicine. This point is an important safeguard against any temptation to present a biased account of the evidence or to lie intentionally in order to benefit from one of the parties in the case. A physician who knowingly presents false information in court can be punished for perjury, which is defined as the willful making of verifiably false statements under oath in a court of law. Perjury does not include unintentional errors or offering an interpretation of the evidence that later turns out to be incorrect.

Work settings

From the standpoint of legal definitions and tax regulations, there are six basic types of medical practice:

• Solo practice. In a solo practice, one doctor practices alone. Many dentists still maintain solo practices; physicians, however, are increasingly reluctant to set up solo practices because of the need to repay loans for their medical education and the high cost of maintaining an independent office.

• Sole proprietorship. In this type of practice, one doctor employs other physicians as salaried professionals, pays all the expenses of the practice, and retains control of all assets.

• Partnership. In a partnership, two or more physicians draw up a legal agreement to share in the business operation of a medical practice. Each partner is legally responsible for the actions of all the other partners.

• Associate practice. In this type of practice, the physicians share staff and facilities but not the profits and losses. They also do not share legal responsibilities for one another's actions.

• Group practice. In a group practice, three or more physicians share the same facilities and practice medicine together. They share all expenses, income, staff, equipment, and records. Group practices may be legally defined as either **health maintenance organizations (HMOs)** or independent practice

KEY TERMS

Controlled Substances Act (CSA)—A law passed by Congress in 1970 to regulate the manufacture, distribution, and possession of narcotics and certain other drugs. Drugs are divided into five schedules (categories) according to their potential for abuse, potential for addiction, and accepted medical use(s). The classification of drugs is administered jointly by the Department of Justice and the Food and Drug Administration (FDA).

Coroner—An officer who holds inquests regarding violent, sudden, or unexplained deaths. Coroners in the United States may be elected officials who are finders of fact or they may be physicians. In the latter case, they are usually called medical examiners. The name is derived from "crown," because coroners in medieval England were minor officials of the Crown.

Ethics—The rules or principles governing right conduct. The term is also used to refer to the branch of philosophy that studies these rules.

Expert witness—A person called to appear in court in order to explain certain facts or points of information relevant to the case that lie outside the general knowledge of most nonspecialists.

Fee splitting—Accepting payment for referring patients to another physician.

Forensic—Referring to legal or courtroom matters.

Impairment—A condition of incompetence to practice medicine resulting from a physical injury or disease, psychiatric disorder, or substance abuse.

Liability—The state or condition of being legally responsible for an act or event.

Medical malpractice—Intentional abandonment of duty or failure to exercise medical skill on the part of a physician rendering services that results in loss, injury, or damage.

Negligence—Failure to perform one's professional duties according to an accepted standard of care.

Perjury—The making of verifiably false statements under oath in a court of law.

Respondeat superior—The legal principle that holds an employer responsible for the actions of employees performed in the course of employment.

Tort—A wrongful act against another person or property that results in harm. Torts are considered civil cases and are settled by common law (court decisions) rather than by statutory law.

associations (IPAs). Large group practices of over 100 physicians are no longer unusual.

• Professional corporation. Professional corporations for physicians were made possible by changes in state legislation in the 1960s. The physicians who participate in the corporation become shareholders and are eligible for fringe benefits such as disability insurance or profit-sharing arrangements. Another advantage of forming a corporation for many physicians is that members are protected from losing their individual assets if the corporation is sued.

Education and training

Because of the increasingly complex network of regulations and other legal considerations surrounding the practice of medicine, a number of medical schools in the United States and Canada now offer or require courses in law as part of the course work for the MD degree. Many medical schools in the United States required students to take a course in medical jurisprudence or offer the subject as part of an existing required course. Other schools offer courses in health

law as electives. One law professor states that at the minimum level, all medical students should acquire a familiarity with laws that affect their patients and those that affect their relationships with their patients. In addition, she maintains that courses offered jointly to law and medical students are helpful in helping students in both fields come to a clearer understanding of the patterns of reasoning and analysis used by members of the other profession.

A growing number of physicians choose earn a second degree in law. The American College of Legal Medicine (ACLM) was founded in 1960 to meet the growing demand for interprofessional cooperation as well as better understanding of medico-legal issues among attorneys as well as physicians. Seventeen medical schools in the United States and Canada offer joint MD/JD programs. These programs typically take six years to complete. The usual pattern for joint degree programs consists of two years of preclinical course work at the medical school, followed by two years of courses in the law school and completed by two years of clinical rotations at the medical school. MD/JD programs are particularly attractive to four groups of students:

- Those interested in a career in government healthcare policy
- Those who wish to serve on the executive board of a hospital
- Those who wish to specialize in forensic medicine
- Those who want to practice law with a focus on medical issues

Resources

BOOKS

Allen, James. *Health Law and Medical Ethics.* Upper Saddle River, NJ: Prentice Hall, 2012.

Herring, Jonathan. *Medical Law and Ethics,* 4th ed. New York, NY: Oxford, 2012.

Hester, D. Micah., and Toby Schonfeld., eds. *Guidance for Healthcare Ethics Committees.* New York, NY: Cambridge University Press, 2012.

PERIODICALS

Feldman, Yuval, Gauthier, Rebecca L., and Schuler, Troy H. "Curbing Misconduct in the Pharmaceutical Industry: Insights from Behavioral Ethics and the Behavioral Approach to Law." *American Journal of Law and Medicine* 14 no. 3 (2013).

Hasday, Lisa R. "The Hippocratic Oath as Literary Text: A Dialogue Between Law and Medicine." *Yale Journal of Health Policy, Law, and Ethics* 2 no. 2 (2013): 4.

Penn, C. L. "The Law of Medicine: Mitchell Blackstock Ivers Sneddon, PLLC: A Closer Look at the Medical Society's Legal Counsel." *The Journal of the Arkansas Medical Society* 109 no. 5 (2012): 80.

ORGANIZATIONS

American Bar Association, 321 N. Clark St., Chicago, IL 60654-7598, (800) 285-2221, www.abanet.org.

American College of Legal Medicine, Two Woodfield Lake, 1100 E. Woodfield Road, Suite 350, Schaumburg, IL 60173, (800) 969-0283, www.aclm.org.

American Medical Association, 515 N. State Street, Chicago, IL 60610, (800) 621-8335, http://www.ama-assn.org.

National Board of Medical Examiners, 3750 Market Street, Philadelphia, PA 19104, (215) 590-9500, http://www.nbme.org.

Rebecca J. Frey, Ph.D.
Tish Davidson, AM

Medical Loss Ratio (MLR)

Definition

The Medical Loss Ratio (MLR) is the percentage of overall premium revenues that insurance companies spend on medical costs and activities to improve healthcare quality. Under the **Patient Protection and Affordable Care Act** of 2010 (ACA), insurers who do not meet minimum MLR standards for a given year must provide financial rebates to their policyholders.

Description

Also known as the 80/20 rule, MLR is a financial measurement first introduced in the Affordable Care Act as part of a large-scale initiative to increase the value and affordability of health insurance in the United States. Commonly referred to as the Affordable Care Act or "Obamacare", the ACA was signed into law on March 23, 2010 and mandates a broad range of reforms to be rolled out over a four-year period.

As part of a series of measures to control healthcare costs and make health insurance more affordable, the MLR provision of the ACA holds insurance companies more accountable for how they spend the fees collected from their policyholders. A significant proportion of these premiums have typically been spent on operating expenses such as administrative costs, marketing, and executive salaries. A 2010 report from the Center for Consumer Information and Insurance Oversight (CCIIO) noted that more than 45 percent of consumers are covered by individual plans that spend at least one-quarter of premium revenues on administrative expenses.

Effective January 1, 2011, insurers are required to report what proportion of premium revenues are spent on medical claims, clinical services, and programs to improve quality of healthcare. Under the ACA, this percentage must exceed 80 percent for individual and small group plans and 85 percent for large employer plans. Insurance companies that do not meet the MLR target for a given year are required to pay a rebate to their policyholders.

MLR requirements and exemptions

MLR is calculated from two key financial measurements: The medical numerator, or the amount insurance companies spend on medical claims and quality improvement activities; and the premium denominator, or total amount of revenues generated from member premiums after certain taxes, fees, and risks have been subtracted. To determine MLR, the medical numerator is divided by the premium denominator.

The ACA outlines several exemptions to the MLR requirement to further protect consumers and ensure consistent access to health coverage. Only fully insured individual and group plans are required to meet minimum MLR criteria; self-insured plans are excluded

KEY TERMS

Medical numerator—The amount insurance companies spend on medical claims and quality improvement activities. Used in calculating the MLR.

Patient Protection and Affordable Care Act (ACA)—Legislation signed into law in 2010 as part of a large-scale initiative to increase the availability, value, and affordability of health insurance in the United States.

Premium—Fees paid to an insurance company in exchange for coverage under a specific insurance plan.

Premium denominator—The total amount of revenues generated by member premiums after certain taxes, fees, and risks have been subtracted. Used in calculating the MLR.

from the requirement. Non-medical plans such as dental or vision are also not included. Additional considerations may be made for small plans, new plans, student health plans, or other unique circumstances.

Why this is important to the consumer

Nearly 9 million Americans were estimated to receive insurance rebates in 2012, with an average rebate of $100 and total returns of $500 million. A study published in *Insurance Journal* reported that the savings conferred to consumers as a result of insurer rebates and reduced administrative costs totaled nearly $1.5 billion for the same time period.

Rebate amounts are calculated based on a policyholder's share of total premium revenues and must be paid by August 1 each year. For both small and large group plans, rebates are usually paid to the employer, who can then determine how to best apply the rebate to its employees; individual policyholders receive rebates directly from the insurance company. Rebates may be paid by check, direct deposit, or a reduction in future premiums.

Resources

BOOKS

Obama, Barack and the 111th Congress. *The Patient Protection and Affordable Care Act.* Dallas, TX: Primedia eLaunch Publishing, 2010.

PERIODICALS

Williams, Claudia, et al. "From the Office of the National Coordinator: The Strategy for Advancing the Exchange of Health Information." *Health Affairs* 31, no. 3 (March 2012): 527–36.

WEBSITES

Center for Consumer Information and Insurance Oversight. "Medical Loss Ratio: Getting Your Money's Worth on Health Insurance." CMS.org. http://www.cms.gov/CCIIO/Resources/Fact-Sheets-and-FAQs/medical-loss-ratio.html (accessed October 20, 2013).

Commonwealth Fund. "Obamacare Medical Loss Ratio Saved $1.5 Billion in 2011: Report." InsuranceJournal.com. http://www.insurancejournal.com/news/national/2012/12/05/272875.htm (accessed October 20, 2013).

HealthCare.gov. "How Does the Health Care Law Protect Me?" HealthCare.gov. http://www.healthcare.gov/how-does-the-health-care-law-protect-me (accessed October 20, 2013).

Young, Jeffrey. "Health Insurance Rebates Sending $500 Million Back To Consumers, Federal Report Says." HuffingtonPost.com. http://www.huffingtonpost.com/2013/06/20/health-insurance-rebates_n_3472978.html (accessed October 20, 2013).

ORGANIZATIONS

Centers for Medicare and Medicaid Services, 7500 Security Blvd., Baltimore, MD 21244, (410) 786-0727, (877) 267-2323, http://www.cms.gov.

Health Resources and Services Administration, 5600 Fishers Ln., Rockville, MD 20857, (888) 275-4772, ask@hrsa.gov, http://www.hrsa.gov.

Stephanie Dionne

▌Medical malpractice lawsuits

Definition

Medical malpractice is a form of tort, a legal term for civil actions that can be brought in cases where the negligence or intentional acts of one person result in injury or other harm to another person. Medical malpractice is a specific tort niche used to define cases in which a doctor or other healthcare provider displays professional negligence and fails to meet his or her medical community's recognized "standard of care," resulting in medical harm to a patient. Medical malpractice can take a variety of forms, including misdiagnosis of illness or condition; careless or improper treatment; delays or total failure in providing treatment; prescribing improper medication or therapeutic interventions; and failure to perform necessary follow-up with patients.

Medical malpractice laws are thus recognized to have two main goals: to provide financial redress to patients or patients' families who have suffered injury as a result of poor medical care, and to provide financial incentives for healthcare professionals and facilities to maintain a high standard of care. Considerable disagreement exists about whether medical malpractice laws, as currently constituted, meet either of these goals.

Description

Medical malpractice is one of the more controversial and emotional subjects swirling around the U.S. healthcare system. Studies indicate that it is both a significant public health issue and a contributor to the steep cost of American health care. But key constituencies, from physicians to attorneys to consumer advocates, have historically found it extremely difficult to arrive at common ground on proposed remedies. In addition, although there is widespread agreement that medical malpractice contributes to overall healthcare costs, researchers and various industry stakeholders are deeply divided about the extent to which it drives up those costs. Some see it as a major factor, while others believe it is only a minor element in the overall **cost of health care**.

U.S. healthcare professionals and organizations provide valuable, life-saving medical interventions to millions of Americans every year. However, errors in treatment do occur. The exact number of deaths that occur every year from medical malpractice is impossible to determine. A 1999 report by the **Institute of Medicine** estimated the number of iatrogenic deaths at about 98,000 annually. Other researchers have placed the figure higher, at more than 200,000 each year. If these latter figures are correct, deaths from unnecessary or botched surgeries, infections incurred in hospitals, medication errors, and other mistakes by healthcare providers would make medical negligence the third-leading cause of death in the United States, behind only heart disease and cancer. The number of illnesses or health complications stemming from poor medical care is even harder to quantify, but analysts believe that medical errors that result in temporary or even chronic health conditions are far more commonplace than patient deaths from iatrogenic factors.

The Financial Cost of Malpractice

Medical malpractice has economic consequences as well. Payouts to plaintiffs in medical malpractice cases exceeded $3 billion in 2012. Medical malpractice lawsuits also cost healthcare systems and healthcare professionals money in two other ways. The first is malpractice insurance coverage. The malpractice premiums paid by doctors and other healthcare providers can be quite high, and it is not uncommon for some

specialists, such as surgeons and obstetricians, to shoulder policies that cost them more than $100,000 annually. The comparatively high cost of their policies stems from the fact that they practice higher-risk procedures and are more likely to be sued. Many healthcare professionals have stated that their malpractice insurance premiums are so high that they have no choice but to pass on some of this operating expense on to their patients. Some have even stopped performing certain procedures or services because of associated insurance premium costs.

Medical malpractice cases also increase overall costs in the healthcare system because they encourage healthcare providers to practice what is known as "defensive medicine." This term refers to diagnostic tests and treatment procedures that doctors order to protect themselves from litigation rather than because they are medically justified. Health policy experts say that these unnecessary tests not only add billions of dollars to medical bills, they may also have the ironic effect of *worsening* treatment outcomes for some patients. After all, they explain, every additional test, procedure, or drug increases the risk—however slightly—of an adverse drug reaction, a post-operative infection, or some other health problem for a patient.

In 2010 a *Health Affairs* overview of tort reform in the field of health care reported that defensive medicine practices and other efforts to reduce medical liability exposure cost nearly $56 billion in 2008, about 2.4% of total health care spending. Other studies differ on the severity of the defensive medicine problem, with some indicating that it accounts for as much as 8–10% of total healthcare spending, and others estimating that it accounts for less than 1%. Tellingly, surveys of physicians and other healthcare providers who are the main targets of medical malpractice lawsuits indicate that they operate under the belief that defensive medicine accounts for 30% or more of annual healthcare costs in the United States.

Proposed Malpractice Reforms

Most medical malpractice lawsuits in the United States are governed by state rather than federal laws, even though doctors and other stakeholders involved in the provision of healthcare have been urging federal tort reform in this area since the 1970s. These calls for federal laws that would curb their impact intensified in the late 1970s and 1980s, when malpractice litigation cases, financial awards to patients, and malpractice insurance premiums all surged skyward. The American Medical Association (AMA) and other healthcare provider organizations attributed this jump to unrealistic patient expectations and the greed of personal injury lawyers. Consumer advocate groups and the American Bar Association (ABA) rejected these claims. They laid the blame at the feet of careless, corner-cutting hospitals and medical specialists.

Since the late 1980s, Democrats and Republicans in Washington have repeatedly tried to pass reforms that would reduce medical malpractice lawsuits and improve patient safety and health. All of these efforts have thus far become mired in partisan gridlock, though, in large part because the healthcare industry is a big supporter of the Republican Party, and lawyers are an important constituency for the Democratic Party.

The reform proposals floated by groups and lawmakers who feel that medical malpractice lawsuits are out of control typically include some blend of the following, many of which have been adopted by individual states:

- Caps on financial damages

- Creation of special "health courts" to adjudicate malpractice claims and toss out "frivolous" complaints

- Establishment of special statutes of limitations on malpractice filings

- Heightened expert witness requirements

- Sliding scale of attorney fees in malpractice cases.

Supporters of these reforms argue that they will not only reduce the cost of health care, they will ultimately improve patient safety. Proponents assert that if the threat of crippling malpractice awards is reduced, healthcare providers will become more transparent in discussing strategies for reducing medical error with one another.

Legal and consumer groups remain adamantly opposed to these changes to tort law. They argue that caps on financial awards for medical errors have the greatest impact on precisely those patients who suffer most egregiously from medical negligence. Critics say that these proposed reforms would also unfairly shift the burden of paying for catastrophic medical errors from responsible doctors, hospitals, and other healthcare providers to public programs, like **Medicaid** or **Medicare**, that are supported by American taxpayers. Finally, they say that the medical profession has never shown much interest in holding members responsible for negligent behavior or actions. In light of such inaction, say consumer and legal groups, malpractice lawsuits (or the threat thereof) provide an important incentive for medical practitioners to carry out their duties and provide care to the absolute best of their abilities.

KEY TERMS

Iatrogenic—Illness or other adverse health impact resulting from medical treatment.

Liability—Financial obligation or debt.

Premium—Amount paid for insurance coverage.

Tort—The civil branch of U.S. law that addresses accidental and intentional injuries to people or property.

A 2009 tort reform analysis by the nonpartisan Congressional Budget Office (CBO) provided comfort to both sides. The CBO estimated that if the United States were to introduce damage caps and other tort reforms favored by the AMA on a nationwide basis, they would only reduce total U.S. healthcare spending by about 0.5% (0.2% from lower insurance premiums and 0.3% from reductions in defensive medicine). These percentages are much lower than the claims made by most proponents of tort reform. On the other hand, the CBO concluded that even these savings would reduce total national healthcare spending by about $41 billion over the next decade—a considerable sum in an era when the long-term financial viability of programs like Medicare and Medicaid is under close scrutiny.

Why this is important to the consumer

Considerable disagreement exists about whether medical malpractice lawsuits are a positive or negative force in terms of healthcare quality and healthcare costs. Although a political consensus to make significant tort changes at the federal level remains elusive, individual states continue to revise and update their own medical liability laws. Any and all such revisions are relevant to healthcare consumers because they involve trade-offs. In states that have placed AMA-endorsed restrictions on the legal liability of primary care and specialty physicians, nurses, and hospitals, for example, patients who are the victims of medical negligence have only limited recourse to financial compensation for their injuries and suffering. Supporters of tort reform say, though, that these same liability restrictions may contribute to lower-priced healthcare services for consumers in the state. Advocates of tort reform also say that states that reduce the legal vulnerability of surgeons, obstetricians, and other healthcare specialists also are more attractive to those specialists, ultimately resulting in a greater choice of doctors for healthcare consumers.

Resources

BOOKS

Sloan, Frank A., and Lindsey M. Chepke. *Medical Malpractice*. Cambridge, MA: MIT Press, 2008.

PERIODICALS

Colchamiro, Eric. "Understanding the legislative and regulatory climate for medical errors." *Physician Executive* (November-December 2012): 61.

Fleeter, Thomas B. "Pearls and pitfalls in medical liability lawsuits: plaintiff and defense attorneys answer commonly asked questions." *AAOS Now* (2012): 38.

Gupta, Sanjay. "More Treatment, More Mistakes." *New York Times,* July 31, 2012. http://www.nytimes.com/2012/08/01/opinion/more-treatment-more-mistakes.html?_r=0 (accessed August 31, 2013).

Hyman, Chris Stern, et al. "Interest-based mediation of medical malpractice lawsuits: a route to improved patient safety?" *Journal of Health Politics, Policy and Law* (October 2010): 797-828.

Mello, M.M., et al. "National Costs of the Medical Liability System." *Health Affairs* 29, no. 9 (September 2010): 1569-1577.

WEBSITES

Kaiser Family Foundation. "Medical Malpractice Policy." KaiserEdu.org. http://www.kaiseredu.org/Issue-Modules/Medical-Malpractice-Policy/Background-Brief.aspx (accessed August 31, 2013).

ORGANIZATIONS

American Bar Association (ABA), 321 North Clark Street, Chicago, IL 60654, (312) 988-5000, http://www.americanbar.org.

American Medical Association (AMA), 330 North Wabash Ave., Ste. 39300, Chicago, IL 60611-5885, (312) 464-5000, http://www.ama-assn.org.

Kevin Hillstrom

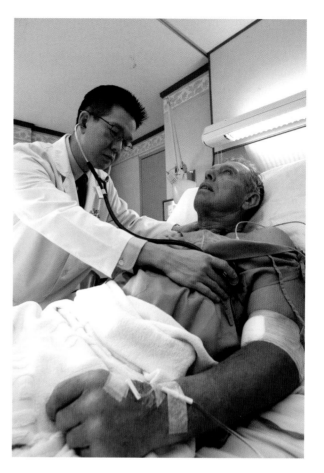

A Thai cardiologist examines a Norwegian patient at the cardiology ward of Bumrungrad International Hospital in Bangkok, Thailand. Of the one million patients each year at Bumrungrad, nearly 50 percent are foreigners, mostly medical tourists from the United States. *(AFP/Getty Images)*

Medical tourism

Definition

Medical tourism refers to the practice of seeking health care—most often elective surgical procedures—outside one's own country. It is also known as "health tourism," "medical travel,"and "global health care." In the past, the term was usually applied to wealthy or famous people from less-developed countries traveling to the United States, Canada, or Western Europe for surgery or other treatments not available in their homelands. More recently, however, medical tourism also refers to people from the developed countries traveling to less-developed parts of the world for elective procedures.

Medical tourism should not be confused with travel medicine, which is a medical specialty that deals with the prevention of disease and the treatment of medical emergencies in international travelers.

Description

Medical tourism has become a multibillion-dollar industry since the early 2000s, facilitated by the speed and relative affordability of international travel; the ease and widespread availability of Internet communication; improvements in the medical technology, technical skill of medical personnel, and standards of care in many foreign countries; and the emergence of international bodies that inspect and accredit hospitals. The **Joint Commission International** (JCI) is a subgroup of the **Joint**

Commission (formerly the Joint Commission on Accreditation of Healthcare Organizations or JCAHO), a nonprofit organization based in the United States that develops standards of patient care and safety that hospitals must meet in order to be certified. The JCI has accredited hospitals outside the United States since 1999, and hospitals in other countries often seek JCI accreditation in order to attract American medical tourists. Other international accrediting bodies include Accreditation Canada, La Haute Autorité de Santé (HAS) in France, and the Australian Council for Healthcare Standards International (ACHSI).

It is difficult to obtain accurate statistics in regard to medical tourism, in that the industry is highly competitive. Over 50 countries worldwide regard medical tourism as a national industry as of 2013, and medical tourism providers tend to exaggerate the numbers of persons they serve, in order to attract new patients. One contributor to *International Medical Travel Journal*, an online publication, noted in late 2012 that the numbers of medical tourists are often inflated by counting ordinary vacationers who need medical assistance, diplomats, foreign students, business travelers, military personnel, foreign nationals who are living in but not citizens of the country, visitors to health spas, and long-term expatriates. The **Centers for Disease Control and Prevention (CDC)** reports that estimates of the number of American medical tourists vary from 66,000 per year to 750,000, depending on the definition of "medical tourism" and the method of calculation.

There are five major reasons why consumers may choose medical tourism:

• To save money on elective procedures. Many medical tourism providers point out that the price of elective surgeries in the United States is high because of the costs imposed on doctors and hospitals by health insurance and government paperwork on the one hand, and malpractice insurance on the other. Hospitals and physicians abroad can charge lower fees because they do not incur these regulatory and legal costs. One study completed in 2012 estimated that the United States lost between $1.3 and $2 billion in 2005 alone to just two countries, India and Thailand, for only three procedures (hip replacement, knee replacement, and coronary artery bypass) because of inefficiencies in the U.S. health care system. By 2011, the estimated loss had risen to $20 to $30 billion because of the growing popularity of medical tourism.

• To avoid long waiting times for elective procedures. This consideration is often mentioned by Canadians and citizens of the United Kingdom, whose health systems require people to wait several months, or even years, for non-urgent procedures like hip replacement or cataract surgery.

• To have procedures that are not covered by the patient's present health insurance.

• To obtain access to procedures that are considered experimental or are not performed in the person's home country. Stem cell therapies are one type of experimental treatment that is growing rapidly in popularity as a reason for medical tourism.

• To spend some time either before or after the procedure, sightseeing in the destination country.

As of 2013, the most common elective procedures sought by medical tourists from the United States are cosmetic surgery; dental work; cardiac surgery; knee and hip replacement; other types of orthopedic surgery; and fertility or assisted reproductive services, including surrogate pregnancy. The most popular destinations at present for American medical tourists are Thailand, Mexico, Singapore, India, Malaysia, Cuba, Brazil, Argentina, Panama, and Costa Rica.

Why this is important to the consumer

Financial considerations

Although surgical procedures abroad may cost less than in the United States (for example, a liver transplant costing $300,000 in the United States is performed for $91,000 in Taiwan), a prospective medical tourist must take into consideration the costs involved in working with a medical tourism provider—an organization that acts as an intermediary between the patient and the foreign hospital or clinic. Sometimes called a "medical concierge service," the medical tourism provider generally requests medical information from the patient, including the long-term medical history and diagnosis as well as the desired treatment. The information is then shared with the company's medical consultant, who offers advice regarding the patient's fitness for travel and the appropriateness of the desired procedure. If the consultant approves the patient for treatment abroad, American-based medical tourism providers usually provide a **case manager** in the United States, who draws up a list of possible destinations for the treatment, travel dates, facilities abroad, hotel choices, visa or passport requirements, and similar matters. A price is then quoted. If the patient agrees with the price estimate, he or she then signs a contract with the medical tourism provider, who will then book the designated surgeon, hospital or clinic, and local hotel. When the tourist arrives at the destination, he or she is met by a destination program manager to assist with language issues and cultural differences. After the tourist returns home, the American case manager is available to help with any remaining problems or questions. In any case, consumers should recognize that at least some of the savings from the cost of the operation itself will be spent to cover the services of the medical tourism provider and out-of-pocket costs incurred during the stay in the destination country.

American insurance companies and hospitals have responded in several ways to the loss of income to foreign health care providers. In recent years, some American health insurance companies have entered the field of medical tourism, and some employers who offer health insurance to their employees have suggested surgery abroad for elective procedures in order to cut costs. Other employers have offered to pay for air travel and out-of-pocket expenses if the employee chooses surgery outside the United States; and at least two Blue Cross Blue Shield programs have entered into medical tourism agreements with certified hospitals in Mexico, Thailand, Singapore, Turkey, Ireland, Costa Rica, and India. Lastly, several American university-related medical centers—in particular Johns Hopkins, Harvard, and Duke—have developed joint initiatives with hospitals in Dubai and Singapore in order to encourage American medical tourists to consider these hospitals as destinations.

Time considerations

Medical tourism demands a considerable time commitment as well as a significant monetary outlay. Most medical tourism providers recommend allowing a minimum of 30 to 45 days from the time the patient begins the process of working with the tourism provider until he or she travels to the destination hospital or clinic; the **CDC** also recommends six weeks for planning and travel preparation.

Medical tourists must also allow time to recuperate after the procedure; the Aerospace Medical Association states that patients who have traveled abroad for thoracic or abdominal surgery should wait for at least 10 days after the operation to fly, as the pressurized air in an airplane cabin increases the risks of a pulmonary embolus or deep vein thrombosis. Similarly, the American Society of Plastic Surgeons (ASPS) advises patients who have had laser treatments or cosmetic surgery of the face, nose, or eyelids to wait 7 to 10 days before traveling by air.

Health considerations

One major risk to health involved in medical tourism is the possibility of contracting an infectious disease that is rare in the United States but is endemic or more commonly encountered abroad, such as malaria, tuberculosis, HIV infection, methicillin-resistant staphylococcal infections, influenza, hepatitis A, and typhoid fever. In addition, the patient's body will be weakened by the stress of travel and surgery, and thus more susceptible to infection. Some countries have considerably lower standards of postoperative care than American and European patients are accustomed to.

Persons considering medical tourism should consult the International Association for Medical Assistance to Travelers (IAMAT), which has downloadable information about specific infectious diseases on its website; or the CDC's *Yellow Book: CDC Health Information for International Travel*, which is published every two years and contains information about required immunizations and health dangers in specific countries. The 2012 edition of the *Yellow Book* is available online at the CDC website.

Several major American medical organizations, including the American Dental Organization (ADA), the American Society of Plastic Surgeons (ASPS), and the American Medical Association (AMA), have published guidelines and safety checklists for persons considering surgery or other procedures abroad. URLs for these documents are listed under resources below, and the checklists are also reproduced at the CDC web page for medical tourism listed below. These documents include the types of questions that prospective medical tourists should consider when selecting a health care destination abroad.

Legal and ethical considerations

Legal considerations are another important factor in the decision to seek health care abroad. Most other countries allow only limited litigation in the event of malpractice or an unsatisfactory outcome; moreover, many medical tourism providers ask patients to sign a document stating that they will not sue the foreign hospital or clinic if they are dissatisfied with the treatment received. In addition, medical tourists usually have to pay out of pocket for follow-up care if complications develop after they return home.

Ethical issues should also be kept in mind. In some countries, such as India and Thailand, medical tourists have a major impact on the health services available to the local population. Some physicians and public health experts in these countries have expressed concern that the rapid influx of medical tourists from the West has worsened the scarcity of health care for the inhabitants of low-income countries. Other observers have argued that wealthy countries should adopt

KEY TERMS

Embolus—The medical term for any solid, liquid, or gaseous mass that can travel through the bloodstream and block a blood vessel.

Medical tourism provider—A group or organization that acts as an intermediary between the prospective patient and the foreign physician, hospital, or clinic. Such providers are also known as "medical concierge services."

Organ trafficking—The illegal trade in organs for transplantation, often involving the kidnapping, coercion, or deception of people for the purpose of organ removal and exploitation.

Travel medicine—A medical specialty that focuses on preventing injuries, medical emergencies, and the spread of infectious diseases among international travelers. It should not be confused with medical tourism.

public policies to curb the demand of their citizens for medical services abroad at the expense of the poor in the destination countries.

Another major ethical concern is organ transplantation. The practice of "transplant tourism," or travel for the purpose of receiving an organ purchased from an unrelated donor for transplant, has led to organ trafficking; a few countries permit the sale of one's own organs for profit, and China still procures organs for transplantation from executed prisoners. In 2008, the **World Health Organization (WHO)** and several leading international transplant societies issued the *Declaration of Istanbul on Organ Trafficking and Transplant Tourism* in an effort to protect the poorest citizens in developing countries from transplant tourism. Although government regulations worldwide have been tightened following the Istanbul declaration to prevent illegal trade in organs for transplantation, it is estimated that about 11% of all transplants still involve illegally obtained organs. The lengthy median waiting times for organ transplants—over three years in the United States alone—unfortunately encourage transplant tourism. As the CDC notes, however, there are several additional problems to consider before receiving a transplanted organ abroad: the donor and place of donation may lack proper documentation; the foreign facility is likely to use fewer immunosuppressive drugs than is currently the practice in the United States; and the patient might not receive adequate antibiotic prophylaxis (preventive treatment).

Resources

BOOKS

Centers for Disease Control and Prevention (CDC). *The Yellow Book: CDC Health Information for International Travel 2014.* New York: Oxford University Press, 2013.

Connell, John. *Medical Tourism.* Cambridge, MA: CABI, 2011.

Hall, Michael, ed. *Medical Tourism: The Ethics, Regulation, and Marketing of Health Mobility.* New York: Routledge, 2013.

Hodges, Jill R., Leigh Turner, and Ann Marie Kimball, eds. *Risks and Challenges in Medical Tourism: Understanding the Global Market for Health Services.* Santa Barbara, CA: Praeger, 2012.

PERIODICALS

Chen, Y.Y., and C.M. Flood. "Medical Tourism's Impact on Health Care Equity and Access in Low- and Middle-income Countries: Making the Case for Regulation." *Journal of Law, Medicine and Ethics* 41 (Spring 2013): 286–300.

Danovitch, Gabriel M., et al. "Organ Trafficking and Transplant Tourism: The Role of Global Professional Ethical Standards—The 2008 Declaration of Istanbul." *Transplantation* 95 (June 15, 2013): 1306–1312.

Davis, X.M., et al. "International Travelers as Sentinels for Sustained Influenza Transmission during the 2009 Influenza A(H1N1)pdm09 Pandemic." *Journal of Travel Medicine* 20 (May-June 2013): 177–184.

Einsiedel, E.F., and H. Adamson. "Stem Cell Tourism and Future Stem Cell Tourists: Policy and Ethical Implications." *Developing World Bioethics* 12 (April 2012): 35–44.

Gan, L.L., and J.R. Frederick. "Medical Tourists: Who Goes and What Motivates Them?" *Health Marketing Quarterly* 30, no. 2 (2013): 177–194.

Kumar, S., et al. "Globalization of Health Care Delivery in the United States through Medical Tourism." *Journal of Health Communication* 17 (February 2012): 177–198.

McGuire, M.F. "International Accreditation of Ambulatory Surgical Centers and Medical Tourism." *Clinics in Plastic Surgery* 40 (July 2013): 493–498.

Shetty, P. "India's Unregulated Surrogacy Industry." *Lancet* 380 (November 10, 2012): 1633–1634.

Turner, L. "Making Canada a Destination for Medical Tourists: Why Canadian Provinces Should Not Try to Become 'Mayo Clinics of the North.'" *Healthcare Policy* 7 (May 2012): 18–25.

Youngman, Ian. "Those Medical Tourism Numbers . . . Revisited." *International Medical Travel Journal,* December 2012. Available online at http://www.imtjonline.com/articles/2012/medical-tourism-statistics-30151/ (accessed July 27, 2013).

WEBSITES

American Dental Association (ADA). "Dental Care Away from Home." http://www.ada.org/371.aspx (accessed July 29, 2013).

American Medical Association (AMA). "New AMA Guidelines on Medical Tourism." http://www.

ama-assn.org/ama1/pub/upload/mm/31/medical tourism.pdf (accessed July 29, 2013).

American Society of Plastic Surgeons (ASPS). "Cosmetic Surgery Tourism Briefing Paper." http://www.plastic surgery.org/news-and-resources/briefing-papers/ cosmetic-surgery-tourism.html (accessed July 29, 2012).

Centers for Disease Control and Prevention (CDC). *The Yellow Book 2012*, Chapter 2, "Medical Tourism." http://wwwnc.cdc.gov/travel/yellowbook/2012/chapter-2-the-pre-travel-consultation/medical-tourism (accessed July 28, 2013).

International Association for Medical Assistance to Travelers (IAMAT). "How To ... Know Travel Medicine from Medical Travel." http://www.iamat.org/pdf/elibrary/ Travel%20Medicine%20and%20Medical%20Travel. pdf (accessed July 29, 2013).

ORGANIZATIONS

American Dental Association (ADA), 211 East Chicago Ave., Chicago, IL, United States 60611-2678, (312) 440-2500, http://www.ada.org/.

American Society of Plastic Surgeons (ASPS), 444 E. Algonquin Rd., Arlington Heights, IL, United States 60005, (847) 228-9900, http://www.plasticsurgery.org/.

Centers for Disease Control and Prevention (CDC), 1600 Clifton Rd., Atlanta, GA, United States 30333, (800) CDC-INFO (232-4636), http://www.cdc.gov/cdc-info/ requestform.html, www.cdc.gov.

International Association for Medical Assistance to Travelers (IAMAT), 1623 Military Rd., #279, Niagara Falls, NY, United States 14304-1745, (716) 754-4883, http://www.iamat.org/contact.cfm, http://www.iamat. org/index.cfm.

Joint Commission International (JCI), 1515 West 22nd Street, Suite 1300W, Oak Brook, IL, United States 60523, (630) 268-4800 (accreditation), http:// www.jointcommissioninternational.org/.

Rebecca J. Frey, Ph.D.

Medicare

Definition

Medicare is a federal health insurance program in the United States. It is only available to adults aged 65 and older and some younger people with certain disabilities. It is one of the largest health insurance programs in the United States.

Purpose

Medicare is the healthcare lifeline for the majority of senior citizens. It is available to almost all Americans over age 65, regardless of income or medical history; however, in 2012, 50% of all Medicare recipients had annual incomes of less than $22,000. Furthermore, 50% of all Medicare beneficiaries had less than $78,000 in personal savings; thus, medical bills for one serious illness could potentially wipe out their retirement funds.

Demographics

As of 2013, Medicare covered more than 50 million people in the United States. That number is increasing rapidly, with rising life expectancies and with approximately 10,000 U.S. baby boomers turning age 65 each day. Along with an aging population, the prevalence of chronic conditions and risk factors for chronic conditions, such as obesity and type 2 diabetes, is increasing among Medicare recipients. Of all Medicare recipients, approximately:

- 40% suffer from three or more chronic conditions
- 27% are in fair or poor health
- 23% have cognitive or other mental impairments
- 15% have at least two limitations in activities of daily life
- 13% are over age 85
- 5% are residents of long-term care facilities Therefore, the demand for Medicare-covered healthcare services is rising rapidly.

Most Americans aged 65 and older are eligible for Medicare. Those under age 65 who receive Social Security Disability Insurance (SSDI) payments are generally eligible for Medicare following a two-year waiting period. This latter population accounts for 17% of Medicare recipients and is included in the 20% of Medicare recipients who are also eligible for **Medicaid**. Patients diagnosed with end-stage renal disease (ESRD) or amyotrophic lateral sclerosis (ALS) are eligible for Medicare immediately upon diagnosis. People in some of these and certain other categories are automatically enrolled in Medicare as soon as they become eligible.

Description

Medicare eligibility is not based on income or assets, although premiums and co-payments may be based on income and assets. People can only enroll in Medicare or change their Medicare coverage at specific times during the year.

There are four distinct Medicare programs, and they have different costs associated with them:

- Medicare Part A, also called Original Medicare, is hospital insurance that covers inpatient hospital stays, short-term stays in a skilled nursing facility, some home health care, and hospice care for the terminally ill. Enrollment in Part A is usually automatic. Although most people do not pay Part A premiums because they or their spouses paid payroll taxes while working, Part A medical expenses are subject to deductibles and to other insurance.

- Medicare Part B is medical insurance that covers visits to physicians and other healthcare providers, outpatient services, preventive care, home health visits, durable medical equipment, and some physical and occupational therapies. Enrollment in Part B is optional and requires payment of a monthly premium. In 2013, most people paid just over $100 per month for Part B, with a $147 annual deductible. People with higher incomes may pay more for Medicare Part B.

- Medicare Part C, or Medicare Advantage Plans, are for beneficiaries enrolled in a private health plan, such as a health maintenance organization (HMO), who receive all of their Part A and Part B benefits through Part C. Private Medicare Advantage and other private Medicare plans must provide at least the same coverage as Medicare Parts A and B. They may offer various types of extra coverage, such as vision and dental, and most of them include Medicare prescription drug coverage (Part D). In 2012, 27% of all beneficiaries were enrolled in a Medicare Advantage program. Medicare Advantage Plans set their own rules and payments, including Part B premiums and additional premiums for other covered services.

- Medicare Part D is an optional, subsidized, outpatient prescription drug benefit, and also includes additional subsidies for low-income beneficiaries with only modest assets. Drug benefits are provided either through a Medicare Advantage drug plan or a private, stand-alone drug plan. There is a monthly premium for Part D.

Origins

Medicare was created by the 1965 Social Security Act, which also established Medicaid. It was expanded in 1972 to cover people younger than 65 with permanent disabilities and people with permanent kidney failure who need dialysis or a kidney transplant. Medicare Part C or **Medicare Advantage** was established in 1997. Part D, the prescription drug benefit, was added in 2003. Although originally administered by the Social Security Administration, Medicare is now administered by the **Centers for Medicare and Medicaid Services (CMS)**, within the U.S. **Department of Health and Human Services (HHS)**.

The **Patient Protection and Affordable Care Act** (ACA) of 2010 (also called "Obamacare") brought about further changes to Medicare, including enhanced benefits, such as free preventive services, and the phasing out of the Part D coverage gap, the so-called "**donut hole**." The ACA also instituted changes in the delivery of services and payments to Medicare providers and ramped up efforts to reduce **Medicaid/Medicare fraud, abuse**, and waste.

Medicare costs

General federal government revenues and payroll tax contributions each cover approximately 40% of Medicare costs. Monthly premiums paid by beneficiaries cover 13% of the costs. Individuals with higher incomes pay higher Part B and Part D premiums. Furthermore, in 2013, the Medicare payroll tax for high-income taxpayers increased by 0.9%. In addition to the increase in the elderly population, Medicare costs are affected by rising healthcare costs, which include increased services and expensive medical technologies. Therefore, Medicare costs are expected to continue to rise at a rapid rate, and, as of 2013, Medicare Part A was expected to run out of money by 2024.

Medicare spending in 2012 was $551 billion, accounting for 16% of total federal spending and 21% of total healthcare spending in the United States. Medicare spending in 2012 was allocated as follows:

- 26% for hospital inpatient services and 5% for skilled nursing facilities under Part A
- 13% for physician payments and 6% for hospital outpatient services under Part B
- 13% for other services and 4% for home health care under Parts A and B
- 23% for Part C Medicare Advantage
- 10% for Part D outpatient prescription drugs

Medicare has relatively high deductibles and patient cost-sharing, with no limit on out-of-pocket expenses, and the Part D "donut hole" gap in coverage will continue until 2020. Most Medicare recipients have more out-of-pocket health care expenses than people covered by private insurance. In 2010, healthcare costs, including Medicare premiums and other insurance premiums, accounted for 15% of expenses in Medicare-covered households, compared to 5% of expenses in other households. Furthermore, most people who do not sign up for Parts B and D when they first become eligible for Medicare pay a late enrollment fee if they sign up at a later time. However, people with low incomes and limited resources may receive help from their state in paying for Medicare Parts A, B, and D. About 20% of all Medicare beneficiaries—those with low incomes and

Affordable Care Act (ACA)—The Patient Protection and Affordable Care Act ("Obamacare"); signed into law by President Barack Obama in March of 2010, the ACA overhauled the U.S. healthcare system, including major changes to Medicare.

Centers for Medicare & Medicaid Services (CMS)—The division within the U.S. Department of Health and Human Services that administers Medicare and Medicaid.

Co-payment—The amount that an insured individual pays out-of-pocket for healthcare services.

Deductible—The amount that an insured person is required to pay on each claim or over the course of a year.

Medicaid—Government-financed health insurance for low-income Americans that is administered by individual states.

Medicare Part A—Original Medicare; hospitalization insurance that is provided for free to most Americans aged 65 and older.

Medicare Part B—Health insurance that pays for some services not covered by Medicare Part A

and that requires recipients to pay a monthly premium.

Medicare Part C—Also known as Medicare Advantage Plans; private healthcare plans that include all Medicare Part A and Part B benefits and usually some additional benefits.

Medicare Part D—An optional, subsidized, outpatient prescription drug benefit provided through a private insurer.

Medigap—Supplemental healthcare insurance policies that cover services not included in Medicare.

Premium—The amount paid by a beneficiary for insurance coverage, usually on a monthly basis.

Prescription drug "donut hole"—The coverage gap in Medicare Part D that requires participants to pay all of their annual prescription drug costs that fall between approximately $3,000 and $5,000 annually.

Social Security Disability Insurance (SSDI)—A federal program that pays benefits and provides Medicare to disabled workers under age 65.

modest assets—receive help paying for Medicare premiums and cost sharing, as well as receiving full Medicaid benefits, including long-term care.

The ACA aims to reduce Medicare spending, primarily by reducing overpayments to private Medicare plans. However, the insurance companies that operate these plans have lobbied hard to hold on to their relatively high payments from the federal government. The ACA has instituted a payroll tax for higher-income earners and will charge higher Medicare premiums for higher-income recipients, reduce payments to Medicare providers, and attempt to slow the overall growth in Medicare spending. Nevertheless, Medicare spending is expected to increase to more than $1 trillion by 2022. Per-capita Medicare spending, however, is expected to grow at a rate of 3.6% per year, which is less than the per-person growth in private health insurance spending.

Medicare gaps

Medicare does not cover many facets of health care that the elderly and disabled require, including long-term care and dental services. Thus, most Medicare beneficiaries have some form of **supplemental**

insurance to cover gaps and cost sharing. Although about one-third of Medicare beneficiaries have employer-sponsored supplemental coverage for retirees, the percentage of employers that offer retiree health benefits dropped from 66% in 1988 to 25% in 2012, and this trend is expected to continue. Beneficiaries who have only Medicare Part A may choose to buy Medicare Supplement Insurance or Medigap from a private company. People with Medicare Part C cannot purchase **Medigap insurance**. Approximately one-quarter of Medicare beneficiaries purchase a Medigap plan. In 2009, 12% of Medicare recipients had no supplemental coverage. The majority of those without supplemental coverage were non-elderly disabled recipients, people with incomes at 100%–200% of the poverty level, recipients in rural areas, and African Americans.

Precautions

Many people turn 65 believing that Medicare is free, and they are surprised to learn they have to pay Medicare premiums as well as pay for services and medications not covered by their Medicare plan. Furthermore, while Medicare covers treatments that are considered to be medically necessary for a given disease or condition, Medicare or private Medicare insurers may disagree with patients and physicians over what constitutes medically necessary treatment.

The Medicare system is very complicated, and seniors may be confused about how to choose a Medicare plan. For example, the official 2013 handbook, "Medicare & You," is 140 pages long. The ACA instituted a five-star rating system for Medicare Advantage or Part C plans. However, there were only about 11 five-star plans available in 2013, out of an average of 22 Medicare Advantage plans available in each market of the country.

Another issue with Medicare is that physicians generally view Medicare reimbursement rates as too low. Although most physicians accept some Medicare patients, approximately 20% of all physicians, including 31% of primary care physicians, limit the number of Medicare patients they will accept.

Results

Despite its many problems, Medicare has proved to be both a successful and cost-effective program, providing essential health care for millions of seniors who could otherwise not afford it. Out-of-pocket costs for Medicare remain far lower than private insurance costs for people in the 55–64 age bracket. Studies have found that Medicare beneficiaries have lower health care costs and better access to health care than those with private insurance.

Resources

BOOKS

Altman, Stuart H., and David Shactman. *Power, Politics, and Universal Health Care: The Inside Story of a Century-Long Battle*. Amherst, NY: Prometheus, 2011.

Béland, Daniel, and Alex Waddan. *The Politics of Policy Change: Welfare, Medicare, and Social Security Reform in the United States*. Washington, DC: Georgetown University, 2012.

Lynch, Frederick R. *One Nation Under AARP: The Fight Over Medicare, Social Security, and America's Future*. Berkeley, CA: University of California Press, 2011.

Madrick, Jeff. "Medicare for All." In *The Occupy Handbook*, edited by Janet Byrne and Robin Wells. New York: Back Bay, 2012.

McDonough, John E. *Inside National Health Reform*. Berkeley: University of California, 2011.

Miller, Debra A. *Medicare*. Detroit: Greenhaven, 2013.

Prohaska, Thomas R., and Lynda A. Anderson. *Public Health for an Aging Society*. Baltimore: Johns Hopkins University Press, 2012.

PERIODICALS

Baicher, Katherine, and Helen Levy. "The Insurance Value of Medicare." *New England Journal of Medicine* 367, no. 19 (2012): 1773–75.

Davis, Karen, et al. "Medicare Beneficiaries Less Likely To Experience Cost—and Access-Related Problems than Adults with Private Coverage." *Health Affairs* 31, no. 8 (2012): 1866–75.

Hill, Catey, and Elizabeth O'Brien. ". . . Medicare Won't Tell You." *Wall Street Journal*, March 10, 2013.

Pear, Robert. "Despite Democrats' Warnings, Private Medicare Plans Find Success." *New York Times*, August 26, 2012.

OTHER

American College of Physicians. *Reforming Medicare in the Age of Deficit Reduction*. Policy Paper. Philadelphia: American College of Physicians, 2012. http://www. acponline.org/advocacy/current_policy_papers/assets/ reforming_medicare.pdf (accessed July 22, 2013).

American Hospital Association. "Are Medicare Patients Getting Sicker?" *TrendWatch* (December 2012). http:// www.aha.org/research/reports/tw/12dec-tw-ptacuity. pdf (accessed July 22, 2013).

WEBSITES

"The Affordable Care Act & Medicare." Medicare.gov. http://www.medicare.gov/about-us/affordable-care-act/affordable-care-act.html (accessed July 22, 2013).

American Medical Association. "Medicare and Medicaid." http://www.ama-assn.org/ama/pub/physician-resources/ legal-topics/business-management-topics/medicare-medicaid.page (accessed July 22, 2013).

Center for Medicare Advocacy, Inc. "Medicare Facts & Fiction." http://www.medicareadvocacy.org/medicare-facts-fiction-quick-lessons-to-combat-medicare-spin (accessed July 22, 2013).

Centers for Medicaid & Medicare Services. "Hospital Compare." Medicare.gov. http://www.medicare.gov/ hospitalcompare (accessed July 22, 2013).

Centers for Medicaid & Medicare Services. "Medicare Program—General Information." http://cms.hhs.gov/ Medicare/Medicare-General-Information/Medicare GenInfo/index.html (accessed July 22, 2013).

Kaiser Family Foundation. "Medicare at a Glance." http:// kff.org/medicare/fact-sheet/medicare-at-a-glance-fact-sheet (accessed July 22, 2013).

"Key Features of the Affordable Care Act, By Year." HealthCare.gov. http://kff.org/medicare/fact-sheet/ medicare-at-a-glance-fact-sheet (accessed July 22, 2013).

Medicare Rights Center. "Medicare Answers." http:// www.medicarerights.org/medicare-answers (accessed July 22, 2013).

ORGANIZATIONS

American College of Physicians (ACP), 190 N. Independence Mall West, Philadelphia, PA 19106-1572, (215) 351-2400, (800) 523-1546, http://www.acponline.org.

American Hospital Association, 155 N. Wacker Dr., Chicago, IL 60606, (312) 422-3000, (800) 424-4301, http://www.aha.org.

American Medical Association, 515 N. State St., Chicago, IL 60654, (800) 621-8335, http://www.ama-assn.org.

Center for Medicare Advocacy, P.O. Box 350, Willimantic, CT 06226, (860) 456-7790, Fax: (860) 456-2614, http://www.medicareadvocacy.org.

Centers for Medicare & Medicaid Services, 7500 Security Blvd., Baltimore, MD 21244, (410) 786-3000, (877) 267-2323,TTY: (866) 226-1819, http://www.cms.gov., http://www.medicare.gov.

Kaiser Family Foundation, 2400 Sand Hill Rd., Menlo Park, CA 94025, (650) 854-9400, Fax: (650) 854-4800, http://www.kff.org.

Medicare Rights Center, 520 Eighth Ave., N. Wing, 3rd Fl., New York, NY 10018, (212) 869-3850, (800) 333-4114, Fax: (212) 869-3532, info@medicarerights.org, http://www.medicarerights.org/.

L. Fleming Fallon, Jr., MD, DrPH
Margaret Alic, PhD

Number of Medicare enrollees age 65 and over who enrolled in Part D prescription drug plans or who were claimed for retiree drug subsidy payments, June 2006 and September 2007

Part D benefit categories	June 2006	September 2007
All Medicare enrollees age 65 or over	36,052,991	36,917,978
Enrollees in prescription drug plans	18,245,980	19,747,718
Type of plan		
Stand-alone plan	12,583,676	13,171,983
Medicare Advantage plan	5,662,304	6,575,735
Low income subsidy		
Yes	5,935,532	5,906,610
No	12,310,448	13,841,108
Retiree drug subsidy	6,498,163	6,454,729
Other	11,308,848	10,715,531

SOURCE: Centers for Medicare and Medicaid Services, Management Information Integrated Repository

(Illustration by GGS Information Services. Cengage Learning, Gale)

Medicare Advantage

Definition

A **Medicare** Advantage Plan (sometimes referred to as a "Medicare Health Plan"or a "Medicare Part C Plan") is a type of Medicare health plan offered by a private company that contracts with Medicare to provide Medicare beneficiaries with all Part A and Part B benefits. For patients enrolled in a Medicare Advantage Program, Medicare services are covered through the plan and are not paid for by Original Medicare. A Medicare Advantage Plan must offer at least the same benefits as Original Medicare but can do so with different rules, costs, and restrictions. Most Medicare Advantage Plans offer prescription drug coverage.

Description

Medicare pays a fixed amount each month for each patient to companies that offer Medicare Advantage Plans. The companies must follow rules set by Medicare. However, each Medicare Advantage Plan can charge different out-of-pocket costs. In general, Medicare Advantage plans offer additional benefits or require smaller co-payments or deductibles than original Medicare. Sometimes beneficiaries pay for these additional benefits through a higher monthly premium, but sometimes they are financed through plan savings. Medicare Advantage Plans also have rules for how patients access services. For example, the plan can require that a patient obtain a referral to see a specialist or require that a patient only utilize doctors, facilities, or suppliers that belong to the plan for non-emergency or non-urgent care. As of January 2009, all Medicare beneficiaries had access to a Medicare Advantage Plan, with 23 percent of beneficiaries enrolled in one.

There is usually Medicare prescription drug coverage (Part D) through a Medicare Advantage Plan. If the Plan does not offer prescription drug coverage, the patient is allowed to join a Medicare Prescription Drug Plan. However, a patient is not allowed to have prescription drug coverage through both a Medicare Advantage Plan and a Medicare Prescription Drug Plan at the same time. If a patient in a Medicare Advantage Plan that includes drug coverage joins a Medicare Prescription Drug Plan, the patient will be disenrolled from the Medicare Advantage Plan and changed to coverage through Original Medicare.

There are several types of Medicare Advantage Plans available, including:

• Health Maintenance Organization (HMO) Plans
• Preferred Provider Organization (PPO) Plans
• Private Fee-For-Service (PFFS) Plans
• Special Needs Plans

Why this is important to the consumer

A person must meet a few conditions to eligible for a Medicare Advantage Plan. If a patient wants to enroll in a Medicare Advantage Plan, he or she must be:

Beneficiaries—Persons determined by the Social Security Administration to be eligible for Medicare benefits.

Coinsurance—The amount a patient may be required to pay for services after any plan deductibles are paid. In Original Medicare, this is a percentage (such as 20 percent) of the Medicare approved amount.

End-stage kidney disease (ESRD)—A disease where the kidneys are no longer able to work at a level needed for day-to-day life. The most common causes of ESRD in the United States are diabetes and high blood pressure. A person with ESRD will usually get health care coverage through Original Medicare, although in certain situations, the patient may be able to join a Medicare Advantage Plan, which might include a Medicare Special Needs Plan.

Health Maintenance Organization (HMO) Plan—A health organization that contracts with Medicare to provide a patient with access to a network of doctors and hospitals that coordinate the patient's care, with an emphasis on prevention. In most cases, the patient must choose a primary care doctor and must get a referral to see a specialist. An HMO allows a patient to get more benefits than the Original Medicare Plan and many Medicare Supplement plans. An HMO has the tightest or most restrictive network where the patient's care may not be covered outside the HMO network without obtaining prior approval.

Health Maintenance Organization Point of Service Plan (HMOPOS)—A less common variation on an HMO plan that may allow the patient to receive services out-of-network for a higher cost.

Medicare prescription drug coverage (Part D)—A federal program to subsidize the costs of prescription drugs for Medicare beneficiaries in the United States.

Medical Savings Account (MSA) Plan—A less common type of health plan that combines a high deductible health plan with a bank account. Medicare deposits a certain amount of money per year, which is used to pay for Medicare Part A and Medicare Part B expenses, and when the Plan deductible is met, the Plan pays for any further Medicare-covered services. MSAs do not offer Medicare Part D prescription drug coverage.

Medicare Supplemental Insurance (Medigap)—An insurance policy sold by private companies that can help pay some of the health care costs that Original Medicare does not cover, such as copayments, coinsurance, and deductibles. Some Medigap policies also offer coverage for services that Original Medicare does not cover, such as medical care when the patient travels outside the United States. When a patient has Original Medicare and buys a Medigap policy, Medicare will pay its share of the Medicare-approved amount for covered health care costs, and then the Medigap policy pays its share.

Original Medicare—A fee-for-service health plan that lets a patient go to any doctor, hospital, or other health care supplier who accepts Medicare and is accepting new Medicare patients. Medicare pays its share of the Medicare-approved amount, and the patient pays a coinsurance.

Preferred Provider Organization (PPO) Plan—A type of Medicare Advantage Plan offered by a private insurance company. In a PPO Plan, the patient pays less when doctors, hospitals, and other health care providers that belong to the plan's network (preferred providers) are chosen for care, while the costs are higher when the patient uses doctors, hospitals, and providers outside of the network. The patient does not need to select a primary care physician and does not need referrals to see other providers in the network.

Private Fee-For-Service (PFFS) Plan—A type of Medicare Advantage Plan in which you may go to any Medicare-approved doctor or hospital that accepts both Medicare and the plan's payment terms and conditions. The insurance plan, rather than the Medicare Program, decides how much it will pay and what the patients pays for the services received. The patient may pay more or less for Medicare-covered benefits and may have extra benefits that the Original Medicare Plan does not cover. The PFFS Plans are the most flexible, but a doctor or hospital can make patient-by-patient or visit-by-visit decisions of whether to accept the PFFS Plan Member.

Special Needs Plan (SNP)—A Medicare Advantage Plan with coverage designed especially for Medicare beneficiaries with certain chronic conditions (like diabetes) or some other specific need. Usually, only people with certain conditions or needs are allowed into a SNP.

- Eligible for Medicare;
- Enrolled in both Medicare Part A and Medicare Part B (date of enrollment can be checked by referring to the patient's Red, White, and Blue Medicare Card);
- Living within the Plan's service area, which is county-by-county and not state-by-state (if a person lives in different areas or states throughout the year, the patient should check to see that the plan selected will cover all resident locations); and
- Not living with end-stage renal disease (ESRD).

Since all plans are different, Medicare patients should carefully evaluate the health plans available in the patient's area. Medicare provides a plan finder online at https://www.medicare.gov/find-a-plan/ques tions/home.aspx. To join a Medicare Advantage Plan, patients must provide their Medicare number and the date their Part A and/or Part B coverage started. Medicare providers are not allowed to call without the patient's permission, and the patient should not provide financial information, including credit card or bank account numbers, over the telephone. During open-enrollment periods, a patient can switch Medicare Advantage Plans or switch to Original Medicare. In some cases, enrolling in a Medicare Advantage Plan could result in loss of other coverage from an employer, union, or other benefits administrator for the patient and possibly other family members. Rules for maintaining other coverage should be checked before enrolling in a Medicare Advantage Plan.

If a Medicare Advantage Plan provider decides to leave the Medicare Program, the patient's coverage will be returned to Original Medicare if another Medicare Advantage Plan is not selected. The patient will also then have the right to purchase Medicare **Supplemental Insurance**.

Medicare Supplemental Insurance (Medigap) policies do not work with Medicare Advantage Plans, as Medigap policies cannot be used to pay Medicare Advantage Plan copayments, deductibles, or premiums.

Resources

BOOKS

Baylis, Charles V. *Medicare Advantage: The Alternate Medicare Program* (Public Health in the 21st Century). Hauppauge. N.Y.: NOVA Science Publishers, 2010.

Omdahl, Diane J., *A Guide to Choosing a Medicare Advantage Plan: Using the Plan Finder: Supplemental Educational Materials*. Seattle, WA: CreateSpace Independent Publishing Platform, 2014.

Stevenson, D.I. 2013 *Medicare Advantage?: An Inside Look on What You Should Know Before Choosing a Medicare Advantage Plan*. Seattle, WA: CreateSpace Independent Publishing Platform, 2012.

PERIODICALS

WEBSITES

Medicare Advantage Plans. http://www.medicare.gov/sign-up-change-plans/medicare-health-plans/medicare-advantage-plans/medicare-advantage-plans.html

ORGANIZATIONS

Centers for Medicare & Medicaid Services, 7500 Security Boulevard, Baltimore, MD, USA 21244, (248) 699-8524, (800) 633-4227, Medicare.gov.

Judith L Sims, MS

Medigap insurance

Definition

Medigap, or **Medicare** Supplement Insurance, is insurance that can be purchased by the consumer to pay for some of the health coverage that Medicare Part A and Part B do not cover. Medigap may cover prescription drugs (if the policy was purchased before 2006), copayments, coinsurance, and deductibles. Medigap is an alternative to **Medicare Advantage**. The consumer cannot be enrolled in the Medicare Advantage Plan and Medigap at the same time.

Description

Medigap insurance is provided by private insurance companies; however, it is regulated by the federal government and individuals can only purchase policies that are licensed by their respective states. The individual pays the private company a monthly premium for Medigap. There are 10 standardized types of Medigap policies available, except in Massachusetts, Minnesota, and Wisconsin, which have their own standardized Medigap policies. A description and comparison of the Medigap policies can be found on the Medicare site at http://www.medicare.gov/supplement-other-insurance/compare-medigap/compare-medigap.html. Other than the exceptions of the three states noted above, the only thing that really varies about Medigap policies is the price. Costs vary depending upon the consumer's age, where he or she lives, and the particular insurer and the type of plan selected. Therefore, it is important that the individual research the costs of Medigap plans from various insurance companies to find the one that is best for his or her lifestyle and budget.

Why this is important to the consumer

Medigap is not as popular as the less-expensive Medicare Advantage. Also, Medigap policies usually do not cover long-term care, prescriptions, vision or dental care, hearing aids, eyeglasses, or private-duty nursing. Married consumers must have their own plans, unlike Medicare Advantage. However, Medigap has some advantages:

• Medigap policies are guaranteed renewable, even if one has serious health problems.

• An insurance company cannot terminate a policy as long as the monthly premiums are paid.

• Medigap policies allow the individual to have a larger network of providers to choose from.

• If the consumer has a health condition, a Medigap plan may offer greater access to providers and better ways to pay for medical expenses.

Therefore, if a consumer can afford to spend more on a Medigap policy, it may be a better choice in the long run. To be eligible for Medigap, an individual must have Medicare Part A and Part B.

Resources

WEBSITES

"Compare Medigap policies." Medicare.gov. http://www.medicare.gov/supplement-other-insurance/compare-medigap/compare-medigap.html (accessed October 18, 2013).

Heilbrunn, Evi. "Medicare and Medigap: What's the Difference?" Yahoo News. October 15, 2013. http://news.yahoo.com/medicare-medigap-whats-difference-143827890.html;_ylt = A2KJ3CYrpl1S4E-cAq0vQtDMD (accessed October 18, 2013).

"Medigap (Medicare Supplement Health Insurance)." Centers for Medicare & Medicaid Services. March 26, 2012. http://www.cms.gov/Medicare/Health-Plans/Medigap/index.html (accessed October 18, 2013).

"What's Medicare supplement (Medigap) insurance?" Medicare.gov. http://www.medicare.gov/supplement-other-insurance/medigap/whats-medigap.html (accessed October 18, 2013).

Cara Mia Massey

▌Medihotel

Definition

A medihotel is a hotel or studio apartment building adjacent to a medical center or hospital. It allows the family of patients, or patients who do not require inpatient treatment, to stay proximate to the hospital so that they can return for re-evaluation or treatment as indicated.

Description

Medihotels are accommodations that cater to patients and their families. In many cases, the patient is ill enough to require ongoing treatment but not ill enough to necessitate inpatient care. The medihotel is located close enough to the hospital to make repeated trips back and forth easy on patients and families. In fact, some medihotels have walkways that go directly to the hospital or are built within the actual hospital complex. Others are simply across the street or within a few blocks.

Usually, patients who stay in medihotels are expected to be completely self-sufficient and able to administer all their own medications. There may or may not be a nurse onsite in case of emergencies.

Some medihotels are an offshoot of **medical tourism**, a kind of healthcare that occurs when people travel outside of their country of origin to attain healthcare in a distant location. While an older model saw patients from developing countries seek unavailable, more technically advanced care in developed countries, the new medical tourism sees patients from developed countries seeking care in developing countries, where the costs can be significantly less. This is usually done in order to obtain cheaper services than those available in the patient's home country.

Why this is important to the consumer

Medical tourism, and thus medihotels, have grown exponentially in recent years. As healthcare costs in the United States have skyrocketed, more and more people have sought healthcare overseas, particularly for elective surgeries. Savings in remote locations, compared to U.S. costs, can be substantial. Projections by **Patients Beyond Borders** suggest that, compared to costs in the United States, savings run

• 25-40% in Brazil

• 40-50% in Costa Rica

• 65-90% in India

• 30-45% in Korea

• 65-80% in Malaysia

• 40-65% in Mexico

• 30-45% in Singapore

• 40-55% in Taiwan

• 50-70% in Thailand

• 50-65% in Turkey

Projections suggest that the number of people seeking healthcare overseas may increase by as much as 15% over the next decade. As this increases, so will the number of available medihotels, as they will be needed to accommodate families and friends of patients, as well as the patients themselves, either pre-operatively, during post-operative convalescence, or when patients are seeking nonsurgical treatment abroad.

Resources

BOOKS

Kovner Anthony R. et al. *Health Care Delivery in the United States* 10th ed. New York: Springer Publishing Company, 2011.

Schulte, Margaret F. *Health Care Delivery in the U.S.A.: An Introduction* 2nd ed. New York: Productivity Press, 2012.

Sultz, Harry A. et al. *Health Care USA: Understanding Its Organization and Delivery* 7th ed. Sudbury, MA: Jonas & Bartlett Learning, 2010.

WEBSITES

National Caregivers Library. Types of Care Facilities [accessed September 22, 2013]. http://www.caregivers library.org/caregivers-resources/grp-care-facilities/types-of-care-facilities-article.aspx.

USA.gov. Choosing a Health Care Facility. 2013 [accessed September 22, 2013]. http://www.usa.gov/topics/health/caregivers/health-care-facility.shtml/.

ORGANIZATIONS

American Hospital Association, 155 N. Wacker Dr., Chicago, IL 60606, (312) 422-3000, http://www.aha.org/.

Patients Beyond Borders, P.O. Box 17057, Chapel Hill, NC 27516, (919) 924-0636, http://www.patientsbeyond borders.com/.

United States Department of Labor, 200 Constitution Ave. NW, Washington, DC 20210, (800) 321-6742, https://www.osha.gov/.

Rosalyn Carson-DeWitt, MD

Mental health assessment

Definition

Mental health assessment is the process by which the physician reaches a decision regarding the degree to which a threat to the patient's mental health is interacting with reported symptoms or interfering with treatment. This assessment takes place indirectly with all patients but follows specific standards and criteria when the threat appears substantial.

Description

Physicians have to make many decisions about their patients, particularly new patients. Diagnoses are based on symptoms self-reported by the patient; therefore, the patient's veracity has to be evaluated to identify the legitimacy of the symptoms. If the patient is exhibiting a mental health disorder or even a minimal abnormality (such as exaggerating pain), the doctor has to consider the patient's mental health as a factor in developing a diagnosis. With the new patients, the physician uses some basic questions to understand the patient's communication and adaptation to life challenges. If the physician has some concern about the patient's mental health, the physician may rely on a screening process for mental disorders. If this screening process suggests that the patient was at a high risk of a mental disorder, the physician may rely on a formal standardized instrument for identifying mental disorder. The physician may also want to consider referring the patient to a mental health professional to determine completely the patient's mental health status.

Mental health assessment is particularly important when the physician is seeing a young child as a patient. The physician is in a better position than any other professional to diagnose developmental delays in a child. First of all, the physician will notice whether the child has a delay in language or in gross motor skills. If the physician is concerned about the child in these easy-to-notice areas of development, the physician can rely on developmental schedules to determine whether the child is at age level in all areas of development. Developmental schedules are instruments that are normed for children from birth to six years old. These instruments involved simple tasks that mark the half-year milestones of development in the first six years. If the child cannot perform age-related tasks, the physician will rely on a more precise instrument or refer the child to a mental health professional.

There are many physical conditions related to mental health from which adults can suffer, such as anxiety, eating disorders, and depression. A person who is suffering from insomnia or other sleeping problems will see the medical doctor but may have a condition related to anxiety. Before determining that the person's condition is physical in nature, the physician would have to rule out any mental disorder. Therefore, mental health assessment techniques would be used by the physician to make a complete diagnosis. Eating disorders have a psychological basis but result in physical problems. Although a mental health professional needs to work with the person suffering from an eating disorder, the medical doctor is usually the first to identify symptoms.

The medical doctor has to be part of the therapy team treating eating disorders. As depression also manifests itself in physical conditions, a person is more likely to see a medical doctor before a mental health professional. The physician will conduct a mental health assessment for this patient before prescribing treatment or referral to a mental health professional. Many people are more comfortable talking about mental health problems with the medical doctor than seeking out a mental health professional.

There are several conditions under which the physician would be required to conduct a mental health assessment. The first would be if a patient were recently incarcerated. This assessment would focus on any possible antisocial disorder that led to the incarceration or were developed while incarcerated. Another condition would be known substance abuse. This assessment would focus on the problems of continued use and of adapting to life challenges. A third condition would be for a patient who has a known mental disorder. This assessment would identify any change in the disorder or any development of comorbidity. These are three conditions in which the patient's mental health problem could interfere with a complete diagnosis or with the treatment processes. Whether the medical doctor is on the therapy team for mental disorder or not, heor she still needs to be aware of the patient's mental health status.

The Substance Abuse and Mental Health Services Administration recommends that physicians regularly screen for mental health problems. It advises physicians on the various instruments for mental health assessment that are available. These instruments are chosen by taking into consideration the four characteristics of all psychological instruments: reliability, validity, sensitivity, and specificity. Reliability is the measure of consistency of the instrument. Validity is the degree to which the instrument is appropriate for the given situation. Sensitivity is the ability to recognize when a small threat of mental disorder is present. Specificity is the ability to recognize when a patient does not have any mental health problems. The physician must recognize the purpose of each instrument and use it appropriately. The physician should also recognize when the results for mental health assessment are not clear enough for him or her to take action. In such a situation, the medical doctor should refer the patient to a mental health professional.

Why this is important to the consumer

It is important for healthcare consumers to recognize that mental health assessment can be performed by a medical doctor. For many people, dealing with any

---

KEY TERMS

Comorbidity—The occurrence of two or more mental health challenges simultaneously.

Developmental schedules—A type of assessment instrument designed to identify developmental delays by comparing a child's behavior to the typical behavior of a child of the same age, usually normed in months or half years.

Reliability—The quality of a test or measurement instrument to produce consistent results under comparable conditions.

SAMHSA—The Substance Abuse and Mental Health Services Administration, the agency within the Department of Health and Human Services responsible for initiatives related to public mental health.

Screening—An assessment instrument designed to give a quick and general diagnosis of a possible threat to mental health.

Sensitivity—The quality of a test or instrument to reduce the occurrence of false negatives.

Specificity—The quality of a test or instrument to reduce the occurrence of false positives.

Validity—The quality of a test or measurement instrument to produce results appropriate to its purpose.

---

threat to mental health can be very intimidating, even when the threat is normal and not very severe. Mental health diagnosis and treatment are perceived as threatening to such people, particularly because there is a social stigma attached to seeking mental health services. On the other hand, most people have a trust for the regular physician. Going to a primary care doctor's office does not hold a social stigma as going to a psychiatrist's office might. Therefore, it is better for people to seek a screening or preliminary mental health assessment from their medical doctor than to allow a condition to go undiagnosed and untreated.

It is also important for a person who might suspect that he or she has a mental condition to have the medical doctor rule out any physical problems first. Problems with digestion or with the thyroid gland could have similar symptoms to anxiety or depression. The patient should know the real source of his or her health problems before suggesting that it is a mental health problem. The medical doctor relying on a mental health assessment is in a position to make a holistic diagnosis.

A patient who is in a situation that would require a mental health assessment before any medical treatment should know how ordinary such a procedure is. The patient should know that the procedure is not invasive or mysterious. Patients would want to know what instrument is being used, what its designed purpose is, and what its ratings are for reliability and validity. Using mental health assessment in the proper manner can identify problems before they become more serious. Mental health assessment ensures greater efficacy of diagnosis techniques and treatment of medical problems.

Resources

BOOKS

Hagan J.F., Shaw, J. S., Duncan, P. M., eds. (2008) Bright Futures: Guidelines for Health Supervision of Infants, Children, and Adolescents, Third Edition. Elk Grove Village, IL: American Academy of Pediatrics; 2008.

Hales R.E., Yudofsky S.C., eds. (2008). The Psychiatric Interview And Mental Status Examination. Textbook Of Clinical Psychiatry, Fifth Edition. Washington, D.C.: American Psychiatric Publishing.

PERIODICALS

Ai, A., Rollman, B., & Berger, C. (2010). Comorbid mental health symptoms and heart diseases: can health care and mental health care professionals collaboratively improve the assessment and management? Health & Social Work, 35, 27-38.

Fossey, E., Harvey, C., Mokhtari, M., & Meadows, G. (2012). Self-Rated Assessment of Needs for Mental Health Care: A Qualitative Analysis. Community Mental Health Journal, 48(4), 407-419.

Mental Health Screening and Assessment Tools for Primary Care. http://www.aap.org/en-us/advocacy-and-policy/aap-health-initiatives/Mental-Health/Documents/MH_ScreeningChart.pdf.

Substance Abuse and Mental Health Services Administration Clinical Practice Screening Tools. http://www.integration.samhsa.gov/clinical-practice/screening-tools.

ORGANIZATIONS

Substance Abuse and Mental Health Services Administration, 1 Choke Cherry Road, Rockville, MD 20857, 240-276-2130, 877-726-4727, samhsa.media@ees.hhs.gov, http://www.samhsa.gov.

Ray F Brogan, Ph.D.

| Mental health/behavioral health facility

Definition

A mental or behavioral health facility is a setting in which people can receive counseling or treatment for mental, emotional, or psychological conditions. The terms are often used interchangeably.

Description

Such centers vary widely in the treatments and services they offer and the types of patients they see. They range from residential facilities that provide medication and intensive psychiatric treatment to people with severe mental illnesses such as schizophrenia, to simpler outpatient community clinics that provide counseling to people with less serious conditions, along with related services such as marriage and family therapy. Some facilities also treat people with developmental disabilities such as autism.

Some places specialize in one particular type of problem, such as eating disorders or drug or alcohol rehabilitation, while others may treat a range of conditions. There are facilities that treat all comers, and those that cater to a particular type of patient, such as children or people in the lesbian, gay, bisexual, or transgender (LGBT) communities. Some of these programs are affiliated with larger hospitals or medical schools; some are freestanding, privately run institutions; others are run by state or county governments. In many cases, they also serve as teaching facilities in which students and interns in fields such as psychiatry, psychology, and social work can get the clinical experience they need in order to graduate from their school programs or obtain licensure in their field.

In addition to the range of people and conditions these facilities accept, they vary widely with respect to the scope of treatments and services they offer. For example, inpatient programs that treat more severely ill people may offer classes in social or occupational skills along with their psychiatric and psychological therapies. Some private drug-rehabilitation facilities are almost like exclusive spas: they are located in upscale communities and provide luxurious private rooms and gourmet meals, as well as services such as acupuncture and massage. At the other end of the spectrum are no-frills community mental-health clinics that may offer counseling to the local population at affordable rates, but are not equipped to serve people who may be actively psychotic or suicidal.

Why this is important to the consumer

Anyone searching for a mental health facility for themselves or someone else should take into account the patient's needs, the resources available in the community, and the type of treatment their medical insurance will cover. Someone with severe mental illness may require an inpatient facility, while people with certain types of conditions, such as eating disorders, often feel more comfortable in a specialized program, where they can encounter patients with issues similar to their own. People who are simply seeking more insight into their problems and are not seriously mentally ill, but have a limited budget, may find help at a teaching facility where students and interns work for free in exchange for school credit or clinical hours. Regardless of the type of facility chosen, doctors and counselors should be graduates of accredited academic programs and licensed or practicing under the direction of a licensed supervisor.

The plethora of facilities available today is the result of several trends. The 1950s saw the development of drugs that could keep the more florid symptoms of psychosis in check. The drugs were controversial, as they were often associated with severe and sometimes permanent side effects, but by reducing symptoms, they offered hope that the mentally ill could be rehabilitated and did not have to languish in institutions. Over the years, newer generations of drugs have been developed, and doctors have become better at prescribing them, which has somewhat reduced the risk of side effects.

There was also a growing interest in liberating patients from the notorious "lunatic asylums" of the past, in favor of care at home or in more intimate, less impersonal surroundings. In 1963, President John F. Kennedy signed the Community Mental Health Centers Act. Kennedy had a special interest in the plight of the mentally ill because his sister, Rosemary, had undergone a lobotomy a few years before, and required institutionalization for the rest of her life. He urged Congress to provide funding to train more mental health professionals and to study the possibility of housing mentally ill patients in small community settings rather than warehousing them in hospitals. Thanks to improvements in drug and psychiatric treatment as well as the establishment of smaller care centers, the number of people in mental institutions dropped from about 560,000 in 1955 to about 160,000

by 1977. Those who remained hospitalized were the most severely ill patients.

Progress in mental health treatment hit a roadblock in the 1980s, as federal funds for programs such as Kennedy's were withdrawn, leaving many patients homeless. By the end of the decade, it was clear that this experiment had failed, and the 1990s ushered in an era of rebuilding resources for this patient population, including the establishment of many local clinics.

Resources

WEBSITES

"A History of Mental Institutions in the United States." University of Maryland, Philip Merrill School of Medicine. http://www.tiki-toki.com/timeline/entry/37146/A-History-of-Mental-Institutions-in-the-United-States/#vars!date=1806-05-04_05:59:26! (accessed September 28, 2013).

"Mental Illness and the Family: Is Hospitalization Necessary?" Mental Health America. http://www.nmha.org/go/information/get-info/mi-and-the-family/is-hospitalization-necessary (accessed September 11, 2013).

ORGANIZATIONS

Mental Health America, 2000 North Beauregard Street, 6th Floor, Alexandria, VA 22311, (703) 683-7733, (800) 969-6642, Fax: (703) 684-5968, http://www.mentalhealthamerica.net.

National Alliance on Mental Illness, 3803 N. Fairfax Drive, Suite 100, Arlington, VA 22203, (703) 524-7600, (800) 950-6264, Fax: (703) 524-9094, http://www.nami.org/.

Norra MacReady

Mental health/behavioral health insurance plans

Definition

Mental health insurance is a type of health insurance designed to cover mental health and behavior issues. Most health insurance policies provide mental health coverage, and, since 2008, U.S. law has required that mental health coverage be comparable to insurance coverage provided for general health.

Description

Mental health insurance is a type of insurance designed to cover issues related to emotional, mental, and behavioral health issues. Coverage includes such services as psychological counseling, substance abuse treatment, and inpatient mental health treatment. Most often, this coverage is included in general health insurance policies, but mental health coverage may also be purchased as a separate, specialized insurance plan.

Mental health insurance typically covers mental health counseling, treatment for alcoholism and drug addiction, and mental illness such as depression, anxiety disorders, eating disorders, schizophrenia, and bipolar disorder. Mental health insurance is designed to cover only mental health issues and will not generally cover physical illnesses or other health conditions that are not related to a mental health or addiction issues.

Why this is important to the consumer

Types of Coverage

There are many types of mental health insurance plans. Some benefits are covered under standard health insurance plans. Other plans may be administered by managed care systems. The four most common types of mental health insurance include Fee-for-Service (FFS), **Health Maintenance Organization** (HMO), **Preferred Provider Organizations (PPO)**, and Point-of-Service plans (POS).

FFS plans allow patients to select the licensed mental health care provider of their choice. HMO plans require patients to choose from providers within an insurance company select network. PPOs allow lower co-pays and may provide a higher benefit for the selection of mental health providers who choose to join the PPO network.

MENTAL HEALTH INSURANCE PARITY. The Mental Health Parity and Addiction Equity Act of 2008 mandates that, when coverage for mental health and substance use treatment is provided in conjunction with heath coverage, it is comparable to coverage for medical and surgical care. The **Patient Protection and Affordable Care Act** (PPACA) expands the parity law by requiring that mental health and substance abuse disorders be covered in insurance plans offered within the individual and small group markets. The PPACA also mandates preventive mental health services like depression screening for adults and behavioral assessments for children at no cost. Beginning January 1, 2014, insurance providers are prohibited from denying coverage due to pre-existing health conditions, including mental illnesses.

SPECIFIC MENTAL HEALTH BENEFITS MAY VARY STATE TO STATE. February 20, 2013, the Obama administration defined the specific rules for **essential health benefits** that states must follow when establishing insurance coverage in the states' insurance exchanges. These rules include guidelines for mental health

---

KEY TERMS

Mental Health Parity and Addiction Equity Act of 2008 (MHPAEA, or the federal parity law)—Law that requires group health plans and insurers that offer mental health and substance use disorder benefits to provide coverage that is comparable to coverage for general medical and surgical care.

---

and behavioral insurance coverage and require that these services be provided. These rules attempt to limit costs to consumers. Health plans offered through the state insurance exchange markets will be limited to deductibles (the amount of money that must be paid out-of-pocket before an insurance plan begins to pay) of no more than $2,000 for individuals, and no more than $4,000 for families. There will also be out-of-pocket maximums consumers will have to pay.

Resources

BOOKS

Sultz, Harry A. and Kristina M. Young. "Mental Health Services." In *Health Care USA: Understanding Its Organization and Delivery, Seventh Edition*, 305–338. Sudbury: Jones & Bartlett Learning, LLC, 2011.

WEBSITES

Centers for Medicare and Medicaid Services. "Medicare and your mental health benefits." June 2012. http://www.medicare.gov/Pubs/pdf/10184.pdf (accessed September 20, 2013).

Centers for Medicare and Medicaid Services. "The Mental Health Parity and Addiction Equity Act." Accessed September 19, 2013. http://www.cms.gov/CCIIO/Programs-and-Initiatives/Other-Insurance-Protections/mhpaea_factsheet.html. (accessed September 20, 2013).

Office of the Assistant Secretary for Planning and Evaluation, US Department of Health and Human Services. "Affordable Care Act Expands Mental Health and Substance Use Disorder Benefits and Federal Parity Protections for 62 Million Americans." February 20, 2013. http://aspe.hhs.gov/health/reports/2013/mental/rb_mental.cfm. (accessed September 20, 2013).

US Department of Health and Human Services. "Health care law allows consumers to easily find and compare options starting in 2014." February 20, 2013. http://www.hhs.gov/news/press/2013pres/02/20130220a.html. (accessed September 20, 2013).

US Department of Health and Human Services. "The Affordable Care Act, Section by Section." http://www.hhs.gov/healthcare/rights/law/index.html (accessed September 19, 2013).

Deborah L. Nurmi, MS

Midwife

Definition

A midwife is an independent health care provider who offers services to women of all ages and stages of life, especially during pregnancy, labor, and the postpartum period, along with care for the newborn. Midwives also assist mothers with breastfeeding. Midwifery is aimed at preventing health problems during pregnancy, detecting abnormal conditions, providing medical assistance when necessary, and executing emergency measures in the absence of medical help.

Description

A practitioner of midwifery is known as a midwife. The term was coined in the 1300s, with "wife" referring to the mother, and "mid" meaning "together with." In Scots, the term "midwife" is translated as "kneeling woman," suggesting that she kneels in front of the mother to catch her baby.

In the United States, nurse-midwifery dates back to 1925. During that time, Mary Breckenridge developed the Frontier Nursing Service in Kentucky. The program used public health registered nurses, who were educated in England, to staff nursing centers in the Appalachian Mountains. The centers offered family health care services, as well as childbearing and delivery care, to residents in the area. The first nurse-midwifery education program in the United States began in 1932 at the Maternity Center Association of New York City. The program enrolled public health nurses and awarded its graduates a certificate in nurse-midwifery. Today, all nurse-midwifery programs are in colleges and universities.

Types of Midwives

In the United States, there are three main types of midwives:

• Certified Nurse-Midwife (CNM)
• Certified Midwife (CM)
• Certified Professional Midwife (CPM)

A midwife holds a twenty-minutes old newborn. *(Joe Raedle/Getty Images)*

CERTIFIED NURSE-MIDWIFE (CNM). A Certified Nurse Midwife (CNM) is a registered nurse with graduate education in midwifery. He or she has graduated from a nurse-midwifery education program accredited by the Accreditation Commission for Midwifery Education (ACME) and has received a university degree along with hands-on clinical training by practicing CNMs. A Certified Nurse Midwife has also passed the national certification exam of the American Midwifery Certification Board (AMCB). CNMs provide general women's health care throughout a woman's lifespan through menopause. The services they provide include check-ups and physical exams; pregnancy, birth, and postpartum care; well woman gynecologic care; and treatment of sexually transmitted infections. CNMs are able to prescribe a full range of substances, medications, and treatments, including pain control medications. CNMs work in several different settings, including hospitals, health care centers, private practices, birth centers, and private homes. Most Certified Nurse-Midwives (CNMs) are women, however, in recent years more male nurses have chosen to become nurse-midwives. Most midwives in the United States are CNMs. Recertification for a CNM is every five years.

CERTIFIED MIDWIFE (CM). Unlike a CNM, Certified Midwives (CMs) have obtained a bachelor's degree in a field other than nursing. However, they have graduated from a graduate-level midwifery education program accredited by the Accreditation Commission for Midwifery Education (ACME). These programs include health-related skills and training in addition to midwifery education, which is the same as that of Certified Nurse-Midwives. CMs have also passed the national certification exam of the American Midwifery Certification Board (AMCB) and provide the same services as CNMs, along with prescribing medications and treatments. CMs assist with menopause as well. They must recertify every five years.

CERTIFIED PROFESSIONAL MIDWIFE (CPM). A Certified Professional Midwife (CPM) is a knowledgeable, skilled, and professional independent midwifery practitioner who has met the standards for certification set by the North American Registry of Midwives (NARM) and is qualified to provide the Midwives Model of Care. The CPM is the only midwifery credential that requires knowledge about and experience in out-of-hospital settings.

LAY MIDWIFE. The lay midwife is an individual who is not certified or licensed as a midwife but has been trained informally through self-study or apprenticeship. Their services are usually focused on pregnancy and birth, and they are unable to prescribe medications. The lay midwife does not imply a low level of education or skill, only that the midwife either chose not to become certified or licensed, or began practicing as a midwife before the CPM certification was available.

Demographics

According to the National Center for Health Statistics, certified nurse-midwives (CNMs) and certified midwives (CMs) attended 309,514 births in 2011. This represents 11.7% of all vaginal births, or 7.8% of total US births. That same year, CNMs/CMs attended 92.2% of midwife-attended births, and the majority of CNM/CM-attended births occurred in hospitals (95.2%), while 2.3% occurred in freestanding birth centers, and 2.4% occurred in homes. According to the World Health Organization (WHO), midwifery services are key to a healthy and safe pregnancy and childbirth. Worldwide, approximately 287,000 women die every year due to pregnancy and childbirth related complications. Most of these largely preventable deaths occur in low-income countries and in poor and rural areas. Many maternal and newborn deaths can be prevented if competent midwives assist women before, during, and after childbirth and are able to refer them to emergency obstetric care when severe complications arise.

Why this is important to the consumer

Midwives play an important role in the well-being of both the mother and child as an alternative to an obstetrician. Several studies have shown that midwife-supervised births produce excellent outcomes with fewer medical interventions than average. Midwives' patients use electronic fetal monitoring less often and tend to have a reduced need for epidurals, episiotomies, and C-sections for successful deliveries. To some degree, this stems from the fact that midwives see only low-risk patients with uncomplicated pregnancies. But some researchers attribute the need for a minimum of medical intervention to the midwives' natural approach to the management of labor and delivery, which may reduce a woman's fear, pain, and anxiety during birth. Midwives generally spend a lot of time during prenatal visits addressing a woman's individual concerns and needs, and will stay with her as much as possible throughout labor. They sometimes encourage physical positioning during labor

KEY TERMS

Alphafetoprotein (AFP)—A substance present in the blood of pregnant women. You may need further tests if levels are higher or lower than normal.

APGAR—A wellness assessment tool used to measure how well a neonate is doing and if intervention is necessary. Babies get two points each for color, heartbeat, respiration, muscle tone and grimace, or response to stimuli. Named for pediatric anesthesiologist Virginia Apgar.

APH (Antepartum Hemorrhage)—Bleeding before the birth.

Braxton-Hicks—Light, usually painless uterine contractions. Sometimes called "false labor." Women can experience these throughout pregnancy and often note they increase in the last weeks before birth.

Dilation—Opening, specifically in birthing of the cervix. Cervical dilation happens in the first stage of labor and is measured in centimeters, with 10 cm considered "complete" and ready for a woman to begin the second stage of labor (pushing and birth).

Episiotomy—A cut made in the mother's perineum (area between the vagina and anus) to allow the baby to be born more quickly and prevent tearing.

Fetus—Medical name for the baby before it is born.

HBAC—Home Birth After Cesarean.

Oedema—Swelling or fluid retention, usually in your ankles, fingers, or feet during pregnancy.

Quickening—The first movements of the baby that you can feel.

VBAC—Vaginal Birth After Cesarean.

such as walking around, showering, rocking, or leaning on birthing balls. Midwives also usually allow women to eat and drink during labor.

The Midwifery Model of Care is based on the fact that pregnancy and birth are normal life events. The Midwifery Model of Care includes:

- Monitoring the physical, psychological, and social well-being of the mother throughout the childbearing cycle
- Providing the mother with individualized education, counseling, and prenatal care, continuous hands-on assistance during labor and delivery, and postpartum support
- Minimizing technological interventions
- Identifying and referring women who require obstetrical attention

Finding a midwife

Women can decide whether they want a midwife during most stages of pregnancy. However, most patients turn to midwifery a few months prior to their due dates, when they begin to seriously consider their birthing plan. Few midwives will accept a patient who is well along in pregnancy unless she has had adequate prenatal care. Therefore, most midwives will require that you bring your prenatal care records to the first meeting with them. Women should begin the process by asking their obstetrician/gynecologist (OB/GYN), family doctor, and friends for a referral. Thereafter, interview prospective midwives carefully. Investigate their background, certifications, experience, back-up practitioners/obstetricians, and ability to handle emergency situations and procedures.

Resources

BOOKS

Ehrenreich, Barbara and Deidre English. *Witches, Midwives, and Nurses: A History of Women Healers, 2nd Edition.* Feminist Press, pp. 85-85, 2010.

Gabbe, Steven G., et al. *Obstetrics: Normal and Problem Pregnancies, 6th Edition.* Saunders, 2012.

Rogoff, B. *Developing Destinies: A Mayan midwife and town.* New York: Oxford University Press, 2011.

ORGANIZATIONS

American College of Nurse-Midwives, 8403 Colesville Rd, Ste 1550, Silver Spring, MD 20910-6374, (240) 485-1800, www.midwife.org, http://www.midwife.org.

American Midwifery Certification Board, 849 International Drive, Suite 120, Linthicum, MD 21090, (866) 366-9632, www.amcbmidwife.org, http://www. amcbmidwife.org.

Midwife Alliance of North America, 1500 Sunday Drive, Suite 102, Raleigh, NC 27607, (888) 923-MANA(6262), info@mana.org, http://www.mana.org.

National Association of Certified Professional Midwives, 243 Banning Road, Putney, VT 05346, admin@nacpm. org, http://www.nacpm.org.

National Association of Certified Professional Midwives, 243 Banning Road, Putney, VT 05346, admin@nacpm. org, http://www.nacpm.org.

North American Registry of Midwives, 5257 Rosestone Dr., Lilburn, GA 30047, (888) 842-4784, info@narm.org, http://narm.org.

Karl Finley

MLR *see* **Medical Loss Ratio (MLR)**

National Health Insurance Program (Canada)

Definition

The Canadian National Health Insurance Program, often called Medicare, provides tax-supported, pre-paid access to medically necessary physician and hospital services for all Canadian residents.

Description

Canadian Medicare is a healthcare program linking thirteen provincial and territorial government programs and the federal government. Although the program varies slightly across the thirteen governmental regions, basic features and standards of care are the same as defined under the 1984 Canada Health Act (CHA). The Act states that the objective of Canadian healthcare policy is "to protect, promote and restore the physical and mental well-being of residents of Canada and to facilitate reasonable access to health services without financial or other barriers." To receive federal healthcare money under the Canada Health Transfer (CHT), the provinces and territories must provide the healthcare services defined in the CHA.

In the 1950s, the provinces of Alberta and Saskatchewan developed successful pre-paid healthcare programs that eventually served as the basis for current national plan. By 1966, all provinces were directed to establish universal healthcare plans in which the cost was shared by the provincial and federal government. The 1984 Canada Health Act serves as the basis for the present system. The system is designed to be comprehensive, universal, portable (i.e., not tied to employment), accessible, and publicly administered.

Healthcare in Canada is funded through taxes (thus, it is considered a universal pre-paid system), although in British Columbia, individuals also pay a small monthly premium. Necessary physician visits and hospitalization are completely covered; the individual has no co-pays, deductibles, or out-of-pocket expenses. Dental care, vision care, prescription medicines, and elective surgery (e.g., cosmetic surgery) are not covered. Exceptions apply to the elderly and the poor. About 70% of Canadians have either employer-provided or private insurance that cover some or all of these costs.

Prescription medicine costs are negotiated by the federal government and usually are significantly lower than in the United States. Physicians are not salaried employees of the government. Instead, they are independent contractors and are paid a fee that is negotiated annually for each patient visit. Individuals access the healthcare system through a **primary care physician** (general practitioner) who can make referrals to specialist physicians as needed.

Why this is important to the consumer

Canadian Medicare provides pre-paid health insurance for residents of Canada. All billing is done by the physicians and hospitals. Individuals do not have to lay out any cash when they receive physician or hospital services. This relieves Canadians from unexpected expenses and crushing debt related to healthcare treatment. In addition, the program emphasizes primary and preventive care. Because healthcare is pre-paid through tax dollars, there are fewer barriers to seeking well-person physicals, immunizations, and routine care for chronic diseases.

Various studies have shown that between 85% and 91% of Canadians are satisfied with their healthcare system and the care it provides. In addition, health outcomes are about the same in the United States and Canada, but Canada spends significantly less per person on healthcare than does the United States.

Limitations

Generally, the provincial government is responsible for the bulk of administering and paying for healthcare. One exception to this is that the federal government provides coverage to about 850,000 Inuit and First Nations individuals for:

• prescription drugs

• dental care

• vision care

• medical transportation

• medical supplies and equipment

• short-term mental health crisis counseling

The biggest complaint about the Canadian healthcare system is that the wait for specialty diagnosis or to see a specialist physician may be prolonged in non-emergency situations. Various studies have shown the median wait time for a CAT scan or MRI is two weeks, while the median wait time to see a specialist is four weeks, and another four weeks wait for surgery. These are median times, meaning half the individuals waited less long and half waited longer. Waiting time for non-emergency surgery such as hip replacement surgery can stretch to as long as four to six months. Even though waits are much shorter in the United States, almost all Canadians say they prefer their tax-funded, portable healthcare program to the private, employer-based healthcare prevalent in the United States.

Resources

BOOKS

Fierlbeck, Katherine. *Healthcare in Canada: A citizen's Guide to Policy and Politics.* Toronto; Buffalo, NY: University of Toronto Press, 2011.

Thompson, Valerie D. *Health and Healthcare Delivery in Canada.* St. Louis: Mosby, 2010.

WEBSITES

Health Canada. "Canada's Healthcare System (Medicare)." http://www.hc-sc.gc.ca/hcs-sss/medi-assur/index-eng. php (accessed July 27, 2013).

Health Canada. "Canada Health Act." http://www.hc-sc.gc. ca/hcs-sss/medi-assur/cha-lcs/index-eng.php (accessed July 27, 2013).

Health Canada. "About Health Canada." http://www.hc-sc. gc.ca/ahc-asc/index-eng.php (accessed July 27, 2013).

Institute for Clinical Evaluative Sciences. "Healthcare Delivery in Canada and the United States: Are There Relevant Differences in Healthcare Outcomes" http://www.ices.on.ca/file/health%20care%20delivery%20in%20canada%20and%20the%20united%20states%20-%20are%20there%20relevant%20differences%20in%20health%20care%20outcomes.pdf (accessed July 28, 2013).

Rosenthal, Elizabeth. "Canada's National Health Plan Gives Care to All with Limits." http://www.nytimes.com/1991/04/30/us/canada-s-national-health-plan-gives-care-to-all-with-limits.html?pagewanted=all&src=pm (accessed August 3, 2013).

ORGANIZATIONS

Health Canada, Address Locator 0900C2, Ottawa, Ontario, Canada K1A 0K9, 1(613) 957-2991, 1(866) 225-0709, Fax: 1(613) 941-5366, info@hc-sc.gc.ca, http://www.hc-sc.gc.ca.

Tish Davidson, AM

National Health Service Corps

Definition

The National Health Service Corps (NHSC) is a U.S. federal government program that helps to connect primary health care providers to underserved areas throughout the United States. The NHSC is part of the U.S. **Department of Health and Human Services** (DHHS) and is administered by the Health Resources and Services Administration (HRSA), Bureau of Clinician Recruitment and Service (BCRS).

Each year about 10,000 NHSC participants deliver health care services to more than 10 million people who live in one of more than 14,000 NHSC-approved sites. These sites, located in urban, rural, or frontier areas, are designated as health professional shortage areas (HPSAs) because they do not have a sufficient number of primary care practitioners to meet the needs of their communities. About half of the sites are **federally qualified health centers** (FQHS), which are supported by the Health Resources and services Administration of DHHS. Other sites include rural health clinics, hospital-affiliated clinics, Indian Health Service clinics, state or federal correctional facilities, community mental health centers, free clinics, school-based health programs, and state and county department-of-health clinics

Purpose

The NHSC was developed in response to a growing **shortage of primary care physicians** that started during the 1950s and 1960s when physicians in training began to choose specialization instead of general practice. By the 1970s there was a shortage of primary care physicians in many parts of the United States. The NHSC estimates that one in five people in the United States lives in an area with a shortage of primary care physicians, and as a result must travel great distances to obtain needed medical care.

The NHSC supplies qualified health care providers to areas of the United States with limited access to care. Since its inception in 1972, more than 40,000 primary care medical, dental, and mental and behavioral health professionals, including 5,483 since passage of the **Patient Protection and Affordable Care Act**, have served in the NHSC.

Programs

There are three different ways for health professionals to participate in the NHSC. The first way is via the NHSC Scholarship Program. This program gives scholarships to students pursuing primary health care professions training in medicine or dentistry or as a **nurse practitioner**, certified nurse **midwife**, or physician assistant. In return for scholarships that cover tuition, other required fees and provide a monthly living stipend intended to defray expenses associated with room and board, students must commit to provide health care to communities in need once they have graduated and completed their training.

In exchange for each school year, or partial school year, of financial support received, students agree to provide primary health care services for one year at an NHSC-approved site located in a high-need health professional shortage area (HPSA). For the first year, or partial school year, of financial support, students must commit to a minimum of two years of service.

Scholarship students have the chance to choose where they will serve from hundreds of NHSC-approved sites in high-need urban, rural, and frontier communities across the United States. The NHSC not only connects participating students to a list of sites with job openings but also supports travel to and from interviews.

The second way to participate is through the NHSC Students to Service Loan Repayment Program (S2S LRP), which offers student loan repayment assistance to medical students in their last year of school in exchange for a commitment to provide primary health care services in eligible Health Professional Shortage Areas (HPSAs) of greatest need. To be eligible, students must be committed to pursuing postgraduate residency training and a career in a primary care specialty—family medicine, internal medicine, general pediatrics, geriatrics, or obstetrics-gynecology. Participants must commit to three years of full-time or six years of half-time service upon completion of their residencies. This time commitment makes participants eligible for loan repayment assistance up to $120,000.

The third way to participate is via the NHSC Loan Repayment Program. This program gives health care providers initial loan repayment awards of as much as $60,000 to help repay student loans in exchange for two years of service at an NHSC-approved site. After they have completed the two-year commitment, participants may continue to work at their sites and receive loan repayment of up to $30,000 per year. Over time and with continued service, health care providers are able to repay all of their education loans.

Eligible physicians can continue to work in underserved areas until all of their qualified student loans are repaid. Many NHSC participants opt to remain in underserved communities long after their service commitment has ended.

The NHSC also offers participants opportunities for continuing education and training as well as the chance to network with a community of health care providers dedicated to improving access to care.

NHSC Provider Retention

Retention in the NHSC is defined as "the percentage of NHSC clinicians who remain practicing in underserved areas after successfully completing their service commitment to the Corps." The NHSC does not offer participating providers any additional financial incentives to remain in these underserved communities. It does, however, actively encourage providers to continue to work in underserved areas and analyzes retention rates.

A survey conducted by the NHSC in 2012 survey found that 82% of NHSC participating providers who completed their service commitment continued to practice in underserved communities for up to one year after their service completion. More than half (55%) continued to practice in underserved areas 10 years after completing their service commitment.

The 2012 survey also found that retention rates were increasing. Retention for up to one year after service completion increased 28% from the rate reported in 2000. The 2012 long-term retention (10 years after

Certified nurse midwife—An advanced practice nurse with specialized education and training in nursing and midwifery. Certified nurse midwives care for women and/or newborns before, during, and after birth and provide well-woman health care.

Community Mental Health Center—A facility that provides core services as described in the Public Health Service Act, including outpatient services, 24-hour emergency care, day treatment, or other partial hospitalization services, psychosocial rehabilitation services, and screening for patients being considered for admission to state mental health facilities.

Department of Health and Human Services (DHHS)—The U.S. government's principal agency charged with protecting the health of all Americans and providing essential human services, especially for vulnerable populations. DHHS is responsible for nearly 25% of all federal expenditures and administers more grant funding than all other federal agencies combined.

Health Professional Shortage Area (HPSA)—A federally designated area in which residents lack adequate access to primary health care providers and services.

Health Resources and Services Administration (HRSA)—The primary federal agency within the Department of Health and Human Services (DHHS) that acts to improve access to health care services for vulnerable individuals and populations.

Indian Health Service—The agency of the Department of Health and Human Services that is responsible for providing federal health services to American Indians and Alaska Natives.

Nurse practitioner—An advanced practice nurse who is trained to provide primary health care. Nurse practitioners perform many of the functions previously assumed by physicians.

Physician Assistant—A health care professional licensed to practice medicine under the supervision of a physician. Like nurse practitioners, physician assistants perform many of the functions previously assumed by physicians.

Primary care physicians—Medical doctors, including general practitioners, internists, pediatricians, family practitioners, and obstetrician-gynecologists who diagnose and treat a variety of health-related problems and refer patients to specialists as needed.

Primary care provider—A health practitioner who identifies, prevents, and treats common illnesses. Primary care providers may be physicians, nurse practitioners, or physician assistants.

service completion) was up 6% from the 2000 rate of 52%. The survey also found that long-term retention rates are higher for providers serving in rural rather than inner city communities.

Retention Rates by Type of Provider

The 2012 survey found the highest retention rate—60%—among physicians who completed their NHSC commitment more than 10 years ago. Ten years after their service commitment was completed, the retention rate for nurse practitioners and certified nurse midwives was comparable to that of physicians—59%—and for physician assistants it was 42%.

Nearly half (48.1%) of dentists and registered dental hygienists participating in the NHSC still practiced in health professional shortage areas (HPSAs) 10 years after their service commitment was completed.

Other health care professionals, such as psychologists, licensed clinical social workers, psychiatric nurse specialists, marriage and family therapists, and licensed professional counselors, are eligible to participate in the NHSC. Four years after completing their NHSC service commitment, 61.1% of these mental and behavioral health clinicians remained in practice in HPSAs.

Factors Influencing Retention

Several factors influence whether providers will remain in underserved areas. The 2012 survey found that major factors affecting NHSC retention rates include the participant's motivation and timing when joining the NHSC and his or her experience at the practice site. The participants most likely to remain in the underserved areas were those whose social, professional, and educational needs were met by the community. Ongoing engagement with NHSC educational programs and other non-financial involvement also favored remaining in practice in an underserved area. To improve retention rates, the NHSC focuses on intensifying support in the areas known to influence health care providers' decisions about whether to remain in underserved communities.

Resources

BOOKS

Barton, Phoebe L. *Understanding the U.S. Health Services System, Fourth Edition* . Chicago, IL: Health Administrations Press, 2009.

Longest, B.B. *Health Policymaking in the United States, Fifth Edition*, Chicago, IL: Health Administrations Press, 2010.

McDonough, J.E. *Inside National Health Reform (California/Milbank Books on Health and the Public)*. Berkeley, CA: University of California Press, 2011.

PERIODICALS

Benson Gold, R. "The National Health Service Corps: An Answer to Family Planning Centers' Workforce Woes?." *Guttmacher Policy Review* 14 (Winter 2011).

Cullen T.J., Hart L.G., Whitcomb M.E., Rosenblatt R.A."The National Health Service Corps: rural physician service and retention." *Journal of the American Board of Family Medicine* 10 (July–August 1997): 272–279.

Kerry, V.B., Auld, A. and Farmer, P. "An International Service Corps for Health &mdash An Unconventional Prescription for Diplomacy." *The New England Journal of Medicine* 362 (September 2010): 1199–1201.

Pathman, D.E., et al. "American Recovery and Reinvestment Act and the Expansion and Streamlining of the National Health Service Corps: A Great Opportunity for Service-Minded Family Physicians." *Journal of the American Board of Family Medicine* 22 (September–October 2009): 582–584.

Pathman, D.E., Konrad, T.R., Ricketts, T.C. "The Comparative Retention of National Health Service Corps and Other Rural Physicians: Results of a 9-Year Follow-up Study." *JAMA* 268 (September 23, 1992): 1552–1558.

Saxton, J.F., Johnd, M.M.E. "Grow the U.S. National Health Service Corps" *JAMA* 301 (May 2009): 1925–1928.

WEBSITES

U.S. Department of Health & Human Services National Health service Corps. http://http://nhsc.hrsa.gov (accessed August 20, 2013).

ORGANIZATIONS

National Advisory Council on the National Health Service Corps, 5600 Fishers Lane, Parklawn Building, Room #13-92, Rockville a, MD 20857

National Health Service Corp (NHSC), (800) 594-4000, Fax: (301) 451-5612

Barbara Wexler, MPH.

National Health Service (United Kingdom)

Definition

The National Health Service (NHS) in the United Kingdom (UK) is the largest publically funded healthcare system in the world. It provides comprehensive healthcare services to all residents of the United Kingdom.

Description

The National Health Service in the United Kingdom is administered as four independent systems:

- National Health Service (England)
- Health and Social Care in Northern Ireland (HSCNI)
- NHS ScotlandNHS Wales

Universal publicly funded healthcare in the United Kingdom began in 1948 after the passage of three Acts. The National Health Service Act created the National Health Service in England and Wales in 1946. The National Health Service (Scotland) created the National Health Service in Scotland in 1947. The Health Services Act (Northern Ireland) of 1948 created the Health Service in Northern Ireland. Although all four health services are administered independently, UK residents can receive necessary services in any of the four countries.

There are slight differences in the organization and benefits of the four separate healthcare services, but they share many common features. Patients access services through a general practice physician (GP) who handles preventative and routine medical needs. The GP and all other service providers must hold a license from the Quality Care Commission and provide a defined level of safety and care. The GP can make referrals to specialist physicians as needed and to NHS hospitals. Costs are covered by monies raised by general taxation. The patient pays nothing at the point of service, and, except in motor vehicle accidents, when the insurer of the vehicle is charged, the patient is not involved in the billing process. Patients cannot be excluded from treatment because of a pre-existing condition.

Almost all healthcare services are covered. This includes care such as:

- prenatal testing
- routine physicals and preventive care
- treatment of illness or injury by a GP, specialist physician, Accident & Emergency department.

Secretary of the United Kingdom's National Health Service, Jeremy Hunt. *(Getty Images)*

- ongoing treatment of chronic illnesses
- hospitalization, including drugs prescribed during hospital stay
- necessary surgery
- rehabilitative services
- mental health services
- learning disability services
- necessary dental care
- necessary ambulance transportation

NHS England requires the patient pay a standard fee for prescription medicines prescribed by a GP. This fee is waived for youth, the elderly, and the poor and for drugs for contraception. The other three health services do not charge a prescription medicine fee. Some vision services may not be covered.

In April 2013, NHS England re-organized internally in an effort to become more cost-efficient and more responsive to local needs. The changes did not affect covered service the way patients accessed care.

Why this is important to the consumer

Universal, publicly funded healthcare relieves the individual of concerns about unexpected expenses and crushing debt related to healthcare treatment. In addition, the program emphasizes primary and preventive care, which has extended life expectancy in the UK. Because the healthcare program is universal and not tied to employment, uniform across the country, and requires no point-of-service payment, barriers to access are removed. In 2010, the Commonwealth Fund surveyed seven first-world healthcare systems and ranked the UK system second overall and first in effective care, efficiency, and cost-related problems.

Limitations

Residents of the UK tend to be satisfied with their healthcare system. There are, however, some concerns about the delay in receiving service for non-emergency events. Patients may have to wait several weeks for specialized diagnostic tests, and even longer for treatments such as hip and knee replacements. The growing shortage of GPs and nurses is a particular threat to the delivery of timely, easily accessible service. The Royal College of General Practitioners predicts that there will be a deficit of 16,000 GPs by 2021. The Royal College of Nursing predicts a shortfall of 47,500 nurses by 2016 and 100,000 nurses by 2022.

Resources

WEBSITES

National Health Service. "About the National Health Service (NHS)." http://www.nhs.uk/NHSEngland/thenhs/about/Pages/overview.aspx (accessed July 27, 3013).

National Health Service. "The NHS." http://www.nhs.uk/choiceintheNHS/Rightsandpledges/NHSConstitution/Pages/Overview.aspx (accessed July 27, 2013).

National Health Service. "The NHS Structure Explained." http://www.nhs.uk/NHSEngland/thenhs/about/Pages/nhsstructure.aspx (accessed July 27, 2013).

NHS Northern Ireland. "Health and Social Care in Northern Ireland." http://www.n-i.nhs.uk (accessed July 27, 3013).

NHS Scotland. "Health in Wales." http://www.show.scot.nhs.uk (accessed July 27, 2013).

NHS Wales. "Health in Wales." http://www.wales.nhs.uk (accessed July 27, 2013).

ORGANIZATIONS

HSC Business Services Organisation Headquarters, 2 Franklin Street, Belfast, Northern Ireland BT2 8DQ, 44 028 (9032) 4431, Admin.Office@hscni.net, http://www.hscbusiness.hscni.net.

NHS England, P.O. Box 16738, Redditch, United Kingdom B97 9PT, 44 0300 311 22 33, england.contactus@nhs.net, http://www.england.nhs.uk.

NHS Scotland Patient/Customer Relations Department, NHS 24, Caledonia House, Cardonald Park, Glasgow, United Kingdom G51 4EB, 44(0800) 377 7330, ask@spso.org.uk, http://www.nhs24.com/.

NHS Wales, http://www.wales.nhs.uk.

Tish Davidson, AM

▌National Institutes of Health

History

The National Institutes of Health (NIH) is part of the United States **Department of Health and Human Services**. The NIH is "the nation's medical research agency" and provides the largest amount of funding for medical research in the world, according to the agency's website, www.nih.gov. The NIH occupies an extensive campus north of Washington, D.C., in Bethesda, Maryland, that occupies approximately 300 acres and includes 75 buildings. The NIH dates from 1887, when the Marine Hospital Service (the predecessor of the U.S. Public Health Service) created a one-room laboratory to assist in its treatment of sailors.

Structure and Functions

The Office of the Director sets policies and coordinates the activities of the 27 different institutes and centers that make up the NIH. The institutes include the National Cancer Institute, National Eye Institute, Heart, Lung, and Blood Institute, National Human Genome Research Institute, National Institute on Aging, National Institute on Alcohol Abuse and Alcoholism, National Institute of Allergy and Infectious Diseases, National Institute of Arthritis and Musculoskeletal and Skin Diseases, National Institute of Biomedical Imaging and Bioengineering, Eunice Kennedy Shriver National Institute of Child Health and Human Development, National Institute on Deafness and Other Communication Disorders, National Institute of Dental and Craniofacial Research, National Institute of Diabetes and Digestive and Kidney Diseases, National Institute on Drug Abuse, National Institute of Environmental Health Sciences, National Institute of Mental Health, National Institute on Minority Health and **Health Disparities**, National Institute of Neurological Disorders and Stroke, National Institute of Nursing Research, and the **National Library of Medicine**. The centers include the Center for Information Technology, Center for Scientific Review, Fogarty International Center, National Center for Advancing Translational Sciences, National Center for Complementary and Alternative Medicine, National Center for Research Resources, and NIH Clinical Center.

Why is the NIH important to the consumer?

Thanks in part to research supported by the NIH, Americans are living approximately 30 years longer than they did in 1900, and the quality of life has dramatically improved. Advances in health that have been impacted by NIH research include a 60% reduction in death rates from heart disease and stroke over the last 50 years, significant improvements in prenatal care that have reduced the risk of maternal death and child mortality, and the development of anti-viral therapies that allow young individuals infected with the HIV virus to expect a normal lifespan of 70 years or longer.

Consumer Education

In partnership with the National Library of Medicine, the NIH maintains the MedlinePlus website, www.nlm.nih.gov/medlineplus, to provide consumer health information. The website includes health and medical data on common topics, such as cancers, pregnancy, diabetes, infections, sexual health, fitness, and complementary/alternative therapies. The site includes links to other organizations for specialized information on health topics for men, women, children, and seniors, and it also includes interactive quizzes and videos of actual surgical procedures.

Public Health

The NIH plays an active role in many aspects of public health. For example, in outbreaks of foodborne bacterial infections, NIH researchers are able to use genetic sequencing to help identify the bacteria, confirm the source of infection, and develop strategies to control the outbreak. Another notable ongoing NIH research effort involves the development of a universal flu vaccine that will protect people from many different strains of flu over a long time, eliminating the need for a yearly flu shot.

Health and Wellness Resources

In addition to co-sponsoring the consumer health website MedlinePlus, the NIH offers a variety of additional online health and wellness resources for consumers, in keeping with the NIH's overall mission to improve the nation's health through quality scientific research. For example, the NIH-sponsored website smokefree.gov provides extensive information for anyone who wants to quit smoking, knows someone who wants to quit, or is struggling with the challenge of quitting. The site links to an option for downloading an associated app, smokefreetxt, which delivers tips, support, and advice to an individual's smartphone.

"It's a Noisy Planet" is an example of an NIH consumer health initiative specifically for children. The Noisy Planet program is designed to educate children and teens about the importance of protecting their hearing and how to control exposure to excessive noise.

Health Literacy

Another important aim of the NIH is to make it easier for patients to talk to their doctors. The NIH **health literacy** initiative, called Clear Communication, is designed to help patients understand and communicate about their health. Effective communication between doctors and patients is important so patients understand instructions for prescriptions to avoid taking too much or too little medication, and instructions for care after a medical procedure or a hospital stay. But patients have to do their part. The NIH site includes tips on preparing for a doctor visit, such as making a list of symptoms associated with a problem, questions about medication or treatment, or other specific concerns to discuss.

NIH's Clinical Trials

The medical research conducted by the NIH has contributed to vast improvements in health and will continue to do so with the help of volunteers. Individuals can participate in clinical trials of medications, devices, or health intervention strategies such as changes in diet or exercise. Some clinical trials involve healthy volunteers, as well as people who are ill, while others focus on people with specific conditions, such as cancer or diabetes. The clinical trials information section on the NIH website describes different types of trials, and what may be expected of participants. In addition, ClinicalTrials.gov, a website co-sponsored by the NIH, the National Library of Medicine, and the U.S. Department of Health and Human Services, allows consumers, as well as doctors and scientists, to search for clinical trials by topic, such as diabetes, heart attack, or asthma, or by location, such as Los Angeles, Boston, or Canada. The ClinicalTrials.gov site also includes general information about clinical trials, aimed at a consumer audience.

Resources

WEBSITES

National Institutes of Health. "About NIH." September 18, 2013. http://www.nih.gov/about/ (accessed November 24, 2013).

National Institutes of Health. "Clear Communication." August 28, 2013. http://www.nih.gov/clear communication/talktoyourdoctor.htm (accessed November 24, 2013).

National Institutes of Health. "NIH Clinical Research Trials and You." September 27, 2013. http://www.nih.gov/health/clinicaltrials/index.htm (accessed November 24, 2013).

National Institutes of Health. "Our Health." September 10, 2013. http://www.nih.gov/about/impact/health.htm (accessed November 24, 2013).

National Institutes of Health. "Science-Based Health & Wellness Resources for Your Community." March 13, 2013. http://www.nih.gov/health/wellness/ (accessed November 24, 2013).

National Institutes of Health. "Videos from NIH." November 22, 2013. http://www.nih.gov/news/videos/index.htm (accessed November 24, 2013).

Noisy Planet. November 6, 2013. http://www.noisypla net.nidcd.nih.gov/Pages/Default.aspx (accessed November 24, 2013).

Smokefree.gov. http://smokefree.gov/ (accessed November 24, 2013).

Heidi Splete

National Library of Medicine

History

The National Library of Medicine (NLM) was founded in 1836, and it is part of the **National Institutes of Health**. The NLM is located on the National Institutes of Health campus in Rockville, Maryland, just north of Washington, D.C. It is the largest biomedical library in the world, with resources that include print and online materials on a range of health and medical topics. These resources are accessed by millions of consumers, scientists, and health professionals worldwide each year, according to the NLM's website.

The NLM began as the library of **Surgeon General** Thomas Lawson, who served from 1862 to 1864. The library existed and expanded in several locations in downtown Washington, D.C., until 1962, when it moved to its current location in Maryland.

Structure and Functions

In addition to serving as a library, the NLM administers a medical library system across the United States (the 6,000-member National Network of Libraries of Medicine) and coordinates extramural programs to train people in health information technology and biomedical informatics.

Why is the NLM important to the consumer?

The NLM is, at its heart, a library, and as such it serves as a resource for consumers as well as scientists, clinicians, and researchers. The NLM, in partnership with the National Institutes of Health, has developed a health website specifically for consumers: MedlinePlus.

MedlinePlus Overview

The MedlinePlus website, www.nlm.nih.gov/medlineplus, is designed to provide health information to the consumer. The site is maintained by the NLM in partnership with the National Institutes of Health. The website includes health and medical data divided into three sections: "Health Topics," "Drugs & Supplements," and "Videos and Cool Tools." The Health Topics section allows users to search for health information by keyword, such as "back pain," but it also provides a list of common topics, such as cancers, pregnancy, diabetes, infections, sexual health, fitness, and complementary/alternative therapies. MedlinePlus also features a news section that is updated regularly with the latest consumer health news, and the home page features tabs with general health topics and topics categorized as seniors', children's, men's, and women's health issues. The Drugs & Supplements section allows users to search for information about prescription drugs and over-the-counter medications using either brand or generic names. This section also allows consumers to search for types of dietary supplements and herbal remedies. The Videos and Cool Tools section includes interactive tutorials for consumers about common medical conditions, diagnostic tests, and surgical procedures. The website also features an archive of hour-long videos of actual surgical procedures performed at various facilities across the United States.

Just for Kids

The National Library of Medicine has something for everyone, including children. The NLM consumer website, MedlinePlus, includes a special kids' page with a range of health resources and links to sites that provide information on topics ranging from the basics of how different body systems work to advice for managing conditions such as asthma, social issues such as bullying, and overviews of what kids can expect during a hospital visit.

Resources and Research

The NLM offers access to resources about the history of health and medicine as well contemporary research, most of which are available online to consumers, scientists, and clinicians. The NLM's digital projects include Historical Anatomies on the Web, a collection of images from anatomy atlases in the NLM's permanent collection; Profiles in Science, biographical information about 20th-century pioneers in

(National Library of Medicine)

health and medical research (such as C. Everett Koop, Virginia Apgar, and Linus Pauling); and the Visible Human Project, a complete, 3-D illustration of male and female human anatomy.

What's Toxic?

The NLM maintains databases of information about hazardous chemicals and environmental health, as well as details about potential problems with drugs and other consumer health products. This information is available to everyone through Toxnet, a database that is part of the NLM's division of specialized information services. Concerned about reports of fever related to ibuprofen use? Type "ibuprofen fever" into Toxnet, and you will get links to clinical trials.

Find Out About Clinical Trials

One of the functions of the NLM is to provide information about past, ongoing, and future clinical trials to test new drugs, medical devices, or other treatments. Doctors, scientists, and consumers can read about the design and results of medical trials through ClinicalTrials.gov, and website co-sponsored by the NLM, the National Institutes of Health, and the U.S. **Department of Health and Human Services**. Consumers can search for clinical trials by topic, such as diabetes, heart attack, or asthma, or by location, such as Los Angeles, Boston, or Canada. The ClinicalTrials.gov site also includes general information about clinical trials aimed at a consumer audience. The Q&A format addresses such topics as how long clinical trials last, who conducts them and why, and details about participation in clinical trials.

Resources

WEBSITES

National Library of Medicine. http://www.va.gov/health/ (Accessed September 1, 2013.)

National Library of Medicine. http://www.nlm.nih.gov/about/index.html(Accessed September 1, 2013.)

National Library of Medicine. http://www.nlm.nih.gov/medlineplus/(Accessed September 1, 2013.)

National Library of Medicine. http://www.nlm.nih.gov/medlineplus/childrenspage.html(Accessed September 1, 2013.)

National Library of Medicine. http://toxnet.nlm.nih.gov/ (Accessed September 1, 2013.)

National Library of Medicine. http://clinicaltrials.gov/ (Accessed September 1, 2013.)

Heidi Splete

National Quality Forum (NQF)

Definition

The National Quality Forum (NQF) is a non-profit organization whose mission is to improve the quality of healthcare for all Americans.

Description

NQF was founded in 1999 on the recommendation of the President's Advisory Commission on **Consumer Protection** and Quality in the Healthcare Industry. It is a public-private partnership funded by the federal government and corporate and foundation grants.

The mission of NQF is

- building consensus on national healthcare priorities and goals for performance improvement and working in partnership to achieve them.
- endorsing national consensus standards for measuring and publicly reporting on performance.
- promoting the attainment of national goals through education and outreach programs.

The membership of NQF is composed of stakeholders representing governmental agencies, corporate interests, medical practitioners, and patients. Members can participate through eight councils representing various aspects of healthcare that advise the board of directors. These eight councils are:

- Consumer Council
- Health Plan Council
- Health Professionals Council
- Provider Organizations Council
- Public/Community Health Agency Council
- Purchasers Council
- Quality Measurement, Research, and Improvement Council
- Supplier and Industry Council Through these councils, the NQF addresses topics such as health and well-being, disease prevention, **patient-centered care**, effective communication and coordination of care, patient safety, cost of care, **end-of-life care**, disparities in care across diverse communities, and the use of information technology in healthcare.

Why this is important to the consumer

The NQF reviews, endorses, and recommends standardized healthcare performance measures (best practices) to improve the quality of healthcare and its equitable delivery across diverse communities. The results of these performance measures are made available to the public. Many of these performance measures are concerned with patient safety, affordability, and equitable delivery of healthcare and are not readily visible to the consumer. However, the work of the NQF benefits consumers in the following ways:

- By collecting information on performance measures, they make the healthcare system more information-rich.
- The information collected indicates steps that healthcare professionals can take to make care safer, more equitable, and more cost-effective.
- By publicizing the information collected, the healthcare system becomes more transparent.
- Healthcare providers are held more accountable to consumers.
- Consumers have access to information that helps them make informed decisions about their care.

Resources

WEBSITES

Agency for Healthcare Research and Quality. "30 Safe Practices for Better Healthcare." http://www.ahrq.gov/ research/findings/factsheets/errors-safety/30safe/ index.html (accessed July 24, 2013).

National Quality Forum. "Field Guide to NQF Resources." http://www.qualityforum.org/Field_Guide (accessed July 26, 2013).

National Quality Forum. "Safe Practices for Better Healthcare." http://www.ahrq.gov/professionals/quality-patient-safety/patient-safety-resources/resources/ nqfpract.pdf (accessed July 24, 2013).

ORGANIZATIONS

National Quality Forum, 1030 15th Street NW, Ste 800, Washington, DC 20005, (202) 783-1300, Fax: (202) 783-3434, info@qualityforum.org, http://www.quality forum.org.

Tish Davidson, AM

Naturopathy

Definition

Naturopathy is a form of alternative medicine that combines a belief in vitalism (the notion that the human body contains a vital force or energy that governs respiration, metabolism, growth, and the immune system; and that it can maintain health without unnatural interventions) with a holistic approach to health care. It is also known as "natural medicine." The National Center for Complementary and Alternative Medicine (NCCAM)

classifies naturopathy as a "medical system" rather than a specific practice or type of intervention. The English word *naturopathy* was coined by a homeopathic physician, John H. Scheel, in 1895. It is derived from the Latin word for "nature" and the Greek word for "disease."

Naturopathy grew out of the nature cure (also called "natural medicine cure") movement in nineteenth-century Germany and the United Kingdom, which was more of a philosophy of healing or a way of life than a set of specific therapies. As a result, contemporary naturopathy includes treatments and interventions drawn from a range of other medical systems, including **Ayurveda**, **homeopathy**, Western **herbal medicine**, acupuncture, **traditional Chinese medicine**, and mainstream psychology and nutritional science. None of these approaches is unique to naturopathy, and some are considered pseudoscience by conventional physicians. It is telling that Bastyr University, the flagship school for training naturopaths in the United States and Canada, offers courses in midwifery, herbal sciences, Oriental medicine, Ayurvedic sciences, counseling and health psychology, and holistic landscape design as well as naturopathic medicine.

Description

The practice of naturopathy in the contemporary United States, Canada, Germany, and Australia (the countries where it is most widely used as of 2013) varies according to the training of the individual practitioner and his or her interest in non-Western medical systems. In North America, most naturopaths offer a form of primary health care combined with some complementary and alternative (CAM) therapies, with an overall emphasis on wellness and preventive medicine.

Naturopathy claims to be based on six principles of healing:

- First, do no harm. This principle, first enunciated by Hippocrates in the fifth century B.C., is interpreted by naturopaths to imply that medicines and other therapies should be chosen to minimize the risk of harmful side effects and that the least force necessary to treat illness should be employed.
- Respect the healing power of nature. Naturopaths frequently quote the Latin phrase *vis medicatrix naturae* as a summary of their belief that the body has an orderly and intelligent ability to heal itself, and that the naturopath's task is to remove obstacles to this natural ability.
- Identify and treat the causes of the patient's illness rather than merely suppressing symptoms.
- Counsel patients about the importance of a healthful lifestyle. To naturopaths, the healer's proper role is that of a teacher or lifestyle coach, helping the patient

to take responsibility for his or her own health. Naturopaths often refer to the fact that the English word *doctor* comes from the Latin *docere*, "to teach."

• Treat the whole person, not just the body. Naturopathy is a holistic approach to health that seeks to take into account the physical, mental, emotional, genetic, and social dimensions of each patient's life. Naturopaths will typically advise patients to follow a spiritual practice or path of some kind as well as take care of their physical health.

• Emphasize the role of preventive health care, not just the treatment of illness, in maintaining the patient's health and well-being.

Background

Naturopathy came to the United State from Europe at the beginning of the twentieth century with the arrival of Benedict Lust (1872–1945), an immigrant from Germany who claimed that he had been cured of tuberculosis by taking the "water cure" (hydrotherapy) popularized by Sebastian Kneipp (1821–1897), a Bavarian Roman Catholic priest who had devised a system of hydrotherapy combined with herbal remedies and advice about exercise and diet to treat the monks in a nearby monastery as well as the local villagers.

Lust settled in New York City, where he opened a health food store and published newsletters in both German and English advocating natural treatments for illness—primarily herbal remedies, homeopathic medicines, hydrotherapy, and exercise. Lust purchased the right to use the term *naturopathy* from John Scheel in 1902, and shortly afterward founded the first school of naturopathy in the United States, the American School of Naturopathy. In addition to establishing health resorts in New Jersey and Florida, Lust introduced yoga and Ayurvedic medicine to the American public. This combination of European nature cures with alternative medical systems developed in Asia continues to characterize the practice of naturopathy in North America.

Naturopathy went into decline in the 1920s and 1930s, partly because of the standardization of mainstream medical education following the reforms suggested by Abraham Flexner's famous report in 1910, and partly because Benedict Lust was arrested by federal authorities several times for promoting nude sunbathing at his health resorts. In the 1970s, however, naturopathy underwent a revival as part of the growing interest in holistic and traditional medicine that characterized the New Age movement. One of the leaders of this revival was John Bastyr (1912–1995), a naturopath, homeopath, and chiropractor practicing in the Seattle area. Bastyr became the president of the National College of Natural Medicine (NCNM) in Portland, Oregon. Founded in 1956,

NCNM is the oldest of the seven accredited naturopathic medical schools in North America, six in the United States and one in Toronto, Canada. Bastyr University, named after John Bastyr, was founded in Seattle in 1978 and opened a second campus in San Diego in 2012. The seven schools are accredited by the Council on Naturopathic Medical Education (CNME) and confer the degree of doctor of naturopathy (N.D.) or doctor of naturopathic medicine (N.M.D.). The CNME is recognized for accreditation purposes by the U.S. Department of Education.

Education and credentialing

Naturopaths vary in their academic preparation and credentialing. While the seven schools accredited by the CNME require four years of coursework beyond the college level for the N.D. or N.M.D. degree, they also offer master's degrees in such fields as acupuncture, Ayurveda, nutrition, midwifery, and other fields. In addition, Bastyr offers bachelor's degrees in nutrition, health psychology, exercise science, and human biology. NCNM offers online courses of study as well as residential programs, leading to what are called "certificates" rather than academic degrees, while Bastyr offers certificates in holistic landscape design and Chinese herbal medicine.

Candidates for the N.D. or N.M.D. are required to hold a bachelor's degree from an accredited college or university with a 3.0 grade point average, and to have completed a standard undergraduate premedical curriculum. They receive training in basic sciences, diagnostic imaging, and standard medical testing as well as naturopathic therapies and clinical practice. Although some N.D.s or N.M.D.s pursue residencies in naturopathic medicine after graduation, completion of a residency is not required to qualify as a practitioner. Following completion of the degree, N.D.s or N.M.Ds in jurisdictions that regulate naturopathy must pass the Naturopathic Physicians Licensing Examinations, or NPLEX, administered by the North American Board of Naturopathic Examiners (NABNE).

American jurisdictions that require licensing for naturopaths as of 2013 include Alaska, Arizona, California, Connecticut, Hawaii, Idaho, Kansas, Maine, Minnesota, Montana, New Hampshire, North Dakota, Oregon, Utah, Vermont, the state of Washington, Washington, D.C., Puerto Rico, and the U.S. Virgin Islands. Five Canadian provinces—Alberta, British Columbia, Manitoba, Ontario, and Saskatchewan—similarly require naturopaths to be licensed and to pass continuing education examinations. The scope of practice varies somewhat across jurisdictions: in some, naturopaths may perform minor surgery, deliver babies, practice acupuncture, or prescribe medications.

Types of naturopaths

Not all persons who call themselves naturopaths have completed a doctoral degree in naturopathy from a residential program accredited by the CNME. There are several thousand so-called traditional naturopaths in North America who are not graduates of accredited schools, or have obtained degrees or certificates only through correspondence or online schools. The CNME states on its website, "Although correspondence courses can be effective in many disciplines, naturopathic licensing agencies do not believe they are adequate for preparing students to practice as licensed physicians. The American Association of Naturopathic Physicians and the Canadian Association of Naturopathic Doctors do not consider those who obtain N.D. or N.M.D. degrees from correspondence schools to be part of the naturopathic medical profession." Traditional naturopaths do not use or offer prescription medications, surgery, x-ray imaging, or injections of any kind; they emphasize cleansing and strengthening the body by noninvasive treatments.

In addition to licensed and traditional naturopaths, there is a third type of practitioner, namely chiropractors, practitioners of traditional Chinese medicine, osteopathic physicians, and some mainstream dentists and physicians who have added naturopathic treatments to their standard practices. Some of these practitioners have pursued specialized study at one of the accredited naturopathic medical colleges.

Why this is important to the consumer

There are several major reasons for consumers to inform themselves about naturopathy and its practitioners. Although some of the individual therapies recommended by naturopaths (such as acupuncture) have been investigated in clinical trials, naturopathy as an overall approach to health care has not been thoroughly researched and is regarded with skepticism by many conventional physicians. There are only 10 trials of naturopathy in the United States registered with the **National Institutes of Health** as of late 2013.

Know the naturopath

As the foregoing discussion of the lack of standardized educational and licensing standards for naturopaths indicates, consumers must find out what their particular state or province requires, and the scope of practice it allows, before they consult a naturopath. NCCAM suggests asking the naturopath not only about his or her education and training, but also about his or her referral network and coordination

---

KEY TERMS

Ayurveda—The traditional medical system of India.

Holistic—In medicine, an approach that takes all dimensions of a human being into account, the psychosocial and spiritual as well as the physical. Naturopathy is based on a holistic approach to health care.

Hydrotherapy—The use of water to relieve pain and treat various diseases. Hydrotherapy may involve drinking the water, bathing in it, or having water at various temperatures applied under pressure to the body.

Pseudoscience—A belief or practice that claims to be scientific but cannot be tested by any known scientific method and lacks supporting evidence or credibility.

Vitalism—A term used to describe a set of beliefs that bodily functions in humans (and other animals) are governed by a vital force or energy that is distinct from all chemical or physical substances or processes and cannot be explained in material terms.

---

with mainstream health care providers. In addition, wise consumers will inform their **primary care physician** or any specialists who treat them that they are receiving treatment from a naturopath.

Costs and insurance coverage

As of 2013, the Canadian public health insurance system does not cover naturopathy. **Medicare** and **Medicaid** in the United States also do not cover the costs of naturopathic treatment, although some **private insurance plans** do pay for it. Consumers should find out whether their present health insurance policy does, in fact, cover naturopathy before consulting a practitioner, and they should ask the practitioner about any out-of-pocket costs.

Benefits and risks of naturopathic treatment

Consumers who prefer to take charge of their own health care and to have a relatively egalitarian relationship with their health care provider are often attracted to naturopathy because of its emphasis on the naturopath's role as a teacher. Others like naturopathy's emphasis on wellness and preventive medicine, and its holistic approach to treating patients as full human beings rather than focusing on the symptoms of physical disease.

There are, however, risks to using a naturopath as a primary care physician. One is the emphasis on herbal medicine in naturopathy. The fact that herbs are natural products does not mean that they cannot produce side effects as severe as those of conventional prescription drugs, and they can interact in problematic ways with surgical anesthesia as well as other medications. Moreover, many naturopaths discourage patients from receiving vaccinations on the grounds that these are unnecessary or unnatural interventions, which may expose patients to preventable illnesses, particularly if they travel abroad. A third risk to health is the recommendation of unusual or highly restrictive diets, which may be harmful to some people. Last, relying exclusively on naturopathy to the exclusion of mainstream medical care for severe infections or broken bones and other traumatic injuries can have serious health consequences.

Resources

BOOKS

Crawford, Gregory A. *The Medical Library Association Guide to Finding Out about Complementary and Alternative Medicine: The Best Print and Electronic Resources.* New York: Neal-Schuman Publishers, 2010.

Murray, Michael T., and Joseph E. Pizzorno. *Encyclopedia of Natural Medicine*, 3rd ed., revised. New York: Atria Books, 2012.

Pizzorno, Joseph E., and Michael T. Murray, eds. *Textbook of Natural Medicine*, 4th ed. St. Louis, MO: Elsevier/ Saunders, 2013.

PERIODICALS

Arankalle, D.V. "Integrating Naturopathy and Yoga in Management of Musculoskeletal Disorders." *International Journal of Preventive Medicine* 4 (January 2013): 120–121.

Braun, L.A., et al. "Naturopaths and Western Herbalists' Attitudes to Evidence, Regulation, Information Sources and Knowledge about Popular Complementary Medicines." *Complementary Therapies in Medicine* 21 (February 2013): 58–64.

Eggertson, L. "The New Rules of Naturopathy." *Canadian Medical Association Journal* 184 (October 2, 2012): E743–E744.

Fok, M.C., et al. "A Naturopathic Cause of Portal Venous Gas Embolism. Hydrogen Peroxide Ingestion Causing Significant Portal Venous Gas and Stomach Wall Thickening." *Gastroenterology* 144 (March 2013): 509, 658–659.

Leach, M.J. "Profile of the Complementary and Alternative Medicine Workforce across Australia, New Zealand, Canada, United States and United Kingdom." *Complementary Therapies in Medicine* 21 (August 2013): 364–378.

Litchy, A.P. "Naturopathic Physicians: Holistic Primary Care and Integrative Medicine Specialists." *Journal of Dietary Supplements* 8 (December 2011): 369–377.

WEBSITES

American Association of Naturopathic Physicians (AANP). "Definition of Naturopathic Medicine." http://www.naturopathic.org/content.asp?pl = 16&sl = 59& contentid = 59 (accessed September 7, 2013).

Bastyr University. "Principles of Naturopathic Medicine." http://www.bastyr.edu/academics/areas-study/study-naturopathic-medicine/about-naturopathic-medicine# Principles (accessed September 7, 2013).

Bastyr University. "What Is Naturopathic Medicine?" http://www.bastyr.edu/academics/areas-study/study-naturopathic-medicine/about-naturopathic-medicine (accessed September 7, 2013).

National Center for Complementary and Alternative Medicine (NCCAM). "Naturopathy: An Introduction." http://nccam.nih.gov/health/naturopathy/naturopathyintro.htm (accessed September 7, 2013).

ORGANIZATIONS

American Association of Naturopathic Physicians (AANP), 818 18th Street, NW, Suite 250, Washington, DC, United States 20006, (202) 237-8150, (866) 538-2267, Fax: (202) 237-8152, member.services@naturopathic.org, http://www.naturopathic.org/index.asp.

Bastyr University, 14500 Juanita Drive N.E., Kenmore, WA, United States 98028-4966, (425) 602-3000, Fax: (425) 823-6222, http://www.bastyr.edu/.

Council on Naturopathic Medical Education (CNME), P.O. Box 178, Great Barrington, MA, United States 01230, (413) 528-8877, http://www.cnme.org/contact.html, http://www.cnme.org/.

National Center for Complementary and Alternative Medicine (NCCAM), 9000 Rockville Pike, Bethesda, MD, United States 20892, (888) 644-6226, http://nccam.nih.gov/tools/contact.htm, http://nccam.nih.gov/.

National College of Natural Medicine (NCNM), 049 S.W. Porter Street, Portland, OR, United States 97201, (503) 552-1555, reception@ncnm.edu, http://www.ncnm.edu/.

Rebecca J. Frey, Ph.D.

NIH *see* **National Institutes of Health**

NLM *see* **National Library of Medicine**

Nurse practitioner

Definition

A nurse practitioner (NP) is a nurse with advanced training who can provide medical services with or without physician supervision, depending on the laws of the state.

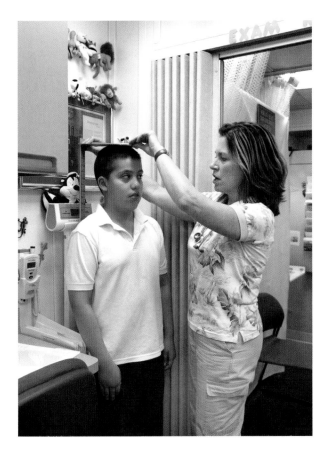

A nurse practitioner (NP) is a nurse with advanced training who can provide medical services with or without physician supervision. *(Tim Boyle/Getty Images)*

Description

An NP is a nurse who has received additional education, usually a graduate degree, and passed a national certification exam. The NP then can provide a range of health care services, depending on the state regulations and licensing requirements in the state in which the NP is located. More than 170,000 NPs practiced in the United States as of 2012, and the profession has been growing. Nurse practitioners work in a number of health care settings and specialty areas, but most are employed in physician offices and hospitals.

The first program to educate this advanced level of nurse was opened at the University of Colorado at Boulder in 1965. By 1993, the American Association of Nurse Practitioners (AANP) had formed a certification program separate from the growing number of educational programs. Today, more than 97% of all NPs maintain national certification in addition to required state licenses. Nearly 90% of NPs were educated in primary care practice, and nearly all NPs prescribe medications.

Education

Most NPs enter their advanced education program following completion of a bachelor's degree program in nursing, and sometimes following several years of working as a registered nurse (RN). Coursework depends on the specialty chosen but usually covers areas such as research, pharmacology, primary care, and diagnosis of disease. Some NPs enter programs from other fields; they might have a bachelor's degree but no nursing experience. In those cases, the NP candidate might have to take certain prerequisites, such as chemistry or microbiology, before beginning the NP graduate coursework. Some NPs receive doctoral degrees. Most then pass a national certification examination and continue to take courses after beginning practice to maintain their skills. The number of continuing-education hours they must take each year depends on state licensing requirements.

Typical role of the NP

Many NPs work alongside physicians, helping to provide care to patients in busy offices. For example, NPs often assist obstetrics and gynecology specialists by seeing patients, providing education, and counseling patients. Some NPs work in clinics without having physician supervision. The requirement for supervision and the extent of the NP's practice depends on the state's laws. Several states allow NPs to practice without supervision, so that they can evaluate, diagnose, and treat patients. NPs in these states can order and interpret imaging or laboratory tests and prescribe medications. In other states, NPs have reduced practice, or engage in one or more of these practices without supervision, but not all of them. Other states restrict NP practice, requiring a team approach or supervision by a physician. Every state and the District of Columbia license NPs in some capacity.

Nurse practitioners might help patients in physician offices, hospitals, specialty clinics, public health clinics, community health centers, emergency departments, urgent care centers, or nursing homes, or in schools and college health centers. Specialty areas for NPs include:

- acute care
- adult health
- family health
- oncology
- pediatrics
- neonatal health
- women's health
- mental health

Role of the nurse practitioner in health care reform

Many areas, such as rural communities and urban neighborhoods, have too few primary care providers for the residents who need health care. Health care reform hopes to improve access to care, especially for those who currently do not have access or insurance coverage. This means there will be an even greater need for primary care providers, a gap that NPs could help fill. NPs can only help to the extent that state laws will allow, however.

Why they are important to the consumer

Use of nurse practitioners helps to lower costs at physician offices, health clinics, and community health centers. Having nurse practitioners provide primary care also can lower overall health care costs by providing care to patients who might otherwise not receive preventive or education services close to their homes. NPs often help to educate and counsel patients, which can help patients better prevent disease or manage chronic illness.

NPS can be integral to a new focus on **patient-centered care** and the teamwork approach that makes up the **patient-centered medical home**. Since the 1970s, community-based health centers have provided much-needed primary care and mental health services to people in underserved communities. As many as 21% of the visits made to community health centers each year are to NPs, and more than one-third of the patients whom the NPs see have chronic illnesses.

In addition to helping ease the problem of a primary care provider shortage, NPs can help keep patients satisfied with their health care. The AANP reports that about 600 million visits are made to NPs in the United States each year, but that patient satisfaction with the care they receive is extremely high.

Resources

BOOKS

Institute of Medicine of the National Academies. *Living Well with Chronic Illness*. Washington, D.C.: National Academies Press, 2012.

WEBSITES

"Occupational Employment and Wages, May 2012. 29-1171 Nurse Practitioners." Bureau of Labor Statistics. http://www.bls.gov/oes/current/oes291171.htm (accessed September 25, 2013).

"What's an NP?" American Association of Nurse Practitioners. http://www.aanp.org/all-about-nps/what-is-an-np (accessed September 25, 2013).

Yee, Tracy, Ellyn R. Boukus, Dori Cross, and Divya R. Samuel. "Primary Care Workforce Shortages: Nurse Practitioner Scope-of-Practice Laws and Payment Policies." National Institute for Health Care Reform. http://www.nihcr.org/PCP-Workforce-NPs (accessed September 25, 2013).

ORGANIZATIONS

American Association of Nurse Practitioners, P.O. Box 12846, Austin, TX 78711, (512) 442-4262, Fax: (512) 442-6469, admin@aanp.org, www.aanp.org.

Teresa G. Odle

Nursing home

Definition

A nursing home is a facility that provides 24-hour-a-day custodial and nursing care for individuals who cannot care for themselves. Most nursing home residents are elderly, although younger people with physical or cognitive deficits may also live in nursing homes.

Description

Nursing homes, also called "skilled nursing facilities," care for people who have severe deficits in their ability to attend to the activities of daily living. These activities include toileting, feeding, bathing, dressing, transferring (getting out of bed or into a chair, for example), walking, and climbing stairs. Instrumental activities of daily living are more complex tasks that also become difficult for people as they age or become debilitated. These include shopping, cooking, managing finances, driving, and doing laundry. When people can no longer reliably and safely do these activities, they are often candidates for a more supervised living environment, such as a nursing home.

A nursing home is a living center that cares for a minimum of three individuals who are unrelated to the home licensee. Nursing homes can care for people with permanent disabilities or chronic conditions, or can be a brief convalescent or rehabilitative stop after surgery, an illness, or an injury. Federal law regulates nursing homes very closely, and funding for these facilities may be accomplished through private insurance, **long-term care insurance**, or the government's **Medicare** or **Medicaid** programs. While nursing home costs can vary widely among facilities, the median daily cost in the United States is $206.

Nursing homes are responsible for custodial care, which generally addresses the resident's Activity of Daily Living Deficit and provides assistance for them to get into and out of bed, dress, bathe, toilet, and feed themselves (or be fed). Additionally, medical care is immediately available in nursing homes. Many nursing home residents have significant medical conditions which require attention. The most common medical diagnoses among nursing home residents include conditions involving the circulatory system (about 25%), mental conditions (around 20%), and conditions involving the nervous/sensory system (about 15%). Dementia is particularly common among nursing home residents; fully 60% of them

suffer from some form of this disabling condition, including Alzheimer's disease. About 40% of nursing home residents arrive at the facility after a disabling fall.

While individuals with brief conditions that cause disability may temporarily live in a nursing home while recovering, the majority of individuals living in nursing homes are permanent residents. Most are elderly, and about 50% are 85 or older. The majority are women, and difficulties with mobility, frailty, and behavioral issues are common.

Medical personnel working in nursing homes include nursing assistants, who take vital signs and test blood sugar for patients who are diabetic, as well as assisting with general care. Licensed practical or registered nurses are always on site. They are often responsible for passing out medications, providing wound care and dressing changes, and supervising other medical procedures that residents require. Federal law mandates that nursing homes be overseen by a licensed physician. Other ancillary staff provide physical therapy, occupational therapy, speech therapy, and nutrition consultations.

Why this is important to the consumer

The population of the United States is rapidly aging. While there were 39.6 million individuals aged 65 or more in 2009, projections suggest that there will be 72.1 million people in that age bracket by the year 2030. While the elderly made up 12.4% of the population in 2000, they will be

Personal health care expenditures, by source of funds and type of expenditure: United States, selected years 1960–2010

	1960	1970	1980	1990	2000	2008	2009	2010
					Amount in billions			
Nursing care facilities and continuing care retirement communities expenditures	$0.8	$4.0	$15.3	$44.9	$85.1	$132.7	$138.7	$143.1
					Percent distribution			
All sources of funds	100.0	100.0	100.0	100.0	100.0	100.0	100.0	100.0
Out-of-pocket payments	74.8	49.5	40.7	40.3	31.9	29.1	28.5	28.3
Health insurance	0.0	28.5	51.9	48.8	61.1	64.7	65.3	65.5
Private health insurance	0.0	0.2	1.3	6.2	8.8	8.2	8.5	8.9
Medicare	—	3.5	2.0	3.8	12.7	20.8	21.6	22.3
Medicaid	—	23.3	46.2	36.6	37.4	33.0	32.4	31.5
Federal	—	12.5	26.1	20.6	21.7	19.3	21.6	21.4
State and local	—	10.8	20.1	16.0	15.7	13.7	10.8	10.1
Other health insurance programs*	0.0	1.5	2.4	2.2	2.2	2.8	2.9	2.8
Other third-party payers and programs**	25.2	21.9	7.4	10.9	6.9	6.2	6.2	6.3

*Includes Department of Defense and Department of Veterans Affairs
**Includes worksite health care, Indian Health Service, workers' compensation, among others.

(Table by PreMediaGlobal. Copyright © 2014 Cengage Learning®.)

KEY TERMS

Fellow—An M.D. who has completed a residency and is undergoing further training in a particular medical subspecialty.

Medical resident—An individual who has received an M.D. and is undergoing further training in a particular medical specialty.

Nurse practitioner—An advanced practice nurse whose practice scope includes diagnosis and treatment, in some cases outside of the direct supervision of a physician.

Physician assistant—A healthcare provider whose practice scope includes diagnosis and treatment, which must be provided under the direct supervision of a physician.

Nursing and medical care in nursing homes is more extensive than that offered in assisted living and independent living facilities. *(Stockbyte/Getty Images)*

fully 19% in 2030. This rapidly growing group of elderly will require care as they continue to age. The U.S. currently has 16,100 nursing homes, with a total of 1.7 million beds; this represents an 86% occupancy rate. As the population of individuals who are aging out of their own homes grows, more of these types of facilities will be needed.

Resources

BOOKS

Kovner Anthony R. et al. *Health Care Delivery in the United States* 10th ed. New York: Springer Publishing Company, 2011.

Schulte,Margaret F.*Health Care Delivery in the U.S.A.: An Introduction* 2nd ed. New York: Productivity Press, 2012.

Sultz, Harry A. et al. *Health Care USA: Understanding Its Organization and Delivery* 7th ed. Sudbury, MA: Jonas & Bartlett Learning, 2010.

WEBSITES

National Caregivers Library. Types of Care Facilities [accessed September 22, 2013]. http://www.caregivers library.org/caregivers-resources/grp-care-facilities/types-of-care-facilities-article.aspx.

USA.gov. Choosing a Health Care Facility. 2013 [accessed September 22, 2013]. http://www.usa.gov/topics/health/caregivers/health-care-facility.shtml/.

ORGANIZATIONS

Administration on Aging, One Massachusetts Avenue NW, Washington, DC 20001, (202) 619- 0724, http://www.aoa.gov/.

National Care Planning Council, P.O. BOX 1118, Centerville, UT 84014, (801) 298-8676

National Institute on Aging, National Institutes of Health, Health & Human Services, 31 Center Drive, MSC 2292., Bethesda, MD 20892, (301) 496-1752, http://www.nia.nih.gov/.

United States Department of Labor, 200 Constitution Ave. NW, Washington, DC 20210, (800) 321-6742, https://www.osha.gov/.

Rosalyn Carson-DeWitt, MD

Nutritional labeling

Definition

Nutritional labeling tells consumers about the amount, ingredients, and nutrients in packaged food for sale. Some cities and states also require that calorie content and other nutritional information be available for food served in restaurants.

Description

The requirements for nutritional labeling are determined by law and vary from country to country. In the United States, the **Food and Drug Administration** (FDA) regulates food labeling under the Nutritional Labeling and Education Act (NLEA) of 1990 and subsequent revisions. This law does not apply to

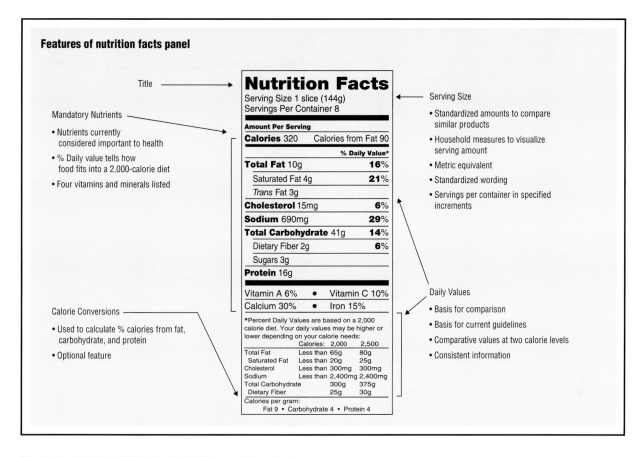

Features of nutrition facts panel

(Illustration by PreMediaGlobal. © 2013 Cengage Learning.)

meat and poultry, raw fruits and vegetables, ready-to-eat food such as cookies or cakes sold at a bakery, food sold by sidewalk vendors, and a few other exceptions.

Mandatory Information

The mandatory nutritional facts that must be included on a food label are: calories, calories from fat, total fat, saturated fat, *trans* fat, cholesterol, sodium, total carbohydrates, dietary fiber, sugars, protein, vitamin A, vitamin C, calcium, and iron. This information must be listed for a single serving of the food. In addition, all labels must contain an ingredients list, with every ingredient listed in order from the greatest to least by weight. There are exceptions for certain artificial colors and flavorings, which may be listed generically by terms such as "artificial coloring.". None of this information is required on fresh meat, fresh poultry, fresh seafood, or fresh fruit and vegetables.

Other non-nutritional information is also required on food labels in the United States, including:

• Name of the product. Laws regulate what some products may be called, based on their content and processing. This explains why some substances that look like cheese are called "cheese food"or "processed cheese product," and some juice-like products are called "fruit drinks"or "fruit beverages" and not "juice."

• Net quantity. This is the amount of food by weight in the package. This does not include the weight of the packaging. Meat and poultry labels are required to give the weight in English (avoirdupois) measures such as pounds or ounces. Other foods are required to give the weight in both English and metric (grams, kilograms) units.

• Serving size. The number of servings the package contains except for single-serving packages.

• Name of manufacturer or distributor. In some cases, a full street address also is required.

Certain foods are required to have additional nutritional information on the label. Some of these requirements are listed below.

- Foods containing the fat replacers such as olestra must state this on the label.
- Foods containing sorbital or mannitol, both artificial sweeteners, must list the amount.
- Juices must show the percentage of real juice the product contains (e.g., 100% grapefruit juice.
- Foods to which vitamins and minerals have been added must be labeled as enriched with the appropriate nutrient(s).

Optional information

Food labels contain optional nutritional information to help consumers make educated nutritional choices. Any optional information on the label must be correct and not be misleading. For example, foods that are labeled as "low fat," "reduced calorie," or "sugar free," or that make similar claims must meet the official FDA definition of these words (see below). Foods may list a specific amount of a particular nutrient, such as "3 grams of carbohydrates," so long as it is not done in a misleading way. The FDA must approve any health claims the label makes that relate a specific ingredient to a specific disease (such as calcium helping to prevent osteoporosis).

Finally, food labels may contain optional information that is not directly related to nutrition but that helps consumers make educated choices. This information concerns the conditions under which the food was grown or processed. For example, plant foods labeled "organic" are made from crops raised without synthetic fertilizers or sewage sludge fertilizer, and they have not been treated with most conventional pesticides or are not raised from genetically modified seed. Note that, nutritionally, organic and non-organic foods are equivalent.

Animal products labeled "organic" come from livestock that has been fed 100% organic feed and raised without growth hormones or antibiotics in an environment where they have access to the outdoors. Debate continues to about the exact requirements to label animal products "cage-free," "free-range," or "grass-fed."

Other optional information, such as kosher or halal, indicates that the food is approved for use by followers of religions with specific dietary requirements. In addition, use of the word "natural" indicates that the food contains no artificial ingredients or added color and has been processed in a way that does not alter the raw product.

Reading a food label

Many descriptive words on a food label cannot be used unless they meet very specific legal requirements. Some of the common descriptions found on FDA-regulated foods are listed below.

- Fat-free: less than 0.5 grams of fat per serving.
- Low fat: no more than 3 grams or less of fat per serving.
- Less fat: A minimum of 25% less fat than the comparison food.
- Light (fat) A minimum of 50% less fat than the comparison food.
- Cholesterol-free: Less than 2 mg of cholesterol and 2 g of saturated fat per serving.
- Low cholesterol: no more than 20 mg of cholesterol and 2 grams of saturated fat per serving.
- Reduced calorie: A minimum of 25% fewer calories than the comparison food.
- Low calorie: No more than 40 calories per serving.
- Light (calories): A minimum of one-third fewer calories than the comparison food.
- Sugar-free: Less than 0.5 grams of sugar per serving.
- Low sodium: No more than 140 mg of sodium per serving.
- Very low sodium: No more than 35 mg of sodium per serving.
- High fiber: 5 or more grams of fiber per serving.
- High, rich in, excellent source of: 20% or more of the Daily Value of the nutrient.
- Good source of: 10% or more of the Daily Value of the nutrient than the comparison food.
- Less, fewer, reduced: 25% or less of the named nutrient than the comparison food.

Understanding the nutrition facts panel

The nutrition facts panel of a food label is designed to encourage healthy eating. It gives consumers a way to compare the nutritional value of products and to see how specific products can meet their dietary needs. The panel consists of several sections. The serving size is given in both familiar units, such as cups or ounces, and metric units. Serving sizes are standardized for similar foods, so that consumers can make easy comparisons. If the package contains a single serving, the serving size is not required. Under the serving size, the servings per container lists the total number of servings contained in the package.

All information listed below the servings per container is given per single serving. People who eat more than one serving will take in more calories and nutrients than the amount listed on the label. Calories and calories from fat, the first nutrient listed, give the consumer a quick idea of how much energy the food provides and how healthful it is or is not.

The next section of the nutrition facts panel deals with specific nutrients. The information is given by weight in metric units (grams or mg) and as a percent daily value. The percent daily value shows how much of each nutrient the food contributes toward meeting the daily recommended amount of each specific nutrient. Percent daily values are based on the recommended dietary allowances (RDAs) of the nutrient for a person who is eating a 2,000-calorie diet. Percent daily values of 5% or less are considered low, and values of 20% or greater are considered high.

The nutrients listed next on the panel are ones that Americans generally eat enough or too much of and that they should try to limit. The first of these are total fat, saturated fat, and *trans* fat. High consumption of saturated fat and *trans* fat are linked to the development of cardiovascular disease. People should try to consume as little of these fats as possible. *Trans* was not part of the original nutrient facts panel but was added beginning January 1, 2006. Not enough information is available to calculate a percent daily value for *trans* fat. Cholesterol and sodium complete the list of nutrients that Americans consume in large amounts and should try to consume less of.

The nutrient panel also lists total carbohydrates, dietary fiber, sugars, and proteins. Americans should try to increase the amount of dietary fiber they consume. A percent daily value for protein is not required unless the food makes the claim "high in protein." In that case, the daily value must be 20% or greater. No recommendations have been made about how much sugar should be consumed in a day, so no percent daily value can be calculated.

At the bottom of the label, percent daily values, but no weights, are listed for four nutrients: vitamin A, Vitamin C, calcium, and iron. These percentages give consumers an idea how low or high the food is in these particular nutrients.

Why this is important to the consumer

The purpose of nutritional labeling is to allow consumers to

• know what ingredients are in the food they choose

• determine the relative amounts of each ingredient

• determine how much of selected vitamins, minerals, and other nutrients a food contains.

• examine foods for potential allergens, additives, or ingredients that they wish to avoid

> ## KEY TERMS
>
> **Allergen**—something that causes an allergic reaction
>
> **Mineral**—an inorganic substance found in the earth that is necessary in small quantities for the body to maintain health. Examples: zinc, copper, iron.
>
> **Vitamin**—a nutrient that the body needs in small amounts to remain healthy but that the body cannot manufacture for itself and must acquire through diet

• determine whether nutrients have been added or removed from the base food (e.g., enriched, reduced fat)

By using all the information available on food labels, consumers can make informed decision about the nutritional content of what they eat, and maintain a healthy diet. They can also avoid allergens and foods unacceptable to their religious beliefs. In addition, they can choose to eat food produced under certain conditions, based on their personal health values.

Resources

BOOKS

Shelton, C.D. *Nutrition (Know What You're Buying: How to Read Food Labels.* Choice PH, Amazon Digital Services, 2012.

Stewart, Kimberly L. *Eating Between the Lines: The Supermarket Shopper's Guide to the Truth Behind Food Labels.* New York: St. Martin's Griffin, 2007.

Taub-Dix, Bonnie. *Read It Before You Eat It: How to Decode Food Labels and Make the Healthiest Choice Every Time.* New York: Plume Books/Penguin Group, 2010.

WEBSITES

United States Food and Drug Administration. "Food Labels." http://www.nutrition.gov/shopping-cooking-meal-planning/food-labels (accessed July 23, 2013).

United States Food and Drug Administration. "Make Your Calories Count: Use the Nutrition Facts Label for Healthy Weight Management." http://www.fda.gov/Food/IngredientsPackagingLabeling/LabelingNutrition/ucm275438.htm (accessed July 23, 2013).

United States Food and Drug Administration. "Labeling & Nutrition." http://www.fda.gov/Food/IngredientsPackagingLabeling/LabelingNutrition/default.htm (accessed July 23, 2013).

ORGANIZATIONS

Center for Food Safety and Applied Nutrition (CFSAN), U.S. Food and Drug Administration, 5100 Paint

Branch Pkwy., College Park, MD 20740, (888) SAFE-FOOD (723-3366), consumer@fda.gov, http://www.fda.gov/Food/default.htm.

Tish Davidson, AM

Nutritionist

Definition

A nutritionist specializes in the study of food and nutrition, including sources of nutrition, nutritional deficiencies, and nutritional challenges. They are concerned about the prevention and treatment of illnesses through proper dietary care.

Description

Some use the terms "nutritionist" and "dietitian" interchangeably. However, in many countries, a nutritionist is not subject to professional regulations like a **dietician**. In the United States, the term "nutritionist" is a non-accredited title that is not legally protected; whereas a dietician should have a bachelor's degree in nutrition and should have spent some time as an intern and passed all the relevant exams and tests. A nutritionist may have only taken a few courses in nutrition or may have a graduate degree in nutritional science. Dietitians are considered to be nutritionists, but not all nutritionists are dietitians.

In the early 1900s, the science of nutrition commenced for the Modern Age when Carl Von Voit and Max Rubner measured the expenditure of caloric energy in animals. As the century progressed, nutritionists' began to more closely study vitamins, their effect on the body, and how they could be effectively added to food. The first vitamin pills were marketed in the 1930s, and created a new industry around science-based health products. In 1941, the National Research Council established the first Recommended Daily Allowances (RDA) as a guide for people to consume a healthy diet. In October of 1994, the Dietary and Supplement Health and Education Act was approved by Congress. It sets forth what may and may not be said about nutritional supplements without prior **Food and Drug Administration** (FDA) review.

As the science of nutrition became more complex, the need for education, training, and certification arose. In the United States, several states now mandate that a nutritionist meet requirements through a licensing procedure. In 1993, the American College of Nutrition established the Certification Board of Nutrition Specialists, where qualified nutritionists are given the designation of Certified Nutrition Specialist.

Nutritionists typically:

- Assess clients' health needs and diet
- Explain nutrition issues
- Develop affordable meal plans
- Evaluate the effects of meal plans and change course, if needed
- Promote better nutrition
- Keep up with the latest nutritional science research

Many nutritionists work in private or public service. Others may work in prisons, nursing homes, or schools to ensure that prison inmates, retirees, and students are getting the proper nutrients in their diet. Nutritionists have knowledge of food and the various vitamins and minerals that people need in order to be healthy. Mostly, nutritionists help others make informed decisions about the food they put inside their bodies.

Nutritionists usually specialize in one of three major areas of practice: clinical, community, or administrative management. Clinical nutritionists service clients who are institutionalized. They develop nutritional programs for clients in hospitals, nursing homes, retirement communities, day care centers, and prisons. Before proposing or implementing any dietary program, nutritionists must consult with doctors or other health professionals to ensure that medical and dietary needs are met. Community nutritionists usually service health clinics, clubs, agencies, and **Health Maintenance Organizations** (HMOs). They advise individuals and groups and structure diet plans for whole families, including meal preparation and shopping for the right foods. Administrative or management nutritionists provide large-scale meal planning and preparation for a school district. Their responsibilities include preparing food budgets, purchasing food, ensuring that health and safety codes are strictly observed, maintaining records, and writing reports. In this environment, the primary concern of the nutritionist is to bring the work environment up to standard by enforcing health and safety codes and improving the overall production capacity.

Why this is important to the consumer

Nutritionists are generally well respected for their knowledge and can help others achieve a healthier life. Nutritionists don't just look at food from a taste

KEY TERMS

Basal Metabolic Rate (BMR)—The lowest rate of body metabolism (rate of energy use) that can sustain life, measured after a full night's sleep in a laboratory under optimal conditions of quiet, rest, and relaxation.

Malnutrition—A condition resulting when a person's diet does not provide adequate nutrients for growth and maintenance or if they are unable to fully utilize the food they eat, due to illness.

Micronutrients—Essential vitamins and minerals required by the body throughout the lifecycle in minuscule amounts.

Minerals—Inorganic (non-living) elements that are essential to the nutrition of humans, animals, and plants.

Nutrients—Substances obtained from food and used in the body to provide energy and structural materials and to regulate growth, maintenance, and repair of the body's tissue.

Recommended Dietary Allowance (RDA)—The amount of an essential nutrient, as a vitamin or mineral, that has been established by the Food and Nutrition Board of the National Academy of Sciences as adequate to meet the average daily nutritional needs of most healthy persons according to age group and sex.

Reference Daily Intakes (RDI)—Food labeling values for protein, vitamins and minerals based on population-adjusted means of the RDA.

Undernutrition—An insufficient intake and/or inadequate absorption of energy, protein, or micronutrients that, in turn, leads to nutritional deficiency.

Vitamin—A substance, required in a small amount, that is essential for normal growth and activity of the body. Vitamins are obtained through the foods you eat. They are classified as fat-soluble vitamins or water-soluble vitamins.

perspective, they know what foods and nutrients are needed to achieve a good balance for the physical body. For consumers seeking advice about nutrition, it is a good idea to ask about qualifications, such as education and field of study, when consulting a nutrition professional. Ideally, people should seek a recommendation from a physician or another medical professional. Since the title "nutritionist" has been used by many unqualified people to describe their involvement in food- and nutrition-related practice, one should be careful when choosing a qualified nutritional professional.

Resources

BOOKS

Hornick, Betsy, Roberta Larson Duyff, Alma Flor Ada. *American Dietetic Association Complete Food and Nutrition Guide, Revised and Updated 4th Edition.* Houghton Mifflin Harcourt, 2012.

Wildman, Robert E.C.*The Nutritionist: Food, Nutrition, and Optimal Health, 2nd Edition.* Routledge, 2009.

PERIODICALS

Post, RC, Eder, J, Maniscalco, S, Johnson-Bailey, D, and Bard, S. "MyPlate is now reaching more consumers through social media." *Journal of the Academy of Nutrition and Dietetics* 113, no. 6 (June 2013): 754-5.

WEBSITES

United States Food and Drug Administration. "Food Labels." http://www.nutrition.gov/shopping-cooking-meal-planning/food-labels (accessed August 12, 2013).

ORGANIZATIONS

Academy of Nutrition and Dietetics, 120 South Riverside Plaza, Suite 2000, Chicago, IL 60606-6995, (800) 877-1600, (312) 899-0040, foundation@eatright.org, http://www.eatright.org.

American Society for Nutrition, 9650 Rockville Pike, Bethesda, MD 20814, (301) 634-7050, info@nutrition.org, http://www.nutrition.org.

Center for Food Safety and Applied Nutrition (CFSAN), U.S. Food and Drug Administration, 5100 Paint Branch Pkwy, College Park, MD 20740, (888) SAFEFOOD (723-3366), (312) 899-0040, consumer@fda.gov, http://www.fda.gov/Food/default.htm.

Clinical Nutrition Certification Board (CNCB), 115280 Addison Road, Suite 130, Addison, TX 75001, (972)250-2829, ddc@clinicalnutrion.com, http://www.cncb.org.

Karl Finley

O

Obamacare *see* **Patient Protection and Affordable Care Act**

Occupational medicine

Definition

Occupational medicine is a branch of clinical medicine that works to prevent and treat work-related injuries and illnesses.

Description

The purpose of occupational medicine is to prevent and treat work-related injury, illness, and disability by focusing on managing the physical, chemical, and social environment. Occupational health specialists work for corporations, trade unions, government agencies, and nonprofit organizations on either a part- or full-time basis. While certified occupational health specialists can treat illness and injuries, the focus is on prevention. Specialists take into consideration the work environment, including physical and chemical stresses and workers' mental health. Typically, occupational health specialists develop a comprehensive occupational health policy and program for a company or organization. Policies and programs focus on areas such as stress management, industrial hygiene, toxicology, and epidemiology.

Occupational health specialists can be physicians, **physician assistants,** or registered nurses who have received additional training and certification to practice occupational medicine. With the correct education and certification, a physician can become board certified in preventive medicine and can specialize in occupational medicine. Between 1955 and 2012, the American Board of Preventive Medicine certified 3,961 physicians in occupational medicine. A registered nurse with the correct training and certification can become a certified occupational health nurse.

Origins

Occupational medicine can be traced back as far as 1700 BC. The Edwin Smith Papyrus, written in ancient Egypt, mentioned the impact work has on health. The Greeks and Romans recorded observations about increased rates of illness and death of miners. In 1556, Georg Bauer, also known as Georgius Agricola, published the book, *De re metallicus* in which he discussed the dangers and diseases miners face. At this time, however, there was still no area of study known as occupational medicine.

In 1700, the Italian physician Bernardino Ramazzini published his book, *Diseases of Workers.* In this book, Ramazzini discusses health hazards such as chemicals, dust, repetitive motions, and odd postures in 52 occupations. Ramazzini believed that physicians should ask patients their occupation because their work played a role in their health. His book and other works regarding work-related health problems played a major role in the foundation of the field of occupational medicine.

Alice Hamilton is another important name in the field of occupational medicine. She was the first woman appointed to the faculty at Harvard University and specialized in the effect industrial metals and chemical compounds have on workers. In 1908, Hamilton became part of the first body in the United States to investigate occupational hazards, called the Occupational Diseases Commission of Illinois. Throughout her life, Hamilton was an advocator for the protection of workers' health.

As more researchers and physicians focused on occupational health and medicine, the field grew. The American Board of Preventive Medicine and Public Health was created in 1948. In 1955, the

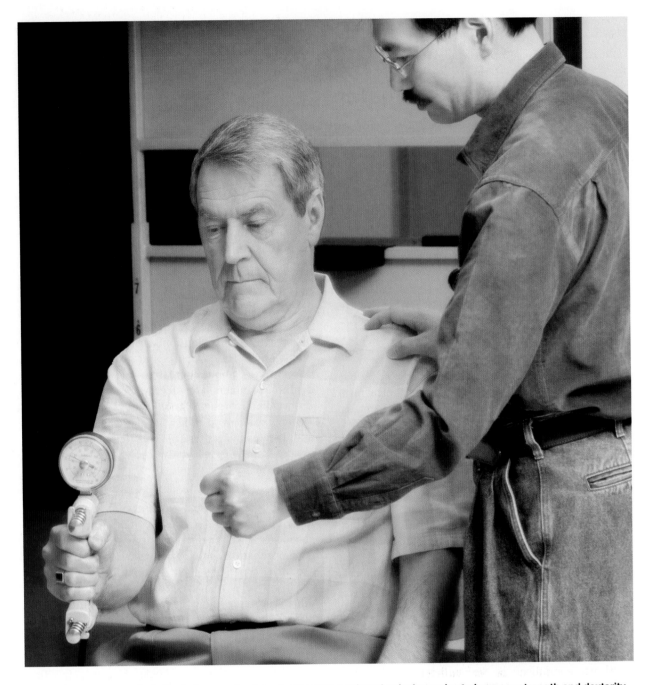

An occupational therapist helps to improve basic motor functions using physical exercise to increase strength and dexterity.
(Design Pics/Kristy-Anne Glubish/Getty Images)

certification in occupational medicine was authorized. In 1970, the U.S. Congress passed the **Occupational Safety and Health Act.**

Occupational medicine and related occupational health fields continue to grow as researchers and employers recognize the importance of employee health and **workplace safety.** A growing number of universities and colleges offer degrees in occupational health fields and occupational health organizations continue to increase their memberships.

To become an occupational medicine physician, a person must graduate from an accredited medical school, followed by a four-year residency to become a licensed physician. Once licensed, a person who wants to become an occupational medicine physician must complete additional occupational medicine training or on-site experience. Completion of residency training during which the physician also earns a master's in **public health** (MPH degree) enables a physician to participate in an examination by the American Board of Preventive Medicine. Certification as an occupational medicine physician occurs when the examination is successfully completed.

Occupational health nurses are either registered nurses or **nurse practitioners** who have received additional training or on-site experience in the field of occupational health. Education requirements depend on the position the nurse holds. Some occupational health nurses may have only an associate's or bachelor's degree, while others may have a master's degree. Nurses who have received additional education and have extensive on-site experience may take the occupational health nursing examination to become a certified occupational health nurse through the American Board for Occupational Health Nurses.

Why this is important to the consumer

The United States Congress passed the Occupational Safety and Health Act of 1970 to ensure that work environments are safe and free of dangerous hazards for both employees and their employers. The Occupational Safety and Health Administration (OSHA) is the regulating governmental body that inspects workplaces for unsafe and unhealthy conditions.

Enforcement by OSHA attempts to assure that products are manufactured in a safe environment and that employees are not exposed to hazardous chemicals, excessive noise, excessive dust, and other unsafe conditions. OSHA oversees not only manufacturing sites, but other types of workplaces including construction sites and offices. A myriad of regulations determine what safety measures must be in place in order for workers to perform their job without endangering their health. The role of occupational medicine specialists is to anticipate workplace hazards, see that any existing hazards are corrected, be familiar with and provide guidance on OSHA regulations applicable to the specific workplace, and in some cases to treat workplace injuries.

Occupational medicine specialists benefit employees by preventing conditions that create both short- and long-term disability. They also benefit employers by creating a better working environment and decreasing legal and financial liabilities of the employer. Consumers should be aware that many items manufactured in the developing world are made under conditions that do not meet OSHA

KEY TERMS

Epidemiology—A branch of medicine that focuses on the distribution, spread, and control of diseases.

Toxicology—A branch of science that focuses on the effects of chemicals and poisons on the body.

standards. In the 2010s, sporadic attempts have been made by consumers to pressure American companies that manufacture products overseas in dangerous and unhealthful environments to improve the health and safety conditions in these foreign plants. This movement has met with only minor successes as of 2013.

Resources

BOOKS

Guidotti, Tee L. *The Praeger Handbook of Occupational and Environmental Medicine.* Praeger: 2010.

Smedley, Julia, Finlay Dick and Steven Sadhra. *Oxford Handbook of Occupational Health.* Oxford University Press: 2013.

Snashall, David, and Dipti Patel, eds. *ABC of Occupational and Environmental Medicine.* BMJ Books: 2013.

PERIODICALS

Franco, Giuliano. "Research evaluation and competition for academic positions in occupational medicine." *Archives of Environmental and Occupational Health* (April–June 2013): 123-127.

Harber, Philip, et al. "Career paths in occupational medicine." *Journal of Occupational and Environmental Medicine* (November 2012): 1324.

Harber, Philip, et al. "Value of occupational medicine board certification." *Journal of Occupational and Environmental Medicine* (May 2013): 532.

Kuhle, Carol S., et al. "Improving patient-centered care: agenda-setting in occupational medicine." *Journal of Occupational and Environmental Medicine* (May 2013): 479.

WEBSITES

"Archive of Journal of Occupational Medicine and Toxicology (London, England)" National Center for Biotechnology Information. http://www.ncbi.nlm.nih.gov/pmc/journals/399/ (accessed December 10, 2013).

"Occupational Health." MedlinePlus. December 9, 2013. http://www.nlm.nih.gov/medlineplus/occupational health.html (accessed December 10, 2013).

"Occupational Health and Safety Specialists: Occupational Outlook Handbook." U.S. Bureau of Labor Statistics. March 29, 2012. http://www.bls.gov/ooh/healthcare/occupational-health-and-safety-specialists.htm (accessed December 10, 2013).

"Total Worker Health." CDC, National Institute for Occupational Safety and Health. November 15, 2013. http://www.cdc.gov/niosh/TWH/ (accessed December 10, 2013).

ORGANIZATIONS

American Board of Preventive Medicine, 111 West Jackson Boulevard, Suite 1110, Chicago, IL 60604, (312) 939-ABPM [2276], Fax: (312) 939-2218, abpm@theabpm.org, https://www.theabpm.org.

American College of Occupational and Environmental Medicine (ACOEM), 25 Northwest Point Blvd. Suite 700, Elk Grove Village, IL 60007, (847)818-1800, Fax: (847) 818-9266, memberinfo@acoem.org, http://www.acoem.org.

The American Osteopathic College of Occupational and Preventive Medicine (AOCOPM), PO Box 3043, Tulsa, OK 74101, (800) 558-8686, AOBPM@osteopathic.org, http://www.aocopm.org.

International Labour Organization, 4 route des Morillons, Geneva 22, Switzerland CH-1211, 41 22 799 6111, Fax: 41 22 798 8685, ilo@ilo.org, http://www.ilo.org.

United States Department of Labor Occupational Safety & Health Administration, 200 Constitution Avenue, Washington, DC 20210, (800) 321-OSHA (6742); TTY: 877-889-5627, http://www.osha.gov/.

Tish Davidson, AM

Occupational Safety and Health Act

Definition

The United States Congress passed the Occupational Safety and Health Act of 1970 to ensure that work environments are safe and free of dangerous hazards for both employees and their employers. Small amendments have been made to the Act since its passage. For example, the dollar value of fines has been increased.

Description

When the Act was signed into law by President Richard M. Nixon on December 29, 1970, it called for the creation of the Occupational Safety and Health Administration (OSHA) under the Department of Labor. OSHA is the regulating governmental body that inspects workplaces for unsafe and unhealthy conditions. The first standards were adopted by OSHA in 1971. The Act also created the National Institute for Occupational Safety and Health (NIOSH), a federal agency under the **Centers for Disease Control and Prevention (CDC)** that researches work-related injuries and workplace hazards. NIOSH also is charged with making recommendations on how to prevent accidents in the workplace and, at the request of business owners or its employees, investigates businesses where hazards may exist. The agency is the clearinghouse for dissemination of workplace safety information and trains occupational safety and health professionals. NIOSH follows the National Occupational Research Agenda (NORA), a research agenda developed by 500 organizations that outlines the top 21 research priorities among workplace safety issues.

The law applies to all employers and employees in the United States, District of Columbia, Puerto Rico, and any other jurisdiction of the U.S. federal government. The law is not enforceable among federal or state employees, or farms where only immediate family members are employed. Those who are self-employed or whose workplaces are covered under other federal regulations, such as nuclear energy, mining, or nuclear weapons manufacturing, also are exempt from the Act.

Employers covered by the law are required to implement policies and procedures within their businesses that comply with the regulations. Regulations cover, but are not limited to, hazardous waste handling, fall protection at construction sites, asbestos, ergonomics, and respiratory protection. States have the option of enforcing the federal regulations or adopting their own job safety programs that are at least as strict as the OSHA regulations. In 1972, South Carolina, Montana, and Oregon were the first states to approve their own programs.

Employees who work in environments covered by the Act have certain rights under the law. Employees are permitted to file complaints with OSHA regarding the safety conditions of their workplaces. Complaints are kept confidential from employers. In order to enforce the Act, OSHA employs compliance safety and health officers (CSHOs) who are authorized to perform inspections of workplaces covered under the law. OSHA conducts two kinds of inspections, programmed and unprogrammed. Unprogrammed inspections are triggered when a complaint is filed or when a fatality or catastrophe occurs.

Violations

A violation of an OSHA standard covered under the Act carries several penalties depending on the severity of the violation. Violations are classified as "other than serious," "serious," "willful," or "repeated":

Employers covered by the Occupational Safety and Health Act are required to implement proper policies and procedures that comply with the regulations. *(©J.D.S/Shutterstock.com)*

- Other-than-serious violation. An other-than-serious violation directly affects job safety, but likely would not cause serious injury or death. It is within the CSHO's discretion to impose up to a $7,000 penalty for each violation. However, if the business owner shows a good-faith effort to make the appropriate corrections to comply with the law, the $7,000 penalty can be reduced by up to 95%. The size of the business and whether there have been previous violations also are taken into consideration when reducing a penalty.

- Serious violation. A serious violation is one that would likely cause serious injury or death; it is also a violation that the employer knows or should know is harmful or hazardous. In cases of serious violations, up to a $7,000 penalty can be imposed. But, again, the penalty can be decreased on the basis of previous violations, how serious the violation, good-faith effort to correct the problem, and the size of the business.

- Willful violation. An employer willfully commits a violation when he or she is aware the violation exists. Either the employer knows a violation is being committed or does not try to eliminate a dangerous condition that exists. An employer who commits a willful violation faces a penalty of at least $5,000 and not more than $70,000. The only considerations taken into account when decreasing the penalty for a willful violation is the number of previous violations and the size of the business. If a death has occurred because of a willful violation, an employer could face up to six months of prison and/or a fine imposed by the courts. If criminal charges are levied and a conviction results, the employer's corporation could face a $500,000 fine and the individual a $250,000 fine, enforceable under the Comprehensive Crime Control Act of 1984.

- Repeated violation. If upon re-inspection by OSHA officers a similar violation is found, a $70,000 penalty may be imposed.

• Other violations. Once a violation is found and a deadline is imposed for the violation's correction, employers could face a $7,000 penalty for every day the problem goes uncorrected. Additionally, employers found doctoring records or applications could face a fine of up to $10,000 and/or six months in prison. Any kind of interference with an OSHA compliance officer who is attempting to perform an inspection, whether it be by resisting or intimidating the officer, is considered a crime and could carry up to a $250,000 penalty for an individual and $500,000 for a corporation.

Why this is important to the consumer

Consumers as well as employees benefit from the ACT. OSHA works with other federal and state agencies such as NIOSH and the Environmental Protection Agency (EPA) to evaluate research on pollutant exposure and to enforce OSHA and EPA regulations. This creates a higher awareness of workplace hazards and a cleaner environment for all Americans while reducing medical conditions that result from unsafe work environments.

Resources

BOOKS

Connolly, Walter B., and Donald R. Crowell II. *A Practical Guide to the Occupational Safety and Health Act*. Law Journal Seminars Press: 2012.

Moran, Mark. *The OSHA Answer Book*, 11th edition. Moran Associates, 2011.

PERIODICALS

"Applying the Law to Workplace Health: Health Surveillance Programmes." *Occupational Health* 1 (November 2013).

Miller, G. Klaud. "How safe is your office? An office safety program is key to reducing risk." *AAOS Now* (2012): 35.

WEBSITES

United States Department of Labor. "OSHA Law and Regulations." (accessed November 26, 2013).

ORGANIZATIONS

American College of Occupational and Environmental Medicine (ACOEM), 25 Northwest Point Blvd. Suite 700, Elk Grove Village, IL 60007, (847)818-1800, Fax: (847) 818-9266, memberinfo@acoem.org, http://www.acoem.org.

The American Osteopathic College of Occupational and Preventive Medicine (AOCOPM), PO Box 3043, Tulsa, OK 74101, (800) 558-8686, AOBPM@osteopathic.org, http://www.aocopm.org.

United States Centers for Disease Control and Prevention (CDC)/ National Institute for Occupational Safety and Health, 1600 Clifton Road, Atlanta, GA 30333, (404) 639-3534, (800) CDC-INFO (800-232-4636), TTY: (888) 232-6348, inquiry@cdc.gov, http://www.cdc.gov.

United States Department of Labor Occupational Safety & Health Administration, 200 Constitution Avenue, Washington, DC 20210, (800) 321-OSHA (6742), TTY: (877) 889-5627, http://www.osha.gov/.

United States Environmental Protection Agency (EPA), Ariel Rios Building, 1200 Pennsylvania Avenue, N.W., Washington, DC 20460, (202) 272-0167, TTY: (202) 272-0165, http://www.epa.gov.

Meghan M. Gourley
Tish Davidson, AM

Osteopathy

Definition

Osteopathy is a holistic approach to health care that emphasizes the close relationship between the body's structure and its functions, and the body's ability to heal itself when its structures are properly aligned. Although osteopathy is sometimes described as a form of complementary and alternative medicine (CAM) because of its early history, the National Center for Complementary and Alternative Medicine (NCCAM) explicitly lists osteopathic medicine together with mainstream medicine as a form of modern conventional medical practice. As of 2013, doctors of osteopathic medicine in the United States are licensed to practice the full scope of medicine and surgery in all 50 states, and are recognized as physicians in all Canadian provinces.

The complicated historical relationship between so-called scientific medicine and osteopathy in the United States will be further explained below. Here the reader should note that current American usage prefers the term *osteopathic medicine* to *osteopathy*, and *doctor of osteopathic medicine* or *osteopathic physician* to *osteopath*. The American Osteopathic Association (AOA) explains, "Both the terms *osteopathy* and *osteopath* are primarily used in historical context when describing the profession and its practitioners [in the United States] before 1960. These terms are also used to describe the profession as it is practiced outside the United States by practitioners who have not been trained at AOA-accredited osteopathic medical colleges."

Another term that often appears in discussions of osteopathic medicine in contemporary American health care is *allopathic*, a word derived from two Greek words that mean "different [from]" and "disease." The term was coined by Samuel Hahnemann

(1755–1843), the founder of **homeopathy**, as an uncomplimentary term for medicine as it was practiced in the late eighteenth century. *Allopathic* was also used by other nineteenth-century practitioners of what would now be considered alternative medicine to describe mainstream physicians, who angrily resented the label. The recent usage of *allopathic* to distinguish doctors of medicine (M.D.s) from doctors of osteopathic medicine (D.O.s) within the larger framework of conventional or mainstream medicine indicates that the history of the word is largely forgotten and its negative overtones have disappeared.

Description

Background

To fully understand the relationship between osteopathic and **allopathic medicine** in the United States, one should know that osteopathy not only developed in the United States (and subsequently expanded into Europe rather than the other way around) but that it developed *before* the present distinction between "scientific" and "alternative" medicine came about. That distinction was made as a result of changes in medical education and government licensing of physicians at the end of the nineteenth century. These changes began in Europe and spread to the United States

EMERGENCE OF SCIENTIFIC MEDICINE. In Europe, the development of antiseptic surgical technique and the emergence of such fields as bacteriology, organic chemistry, anesthesiology, and radiology led to the separation of "scientific" medicine from such rival systems as homeopathy, **naturopathy**, folk medicine, and herbalism. Scientific medicine was taught as well as practiced in the medical faculties of British, French, and German universities, and was followed by state approval or licensure of practicing physicians. Government recognition and regulation of medical practice became a major factor in the separation of "mainstream" medicine from alternative practices.

The European pattern was imported to the United States in the 1890s, when the Johns Hopkins University School of Medicine was founded explicitly to teach "German scientific medicine." Older university-based medical schools, such as those of Harvard, Yale, and the University of Pennsylvania, had also adopted changes in their curricula borrowed from the European models. At the turn of the twentieth century, however, the United States still had over 150 medical schools, some of which taught homeopathy, **chiropractic**, or what was then called "eclectic medicine." In 1908, the Carnegie Foundation hired Abraham Flexner, who was not a physician, although he was a college graduate, to visit all 155 medical schools in the United States and report on the quality of their instruction. Flexner's report, issued in 1910, recommended the closing of most of these schools; basing the educational standards of the remainder on the German model; requiring at least two years of college prior to admission to medical school; and strengthening state examination and licensing of physicians. In addition to forcing the closure of all but 66 medical schools by the 1930s, the Flexner Report made scientific medicine the sole model for American medical practice, driving other approaches to health care into the shadows.

ORIGINS OF OSTEOPATHY. Osteopathy grew out of the life experiences as well as the medical practice of Andrew Taylor Still (1828–1917), a Civil War veteran as well as a physician. Still became a doctor in the 1850s by serving as an apprentice to his father, a Methodist clergyman as well as a physician in rural Virginia. This informal pattern of medical education was commonplace in nineteenth-century America. Still's experiences as a battlefield surgeon, followed by the deaths of three of his children from spinal meningitis in 1864, convinced him that medicine as it was then practiced was more harmful than helpful. His conclusion is understandable in light of the way medicine was then practiced. The period from the 1790s through the 1870s is sometimes called the "age of heroic medicine," "heroic" referring to the "heroic measures" that were taken to cure patients. These heroic measures included aggressive practices that were not scientifically proven, such as bloodletting, administering calomel (dimercury dichloride, a form of mercury) to purge the digestive tract or treat syphilis, and using such dangerous substances as arsenic and opium to treat disease. Surgery was performed without any attempts at antisepsis; thus, it was no wonder that many people died from treatments intended to help them. In other words, Still reacted, not against scientific medicine as the twentieth century came to define it, but against an approach to medicine that dominated nineteenth-century American practice but was not scientific.

Still set about investigating other forms of therapy that were used at the time, including dietary and nutritional treatments, bonesetting, and magnetic therapy, and recognized that these treatments produced only minor side effects, compared to the adverse effects of heroic medicine. In his search for what he called "rational medical therapy," Still decided that the musculoskeletal system is the key to human health and disease, and that a thorough knowledge of its

Osteopathy

anatomy is essential to a doctor's training. Still coined the term *osteopathy* to define his new approach to medicine. The English word comes from two Greek words for "bone" and "disease", and summarizes Still's belief that human illness derives from disorders and dysfunctions of the muscles and bones. In addition to developing a form of hands-on therapy now known as osteopathic manipulative treatment or OMT, Still also emphasized the importance of preventive medicine and a holistic approach to treatment—that is, that the physician should treat the whole person and not just the symptoms of the patient's disease.

Still moved from his practice in rural Kansas to Kirksville, Missouri, where he founded the first school of osteopathic medicine in 1892. Now called the A.T. Still University-Kirksville College of Osteopathic Medicine, the school's foundation coincided with the establishment of Johns Hopkins and the introduction of the German model of medical education in the United States. The result was that osteopathy in its early years was rejected by the practitioners of "scientific" medicine. The American Medical Association (AMA) went so far as to call osteopathy a "cult" and drew up a code of ethics that forbade M.D.s to associate professionally with osteopaths.

The early twentieth century was a period of struggle on the part of osteopaths for full recognition by the federal government. During this period, the various schools of osteopathic medicine in the United States adopted curricula that closely resembled the courses of instruction in university-related medical schools, and required the same level of college preparation as an admission requirement. Between 1901 and 1930, 22 states granted osteopaths the same license to practice medicine as M.D.s. Nebraska became the last state to grant osteopaths this privilege in 1989. In 1966, the federal government permitted osteopathic physicians to serve in the U.S. Military Medical Corps on an equal basis with M.D.s; and in 1969, the AMA admitted D.O.s as full members of the association alongside M.D.s. The American Medical Student Association (AMSA) admitted students of osteopathic medicine as equal members in 2006.

One distinctive aspect of osteopathic medicine in the first half of the twentieth century was its openness to women and minorities at a time when allopathic medical schools either refused to admit women and African Americans altogether or maintained a strict quota on their numbers. In 1993, Barbara Ross-Lee, D.O., made history when she became the first female African American dean of an American medical school, the Ohio University College of Osteopathic Medicine.

Current practice of osteopathic medicine

As of 2013, the education and training of osteopathic physicians is virtually identical to that of their allopathic colleagues. There are currently 30 accredited colleges of osteopathic medicine in 37 locations across the United States, compared to 141 accredited allopathic medical schools. D.O.s have always been a minority within the medical profession in the United States, accounting for about 11% of all practicing physicians. This proportion is changing, however, as osteopathic colleges of medicine are undergoing rapid expansion and increasing their class sizes. In 1980, there were about 1,000 D.O.s graduating from osteopathic medical colleges each year; this number is expected to reach 5,000 per year by 2015. In contrast, the number of M.D.s graduating each year from American medical schools has remained steady at about 19,000 per year. The sex and racial distribution of students is almost identical in both types of schools.

The requirements for licensure and board certification are virtually the same for D.O.s and M.D.s as of 2013. Both branches of mainstream American medicine require practitioners to complete four years at an accredited undergraduate institution, followed by four years of medical school. Following completion of the D.O. degree, osteopathic physicians complete internships and residencies alongside M.D.s. As of 2013, about 60% of D.O.s enter residencies accredited by the Accreditation Council for Graduate Medical Education (ACGME), which oversees all residencies approved for M.D.s; the remaining 40% enter residencies accredited by the American Osteopathic Association (AOA). By 2015, the two residency accreditation programs will merge, and all American residencies will be accredited by the ACGME. Following completion of the residency, both D.O.s and M.D.s can seek board certification in medical or surgical specialties.

One major difference between D.O.s and M.D.s up through the 1970s was the greater emphasis in osteopathic medicine on primary care (family practice) as compared to specialization. In recent years, however, the number of D.O.s entering family practice has begun to decline in the same way as it has for M.D.s.

Osteopathic manipulative treatment

Osteopathic manipulative treatment (OMT), sometimes called "manual therapy" or "manual medicine," is the remaining distinctive aspect of osteopathic medical education. As noted earlier, OMT was developed by A.T. Still out of his conviction that the structure and function of the body influence each other, and that correction of the body's musculoskeletal structure releases and strengthens the body's innate self-healing abilities. Colleges of osteopathic medicine presently require students to complete about eight weeks of clerkships in OMT during their third and fourth years.

OMT includes several different techniques for releasing tight or sore muscles and improving the circulation of lymph within the lymphatic system. These techniques include gentle pressure, stretching of the affected muscles, and myofascial release, a form of soft-tissue manipulation. OMT is used primarily to treat lower back pain and other muscular disorders as of 2013, but has also been found to be helpful in treating dysmenorrhea (painful menstruation), migraine headaches, back problems associated with pregnancy, and depression. The American Pain Society has reported that patients receiving OMT for back pain do not need as much medication for pain relief as those who take drugs only.

Why this is important to the consumer

Competence and qualifications

The close similarities between the education and certification of D.O.s and M.D.s mean that consumers can trust that an osteopathic physician educated and licensed in the United States has the same skills and expertise as an allopathic physician. Although osteopathic physicians were at one time considered less intelligent or less thoroughly trained than M.D.s, that is no longer the case. The chief distinction that matters to consumers in 2013 is the difference between graduates of American colleges of osteopathic medicine and osteopaths trained in Europe or Asia. The reason for the difference is that while osteopathic practice in the United States has become almost identical to allopathic medicine, osteopathy in Europe and other parts of the world has remained a form of manual medicine practiced by non-physicians. The United States does not recognize or license non-physician osteopaths trained abroad. The distinction between the two forms of osteopathy is the reason why the AOA insists on referring to D.O.s as osteopathic physicians rather than osteopaths, and to the profession as osteopathic medicine rather than osteopathy.

Distinctiveness of osteopathic medicine

Some consumers may be attracted to the holistic, patient-centered approach of osteopathic physicians and the practice of OMT. Interestingly, many M.D.s

have recently come to reconsider the benefits of manual therapy in treating musculoskeletal disorders, and have increased their own use of manual therapy in treating lower back pain and similar problems. Consumers who are interested in osteopathic treatment can consult the AOA website at http://www.osteopathic.org/Pages/default.aspx under the heading "Find a DO" to locate an osteopathic physician in their area.

Resources

BOOKS

American Association of Colleges of Osteopathic Medicine (AACOM). *Glossary of Osteopathic Terminology.* Chevy Chase, MD: AACOM, 2009.

American Osteopathic Association. *Foundations of Osteopathic Medicine*, 3rd ed. Philadelphia: Wolters Kluwer Health/Lippincott Williams and Wilkins, 2011.

Nicholas, Alexander S., and Evan A. Nicholas. *Atlas of Osteopathic Techniques*, 2nd ed. Philadelphia: Wolters Kluwer Health/Lippincott Williams and Wilkins, 2012.

PERIODICALS

Cruser, dA., et al. "A Randomized, Controlled Trial of Osteopathic Manipulative Treatment for Acute Low Back Pain in Active Duty Military Personnel." *Journal of Manual and Manipulative Therapy* 20 (February 2012): 5–15.

Genese, J.S. "Osteopathic Manipulative Treatment for Facial Numbness and Pain after Whiplash Injury." *Journal of the American Osteopathic Association* 113 (July 2013): 564–567.

Gross, C., and E.C. Bell. "AOA Specialty Board Certification." *Journal of the American Osteopathic Association* 113 (April 2013): 339–342.

Iglehart, J.K. "The Residency Mismatch." *New England Journal of Medicine* 369 (July 25, 2013): 297–299.

Johnson, C. "Back to Back: Postnatal Osteopathic Care." *Practising Midwife* 16 (May 2013): 26–27.

Licciardone, J.C., et al. "Osteopathic Manual Treatment and Ultrasound Therapy for Chronic Low Back Pain: A Randomized Controlled Trial." *Annals of Family Medicine* 11 (March-April 2013): 122–129.

Williams, A., and K.C. Miskowicz-Retz. "New Colleges of Osteopathic Medicine: Steps in Achieving Accreditation—An Update." *Journal of the American Osteopathic Association* 113 (April 2013): 296–302.

WEBSITES

American Association of Colleges of Osteopathic Medicine (AACOM). "Difference between U.S.-Trained Osteopathic Physicians and Osteopaths Trained Abroad." http://www.aacom.org/about/osteomed/Pages/TheDifference.aspx (accessed August 16, 2013).

American Association of Colleges of Osteopathic Medicine (AACOM). "History of Osteopathic Medicine." http://www.aacom.org/about/osteomed/Pages/History.aspx (accessed August 16m 2013).

American Osteopathic Association (AOA) History of Osteopathic Medicine Virtual Museum. http://history.osteopathic.org/ (accessed August 16, 2013).

MedlinePlus. "Doctor of Osteopathic Medicine." http://www.nlm.nih.gov/medlineplus/ency/article/002020.htm (accessed August 17, 2013).

University of Maryland Medical Center. "Osteopathy." http://umm.edu/health/medical/altmed/treatment/osteopathy (accessed August 16, 2013).

Via Christi Health System. "What Is Osteopathic Manipulative Therapy?" This is a 5-minute video in which an osteopathic physician demonstrates some of the basic techniques of OMT. http://www.youtube.com/watch?v=KQR1UPHRY4o (accessed August 17, 2013).

ORGANIZATIONS

American Association of Colleges of Osteopathic Medicine (AACOM), 5550 Friendship Boulevard, Suite 310, Chevy Chase, MD, United States 20815-7231, (301) 968-4100, Fax: (301) 968-4101, http://www.aacom.org/Pages/default.aspx.

American Osteopathic Association (AOA), 142 E. Ontario St., Chicago, IL, United States 60611, (312) 202-8000, (800) 621-1773, Fax: (312) 202-8200, info@osteopathic.org, http://www.osteopathic.org/Pages/default.aspx.

Kirksville College of Osteopathic Medicine (KCOM), 800 W. Jefferson St., Kirksville, MO, United States 63501, (660) 626-2121, (866) 626-2878, admissions@atsu.edu, http://www.atsu.edu/kcom/.

National Center for Complementary and Alternative Medicine (NCCAM), 9000 Rockville Pike, Bethesda, MD, United States 20892, (888) 644-6226, http://nccam.nih.gov/tools/contact.htm, http://nccam.nih.gov/.

Rebecca J. Frey, Ph.D.

Palliative care

Definition

Palliative care is holistic care given to improve the quality of life of persons with serious or life-threatening illnesses; it comprises psychological, spiritual, and social interventions as well as medical treatments given to relieve physical distress. The term was coined by Balfour Mount (1939–), a Canadian physician credited as the father of palliative care in North America. The English word *palliative* is derived from the medieval Latin *palliare*, which can mean either "to cloak or cover" or "to relieve." Palliative care is also known as comfort care, symptom management, and supportive care.

The basic goal of palliative care is to prevent or relieve the symptoms of serious disease rather than to cure it. It is important to keep in mind, however, that palliative care can be given alongside curative therapies; it is not a replacement for surgery, chemotherapy, or other treatments given to cure disease. In fact, in many cases palliative care is recommended to relieve the side effects of curative treatments, such as the nausea caused by cancer chemotherapy.

Description

Background

Palliative care in its present form is a relatively recent form of patient care, associated with the hospice movement of the 1970s and 1980s. Because of this close historical association, many people think of palliative care as given only to patients with a terminal illness. As of 2013, however, palliative care is available in North America to patients with such serious and complex illnesses as HIV infection, kidney or lung disease, progressive disorders of the nervous system, and chronic heart failure as well as cancer. While palliative care shares the same goals as hospice, it is not identical with it; palliative care is given as soon as the patient receives a diagnosis of cancer or other serious illness, and it continues throughout the patient's course of treatment and follow-up visits without regard to the patient's prognosis.

The concept of symptom relief is not new, but for most of the history Western medicine, doctors have been trained to focus on the cure of disease rather than preventing physical and emotional suffering. What is new about the development of palliative care in Canada and the United States since the 1980s is the rapid expansion of hospital and long-term care facilities as well as hospices for the provision of palliative care; the increase in federal and private insurance funding for such care, and the emergence of specialized training and licensing of doctors and nurses in the field of palliative care. The first hospital-based programs for palliative care were started at the Medical College of Wisconsin and the Cleveland Clinic in the late 1980s; as of 2013, there are over 1,400 programs for palliative care across the United States. About 80% of hospitals with 300 or more beds have palliative care programs, while 55% of smaller community hospitals have such programs.

With regard to physician training and credentialing, what is now the American Academy of Hospice and Palliative Medicine (AAHPM) was founded in 1988. The American Board of Hospice and Palliative Medicine was incorporated in 1996 to offer board certification in the specialty of palliative medicine and administered its first qualifying examination that same year. As of 2013, board certification in palliative medicine is offered through 10 specialty boards of the American Board of Medical Specialties (ABMS), namely internal medicine, anesthesiology, family medicine, physical medicine and rehabilitation, psychiatry and neurology, surgery, pediatrics, emergency medicine, radiology, and obstetrics/gynecology. The American Osteopathic Association also recognizes palliative medicine as a specialty. About 5,000 physicians in North America are board-

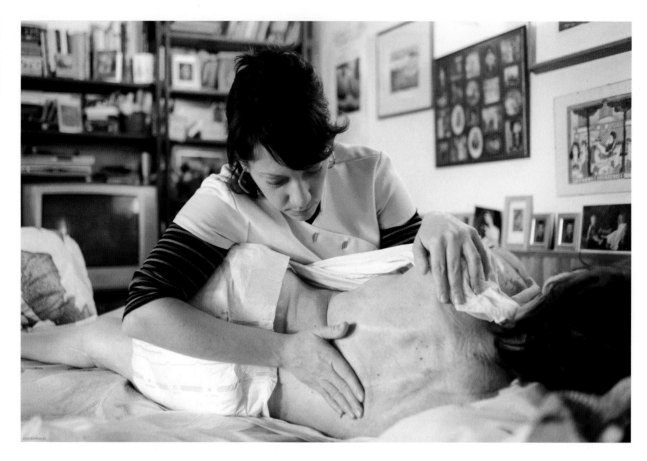

Palliative care is also known as comfort care, symptom management, and supportive care. *(© RGB Ventures LLC dba SuperStock / Alamy)*

certified in palliative medicine as of 2013, and almost all medical schools in Canada and the United States include palliative care in their courses of study.

Present practice

As the number of medical specialties that now offer certification in palliative care indicates, this form of health care is multidisciplinary. In addition to running across a variety of medical fields, palliative care involves persons in a wide range of helping professions as well as doctors, nurses, pharmacists, physical therapists, and other health care professionals. A patient receiving palliative care is usually treated by a team headed by a physician certified in palliative medicine, but the team also includes psychologists, chaplains, social workers, registered dietitians, and the patient's **primary care physician**. Patients do not have to give up their primary health care provider to receive palliative care. In addition, palliative care is not limited to a hospital, outpatient clinic, or hospice setting; it may be given in the patient's home when circumstances allow.

The primary purpose of palliative care is to offer the patient the best possible quality of life over the course of his or her illness. Because no two patients are alike in their diagnosis, symptom severity, family situation, cultural background, spiritual beliefs, and other factors, palliative care is individualized. Palliative care may address any or all of the following concerns:

• Physical symptoms caused by the disease. Patients suffering from any serious illness may experience pain in the muscles or joints, skin rashes or itching, fatigue, loss of appetite, nausea, vomiting, diarrhea, shortness of breath, and insomnia or other sleep disturbances. While patients may be given medications to relieve these and other symptoms, they may also be given physical or nutritional therapy to ease their discomfort. Cancer patients in particular may be treated with surgery or radiation therapy to reduce the size of the tumors that are causing the illness.

• Emotional distress. Most patients undergoing treatment for a severe or complex illness experience fear, anxiety, depression, anger, or other strong emotions along with physical symptoms. Palliative care may include counseling, meetings with family members, support group meetings, or referral to mental health professionals. It may also include complementary and alternative (CAM) approaches, including relaxation techniques, meditation, guided visualization, hypnosis, massage therapy, music therapy, and pet therapy.

• Spiritual issues. Severe illness often prompts people to turn to their core beliefs about the meaning of life and faith in a personal God or some source of spiritual power. Some patients feel upheld by their lifelong beliefs and practices, while others find themselves struggling with doubt and despair. Most palliative care programs have chaplains as part of the care team for patients whose own spiritual leaders are not available or who do not belong to any faith group but wish to discuss their spiritual concerns.

• Financial and legal matters. Palliative care teams can help patients cope with concerns about employment, housing, legal documents, insurance claims, transportation, ethical decisions related to the end of life, and similar matters.

• The patient's family. Contemporary palliative care includes the patient's family and friends affected by the patient's illness. Care may range from providing respite care for family members caring for a patient at home to helping the family with home health care, transportation, and shopping, to educating friends and family members about the patient's illness, treatments, and prognosis. In some cases, the palliative care team can assist patients in reaching out to former spouses, children, or other relatives who have become estranged. Many patients feel a strong need to heal damaged relationships as a result of their illness.

Why this is important to the consumer

Quality of life

Palliative care is important to consumers, first of all, because of its demonstrated benefits to the patient's quality of life. To begin with, the individualized character of palliative care means that each patient can define quality of life for him- or herself, and identify his or her priorities for supportive care. Some patients may prefer relief from physical pain above all else, while others may desire to live as long as possible even if they are in pain. Some may want to take a long-awaited trip or complete a course of study or other project, and need the kind of palliative care that will allow them to do that if possible.

Patients also vary in their desire for information about their disease and its treatment. Some want their doctors to tell them as much as possible, while others prefer limited communication, and at a time of their choosing. Some family members may also prefer not to be overwhelmed with all the medical details of the patient's symptoms and therapies. It is important to discuss this aspect of palliative care with the care team at the beginning of the patient's treatment.

Several studies have shown that palliative care extends the length of life for many patients as well as improving their quality of life. A 2007 report published by the **Institute of Medicine** (IOM) stated that patients are better able to comply with their treatment regimens and take care of household and family matters when they are not in constant physical pain or emotional distress. Other studies, specifically of cancer patients, have found that such patients live two to three months longer with increased quality of life than those receiving medical treatment alone.

Palliative care also improves family members' quality of life. Researchers have recognized since the late 1990s that the stress of caring for a family member with Alzheimer's disease, HIV infection, multiple sclerosis, or cancer takes a heavy physical as well as emotional toll on caregivers. These relatives and friends are at increased risk of heart disease, depression, acute stress disorder, sleep disturbances, and strained relationships with people other than the patient. Palliative care can provide needed social support for family members as well as respite care and other forms of direct assistance in caring for the patient.

Financial considerations

According to the National Cancer Institute (NCI), as of 2013 palliative care in the United States is usually covered by private insurance. **Medicare** and **Medicaid** also pay for palliative care, depending on the patient's specific situation. Patients who do not have insurance or are unsure about their coverage should check with the hospital's financial advisor or **social worker**.

Information gathering

Because palliative care is tailored to each patient's unique situation, patients and family members should gather information about their options for palliative care in their particular location. The AAHPM maintains a web page at http://www.palliativedoctors.org/resources/find-a-hospice-a-palliative-medicine-physician.html that allows patients to search for board-certified palliative care specialists on either the ABMS

KEY TERMS

Holistic—In medicine, an approach that takes all dimensions of a human being into account, the psychosocial and spiritual as well as the physical.

Hospice—A term that refers both to institutions that provide palliative care for the terminally ill, and to the philosophy of care that guides these institutions.

Prognosis (plural, prognoses)—The medical term for predicting the likely outcome of a patient's present health condition.

Respite care—Provision of short-term or temporary care to relieve family members caring for seriously ill patients.

website or the American Osteopathic Association's database. Similarly, the Center to Advance Palliative Care (CAPC) maintains a database of hospitals offering palliative care, searchable by state, at http://www.getpalliativecare.org/providers/. The site also includes a quiz to determine whether palliative care is a good choice for a specific patient.

Resources

BOOKS

Moore, Rhonda J., ed.*Handbook of Pain and Palliative Care: Biobehavioral Approaches for the Life Course*. New York: Springer, 2012.

Perrin, Kathleen Ouimet, et al. *Palliative Care Nursing: Caring for Suffering Patients*. Sudbury, MA: Jones and Bartlett Learning, 2012.

Quill, Timothy E., et al. *Primer of Palliative Care*, 5th ed. Chicago: American Academy of Hospice and Palliative Medicine, 2010.

PERIODICALS

Chur-Hansen, A., et al. "Furry and Feathered Family Members—A Critical Review of Their Role in Palliative Care." *Journal of Hospice and Palliative Care*, July 26, 2013 [e-publication ahead of print].

Drisdom, S. "Barriers to Using Palliative Care." *Clinical Journal of Oncology Nursing* 17 (August 1, 2013): 376–380.

Evans, D., and E. Lee. "Respite Services for Older People." *International Journal of Nursing Practice* 19 (August 2013): 431–436.

Gaertner, J., et al. "Early Palliative Care for Patients with Advanced Cancer: How to Make It Work?" *Current Opinion in Oncology* 25 (July 2013): 342–352.

Litrivis, E., and C.B. Smith. "Palliative Care: A Primer." *Mount Sinai Journal of Medicine* 78 (July-August 2011): 627–631.

Payne, C., et al. "Exercise and Nutrition Interventions in Advanced Lung Cancer: A Systematic Review." *Current Oncology* 20 (August 2013): e321–e337.

Ritchie, C.S. "Ushering in an Era of Community-based Palliative Care." *Journal of Palliative Medicine* 16 (August 2013): 818–819.

Strand, J.J., et al. "Top 10 Things Palliative Care Clinicians Wished Everyone Knew About Palliative Care." *Mayo Clinic Proceedings* 88 (August 2013): 859–865.

WEBSITES

Center to Advance Palliative Care (CAPC). "Palliative Care and Hospice Care Across the Continuum." http://www.capc.org/palliative-care-across-the-continuum/ (accessed august 7, 2013).

Mayo Clinic. "Palliative Care: Symptom Relief During Illness." http://www.mayoclinic.com/health/palliative-care/MY01051 (accessed August 7, 2013).

National Cancer Institute (NCI). "Fact Sheet: Palliative Care in Cancer." http://www.cancer.gov/cancertopics/factsheet/support/palliative-care (accessed August 7, 2013).

WebMD. "What Is Palliative Care?" http://www.webmd.com/palliative-care/what-is-palliative-care (accessed August 7, 2013).

ORGANIZATIONS

American Academy of Hospice and Palliative Medicine (AAHPM), 8735 West Higgins Road, Suite 300, Chicago, IL, United States 60631, (847) 375-4712, Fax: (847) 375-6475, info@aahpm.org, http://www.aahpm.org/.

Center to Advance Palliative Care (CAPC), 1255 Fifth Avenue, Suite C-2, New York, NY, United States 10029, (212) 201-2670, capc@mssm.edu, http://www.capc.org/.

National Cancer Institute (NCI), BG 9609 MSC 9760, 9609 Medical Center Drive, Bethesda, MD, United States 20892-9760, Fax: (800) 4-CANCER (422-6237), http://www.cancer.gov/global/contact/email-us, http://www.cancer.gov/.

National Hospice and Palliative Care Organization (NHPCO), 1731 King Street, Alexandria, VA, United States 22314, (703) 837-1500, Fax: (703) 837-1233, http://www.nhpco.org/.

Rebecca J. Frey, Ph.D.

Patient-centered care

Definition

Patient-centered care is health care that respects and responds to an individual patient's values and needs.

Description

For many years, medical care has revolved around the physician; patients and their families have taken the word of the physician as final, seldom questioning or refuting a physician's decision. Patient-centered care is not a new approach that makes the relationship adversarial or questions physician judgment, but rather places the patient in more control. Patient-centered care reminds physicians and other providers to consider patients as individuals and consult with them on health care decisions.

The idea of patient-centered health care first was introduced in the late 1960s. The term "patient-centered care" was coined in 1988 by a group that came to be known as the Picker Institute. The group was conducting research on patient needs and preferences to define quality. Family-centered care is another term that has evolved to recognize the role families play in making decisions on behalf of young children and sometimes older relatives who might be receiving help with care from family members. The major principles of patient-centered care are:

- dignity and respect, or listening to patients and family members when appropriate, and honoring their concerns and choices
- sharing information among patients and families so they can actively participate in decisions about health care
- encouraging patient and family participation in care and making decisions
- sharing information among patients and families so they can actively participate in decisions about health care
- collaboration between physicians and patients or families, but also between physicians and other clinicians in planning and delivering a patient's care

With patient-centered care, patients receive enough information and education to participate in decisions about their health care, such as which treatment might best suit their lifestyle, or which seems worth the risk for the benefits it promises. In patient-centered care, patients and their families partner with physicians and other health care providers instead of strictly following a prescribed course of diagnosis or treatment. A fundamental strength of patient-centered care comes from improving communication between patients and their providers.

There are many different definitions of patient-centered care that have evolved over recent years. One definition includes "medical home" in the description.

The **patient-centered medical home** is a philosophy that delivers care in a patient-centered and coordinated way with providers working together as a team.

Regardless of whether a patient's care is coordinated formally as a medical home, improved care coordination is another essential component of patient-centered care. The idea is to overcome some of the communication problems caused by specialization in health care and help organize activities on behalf of patients. Primary care physicians also try to do this for patients, but many are too busy or do not have the tools. One example of a patient-centered care plan is survivor care plans that have been developed for many cancer survivors. The plans list the cancer patient's diagnosis, all treatments the patient receives, and follow-up care the patient should receive.

Examples of patient-centered care strategies

Aside from the patient-centered medical home, improving communication with patients and between health care providers is an important strategy for establishing patient-centered care. Use of electronic health records, electronic communication between clinicians, patient self-management for chronic disease, shared decision-making between physicians and patients, and use of Web-based communication or applications for patients are some examples of programs to reinforce patient-centered care.

Why patient-centered care is important to the consumer

One reason patient-centered care has evolved is because patients are more informed today and want to be more involved in decisions about their treatment options. Studies have shown that patients who perceived their care as patient-centered care recovered better and had better emotional health a few months following their physician visits. They also received fewer referrals to specialist physicians or diagnostic tests. A 2013 study reported reduced use of emergency care because of fewer problems in coordinating care and fewer delays in care. On the other hand, studies have shown that physicians order more diagnostic tests, referrals to specialists, or hospitalizations when they communicate poorly with their patients.

Patient safety also is a priority under patient-centered care. Communication can improve safety, such as making sure a patient understands instructions about preparing for a procedure or for taking medications at home. Physicians and other health care providers also can emphasize patient safety as part of patient-centered care.

KEY TERMS

Medical home—A patient-centered concept that delivers coordinated, team-based medical care.

Primary care physician—A physician who is the first contact for medical care for a patient and who coordinates the use of specialty care.

To many patients and family members, patient-centered care is about dignity and respect. They feel that physicians listen to them and that health care providers have empathy for them as patients. To clinicians and policymakers, patient-centered care also is about improving patient safety and quality, and about saving money for the health care system by improving patient health and preventing complications.

Patient-centered care and health care reform

It has been difficult for many physicians to fully adopt the principles of patient-centered care because of how health care delivery and reimbursement currently work. For example, reimbursement models can reward physicians for quantity of patients seen, which makes it more difficult to spend time listening, educating, and discussing options. The **Patient Protection and Affordable Care Act** aims to strengthen primary care for patients and the role of the patient-centered medical home. Funding for new medical home models and health teams to support medical homes will be available, as will dollars to increase the number of primary care physicians in underserved areas.

Resources

PERIODICALS

Hearld, Larry R., and Jeffrey A. Alexander. "Patient-Centered Care and Emergency Department Utilization: a Path Analysis of the Mediating Effects of Care Coordination and Delays in Care." *Medical Care Research and Review* 69, no. 5 (2012):560-580.

WEBSITES

Conway, Jim, et al. "Partnering with Patients and Families to Design a Patient- and Family-Centered Health Care System." Institute for Patient-and Family-Centered Care. http://www.ipfcc.org/pdf/Roadmap.pdf (accessed September 12, 2013).

Rickert, James. "Patient-Centered Care: What It Means and How to Get There." *Health Affairs* Blog. http://health affairs.org/blog/2012/01/24/patient-centered-care-what-it-means-and-how-to-get-there/ (accessed September 12, 2013).

Rodack, Sabrina. "10 Guiding Principles for Patient-Centered Care." Becker's Clinical Quality and Infection Control website. http://www.beckershospitalreview.com/quality/10-guiding-principles-for-patient-centered-care.html (accessed September 12, 2013).

Stanton, Mark W. "Expanding Patient-Centered Care to Empower Patients and Assist Providers." Agency for Healthcare Research and Quality http://www.ahrq.gov/research/findings/factsheets/patient-centered/ria-issue5/index.html (accessed September 12, 2013).

ORGANIZATIONS

Institute for Patient-and Family-Centered Care, 6917 Arlington Road, Suite 309, Bethesda, MD 20814, (301) 652-0281, institute@ipfcc.org, www.ipfcc.org.

Teresa G. Odle

Patient-centered medical home (PCMH)

Definition

The patient-centered medical home (PCMH) is a model for delivering primary care that facilitates the development of a relationship between the patient and the patient's **primary care physician**, and when appropriate, the patient's family. Beyond the delivery of primary care, it supports coordination of health-supporting services to meet the patient's changing needs.

Description

The PCMH model is designed to improve and streamline the delivery of healthcare services by addressing the patient's comprehensive medical needs, including acute care, chronic care, preventative care, and wellness services. To do this, the PCMH model uses a team approach that can include physicians, physician assistants, nurses, nurse practitioners, pharmacists, nutritionists, social workers, addiction counselors, educators, and care coordinators.

The concept of a "medical home" was first introduced by the American Academy of Pediatrics in 1967. It defined a comprehensive practice that was patient-centered, accessible, coordinated, and culturally sensitive. Over the next 20 years, the **World Health Organization (WHO)** and the United States **Institute of Medicine** (IOM) instituted changes that encouraged primary care practices to become more accessible and integrated.

The PCMH model received more support in 2005, when researcher Dr. Barbara Starfield published information showing that health is improved when primary health care systems provide a better quality of care, are easily accessible, focus on prevention and early management of health problems, and reduce unnecessary hospitalizations. This research encouraged several physician groups, including the American College of Physicians and the American Academy of Family Physicians, to promote the PCMH model.

Over the next five years, the PCMH model became widely accepted. Incentives to move primary care to the PCMH model were incorporated into the 2010 **Patient Protection and Affordable Care Act** (Obamacare). By 2012, 47 states had adopted policies to promote the medical home model.

One highlight of the PCMH model is that care is coordinated across all aspects of the healthcare system whether or not the services are physically located in the same place or dispersed throughout the community. In practice, this means coordinating primary care, specialty care, hospital stays, **home health care**, and community support services. The goal is to deliver seamless healthcare to meet the patient's changing needs. For example, before an elderly patient is discharged from the hospital, a care coordinator might set up visits at the patient's home by a home health care nurse and a physical therapist and enroll the patient in a community support system such as Meals on Wheels.

In addition to coordinating care across a variety of healthcare services, the PCMH model works to build a relationship between the patient, the patient's family, and the patient's primary care physician. The goal is to involve the patient, and where appropriate, the patient's family in the management of health and wellness issues. This is done by recognizing each patient's unique needs, values, culture, and individual preferences.

By making members of the patient's health care team easily available by telephone or electronically outside normal business hours (and ideally, twenty-four hours a day), the PCMH model can reduce wait times for services and more efficiently address urgent needs. By giving patients the tools to share in decision making, responding to the patient's experiences and needs, and practicing evidence-based medicine, healthcare quality, safety, and patient satisfaction can be improved.

Why this is important to the consumer

When the PCMH model is fully implemented, it can deliver consumers higher-quality, more personalized, and more efficient health care in the most timely manner possible. This benefits the consumer in several ways.

KEY TERMS

Acute care—Treatment of a short-term illness such as bronchitis or a urinary tract infection.

Chronic care—Treatment of ongoing diseases, such as high blood pressure or diabetes.

Primary care physician—A medical doctor (MD) or osteopathic doctor (DO) who provides the first contact for an individual with a new health concern and who provides continuing care for an ongoing medical conditions.

• The primary care physician knows and understands the patient's values and preferences and can better deliver more effective and personalized healthcare solutions.

• Tests and assessments are less likely to be duplicated when a coordinated team approach is used, saving time and money.

• Increased accessibility to members of the PCMH team can result in swifter treatment of health problems. This may prevent a health condition from worsening and requiring more extensive or emergency treatment.

• Patients can be linked to social service organizations that provide support beyond direct healthcare, such as meals, transportation to doctor visits, and support groups.

• A high level of coordinated care prevents patients from "falling through the cracks" of the healthcare system. This is especially important for the mentally ill, individuals with addictions or dementia, and non-English speakers who might not be able to negotiate the social service network on their own.

Resources

BOOKS

United States Department of Health and Human Services Agency for Healthcare Research and Quality. *The Patient-Centered Medical Home: Closing the Quality Gap: Revisiting the State of the Science (Evidence Report/Technology Assessment Number 208)*. Create-Space Independent Publishing Platform, 2013.

PERIODICALS

Rittenhouse, Diane and Stephen M. Shortell. "The Patient-Centered Medical Home: Will It Stand the Test of Health Reform?" *Journal of the American Medical Association* 301,no.19(2009)2038–2040. (accessed July 21, 2013).

WEBSITES

Agency for Healthcare Research and Quality. "Patient-Centered Medical Home Resource Center." http://pcmh.ahrq.gov/portal/server.pt/community/pcmh__home/1483/PCMH_Defining%20the%20PCMH_v2 (accessed July 21, 2013).

Patient-Centered Primary Care Collaborative. "Defining the Medical Home." http://www.pcpcc.org/about/medical-home (accessed July 21, 2013).

ORGANIZATIONS

Agency for Healthcare Research and Quality, 540 Gaither Road, Suite 2000, Rockville, MD 20850, (301) 427-1104, http://pcmh.ahrq.gov/portal/server.pt/community/pcmh__home/1483.

National Committee for Quality Assurance, 1100 13th St., NW Suite 1000, Washington, DC 20006, (202) 992-3500, Fax: (202) 992-3599, customersupport@ncqa.org, http://www.ncqa.org.

Patient-Centered Primary Care Collaborative, 601 Thirteenth Street, NW, Suite 430 North, Washington, DC 20005, (202) 2081, Fax: (202) 2082, http://www.pcpcc.org.

Tish Davidson, AM

Patient confidentiality

Definition

Patient confidentiality is a patient's right to have all personal and identifiable medical information kept private. Such information should be available only to the physician and other healthcare and insurance personnel. It is a physician's duty not to disclose any medical information revealed by a patient or discovered by the physician in the course of diagnosis or treatment. Patient confidentiality is sometimes called doctor-patient confidentiality or physician-patient privilege, although it applies to any healthcare provider. However, in this age of healthcare provider teams, managed care, **electronic health records (EHRs),** and data mining and marketing, patient confidentiality is becoming ever more difficult to protect.

Purpose

The purpose of patient confidentiality goes beyond a person's right to privacy. Disclosure of confidential medical information, including genetic information, can lead to discrimination or other difficulties in education, employment, insurance coverage, access to credit, personal relationships, and other aspects of life. The disclosure of such information can seriously jeopardize an individual's well-being. The dissemination of personal information without the patient's permission can erode confidence in the medical profession and expose healthcare professionals to legal action.

Description

Patient confidentiality means that personal and medical information given to a healthcare provider or uncovered by the provider in the course of examination, diagnosis, or treatment will not be disclosed to others unless the patient has given specific permission for its release. Ethical and legal principles of confidentiality are rooted in age-old values underlying the patient-physician relationship. It is essential that patients trust their caregivers, and patient confidentiality is a requirement for that trust. Private information learned within the patient-doctor relationship that is disclosed to a third party by any means—oral, written, or electronic—is a breach of patient confidentiality, unless it is released with patient consent or by court order.

Although patients rely on healthcare providers to keep their medical information private, it is rare for medical records to remain completely sealed. The most benign breach of confidentiality occurs when clinicians share medical information in the form of case studies. However, when case studies or other patient data are published in professional journals, the identity of patients is never divulged, and all identifying information is either eliminated or changed. If this confidentiality is breached in any way, patients may have the right to sue.

Health records are routinely viewed, not only by physicians and other healthcare providers, but by the employees of insurance companies, medical laboratories, public **health departments,** researchers, and others. The greatest threat to patient confidentiality occurs because most medical bills are paid by some form of health insurance, either private or public. This makes it difficult, if not impossible, to keep information truly confidential. Furthermore, if an employer is providing health insurance, the employer and designated staff may have access to employee medical information.

Origins

Patient confidentiality has been an important feature of medical practice since the formulation of the Hippocratic Oath in ancient Greece. Over the last century, the U.S. government and individual states have enacted laws to protect the confidentiality of healthcare information generally, with particular attention to information about communicable diseases and mental health. For example, throughout the 1960s, substance and alcohol abuse were treated as mental illnesses, and patient confidentiality was determined by the laws in each state, since the states were responsible for mental health care and treatment. In the early 1970s, however, the increasing need for substance abuse treatment came to the attention of the federal government, because drug-related activities, including treatment for substance abuse, could be the basis for criminal prosecution at the federal level. Confusion ensued when practitioners who were treating substance abusers were required to follow two different sets of requirements—one mandated by the state and one by the federal government. Furthermore, state mental health laws varied in their degree of protection. There was growing concern that this situation deterred people from seeking treatment for substance abuse.

Beginning in the 1970s and 1980s, despite state and federal laws and voluntary safeguards, patient confidentiality was eroded by the near-complete dominance of **health maintenance organizations (HMOs)** and other managed care plans and third-party payers. This led to the passage of the federal **Health Insurance Portability and Accountability Act (HIPAA)** of 1996, which aimed to ensure privacy and protection of personal records and data in an environment of electronic health records (EHRs) and third-party insurance payers.

HIPAA

HIPAA, which went into effect in 2003, requires all healthcare workers and organizations to guard the privacy of their patients, clients, and customers. Employees at all levels are required to maintain confidentiality. Individuals must provide written consent for any and all releases of medical or health-related information. Patient consent must identify the types of information that can be released, the people or groups that are permitted access to the information, and the period of time for which the release is valid. Although similar policies had been in place for some time and were a requirement of the **Joint Commission** that accredits healthcare facilities, HIPAA was the first comprehensive regulation of health information by the federal government.

The HIPAA Privacy Rule established basic protections for health information, while allowing more stringent state laws to remain in effect. The Privacy Rule broadly defines protected health information (PHI), including information about past, present, and future physical and mental health and conditions, healthcare services provided, and healthcare payments that could be traced to an identifiable individual. It is generally accepted as also protecting the privacy of an individual's genetic information. The Privacy Rule prohibits disclosure of health information for employment-related decisions without the individual's consent and prevents PHI from being sold or used for marketing purposes. Under the Privacy Rule, individuals have the right to:

- access and copy their PHI held by clinics, hospitals, health plans, and certain other entities

- request amendments to their PHI

- request an accounting of unauthorized disclosures of PHI for purposes other than treatments, payments, and healthcare operations

- receive a Notice of Privacy Practices from physicians, hospitals, health plans, and others in the healthcare system

- request confidential communication of their PHI

- request restrictions on uses or disclosures of their PHI

- complain about privacy practices

The HIPAA Security Rule, which went into effect in 2005, set standards for protecting EHRs. HIPAA rules were substantially revised again in 2013. One result of HIPAA has been an increase in patient lawsuits against physicians who release information without the patient's permission.

Medical records

A major threat to patient confidentiality is the variety of purposes for which medical records are used, in addition to providing patient health care. Life and health insurance companies, especially private insurance outside of employer-sponsored plans, generally require the release of medical records before issuing a policy or providing payment under an existing plan. Insurance companies often subscribe to databases that provide prescription purchase histories. Government agencies may require medical charts to verify claims under **Medicaid, Medicare,** Social Security Disability, or Workers' Compensation. Employers often ask employees to authorize the release of their medical records. Medical charts can be subpoenaed and used as evidence in legal proceedings. Medical records are also used when hospitals, clinics, and individual healthcare providers are evaluated. Medical records from informal health screenings can even be released to direct marketers.

Increasingly, institutions are adopting standardized computer systems for clearer and more comprehensive documentation, enhanced access and searching, and more efficient storage and retrieval of individual records. These EHRs enable healthcare providers to consolidate, store, retrieve, and share a patient's complete medical history. Medical charts may contain far more than simple medical histories. The incorporation into EHRs of genetic information and the results of genetic testing is expected to increase dramatically in coming years. EHRs may also include family medical information, lifestyle details such as smoking or sports activities, participation in research projects, and information from applications for disability, life or accident insurance, or government programs. Medical records may include information about a patient's family, sexual behaviors, substance use or abuse, and even private thoughts and feelings divulged during psychotherapy.

Regulatory protections for medical charts have multiplied along with the rapid increase in the uses of medical information. Institution and government policies dictate the information included in medical charts, how that information is documented, personnel access to charts, and policies regulating access and protecting the integrity and confidentiality of medical charts. Patients or their personal representatives must consent to the release of medical charts outside of the immediate healthcare system, including release to caregivers in a new clinical setting. Some privacy regulations apply only to certain information, such as psychiatric records, HIV/AIDS or other communicable disease status, substance abuse records, or information held by government agencies or specific groups.

Breaches of confidentiality

Despite legal and ethical obligations and prohibitions, patient confidentiality continues to erode, particularly with the widespread establishment of electronic health information systems. Physicians in integrated healthcare systems and networks have access to confidential information on all patients in their system or network. Patient confidentiality is also threatened by the increase in clinical data repositories and shared databases. These data sources have the potential to improve overall health care, but sometimes at the expense of patient confidentiality.

Institutional policies and state laws govern the onsite and offsite storage of medical charts and required storage times. However, information in medical charts is now utilized by various individuals and organizations who are not bound by medical codes of ethics, including insurance companies, government agencies, employers, and attorneys. Researchers, quality assurance and regulatory organizations, and legal bodies may have access to medical charts for specific purposes, such as research studies, documentation, institutional audits, legal proceedings, or verification of information for insurance reimbursement. EHRs make this information readily accessible. In the United States, the frequent keying of medical information to social security numbers is also a serious threat to confidentiality.

Much personal health information exists outside of HIPAA regulations. Medical information in financial, school, and employment records is not covered by the HIPAA Privacy Rule, although Substance Abuse Confidentiality Requirements are more protective of patient privacy than HIPAA. To help maintain the confidentiality of their medical records, patients should:

- protect their social security numbers
- avoid disclosing personal information to healthcare providers if it has no bearing on health
- ask healthcare providers about outside access to their medical records
- ask to review medical records before they are sent to another entity, such as an insurance company
- ask for notification if their medical records are subpoenaed

Exceptions to patient confidentiality

While all states have specified exceptions to confidentiality, few states have spelled out the necessary elements of valid consent for disclosure of mental health information. Some states allow disclosure of mental health information without patient consent to:

- other treatment providers
- healthcare services payers or other sources of financial assistance to the patient
- agencies charged with oversight of the healthcare system or the system's practitioners
- third parties that the mental health professional believes might be endangered by the patient
- families, under certain circumstances
- law enforcement officials, under certain circumstances
- public health officials
- researchers

Prior to the 2003 enactment of HIPAA provisions, providers had become increasingly concerned that these exceptions were not addressed uniformly,

KEY TERMS

Electronic health records (EHRs)—A system for consolidating, storing, accessing, and sharing complete medical histories without the use of paper medical charts.

Health Insurance Portability and Accountability Act (HIPAA)—U.S. federal law that governs the privacy and security of personal health information.

Joint Commission—The accrediting organization that evaluates virtually all U.S. healthcare facilities and programs. Accreditation is maintained with on-site surveys every three years; laboratories are surveyed every two years.

Managed care—The integration of financing and delivery of health care.

Protected health information (PHI)—Information that is protected by law that relates to an individual's past, present, or future physical or mental health, as well as conditions, treatments, services, and payments that can be traced to an identifiable individual.

particularly when providers and payers were operating in different states. This resulted in open-ended disclosures that specified neither the parties to whom disclosure was to be made nor the specific information to be revealed. Implementation of HIPAA requirements have rectified this problem to some extent.

However, these exceptions to patient confidentiality remain a gray area fraught with ethical concerns. The effectiveness of these exceptions is also unclear. For example, a month before James Holmes killed 12 people and wounded 58 in a July 2012 attack in a movie theater in Aurora, Colorado, his psychiatrist at the University of Colorado broke doctor-patient confidentiality to inform the campus police that Holmes was fantasizing about killing large numbers of people. However, this disclosure did nothing to prevent the massacre.

Resources

BOOKS

Fremgen, Bonnie F. *Medical Law and Ethics.* Upper Saddle River, NJ: Pearson, 2012.

Landreneau, Raphael J. "Protecting Patient Confidentiality." In *Heart of the OR: Stories of Growth, Discovery, and Innovation by Perioperative Nurses,* edited by Carina Stanton. Denver, CO: AORN, 2011.

Stauch, Marc, et al. *Text, Cases, and Materials on Medical Law and Ethics.* New York: Routledge, 2012.

PERIODICALS

Barker, Richard W., David A. Brindley, and Anna Schuh. "Establish Good Genomic Practice to Guide Medicine Forward." *Nature Medicine* 19, no. 5 (May 2013): 530.

Pi, Diana. "Hiding Behind the Hippocratic Oath." *Journal of General Internal Medicine* 28, no. 4 (April 2013): 596–7.

Taylor, Paul. "Caldicott 2 and Patient Data." *British Medical Journal* 346, no. 7905 (April 27, 2013): 7.

WEBSITES

American Academy of Family Physicians. "AAFP, Other Physician Organizations Call for Ending Laws That Infringe on Patient-Physician Relationship." October 23, 2012. http://www.aafp.org/news-now/government-medicine/20121023nejmlawsarticle.html (accessed September 1, 2013).

American Medical Association. "Patient Confidentiality." http://www.ama-assn.org/ama/pub/physician-resources/legal-topics/patient-physician-relationship-topics/patient-confidentiality.page (accessed September 1, 2013).

Center on Medical Records Right and Privacy. "Your Medical Record Rights." http://ihcrp.georgetown.edu/privacy/records.html (accessed September 1, 2013).

Electronic Privacy Information Center. "Medical Record Privacy." http://epic.org/privacy/medical (accessed September 1, 2013).

Privacy Rights Clearinghouse. "Medical Privacy Resources." https://www.privacyrights.org/medical.htm (accessed September 1, 2013).

U.S. Department of Health and Human Services. "Health Information Privacy." https://www.privacyrights.org/medical.htm (accessed October 23, 2013).

ORGANIZATIONS

American Academy of Family Physicians, PO Box 11210, Shawnee Mission, KS 66207-1210, (913) 906-6000, Fax: (913) 906-6075, (800) 274-2237, http://www.aafp.org.

American Medical Association, 515 N. State St., Chicago, IL 60654, (800) 621-8335, http://www.ama-assn.org.

Center on Medical Record Rights and Privacy, Health Policy Institute, Georgetown University, Box 57144, Washington, DC 20057-1485, (202) 687-0880, Fax: (202) 687-3110, http://hpi.georgetown.edu/privacy.

Electronic Privacy Information Center (EPIC), 1718 Connecticut Ave. NW, Ste. 200, Washington, DC 20009, (202) 483-1140, Fax: (202) 483-1248, http://epic.org.

Privacy Rights Clearinghouse, 3108 Fifth Ave., Ste. A, San Diego, CA 92103, (619) 298-3396, https://www.privacyrights.org.

L. Fleming Fallon, Jr., MD, DrPH
Margaret Alic, PhD

Patient education

Definition

Patient education involves helping patients become better informed about their condition, medical procedures, and choices they have regarding treatment.

Description

Patients acquire information about their condition in a variety of ways, including: by discussing their condition with health professionals; by reading written materials or watching films made available in hospitals or doctors' offices; through specific health care organizations, such as the American Cancer Association; and through drug advertisements on television and in popular magazines. With the explosion of information on the Internet, patients can access a wide range of medical information, from professional medical journals to online support and chat groups with a health focus.

In addition to acquiring general information, patients may wish to ask their health practitioners questions about **evidence-based practice** and about prior process and outcomes, in reference to proposed treatment options and their plan of care.

Being informed about one's health care options is essential to a patient's health and well-being. Especially with the increase in **managed care,** in which economics and efficiency are sometimes paramount, patients may be able to obtain better health care if they are knowledgeable and assertive about their needs and wishes. Informed patients may benefit, for example, by realizing they have a choice of a variety of medications, a variety of treatments, and of various lifestyle patterns that may impact or affect their condition.

Professional health care providers have traditionally borne the responsibility for patient education. In recent years, however, patients independently have easy access to a wide range of health information. However, many patients cannot easily obtain or understand relevant information, especially if they lack the education or experience with the issues, or if

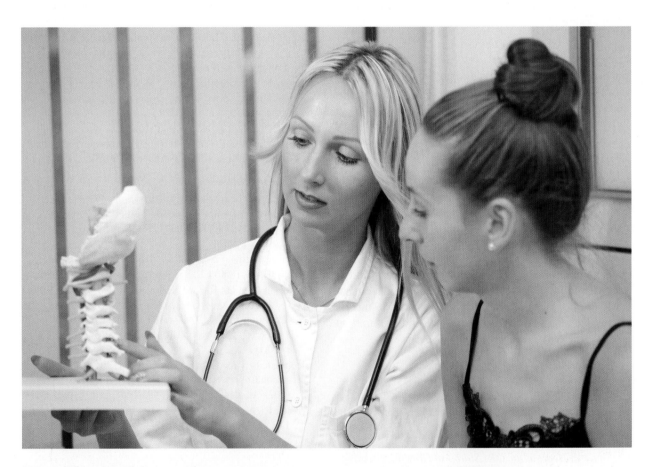

Patient education is important to enable individuals to make informed decisions regarding medical care.
(©Edw/Shutterstock.com)

KEY TERMS

Evidence-based practice—The process by which health care providers incorporate the best research or evidence into clinical practice in combination with clinical expertise and within the context of patient values.

Outcomes—Results or consequences of care or treatment.

Process—The steps, actions, or operations used to bring about the desired outcome.

they are not fluent in English. In addition, many patients may not understand enough about their condition to ask relevant questions. Finally, a significant amount of popular information is inaccurate or publicized for a profit motive rather than for education purposes. Patients may not be able to sort out what is true or what is relevant to their own condition. This is why consumers should do all they can to increase their **health literacy.**

Another relatively recent aspect of patient education centers on legal ramifications. When a patient is fully informed about the risks and benefits of a particular procedure or therapeutic approach, the likelihood of a lawsuit resulting from a complication is sharply reduced.

Nurses play an important role in providing health education. They are often the best sources of information regarding caring for patients, such as learning to breast feed, soothing fussy babies, or staying comfortable in the hospital. They may be more accessible than doctors, both because they may spend more time with patients and because patients may feel less intimidated by nurses and more comfortable asking questions and sharing fears.

Why this is important to the consumer

Healthcare can require consumers to deal with complex topics and issues at a time when they are upset, unwell, or in pain. Patient education is especially important for consumers at these times because it can help them make well-informed decisions that accurately reflect their preferences and beliefs. Even for more minor issues such as how to treat a cold, patient education can help consumers take care of themselves in a way that best promotes their health and well-being.

Consumers should never be afraid to ask for more information about a diagnosis, procedure, test, or any other issue that is raised in a health care setting. If the health care practitioner does not have the information immediately available, he or she should be able to point the consumer to a reputable website, book, or pamphlet for additional information. Consumers should speak up if they are presented with information that they do not understand or that feels incomplete. In a health care world of many different specialists all treating one patient, overworked practitioners, and crowded hospitals, consumers who take the initiative to read and understand educational materials that are offered and ask for materials if they are not made readily available can help to ensure their best health outcome.

Resources

BOOKS

Muma, Richard D., and Lyons, Barbara Ann. *Patient Education: A Practical Approach,* 2nd ed., Sudbury, MA: Jones and Bartlett Learning, 2012.

Schutte, Adam, Ed. *Patient Education and Management: Practices, Challenges, and Outcomes.* Hauppauge, NY: Nova Science Publishers, 2013.

Stewart, Melissa N. *Practical Patient Literacy: The Medagogy Model.*New York: McGraw-Hill Medical, 2012.

PERIODICALS

Beitz, Janice M. "Power up your patient education with analogies and metaphors: these creative teaching tools can make education more effective." *Wound Care Advisor* 2.5 (2013): 12.

Fink, Christine, et al. "Impact of preoperative patient education on prevention of postoperative complications after major visceral surgery: study protocol for a randomized controlled trial (PEDUCAT trial)." *Trials* 14 (2013): 271.

Hayek, Ayman Al, et al. "Impact of an education program on patient anxiety, depression, glycemic control, and adherence to self-care and medication in Type 2 diabetes." *Journal of Family and Community Medicine* 20.2 (2013): 77.

Schwartz, LM, and Woloshin, S. "The Drug Facts Box: Improving the Communication of Prescription Drug Information." *Proceedings of the National Academy of Sciences of the United States of America.* (August 20, 2013): 14069–74.

WEBSITES

United States Centers for Disease Control and Prevention. "Vaccination and Immunization Patient Education." http://www.cdc.gov/vaccines/ed/patient-ed.htm (accessed December 1, 2013).

University of Pittsburg Medical Center. "UPMC Patient Education Materials." http://www.upmc.com/patients-visitors/education/pages/default.aspx (accessed December 1, 2013).

ORGANIZATIONS

Agency for Healthcare Research and Quality, 540 Gaither Road, Suite 2000, Rockville, MD 20850, (301) 427-1104, http://www.ahrq.gov.

Directors of Health Promotion and Education, 1015 18th Street NW, Suite 300, Washington, DC 20036, (202) 659-2230, http://www.dhpe.org.

United States Centers for Disease Control and Prevention (CDC), 1600 Clifton Road, Atlanta, GA 30333, (404) 639-3534, (800) CDC-INFO (800-232-4636); TTY: (888) 232-6348, inquiry@cdc.gov, http://www.cdc.gov.

National Institutes of Health (NIH), 9000 Rockville Pike, Bethesda, MD 20892, (301) 496-4000, http://www.nih.gov/index.html.

U.S. National Library of Medicine, 8600 Rockville Pike, Bethesda, MD 20894, http://www.nlm.nih.gov/.

Jacqueline N. Martin, M.S.
Tish Davidson, AM

Patient navigator

Definition

A patient navigator (sometime called a "patient advocate") serves as a guide to people in the health-care system, determining what factors impede their access to quality care and helping them dispense with obstacles so that they can obtain the care they need.

Description

Patient navigation or advocacy was started with the desire to decrease **health disparities** that occur due to economics, race, geography, or other potential impediments to good care. The first patient navigation programs were designed to decrease mortality due to cancer, but the same concepts are now being success-fully applied to patient navigation for clients with other medical conditions. Patient navigation seeks to provide care across the full spectrum of a client's medical trajectory: from prevention, to screening, to diagnosis, to treatment, to **end-of-life care**.

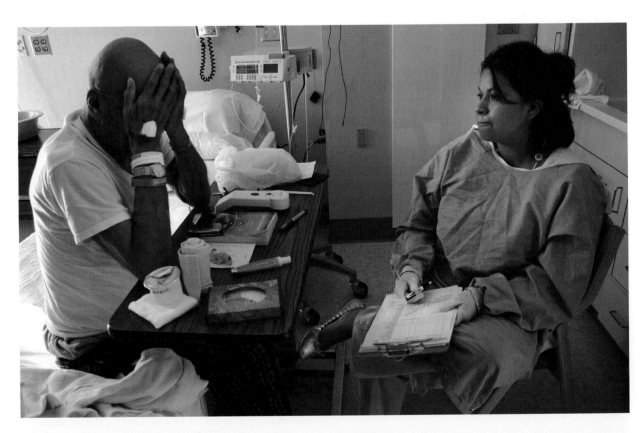

Patient navigation or advocacy was started with the desire to decrease healthcare disparities that occur due to economics, race, geography, or other potential impediments to good care. (© ZUMA Press, Inc. / Alamy)

Among other things, access to quality healthcare depends on an individual's understanding of the system, the capacity to ask knowledgeable questions about treatment options (and the ability to understand the answers), the ability to fill out appropriate paperwork, and the client's comprehension of how to receive appropriate reimbursement for services. Barriers to care can include English as a second language (and the subsequent need for medical translation), unfamiliarity and/or difficulty understanding medical vocabulary and concepts, lack of understanding of community resources, confusion about insurance reimbursement and what is covered care, cultural differences, psychological and emotional responses to illness, and difficulties with transportation and childcare. Patient navigators attempt to identify and circumvent obstacles, guiding their clients through the complicated healthcare system so that they can access quality care.

Some patient navigators deal primarily with paperwork and insurance reimbursement issues; others attend appointments with their clients, providing on-the-spot support and translation of medical vocabulary into layperson's terms, and helping the client understand the risks and benefits of proffered treatments.

Education, certification and skills

There is no clear cut educational pathway for people who wish to be a patient navigator or advocate. There is also neither a specific set of national standards nor any universally sanctioned certification or licensure program. Some patient navigators have some background in healthcare, social work, or some other area of social services. A number of programs have sprung up offering training that ranges from several weeks all the way up to a master's degree. As mentioned, there are some research programs that are funding access to patient navigators, in order to ascertain the potential benefits that might come from such programs.

A patient navigator should be knowledgeable about the health areas on which he or she is planning to focus, as well as the medical system and community in which he or she is based. The patient navigator needs to understand reimbursement and insurance. Cultural sensitivity, an understanding of psychological dynamics, and excellent communication skills are critical.

Places of employment

Patient navigators may be employees of hospitals, medical centers, physician's offices, public or private

health clinics, corporations, or other organizations. Patient navigators employed by the American Cancer Society are available in some locations, as are navigators trained and employed in a research capacity by the **National Institutes of Health** National Cancer Institute.

Tasks of a patient navigator

Patient navigators must build trust and rapport with their clients. This requires sensitivity and an understanding of the cultural context in which the client's medical needs occur. The patient navigator should have a fundamental understanding of disease processes and treatments, as well as the ability to translate technical medical information into language understood by most laypeople (perhaps with the help of a medical translator). The patient navigator may need to meet with the client in his or her home to help procure home-based services and/or to fill out necessary paperwork.

Why this is important to the consumer

Originally conceived of to decrease the disparities in healthcare wrought by race, gender, socioeconomic status, or level of educational attainment, patient navigators are still needed in our world of rapidly changing, complicated healthcare systems, technologies, and reimbursement policies. Research in 2013 showed that only 14% of people polled were clear about the meaning of very basic insurance terms that included copayments, co-insurance, and deductibles. Furthermore, about 48.61 million people in the United States were without health insurance in 2011; lack of insurance has been shown to decrease the likelihood of receiving appropriate and timely medical care, increase the likelihood of having a poor health status, and increase the likelihood of early death. Patient navigation can help obviate some of these consequences, by matching up people in need of care with the community resources that will allow them to receive that care, and by ensuring that patients have the best background possible to make educated healthcare choices.

Resources

BOOKS

EZ Occupational Outlook Handbook, 2nd ed. St. Paul, MN: JIST Publishing, 2011.

U.S. Department of Labor. *Occupational Outlook Handbook.* St. Paul, MN: JIST Publishing, 2013.

Wischnitzer, Saul. *Top 100 Health-Care Careers.* St. Paul, MN: JIST Publishing, 2011.

ORGANIZATIONS

Colorado Patient Navigator Training, Cancer Center (UCD) - Cancer Prevention & Control Division, Room W6111-F, Building 500, Anschutz Medical Campus, 13001 E. 17th Place, Aurora, CO 80045, (856) 380-6836, http://www.patientnavigatortraining.org/index.htm/.

Commission for Case Manager Certification, 15000 Commerce Parkway, Suite C, Mount Laurel, NJ 08054, (856) 380-6836, http://ccmcertification.org/.

ExploreHealthCareers.org, American Dental Education Association, 1400 K Street, NW, Suite 1100, Washington, DC 20005, (202) 289-7201, cmsa@cmsa.org, http://explorehealthcareers.org/en/home/.

Harold P. Freeman Patient Navigation Institute, 55 Exchange Place, Suite 405, New York, NY 08054, (646) 380-4060, http://www.hpfreemanpni.org/.

National Health Institutes Center to Reduce Cancer Health Disparities, 9609 Medical Center Dr., MSC 9746, Sixth Floor, West Tower, Bethesda, MD 20892, (856) 380-6836, nci-crchd@mail.nih.gov, http://crchd.cancer.gov/pnp/what-are.html.

Patient Navigation in Cancer Care, patientnavigation@paladinhealthcom.com, http://www.patientnavigation.com/content/default.aspx/.

U.S. Bureau of Labor Statistics, Postal Square Building, 2 Massachusetts Ave., NE, Washington, DC 20212, (202) 691-5200, http://www.bls.gov.

U.S. Department of Labor, Frances Perkins Building, 200 Constitution Ave., NW, Washington, DC 20210, (866) 487-2365, http://www.dol.gov/.

Rosalyn Carson-DeWitt, MD

Patient Protection and Affordable Care Act

Definition

The Patient Protection and Affordable Care Act (PPACA)—signed into law by President Barack Obama on March 23, 2010 and commonly referred to as "Obamacare"—is the most sweeping overhaul of the U.S. healthcare system since the establishment of **Medicare** and **Medicaid** in 1965.

Why this is important to the consumer

The ultimate goal of the PPACA is to expand healthcare coverage to an estimated 53 million uninsured Americans, while controlling increasing healthcare costs and improving healthcare delivery. Over the last decades of the twentieth century, the American employer-based health insurance model began to fail, as an increasing number of employers reduced or eliminated employee healthcare benefits, and private health insurance became increasingly unaffordable. Not only were tens of millions of Americans uninsured, but millions more were underinsured, without enough coverage to meet their healthcare needs. By 2007, medical expenses became the most common cause of personal bankruptcy.

The PPACA aims to make healthcare insurance affordable to individuals and small employers through major expansion of the Medicaid system in addition to marketplace **health insurance exchanges** organized by state. It increases competition within private insurance markets and offers a minimum standard of baseline coverage for consumers. In particular, under PPACA, insurance companies cannot deny coverage due to pre-existing conditions or cancel policies because of illness.

President Barack Obama signs the Patient Protection and Affordable Care Act during a ceremony in the East Room of the White House on March 23, 2010. *(AFP/Getty Images)*

No health insurance coverage among persons under age 65, by selected characteristics: United States, selected years 1984–2011

Characteristic	1984	1989	1995	1997	2000	2001	2004 (1)	2004 (2)	2010	2011
					Number in millions					
Total	**29.8**	**33.4**	**37.1**	**41.0**	**41.4**	**40.3**	**42.1**	**41.6**	**48.3**	**45.8**
					Percent of population					
Total	**14.5**	**15.6**	**16.1**	**17.5**	**17.0**	**16.4**	**16.6**	**16.4**	**18.2**	**17.2**
Age										
Under 19 years	14.1	15.0	13.7	14.4	12.9	11.6	10.1	9.6	8.3	7.4
Under 6 years	14.9	15.1	11.8	12.5	11.8	9.9	8.9	8.2	6.3	5.0
6–18 years	13.8	15.0	14.6	15.2	13.4	12.4	10.6	10.3	9.2	8.5
18–64 years	14.8	16.0	17.3	19.0	18.9	18.5	19.4	19.3	22.3	21.2
18–44 years	17.1	18.4	20.4	22.4	22.4	22.2	23.6	23.5	27.1	25.4
18–24 years	25.0	27.1	28.0	30.1	30.4	29.9	30.1	30.0	31.4	25.9
19–25 years	25.1	27.9	28.8	31.5	32.3	31.8	32.3	32.2	33.8	27.9
25–34 years	16.2	18.3	21.1	23.8	23.3	23.1	25.7	25.5	28.3	28.1
35–44 years	11.2	12.3	15.1	16.7	16.9	16.8	17.6	17.5	22.6	22.2
45–64 years	9.6	10.5	10.9	12.4	12.6	12.2	12.6	12.8	15.7	15.4
45–54 years	10.5	11.0	11.6	12.8	12.8	13.0	13.7	13.6	17.9	17.4
55–64 years	8.7	10.0	9.9	11.8	12.4	11.0	11.7	11.6	12.8	13.0
Sex										
Male	15.3	16.8	17.4	18.7	18.1	17.5	18.1	17.9	20.3	18.8
Female	13.8	14.4	14.8	16.3	15.9	15.3	15.2	14.9	16.1	15.6
Sex and marital status										
Male:										
Married	11.1	12.5	15.0	13.9	14.1	13.5	14.5	14.4	17.2	16.5
Divorced, separated, widowed	24.9	25.0	24.0	28.8	25.8	25.6	27.1	27.0	31.4	30.0
Never married	22.4	25.0	25.6	27.9	27.2	27.1	27.6	27.5	31.1	28.0
Female:										
Married	11.2	11.8	13.6	13.0	13.3	13.1	13.2	13.1	14.7	14.4
Divorced, separated, widowed	19.2	19.1	18.1	23.2	21.3	21.2	23.3	23.0	23.6	24.0
Never married	16.3	18.0	17.5	20.5	21.1	20.0	19.6	19.3	21.9	20.5
Race										
White only	13.6	14.5	15.5	16.4	15.4	14.9	16.3	16.1	17.6	16.7
Black or African American only	19.9	21.6	18.0	20.1	19.5	18.8	18.1	17.6	20.6	19.0
American Indian or Alaska Native only	22.5	28.4	34.3	38.1	38.4	33.1	35.0	34.6	44.0	34.2
Asian only	18.5	16.9	18.6	19.5	17.6	17.3	16.7	16.5	17.1	16.5
2 or more races	—	—	—	—	16.8	16.6	12.6	12.3	15.8	16.0
Hispanic origin										
Hispanic or Latino	29.5	33.7	31.4	34.5	35.6	35.0	35.1	34.4	32.0	31.1
Mexican	33.8	39.9	35.6	39.4	39.9	39.4	38.1	37.6	34.8	33.0
Puerto Rican	18.3	24.7	17.6	19.0	16.4	15.5	21.0	20.4	13.7	15.8
Cuban	21.6	20.6	22.3	21.1	25.4	20.4	22.8	22.8	26.5	28.1
Other Hispanic or Latino	27.4	25.8	30.2	33.0	33.4	33.2	33.3	32.3	32.4	31.8
Age and percent of poverty level										
Under 65 years:										
Below 100%	33.9	35.2	29.6	33.7	34.2	33.1	31.8	31.0	30.3	28.4
100%–199%	21.8	25.6	28.3	30.6	31.0	29.1	29.4	29.0	32.4	30.0
100%–133%	28.8	32.3	34.1	36.6	35.7	32.9	32.3	31.7	34.9	32.0
134%–199%	18.7	22.6	25.1	27.7	28.7	27.3	28.0	27.6	31.0	28.9
200%–399%	7.6	8.3	10.0	14.2	15.4	14.9	15.7	15.6	17.4	16.5
400% or more	3.2	4.2	5.4	6.1	5.9	6.1	5.9	5.9	5.6	5.2
Under 18 years:										
Below 100%	28.9	31.6	20.0	23.2	22.0	20.7	16.5	15.0	10.6	8.8
100%–199%	17.5	20.2	22.0	23.2	21.7	18.6	15.8	15.1	12.7	11.4
100%–133%	24.0	27.1	26.1	28.1	26.4	21.3	17.9	17.1	15.1	11.5
134%–199%	14.4	16.9	19.5	20.7	19.1	17.1	14.7	14.1	11.3	11.3
200%–399%	4.9	4.7	6.6	9.4	9.3	8.3	7.7	7.6	7.0	6.4
400% or more	1.8	1.9	4.6	3.9	3.3	3.2	2.6	2.6	2.1	2.0

(Table by PreMediaGlobal. Copyright © 2014 Cengage Learning®.)

No health insurance coverage among persons under age 65, by selected characteristics: United States, selected years 1984–2011 [CONTINUED]

Characteristic	1984	1989	1995	1997	2000	2001	2004 (1)	2004 (2)	2010	2011
					Percent of population					
18–64 years:										
Below 100%	37.6	38.2	37.0	41.2	42.4	41.3	41.4	41.0	42.7	40.4
100%–199%	24.4	28.8	32.0	34.7	36.4	35.0	36.7	36.5	42.1	39.3
100%–133%	31.9	35.6	39.7	41.7	41.7	39.8	40.4	40.0	45.7	42.5
134%–199%	21.1	25.9	28.2	31.5	34.0	32.8	35.0	34.8	40.3	37.6
200%–399%	8.9	10.0	11.7	16.4	18.2	17.8	19.1	19.1	21.3	20.4
400% or more	3.4	4.4	5.5	6.7	6.6	6.9	6.8	6.8	6.5	6.1
Geographic region										
Northeast	10.2	10.9	13.3	13.5	12.2	11.7	11.9	11.8	12.4	11.8
Midwest	11.3	10.7	12.2	13.2	12.3	11.7	12.6	12.4	14.1	13.4
South	17.7	19.7	19.4	20.9	20.5	20.2	20.2	19.9	21.9	20.4
West	18.2	18.8	17.9	20.6	20.7	19.0	19.1	18.9	20.6	20.0

(Table by PreMediaGlobal. Copyright © 2014 Cengage Learning®.)

The PPACA also prohibits annual and lifetime caps on coverage.

Description

At almost 1,000 pages, the PPACA, along with accompanying legislation, represents a comprehensive restructuring of the U.S. healthcare system. Its passage by the U.S. Congress was the result of countless compromises on everything from coverage of contraceptives and abortion to protecting the interests of private insurers. Proponents of a single-payer system, similar to those of many other developed countries, viewed the PPACA as a giveaway to insurance and pharmaceutical companies. President Obama backed off from a public option that would have competed directly with private insurance. On the other side, opponents continued their efforts to repeal the PPACA, preferring a return to a total free-market-based system. In June 2012, the U.S. Supreme Court upheld the PPACA **individual mandate**, which requires most citizens and legal residents to obtain health insurance in 2014 or pay an annual fine. This is a key provision because it enlarges the health insurance pool to include the young and healthy as well as those with expensive medical needs, thereby spreading the cost of healthcare over the entire population. Approximately 30 million Americans who would otherwise be uninsured are expected to obtain coverage through either the private insurance market or Medicaid expansion.

Important PPACA provisions that directly benefit many Americans are in effect as of January 2014:

• Annual and lifetime dollar limits on essential healthcare services are abolished.

• Insurance companies can no longer deny coverage because of pre-existing health conditions.

• Coverage cannot be terminated or premiums increased because of illness, a health condition, or an honest mistake on an insurance application.

• Women can no longer be charged more than men for health insurance.

• Children can remain on a parent's policy or plan until age 26.

• New plans must offer a baseline of essential benefits, including free preventative screening and immunizations, and coverage of contraception counseling and methods.

• Emergency care outside a plan network must be provided without financial penalty.

• Consumers are free to choose their primary care doctor or pediatrician within their plan's network.

• Women do not require a referral for obstetrical and gynecological care.

• Healthcare plans must provide an easily understood, standardized Summary of Benefits and Coverage (SBC) for ready comparison, including a Uniform Glossary of terms.

• Consumers have the right to appeal healthcare plan decisions.

• Consumers have the right to a 30-day notice before a policy is canceled for cause, such as intentionally false or incomplete information on an insurance application or failure to pay premiums.

Some of these provisions apply only to new healthcare plans. Many existing plans are not required to follow all of these rules, and many managed-care plans have requested exceptions. Thus, it may be years before all of these new rights apply to all healthcare consumers.

Personal health care expenditures, by source of funds and type of expenditure: United States, selected years 1960–2010

(Data are compiled from various sources by the Centers for Medicare & Medicaid Services)

Type of personal health care expenditures and source of funds	1960	1970	1980	1990	2000	2008	2009	2010
					Amount			
Per capita	$125	$300	$943	$2,430	$4,128	$6,615	$6,886	$7,082
					Amount in billions			
All personal health care expenditures	$23.4	$63.1	$217.2	$616.8	$1,165.4	$2,010.2	$2,109.0	$2,186.0
Out-of-pocket payments	13.1	25.0	58.4	138.7	201.8	294.0	294.4	299.7
Health insurance	6.6	29.6	132.0	403.3	844.8	1,544.9	1,637.1	1,703.0
Private health insurance	4.9	14.0	61.4	205.1	407.1	707.5	734.0	746.0
Medicare	—	7.3	36.3	107.3	215.8	442.0	471.2	493.8
Medicaid	—	5.0	24.7	69.7	186.9	317.1	345.9	371.6
Federal	—	2.7	13.7	40.3	109.3	187.8	230.5	251.5
State and local	—	2.3	11.0	29.4	77.6	129.3	115.4	120.1
Children's Health Insurance Program (CHIP; Medicaid)	—	—	—	—	2.5	8.7	9.6	10.0
Federal	—	—	—	—	1.8	6.1	6.7	7.0
State and local	—	—	—	—	0.8	2.6	2.8	3.0
Other health insurance programs*	1.7	3.3	9.6	21.2	32.4	69.6	76.5	81.6
Other third-party payers and programs**	3.7	8.5	26.8	74.9	118.8	171.4	177.4	183.3
					Percent distribution			
All sources of funds	100.0	100.0	100.0	100.0	100.0	100.0	100.0	100.0
Out-of-pocket payments	55.9	39.6	26.9	22.5	17.3	14.6	14.0	13.7
Health insurance	28.3	46.9	60.8	65.4	72.5	76.8	77.6	77.9
Private health insurance	21.1	22.2	28.3	33.3	34.9	35.2	34.8	34.1
Medicare	—	11.5	16.7	17.4	18.5	22.0	22.3	22.6
Medicaid	—	8.0	11.4	11.3	16.0	15.8	16.4	17.0
Federal	—	4.3	6.3	6.5	9.4	9.3	10.9	11.5
State and local	—	3.7	5.1	4.8	6.7	6.4	5.5	5.5
Children's Health Insurance Program (CHIP; Medicaid)	—	—	—	—	0.2	0.4	0.5	0.5
Federal	—	—	—	—	0.2	0.3	0.3	0.3
State and local	—	—	—	—	0.1	0.1	0.1	0.1
Other health insurance programs*	7.2	5.2	4.4	3.4	2.8	3.5	3.6	3.7
Other third-party payers and programs**	15.8	13.5	12.3	12.1	10.2	8.5	8.4	8.4

*Includes Department of Defense and Department of Veterans Affairs.
**Includes worksite health care, Indian Health Service, workers' compensation, among others.

(Table by PreMediaGlobal. Copyright © 2014 Cengage Learning®.)

Medicaid and Medicare

The PPACA expands Medicaid coverage to most adults under age 65 with incomes up to 133% of the federal poverty level (FPL). Because of exemptions, the limit is effectively 138% of the FPL. In 2013, the FPL was $19,530 for a family of three. It is projected that by 2019, an additional 16 million Americans will be covered by Medicaid or the **Children's Health Insurance Program (CHIP)**. Thus, Medicaid will likely become the foundation of healthcare financing and the healthcare economy in most of the United States.

Although in its 2012 decision the U.S. Supreme Court ruled that states could decide whether or not to participate in PPACA-legislated Medicaid expansion, in most cases it is to states' advantage to do so, since the federal government will pay 100% of Medicaid coverage for newly eligible adults for the first three years and at

least 90% thereafter. The PPACA also increases Medicaid payments to fee-for-service and managed-care providers for primary care services, and it increases Medicaid prescription drug reimbursements to states. There are incentives for states to adopt homecare-based and community-based programs for disabled Medicaid recipients requiring long-term care. Nevertheless, 15 states have opted out of participation and another seven are likely to not participate as of late 2013. Over half of the nation's working uninsured are included in these states.

The PPACA enhances Medicare benefits, including free preventive services and the phasing out of the Part D prescription drug coverage gap or **"donut hole."** The legislation aims to slow the overall growth in Medicare spending, primarily by reducing overpayments to private Medicare plans. It levies a

Ten characteristics of the Affordable Care Act

1. Provides insurance through the Health Insurance Marketplace
2. Requires insurance companies to cover patients with pre-existing conditions
3. Provides for free preventive care
4. Guarantees young adults coverage until age 26
5. Mandates uniform and simplified summary of benefits and coverage documents
6. Reviews increases in insurance rates
7. Prevents insurance companies from cancelling health insurance because of illness
8. Allows patients to choose their own doctors
9. Ends coverage limits for essential health benefits
10. Grants patients the right to appeal health plan decisions

SOURCE: U.S. Centers for Medicare & Medicaid Services, "10 Ways the Health Care Law Protects You," *Health Insurance Blog*, HealthCare.gov, June 21, 2013. Available online at: https://www.healthcare.gov/blog/10-ways-the-health-care-law-protects-you.

(Table by PreMediaGlobal. Reproduced by permission of Gale, a part of Cengage Learning.)

payroll tax on higher-income earnings and will charge higher Medicare premiums for higher-income recipients. The PPACA increases efforts to reduce Medicare fraud and waste and establishes a five-star rating system for **Medicare Advantage** Plans. The provisions include an Independence at Home demonstration program for high-need Medicare beneficiaries to reduce hospitalizations, improve patient outcomes, and reduce costs.

One of the most significant groups affected by the PPACA is people who qualify for both Medicare and Medicaid—largely low-income senior citizens and individuals with significant physical and mental healthcare needs. Caring for these 9.2 million Americans cost $319.5 billion in 2011. In terms of sheer numbers, these "dual-eligibles" only accounted for 15% of all Medicaid recipients and 16% of all Medicare participants, but they accounted for 39% of all Medicaid spending and 27% of all Medicare spending. Under the PPACA, care for these dual-eligible individuals will be coordinated and streamlined through a new office within the **Centers for Medicare and Medicaid Services**.

Health insurance exchanges and CO-OPs

Under the PPACA, states are required to establish Health Benefit Exchanges and **Small Business Health Options Program (SHOP)** exchanges, through which individuals and businesses with up to 100 employees can purchase coverage. The exchanges will be administered by state agencies or nonprofit organizations.

Access to available health insurance by state, along with potential PPACA benefits, is centralized in a Healthcare Marketplace website available at www.healthcare.gov. Despite an unsuccessful last-minute filibuster in the U.S. Senate aimed at derailing funding for the PPACA, the exchanges opened for enrollment on October 1, 2013 for coverage commencing January 2014. Beginning in 2017, states can choose to allow businesses with more than 100 employees to use SHOP exchanges.

It is estimated that approximately 24 million Americans will obtain insurance through the exchanges by 2016, with another 24 million obtaining individual coverage outside of the exchanges. Families with incomes between 133% and 400% of the FPL will be eligible for financial help to purchase coverage through an exchange. Tax credits will be available for insurance purchased through an exchange by people without job-based health coverage or with job-based coverage that costs more than 9.5% of their income. Small businesses that purchase health insurance for their employees will receive tax credits. Individuals without coverage will pay a phased-in annual penalty. Employers with 50 or more full-time employees who do not offer healthcare coverage will be subject to fines.

The PPACA will help finance the creation of Consumer Operated and Oriented Plans (CO-OPs). These are independent, nonprofit, member-owned and operated health insurance companies whose sole purpose will be to offer qualified consumer-oriented benefit plans. Any and all profits must be used to lower premiums or improve benefits and healthcare quality. States are also permitted to establish basic health plans for uninsured Americans with incomes of 133%–200% of the FPL and who would otherwise be eligible for premium subsidies in an exchange.

Private insurance

The PPACA establishes new regulations for private health insurance companies. Those operating in the individual and small group markets and exchanges are required to guarantee the issuing and renewing of policies. Variations in the rates charged consumers can be based only on residence in a high-rate area, family composition, age, which is limited to a 3:1 differential in rates, and tobacco use, which is limited to a 1.5:1 ratio.

PPACA requires that all new **private insurance plans** and new coverage periods cover preventive services for women without co-payments or other additional costs. These services include well-woman visits, mammograms, contraceptives, contraceptive and breastfeeding counseling and equipment, HIV testing

Children's Health Insurance Program (CHIP)— Children's Medicaid; a federal program administered by the states that provides low-cost or free health insurance to children from families with incomes that have traditionally been too high to qualify for Medicaid.

Consumer Operated and Oriented Plans (CO-OPs)—Independent, nonprofit, member-owned, and member-operated health insurance companies established under the PPACA.

Co-payment—The amount that an insured individual pays out-of-pocket for healthcare services.

Deductible—The amount that an insured person is required to pay on each claim or over the course of a year.

Dual eligibles—Low-income elderly and those with physical or mental disabilities who are eligible for both Medicaid and Medicare.

Essential health benefits (EHB)—Minimum services that must be provided by health insurance plans under the PPACA.

Exchanges—American Health Benefit Exchanges; state systems through which individuals can compare and purchase health insurance under the PPACA.

Federal poverty level; FPL—The U.S. government's definition of poverty for families of a given size, adjusted annually for inflation and used as the

reference point for determining eligibility for Medicaid and health insurance subsidies under the PPACA.

Managed care—The integration of financing and delivery of health care.

Medicaid—U.S. government-financed health insurance for low-income Americans that is administered by individual states and is being greatly expanded under the PPACA.

Medicare—The U.S. government health insurance system for those aged 65 and over.

Medicare Advantage Plans—Medicare Part C; private managed-care plans that include all Medicare Part A and Part B benefits and usually some additional benefits.

Medicare Part D—An optional, subsidized, outpatient prescription drug benefit provided through a private insurer.

Premium—The amount paid by a beneficiary for insurance coverage, usually on a monthly basis.

Small Business Health Options Program; SHOP—State systems under the PPACA through which small businesses can compare and purchase health insurance for their employees.

Summary of Benefits and Coverage (SBC)—A standard form that health insurance companies and plans must use under the PPACA to explain their plans and allow for easy comparisons of plans.

---

and counseling, and screening for gestational diabetes, breast and cervical cancer, sexually transmitted infections, and intimate partner violence.

Almost all individual insurance plans, including those in exchanges and those in individual and small group markets outside of the exchanges, were required to offer defined essential services by 2014. These include hospitalization, physicians' services, prescription drugs, rehabilitation, mental health services, and pregnancy and newborn care. Although there are exceptions for some existing individual and employer-sponsored plans, most plans that did not meet the new minimum standards will be eliminated. Approximately half of all individual plans available prior to 2014 did not meet the new standards.

The 80/20 rule requires that insurance companies spend at least 80% of their income from premiums on healthcare services or quality improvement rather than on administration, overhead, or marketing.

This increases to 85% for companies selling insurance to large groups, such as to employers with more than 50 employees. Large-group market plans that spend less than 85% of premiums on services and quality improvement, and individual and small group plans that spend less than 80%, must rebate the difference to consumers. Insurance companies must publicly justify premium rate increases of 10% or more.

Other provisions

The PPACA establishes four benefit tiers that apply to all new health insurance plans inside and outside of exchanges. All of the tiers include **essential health benefits** (EHB), as well as mental health and addiction services. They have out-of-pocket expense limits of $5,950 for individuals and $11,900 for families. These limits are lower for people with incomes up to 400% of the FPL. People with annual incomes up to 499% of the FPL—about $95,000 for a family of four—are eligible for federal subsidies to help pay the premiums. Catastrophic plans are available through the individual market only for people up to the age of 30 and those who are exempt from the health insurance mandate:

- Bronze plans are minimum coverage plans that pay 60% of the costs of benefits.
- Silver plans cover 70% of benefit costs.
- Gold plans cover 80% of benefit costs.
- Platinum plans cover 90% of benefit costs.

Among the benefit tiers, bronze plans have the lowest premiums but high deductibles and co-payments, and platinum plans have the highest premiums but the lowest out-of-pocket expenses.

The PPACA includes a number of provisions for improving health and health care in the nation as a whole and among specific at-risk populations. It emphasizes prevention, reducing rates of chronic disease, and addressing disparities in health and health care. It includes incentives for developing the professional healthcare workforce, especially primary care professionals and general surgeons in underserved communities and rural areas. It increases funding for community, school-based, and nurse-managed health clinics and for improvements to emergency departments and trauma facilities. The legislation provides grants to small employers for establishing wellness programs. A nonprofit Patient-Center Outcomes Research Institute will identify and conduct research comparing the clinical effectiveness of medical treatments. The PPACA even requires chain restaurants and food vending machines to disclose the nutritional content of each item it sells.

Risks

It remains too soon to know whether the PPACA will reach its goals of significantly expanding healthcare coverage while improving quality of care and reducing costs. Its funding comes from numerous changes to the federal tax code, annual fees imposed on insurance and pharmaceutical companies, new participants (especially young adults), and new programs to reduce waste, fraud, and abuse.

Medicaid eligibility for people under age 65 is now based solely on income, extending coverage to millions of lower-income people. It is hoped that Medicaid enrollment will be simplified and access to care will improve. However, just as pre-PPACA Medicaid implementation varied by state, it remains to be seen how well individual states will succeed in implementing Medicaid expansion and other provisions of the PPACA. Some experts believe that the ultimate success

of the PPACA will depend on the design and affordability of the essential health benefits package.

Resources

BOOKS

Feldman, Arthur M. *Understanding Health Care Reform: Bridging the Gap Between Myth and Reality.* Boca Raton, FL: CRC, 2012.

Gold, Susan Dudley. *Health Care Reform Act.* New York: Marshall Cavendish Benchmark, 2012.

Gruber, Jonathan, and H. P. Newquist. *Health Care Reform: What It Is, Why It's Necessary, How It Works.* New York: Hill and Wang, 2011.

Haugen, David M., and Susan Musser. *Health Care Legislation.* Detroit: Greenhaven, 2012.

Jacobs, Lawrence R., and Theda Skocpol. *Health Care Reform and American Politics: What Everyone Needs to Know.* New York: Oxford University, 2012.

Kirsch, Richard. *Fighting for Our Health: The Epic Battle to Make Health Care a Right in the United States.* Albany, NY: Rockefeller Institute, 2011.

Maxwell, Nan L. *The Health and Wealth of a Nation: Employer-Based Health Insurance and the Affordable Care Act.* Kalamazoo, MI: W. E. Upjohn Institute for Employment Research, 2012.

Miller, Debra A. *The Uninsured.* Detroit: Greenhaven, 2011.

Ulmer, Cheryl. *Essential Health Benefits: Balancing Coverage and Cost.* Washington, DC: National Academies, 2012.

PERIODICALS

Brandon, William P. "Medicaid Transformed: Why ACA Opponents Should Keep Expanded Medicaid." *Journal of Health Care for the Poor and Underserved* 23, no. 4 (November 2012): 1360–82.

Cartwright-Smith, Lara, and Sara Rosenbaum. "Controversy, Contraception, and Conscience: Insurance Coverage Standards Under the Patient Protection and Affordable Care Act." *Public Health Reports* 127, no. 5 (September/ October 2012): 541.

Decker, Sandra L. "In 2011 Nearly One-Third of Physicians Said They Would Not Accept New Medicaid Patients, but Rising Fees May Help." *Health Affairs* 31, no. 8 (August 2012): 1673–9.

Dolan, Elizabeth M., and Mitch Manouchehr Mokhtari. "The Patient Protection and Affordable Care Act (ACA): Pros and Cons." *Journal of Family and Economic Issues* 34, no. 1 (March 2013): 1–2.

Giaimo, Susan. "Behind the Scenes of the Patient Protection and Affordable Care Act: The Making of a Health Care Co-op." *Journal of Health Politics, Policy and Law* 38, no. 3 (June 2013): 500.

Graves, John A. "Medicaid Expansion Opt-Outs and Uncompensated Care." *New England Journal of Medicine* 367, no. 25 (December 20, 2012): 2365–7.

Pear, Robert, and Peter Baker. "Health Law is Defended with Vigor by President." *New York Times* (May 11, 2013): A11.

Tanner, Michael. "The Patient Protection and Affordable Care Act: A Dissenting Opinion." *Journal of Family and Economic Issues* 34, no. 1 (March 2013): 3–15.

WEBSITES

AARP. "Fact Sheet: The Health Care Law and You: Key Improved Health Insurance Practices." http://www.aarp.org/health/health-care-reform/info-06-2010/fact_sheet_health_law_improved_health_insurance_practices.html (accessed October 10, 2013).

Centers for Medicare & Medicaid Services. "Affordable Care Act." Medicaid.gov. http://www.medicaid.gov/AffordableCareAct/Affordable-Care-Act.html (accessed October 10, 2013).

Centers for Medicare & Medicaid Services. "Healthcare Marketplace." https://www.healthcare.gov.html (accessed October 10, 2013).

Centers for Medicare & Medicaid Services. "How Does the Health Care Law Protect Me?" https://www.healthcare.gov/how-does-the-health-care-law-protect-me (accessed October 10, 2013).

Henry J. Kaiser Family Foundation. "Focus on Health Reform: Summary of the Affordable Care Act." http://kaiserfamilyfoundation.files.wordpress.com/2011/04/8061-021.pdf (accessed October 10, 2013).

Luhby, Tami. "Most Individual Health Insurance Isn't Good Enough for Obamacare." CNNMoney. April 3, 2013. http://money.cnn.com/2013/04/03/news/economy/health-insurance-exchanges/index.html (accessed October 10, 2013).

Rural Assistance Center. "Medicaid Frequently Asked Questions."http://www.raconline.org/topics/medicaid/faqs (accessed October 10, 2013).

ORGANIZATIONS

Centers for Medicare & Medicaid Services, 7500 Security Blvd., Baltimore, MD 21244, (410) 786-3000, (877) 267-2323,TTY: (866) 226-1819, http://www.cms.gov.

Henry J. Kaiser Family Foundation, 2400 Sand Hill Rd., Menlo Park, CA 94025, (650) 854-9400, Fax: (650) 854-4800, http://www.kff.org.

Rural Assistance Center, 501 N. Columbia Rd., Stop 9037, Grand Forks, ND 58202-9037, (800) 270-1898, Fax: (800) 270-1913, info@raconline.org, http://www.raconline.org.

U.S. Department of Health and Human Services, 200 Independence Ave. SW, Washington, DC 20201, (877) 696-6775, http://www.hhs.gov.

Margaret Alic, PhD

Patient satisfaction surveys and scores

Definition

Patient satisfaction surveys are short questionnaires that health care providers offer to patients, asking them to rate the quality of care they received. These surveys produce scores that may be used to improve the quality of health care and to compare facilities.

Description

Patient satisfaction surveys are brief questionnaires completed by patients. They are used to rate or score the services of health care providers and health centers. These surveys are primarily used to help to improve the quality of care at individual facilities; however, since 2002, the federal government has been standardizing these surveys in the hopes of providing meaningful comparisons of hospitals, incentives for improving the quality of patient care, and opportunities to increase the accountability of heal care facilities. Patient satisfaction survey scores may be used to compare health centers within communities, across the country, or around the world. Surveys are available in many languages and are most typically offered in English and Spanish. Since 2008, the CAHPS Survey has provided data that have made it possible to compare patient experiences from hospitals located within local communities and states and nationwide.

Why this is important to the consumer

Grading Your Doctor

Patient surveys are particularly beneficial to patients because they provide a direct and immediate means for patients to impact the quality of care within their community. These surveys may range from five questions to 30 or more. Topics include such things as the amount of time spent waiting for a doctor, the cleanliness of the facility, the time spend with the provider, ease of payment, and effectiveness of treatment.

National Standards

Doctors' offices and hospitals collect this information for internal review and to assess and measure their patients' experience. In 2002, the **Hospital Consumer Assessment of Healthcare Providers and Systems (HCAHPS)** designed a standardized, national survey called the CAHPS Survey.

According to HCAHPS, they developed this form with three goals in mind:

- To produce data about patients' perspectives of care that allow objective and meaningful comparisons of hospitals on topics that are important to consumers
- To create new incentives for hospitals to improve quality of care
- To enhance accountability in health care by increasing transparency of the quality of hospital care provided in return for the public investment to enhance accountability in health care through public reporting

EASY TO COMPLETE. The CAHPS Survey is available at no cost to health care providers. The forms are in an electronic format that may be printed by providers to give to patients to complete, or, with the conversion to electronic medical record systems, these forms may be administered in a portable electronic format that allows for rapid analysis and an easy way to produce reports.

To make it easier for patients to complete satisfaction surveys, they are most often administered in the following ways:

- Paper surveys are available at check-out and include an envelope with return postage or a clearly labeled box for returned surveys.
- Staff members personally deliver the survey and provide a confidential way for patients to return survey forms.
- Patients with impaired vision or limited literacy are provided with a non-health care assistant to help them complete the survey.

IMPROVING THE QUALITY OF PATIENT CARE. Patient satisfaction surveys are an important tool to help health care providers discover how well they are achieving the main goals of patient care: providing quality health care, making sure that care is accessible to all, and ensuring that patients are treated with respect, compassion, and courtesy. Patient satisfaction surveys provide the health care consumer with an important tool to share their experiences and impact the quality of care provided in the future.

Resources

BOOKS

Studer, Quint, Brian Robinson, and Karen Cook. *The HCAHPS Handbook: Hardwire Your Hospital for Pay-For-Performance Success.* Gulf Breeze: Fire Starter Publishing, 2010.

WEBSITES

American Academy of Family Physicians. "American Academy of Family Physicians Patient Satisfaction Survey." http://www.aafp.org/fpm/1999/0100/fpm 19990100p40-rt1.pdf (accessed September 19, 2013).

Centers for Medicare and Medicaid Services. "HCAHPS: Patients' Perspectives of Care Survey." http://www. cms.gov/Medicare/Quality-Initiatives-Patient-Assess ment-Instruments/HospitalQualityInits/Hospital HCAHPS.html (accessed September 19, 2013).

"HCAHPS Fact Sheet (CAHPS Hospital Survey), August 2013." http://www.HCAHPSonline.org/files/August %202013%20HCAHPS%20Fact%20Sheet2.pdf (accessed September 20, 2013).

Deborah L. Nurmi, MS

Patients Beyond Borders

Definition

Patients Beyond Borders is the publisher of international **medical tourism** guidebooks that help individuals find lower-cost medical procedures in countries outside the United States.

Description

Patients Beyond Borders publishes books designed to help individuals seeking to avoid the high cost of medical care in the United States by traveling to countries where the cost of medical care is substantially lower. This practice is known as "medical tourism." As of 2013, Patients Beyond Borders estimates 2013 that medical tourism is a $40 million business with 7 million Americans traveling abroad for medical care each year. Most people who practice medical tourism do so because they are uninsured or they desire a procedure such as cosmetic surgery or dental work that is not covered by their insurance plan.

Josef Woodman is the CEO and founder of Patients Beyond Borders. Woodman is an entrepreneur who has founded several digital companies. He is not a physician. Patients Beyond Borders researches overseas hospitals and clinics and recommends those that meet various health and safety standards. Many of the recommended hospitals are accredited by **Joint Commission International** (JCI), an international branch of the **Joint Commission** that accredits American hospitals. To be accredited by the JCI, a hospital must meet the same standards set forth in the United States by the Joint Commission. Internationally trained physicians, stability of the country, and attractiveness of fees are also taken into consideration in making recommendations.

KEY TERMS

Medical tourism—The act of traveling to a foreign country specifically to obtain medical care at a lower cost than is available in one's home country.

As of 2013, Patients Beyond Borders has published eight country-specific guides as well as a general international guidebook. The leading medical tourist destinations are Brazil, Costa Rica, India, Korea, Malaysia, Mexico, Singapore, Taiwan, Thailand, and Turkey. Cost savings are considerable, often around 50% and for some procedures in some countries as high as 90%. These savings do not include the cost of airfare and accommodations before and after the procedure. The most common medical tourism procedures are cosmetic surgery, dental procedures, cardiovascular surgery, joint and spine surgery, cancer treatment, fertility treatment, and weight-loss surgery.

Why this is important to the consumer

Health care in the United States is some of the best in the world, but it can be extremely expensive. People without insurance or whose policies have high deductibles may be saddled with crushing debt from medical procedures. Others forgo needed care because of the cost. Medical tourism offers an alternative to the high cost of American health care.

When considering traveling abroad for health care, patients need to consider not only the cost of the procedure, but also the cost of transportation for themselves and often for a companion, accommodations during recovery, the riskiness of the procedure, their comfort level with a foreign culture, and the political stability of the country they plan to visit. Although many physicians are fluent in English, their support staff might not be. Patients also must consider the possibility that if something goes wrong, they will not have the same legal recourse available to them as they would in the United States.

Despite these considerations, medical tourism offers some patients a legitimate alternative for some procedures. For example, many people living near the Mexican border have found they save substantially by having low-risk dental work done in Mexico.

As of this writing, the 2010 **Patient Protection and Affordable Care Act** (Obamacare) has not been fully implemented. It remains to be seen whether medical tourism will maintain its popularity after all Americans are required to have health insurance or pay a penalty for refusing to be insured.

Resources

BOOKS

Marsek, Patrick and Frances Sharpe. *The Complete Idiot's Guide to Medical Tourism.* New York Alpha, 2009.

Woodman, Josef. *Patients Beyond Borders: Everybody's Guide to Affordable, World-Class Medical Travel,* 2nd ed. Chapel Hill, NC: Healthy Travel Media, 2008.

PERIODICALS

Alsharif, Mohd. J., Robert Lebonté and Zuxun Lu. "Patients Beyond Borders: A study of Medical Tourists in Four Countries." *Global Social Policy* 10, no. 3 (December 2010): 315-35.

Robertson. Jordan. "Top Destinations for Medical Tourism." Bloomberg News June 25, 2013. http://www.bloomberg.com/slideshow/2013-06-25/top-travel-destinations-for-medical-tourism.html (accessed July 21, 2013).

ORGANIZATIONS

International Partnership for Innovative Healthcare Delivery, 324 Blackwell Street, Suite 960, Washington Building, Durham, NC 27701, http://www.ipihd.org.

Patients Beyond Borders. P.O. Box 17057. Chapel Hill, NC 27516. (919) 924.0636. http://www.patientsbeyondborders. com.

Tish Davidson, AM

Patient's rights

Definition

In 2001, the Senate and House of Representatives of the United States Congress proposed separate legislation to ensure basic rights and to standardize basic protections for all patients covered by health insurance plans. Unfortunately, the bills could not be reconciled and never materialized as law. However, in 1990 the Association of American Physicians and Surgeons proposed and adopted a list of "patient freedoms" that, in 1995, became modified and known as "a patient's bill of rights." This is a list of guarantees that each patient is entitled to.

Description

All hospitals in the United States have adopted some form of a Patient Bill of Rights. This document, which may be slightly different in wording from institution to institution, contains similar safeguards for patients. The salient features include the right to:

- receive medical care without regard to race, religion, gender, age, or source of payment
- life-saving measures in an emergency without discrimination
- be treated respectfully and without bias
- be informed about one's condition
- know the identity of the people providing treatment
- seek and obtain all information necessary to understanding one's medical condition (may require the services of a translator)
- take part in all decisions regarding one's health care
- privacy in a treatment facility
- access one's medical records
- leave the hospital even if this is against the advice of physicians
- expect confidentiality regarding one's condition (release of information to others requires written consent)
- one's informed consent must be given before treatment can begin
- refuse care
- appoint someone else to make medical decisions on one's behalf
- give permission before participating in clinical research (refusal to participate will not affect the quality of treatment)
- know the cost of services provided

Medical Research and Patient Rights

Medical research is essential and is dependent on patient participation. However, the exploitation of patients for acquiring such information is forbidden. The National Commission for the Protection of Human Subjects in Biomedical and Behavioral Research was created in 1994, to establish guidelines for medical research. The Commission enlisted the American Medical Association to create a framework for the ethical conduct of medical research. This set of guidelines has generally been well accepted and adopted by medical researchers. It consists of:

1. the need to demonstrate the value of the research;
2. a sound methodology for the research;
3. safeguards against risks and expected benefits to the participants;
4. independent review of the proposal by knowledgeable persons unaffiliated with the persons conducting the research;
5. consent of the subjects who are fully informed about the nature of the research and the potential risks and benefits to them;

6. provision for the participant to withdraw from the study without penalty or compromise to future treatment.

Why this is important to the consumer

Patients are protected by law and they are empowered to protect themselves. Health care providers are urged to be vigilant and pro-active and are guided by policies which are designed to ensure patient well-being before, during, and after treatment.

Resources

WEBSITES

"Patient Rights." MedlinePlus. September 17, 2013. http://www.nlm.nih.gov/medlineplus/patientrights.html (accessed October 15, 2013).

"Patient Rights, Responsibilities, Hospitals, HIPAA, Medical Records." eMedicineHealth. http://www.emedicinehealth.com/patient_rights/article_em.htm (accessed October 15, 2013).

"Principles of Patients' Rights and Responsibilities." National Health Council. http://www.nationalhealth council.org/pages/page-content.php?pageid = 66 (accessed October 15, 2013).

Joel C. Kahane, PhD

Personal health record (PHR)

Definition

A personal health record (PHR) is an extensive collection of past and current health and medical information that is compiled by the individual, not by a health care professional, to help track, manage, and share health care information.

Description

HRs can be electronic or paper-based. They are not the same as **Electronic Health Records (EHRs)**. EHRs are complied by a physician and other health care professionals. EHRs contain information used in the treatment of a patient and are the property of the health care provider, although in the United States, patients have the legal right to obtain a copy of their EHR. Similar laws apply in the United Kingdom. PHRs are compiled by the patient, and the patient controls their content and distribution.

PHRs generally contain information about treatment from many different providers and cover a long period. They may also contain information about the individual's diet, exercise, and extended family health history that may have bearing on the individual's own health. The following list suggests information useful to include in a PHR.

- name, address, date of birth
- health insurance information
- names and telephone numbers of the individual's doctors
- blood type
- allergies, especially drug allergies and adverse reactions to drugs
- current medications, including prescription drugs, over-the-counter drugs, herbal medicines, and other supplements; dosage of each item and length of time it has been taken.
- family health history (e.g., hereditary diseases)
- date of last physical
- dates and results of medical tests and screenings
- chronic illnesses
- past major illnesses with dates
- past surgeries with dates
- vaccinations with dates
- physical limitations (e.g., hard of hearing, vision impaired)
- dietary limitations (e.g., vegetarian)
- name and contact information for the person(s) to be notified in case of emergency
- information about the presence of a health care directive or power of attorney and its location
- exercise habits, dietary habits (e.g., alcohol use), personal habits (e.g., tobacco use)

PHRs can be created on paper or electronically. One advantage of an electronic PHR is that it can be transmitted anywhere in the world almost instantly. Multiple companies offer software, fee-based software, to help create and maintain a PHR. Some systems will import data from the health care providers' EHR so that the PHR can easily be kept current. Electronic PHRs can be stored in the cloud, on CD-ROMs, or on a UBS flash drive.

Why this is important to the consumer

PHRs benefit consumers in several ways.

- Health information is gathered in one place, rather than being stored in individual physicians' offices. Easy access to this composite information can be lifesaving.
- The need for duplicate tests by different doctors is reduced or eliminated, saving time and money. One study projected that widespread use of PHRs could

---

> **KEY TERMS**
>
> **Electronic Health Record—**A digital record of treatment created and owned by the health care provider and subject to legal privacy restrictions but accessible upon request to the patient.

save the health care system between $13 billion and $21 billion annually.

- Test results can be viewed over a long period, making it easier for clinicians to spot changes and trends.
- Patients can more easily track when they are due for routine tests and physicals.
- With their health information easily available, patients can ask better questions of their doctors and be a better partner in managing their health care.

Disadvantages of PHRs

PHRs come with some disadvantages. Both paper and electronic PHRs are only as good as the data they contain. Failure to update changes in medications or health status can give a false picture of the individual's medical situation. Paper PHRs can be damaged or destroyed and might not be easily accessible (e.g., if the individual is traveling).

Electronic PHRs that import information from the health care providers' EHRs simplify the chore of updating but require strong encryption to protect the information being transmitted. Any poorly protected electronic document is at risk of being hacked, and the information compromised.

In the United States, neither paper nor electronic PHRs are protected by the privacy regulations of the **Health Insurance Portability and Accountability Act (HIPAA)** that protect health care providers' EHRs.

Resources

BOOKS

Hamilton, Byron. *Electronic Health Records,* 3rd ed. New York: McGraw-Hill, 2013.

Miller, Holly D., William Yasnoff and Howard Burde. *Personal Health Records: The Essential Missing Element in 21st Century Healthcare.* Chicago, IL: HIMSS, 2009.

PERIODICALS

"EHR/PHR Basics." *NIH MedlinePlus.* 4, no.3 (2009):17. http://www.nlm.nih.gov/medlineplus/magazine/issues/summer09/articles/summer09pg17.html (accessed July 20, 2013).

WEBSITES

American Health Management Information Association. "What Is a Personal Health Record (PHR)?" http://www.myphr.com/StartaPHR/what_is_a_phr.aspx (accessed July 20, 2013).

Office of Civil Rights. "Your Health Information Privacy Rights." http://www.hhs.gov/ocr/privacy/hipaa/understanding/consumers/consumer_rights.pdf (accessed July 20, 2013).

"Personal Health Records (PHRs)." Medicare.gov http://www.medicare.gov/manage-your-health/personal-health-records/personal-health-records.html (accessed July 20, 2013).

"Personal Health Records." MedlinePlus July 17, 2013 http://www.nlm.nih.gov/medlineplus/personalhealthrecords.html (accessed July 20, 2013).

ORGANIZATIONS

American Health Information Management Association (AHIMA), 233 N. Michigan Avenue, 21st Floor, Chicago, IL 60601-5809, (312) 233-1100, (800) 335-5535, Fax: (312) 233-1500, myphrinfo@ahima.org, http://www.ahima.org.

Tish Davidson, AM

Personal trainer

Definition

A personal trainer works with someone who has a specific fitness goal, serving in the role of a guide and mentor: educating, encouraging, supporting, and skill-building.

Description

Personal training is a relatively new field. It uses some of the same motivational techniques that are used in successful team coaching, but applies them to one-on-one work with individual clients. The personal trainer serves as an educator, gym teacher, coach, motivator, advocate, drill sergeant, and mentor.

Some personal trainers specialize in specific areas of training, working with children, disabled individuals, or the elderly, for example. Others teach fitness classes to groups.

A number of agencies have created training and certification programs in an effort to standardize the educational background and knowledge level of personal trainers. (© Peter Bernik/Shutterstock.com)

Although the main goals in personal training involve improving physical fitness through exercise, nutrition is obviously integral to these goals. Therefore, many personal trainers also do some nutritional assessment with their clients. Furthermore, smoking cessation may be part of a complete program, as smoking will significantly cut down on an individual's exercise capacity.

Education, certification and skills

There are no educational requirements for becoming a personal trainer. A number of agencies have created training and certification programs in an effort to standardize the educational background and knowledge level of personal trainers.

A personal trainer needs to be in good physical condition, as the job will require a lot of exercise. Additionally, it is difficult to convince clients that they should become more fit if the personal trainer is not fit himself or herself. Personal trainers should possess a good fundamental understanding of human anatomy and exercise physiology, as well as basic knowledge of injuries that can affect the musculoskeletal system. Most fitness centers require that personal trainers have Basic Life Support (BLS or cardiopulmonary resuscitation) training. An understanding of the psychology of behavior change is very useful in this field, and excellent communication skills are critical. Business classes are particularly useful for those personal trainers who intend to open their own business.

Places of employment

Personal trainers may be employed at fitness centers or integrative health practices, or they may start their own business, in which case they may meet at their clients' homes or at a gym or other fitness facility. Many personal trainers work one-on-one with clients, although some personal trainers do some group work and may teach fitness classes or yoga.

Tasks of a personal trainers

Personal trainers begin by determining the client's personal goals, relative to fitness, and then by assessing their client's baseline level of fitness. This may include weighing, caliper measurements of areas of the body, and a variety of methods of determining body fat composition. Fitness testing may include walking, running, squats, weight work, or other ways of quantifying muscle strength, endurance, and balance. Once all of this information is obtained, the personal trainer and the client create a set of fitness

---

KEY TERMS

Fitness—Being physically healthy and capable of carrying out appropriate physical activities with a minimum of fatigue.

Motivational interviewing—Client-centered technique of helping bring about behavioral change by understanding psychological or dynamic impediments, thus helping the client overcome such obstacles.

Nutrition—Providing substances that are necessary for health and growth.

Obese—Weighing considerably too much for a given height. In terms of body mass index, or BMI, obesity is defined as a BMI greater than or equal to 30.

Overweight—Weighing more than is recommended for a given height. In terms of body mass index, or BMI, obesity is defined as a BMI between 25 and 29.9.

---

goals. Most studies suggest that this is most successful if it is done in a collaborative fashion.

Personal trainers must build trust and rapport with their clients; an important part of the process involves helping clients understand what kinds of obstacles may have prevented them from reaching their fitness goals in the past, and then helping them create a plan to master their goal and be successful. The larger goal is usually broken down into much smaller, attainable increments.

At the outset of the program, the personal trainer will demonstrate how to execute the exercises that the client will be undertaking using safe, correct form. The personal trainer and the client decide upon the optimal amount of contact that they will have, as the client works toward his or her fitness goals. Some clients want to meet with the personal trainer for every workout session, and use the relationship to ensure a sense of accountability, to help push and motivate them, to secure regular feedback, and to receive immediate positive reinforcement. Other clients prefer more sporadic contact, and return to the personal trainer on some scheduled basis to be reweighed, remeasured, and retested, thus verifying that they are meeting their fitness goals.

Why this is important to the consumer

Modern day epidemics (e.g., obesity, high blood pressure, high cholesterol, diabetes) are taking a toll on our national health. As of 2010, 35.7% of Americans were clinically obese, meaning that compared to their height, their weight was very far outside of a healthy range. Obesity is considered to be responsible for a number of otherwise preventable medical illnesses, including Type II diabetes, stroke, heart disease, and cancer. Additionally, fewer than 5% of American adults get the recommended 30 minutes of physical activity daily, and only 33% of adults meet the national recommendations for weekly physical activity. Personal trainers can intervene in a useful way, by educating, motivating, and supporting behavioral change that can improve fitness, thereby impacting on overall health.

Resources

BOOKS

EZ Occupational Outlook Handbook, 2nd ed. St. Paul, MN: JIST Publishing, 2011.

U.S. Department of Labor. *Occupational Outlook Handbook*. St. Paul, MN: JIST Publishing, 2013.

Wischnitzer, Saul. *Top 100 Health-Care Careers*. St. Paul, MN: JIST Publishing, 2011.

ORGANIZATIONS

Aerobic and Fitness Association of America, 15250 Ventura Blvd., Suite 200, Sherman Oaks, CA 91403, (877) 968-7263, http://www.afaa.com/.

American Academy of Exercise, 4851 Paramount Drive, San Diego, CA 92123, (888) 825-3636, http://www.acefitness.org/.

ExploreHealthCareers.org, American Dental Education Association, 1400 K Street, NW, Suite 1100, Washington, DC 20005, (202) 289-7201, cmsa@cmsa.org, http://explorehealthcareers.org/en/home/.

National Academy of Sports Medicine, 1750 E. Northrop Blvd., Suite 200, Chandler, AZ 85286, (602) 383-1200, http://www.nasm.org/.

National Federation of Professional Trainers, P.O. Box 4579, Lafayette, IN 47903, (800) 729-6378, http://www.afaa.com/.

U.S. Bureau of Labor Statistics, Postal Square Building, 2 Massachusetts Ave., NE, Washington, DC 20212, (202) 691-5200, http://www.bls.gov.

U.S. Department of Labor, Frances Perkins Building, 200 Constitution Ave., NW, Washington, DC 20210, (866) 487-2365, http://www.dol.gov/.

Rosalyn Carson-DeWitt, MD

▌ Pharmaceutical advertising, impact on consumers

Definition

Pharmaceutical advertising and its impact on consumers is a controversial issue. It involves the practice of advertising new drugs directly to the consumer through television, magazines, websites, and other media. The issue is the degree to which advertising as the basis for consumer decision-making in health care challenges and obstructs doctors' professional assessments of their patients' needs.

Description

The advertising of prescription drugs is not a new practice; however, in recent years the practice has increased in amount of advertisements and in the number of media outlets that run them. In 1939, the law that established the responsibilities of the **Food and Drug Administration** (FDA) anticipated advertising of prescription drugs by making the FDA overseer of the basic regulations for this advertisement. Until late in the twentieth century, most new drug advertising was directed to pharmacists and physicians. Today, it is far more often directed toward the consumer. This direct-to-consumer advertising has three forms. The first type of advertisement explains the disease as if it were newly discovered and does not mention the drug being promoted. The second type names the drug but is directed to those who already have a prescription for it; this type does not explain what the drug is for and makes no claims. The third type of direct-to-consumer advertising actually describes what the drug is for and makes claims about its effectiveness.

When a new disease is described in these advertisements, the symptoms are detailed. The goal is to have people think about whether they have these symptoms and, if so, if maybe they have the disease. It is expected that such people will bring the topic up with their doctor, who would then prescribe the leading drug for treating this disease. Such an advertisement is most likely sponsored by the pharmaceutical company producing the leading prescription drug. Although the goal of the advertisement is ultimately to sell more prescription drugs, this commercial needs no disclaimer because drugs are not mentioned by name. Furthermore, no claim about the effectiveness of the drug is presented.

When the commercial is directed to patients already using the prescription drug, the goal is to build "product loyalty" among these patients. This product loyalty is expected to prevent patients from accepting a generic version. Reminding the patient about the name of the drug should lead the patient to discuss the drug by name with his or her doctor when the time comes to change or renew the prescription. A secondary goal of this type of commercial is to introduce the name of the drug to potential consumers who may become familiar with it through friends or their physician.

For the first two types of drug advertisements to be effective, patients need to discuss with their physician the possibility of a prescription. Because the discussion must take place, the physician is very much in charge of deciding whether the patient gets a prescription or not. However, the direct-to-consumer advertising that includes a description of the indications and claims of effectiveness is designed to encourage the patient to put pressure on the physician for a prescription. Therefore, the commercials related to this type of advertisement are regulated by the FDA. This type of advertising needs to have a disclaimer identifying the major side effects, any counter indications, and any concerns for effectiveness.

Those who favor direct-to-consumer pharmaceutical advertising suggest that there is much good that can come from this type of advertising. In every commercial, there is the message that potential consumers should discuss the possibility of a prescription with their physician. These advocates argue that such guidelines encourage patient-to-doctor discussions and patient empowerment. This is in line with the generally accepted premise that when there is a dialogue with the doctor and the patient is taking responsibility for understanding his or her condition, healthcare is more effective. These advocates also suggest that direct-to-consumer advertising can lead to higher rates of diagnosis and treatment of hard-to-recognize conditions. By constantly discussing specific medical conditions and how people with those conditions can lead normal lives, these advertisements can remove the stigma associated with certain diseases. Another important argument in favor of direct-to-consumer advertising is that the goal of any advertising is to drive demand. With greater demand, the cost of a product is diffused over many consumers; therefore, the product (in this case prescription drugs) can be offered at a lower cost.

The arguments against direct-to-consumer pharmaceutical advertising tend to emphasize that consumers—non-experts usually—can be misled by advertisements. Understanding how and why drugs are prescribed, administered, and monitored cannot be adequately explained in television commercials and magazine ads, for example. The physician has years of education and training and a better understanding of the patient's history, physical condition, and predisposition for disease, and is therefore in a much better position than the patient to recommend treatment options. Another argument against direct-to-consumer advertising is that it tends to misrepresent the seriousness of the condition and the effectiveness of the drug.

Why this is important to the consumer

The goal of direct-to-consumer pharmaceutical advertising is to develop new business. Advertising seeks to increase product demand. There is nothing wrong with this when the need and usefulness of the product can be easily determined. However, direct-to-consumer pharmaceutical advertising promotes a product whose need and usefulness in any given situation can only be evaluated by a professional, an expert such as a physician. On the other hand, if such advertising truly does lead to more dialogue between patient and physician, a positive effect can be the recognition of a condition more clearly and quickly than might otherwise occur. The consumer needs to understand these points when evaluating pharmaceutical advertisements.

Some critics are calling for a ban on advertising that identifies pharmaceutical products by name. These critics argue that such a ban would encourage patient-physician dialogue and would add weight to the physician's professional opinion about a brand name drug, an alternative brand, or a generic drug. Critics also recommend making the disclaimers in all drug advertising complete and more clearly worded. This would require advertisers to present actual data about the risks and effectiveness of their drugs. Implicit in this recommendation is need for effective communication with non-expert consumers. As with all advertising, consumers must use critical thinking. Advertisements always contain arguments that favor the sponsor's point of view.

Resources

BOOKS

Cook, A. G. *Forecasting for the Pharmaceutical Industry: Models for New Product and In-market Forecasting and How to Use Them.* Aldershot, England: Gower, 2006.

Grenada, I. M. and D. A. Mancuso. *Pharmaceutical Industry: Innovation and Developments.* Hauppauge, NY: Nova Science, 2011.

PERIODICALS

Calvert, Sandra L. "Children as consumers: advertising and marketing." *The Future of Children* (Spring 2008): 205.

Cole, Jane. "Marketing contact lenses to the public: boon or bane? Doctors weigh in on the pros and cons of direct-to-consumer advertising for contact lens products, and how it affects their relationships with patients." *Review of Optometry* 15 (April 2013): 56.

Godwin, Dana Moffett, Mathew Joseph, and Deborah F. Spake. "Aging consumers and drug marketing: senior citizens' views on DTC advertising, the medicare prescription drug programme and pharmaceutical retailing." *Journal of Medical Marketing* 8 no. 3 (2008): 221.

Greene, J. A. and A. S. Kesselheim. "Pharmaceutical marketing and the new social media." *New England Journal of Medicine* 363 (2010): 2087–2089.

Mackey, Tim K., and Bryan A. Liang. "Globalization, evolution and emergence of direct-to-consumer advertising: are emerging markets the next pharmaceutical marketing frontier?" *Journal of Commercial Biotechnology* 18 no. 4 (2012): 58.

Ventola, C. L. "Direct-to-Consumer Pharmaceutical Advertising: Therapeutic or Toxic?" *P&T: Journal for Formulary Management* 36 (2011): 669.

WEBSITES

U.S. Food and Drug Administration. "Prescription Drug Advertising—Basics of Drug Ads." September 13, 2012. http://www.fda.gov/Drugs/ResourcesForYou/Consumers/PrescriptionDrugAdvertising/ucm02077.htm (accessed October 4, 2013).

U.S. Government Accountability Office. "Prescription Drugs: Improvements Needed in FDA's Oversight of Direct-to-Consumer Advertising." November 2006. http://www.gao.gov/new.items/d0754.pdf (accessed October 4, 2013).

ORGANIZATIONS

Pharmaceutical Research and Manufacturers of America, 950 F Street NW, Suite 300, Washington, DC 20004, (202) 835-3400, Fax: (202) 835-3414, newsroom@phrma.org, www.PhRMA.org.

Public Citizen's Commercial Alert, 1600 20th Street NW, Washington, DC 20009, (202) 588-7751, http://www.commercialalert.org.

U.S. Food and Drug Administration, 10903 New Hampshire Avenue, Silver Spring, MD 20993, (888) INFO-FDA (888-463-6332), http://www.fda.gov.

Ray F. Brogan, Ph.D.

Pharmacist

Definition

A pharmacist fills medication prescriptions and advises patients on their safe use.

Description

Pharmacists have a vast knowledge of medications, including their chemical composition, actions, duration of action, medical indications, methods of administration, dosages, side effects, interactions with other drugs, and contra-indications to use. Compounding pharmacist may use a variety of ingredients to put together individualized formulas for specific patients. This may be useful for pediatric patients who need a smaller dose than that which is manufactured, for allergic patients who cannot take a mass-produced formulation that contains a particular flavoring or dye, for patients who need multiple medications but have difficulty taking them individually, or for patients who require medications that have been discontinued.

Education, licensing, and skills

Pharmacists must complete two to three years of college (or earn an entire Bachelor's degree) before entering into the actual pharmacy program. These years will see the student taking a variety of prerequisite courses, such as chemistry, mathematics, biology, and physiology. Most pharmacy programs also require that candidates for admission take the Pharmacy College Admissions Test (PCAT). While pharmacists used to be able to practice with a Bachelor's or Master's degree in pharmacy, educational standards were changed in the early 2000s, and the entry-level pharmacist must now possess a doctorate of

Pharmacists used to be able to practice with a Bachelor's or Master's degree in pharmacy, but educational standards were changed in the early 2000s and the entry-level pharmacist must now possess a doctorate of pharmacy, also known as a PharmD. *(Reza Estakhrian/Getty Images)*

pharmacy, also known as a PharmD. Once in pharmacy school, the program will include extensive coursework in the chemistry of pharmaceuticals, biochemistry, physiology, pharmacology, medical ethics, and legal issues in pharmacy. Programs also include extensive internships in various sites, such as hospitals, commercial pharmacies, or laboratories.

In order to be licensed in a given state, a pharmacist needs to take two different examinations. The first will verify his or her knowledge base in the areas of pharmacology and ethics. The second will be specific to the state in which the individual wishes to practice, and will test his or her understanding of laws governing the dispensing and use of pharmaceuticals in that state.

Pharmacists need an excellent fundamental background in chemistry and biology, as well as the ability to read and critically analyze ongoing research in the field. Since pharmacists work closely with patients, they should possess excellent communication skills, an understanding of human psychology, and the

ability to translate more complex science into concepts easily understood by laypeople. Pharmacists who will be involved in education need to have public speaking skills. Pharmacists who are involved in running pharmacies may need to take special courses in business, human resources, and personnel management. Pharmacists who work in research will need specific laboratory skills pertinent to the type of investigations they will be conducting, as well as a good understanding of research design and methods. Some pharmacists go on to complete fellowships or residencies that prepare them further for clinical or research work.

Places of employment

Pharmacists may work in commercial/retail pharmacies, healthcare facilities such as hospitals or nursing homes, private offices or clinics, schools or colleges, research laboratories, private companies, or governmental departments (such as the **Food and Drug Administration**, or the Drug Enforcement Administration).

Ways your pharmacist can help

- Many pharmacists keep track of medicines on their computer. If you buy your medicines at one store and tell your pharmacist all the over-the-counter and prescription medicines or dietary supplements you take, your pharmacist can help make sure your medicines don't interact harmfully with one another.

- Ask your pharmacist to place your prescription medicines in easy-to-open containers if you have a hard time taking off child-proof caps and do not have young children living in or visiting your home. (Remember to keep all medicines out of the sight and reach of children.)

- Your pharmacist may be able to print labels on prescription medicine containers in larger type, if reading the medicine label is hard for you.

- Your pharmacist may be able to give you written information to help you learn more about your medicines. This information may be available in large type or in a language other than English. Your pharmacist can help keep track of your medicines.

SOURCE: Center for Drug Evaluation and Research, Food and Drug Administration, U.S. Department of Health and Human Services

(Illustration by GGS Information Services. Cengage Learning, Gale)

Tasks of a pharmacist

The specific tasks of a pharamacist vary, depending on the practice setting. For example:

- Clinical pharmacists may work in hospitals, nursing homes, clinics, or other patient-care venues. They consult with the health care providers and may do rounds with the entire medical team, supplying the team with their knowledge of medications, dosages, administration methods, and drug interactions, and helping determine the best choice of drug for a given clinical indication and patient.

- Retail pharmacists dispense medications from free-standing pharmacies or pharmacies within clinics or grocery stores, for example. They are responsible for educating their clientele about the medications they are dispensing, verifying that there are no allergies or sensitivities to the prescribed medications, checking on interactions with other medications the individual may be taking, and advising consumers about monitoring for side effects, administration details, and what to do if there is no response to the drug.

- Managed care pharmacists may work for a managed care company, filling prescriptions, determining an appropriate formulary, and reviewing records to verify that medication choices are both clinically appropriate and financially responsible.

- Research pharmacists may be academicians, teaching classes and undertaking research on a university campus, or they may work for a research facility, government agency, or pharmaceutical company.

KEY TERMS

Drug administration—The various ways that a medication may enter the body. Among other avenues, it can include orally, rectally, intravenously, and intradermally (through the skin).

Drug interactions—Side effects that come about when more than one drug is administered at the same time; this can cause one or more medication to be more potent or less potent, or it can cause side effects that are unique to the co-administration of these substances.

Pharmaceutical—A chemical product manufactured for use as a medication.

Pharmacology—The science of drugs, their uses, their effects on the body, and the body's effects on their metabolism.

Side effect—An unwanted effect of a drug, separate from its intended effect.

Toxicology—The study of toxic (or poisonous) effects of a chemical.

- Sales representatives are pharmacists who work for a drug company in marketing. They may work from the company's main office, writing provider or consumer information pamphlets and helping design marketing campaigns, or they may go out into the community and meet with potential prescribers of their company's products to educate them and to try to improve product sales.

Why they are important to the consumer

Pharmacists play an important role in healthcare. Well over 60% of American adults take at least one medication daily, and 25% of our elderly take at least five drugs each day. America is aging rapidly—in 2009, 39.6 million people were aged 65 or older, which was 12.9% of the entire population. Projections are that 2030 will see 72.1 million people aged 65 or older, fully 19% of the population at that time. As our country's population ages, this will mean more prescriptions, and more need for pharmacists.

As of 2011, 4.02 billion prescription were written in the United States on a yearly basis; this comes out to almost thirteen prescriptions per American citizen. Meanwhile, there are about 300,000 types of over-the-counter medications (drugs that can be purchased without a prescription) available. Pharmacists play critical roles in education and safety of both prescribers and consumers of medications.

Resources

BOOKS

EZ Occupational Outlook Handbook, 2nd ed. St. Paul, MN: JIST Publishing, 2011.

U.S. Department of Labor. *Occupational Outlook Handbook*. St. Paul, MN: JIST Publishing, 2013.

Wischnitzer, Saul. *Top 100 Health-Care Careers*. St. Paul, MN: JIST Publishing, 2011.

ORGANIZATIONS

American Pharmacists Association, 2215 Constitution Avenue NW, Washington, DC 20037, (202) 628-4410, http://www.pharmacist.com/.

ExploreHealthCareers.org, American Dental Education Association, 1400 K Street, NW, Suite 1100, Washington, DC 20005, (202) 289-7201, cmsa@cmsa.org, http://explorehealthcareers.org/en/home/.

National Association of Boards of Pharmacy, 1600 Feehanville Dr, Mount Prospect, IL 60056, (847) 391-4406, http://www.nabp.net/boards-of-pharmacy/.

U.S. Bureau of Labor Statistics, Postal Square Building, 2 Massachusetts Ave., NE, Washington, DC 20212, (202) 691-5200, http://www.bls.gov.

U.S. Department of Labor, Frances Perkins Building, 200 Constitution Ave., NW, Washington, DC 20210, (866) 487-2365, http://www.dol.gov/.

Rosalyn Carson-DeWitt, MD

Pharmacologist

Definition

A pharmacologist is a scientist who studies drugs and their effects on organisms (including humans).

Description

Pharmacologists have a vast knowledge of drugs, including their chemical composition, actions, duration of action, medical indications, methods of administration, dosages, side effects, interactions with other drugs, contra-indications to use, pharmacokinetics (how drugs move within an organism; what the organism does to the drug), and pharmacodynamics (how drugs affect an organism, their mechanism of action). Pharmacologists are often involved in research on drugs, ranging from laboratory research at the molecular level, to clinical research involving the testing of a drug in human subjects. Pharmacologists are also involved in drug development and the complex steps that are necessary to receive regulatory approval by the **Food and Drug Administration**, which is necessary for marketing and widespread clinical use.

Education, licensing, and skills

Pharmacologists can enter the field through a number of educational avenues. The first step is a Bachelor's degree, which can be obtained in any number of fields of science, such as biology, physiology, chemistry, or biochemistry. (Some universities even offer a Bachelor's degree in pharmacology.) These initial college years will see the student taking a variety of prerequisite courses, such as chemistry, biochemistry, physics, mathematics, statistics, biology, and physiology, for example. After this, students continue on into a doctoral (PhD) program in pharmacology. Some pharmacologists train first as pharmacists, while others pursue the lengthy, rigorous training of an MD/PhD, which is especially useful for individuals who wish to do research involving human subjects. (Only licensed physicians can administer drugs to people.)

Pharmacologists need an excellent fundamental background in chemistry and biology, the ability to read and critically analyze ongoing research in the field, and expertise in the area of statistical analysis. Since some clinical pharmacologists work closely with patients or research subjects, they should possess excellent communication skills, an understanding of human psychology, and the ability to translate more complex science into concepts easily understood by laypeople. Because pharmacologists may be writing papers for submission to journals, their writing skills must also be strong. Pharmacologists who will be involved in education need to have public speaking skills. Pharmacologists who work in research will need specific laboratory skills pertinent to the type of investigations they will be conducting, as well as a good understanding of research design and methods, and statistical analysis. Some pharmacologists go on to complete fellowships or residencies which prepare them further for clinical or research work, or allow them to subspecialize in specific areas, such as psychopharmacology (the study of pharmacology as it pertains to psychiatry) or neuropharmacology (the study of pharmacology as it pertains to neurology), among other specialty fields.

Places of employment

Pharmacologists may work in academic research settings, clinical research settings (such as hospitals

Some pharmacologists train first as pharmacists, while others pursue the lengthy, rigorous training of an MD/PhD, which is especially useful for individuals who wish to do research involving human subjects. *(Bloomberg/Getty Images)*

or nursing homes), or research laboratories, or for private drug companies or governmental agencies (such as the Food and Drug Administration or the Drug Enforcement Administration).

Tasks of a pharmacologist

The specific tasks of a pharmacologist include:

- Bench research in a laboratory delineating the characteristics of a specific chemical substance

- Research to illustrate the way an organism metabolizes a specific substance, and how that substance affects the organism

- Designing clinical trials

- Evaluation of clinical trials

- Statistical analysis of clinical trials

- Writing clinical guidelines for the use of various medications

- Inquiry into, and tracking of, local and national drug utilization

- Determining rational prescribing guidelines, including appropriate dosage for different clinical circumstances, most efficacious route of administration, frequency of dosing, monitoring drug effects and adverse effects, and discontinuing drugs

Why they are important to the consumer

Pharmacologists play an important role in drug discovery, and in fine-tuning the formulations of currently known medications. Well over 60% of American adults take at least one medication daily, and 25% of our elderly take at least five drugs each day. American society is aging rapidly—in 2009, 39.6 million people were aged 65 or older, which was 12.9% of the entire population. Projections are that 2030 will see 72.1 million people aged 65 or older, fully 19% of the population at that time. There is always call for new medications to better target disease, while avoiding unnecessary side effects and drug interactions.

KEY TERMS

Drug administration—The various ways that a medication may enter the body. Among other avenues, this can include orally, rectally, intravenously, or intradermally (through the skin).

Drug interactions—Side effects that come about when more than one drug is administered at the same time; this can cause one or more medication to be more potent or less potent, or it can cause side effects that are unique to the co-administration of these substances.

Pharmaceuticals—A chemical product manufactured for use as a medication.

Pharmacodynamics—The science of how drugs enter and travel through the body; the ways in which the drug affects the organism.

Pharmacokinetics—The science of how a drug behaves in an organism, including its absorption, distribution, concentration in tissues, and metabolism by the organism.

Side effects—An unwanted effect of a drug, separate from its intended effect.

Toxicology—The study of toxic (or poisonous) effects of a chemical.

Resources

BOOKS

EZ Occupational Outlook Handbook, 2nd ed. St. Paul, MN: JIST Publishing, 2011.

U.S. Department of Labor. *Occupational Outlook Handbook.* St. Paul, MN: JIST Publishing, 2013.

Wischnitzer, Saul. *Top 100 Health-Care Careers.* St. Paul, MN: JIST Publishing, 2011.

ORGANIZATIONS

American College of Clinical Pharmacology, 416 Hungerford Dr., Suite 300, Rockville, MD 20850, (240) 399-9070, http://www.accp1.org/index.shtml.

American Society for Clinical Pharmacology and Therapeutics, 528 N. Washington St, Alexandria, VA 22314, (703) 836-6981, info@ascpt.org, http://www.ascpt.org/.

ExploreHealthCareers.org, American Dental Education Association, 1400 K Street, NW, Suite 1100, Washington, DC 20005, (202) 289-7201, cmsa@cmsa.org, http://explorehealthcareers.org/en/home/.

U.S. Bureau of Labor Statistics, Postal Square Building, 2 Massachusetts Ave., NE, Washington, DC 20212, (202) 691-5200, http://www.bls.gov.

U.S. Department of Labor, Frances Perkins Building, 200 Constitution Ave., NW, Washington, DC 20210, (866) 487-2365, http://www.dol.gov/.

Rosalyn Carson-DeWitt, MD

Pharmacology

Definition

Pharmacology is the branch of medicine that deals with the study of drug actions in living organisms. The English word is derived from two Greek words that mean "drug" and "study of."

Description

Pharmacology is the science of understanding how drugs act on the body and conversely, how the body acts on drugs. Pharmacology is not to be confused with pharmacy, which deals with the preparation and dispensing of drugs. Drugs can be defined as chemical compounds with a specific therapeutic function, such as fever reduction or pain relief. Pharmacology focuses on how a drug enters the body, where the drug acts within the body, and how the body clears (gets rid of) a drug. A **pharmacologist** will also study the therapeutic potential of a drug, the interaction of a drug with other drugs, and analyze adverse drug reactions known as toxicities. There are several subdivisions and subdisciplines of pharmacology that apply the basic principles of pharmacology in different ways.

Pharmacology can be divided into subdivisions based on the body organ being studied. These include, but are not limited to, neuropharmacology, cardiovascular pharmacology, endocrine pharmacology, and chemotherapy:

- Neuropharmacology deals with the effect of drugs on the nervous system, which includes the brain, spinal cord, and nerves. Neuropharmacology includes the study of drugs of abuse such as heroin and also drugs used to treat nervous system disorders such as L-dopa, which is given to Parkinson's disease patients.

- Cardiovascular pharmacology focuses on drugs that modify the heart and vascular system. Blood pressure medications would be studied under this category.

- Endocrine pharmacology focuses on the interaction of drugs with various hormones or hormonal systems. Birth control pills would fall under the division of endocrine pharmacology.

Many Pharmacologists work in a laboratory research setting conducting experiments with various drugs at the biochemical level. *(Jeff Sherman/Getty Images)*

• Chemotherapy studies the pharmacology of drugs used to treat cancer such as tamoxifen, used to treat breast cancer.

In addition to dividing the field of pharmacology on the basis of the targeted organ system, pharmacology can also be divided into subdisciplines. These subdisciplines include but are not limited to molecular pharmacology, behavioral pharmacology, and clinical pharmacology:

• Molecular pharmacology studies the interaction of drugs at the cellular level. This includes studies on the interaction of drugs with protein receptors expressed on the surface of the cell. For example, the asthma drug albuterol interacts with beta receptors in the lungs to increase airflow.

• The effect of drugs on behavior is the basis for the behavioral pharmacology discipline. Behavioral pharmacology includes addiction research, which tries to understand why people become addicted to drugs like alcohol.

• The field of clinical pharmacology focuses more on the therapeutic use of drugs, the interactions of drugs

with one another in the body, and the nature of adverse drug reactions.

Other subdisciplines include:

• Pharmacognosy: the study of drugs derived from plants and other natural sources. Although most researchers in this field investigate botanicals, others study drugs derived from marine organisms and microbes.

• Pharmacogenomics: the application of genomic technologies to the discovery of new drugs and better understanding of older drugs.

• Psychopharmacology: the study of the effects of drugs on the brain and central nervous system, including their effects on mood, cognition, sensation, and behavior.

• Pharmacoepidemiology: the study of the effects of medications in large populations.

• Toxicology: the study of the harmful or poisonous effects of drugs.

• Veterinary pharmacology: the study of how drugs work in animals, safe dosages, the discovery of new drugs, etc. It is more complicated than human pharmacology because researchers must study the effects of medications across a number of species, not in only one.

The various subdivisions and disciplines of pharmacology pursue the discovery and understanding of drugs for the purpose of treating a disease or condition.

The basic principles of pharmacokinetics and pharmacodynamics are universal across the various areas of pharmacology. A significant amount of pharmacology research is spent on identifying new drugs to treat disease. In addition, it is important to predict drug toxicities or adverse reactions. This prediction is accomplished by studying the pharmacokinetics of a drug. Pharmacokinetics is a determination of the ways in which drugs are introduced into the body, how they are used within the body, and how they are cleared (excreted). It describes the relationships between drug dosage and drug blood levels, which can be influenced by individual differences in drug absorption, distribution, metabolism, and elimination. This is important because if a drug is eliminated by the kidneys and a patient has damaged kidneys, then the drug could accumulate in the patient to fatal levels. Pharmacokinetic calculations can be used to determine the dose needed to give safe and effective blood levels in this situation.

A significant amount of pharmacology research is also spent on understanding how drugs act on the body. This is important to understanding adverse reactions, drug interactions, and also for the design of better drugs. This area is known more specifically as pharmacodynamics. Many drugs bind to protein receptors on the surface of a cell. Pharmacodynamics strives to understand how tightly a drug binds to its receptor, what happens inside the cell upon drug binding, and whether the drug has desired or toxic effects on the body.

Lastly, the overall outcome of drugs on the human or animal condition is studied and this is known as efficacy. Efficacy deals with analyzing how well a drug may correct a condition or cure a disease. All three principles, pharmacodynamics, pharmacokinetics, and efficacy, play pivotal roles in pharmacology research.

Work settings

Many pharmacologists work in a laboratory research setting conducting experiments with various drugs. These experiments may be done in animal models of disease or at the biochemical level. Pharmacologists are employed by universities, commercial entities such as pharmaceutical companies, or by the government. University settings are often associated with medical centers and pharmacology research projects are largely funded by grants from outside resources. Many pharmacologists in academic settings study tightly focused areas in which they are interested. Academic labs are headed by a Ph.D. scientist who leads a team of technicians and students. Academic pharmacology projects tend to focus on how different drugs work and why. Veterinary pharmacologists in university settings are usually found only at institutions that have schools of veterinary medicine.

Pharmaceutical company settings usually have a basic pharmacology research division, a **clinical trials** division, a production area, and a quality assurance team. A pharmaceutical company may hire a pharmacologist to discover new drugs or to study existing ones for adverse reactions. Pharmaceutical companies conduct very detailed clinical trials in order to have drugs approved by the United States **Food and Drug Administration (FDA),** part of the **Department of Health and Human Services.** Pharmaceutical companies spend a significant amount of money and employ many scientists in order to prove that a drug is safe and useful in treating a particular disease or condition. A pharmacologist may also be hired by a government agency such as the FDA to conduct research on drugs or to review drug approval applications. The FDA is also responsible for monitoring the safety of already approved drugs and therefore hires pharmacologists

to monitor approved drugs as well as establish guidelines.

A typical workday for a pharmacologist depends on the subdiscipline the pharmacologist works in. A molecular pharmacologist may spend a significant portion of the day at the lab bench conducting experiments in test tubes. A behavioral pharmacologist may spend the day observing animals treated with certain drugs. A clinical pharmacologist is more likely to spend time evaluating data from patients taking certain medications. These workdays are typical of traditional research pharmacologists. Pharmacologists in less traditional careers may be involved in the business or legal side of science. In other words, pharmacologists are not limited to just experimental research in a laboratory setting.

Education and training

A college degree is required to become a pharmacologist. High school students should take biology, chemistry, and math classes. Several undergraduate institutions now offer a bachelor of science degree in pharmacology. College-level courses in biology, biochemistry, anatomy, and physiology are required. The field of pharmacology also requires knowledge of statistics and laboratory mathematics, and students should complete a statistics course. Undergraduate pharmacology majors should also take chemistry courses, including basic chemistry and organic chemistry. The undergraduate science courses should have a practical laboratory component to prepare students for careers in a laboratory research setting. Students should also pursue undergraduate research projects and look for internship opportunities at pharmaceutical or biotechnology companies. Research associate positions in industry are available for pharmacology college majors, but experience in a laboratory research setting is a must for many of these job opportunities. Universities also hire lab technicians with a college-level pharmacology background.

Most pharmacologists have advanced degrees at the master's or doctoral level. More than 120 American and 10 Canadian universities offer graduate degree programs in pharmacology or toxicology. Students pursuing a graduate degree should have an undergraduate degree in biology, chemistry, or a related field. Ph.D. students take in-depth courses in physiology and pharmacology. In addition, a major requirement for a Ph.D. is a dissertation research project that is conducted over several years. The Ph.D. student is required to publish novel findings in peer-reviewed scientific journals. After completing a Ph.D. in pharmacology, many graduates go on to postdoctoral research training. Postdoctoral training may take place in an academic or commercial setting. This training period has an indefinite time length. Many pharmacologists will then go on to become professors at universities or enter the commercial workforce as research scientists.

Why this is important to the consumer

Pharmacology is important to consumers because pharmacologists develop new drugs, and ensure that all drugs are safe and effective. Pharmacologists spend many years in school so that they can work to improve the health and well-being of all people through improved understanding of how drugs work and how they interact with the body and with other drugs or substances. Pharmacologists also work to ensure that there is a good understanding of how drugs may affect special populations, such as individuals with kidney or liver failure, immune system impairments, or women who are pregnant or breastfeeding. Without pharmacologists, there would not be the wide variety of safe and effective drugs available for doctors to prescribe.

Resources

BOOKS

Acosta, W. Renée. *Pharmacology for Health Professionals*, 2nd ed. Philadelphia: Wolters Kluwer/Lippincott Williams and Wilkins Health, 2013.

Edmunds, Marilyn Winterton. *Introduction to Clinical Pharmacology*, 7th ed. St. Louis, MO: Elsevier/Mosby, 2013.

Moini, Jahangir. *Focus on Pharmacology: Essentials for Health Professionals*, 2nd ed. Boston, MA: Pearson Education, 2013.

PERIODICALS

Aronson, J.K. "What Do Clinical Pharmacologists Do? A Questionnaire Survey of Senior UK Clinical Pharmacologists." *British Journal of Clinical Pharmacology* 73 (February 2012): 161–169.

Carpenter, D., and D.A. Tobbell. "Bioequivalence: The Regulatory Career of a Pharmaceutical Concept." *Bulletin of the History of Medicine* 85 (Spring 2011): 93–131.

Mancuso, C., et al. "Pharmacologists and Alzheimer Disease Therapy: To Boldly Go Where No Scientist Has Gone Before." *Expert Opinion on Investigational Drugs* 20 (September 2011): 1243-1261.

WEBSITES

American College of Clinical Pharmacology (ACCP). "Student Outreach." http://www.accp1.org/student_outreach.shtml (accessed December 2, 2013).

American Society for Pharmacology and Experimental Therapeutics (ASPET) Career Center. http://careers.aspet.org/ (accessed December 2, 2013).

U.S. Department of Labor (DOL) Occupational Outlook Handbook. "Medical Scientists." http://www.bls.gov/ooh/life-physical-and-social-science/medical-scientists.htm (accessed December 2, 2013).

U.S. News University Directory. "Pharmacology Majors See Growing Number of Job Opportunities." http://www.usnewsuniversitydirectory.com/articles/pharmacology-majors-see-growing-number-of-job-oppo_12190.aspx (accessed December 2, 2013).

ORGANIZATIONS

American College of Clinical Pharmacology (ACCP), 416 Hungerford Dr., Suite 300, Rockville, MD 20850, (240) 399-9070, Fax: (240) 399-9071, http://www.accp1.org/.

American Society for Pharmacology and Experimental Therapeutics (ASPET), 9650 Rockville Pike, Bethesda, MD 20814-3995, (301) 634-7060, Fax: (301) 634-7061, http://www.aspet.org/.

Food and Drug Administration (FDA), 10903 New Hampshire Avenue, Silver Spring, MD 20993, (888) 463-6332, http://www.fda.gov/default.htm.

Susan M. Mockus, Ph.D.
Tish Davidson, AM

PHR *see* **Personal health record (PHR)**

Physician's assistant

Definition

A physician's assistant (PA) is professionally educated and licensed to practice medicine with a physician's supervision.

Description

Physician's assistants have the equivalent of a master's degree, attending medical training specifically designed for the type of care they provide. They then can take and pass a national certification examination to practice. Once they are

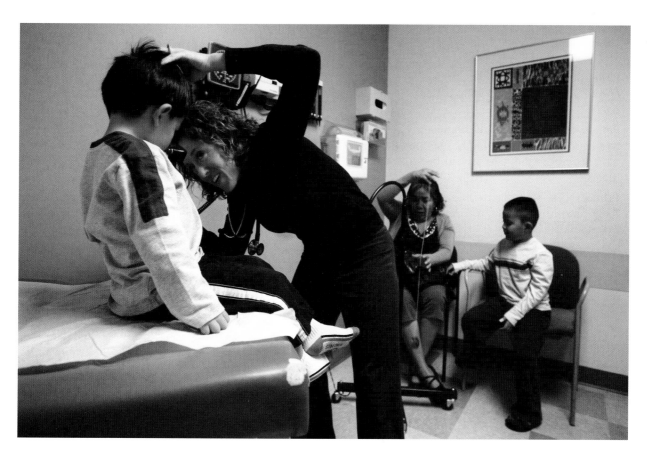

The physician's assistant profession was created to help ease the shortage of primary care physicians. *(John Moore/ Getty Images)*

certified and licensed in the state in which they will practice, PAs work in a number of health care settings, usually helping to provide primary care to patients. PAs also help provide care to inpatients in hospitals.

The PA profession was created to help ease a **shortage of primary care physicians**. The concept was introduced in the 1960s, and the first program for PAs was developed at Duke University Medical Center in Durham, North Carolina. In the 1970s, the federal government began providing funding for PAs, and the medical community backed the concept more completely by supporting standards for PA accreditation and national certification. In 2010, the Bureau of Labor Statistics reported that there were more than 83,000 PAs employed in the United States, but projected that more than 108,000 PAs would be employed by 2020.

Education

Like physicians, PAs attend accredited educational programs that provide both classroom and clinical instruction. The training for PAs is briefer than for

physicians, lasting about 27 months. To enter the programs, candidates usually need to have completed prerequisites such as anatomy, chemistry, or biology. Many PA programs also require that students have some health care experience. Clinical portions of training, which are called "rotations," usually emphasize primary care but can include surgery and emergency medicine. PAs have to complete more than 2,000 hours of clinical rotations for their programs. They also are required to take a set number of continuing education course hours to maintain their licenses.

Typical role of the PA

Physician's assistants examine patients, order imaging or laboratory tests, diagnose patients' illnesses and injuries, and provide treatments for illnesses and injuries, such as setting broken bones. The difference between PAs and physicians is that PAs perform these tasks with physician supervision. They work in all health care settings and roles, such as hospitals where PAs help care for inpatients and outpatients, and in physician offices, providing care alongside physicians. Slightly more than half work in physician offices, and about one-fourth in hospitals. PAs also work in surgical areas with a surgeon's supervision, closing incisions or helping with recovery, and in areas such as psychiatry. In rural and underserved areas, a PA might be the primary provider of care, with a physician present on a part-time and consulting basis. PAs can practice medicine and prescribe medications in all states.

Why PAs are important to the consumer

In underserved and rural areas, residents might not have access to primary care every day if the clinic or health center did not employ a licensed PA. By having the PA present, patients can receive regular care close to home when they need it. One of the biggest advantages to the health care system is that PAs cost less than physicians to hire, which makes them easier to employ in rural and underserved areas, and more cost-effective overall for providing many types of primary care. The National Commission on Certification of Physician Assistants reports that more than 90% of PA employers say that having PAs has increased the number of patients seen in their offices, clinics, or hospitals. Yet, PAs also provide high-quality care, and studies show that patients are satisfied with the care they receive from PAs.

Role of PAs in patient-centered care

Part of **patient-centered care** and the **patient-centered medical home** concept is to put patient needs at the center of care and to improve coordination and communication for more effective care. Aside from the role of PAs in ensuring that patients have access to primary care providers and shorter wait times, PAs are used to working with physicians as part of a health care delivery team. PAs can help manage teams of providers to ensure that patients receive effective, patient-centered care. Their general training also helps to coordinate patient care, effectively using specialist physicians and referrals as needed. Furthermore, studies of care provided at community health centers show that a higher percentage of patient visits to PAs and nurse practitioners include health education and patient counseling than do visits with physicians. Education and counseling are important to preventing disease and to a focus of patient-centered care.

Role of the physician assistant in health care reform

The PA fits in well with the patient-centered medical home, a key concept in the **Patient Protection and Affordable Care Act**. The care coordination, education, and counseling that PAs provide can help patients prevent disease and manage chronic diseases, which should reduce hospital admissions and emergency department visits, especially in areas with fewer primary care physicians than needed to serve the resident population. The Affordable Care Act included language aimed at expanding PA training programs over a period of five years to increase the number of PAs working in primary care around the country.

Resources

BOOKS

Bureau of Labor Statistics. "Physician Assistants." *Occupational Outlook Handbook, 2012-2013 Edition* Washington, D.C.: U.S. Department of Labor, 2012.

WEBSITES

Hanson, Stephen H. "Physician Assistants Play a Key Role in Access to Healthcare." Physicians Practice Website. http://www.physicianspractice.com/blog/physician-assistants-play-key-role-access-healthcare (accessed September 24, 2013).

"NCHS Data Brief. Community Health Centers: Providers, Patients, and Content of Care." Centers for Disease Control and Prevention. http://www.cdc.gov/nchs/data/databriefs/db65.htm (accessed September 24, 2013).

"Professional Issues, Issue Brief: Physician Assistants and the Patient-Centered Medical Home." American Academy of Physician Assistants. http://www.aapa.org/uploadedFiles/content/The_PA_Profession/Becoming_a_PA/Resource_Items/PI_PAs_PCMH_Final.pdf (accessed September 24, 2013).

"The PA's Role." American Academy of Physician Assistants. http://www.aapa.org/the_pa_profession/quick_facts/resources/item.aspx?id=3838 (accessed September 24, 2013).

"Understanding How a Certified PA Can Help You." National Commission on Certification of Physician Assistants. http://www.nccpa.net/public (accessed September 24, 2013).

ORGANIZATIONS

American Academy of Physician Assistants, 2318 Mill Road, Suite 1300, Alexandria, VA 22314, (703) 836-2272, Fax: (703) 684-1924, aapa@aapa.org, www. aapa.org.

National Commission on Certification of Physician Assistants, 12000 Findley Road, Suite 100, Johns Creek, GA 30097, (678) 417-8100, Fax: (678) 417-8135, nccpa@nccpa.net, www.nccpa.net.

Teresa G. Odle

Preferred Provider Organization (PPO)

Definition

A preferred provider organization (PPO) (sometimes also referred to as a "participating provider organization") is a managed care health organization consisting of doctors, hospitals, and other health care providers who have contracted with an insurer or third-party administrator to provide health care at reduced rates to members of the PPO. In most cases, prescription drugs are covered in PPO plans.

In a PPO, the patient does not need to select a **primary care physician** and does not need referrals to see other providers in the network. The patient pays less when doctors, hospitals, and other health care providers that belong to the plan's network (preferred providers) are chosen for care, while the costs are higher when the patient uses doctors, hospitals, and providers outside of the network. These higher costs may be in the form of higher deductibles, co-payments, lower reimbursement percentages, or a combination of these approaches. PPOs differ from health maintenance organizations (HMOs) in that HMO patients who do not use participating health care providers receive little or no benefit from their health plan. PPOs usually require a yearly deductible before the PPO starts paying some or all of the costs. The patient also usually pays a co-payment for a covered service, while the PPO covers the rest of the costs.

The providers associated with a PPO are rewarded by an increased number of patients and more efficient processing of claims. The PPOs profit by charging an access fee to the insurance company for the use of their network. A PPO can also contract with other PPOs to strengthen their position within geographic areas without forming new relationships directly with providers.

Description

PPO administrators negotiate and contract with health care providers, such as primary care physicians, specialists, hospitals, and pharmacies, to create a network of preferred providers. These contracted providers agree to provide health care services at a rate lower than their normal charges. The administrators also serve as liaisons between providers and the insurers. PPOs may contract or hire their own third-party administrators (TPAs), that is, entities that collect and handle premium money and handle claims. Large employer groups, especially when they are self-funded, often contract with a TPA to handle health care administrative functions.

There are three basic types of PPOs:

- Lease-type PPO: Not a health care plan, but an organization that develops provider networks and rents them to one or more payers;
- Managed PPO network: A specific plan design where self-insured employers or payers contract for provider services, and sometimes utilization management;
- Integrated PPO plan: This PPO directly enrolls its patients.

Medicare includes PPOs as a type of health care plan available to Medicare beneficiaries.

Some states regulate what a PPO can and can not do. For example, some states specifically do not allow PPOs to pay contracted providers a capitated amount. These states might only allow PPOs to create a network of contracted providers and to sell the use of this network to companies and other such employer groups.

To achieve quality care and cost savings, PPOs usually develop utilization management programs. Utilization management is the evaluation of the appropriateness, medical need, and efficiency of health care services procedures and facilities according to established criteria or guidelines and under the provisions of an applicable health benefits plan. Typically, it includes new activities or decisions based upon the analysis of a case. Pre-certification and pre-authorization reviews for plan-selected services are often an integral part of a utilization management program in order to provide health care efficiently and cost-effectively before and during health care administration. One means of ensuring quality during the administration of health care activities is by the use of **case management**, which may be triggered by an inpatient admission or a complex outpatient service. A

case manager will meet with the patient and health care providers to develop the best type of care and settings.

After care has been provided, PPOs may use utilization processes to review the outcomes of the health care, for the best measure of quality is medical treatment outcome, that is:

• Were medical resources appropriately used?

• Was the desired treatment outcome achieved?

• Did the patient regain optimal functioning?

These reviews may be conducted by medical directors and a specialty peer review network and may be based on national evidence-based treatment guidelines.

Utilization management often contains a patient education component. Individuals with chronic or high-cost conditions are taught to better understand, learn, and routinely engage in self-management activities to improve their health and long-term quality of life. Often a triage system, designed to help individuals make decisions that will often avoid unnecessary expensive services such as emergency room (ER) visits, is provided. For example, patients may be given 24-hour telephone access to personal one-on-one health counseling with a trained nurse consultant. The nurse can offer medical advice, peace of mind in uncertain situations, and an immediate alternative to an ER or physician visit. Such phone counseling results in improved patient satisfaction and is an inexpensive method to enhance a benefit package, as well as an effective way to reduce unnecessary ER or provider visits. Another educational program used by PPOs is a voluntary and comprehensive on-site health screening with self-reported health risk assessments. This program includes complete confidential reporting to members regarding screening results, interactive website support, nurse follow-up, and health education opportunities.

Why this is important to the consumer

Although premiums may be higher, a PPO plan may be the plan of choice for a patient who wants more flexibility, who wants the freedom to choose almost any medical facility or provider, who wants to have a portion of out-of-network costs covered by the PPO, and who does not want to get referrals before visiting a specialist.

Resources

BOOKS

Steinwald, Bruce, and Cosgrove, James C. *Medicare Demonstration PPOS: Financial And Other Advantages for Plans.* Collingdale, PA: Diane Publishing Company, 2004.

WEBSITES

"Preferred Provider Organization Plans." http://www.medicare.gov/sign-up-change-plans/medicare-health-plans/medicare-advantage-plans/preferred-provider-organization-plans.html (accessed October 3, 2013).

"How do I use my health insurance?" http://www.iom.edu/~/media/files/activity%20files/publichealth/health literacy/background%20documents/q3%20-%20how%20do%20i%20use%20it.pdf (accessed October 3, 2013).

"What are the different types of health insurance?" HealthCare.gov. https://www.healthcare.gov/what-are-the-different-types-of-health-insurance/ (accessed October 3, 2013).

Judith L. Sims, M.S.

Preventable readmissions

Definition

Preventable readmissions are incidents in which an inpatient is readmitted to a hospital within a specified time period—usually 30 days—for medical reasons that could have been prevented if the patient had received better care, either during his or her hospital stay or during post-acute convalescence.

Preventable readmissions, also known more informally in the healthcare industry as "bounce backs," are regarded as a key indicator of hospital performance. Preventable readmissions rates provide a measurement of the quality and safety of medical services that patients receive during their hospital stays. They also serve as a tool for measuring the effectiveness of hospital discharge and post-discharge programs, which are designed to help patients complete their

Tips to avoid medical errors
Make sure your entire healthcare team knows every medicine you are taking, including prescription medications, over-the counter drugs, vitamins, and supplements.
Make sure your healthcare team knows if you have any allergies or have had adverse reactions to medications or substances in the past.
Make sure that you understand what will be done during your surgery and that you, your doctor, and your surgeon all agree on the exact details.
For elective procedures, choose a hospital that performs a high volume of the surgery you need.
Make sure you understand your treatment plan, including what you need to do once you are discharged from the hospital.
Bring a family member or friend to all appointments with you to take notes.
Call to find out test results if you do not hear back from your doctor.
If you have any questions or concerns, do not be afraid to ask, and do not be afraid to seek a second opinion.
SOURCE: Agency for Healthcare Research and Quality, "20 Tips to Help Prevent Medical Errors: Patient Fact Sheet." Rockville, MD: AHRQ, 2011. http://www.ahrq.gov/patients-consumers/care-planning/errors/20tips/index.html.

(Table by PreMediaGlobal. Reproduced by permission of Gale, a part of Cengage Learning.)

recovery at home. Healthcare experts caution, however, that preventable readmissions rates should be viewed with a degree of caution. In some cases, they explain, readmissions take place not because of any shortcomings on the part of the hospital, but because patients fail to follow post-discharge guidelines. Sometimes a patient has to be readmitted because he fails to take prescribed medicines in accordance with hospital instructions, neglects to make dietary or other lifestyle changes urged by his doctors, or otherwise fails to heed post-discharge advice and directives from caregivers.

Description

Patients may be readmitted to hospitals for any number of reasons, from an initial misdiagnosis of their medical condition to complications that often accompany healthcare problems like heart failure or heart disease. Another common source of readmissions is patient confusion about a post-discharge medication regimen. For example, upon discharge, a patient may receive a new prescription for a generic version of a brand-name drug that she is already taking; if she is not instructed to stop taking the brand-name medication—or she simply disregards the instructions to only take one of the medications in the belief that "more is better"—she may end up with health complications from taking too much of the medication. Finally, elderly patients in particular

sometimes require readmission within weeks of discharge for the simple reason that their bodily systems are failing due to the natural aging process. These patients are more likely to need readmission for medical problems completely unrelated to their initial admission.

All of these factors have led hospitals and healthcare experts to caution that some level of readmission is inevitable and proper. Researchers have concluded, though, that about 15-20% of current patient readmissions are avoidable at most hospitals. Experts estimate that even at the nation's highest-performing hospitals, approximately one in ten readmissions may be preventable. A 2007 report by the federal **Agency for Healthcare Research and Quality (AHRQ)** identified nearly 4.4 million hospitalizations nationwide in 2006 that could have been prevented.

The potential implications of a preventable readmission for a patient's well-being are clear. Every preventable readmission is a case in which a patient's health, safety, or comfort is compromised because they did not receive the best possible care, either during their hospital stay or in their transition to home care settings. In addition, readmissions often produce profound disruptions to the personal and work lives of patients and their families, and they can take a heavy financial toll on patients and families with limited or no public or private health insurance coverage.

Preventable readmissions, though, are also a less visible but significant contributor to the overall operating costs of America's taxpayer-funded **Medicare** and **Medicaid** programs. In April 2009, the prestigious *New England Journal of Medicine* published a study estimating that nearly one out of five (19.6%) of Medicare patients was readmitted to the hospital within 30 days of their initial discharge. More than one-third of the Medicare patients (34%) were readmitted within 90 days. Only about 10% of these readmissions were planned in advance. The researchers estimated that the remaining unplanned hospital "bounce backs" cost the Medicare program about $17 billion annually.

Hospital Readmissions and the ACA

Efforts by hospitals to reduce preventable readmissions by improving inpatient care and post-discharge care coordination assumed new urgency in 2010 with the passage of the **Patient Protection and Affordable Care Act** of 2010, also known as "Obamacare." The Affordable Care Act (ACA) included provisions that empowered the **Centers for Medicare and Medicaid Services (CMS)** to begin levying financial

KEY TERMS

Bounce back—Preventable readmission of a patient to a hospital.

Best practices—Professional procedures that are widely recognized as being the most effective in meeting stated goals.

Post-acute care—Medical services that aid a patient's post-hospitalization recovery from illness, surgical procedure, or management of a chronic medical condition.

penalties against hospitals that readmit an excessive number of Medicare patients, who typically account for 25-40% of a hospital's total patient load at any given time.

This penalty takes the form of a reduction in the federal government's reimbursements to hospitals for excess readmission rates of Medicare patients. These penalties are initially based on hospital readmissions rates for three medical conditions—heart failure, heart attack, and pneumonia—but the number of medical conditions monitored by the CMS for this purpose will be expanded by 2015.

When the penalty first went into effect in FY 2013, the maximum penalty was 1% of total Medicare payments for all discharges. By 2015, however, hospitals that fail to meet CMS standards for preventable readmissions could face up to a 3% penalty. The CMS fines translate to billions of dollars in lost revenue for hospitals that do not receive passing grades. Consequently, all hospitals—from those already operating at a loss or with tight profit margins to those with robust financial profiles—have a significant monetary incentive to institute measures to reduce bounce backs.

Hospitals are focusing on a variety of strategies to reduce preventable readmission rates. One of the highest priorities for hospitals is to consistently adhere to evidence-based best practices in every phase of their diagnostic and therapeutic efforts to improve healthcare outcomes for patients. In addition, hospital administrators and staff are examining their admission guidelines to improve the accuracy of initial diagnoses; identifying risk factors for readmissions; working to ensure that all discharged patients meet explicit and measurable standards of "wellness"; revamping their discharge instructions and procedures to reduce medication discrepancies and improve patient self-care competency; shoring up home healthcare services for high-risk populations; and investing in new information technologies to help ensure that medical information about every patient is accurate, up-to-date, and accessible by all parties involved in that patient's care.

Why this is important to the consumer

Reductions in rates of preventable readmissions rest on the capacity of hospitals to improve the quality of medical care they provide in all phases of their caregiving operations. Consumers of hospital services are thus sure to benefit from reforms and practices that reduce bounce backs.

Patient advocates also point out that preventable readmissions rates are a matter of public record. They can thus be a useful tool for consumers interested in researching which hospital is right for them—and which hospitals they should perhaps avoid.

Resources

BOOKS

Acello, Barbara. *Ending Hospital Readmissions: A Blueprint for SNFs.* Danvers, MA: HCPro, 2011.

Institute of Medicine (IOM). *The Healthcare Imperative: Lowering Costs and Improving Outcomes: Workshop Series Summary.* Washington, D.C.: National Academies Press, 2010.

PERIODICALS

Lubell, Jennifer. "Hospitals Cry Foul: Preventable Readmissions Penalty Brings Concerns." *Modern Healthcare* 40, no. 22 (May 31, 2010): 10.

WEBSITES

Abrams, Michael N., and Matt Levy. "Diagnosing and Treating Readmissions." H&HN Daily, January 29, 2013. http://www.hhnmag.com/hhnmag/HHNDaily/HHNDailyDisplay.dhtml?id = 1580005365 (accessed September 5, 2013).

Stone, Julie, and Geoffrey J. Hoffman. *Medicare Hospital Readmissions: Issues, Policy Options and PPACA,* September 21, 2010. Congressional Research Service. http://www.hospitalmedicine.org/AM/pdf/advocacy/CRS_Readmissions_Report.pdf (accessed September 5, 2013).

ORGANIZATIONS

American Hospital Association, 155 N. Wacker Dr., Chicago, IL 60606, (312) 422-3000, (800) 424-4301, http://www.aha.org.

Institute for Healthcare Improvement (IHI), 20 University Road, 7th Floor, Cambridge, MA 02138, (617) 301-4800, (866) 787-0831, Fax: (617) 301-4848, info@ihi. org, http://www.ihi.org.

Kevin Hillstrom

Prevention and Public Health Fund

Definition

The Prevention and Public Health Fund, also known as the Prevention Fund or PPHF, is a mandatory fund for the support of community-based disease prevention and public health programs. It was created by Section 4002 of the **Patient Protection and Affordable Care Act** of 2010. By law, PPHF funds are allocated to wellness and public health programs that improve health and work to reduce the incidence of preventable diseases such as cancer, diabetes, heart disease, high blood pressure, and obesity. Supporters of the PPHF assert that the program's emphasis on preventing chronic illness and disease (rather than treating them after the fact) can improve the health and quality of life of millions of Americans while also reducing the overall financial **cost of health care** in the United States.

Description

The Prevention and Public Health Fund was created in response to research studies indicating that the physical health of Americans and the financial health of the U.S. healthcare system (and especially its **Medicare** and **Medicaid** programs) could be improved through increased investment in wellness and disease-prevention programs. In 2012, for example, an influential **Institute of Medicine** (IOM) report estimated that increased investments in community-based health and wellness programs (such as nutrition, physical fitness, and tobacco cessation initiatives) could produce 40% reductions in cancer rates and 80% reductions in cases of heart disease and type-2 diabetes. A 2011 study published by *Health Affairs* concluded that for every 10% increase in public health spending at county or city levels, mortality rates associated with preventable diseases fell between 1.1 and 6.9%.

Researchers also cited potential improvements in health outcomes as a key element of federal efforts to improve the financial well-being of the U.S. health care system. The health advocacy group Trust for America's Health (TFAH) estimated in 2012 that a mere 5% reduction in American obesity rates could produce $30 billion in health care savings over five years. The IOM, meanwhile, estimated that if the United States were to reduce adult obesity levels by 50%—roughly equivalent to the rate by which tobacco use declined during the second half of the twentieth century—the nation could reduce its total health care bill by about $58 billion every year.

Unlike previous federal disease-prevention and wellness initiatives, the PPHF received a mandatory funding stream when it was created. This arrangement reflected the overall high priority that the Obama administration placed on disease-prevention and wellness programs in the Affordable Care Act. By making PPHF funding mandatory, the program's architects and supporters sought to give the program a stable revenue stream that would not be subject to the usual Congressional wrangling over appropriations. However, the Affordable Care Act did make one important exception to the PPHF's mandatory funding provision. Under the law, Congress retained the power to divert money from the Prevention Fund into already existing wellness and disease-prevention programs that met the primary PPHF goals of promoting health and wellness, reducing rates of preventable disease, and restraining growth in public- and private-sector health costs.

Allocations by Category and Agency

Since its inception, PPHF funds have been funneled into four broad categories of public health activities and programs. The highest percentage of Prevention Fund dollars has gone to "community prevention" programs, which are locally organized and managed programs designed to improve personal behavior and decisions on health-related issues. Examples of community prevention programs include efforts to help people quit smoking, anti-obesity measures that focus on improved nutritional habits and increased physical activity, and other disease-specific efforts. PPHF funds are also being allocated to clinical prevention programs, including **immunization** programs and HIV screening and prevention programs, and to support public health department infrastructure and employee training. Finally, PPHF funds are being used to gather data on public health services across the country and determine which prevention-based practices are most useful and cost-effective.

PPHF allocations are made through the U.S. **Department of Health and Human Services (HHS)**. Six **HHS** agencies or offices have received and dispersed PPHF dollars since the Affordable Care Act was signed into law. These agencies are the Administration on Aging (AoA); the **Agency for Healthcare Research and Quality (AHRQ)**; the **Centers for Disease Control and Prevention (CDC)**; the Health Resources and Services Administration (HRSA); the Office of the Secretary (OS); and the Substance Abuse and Mental health Services Administration (SAMHSA).

In the first two fiscal years of the PPHF's existence, approximately 69% of the program's total allocations went to local and state governments, tribes, and community-based nongovernmental organizations (NGOs) in individual states and the District of Columbia. The remainder was spent at the federal level.

Reductions in Funding

Although the Prevention and Public Health Fund was crafted and passed with language designed to ensure that it remained a strong and stable source of revenue for community-based health, wellness, and disease-prevention programs, funding for the program almost immediately fell victim to deficit concerns and partisan warfare in Washington.

The Affordable Care Act originally authorized $18.75 billion for the PPHF between FY 2010 and FY 2022. Annual funding levels started at $500 million in its first year (FY 2010), then gradually rose over the course of five years to its full annual funding level of $2 billion by FY 2015.

Since PPHF came into being, however, Republican hostility to all aspects of the Affordable Care Act and federal deficit concerns shared by both Republicans and Democrats have resulted in reductions in the pool of PPHF money available for community-based public health programs. Taking advantage of the ACA provision that authorized Congress to use money from the PPHF to fund other federal health programs, lawmakers passed legislation in February 2012 that cut Prevention Fund spending by 33% over ten years starting in FY 2013 in order to "patch" a scheduled cut to Medicare physician payments. President Obama signed the legislation, which also extended payroll tax cuts to workers and jobless benefits to the long-term unemployed, into law on February 22, 2012.

Funding for PPHF was further reduced in the spring of 2013. The deficit-reduction mechanism known as "sequestration" cut $51 million from the Prevention and Public Health Fund's FY2013 funding level of $1 billion, and the Obama administration decided to take another $332 million of PPHF funds to aid in the installation and implementation of the Affordable Care Act's **Health Insurance Exchanges**. These various cuts and diversions, which reduced total PPHF FY2013 funding by 38% from its original FY2013 level, forced HHS agencies to curtail or end their support for a variety of public health programs and services that were reliant on PPHF grants, including ones focused on immunization, mental health, substance abuse, tobacco cessation, prenatal and early childhood care, and nutritional health. These developments led one health policy analyst at the *Washington Post* to describe the PPHF as "the incredible shrinking Prevention Fund."

Critics of the PPHF have applauded these funding reductions. They remain skeptical of the efficacy of federal wellness and disease-prevention programs in general and the PPHF's priorities in particular. They say that spending on such programs is an unaffordable luxury for a nation that already spends too much. Many detractors also contend that such programs are unnecessary, given that Americans are free to improve their dietary habits and get more exercise any time they wish.

Why this is important to the consumer

The Prevention and Public Health Fund is an effort to respond to the heavy physical, emotional, and financial tolls of preventable diseases in the United States. According to the **CDC**, chronic and preventable disease such as obesity, diabetes, high blood pressure, heart disease, cancer, and arthritis are among the most common, costly, and preventable of all health problems in the United States. By some estimates, however, only about 3% of America's healthcare dollars are spent on programs designed to prevent such illnesses and conditions.

The PPHF has been cited by advocates as a pioneering effort to begin addressing this shortfall in prevention efforts. Proponents assert that dollars spent on preventive care and wellness programs now will produce enormous cost savings in the decades to come. These savings will bolster the fiscal health of federal, state, and local governments—as well as the financial security of individual consumers—in the future.

Public health experts also agree that PPHF-funded wellness and public health programs can be a valuable resource for individuals seeking to make major lifestyle changes that improve health and wellness. In many cases, say supporters, these clinical and educational programs act as a catalyst in spurring individuals to immunize their children, quit smoking, get more regular exercise, and curtail other behaviors that increase the risk of chronic disease. Advocates say that the PPHF can thus help millions of Americans lead longer, happier, and more productive lives.

Resources

BOOKS

Holsinger, James W. Jr. *Contemporary Public Health: Principles, Practice, and Policy.* Lexington: University Press of Kentucky, 2013.

PERIODICALS

Haberkorn, Jennifer. "Health Policy Brief: The Prevention and Public Health Fund." *Health Affairs,* February 23, 2012. http://www.healthaffairs.org/healthpolicybriefs/brief.php?brief_id=63 (accessed August 22, 2013).

Mays, Glen P., and Sharla A. Smith. "Evidence Links Increases in Public Health Spending to Declines in Preventable Deaths." *Health Affairs* 30, no. 8 (August 2011): 1585-1593.

WEBSITES

American Public Health Association. "The Prevention and Public Health Fund: A Critical Investment in Our Nation's Physical and Fiscal Health." APHA Issue Brief, June 2012. http://www.apha.org/NR/rdonlyres/D1708E46-07E9-43E7-AB99-94A29437E4AF/0/PrevPubHealth2012_web.pdf (accessed August 22, 2013).

Institute of Medicine. "For the Public's Health: Investing in a Healthier Future." Washington, D.C.: Institute of Medicine, April 2012. http://www.iom.edu/Reports/2012/For-the-Publics-Health-Investing-in-a-Healthier-Future.aspx (accessed August 22, 2013).

Kliff, Sarah. "The Incredible Shrinking Prevention Fund." *Washington Post* Wonkblog, April 19, 2013. http://www.washingtonpost.com/blogs/wonkblog/wp/2013/04/19/the-incredible-shrinking-prevention-fund/ (accessed August 22, 2013).

Knickman, James. "We Should Be in a Race for Prevention, Not Cures." *Atlantic,* May 30, 2012.

Trust for America's Health. "Bending the Obesity Cost Curve." January 2012. http://healthyamericans.org/assets/files/TFAH%202012ObesityBrief06.pdf (accessed August 22, 2013).

ORGANIZATIONS

American Public Health Association, 800 I Street NW, Washington, DC 20001-3710, (202) 777-APHA, Fax: (202) 777-2534, http://www.apha.org.

U.S. Department of Health and Human Services (HHS), 200 Independence Avenue SW, Washington, DC 20201, (877) 696-6775, http://www.hhs.gov.

Kevin Hillstrom

Preventive service coverage

Definition

A preventive service is a type of medical care that focuses on preventing disease and maintaining health. The category includes regular medical examinations, screening tests, immunizations, health education, and other services designed to identify risk factors and avert the development of health problems. Preventive service coverage is the extent to which private health insurance companies and federal health insurance programs pay for this type of medical care. The **Patient Protection and Affordable Care Act** of 2010 required most health insurance plans to cover the full cost of federally recommended preventive services for their customers.

Description

Preventive medical care is intended to help people maintain good health. Although preventive care can be costly, supporters of preventive service coverage argue that it saves money in the long run by allowing people to either avoid or delay the onset of a wide range of diseases and medical conditions. "Preventing illnesses before they become serious and more costly to treat helps Americans of all ages stay healthier," declared Kathleen Sebelius, Secretary of the U.S. **Department of Health and Human Services (HHS)**, in a 2013 press release.

The range of preventive services recommended for Americans is determined by the U.S. Preventive Services Task Force (USPSTF). Established in 1982, the task force is a volunteer panel of national experts in evidence-based medicine. The panel rigorously evaluates peer-reviewed clinical research in order to assess the merits of various preventive measures, such as screening tests, immunizations, medications, and counseling.

Each year, the USPSTF issues a list of preventive services that it recommends the nation's primary-care physicians and healthcare systems offer to their patients. Each recommendation is assigned a letter grade (A, B, C, or D, or I for incomplete) based on the strength of the evidence of its value and the balance of benefits and drawbacks associated with it. The recommendations only apply to preventive services, meaning that patients receiving those services should have no signs or symptoms of the specific disease or condition under evaluation.

USPSTF recommendations have formed the basis of the clinical standards adopted by many professional societies and health organizations. For many years, however, health insurance companies had no obligation to cover the cost of the preventive services that the panel recommended. Although many private insurers did cover at least some of the recommended preventive services, they often required customers to subsidize part of the cost through deductibles, copayments, or coinsurance. In the meantime, studies indicated that even moderate cost-sharing requirements reduced the likelihood that patients would choose to obtain preventive health care. Partly due to the cost involved, Americans used preventive services at about half the recommended rate during the first decade of the twenty-first century.

The major healthcare reform legislation passed by Congress and signed into law by President Barack Obama in 2010, formally known as the Patient Protection and Affordable Care Act, sought to expand access to, and utilization of, preventive services by eliminating cost sharing. The Affordable Care Act required most health insurance plans to provide coverage for a range of preventive services and prohibited them from charging copayments, deductibles, or coinsurance to patients receiving these services from an in-network provider. The law applied to all private health plans except those with "grandfathered" status, meaning that they were in existence prior to March 23, 2010. The majority of the preventive care requirements went into effect for non-grandfathered plans beginning on September 23, 2010.

The Affordable Care Act required private insurers to cover a wide range of preventive services for all adults, as well as additional preventive services aimed at special populations, such as women and children. A fact sheet examining all of the federally recommended preventive services covered under the law is available at https://www.healthcare.gov/what-are-my-preventive-care-benefits/. The following lists summarize this information:

Preventive Health Services for Adults

- Abdominal aortic aneurysm screening for male smokers of specified ages
- Alcohol misuse screening and counseling
- Aspirin use to prevent cardiovascular disease
- Blood pressure screening
- Cholesterol screening
- Colorectal cancer screening for people over 50
- Depression screening
- Diabetes (Type 2) screening

- Diet counseling for people at high risk for chronic disease
- HIV screening
- Immunization vaccines
- Obesity screening and counseling
- Sexually transmitted infection (STI) prevention counseling
- Syphilis screening
- Tobacco use screening and cessation interventions

Preventive Health Services for Women

- Anemia screening for pregnant women
- Breast cancer genetic test counseling
- Breast cancer mammography screenings for women over 40
- Breast cancer chemoprevention counseling for women at high risk
- Cervical cancer screening
- Chlamydia infection screening
- Contraception (does not apply to health plans sponsored by certain "religious employers")
- Domestic violence screening and counseling
- Folic acid supplements for pregnant women
- Gestational diabetes screening for pregnant women
- Gonorrhea screening
- Hepatitis B screening for pregnant women
- Osteoporosis screening for women over 60
- Rh incompatibility screening for pregnant women
- Urinary tract or other infection screening for pregnant women
- Well-woman visits to get recommended services for women under 65

Preventive Health Services for Children

- Autism screening at 18 and 24 months
- Behavioral assessments every five years
- Blood pressure screening every five years
- Cervical dysplasia screening for sexually active girls
- Depression screening for adolescents
- Developmental screening for children under age three
- Dyslipidemia screening for children at high risk of lipid disorders
- Fluoride supplements
- Gonorrhea preventive medication for the eyes of newborns
- Hearing screening for newborns

KEY TERMS

Cost sharing—An effort by insurance companies to make consumers cover part of the cost of their own health care by requiring deductibles and copayments.

Evidence-based medicine—The use of current best practices and medical research in making decisions regarding patient care.

Grandfathered—A health insurance plan that was already in existence before the Affordable Care Act passed in 2010 and is therefore exempt from the law's preventive service coverage requirements.

- Height, weight, and Body Mass Index (BMI) measurements
- Hematocrit or hemoglobin screening
- Hemoglobinopathies or sickle cell screening for newborns
- Hypothyroidism screening for newborns
- Immunization vaccines
- Iron supplements
- Lead screening
- Medical history
- Obesity screening and counseling
- Oral health risk assessment
- Phenylketonuria (PKU) screening for newborns
- Sexually transmitted infection (STI) prevention counseling
- Tuberculin testing
- Vision screening

Why this is important to the consumer

Preventive service coverage plays an important role in promoting individual and public health. In March 2013 the U.S. **Department of Health and Human Services** released a report indicating that the preventive care provisions in the Affordable Care Act had encouraged millions of Americans to get routine checkups, blood pressure screenings, mammograms, colonoscopies, flu shots, and other covered services. **HHS** data showed that about 71 million Americans in private health insurance plans, in addition to an estimated 34 million Americans in **Medicare** programs, received coverage for at least one free preventive health care service in 2011 and 2012.

Resources

BOOKS

Goodwin, Suzanne M. *The Effect of Cost Sharing on Utilization of Preventive Services Among Medicare Beneficiaries.* Ann Arbor, MI: ProQuest, 2009.

PERIODICALS

Goodwin, Suzanne M., and Gerard F. Anderson. "Effect of Cost-Sharing Reductions on Preventive Service Use Among Medicare Fee-for-Service Beneficiaries." *Medicare and Medicaid Research Review* 2, no. 1 (2012). http://www.cms.gov/mmrr/Downloads/MMRR2012_002_01_A03.pdf (accessed September 6, 2013).

WEBSITES

Center for Medicare and Medicaid Services. "What Are My Preventive Care Benefits?" HealthCare.Gov. https://www.healthcare.gov/what-are-my-preventive-care-benefits/ (accessed September 6, 2013).

Kaiser Family Foundation. "Preventive Services Covered by Private Health Plans under the Affordable Care Act." KFF.org, September 2011. http://kaiserfamilyfoundation.files.wordpress.com/2013/01/8219.pdf (accessed September 6, 2013).

U.S. Department of Health and Human Services. "Affordable Care Act Extended Free Preventive Care to 71 Million Americans with Private Health Insurance." HHS.gov, March 18, 2013. http://www.hhs.gov/news/press/2013pres/03/20130318a.html (accessed September 6, 2013).

ORGANIZATIONS

U.S. Preventive Services Task Force, 540 Gaither Road, Rockville, MD 20850, (301) 427-1584, http://www.uspreventiveservicestaskforce.org.

Laurie Collier Hillstrom

Primary care physician

Definition

A primary care physician is a generalist physician who is the first point of entry into the healthcare system for patients, and who provides continuity of care for that patient over time.

Description

As a generalist, the primary care physician is uniquely poised to provide preventive care, as well as to treat uncomplicated, acute, short-term illnesses and to follow patients with reasonably stable chronic illnesses. The three types of physicians who are considered to offer primary care services include internists (specialists in internal medicine), family practitioners,

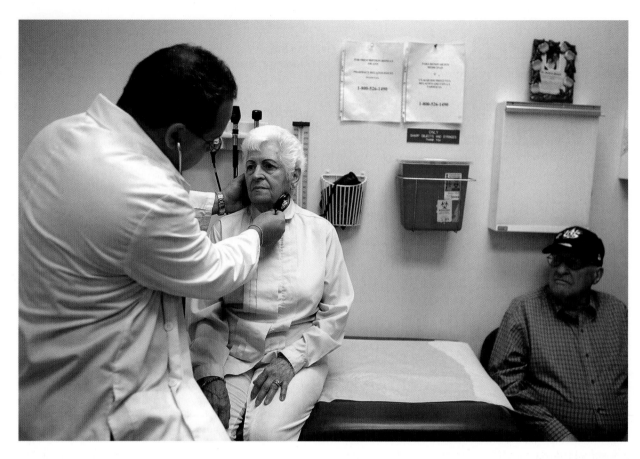

A primary care physician (PCP) is a patient's first point of entry into the healthcare system and provides continuity of care for patients over time. *(Joe Raedle/Getty Images)*

and pediatricians. Internists primarily care for adults; family practitioners provide care for adults and children; and pediatricians care for children and adolescents.

In addition to providing medical care, primary care physicians are responsible for referring patients on to specialty physicians, including

- Cardiologists, for heart problems
- Nephrologists, for kidney problems
- Gastroenterologists, for problems involving the digestive tract
- Dermatologists, for problems involving the skin
- Neurologists, for problems involving the nervous system
- Psychiatrists, for psychiatric problems
- Gynecologists, for problems with the female reproductive system
- Urologists, for problems with the urinary system or the male reproductive system
- Surgeons

Education, licensing, and skills

A primary care physician must have a bachelor's degree, with successful completion of a specific set of premedical prerequisite courses (such as chemistry, organic chemistry, calculus, physics, genetics, microbiology, physiology) prior to taking the medical school entrance examination and applying to medical school. After graduating with the four year M.D., and having passed all three parts of the United States Medical Licensing Exam, an individual pursuing a career in primary care medicine will spend time in a three-year residency receiving further training in order to be board certified in one of the primary care areas (internal medicine, family medicine, pediatrics).

Primary care physicians need a good fundamental background in biochemistry, anatomy, physiology, and microbiology, as well as the ability to read and critically analyze ongoing research in the field. Primary care physicians should also possess excellent interviewing, listening, and communication skills, as well as the ability to translate more complex science into concepts easily understood by laypeople. Primary care physicians also need

Doctors of medicine in primary care, by specialty: United States and outlying U.S. areas, selected years 1949–2010

[Data are based on reporting by physicians]

Specialty	1949	1960	1970	1980	1990	1995	2000	2008	2009	2010
					Number					
Total doctors of medicine	201,277	260,484	334,028	467,679	615,421	720,325	813,770	954,224	972,376	985,375
Active doctors of medicine	191,577	247,257	310,845	414,916	547,310	625,443	692,368	784,199	792,805	794,862
General primary care specialists	113,222	125,359	134,354	170,705	213,514	241,329	274,653	305,264	307,586	304,687
General practice/family medicine	95,980	88,023	57,948	60,049	70,480	75,976	86,312	93,761	94,671	94,746
Internal medicine	12,453	26,209	39,924	58,462	76,295	88,240	101,353	115,314	116,148	113,591
Obstetrics/Gynecology	—	—	18,532	24,612	30,220	33,519	35,922	38,272	38,573	38,520
Pediatrics	4,789	11,127	17,950	27,582	36,519	43,594	51,066	57,917	58,194	57,830
Primary care subspecialists	—	—	3,161	16,642	30,911	39,659	52,294	71,794	74,000	76,122
Family medicine	—	—	—	—	—	236	483	1,193	1,303	1,445
Internal medicine	—	—	1,948	13,069	22,054	26,928	34,831	47,779	49,324	50,730
Obstetrics/Gynecology	—	—	344	1,693	3,477	4,133	4,319	4,363	4,282	4,277
Pediatrics	—	—	869	1,880	5,380	8,362	12,661	18,459	19,091	19,670
					Percent of active doctors of medicine					
General primary care specialists	59.1	50.7	43.2	41.1	39.0	38.6	39.7	38.9	38.8	38.3
General practice/family medicine	50.1	35.6	18.6	14.5	12.9	12.1	12.5	12.0	11.9	11.9
Internal medicine	6.5	10.6	12.8	14.1	13.9	14.1	14.6	14.7	14.7	14.3
Obstetrics/Gynecology	—	—	6.0	5.9	5.5	5.4	5.2	4.9	4.9	4.8
Pediatrics	2.5	4.5	5.8	6.6	6.7	7.0	7.4	7.4	7.3	7.3
Primary care subspecialists	—	—	1.0	4.0	5.6	6.3	7.6	9.2	9.3	9.6
Family medicine	—	—	0.0	0.0	0.0	0.0	0.1	0.2	0.2	0.2
Internal medicine	—	—	0.6	3.1	4.0	4.3	5.0	6.1	6.2	6.4
Obstetrics/Gynecology	—	—	0.1	0.4	0.6	0.7	0.6	0.6	0.5	0.5
Pediatrics	—	—	0.3	0.5	1.0	1.3	1.8	2.4	2.4	2.5

(Table by PreMediaGlobal. Copyright © 2014 Cengage Learning®.)

some understanding of the psychological underpinnings of the kinds of conditions their clients will be confronting, as well as some training in cultural diversity. The ability to be empathic with patients from diverse backgrounds is crucial. Primary care physicians who will be involved in education need to have public speaking skills, while those who work in research will need specific laboratory skills pertinent to the type of investigations they will be conducting, as well as a good understanding of research methods and design.

Licensing is performed by the individual state and generally involves the scrutiny of all academic records, passing all three parts of the United States Medical Licensing Exam, as well as background checks, drug testing, and other paperwork. Becoming board certified means that a physician has passed the specific educational requirements within a residency program, and has then sat for and passed a special exam offered by the certifying body (such as the American Board of Internal Medicine, The American Academy of Family Medicine, or The American Academy of Pediatrics) and testing for a specific specialty.

Places of employment

Primary care physicians may work in healthcare facilities such as hospitals or nursing homes, private offices, student health centers, clinics, government agencies, public health clinics, corporate health services, ambulatory care clinics, urgent care centers, or emergency departments.

Tasks of a primary care physician

The specific tasks of a primary care physician include:

- Interviewing/Taking a medical history: Most appointments begin with the physician asking the patient about his or her past medical history, family medical history, and current health status. If the individual is having a problem, then the focus of the appointment will be on that specific body system.

- Preventive care and screening: A patient's primary care physician is responsible for providing preventive care (such as immunizations), as well as following screening guidelines (such as every-other-year mammograms for women over age 50), so that medical conditions can be diagnosed and addressed at the earliest possible stage.

- Physical examination: A physical examination is an important part of confirming health or illness. If the visit is for an annual, well-person exam, then the primary care physician will do a head-to-toe, complete physical examination. If the office visit is for a

KEY TERMS

Acute—Having a rapid or sudden onset, and often lasting for a short period.

Chronic—Occurring over a long period of time; persistent, recurrent.

Preventive care—Medical care focused on preventing the onset of illness.

Reimbursement—Being repaid for the outlay of money for medical expenses, usually by a health insurance company, or by the government (Medicare or Medicaid).

Screening—Testing an individual for the presence of a condition for which he or she may have a statistically increased risk of developing, although no signs or symptoms.

specific problem, then the exam may be focused only on the specific body system or systems that could be responsible for the patient's symptomatology. Physical exams may also be required for schools, camps, or places of employment.

- Diagnosis: Primary care physicians order diagnostic testing depending on the issues that present during the course of the interview and physical exam. These could include blood tests, x-rays, or urinalysis.

- Acute care: Primary care physicians are trained to treat acute problems, such as sinus or urinary tract infections, uncomplicated headaches, musculoskeletal problems, influenza, gastroenteritis, and ear infections, as well as many other conditions.

- Chronic care: Primary care physicians can care for patients with long-term medical conditions, including high blood pressure, cholesterol issues, uncomplicated diabetes, thyroid problems, asthma and allergies, arthritis, and uncomplicated depression or anxiety.

- Referrals: While primary care physicians may end up diagnosing more complex problems, in many cases they will refer these patients to specialists, either for a brief consultation (in which case, the patient will return to the primary care physician for continuing care) or for long-term treatment and management of the condition. It is in this "gate-keeper" capacity that primary care physicians play an important role in keeping healthcare costs under control. Additionally, the primary care physician will continue to see the patient for routine care, and can serve as a point-person to keep track of all the consulting physicians' recommendations.

- Primary care physicians may also be academicians, teaching medical school classes, supervising resident physicians, and undertaking research on a university campus.

Why this is important to the consumer

Primary care physicians play an important role in the healthcare economy. Often referred to as "gatekeepers," primary care physicians help regulate the flow of patients to more expensive specialty physicians. When patients have complex medical illnesses, the primary care physician can help coordinate the care of several specialists. At the same time, patients have the advantage of seeing a physician who begins to know them well over time, providing continuity of care, an understanding of the patient's personal context of health and illness, and a longitudinal sense of history with the patient and his or her family.

Many studies have shown that primary care allows for improved patient outcomes, lower cost, decreased hospitalization rates, enhanced quality of life scores, increased productivity, and fewer chronic disease complications. As of 2013, projections suggested that the United States could save as much as $2 trillion, and that individual households could save a total of $537 billion over a ten-year period, by adopting recommendations that include an increased focus on expanded and consistent utilization of primary care services.

Unfortunately, the United States is currently experiencing a **shortage of primary care physicians**. Although there are currently around 209,000 in practice, estimates suggest that this is about 50,000 less than needed. Furthermore, this shortage is expected to worsen dramatically as the number of insured individuals increases, and as our population ages.

Resources

BOOKS

EZ Occupational Outlook Handbook, 2nd ed. St. Paul, MN: JIST Publishing, 2011.

U.S. Department of Labor. *Occupational Outlook Handbook.* St. Paul, MN: JIST Publishing, 2013.

Wischnitzer, Saul. *Top 100 Health-Care Careers.* St. Paul, MN: JIST Publishing, 2011.

ORGANIZATIONS

American Academy of Family Practice, P.O. Box 11210, Shawnee Mission, KS 66207, (913) 906-6000, http://www.aafp.org/home.html.

American Academy of Pediatrics, 141 Northwest Point Boulevard, Elk Grove Village, IL 60007, (847) 434-4000, http://www.aap.org/en-us/Pages/Default.aspx.

American College of Physicians, 190 North Independence Mall West, Philadelphia, PA 19106, (215) 351-2400, http://www.acponline.org/.

American Medical Association, AMA Plaze, 330 N. Wabash Ave., Chicago, IL 60611, (800) 621-8335, foundation@ eatright.org, http://www.ama-assn.org/ama.

ExploreHealthCareers.org, American Dental Education Association, 1400 K Street, NW, Suite 1100, Washington, DC 20005, (202) 289-7201, cmsa@cmsa.org, http://explorehealthcareers.org/en/home/.

Society for General Internal Medicine, 1500 King Street, Suite 303, Alexandria, VA 22314, (202) 887-5150, http://www.sgim.org/.

U.S. Department of Labor, Frances Perkins Building, 200 Constitution Ave., NW, Washington, DC 20210, (866) 487-2365, http://www.dol.gov/.

U.S. Bureau of Labor Statistics, Postal Square Building, 2 Massachusetts Ave., NE, Washington, DC 20212, (202) 691-5200, http://www.bls.gov.

Rosalyn Carson-DeWitt, MD

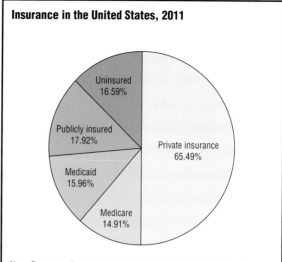

Insurance in the United States, 2011

- Uninsured 16.59%
- Publicly insured 17.92%
- Medicaid 15.96%
- Medicare 14.91%
- Private insurance 65.49%

Note: Some people may receive more than one type of coverage, so numbers may not add up to 100%.

SOURCE: U.S. Census Bureau, "Health Status, Health Insurance, and Medical Services Utilization, 2011." Information available online at: http://www.census.gov/hhes/www/hlthins/hlthins.html (accessed September 3, 2013).

(Table by PreMediaGlobal. Reproduced by permission of Gale, a part of Cengage Learning.)

Private insurance plans

Definition

Private insurance plans include all forms of health insurance that are not administered by federal or state governments.

Purpose

The purpose of private insurance plans is to protect their policyholders from the high costs of health care. Most private health insurance plans in the United States are employment-based or are purchased by individuals for themselves and their families. Some private insurance plans contract with governments to cover recipients of **Medicaid**, **Medicare**, the **Children's Health Insurance Program (CHIP)**, or other state or federal programs.

Private insurance plans can provide individuals, families, and businesses with peace of mind and varying degrees of financial protection from sudden or substantial costs related to medical care. In an effort to lower their costs, private insurance plans increasingly provide prevention and wellness programs to improve the health, safety, and quality of life of their policyholders, as well as to help beneficiaries manage chronic conditions.

Demographics

Most Americans obtain healthcare coverage through private insurance plans, usually through their employers. As of 2013, approximately 15 million Americans—about 6% of non-elderly adults—purchased private insurance on the individual health insurance market. In 2011, 64.2% of Americans between the ages of 18 and 64 had private insurance, 21.3% were uninsured, and the remainder had government-provided insurance such as Veterans, Medicaid, or Medicare. Among children under 18, 53.3% had private insurance, 41% had public insurance such as Medicaid or CHIP, and 7% were uninsured. However, more than 18% of Americans under age 65—48.2 million people—had no health insurance for at least part of 2012. An additional 30 million—16% of the population—were "underinsured" in 2012, with inadequate healthcare coverage that did not protect them from high medical bills. As a result, medical bills are the leading cause of individual bankruptcy in the United States.

Description

The private health insurance market consists of the individual insurance market and the employer-sponsored insurance market. The latter may be part of either

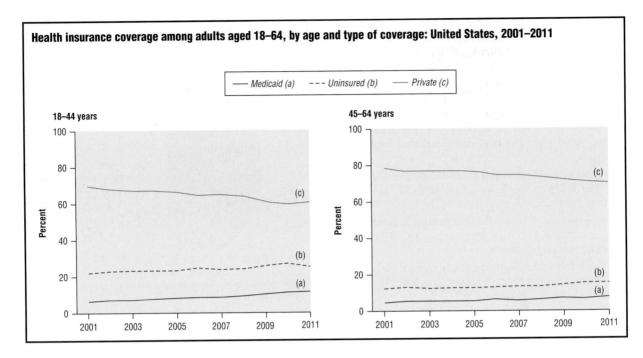

Health insurance coverage among adults aged 18–64, by age and type of coverage: United States, 2001–2011

(Table by PreMediaGlobal. Copyright © 2014 Cengage Learning®.)

the small-group or large-group insurance market. Some group plans are available to individuals through voluntary associations. These private insurance markets differ in their characteristics and operate under different regulations. Individual insurance plans are usually more expensive than group plans and are often more restrictive in their coverage. Furthermore, private insurance plans are regulated by individual states and vary greatly among the states. Many private insurance plans are available only within specific regions of a given state. However, private insurance plans and their costs and benefits are changing dramatically under the **Patient Protection and Affordable Care Act** of 2010 (often shortened to Affordable Care Act, or just called "Obamacare"), with the most substantial changes taking effect starting in 2014.

Origins

In the mid-twentieth century, most American families had employer-based health insurance as a benefit of their jobs. At that time, many workers were employed by large firms, remained with those firms throughout their working lives, and were represented by unions that negotiated good insurance plans as a benefit for their members. With the demise of labor unions, increased employment with small firms that cannot afford health insurance as an employee benefit, increases in part-time and low-wage work, and greater job mobility, the availability of employer-based insurance plans has decreased substantially. During the

1980s, insurance companies began excluding or restricting benefits for people with preexisting conditions. People at high risk of developing cancer or with conditions such as diabetes or HIV/AIDS were often unable to obtain insurance under any circumstances.

The **Health Insurance Portability and Accountability Act** (HIPAA) of 1996 required employer-sponsored insurance plans to accept transfers from other plans without imposing pre-existing-condition clauses on workers who changed jobs. It also introduced **COBRA**, which enabled workers and their families to keep their employee health insurance for a limited time after they left an employer. About 7 million Americans become eligible for COBRA each year, although they usually must pay the full cost of the monthly premiums. In addition, some people who lose job-based insurance are able to convert their coverage to an individual policy with the same insurance company. Finally, some people can buy individual coverage as a "HIPAA eligible individual." Nevertheless, as the cost of private health insurance continued to skyrocket, more and more Americans became uninsured. This trend culminated in the passage of the Affordable Care Act in 2010, with major changes to take effect over the subsequent decade.

Costs

The cost of private insurance plans has risen steadily and dramatically over recent decades, along

Private health insurance coverage obtained through the workplace among persons under age 65, by selected characteristics: United States, selected years 1984–2011

Characteristic	1984	1989	1995	1997	2000	2005	2009	2010	2011
					Number in millions				
Total	141.8	146.3	150.7	153. 6	160.8	160.1	150.2	147.6	146.4
					Percent of population				
Total	69.1	68.3	65.4	66.4	67.1	63.6	58.0	56.6	56.4
Age									
Under 19 years	66.4	65.6	60.5	62.8	63.1	58.7	52.0	50.9	49.9
Under 6 years	62.1	62.3	55.1	58.3	58.9	53.4	46.3	44.9	44.3
6–18 years	68.4	67.3	63.1	64.9	64.9	61.1	54.8	53.8	52.5
Under 18 years	66.5	65.8	60.4	62.8	63.0	58.6	51.8	50.7	49.7
6–17 years	68.7	67.7	63.3	65.1	65.0	61.1	54.7	53.8	52.4
18–64 years	70.3	69.4	67.6	68.0	68.8	65.7	60.4	58.9	59.1
18–44 years	69.6	68.4	65.3	65.7	66.5	62.2	56.6	54.6	55.6
18–24 years	58.7	55.3	53.5	54.9	55.5	52.1	47.4	45.3	51.0
19–25 years	59.0	55.0	53.0	53.7	54.2	50.6	45.9	44.1	50.5
25–34 years	71.2	69.5	65.0	64.6	66.4	61.1	55.5	53.3	53.0
35–44 years	77.4	76.2	72.7	72.7	73.2	69.9	64.3	62.8	61.6
45–64 years	71.8	71.6	72.2	72.8	72.9	70.9	65.7	64.8	63.9
45–54 years	74.6	74.4	74.7	75.6	75.6	72.6	67.1	65.9	64.7
55–64 years	69.0	68.3	68.4	68.4	68.6	68.6	64.0	63.4	63.0
Sex									
Male	69.8	68.7	65.9	66.7	67.3	63.6	57.6	56.1	56.1
Female	68.4	67.9	64.9	66.2	66.9	63.6	58.4	57.1	56.7

(Table by PreMediaGlobal. Copyright © 2014 Cengage Learning®.)

with the rising **cost of health care** in the United States, in part because of increased life expectancy and expensive new medical technologies. As a result, many employers have reduced or eliminated health insurance as an employee benefit. This is particularly true among smaller employers.

The costs of private insurance plans, whether individual or employer-sponsored group plans, include:

- premiums paid by the beneficiary, usually monthly, in addition to any employer-paid premiums

- deductibles—the amount that an individual pays for medical services before any insurance coverage takes effect

- out-of-pocket maximum amounts that an individual pays, usually over the course of a year

The costs for individual insurance plans usually depend on one's health status, age, gender, and other factors. With job-based plans, employers determine how much of the premium their employees will pay for individual and family coverage.

Types of private insurance plans

There are many different types of private insurance plans. Many plans have networks of hospitals, doctors, specialists, pharmacies, and other healthcare providers that are under contract with the insurer to provide care for plan members.

- Traditional **health maintenance organizations (HMOs)** and exclusive provider organizations (EPOs) only pay for services provided within their networks. HMOs usually have no deductibles and only small co-payments. In most HMOs, members select a primary care physician who is responsible for all of their health-care needs, including referrals to specialists.

- **Preferred provider organizations** (PPOs) and point-of-service (POS) plans may allow policyholders to use out-of-network healthcare providers, but beneficiaries usually pay more out-of-pocket for such services.

- **Fee-for-service** insurance plans do not generally have networks. They include indemnity plans that usually pay 70–90% of medical charges from any hospital or physician after the policyholder has paid a deductible amount.

There are other types of private insurance plans. Medigap plans are private insurance plans that supplement Medicare coverage. Medigap policies pay most or all of the co-insurance amounts charged by Medicare. Some Medigap policies cover Medicare deductibles. Long-term care (LTC) insurance covers the cost of custodial or nursing-home care and is usually very expensive.

Eligibility

In general, people with employer-sponsored insurance plans cannot be refused coverage or charged a higher premium because of their health status or a disability. However, employers may deny or restrict coverage to their employees for other reasons, such as part-time employment. Furthermore, until 2014, when new ACA regulations come into effect, insurance companies can continue to restrict or deny individual coverage or charge higher premiums for a variety of reasons, including pre-existing health conditions. Until 2014, under the ACA people with pre-existing conditions who have been uninsured for six months may qualify for the Pre-Existing Condition Insurance Plan (PCIP). Some states also sponsor insurance plans for people with pre-existing conditions.

Changes with the Affordable Care Act

The ACA makes substantial changes in the rules governing private insurance plans. Some of these rule changes went into effect as early as September of 2010:

- Insurance companies can no longer cancel coverage when a beneficiary becomes sick.
- Insurance companies can no longer deny coverage to children with pre-existing conditions.
- New plans must cover preventive care services, such as mammograms and other screenings, free of charge.
- Insurance companies can no longer set limits on lifetime medical benefits.
- Insurance companies must extend coverage to children up to age 26 through their parents' plan.

As of January 1, 2013, the ACA requires that all new private insurance plans and new coverage periods—which usually begin on January 1 of each year—cover preventive services for women without co-payments or other additional costs. These services include well-woman visits, contraceptives, contraceptive and breastfeeding counseling and equipment, HIV testing and counseling, and screening for gestational diabetes, breast and cervical cancer, sexually transmitted infections, and intimate partner violence.

Beginning in 2014, almost all individual insurance plans must offer defined essential services (or **essential health benefits**), including hospitalization, doctors' services, prescription drugs, rehabilitation, mental health services, and pregnancy and newborn care. Although a few existing plans are grandfathered in, most plans that do not meet the new minimum standards will be eliminated. Approximately half of all individual plans available in 2013 do not meet the new

ACA standards. Furthermore, all Americans will be required to have insurance coverage or pay fines that start at $95 per year or 1% of adjusted family income, whichever is larger. Beginning on October 1, 2013, state-based **health insurance exchanges**, also called the "health insurance marketplace" or "affordable insurance exchanges," began offering individuals and small businesses new options and more control over their choice of private insurance plans, with coverage taking effect in January of 2014. Individuals can choose from four levels of coverage: platinum, gold, silver, and bronze. Platinum plans have the highest premiums but the lowest out-of-pocket expenses. Bronze plans have the lowest premiums but high deductibles and co-payments. People with annual incomes of up to 499% of the poverty level—about $95,000 for a family of four—will receive federal subsidies to help pay insurance premiums. Tax credits will become available to help pay for insurance purchased through an exchange for people without job-based health coverage or with job-based coverage that costs more than 9.5% of their income. Marketplace premiums are expected to cost about half of current COBRA premiums. It is estimated that approximately 24 million Americans will obtain insurance through the exchanges by 2016, with another 24 million obtaining individual coverage outside of the exchanges.

In addition to covering essential services, as of 2014, all new individual insurance plans and plans purchased through an exchange must cover certain preventive services free-of-charge, and there are limits on annual out-of-pocket costs for covered services. These plans will not be able to charge higher premiums based on health status, pregnancy, disability, or gender, and there are limits on how much premiums can vary based on age. Insurance companies will not be able to deny coverage to anyone because of a pre-existing condition, and they can no longer place caps on how much they will pay for medical benefits in one calendar year.

Although states have always been allowed to use Medicaid funding to pay for private insurance plans for low-income Medicaid recipients, they have not done so, because private plans have not offered equivalent benefits to Medicaid. However, this may change under the ACA and, as of 2013, some states were proposing to use ACA-mandated Medicaid expansion to contract with private plans to cover low-income recipients.

Risks

Insurance policies tend to be very complex documents, and many people do not understand what healthcare services they are entitled to under their

KEY TERMS

Affordable Care Act (ACA)—The Patient Protection and Affordable Care Act ("Obamacare"); signed into law by President Barack Obama in March of 2010. The ACA overhauled the U.S. healthcare system, including major changes to private insurance plans.

Children's Health Insurance Program (CHIP)—Children's Medicaid; a federal program administered by the states that provides low-cost or free health insurance to children from families with incomes that are too high to qualify for Medicaid.

COBRA—A provision of the Health Insurance Portability and Accountability Act of 1996 that enables people to buy individual insurance coverage from their previous employer-based plan for a limited time period.

Co-payment—The amount that an insured individual pays out-of-pocket for healthcare services.

Deductible—The amount that an insured person is required to pay on each claim or over the course of a year.

Health Insurance Portability and Accountability Act; HIPAA—1996 legislation that attempted to protect health insurance benefits for workers who lost or changed jobs, as well as providing some health insurance standards.

Health maintenance organization (HMO)—A comprehensive private insurance plan that provides a primary care physician who controls referrals to specialists and other services within the HMO's network.

Long-term care (LTC) insurance—Private insurance intended to cover the cost of long-term nursing home or home health care.

Medicaid—Government-financed health insurance for low-income Americans that is administered by individual states.

Medicare—The U.S. government health insurance system for those aged 65 and over.

Medigap—Supplemental healthcare insurance policies that cover services not included in Medicare.

Preferred provider organizations (PPOs)—Private health insurance plans that require beneficiaries to select their healthcare providers from a list approved by the insurance company.

Premium—The amount paid by an insurance policyholder for insurance coverage; most health insurance policy premiums are payable on a monthly basis.

plans. It is not unusual for people with private insurance to find themselves in medical bankruptcy following a major accident or illness, because of extremely high deductibles and medical expenses that are not covered by their plans. Beginning in 2012 under the ACA, all insurance policies are required to be written in clear, comprehensible language, explaining the coverage and how it is implemented. Furthermore, employment-based plans must provide all employees with a summary plan description that explains benefits, employee costs, appeals, and other pertinent information.

Some private health insurance products do not provide comprehensive protection and may mislead consumers. These plans include:

• dread disease policies, which only cover costs for the treatment of specific diseases such as cancer

• accident-only policies, which only pay for care resulting from an accident and not for illness-related services

• supplemental policies, such as supplemental prescription drug coverage, Medigap policies, and hospital indemnity policies that pay cash benefits for

each day spent in a hospital but do not cover the cost of hospital care

• discount plans for a network of healthcare providers, which do not protect consumers from high medical expenses and which are not regulated as health insurance

• stacked policies that combine several limited-coverage products, such as accident-only and hospital supplement policies or dread disease and discount plans

There are additional risks and concerns associated with the ACA as it continues to be implemented. For example, is not yet clear what will happen if states are unable to establish exchanges within the expected time frames, and how people without insurance will be affected as a result. Other concerns surround potential cost increases for insurance companies, employers, and healthcare providers and, in turn, how those changes will affect patient care.

Resources

BOOKS

Beik, Janet I. *Health Insurance Today: A Practical Approach.* St. Louis, MO: Elsevier, 2013.

Green, Michelle A., and Jo Ann C. Rowell. *Understanding Health Insurance: A Guide to Billing and Reimbursement.* Clifton Park, NY: Delmar Cengage Learning, 2011.

Miles, Toni P. *Health Care Reform and Disparities: History, Hype, and Hope.* Santa Barbara, CA: Praeger, 2012.

Ulmer, Cheryl. *Essential Health Benefits: Balancing Coverage and Cost.* Washington, DC: National Academies, 2012.

PERIODICALS

Pear, Robert, and Peter Baker. "Health Law Is Defended with Vigor by President." *New York Times*, May 11, 2013).

OTHER

International Foundation of Employee Benefit Plans. *2013 Employer-Sponsored Health Care: ACA's Impact.* Brookfield, WI: IFEBP, 2013. http://www.ifebp.org/pdf/research/2103ACAImpactSurvey.pdf (accessed July 23, 2013).

WEBSITES

AARP. "Fact Sheet: The Health Care Law and Improved Health Insurance Practices." July 2012. http://www.aarp.org/health/health-care-reform/info-06-2010/fact_sheet_health_law_improved_health_insurance_practices.html (accessed July 23, 2013).

America's Health Insurance Plans (AHIP). "Affordable Care Act." http://www.ahip.org/Issues/Affordable-Care-Act (accessed July 23, 2013).

America's Health Insurance Plans (AHIP). "Private-Market Health Insurance." http://www.ahip.org/Issues/Private-Market-Health-Insurance.aspx (accessed July 23, 2013).

Barry, Patricia. "Ask Ms. Medicare: Medicare's Private Plans." *ARRP Bulletin*. June 4, 2012. http://www.aarp.org/health/medicare-insurance/info-07-2008/ask_ms__medicare_12.html (accessed July 23, 2013).

Luhby, Tami. "Most Individual Health Insurance Isn't Good Enough for Obamacare." CNNMoney. April 3, 2013. http://money.cnn.com/2013/04/03/news/economy/health-insurance-exchanges/index.html (accessed July 23, 2013).

ORGANIZATIONS

AARP, 601 E Street, NW, Washington, DC 20049, (202) 434-3525, (888) OUR-AARP (687-2277), member@aarp.org, http://www.aarp.org.

Agency for Healthcare Research and Quality, Office of Communications and Knowledge Transfer, 540 Gaither Road, Suite 2000, Rockville, MD 20850, (301) 427-1104, http://www.ahrq.gov.

American College of Healthcare Executives, One North Franklin Street, Suite 1700, Chicago, IL 60606-3529, (312) 424-2800, Fax: (312) 424-0023, contact@ache.org, http://www.ache.org.

American Medical Association, 515 North State Street, Chicago, IL 60654, (800) 621-8335, http://www.ama-assn.org.

America's Health Insurance Plans, 601 Pennsylvania Avenue, NW, South Building, Suite 500, Washington, DC 20004, 202) 778-3200, Fax: (202) 331-7487, ahip@ahip.org, http://www.ahip.org.

U.S. Department of Health and Human Services, 200 Independence Avenue, SW, Washington, DC 20201, (877) 696-6775, http://www.hhs.gov.

L. Fleming Fallon, Jr., MD, DrPH
Margaret Alic, PhD

Professional-patient relationship

Definition

The professional-patient relationship is a bond of trust between the patient and the medical professional who is performing treatment.

Description

The relationship established between patients and health care providers is fiduciary in nature, which means that it is based on trust. In this respect, it is similar to the relationships between lawyers and clients or between clergy and their congregations. The professional trusts the patient or client to disclose all the information that may be relevant to his or her condition or illness, and to be truthful while disclosing it. In return, the patient or client trusts the health care professional to maintain high standards of competence; to protect the confidentiality of private information; and to carry out his or her work in the best interests of the patient rather than taking advantage of the patient's vulnerability.

Historical background

Prior to the second half of the twentieth century, the patient-physician relationship was strictly hierarchical. The physician was assumed to know what was best for the patient, and the patient was expected to follow "doctor's orders." After World War II, however, patients in the developed countries began to take a more active role in their health care. This change was related to the larger proportion of high-school students going on to college, and to the rapid spread of medical information via television and health care books written for the public. Patients who were employed in other fields requiring specialized training, or who read widely, were less impressed by the physician's educational credentials and more likely to question his or her advice.

The major emphasis of the professional-patient relationship is on the medical professional and the patient as partners. *(Iconica/Getty Images)*

Ethical principles

Health care professionals are obligated to act according to ethical and legal standards. **"Medical ethics"** refers to the moral standards that are considered to govern health care. The fundamental ethical principles underlying Western medical practice have not changed since they were first enunciated by Hippocrates (460–377 BC). These principles include:

- Honesty. The professional does not withhold necessary information from the patient or lie to the patient about the nature or seriousness of his or her condition.
- Beneficence (doing good). The professional uses his or her knowledge and skills to balance good results and potential harms, and act in the patient's best interests.
- Justice. The professional does not refuse treatment on the basis of a patient's race, religion, nationality, income, or other personal characteristics.
- Avoiding conflicts of interest. This principle means that the professional must not benefit personally from his or her professional actions or influence. For example, a physician should prescribe a particular medication because it is the best choice for the patient, not because the professional owns stock in the company that manufactures the drug.
- Pledging to do no harm. This principle means that the professional must avoid actions detrimental to the patient.

All major organizations of health care providers, including the American Hospital Association, the American Medical Association, the American Dental Association, and the American Nurses Association have formal ethical guidelines for professional-patient relationships. These ethical policy statements are based on the ancient Hippocratic oath.

Legal obligations

In the United States and Canada, the legal obligations of health care providers are based on the traditional ethical standards of good medical practice. These legal obligations include accepting federal and state examination and licensure standards; complying with government mandates regarding the storage and control of confidential medical records; complying with court orders regarding reporting or disclosure of a patient's medical records; providing care that is at or above the commonly accepted standard of care of the profession; and a number of other obligations.

The legal obligations and liabilities of health care professionals have become increasingly complex over the last 30 years. This development is partly the result of technological advances that pose new questions to the legal system. For example, the safe operation of medical lasers depends on proper engineering and maintenance procedures as well as on the surgeon's skill and training in using the laser. A patient injured by a malfunctioning laser might decide to sue the manufacturer and the hospital administration as well as the surgeon. As the government and medical organizations have worked to move to **electronic health records,** to allow for improved ease of sharing between practitioners, among other benefits, a number of new legal and privacy concerns have arisen that are still being addressed.

Social context of contemporary health care

In addition to the rise in education level among the general population in Europe and North America, several other factors have helped to reshape patient-professional relationships. The most important factors include:

• Greater awareness of moral and philosophical differences regarding medical and health issues. At one time, health care professionals acted solely according to their own conception of the best interests of their patients, and patients were unlikely to question them or their authority. Today, however, there is often disagreement both within the professions as well as in the general population about issues such as abortion, euthanasia, organ donation, limitations on medical research, and others. The professional-patient relationship has become more democratized, less one-sided, in this sense.

• The high-pressure education of health care professionals. Over the past thirty years, the training of physicians, nurses, dentists, pharmacists, and other health care professionals has become much more demanding. One factor is the sheer accumulation of scientific knowledge; today's medical, dental, or nursing student must master a much larger body of information than students of previous generations. Another factor is the increased tendency toward professional specialization, which makes it more difficult for health care providers to treat the whole patient on their own.

Managed care. Managed care has changed physician-patient relationships by requiring patients to choose their doctor from a list of providers approved by the **managed care organization.** In many instances, patients have been forced to leave physicians who were trusted and who had cared for them for years. In other instances, managed care organizations have terminated physicians on short notice, thus disrupting continuity of patient care. Some observers have remarked that patients' attitudes toward physicians have become increasingly adversarial because they think doctors are more concerned with pleasing insurance companies than providing good care.

• Changes in communications technology. The widespread use of computers in managed care and health insurance organizations to store databases of patient information has raised questions about preserving **patient confidentiality.** In addition, the increasing popularity of email for communication between patients and professionals opens up concerns about the security and privacy of electronic files.

• Multicultural issues. Hospitals and medical or dental offices have been increasingly confronted with the complications that can arise in cross-cultural professional-patient relationships. Different ethnic and racial groups in the United States have widely varying customs and attitudes toward such matters as expressing physical pain or grief; undressing in front of a professional of the opposite sex; asking questions about their diagnosis and treatment; and other issues that arise in medical settings.

Ongoing issues

Today, the major emphasis of the professional-patient relationship is on the medical professional and the patient as partners making a joint decision about the patient's treatment. Patients have requested and been given more rights concerning their medical treatment. Medical professionals should encourage patients to learn about their medical problems, weigh the benefits of different treatments, and make choices based on their own beliefs and values.

Recent changes in professional-patient relationships have tended to cluster around several specific issues:

INVOLVEMENT OF FAMILY MEMBERS IN PROFESSIONAL-PATIENT RELATIONSHIPS. Although discussions of professional-patient relationships often proceed as if the relationship concerns only two

KEY TERMS

Confidentiality—The protection and maintenance of strict privacy and secrecy in relationships between professionals and their patients or clients.

Ethics—The rules of conduct recognized as governing a particular group, as medical professionals.

Hippocratic Oath—The ethical pledge attributed to Hippocrates that is used as a standard for care by physicians worldwide.

people, the care provider and the patient, in many cases family members are also involved. In the cases of children and elderly patients, family members may be needed to describe the patient's symptoms or provide care at home. With regard to the elderly, family members may have sharp disagreements about the level of health care that is necessary, which can complicate the professional's work.

CONFIDENTIALITY. The computerization of patient information, combined with the increasing involvement of federal and state governments in health care, has led some observers to ask whether present security measures are adequate. Both trends—the use of computers and the expansion of government regulation—increase the number of people who have access to patient records and private information.

In the United States and Canada, the courts generally recognize two limitations on the professional's obligation to preserve confidentiality. The first is a court order that requires the physician to deliver confidential information about a patient. The second limitation concerns situations in which a patient is endangering his or her own life or the lives of others.

Why this is important to the consumer

The consumer-provider relationship is incredibly important to the overall healthcare experience. A consumer who has a medical provider who answers questions, explains options fully, does not appear hurried, is genuinely caring, and keeps the consumer's best interests at heart will have a much better healthcare experience that someone who has a less positive relationship with his or her healthcare provider.

While most professional-patient relationships are positive, consumers should never be afraid to speak up if something is not working. If the healthcare provider will not resolve the issue, consumers should speak to a supervisor or administrator, and/or change providers.

Most medical, dental, and nursing schools in the United States and Canada now include courses in professional ethics, communication skills, and understanding of the social context of professional-patient relationships. Students are taught that mutual respect and clear communication between professionals and patients are the keys to a good relationship.

Resources

BOOK

Mallia, Pierre. *The Nature of the Doctor-Patient Relationship: Health Care Principles Through the Phenomenology of Relationships with Patients*. New York: Springer, 2013.

Purtilo, Ruth B., Haddad, Amy M., and Doherty, Regina *Health Professional and Patient Interaction, 8th Ed*. St. Louis, MO: Elsevier Health Sciences, 2014.

PERIODICAL

Bergeremail, Stephanie, Braehler, Elmar, and Ernst, Jochen. "The health professionalpatient-relationship in conventional versus complementary and alternative medicine." *Patient Education and Counseling* 88, no. 1 (July, 2012): 129–137.

Rathnakar UP, Anjali, Ganesh, Unnikrishnan B., Srikanth D., Ganesh K., Ashok Shenoy K., and Ashwin, Kamath. "Doctor Patient Relationship: Influence of Gender and Role." *International Journal of Medical and Pharmaceutical Sciences* 3(12), no. 1 (2013): 30–36.

ORGANIZATIONS

American Hospital Association, 155 N. Wacker Dr, Chicago, IL, (312) 638-1100, (800) 424-4301 60606, http://www.aha.org.

American Medical Association, 330 N. Wabash Ave., Chicago, IL 60611, (800) 621-8335, http://www.ama-assn.org.

American Nurses Association, 8515 Georgia Ave, Suite 400, Silver Spring, MD 20910, (800) 274-4ANA (4262), Fax: (301) 628-5001, http://www.ana.org.

Peggy Elaine Browning
Tish Davidson, AM

Psychiatrist

Definition

A psychiatrist is a physician who specializes in the diagnosis and treatment of mental disorders.

Description

Psychiatrists treat patients privately and in hospital settings through a combination of psychotherapy and medication. Their training consists of four years of medical school, followed by three or four years of psychiatric residency. Subspecialties usually involve completion of a fellowship that lasts two or more years following the residency. Psychiatrists may receive certification from the American Board of Psychiatry and Neurology (ABPN), which requires two years of clinical experience beyond residency and the successful completion of a written and an oral test. Unlike a medical license, board certification is not legally required to practice psychiatry.

Psychiatrists may practice general psychiatry or choose a specialty, such as child psychiatry, geriatric psychiatry, treatment of substance abuse, forensic (legal) psychiatry, emergency psychiatry, intellectual disabilities, community psychiatry, or public health. Some focus their research and clinical work primarily on psychoactive medication, in which case they are referred to as psychopharmacologists. Psychiatrists may be called upon to address numerous social issues, including juvenile delinquency, family and marital dysfunction, legal competency in criminal and financial matters, and treatment of mental and emotional problems among prison inmates and in the military.

Psychiatrists treat the biological, psychological, and social components of mental illness simultaneously. They can investigate whether symptoms of mental disorders have physical causes, such as a hormone imbalance or an adverse reaction to medication, or whether psychological symptoms are contributing to physical conditions, such as cardiovascular problems and high blood pressure. Because they are licensed physicians, psychiatrists—unlike psychologists and psychiatric social workers—can prescribe medication; they are also able to admit patients to the hospital. Other mental health professionals who cannot prescribe medication themselves often establish a professional relationship with a psychiatrist.

Psychiatrists may work in private offices, private psychiatric hospitals, community hospitals, state and federal hospitals, or community mental centers. Often, they combine work in several settings. In addition to their clinical work, psychiatrists often engage in related professional activities, including teaching, research, and administration. The American Psychiatric Association, the oldest medical specialty organization in the United States, supports the profession by offering continuing education and research opportunities, keeping members informed about new research and public policy issues, helping to educate the public about mental health issues, and serving as an advocate for people affected by mental illness.

Resources

ORGANIZATION

American Psychiatric Association, 1000 Wilson Blvd., Ste. 1825, Arlington, VA 22209-3901, (703) 907-7300, apa@psych.org, http://www.psych.org.

American Board of Psychiatry and Neurology, 2150 E Lake Cook Rd., Ste. 900, Buffalo Grove, IL 60089, (847) 229-6500, Fax: (847) 229-6600, http://www.abpn.com.

Emily Jane Willingham, PhD

Psychologist

Definition

A psychologist is a social scientist who studies behavior and mental processes, generally in a research or clinical setting.

Description

As psychology has grown and changed throughout history, it has been defined in numerous ways. As early as 400 B.C., the ancient Greeks philosophized about the relationship of personality characteristics to physiological traits. Since then, philosophers have proposed theories to explain human behavior. In the late nineteenth century the emergence of scientific method gave the study of psychology a new focus. In 1879, the first psychological laboratory was opened in Leipzig, Germany, by Wilhelm Wundt, and soon afterward the first experimental studies of memory were published. Wundt was instrumental in establishing psychology as the study of conscious experience, which he viewed as made up of elemental sensations. In addition to the type of psychology practiced by Wundt—which became known as structuralism— other early schools of psychology were functionalism, which led to the development of behaviorism, and Gestalt psychology. The American Psychological Association was founded in 1892 with the goals of encouraging research, enhancing professional competence, and disseminating knowledge about the field.

With the ascendance of the Viennese neurologist Sigmund Freud and his method of psychoanalysis early in the twentieth century, emphasis shifted from conscious experience to unconscious processes investigated by means of free association and other techniques. According to Freud, behavior and mental processes were the result of mostly unconscious struggles between the drive to satisfy basic instincts, such as sex or aggression, and the limits imposed by society.

A psychologist is a social scientist who studies behavior and mental processes, usually in a research or clinical setting.
(© Eight Arts Photography / Alamy)

At the same time that Freud's views were gaining popularity in Europe, an American psychology professor, John B. Watson, was pioneering the behavioral approach, which focuses on observing and measuring external behaviors rather than the internal workings of the mind. B. F. Skinner, who spent decades studying the effects of reward and punishment on behavior, helped maintain the predominance of behaviorism in the United States through the 1950s and 1960s. Since the 1970s, many psychologists have been influenced by the cognitive approach, which is concerned with the relationship of mental processes to behavior. Cognitive psychology focuses on how people take in, perceive, and store information, and how they process and act on that information.

Additional psychological perspectives include the neurobiological approach, focusing on relating behavior to internal processes within the brain and nervous system, and the phenomenological approach, which is most concerned with the individual's subjective experience of the world rather than the application of psychological theory to behavior. Although all these approaches differ in their explanations of individual

behavior, each contributes an important perspective to the overall psychological understanding of the total human being. Most psychologists apply the principles of various approaches in studying and understanding human nature.

Along with several approaches to psychology there are also numerous, overlapping subfields in which these approaches may be applied. Most subfields can be categorized under one of two major areas of psychology referred to as basic and applied psychology. Basic psychology encompasses the subfields concerned with the advancement of psychological theory and research. Experimental psychology employs laboratory experiments to study basic behavioral processes, including sensation, perception, learning, memory, communication, and motivation, that different species share. Physiological psychology is concerned with the ways in which biology shapes behavior and mental processes, and developmental psychology is concerned with behavioral development over the entire life span. Other subfields include social psychology, quantitative psychology, and the psychology of personality.

Applied psychology is the area of psychology concerned with applying psychological research and theory to problems posed by everyday life. It includes clinical psychology, the largest single field in psychology. Clinical psychologists—who represent 40% of all psychologists—are involved in psychotherapy and psychological testing. Clinical psychologists are trained in research and often work in university or research settings, studying various aspects of psychology. Like clinical psychologists, counseling psychologists apply psychological principles to diagnose and treat individual emotional and behavioral problems. Other subfields of applied psychology include school psychology, which involves the evaluation and placement of students; educational psychology, which investigates the psychological aspects of the learning process; and industrial and organizational psychology, which study the relationship between people and their jobs. Community psychologists investigate environmental factors that contribute to mental and emotional disorders; health psychologists deal with the psychological aspects of physical illness, investigating the connections between the mind and a person's physical condition; and consumer psychologists study the preferences and buying habits of consumers as well as their reactions to certain advertising.

In response to society's changing needs, new fields of psychology are constantly emerging. One type of specialization, called environmental psychology, focuses on the relationship between people and their physical surroundings. Its areas of inquiry include such issues as the effects of overcrowding and noise on urban dwellers and the effects of building design. Another specialty is forensic psychology, involving the application of psychology to law enforcement and the judicial system. Forensic psychologists may help create personality profiles of criminals, formulate principles for jury selection, or study the problems involved in eyewitness testimony. Yet another emerging area is program evaluation, whose practitioners evaluate the effectiveness and cost efficiency of the programs.

Depending on the nature of their work, psychologists may practice in a variety of settings, including colleges and universities, hospitals and community mental health centers, schools, and businesses. A growing number of psychologists work in private practice and may also specialize in multiple subfields. Most psychologists earn a PhD degree in the field, which requires completion of a four- to six-year post-bachelors' degree program offered by a university psychology department. The course of study includes a broad overview of the field, as well as specialization in a particular subfield, and completion of a dissertation and an internship (usually needed only for applied psychology, such as clinical, counseling, and school psychology). Students who intend to practice only applied psychology rather than conduct research have the option of obtaining a Psy.D. degree, which differs in the limited emphasis that is put on research and a dissertation that does not have to be based on an empirical research study.

Resources

ORGANIZATION

American Psychological Association, 750 1st Street NE, Washington, DC 20002-4242, (202) 336-5500, TTY: (202) 336-6123, (800) 374-2721, http://www.apa.org.

Emily Jane Willingham, PhD

Public education campaigns

Definition

Within the realm of health care, public education campaigns are organized efforts to change unhealthy personal behavior; raise awareness of important public health issues among individuals, families, and the wider community; or inform individuals of healthcare programs, options, and rights of which they may be unaware. These campaigns often utilize a wide range of media technologies to accomplish their goals, including television, radio, mobile phones, magazines and newspapers, billboards and posters, movies, and the Internet.

Description

Government agencies and departments at the local, state, and federal levels are a leading source of public health education campaigns in the United States. These agencies and departments typically have operational mandates to raise general awareness of health issues (such as the value of flu shots), convince individuals to halt or reduce personal behaviors that have negative consequences for the person and wider society (such as smoking), and disseminate information about sources of help for people struggling with different health issues (ranging from cancer to methamphetamine addiction). In addition, federal and state healthcare agencies are responsible for educating consumers about existing and new programs and laws that affect their health care. The **Department of Health and Human**

Services (HHS), for example, has engaged in extensive efforts to educate Americans about the healthcare and insurance provisions contained in the **Patient Protection and Affordable Care Act**, more generally known as "Obamacare."

The educational and outreach efforts of these government agencies are further supplemented by a wide range of public education campaigns sponsored and carried out by nonprofit advocacy organizations and healthcare institutions. The nonprofit American Cancer Society and nonprofit Campaign for Tobacco-Free Kids, for example, both spend millions of dollars every year on anti-smoking advertising campaigns. They have been joined by hospitals and healthcare networks that also target specific health issues. In 2011, for example, Children's Healthcare of Atlanta, one of the most prominent pediatric hospitals in the country, launched a multifaceted wellness campaign called Strong4Life to reverse what the hospital has called an epidemic of childhood obesity and obesity-related diseases in the state of Georgia. Even some insurance companies have invested in health education campaigns, since healthier populations make fewer insurance claims.

Many modern public health education campaigns use graphic words and images and aggressive targeting strategies to get their messages across. Whether these advertisements are meant to foster "safer sex" practices, encourage regular exercise, or convince teens to stay away from methamphetamine, they often employ images and words designed to grab the attention of—or even shock—the viewing audience. Many agencies and organizations say that hard-hitting advertisements are effective precisely because they rise above the level of "background noise" to spark an emotional response. This belief is supported by studies such as a 2008 National Cancer Institute report indicating that public health advertisements with a strong negative message about the consequences of unhealthy personal behavior were more effective than any other form of advertising in eliciting healthier lifestyle choices. Some of these campaigns have been criticized by public health experts and consumers, however, for damaging the self-esteem of precisely the people the ads are trying to help.

As recently as the early 2000s, magazines, newspapers, television, and radio were the primary media formats for public education campaigns concerning health issues. Since that time, television and radio remain important elements of most health education advertising campaigns, but print media have been largely supplanted by digital and online media

---

KEY TERMS

Intervention-style program—A program designed to change the behavior and perspective of the target audience.

Mandate—Official order or responsibility.

---

technologies. The Internet has emerged as a major source for basic health and healthcare information, and online support and discussion groups have become a significant source of comfort for many people and families grappling with substance abuse, chronic health conditions, and other health issues. Meanwhile, many government agencies and nonprofit organizations have made their websites the fulcrum of their wider health education campaigns. Websites are not only ideally suited for low-cost distribution of large volumes of text information, they also are utilized to provide visitors with access to powerful video messages and links to other helpful websites. Public health agencies and health advocacy organizations are also making increasingly extensive use of paid advertising options on social media sites. This approach is attractive because such sites often bring together heavy concentrations of demographic groups that specific campaigns often target (such as ads on parenting sites that remind mothers and fathers about the importance of childhood vaccination).

Why this is important to the consumer

Public education campaigns on health issues benefit consumers in a number of ways, according to health experts. Anti-smoking advertising campaigns and other intervention-style programs have been credited with convincing many people to curtail or end habits and lifestyle choices that threaten their health. Such advertisements have also been cited as motivating factors in keeping people engaged in *positive* lifestyle habits that promote wellness. In addition, studies indicate that public education campaigns often play a key role in keeping consumers of healthcare goods and services educated about patient rights and informed about healthcare programs, laws, and initiatives for which they or their families are eligible.

Resources

BOOKS

Lieberman, D.A. "Using Interactive Media in Communication Campaigns for Children and Adolescents." In R. E. Rice and C. K. Atkin, eds. *Public Communication Campaigns.* 4th ed. Thousand Oaks, CA: Sage, 2013: 273-87.

PERIODICALS

Landen, Rachel, and Ashok Selvam. "Enrollment Challenge: Insurers, Providers Take on Expansion Promotion." *Modern Healthcare* 43, no. 25 (June 24, 2013): 8.

Noar, S.M. "A 10-Year Retrospective of Research in Health Mass Media Campaigns: Where Do We Go From Here?" *Journal of Health Communication* 11, no. 1 (2006): 21-42.

WEBSITES

National Cancer Institute. "Making Health Communication Programs Work: A Planner's Guide." Cancer.gov. 2008. http://www.cancer.gov/cancertopics/cancer library/pinkbook (accessed September 12, 2013).

Rice, Ronald E. "A Brief Overview of the Use of New Media in Health Campaigns and Interventions." Health Games Research, December 2012. http://www.health gamesresearch.org/our-publications/research-briefs/ Use-of-New-Media-in-Health-Campaigns-and-Interventions (accessed September 11, 2013).

ORGANIZATIONS

Johns Hopkins University Center for Communication Programs, 111 Market Place, Ste. 310, Baltimore, MD 21202, (410) 659-6300, Fax: (410) 659-6266, info@ jhuccp.org, http://www.jhuccp.org.

National Prevention Information Network, Centers for Disease Control and Prevention, PO Box 6003, Rockville, MD 20849-6003, (800) 232-4636, info@cdcn pin.org, http://www.cdcnpin.org.

Kevin Hillstrom

Public health

Definition

Public health is the science and clinical practice of population and community-based efforts to prevent disease and disability, and promote physical and mental health. It considers the health of groups, communities, or populations as opposed to the health of individuals.

Description

The science of public health is called epidemiology. It is the study of the occurrence of disease in naturally existing populations, such as nations, cities, or communities. The term "epidemiology" comes from the Greek word epidemic, which means "upon the people." The earliest epidemiologists (public health scientists) worked to prevent the spread of epidemics.

Public health addresses a variety of medical and social issues including:

• environmental health

• nutrition and food safety

• immunization and infectious diseases

• injury and violence prevention

• maternal, infant, and child health

• substance abuse

• chronic disease prevention and treatment

• access, availability, and affordability of health care

• education, screening, and outreach services

Today, epidemiologists gather and analyze information about populations to manage and prevent disease. Epidemiologists are trained in highly specialized research methods: surveillance, investigation, analysis, and evaluation. Surveillance refers to systematic data collection and analysis; it enables the epidemiologists to detect changes that may require investigation. Epidemiological investigation involves observation, detailed descriptions of the problem, documentation of data, and analysis. Evaluation is the process that helps to answer a question, such as "How often should men between the ages of 40 and 60 be screened for hypertension (high blood pressure)?"

By analyzing population data, epidemiologists also are able to describe diseases and determine the factors that cause them. Epidemiology is a quantitative science; it measures rates and proportions. Two commonly used rates are prevalence and incidence rates. Prevalence describes the characteristics of a given population at a specific moment in time; it is like a snapshot.

Incidence describes the rate of development of a disease in a given population over a specified time interval. Incidence offers a longer view of population dynamics, like a video, as opposed to the snapshot offered by the prevalence rate. Epidemiologists also analyze other rates, such as morbidity (disease-related illness) and mortality (death).

Public health practitioners rely on the findings of epidemiologists to develop health services, allocate resources, and determine standards of care. The results of epidemiological studies also influence **health policy.** For example, epidemiological research helps to determine how many health care professionals are needed based on population; the effectiveness of various treatments; and schedules for **immunization** or screening.

History

Historically, public health disease-prevention activities focused primarily on sanitation (also referred to as environmental health) and hygiene. Public health measures aimed to ensure the safety of food and water supplies, and to prevent transmission of communicable (capable of being transmitted) diseases. In some developing countries, these same basic public health problems, such as adequate food supplies and potable (fit to drink) water, continue to threaten health and longevity.

Public health nursing began in the United States during the late 1800s. Public health nurses helped to prevent and manage outbreaks of smallpox, cholera, typhoid, tuberculosis, and other communicable diseases. Today the profession continues to attract nurses interested in community health education and preventive services. Public health nurses (also called community health nurses) work in clinics, schools, voluntary agencies, and provide skilled nursing assessments, visiting nurse services, and **home health care.**

During and after World War II, advances in medicine such as the refinement of antibiotics, cardiac surgery, and physical rehabilitation changed the emphasis of public health in the United States. Federal, state, and local governments enacted legislation to protect public health. Major regulations passed during the twentieth century include:

- the 1938 Food, Drug and Cosmetic Act, which bans distribution of unsafe products and prohibits false advertising
- the 1972 Clean Water Act, which forbids release of pollutants into rivers, streams, and waterways
- the 1974 Safe Drinking Water Acts, which established standards for safe drinking water
- the 1976 Resource Conservation and Recovery Act, which stipulates the safe storage, transport, treatment and disposal of hazardous waste materials
- the 1990 Clean Air Act, which reduced industrial discharge or emission of pollutants into the air and set standards for vehicular emissions

Today, public health practitioners continue to work to prevent disease. However, their efforts are often directed to addressing social issues, such as access to health care and promoting healthy lifestyle change such as smoking cessation, responsible sexual behavior, and violence prevention.

Frequently, public health professionals must work cooperatively with individuals in other disciplines to achieve health-promotion objectives. For example, public health practitioners may work with educators and schools to help combat illiteracy, since persons unable to read may be less able to obtain needed health care services. Similarly, they may work with urban planners and housing specialists to identify health hazards such as lead-based paints or asbestos.

Modern initiatives

The Healthy People 2020 initiative is a national plan to assist states, communities, and professional associations to develop programs to improve health. Coordinated by the Office of Disease Prevention and Health Promotion (ODPHP) of the **Department of Health and Human Services,** the program's goals are to increase quality and years of healthy life and to eliminate **health disparities.** Healthy People 2020 targets many areas for improving the health standards in the United States. They include:

- physical activity
- overweight and obesity
- tobacco use
- substance abuse
- responsible sexual behavior
- mental health
- injury and violence
- environmental quality
- immunization
- access to health care

The goal of "Healthy People 2020" is not only to improve the quality of life for people and help them live longer, but also to eliminate any disparity in health care delivery. The life expectancy of Americans has increased more than 30 years since 1900, with many older Americans living well into their 70s, 80s, and even 90s. Physical health, as well as mental health, has become more and more important as many older adults want to "age in place" and not be forced to live in long-term-care facilities.

Helping Americans maintain good quality of life is only part of the "Healthy People 2020" effort. Disparities still exist among minority groups; minorities have not enjoyed the same health improvement progress as other Americans. Minority Americans have higher rates of diabetes, HIV and AIDS, infant mortality, and heart disease. Life expectancy for these populations is less than that of others, and minority groups living in poverty often do not have access to adequate health care.

The Cooperative Actions for Health Program (CAHP) is a collaborative grant program that is co-sponsored by the American Public Health Association and the American Medical Association (AMA). Its purpose is to build, support, and strengthen state and local collaboration between medical and public health professionals to improve the public's health. The program fosters collaboration through grant funding, developing a communication network to share ideas and coordinate policy-making efforts between the APHA and the AMA.

Providers and agencies

Public health professionals are employed by hospitals, health plans, **managed care organizations,** clinics, medical relief organizations (e.g., American **Red Cross,** American Heart Association, American Cancer Society) and schools as well as federal, state, and local government health departments. Careers in public health include:

- public health nursing
- environmental health technologists and specialists
- restaurant and food safety inspectors
- community health educators
- epidemiologists, biostatisticians, and researchers
- administrators
- patient and consumer health advocates

Federal government agencies that belong to the U.S. Department of Health and Human Services provide many vital public health services. The agencies devoted to health care include the **Health Care Financing Administration (HCFA),** Office of Development Services, **Food and Drug Administration (FDA), National Institutes of Health (NIH),** and the **Centers for Disease Control and Prevention (CDC).**

HCFA administers **Medicare** and **Medicaid,** programs that finance health care services for older adults, persons with disabilities, and those unable to afford medical care. The FDA is the agency responsible for ensuring food, drug, and cosmetic safety. It also enforces labeling practices, so that consumers receive accurate, truthful information about the content, benefits, and risks of products.

Each of the 13 institutes of the NIH is involved in organ or disease-specific research activities. The seven centers of the CDC research and track infectious and other diseases in order to identify sources of disease and prevent their spread.

Why this is important to the consumer

Public health has been fundamental in improving the quality of life and life expectancy of all consumers. From improvements in sewage facilities and refuse collection to safe drinking water and cleaner air, public health has been at the forefront of improvements that help everyone live healthier lives. Public health has also been instrumental in helping to eradicate serious diseases such as polio and small pox that once sickened or killed millions of people. Once such improvements have been made, or diseases have all but disappeared, it is often hard to appreciate what a high toll they once took on health.

Public health professionals continue to monitor to ensure these diseases do not resurface. They also track and study new diseases as they become known, such as bird flu, to help implement policies to reduce or eliminate their spread. Many consumers also benefit from regular public health initiatives such as drives to help consumers stop smoking, exercise more, and eat more healthfully.

KEY TERMS

Communicable—Capable of being transmitted.

Disparity—Inequality or lack of similarity; may be associated with differences in care or treatment.

Epidemiology—The study of disease occurrence in human populations.

Incidence—The rate of development of a disease in a given population over time.

Potable—Safe to drink.

Prevalence—The rate describing the characteristics of a given population at a specific moment in time.

Resources

BOOKS

Gambrill, Eileen. *Critical Thinking in Clinical Practice: Improving the Quality of Judgments and Decisions,*3rd ed. New York, NY: Wiley, 2012.

Mason, Diana J., et al. *Policy & Politics in Nursing and Health Care,*6th ed. New York, NY: Saunders, 2011.

McKenzie, James F., Brad L. Neiger., and Rosemary Thackeray. *Planning, Implementing, & Evaluating Health Promotion Programs.*6th ed., San Francisco, CA: Benjamin Cummings, 2012.

Schimpff, Stephen C., MD.*The Future of Health-Care Delivery: Why It Must Change and How It Will Affect You.*Dulles, VA: Potomac Books Inc, 2012.

PERIODICALS

Edwards, Rhiannon Tudor, Joanna Mary Charles, and Huw Lloyd-Williams. "Public health economics: a systematic review of guidance for the economic evaluation of public health interventions and discussion of key methodological issues." *BMC Public Health* 13 (2013): 1001.

Lurie, Nicole, et al. "Research as a Part of Public Health Emergency Response." *New England Journal of Medicine* 368.13 (2013): 1251-1255.

Price, Julianne R., C. Meade Grigg, and Maggie K. Byrne. "Culture shift: strengthening the role of environmental health in public health performance improvement efforts." *Journal of Environmental Health* 76.3 (2013): 48.

ORGANIZATIONS

American Public Health Association, 800 I. Street, NW, Washington, DC 20001-3710, (202) 777-2532, http://www.apha.org.

United States Centers for Disease Control and Prevention (CDC), 1600 Clifton Road, Atlanta, GA 30333, (404) 639-3534, (800) CDC-INFO (800-232-4636),TTY: (888) 232-6348, inquiry@cdc.gov, http://www.cdc.gov.

U.S. Department of Health and Human Services (USDHHS), Office of Disease Prevention and Health Promotion, 1101 Wootton Parkway, Suite LL100, Rockville, MD 20852, (240) 453-8280, http://odphp.osophs.dhhs.gov.

Meghan M. Gourley
Barbara Wexler
Tish Davidson, AM

Q

Quality improvement initiatives in health care

Definition

Quality improvement (QI) is defined as deliberate, systematic, data-driven activities intended to bring about immediate and lasting improvement in health care delivery in specific settings. Using data to identify quality problems and measure improvements is a hallmark of QI.

QI initiatives are interventions aimed at improving specific dimensions of health care delivery, including population health, outcomes—how patients fare as a result of treatment and the effectiveness and efficiency of health care services and their delivery as well as patients' experiences and satisfaction with care.

QI initiatives address the structure, process, and outcomes of health care services. QI initiatives that are focused on structure seek to improve the characteristics and attributes of settings where care is delivered, in order to improve accessibility, availability, and quality of health care resources. QI initiatives looking at structure might consider the number of primary care physicians serving a population, the bed capacity of an **acute care hospital**, and the number of certified home health aides.

Examples of initiatives that address process—whether evidence-based practices are followed—are the use of clinical practice guidelines to effectively treat patients with hypertension (high blood pressure), development of culturally sensitive health education materials, and efforts to improve patient-provider communication and relationships. Initiatives aimed at improving outcomes generally focus on the impact of care on health status, patient satisfaction, and reducing morbidity (disease) and mortality (deaths).

In health care, quality-improvement initiatives are often instituted in the context of total quality management (TQM) or continuous quality improvement (CQI) programs. TQM is an ongoing, dynamic organizational approach involving management, teamwork, defined processes, systems thinking, and change to create an environment that supports and promotes improvement. It aims to help a health care organization to meet or exceed the needs of health care consumers (patients). TQM requires organization-wide commitment to quality improvement and adherence to a set of management practices to achieve the optimal results.

CQI focuses on the process of care and emphasizes the need to gather and analyze data to improve processes and systems. It is based on the premise that there is an opportunity for improvement in every process and on every occasion. Both TQM and CQI emphasize the importance of management support of quality improvement, clear ongoing communication about challenges and potential solutions and staff empowered to develop and implement quality improvement strategies.

Purpose

QI initiatives focus on effectively addressing and resolving quality problems in health service delivery. The **Agency for Healthcare Research and Quality (AHRQ)** is the **Department of Health and Human Services** agency that supports research to help people make more informed decisions and improves the quality of health care services. AHRQ funding is used to develop research, reports, practical tools, and other initiatives to improve the quality, safety, effectiveness, and efficiency of health care. The AHRQ identifies the types of quality problems in health care that have been documented by research and may be addressed by QI initiatives.

Quality problems in health care include:

- Considerable variation in practice, especially geographic variations, which suggests that **evidence-based practices** are not used uniformly or consistently throughout the nation.
- Underuse of services known to be effective. The AHRQ observes, "Millions of people do not receive necessary care and suffer needless complications that add to costs and reduce productivity."
- Overuse or misuse of services that are unnecessary, duplicative, inappropriate, and even potentially dangerous. Overuse and misuse of services also drive up health care costs.
- Disparities in quality—differences in care and services provide to various populations. Members of ethnic and racial minority populations may be at increased risk of experiencing problems with health care quality.

QI initiatives aim to achieve measurable improvements in the efficiency, effectiveness, performance, accountability, outcomes, and other indicators of quality in services or processes that achieve equity and improve the health of the population served.

Goals and Objectives of QI Initiatives

The goals of QI initiatives are to create an organizational culture of continuous improvement by examining problems, uncovering their root causes, and instituting interventions directly aimed at these root causes. QI initiatives seek to involve staff at all levels of the organization and are continuously assessed—data are collected and analyzed to monitor the progress of the initiatives and determine whether they are resulting in expected outcomes.

Areas for Improvement

The **Institute of Medicine** identifies six domains that identify areas for improvement and serve as goals for QI initiatives. They are:

- Safe—avoiding injuries to patients from the care that is intended to help them.
- Effective—providing services based on scientific knowledge to all who could benefit, and refraining from providing services to those not likely to benefit.
- Patient-centered—providing care that is respectful of, and responsive to, individual patient preferences, needs, and values, and ensuring that patient values guide all clinical decisions.
- Timely—reducing waits and sometimes harmful delays for both those who receive and those who give care.

KEY TERMS

Best practices—Actions that are based on the best evidence available from the relevant literature and clinical experience. New knowledge informs best practices.

Clinical practice guidelines—Recommendations developed by experts intended to optimize patient care that are informed by a systematic review of evidence provide ratings of both the quality of evidence and the strength of the recommendations.

Continuous quality improvement (CQI)—An approach to quality assurance that emphasizes the organization and systems, focuses on processes rather than the individuals, recognizes all stakeholders, and acknowledges the need for objective data to analyze and improve processes.

Quality improvement organization—A group of practicing physicians and other health care experts paid by the federal government to check and improve the care given to people with Medicare.

Total quality management (TQM)—TQM is the integration of an ongoing, dynamic organizational approach involving management, teamwork, defined processes, systems thinking, and change to create an environment that supports and promotes quality improvement.

- Efficient—avoiding waste, including waste of equipment, supplies, ideas, and energy.
- Equitable—providing care that does not vary in quality because of personal characteristics such as gender, ethnicity, geographic location, and socioeconomic status.

Best Practices

One example of a QI initiative is the implementation of best practices, which is the systematic use of the policies, procedures, and actions that have demonstrated the ability to improve outcomes. Although many best practices are based on the results of rigorous research, others are established by professional organizations or collections of experts in a respective field who analyze available data and develop evidence- and consensus-based guidelines for the management of diseases or clinical problems. The use of best practices has been shown to improve patient outcomes and reduce costs.

Public and Private Organizations Champion QI Initiatives

In addition to the QI initiatives instituted by health systems, hospitals, medical groups, and health plans, a number of private and public organizations champion QI initiatives in health care. Private organizations such as the American Medical Association (AMA) Physician Consortium for Performance Improvement (PCPI) and the National Committee for Quality Assurance, along with public initiatives launched and supported by the **Centers for Medicare and Medicaid Services (CMS)**, the **Agency for Healthcare Research and Quality** (AHRQ). The **National Quality Forum (NQF)** has led the development and implementation of QI initiatives. Another ambitious QI initiative, launched in 2006, is the Aligning Forces for Quality (AF4Q) initiative, funded by the Robert Wood Johnson Foundation. AFQ4 is a 10-year initiative with the overarching goals of improving the quality of healthcare and reducing **health disparities** in 16 communities, and providing models for national reform.

Resources

BOOKS

Ransom, E.R., et al. *The Healthcare Quality Book: Vision, Strategy, and Tools.* Chicago, IL: Health Administration Press, 2008.

Shaw, P.L. and C. Elliot. *Quality and Performance Improvement in Healthcare, 5th ed.*, Chicago, IL: American Health Information Management Association, 2012.

Sollecito, W.A. and J.K. Johnson. *Mclaughlin And Kaluzny's Continuous Quality Improvement in Health Care.* Boston, MA: Jones & Bartlett Publishers, 2011.

PERIODICALS

Kaplan, H.C., et al. "The Model for Understanding Success in Quality (MUSIQ): Building a Theory of Context in Healthcare Quality Improvement." *BMJ Quality & Safety* 21 (January 2012):13–20.

Lynn, J., et al. "The ethics of using quality improvement methods in health care." *Annals of Internal Medicine* 146 (May 2007): 666–73.

Muething, S.E., et al. "Quality Improvement Initiative to Reduce Serious Safety Events and Improve Patient Safety Culture." *Pediatrics* 130 (August 2012): 324–35.

Nicolay, C.R., et al. "Systematic review of the application of quality improvement methodologies from the manufacturing industry to surgical healthcare." *British Journal of Surgery* 99 (March 2012): 324–35.

Perla, R.J., E. Bradbury, and C. Gunther-Murphy. "Large-Scale Improvement Initiatives in Healthcare: A Scan of the Literature." *Journal for Healthcare Quality* 35 (January/February 2013): 30–40.

Scanlon, D.P., et al. "Evaluating a Community-Based Program to Improve Healthcare Quality: Research Design for the Aligning Forces for Quality Initiative." *American Journal of Managed Care* 18 (September 22, 2012): 165–76.

WEBSITES

"Identifying Priority Areas for Quality Improvement." Institute of Medicine. http://iom.edu/Activities/Quality/QualityImprovement.aspx (accessed August 31, 2013).

"Improving Health Care Quality: Fact Sheet." Agency for Healthcare Research and Quality. http://www.ahrq.gov/research/findings/factsheets/errors-safety/improving-quality/index.html (accessed August 31, 2013).

"Quality Improvement in Public Health: It Works!" American Public Health Association. http://www.apha.org/NR/rdonlyres/6CC21952-4A55-4E3F-BB51-1BA060BF60FE/0/QI_in_PH_It_Works.pdf (accessed August 31, 2013).

"What Is Quality Improvement?" Health Resources and Services Administration. http://www.hrsa.gov/healthit/toolbox/HealthITAdoptiontoolbox/QualityImprovement/whatisqi.html (accessed August 31, 2013).

ORGANIZATIONS

Agency for Healthcare Research and Quality, (AHRQ), 540 Gaither Road, Suite 2000, Rockville, MD 20850, (301) 427-1104, http://www.ahrq.gov.

The National Quality Forum (NQF), 1030 15th Street NW?Suite 800, Washington, DC 20005, (202) 783-1300, http://www.qualityforum.org.

Barbara Wexler, MPH.

Quality Improvement Organizations (QIOs)

Definition

Quality Improvement Organizations (QIOs) are private contractors that work under the direction of the **Centers for Medicare and Medicaid Services (CMS)** to improve the effectiveness, efficiency, economy, and quality of services delivered to **Medicare** beneficiaries. QIOs review medical care provided through the federal Medicare program, investigate beneficiary complaints about the quality of care, and implement improvements to care-delivery systems. **CMS** maintains a national network of 53 QIOs, one in each state and U.S. territory, staffed by doctors and other medical professionals.

Description

The U.S. Congress established Medicare in 1965 to provide health insurance to Americans age 65 and older, as well as to younger Americans with disabilities.

As of 2010, Medicare covered 48 million people. Congress created the QIO program in 1982 to improve the quality and efficiency of healthcare services provided to Medicare beneficiaries. Under the original legislation (42 U.S.C. § 1320c, et seq.), QIOs were known as "Peer Review Organizations." Although they still perform the traditional function of medical peer review in cases where Medicare providers fail to meet professional standards, QIOs gradually shifted their emphasis toward quality measurement and continuous improvement. Their name was officially changed in the Federal Register in 2002 to reflect this evolving mission.

Most QIOs are private, nonprofit organizations staffed by doctors and other health care professionals who are trained to review medical care, respond to beneficiary complaints, and design and implement improvements to the quality of care. CMS contracts with one QIO in each of the 50 states, as well as one each in the District of Columbia, Puerto Rico, and the U.S. Virgin Islands. All of the QIOs are represented nationally by the American Health Quality Association (AQHA).

The main statutory goals of the Medicare QIO Program include: improving the quality of healthcare services provided to Medicare beneficiaries; safeguarding the Medicare system by ensuring that it pays only for reasonable and necessary medical services; and protecting Medicare beneficiaries by addressing complaints and investigating alleged violations of the Emergency Medical Treatment and Labor Act (EMTALA).

CMS contracts with QIOs in three-year cycles, with the contract start dates for the 53 QIOs staggered into three rounds. During each contract period, CMS identifies specific areas of focus for the QIOs in a Statement of Work (SOW). Varying the emphases of the SOWs every three years enables the Medicare QIO Program to evolve to meet emerging areas of concern in health care.

For example, in the Eighth SOW, which began its first round in August 2005, CMS asked the QIOs to examine necessary clinical and non-clinical measures in nursing homes, home health agencies, and hospital and physician services. It also enlisted the QIOs in rolling out the Doctor's Office Quality Information Technology initiative (DOQ-IT), which assisted small- and medium-sized physicians' offices in adopting **electronic health record** systems to improve access to patient information. The major areas of focus for the Ninth SOW, which took effect in August 2008, included care transitions (improving the quality of care for beneficiaries who transition from one care setting to another),

patient safety, **health disparities** among different demographic groups, and preventive care.

In addition to their work with Medicare providers and beneficiaries, QIOs help CMS coordinate various national healthcare quality improvement initiatives. In 2005, for instance, CMS enlisted the QIOs to launch the Surgical Care Improvement Project (SCIP), which aimed to reduce the rate of adverse outcomes of common surgical procedures performed in hospitals by 25% within five years. QIOs also collect and submit institution-specific quality-measure performance data, which CMS makes available to the public through websites such as **Nursing Home** Compare and Hospital Compare.

In turn, the Medicare QIO Program is required to evaluate its own performance and submit an annual report to Congress detailing its costs and impact. At the conclusion of the Ninth SOW in 2011, CMS hired Mathematica Policy Research to conduct an independent evaluation of the QIO Program. CMS took this step in response to a 2006 report by the **Institute of Medicine** (IOM) entitled *Medicare's Quality Improvement Program: Maximizing Potential*. Following the recommendations of the IOM report and the external review of the Medicare QIO Program, CMS implemented a number of changes designed to strengthen its oversight of the program and align it to meet the future needs of Medicare providers and beneficiaries.

Why this is important to the consumer

The Medicare QIO Program helps ensure the quality, safety, efficiency, and cost-effectiveness of healthcare services provided to 48 million Medicare beneficiaries across the United States and its territories. QIOs bring healthcare quality improvement resources and expertise to the community level, resulting in better health for patients and lower costs for taxpayers.

Resources

BOOKS

Institute of Medicine. *Medicare's Quality Improvement Organization Program: Maximizing Potential.* Washington, D.C.: National Academies Press, 2006.

PERIODICALS

Rollow, William, et al. "Assessment of the Medicare Quality Improvement Organization Program." *Annals of Internal Medicine* 145, no. 5 (2006): 342-53. http://annals.org/article.aspx?articleid = 727999 (accessed September 5, 2013).

Shortell, Stephen M., and William A. Peck. "Enhancing the Potential of Quality Improvement Organizations to Improve Quality of Care." *Annals of Internal Medicine* 145, no. 5 (2006): 388-89. http://annals.org/article.aspx?articleid = 728270 (accessed September 5, 2013).

WEBSITES

American Health Lawyers Association. "QIO: Quality Improvement Organizations." HealthLawyers.org. http://www.healthlawyers.org/hlresources/Health%20Law%20Wiki/QIO%20%28-Quality%20Improvement%20Organizations%29.aspx(accessed September 5, 2013).

American Health Quality Association. "About the QIOs." AHQA.org. http://www.ahqa.org/pub/qios/241_1135_5722.cfm (accessed September 5, 2013).

Centers for Medicare and Medicaid Services. "Quality Improvement Organizations." CMS.gov. http://www.cms.hhs.gov/QualityImprovementOrgs/01_Overview.asp (accessed September 5, 2013).

Quality Net. "QIO Directory." http://www.qualitynet.org/dcs/ContentServer?pagename = QnetPublic%2FPage%2FQnetTier2&cid = 1144767874793 (accessed September 5, 2013).

ORGANIZATIONS

American Health Quality Association, 1776 I Street, NW, 9th Floor, Washington, DC 20006, (202) 331-5790, info@ahqa.org, http://www.ahqa.org.

Laurie Collier Hillstrom

Quality measures in health care
Definition

The **Agency for Healthcare Research and Quality** (the **Department of Health and Human Services** agency that supports research to help people make more informed decisions and improves the quality of health care services) defines two major categories of quality measures in health care: indicators used to assess health care delivery and indicators to assess population health. Assessing the quality of health care delivery entails evaluating the performance of individual providers and practitioners, health care teams, delivery organizations, and health insurance plans in the provision of care to their patients or enrollees.

The **Center for Medicare and Medicaid Services (CMS)** defines quality measures as tools that help to track and quantify the quality of healthcare services. These measures use a variety of data that are associated with a health care provider's ability to deliver quality care and compare these data to evidence-based criteria associated with quality.

Quality measures are used to assess multiple aspects of health care, including health outcomes—how patients fare as a result of treatment, clinical processes—how care is delivered, patient safety, and the efficient use of healthcare resources. Quality measures also consider continuity and coordination of care, population and public health, and adherence to clinical practice guidelines—how closely providers follow recommendations developed by experts intended to optimize patient care. Clinical practice guidelines are informed by a systematic review of evidence, and they generally provide ratings of both the quality of evidence supporting the recommendation and the strength of the recommendation.

Types of Quality Measures

One specific type of quality measure is a clinical performance measure, which is a gauge used to determine the timeliness of service delivery and the extent to which a provider safely and competently delivers the appropriate clinical services. Clinical performance measures are used to assess the actions and conduct of individual health care practitioners, facilities, institutions, organizations, and health insurance plans.

Another type of quality measure is a population health quality measure that evaluates the provision of health care services to an entire population. Assessing population health involves evaluating the impact of health programs or services on the health of a specific population—persons identified by geographic location, organizational affiliation, or other characteristics. Population measures are calculated using persons eligible for a specific public health service or intervention in the denominator, and those who receive the service or intervention in the numerator. For example, the proportion of people age 50 and older who have had a colonoscopy (examination of the inner lining of the colon to detect changes or abnormalities) is a population health quality measure.

Purpose

Quality measures serve several purposes in health care. They may be used to determine baseline values or levels that may be compared to local, regional, or national standards, or they may be used to track the progress of a quality-improvement initiative—to see whether a targeted intervention improves the process or outcome of health care delivery.

Most quality measures examine the structure, process, and outcomes of health care services. Quality measures of structure track and quantify the characteristics and attributes of settings where care is delivered in order to assess accessibility, availability and quality of health care resources. QI measures of structure might consider the number of primary care physicians or specialists serving a population, the bed capacity of an **acute care hospital**, and the number of advanced practice nurses.

Quality measures also are used to evaluate processes—how health care is delivered. For example, these measures seek to determine the extent to which evidence-based practices are followed and to answer questions such as "Are clinical practice guidelines used to effectively manage patients with diabetes?" Process measures also may be used to understand patients' perspectives on the care they receive. For example, they may be used to find out whether patients are satisfied with the communication they have with their health care providers and whether they feel they are treated respectfully.

Another process measure is access to care—the timeliness and appropriateness of care provided to patients or to a population such as the enrollees of a managed care plan or the residents of a particular community. Access measures reflect quality when there is evidence that access to care exerts an influence on health outcomes or patient satisfaction with care.

Examples of quality measures that focus on health outcomes—the impact of care on health status—are utilization rates, hospital admission and readmission rates, morbidity (disease), and mortality (deaths).

How Quality Measures Are Used

Quality measures are crucial elements in quality improvement (QI) programs in institutions or health care systems such as hospitals and health plans or

across institutions or systems to assess quality throughout a geographic region. When quality measures are used in a QI program, the institution or organization usually obtains a baseline measurement to understand the nature and extent of the problem and to establish a basis for comparison after instituting a QI initiative. Ongoing quality measures allow for scrutiny of a problem or issue and its resolution over time.

Quality measures are used for accountability to health care payers and purchasers as well as to regulatory agencies and professional organizations. Agencies such as state or local health departments, independent quality-improvement organizations as well as accreditation and certification boards and organizations use these quality measures to verify that health care providers meet established standards and to select and reward providers based on their performance.

Healthcare consumers also use quality measures to inform their purchases. For example, the Centers for Medicare and Medicaid Services (CMS) operate the Hospital Compare Web site, which provides select hospital performance data to the public. Consumers can compare hospital performance based on a defined set of measures. Other web sites enable consumers to compare physicians and health plans.

Another important use of quality measures is to conduct research about health care delivery and the influence of changes in practice, procedures, and policy of quality of care. For example, many quality measures, such as the number of persons with health insurance and measures of access to care, will help to evaluate the effects of implementation of the 2010 Affordable Care Act on the quality of health care in the United States.

Resources

BOOKS

Dhillon, B.S. *Reliability Technology, Human Error, and Quality in Health Care.* Boca Raton, FL: CRC Press, 2008.

Ransom, E.R., et al. *The Healthcare Quality Book: Vision, Strategy, and Tools.* Chicago, IL: Health Administration Press, 2008.

Shaw, P.L. and C. Elliot. *Quality and Performance Improvement in Healthcare, 5th ed.* Chicago, IL: American Health Information Management Association, 2012.

U.S. Department of Health and Human Services. *Measures of Patient Safety Based on Hospital Administrative Data—The Patient Safety Indicators: Technical Review 5.* CreateSpace Independent Publishing Platform, 2013.

PERIODICALS

Chen, L.M., et al. "Composite Quality Measures for Common Inpatient Medical Conditions." *Medical Care* 51 (September 2013): 832–837.

Kaplan, H.C., et al. "The Model for Understanding Success in Quality (MUSIQ): building a theory of context in healthcare quality improvement." *BMJ Quality & Safety* 21 (January 2012):13–20.

Lynn, J., et al. "The ethics of using quality improvement methods in health care." *Annals of Internal Medicine* 146 (May 2007): 666–673.

Manary, M.P., et al. "The Patient Experience and Health Outcomes." *The New England Journal of Medicine* 368 (January 2013): 201–203.

Muething, S.E., et al. "Quality Improvement Initiative to Reduce Serious Safety Events and Improve Patient Safety Culture." *Pediatrics* 130 (August 2012): 324–335.

Scanlon D.P., et al. "Evaluating a Community-Based Program to Improve Healthcare Quality: Research Design for the Aligning Forces for Quality Initiative." *American Journal of Managed Care* 18 (September 22, 2012): 165–176.

WEBSITES

Agency for Healthcare Research and Quality. Varieties of Measures in NQMC. http://www.qualitymeasures.ahrq.gov/tutorial/varieties.aspx (accessed August 31, 2013).

American Public Health Association. Quality Improvement in Public Health: It Works! http://www.apha.org/NR/rdonlyres/6CC21952-4A55-4E3F-BB51-1BA060BF60FE/0/QI_in_PH_It_Works.pdf (accessed August 31, 2013).

Center for Medicare & Medicaid Services. Clinical Quality Measures (CQM). http://www.cms.gov/Regulations-and-Guidance/Legislation/EHRIncentivePrograms/ClinicalQualityMeasures.html (accessed August 31, 2013).

Health Resources and Services Administration. What Is Quality Improvement? http://www.hrsa.gov/healthit/toolbox/HealthITadoptiontoolbox/QualityImprovement/whatisqi.html (accessed August 31, 2013).

Institute of Medicine. Identifying Priority Areas for Quality Improvement. http://iom.edu/Activities/Quality/QualityImprovement.aspx (accessed August 31, 2013).

ORGANIZATIONS

Agency for Healthcare Research and Quality, (AHRQ), 540 Gaither Road, Suite 2000, Rockville, MD 20850, (301) 427-1104, http://www.ahrq.gov.

The National Quality Forum (NQF), 1030 15th Street NW, Suite 800, Washington, DC 20005, (202) 783-1300, http://www.qualityforum.org.

Barbara Wexler, MPH.

R

Red Cross

Definition

Red Cross is a term referring to organizations under the umbrella of the International Committee of the Red Cross, including the International Red Cross and Red Crescent organizations and individual national societies such as the American Red Cross.

Red Cross organizations are largely independent but remain united under a common goal of providing humanitarian efforts that alleviate human suffering and promote public health.

Description

The International Committee of the Red Cross (ICRC) is an international humanitarian movement

The American Red Cross, part of the International Committee of the Red Cross, provides an extensive range of services both domestically and abroad, with a special emphasis on disaster relief. *(Getty Images)*

with approximately 97 million volunteers, members, and staff worldwide. Headquartered in Geneva, Switzerland, the ICRC operates in five global zones (Africa, Americas, Asia Pacific, Europe, and the Middle East/North Africa) with more than 60 distinct delegations.

The International Red Cross has its roots in a 19th-century movement led by Swiss citizen Jean Henri Dunant to provide better, faster, and more coordinated care for injured soldiers. Founded in 1863, the Red Cross served to provide more humane treatment of the wounded as well as provide a protective measure of neutrality to medical workers by way of an internationally recognized emblem: a red cross on a white background, or the colors of the Swiss flag reversed. Additional emblems were eventually recognized to represent a broader range of nationalities and belief systems, including the Red Crescent (1929) and the Red Crystal (2007).

The membership of the International Red Cross includes representatives from each national society as well as several international committees. Over 180 countries have instituted national Red Cross societies that are self-governing organizations charged to meet the needs of their most vulnerable populations.

The American Red Cross

The American Red Cross was organized in 1881 by Clara Barton, a teacher and nurse who had spent time in Europe volunteering for humanitarian work with the International Red Cross. Upon returning to the United States, Barton set out to create an American chapter of the Red Cross, ultimately becoming its first president and taking personal charge of the organization's relief efforts for more than 23 years. The American Red Cross received its first congressional charter in 1900; while it has been revised several times, the charter has remained true to its founding princi-ples of impartiality, compassion, mobilization, and generosity.

The headquarters of the American Red Cross are located in Washington, DC, and oversee a network of more than 650 chapters and blood services regions. The president of the United States holds the role of honorary chairman of the American Red Cross, and is responsible for the appointment of the organization's president and other board members. The American Red Cross is not a federal agency, however, and is funded by way of voluntary public contributions as well as revenues from fee-based services such as health and safety training courses.

Why this is important to the consumer

The American Red Cross provides an extensive range of services both domestically and abroad, with a

---

KEY TERMS

Automated external defibrillator (AED)—A portable electronic device that has the ability to diagnose and treat several cardiac abnormalities, with only minimal training on the part of the user.

Cardiopulmonary resuscitation (CPR)—A medical technique that can be performed in certain emergency situations (such as cardiac arrest) to create artificial circulation by manually pumping blood through the heart.

---

special emphasis on disaster relief, services to the armed forces and veterans, and public health and safety programs. These services include:

- Disaster relief: Each year the American Red Cross responds to roughly 70,000 natural and man-made disasters in the United States, ranging from fires and transportation accidents to earthquakes and hurricanes. The Red Cross helps to meet immediate emergency needs during a time of disaster, such as shelter for displaced individuals or meals for emergency care workers.

- Support for military families: The American Red Cross works to service members and their families with greater moral and physical support both abroad and stateside. Services include connecting families with advanced communication technology, providing support services to wounded warriors, and helping military families cope with day-to-day challenges.

- Health and safety training: The American Red Cross provides a broad range of safety courses and certification programs to help people in all roles and settings respond to emergency situations. Courses include first aid, cardiopulmonary resuscitation (CPR), automated external defibrillator (AED) training, lifeguard training, and babysitting.

- Blood supply and services: The American Red Cross is the largest blood collection organization in the United States, supplying more than 40 percent of the country's blood and blood products. An extensive network of volunteers and employees helps to collect and distribute 9.5 million blood products each year to patients at approximately 3,000 hospitals and transfusion centers across the country.

- International services: As part of the global Red Cross and Red Crescent network, the American Red Cross helps to respond to overseas disasters, support global vaccination programs, reconnect families in times of war, and educate future humanitarians.

Resources

BOOKS

Irwin, Julia F. *Making the World Safe: The American Red Cross and a Nation's Humanitarian Awakening*. New York, NY: Oxford University Press, 2013.

PERIODICALS

Delano, Jane A. "The Red Cross." *American Journal of Nursing* 11, no. 8 (May 1911): 626–8.

WEBSITES

American Red Cross. "Our History." RedCross.org. http://www.redcross.org/about-us/history (accessed October 20, 2013).

Delbanco, Andrew. "The Angel of the Battlefield." NYT imes.org. http://www.nytimes.com/1994/06/12/books/the-angel-of-the-battlefield.html (accessed October 20, 2013).

International Committee of the Red Cross. "Our History." ICRC.org. http://www.icrc.org/eng/who-we-are (accessed October 20, 2013).

ORGANIZATIONS

American Red Cross, 2025 E St. NW, Washington, DC 20006, (202) 303-4498, (800) 733-2767, http://www.redcross.org.

International Committee of the Red Cross, 19 Avenue de la paix CH, 1202 Geneva, Switzerland, + 41 22 734 60 01, Fax: + 41 22 733 20 57, http://www.icrc.org.

Stephanie Dionne

Rehabilitation hospital

Definition

A rehabilitation hospital is a facility that provides 24-hour-a-day care and therapy to individuals who are recovering from a debilitating illness, injury, or surgery.

Description

Rehabilitation hospitals do not provide care during the acute phase of an illness or injury. People are admitted to rehabilitation hospitals after they have been stabilized in an acute care setting. Most rehabilitation hospitals have specific criteria in place specifying that patients will be considered for admission if

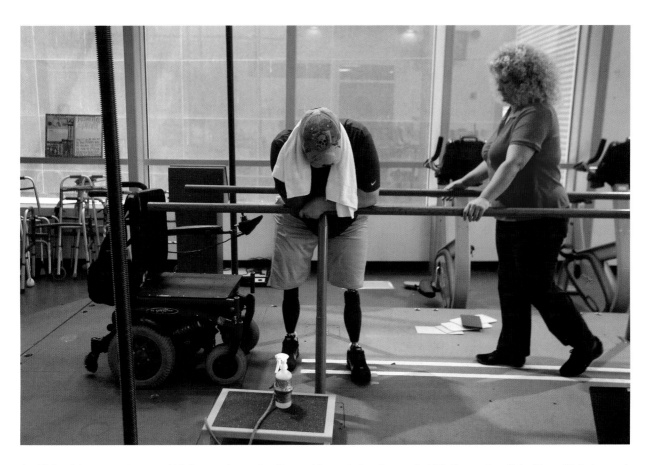

An Afghanistan war veteran and triple amputee rests after working out at an Army rehabilitation center. *(John Moore/Getty Images)*

they have at least two areas of deficit in the domains of mobility, activities of daily living, speech and language, cognitive functioning, and/or swallowing. In addition, patients must have the capacity to be reasonably cooperative and able to engage in the intensive therapy that will be provided.

The goal of a rehabilitation hospital is to help return people to either their baseline level of functioning or the most optimal level possible. Some of the most common reasons for hospitalization in a rehabilitation hospital include:

• Stroke or other neurological event
• Hip replacement surgery
• Amputation
• Severely debilitating medical illness
• Head injury
• Spinal cord injury
• Other orthopedic injury

An individual's time in a rehabilitation hospital is necessarily very active. Days are usually filled with a variety of therapies, including:

• Physical therapy: To improve strength, balance, and the ability to walk; to learn how to safely get in and out of chairs and bed; to learn how to utilize assistive devices such as walkers, crutches
• Occupational therapy: To work on activities of daily living and improve independence with dressing, self-care, cooking, and other household tasks.
• Speech therapy: To work on the ability to talk and understand speech; may also work on swallowing with people whose injury or illness may have left them at risk of choking when eating or drinking.
• Psychological support: Provides individual and/or group psychotherapy to help individuals learn to cope with changes in their level of functioning.

The type of physician who oversees the care in a rehabilitation hospital is termed a "physiatrist." A physiatrist is specially trained in physical medicine and rehabilitation. He or she has a great deal of knowledge of muscle, bone, and nerve disorders, and works collaboratively with the team of physical therapists, occupational therapists, speech therapists, psychologists, and social workers who carry out the specific forms of therapy.

Why this is important to the consumer

Strokes are a leading cause of death and disability in the United States; every year, nearly 800,000 people have a stroke. The American Stroke Association has stated that perhaps 60-80% of stroke victims could

---

KEY TERMS

Occupational therapy—Therapy aimed at recovering the ability to independently attend to the activities of daily living, such as dressing, eating, bathing, and toiling, as well as more complex activities such as shopping, cooking, cleaning, and doing laundry.

Physiatrist—A physician who has specialized training in physical medicine and rehabilitation.

Physical therapy—Therapy aimed at recovering the ability to improve gross motor skills, such as mobility, balance, and muscle strength.

Speech therapy—Therapy aimed at improving an individual's ability to speak and/or understand speech. Speech therapy also assists individuals who have difficulty swallowing and are therefore at risk of aspiration and lung injury while eating or drinking.

---

benefit from intensive rehabilitation aimed at improving functionality and independence. About 11,000 new spinal cord injuries and 1.7 million traumatic brain injuries occur annually. Rehabilitation programs increase functionality and independence, and decrease hospital readmission rates in these individuals.

Resources

BOOKS

Kovner Anthony R. et al. *Health Care Delivery in the United States* 10th ed. New York: Springer Publishing Company, 2011.

Schulte,Margaret F.*Health Care Delivery in the U.S.A.: An Introduction* 2nd ed. New York: Productivity Press, 2012.

Sultz, Harry A. et al. *Health Care USA: Understanding Its Organization and Delivery* 7th ed. Sudbury, MA: Jones & Bartlett Learning, 2010.

WEBSITES

National Caregivers Library. Types of Care Facilities [accessed September 22, 2013]. http://www.caregivers library.org/caregivers-resources/grp-care-facilities/types-of-care-facilities-article.aspx.

USA.gov. Choosing a Health Care Facility. 2013 [accessed September 22, 2013]. http://www.usa.gov/topics/health/caregivers/health-care-facility.shtml.

ORGANIZATIONS

Association of Academic Physiatrists, 7250 Parkway Drive, Suite 130., Hanover, MD 21076, (410) 712-7120, http://www.physiatry.org//.

American Stroke Association, 7272 Greenville Ave., Dallas, TX 20001, (888) 478- 7653, http://www.strokeassociation.org/STROKEORG//.

Brain Injury Association of America, 1608 Spring Hill Rd., Suite 110, Vienna, VA 22182, (703) 761-0750, http://www.biausa.org/.

The National Spinal Cord Injury Association, 75-20 Astoria Blvd., Jackson Heights, NY 11370, (718) 803-3782, http://www.spinalcord.org/.

United States Department of Labor, 200 Constitution Ave. NW, Washington, DC 20210, (800) 321-6742, https://www.osha.gov/.

Rosalyn Carson-DeWitt, MD

Rural healthcare outreach programs

Definition

A rural healthcare outreach program is a general term for programs operated and/or funded by state or federal governmental agencies that seek to help healthcare providers and patients in rural areas of the United States. Prominent examples of these efforts include special **Medicare** payment provisions for rural hospitals and clinics; the Medicare Rural Hospital Flexibility Grant Program and the Small Rural Hospital Improvement Program, both of which are under the purview of the Office of Rural Health Policy (ORHP); the Rural Health Care Program, which is maintained by the Federal Communications Commission (FCC); and state-level Offices of Rural Health. These and other programs are important tools in America's efforts to ensure that residents of the nation's rural communities retain access to needed healthcare services.

Description

Rural hospitals, clinics, and other healthcare providers typically operate under fundamentally different financial conditions from their counterparts in metropolitan areas. Since the pool of patients in lightly populated rural areas is smaller than in big cities or sprawling suburbs, rural healthcare facilities and practices are smaller in size, have smaller financial reserves,

Rural health care outreach programs are operated and/or funded by state or federal governmental agencies and seek to help patients and healthcare providers in rural areas of the United States. This health mobile is operated by the Veterans Administration. (© ZUMA Press, Inc. / Alamy)

and often cannot offer the same range of medical services and staff specialization that patients can find at larger metropolitan healthcare facilities.

The limited capacity of rural medical care facilities to invest in the latest medical technology and retain medical specialists on staff is further exacerbated by the unique challenges of treating rural Americans who need medical interventions. In terms of demographics, rural communities have a higher percentage of elderly patients grappling with medical conditions that emerge with advancing age. These patients usually obtain treatment through Medicare or **Medicaid** rather than through **private insurance plans** that sometimes offer more generous compensation to healthcare providers. In addition, Medicare payments to rural hospitals and physicians have historically not matched those made to their urban counterparts for equivalent services. Rural residents are also less likely than their urban or suburban counterparts to be covered by Medicaid or employer-provided healthcare coverage.

Medical treatment of rural populations poses other challenges as well. Studies indicate that people in rural areas frequently do not seek attention for medical problems until they have become quite serious—and thus more expensive to treat. Experts attribute this dynamic to the fact that rural residents are reluctant to travel the long distances that are necessary to get even routine checkups and screenings. Rural Americans are also at greater risk of certain types of serious injury that require substantial medical intervention, including motor vehicle accidents and gunshot wounds. Finally, rural Americans are, on average, more likely to engage in behavior that can damage health, including drinking and driving, regular use of tobacco (either cigarettes or smokeless), and poor dietary choices.

All of these considerations have led federal lawmakers and agencies to establish a variety of rural healthcare outreach programs designed to help rural healthcare providers and patients.

Special Designations for Medicare Rural Providers

The HHS's **Centers for Medicare and Medicaid Services (CMS)** maintains special payment policies for qualified rural health providers who would struggle to keep their doors open and provide high-quality services if forced to operate under traditional Medicare payment plans. Special designations for rural healthcare facilities are as follows:

- Critical Access Hospital (CAH)—Small rural hospitals with fewer than 25 acute care beds located at least 35 miles from another hospital (or 15 miles over mountainous terrain or via secondary roads).
- Disproportionate Share Hospital (DSH)—Rural hospitals that serve a disproportionate number of low-income patients not covered by Medicare, Medicaid, the Children's Health Insurance Program (CHIP), or other health insurance.
- Rural Health Clinic (RHC)—Rural clinics that receive payment on a cost-related basis for outpatient treatment.
- Rural Referral Center (RRC)—Larger high-volume rural hospitals that receive significant numbers of referrals from other smaller rural hospitals in the region.
- Sole Community Hospital (SCH)—Rural hospitals with fewer than 50 acute care beds located at least 50 miles from the nearest hospital.

ORHP Grant Programs

The ORHP, which is a part of the Health Resources and Services Administration (HRSA) within the **Department of Health and Human Services (HHS)**, administers a variety of financial grant programs for rural hospitals and coordinates other activities related to rural health care. It also advised the HHS Secretary on all healthcare issues related to rural communities, including the impact of Medicare and Medicaid policy changes on rural patients and healthcare providers.

The best-known ORHP financial assistance program for rural healthcare providers is the Medicare Rural Hospital Flexibility Grant Program (Flex). Established in 1997, this program provides funding to individual states to support **critical access hospitals** in rural communities. Rural hospitals that qualify for CAH status receive additional Medicare reimbursements for most inpatient and outpatient services they provide to Medicare patients. The Flex program also provides funding to aid different types of rural healthcare providers, including CAHs, emergency medical services (EMS), clinics, and physicians, in developing cooperative, integrated systems of health care for members of their communities. Flex funds are also used to aid rural hospitals in meeting their operating expenses. One similar but smaller ORHP initiative is the Rural Health Network Development Planning Grant Program, which provides one-year grants for communities to develop integrated clinical, information, administrative, and financial networks that produce cost savings and increased efficiencies for member healthcare organizations.

Another notable ORHP grant program is the Rural Health Care Services Outreach (Outreach) Program, which provides a variety of services that do not involve inpatient care to rural communities. These outreach efforts include health screenings, health fairs and wellness campaigns, and other healthcare education initiatives. Funding priority is given to program models with a proven capacity to improve health in rural communities and practice models that have shown encouraging results in enhancing and sustaining delivery of quality healthcare in rural communities. Outreach dollars may go to programs that meet a wide range of healthcare needs for an assortment of population groups, from **case management** for young HIV patients and prenatal care for pregnant women to expanded oral and mental health services.

The OHRP's Rural Health Network Development Planning Grant (Network Planning) program provides funding to encourage the planning and development of formal healthcare networks in rural areas. Specifically, the Network Planning program provides grants for applicants to develop the necessary intellectual and financial infrastructure for such networks, including business plans, needs assessments, reviews of technology readiness and compatibility, and implementation plans. Network planning funds are not used for the direct delivery of either inpatient or outpatient healthcare services.

Other ORHP grant programs include the Rural Health Information Technology Network Development (RHITND) Program, which supports rural healthcare networks in the adoption and effective use of electronic medical records; special programs to detect and screen black lung disease and radiation exposure; the Small Health Care Provider Quality Improvement (Rural Quality) Grant Program, which seeks to help rural primary care providers develop more effective and beneficial strategies for chronic **disease management**; and the Small Rural Hospital Improvement Program (SHIP), which provides financial support to small rural hospitals (49 beds or fewer) seeking to upgrade their health information technology resources.

ORHP is also the home of the Office for the Advancement of Telehealth, which promotes the use of so-called **telehealth** technologies for healthcare delivery, education, and health information services through financial grants and technical assistance. Telehealth is an umbrella term for digital information and telecommunication technologies that support long-distance clinical health care and health education (for both healthcare professionals and patients). Telehealth technologies include streaming media, videoconferencing, Web-based education, wireless communications, and store-and-forward imaging.

Other ORHP pilot programs of limited duration have also been undertaken in recent years, such as the Rural Health Workforce Development Program. This three-year program, which ended in August 2013, assisted underserved rural communities in recruiting medical students and residents to pursue their education and training at facilities in those communities, with the hope of retaining those young professionals when they establish their careers and practices.

State Offices of Rural Health

The Office of Rural Health Policy also administers grants to rural healthcare providers through its State Offices of Rural Health Grant (SORH) Program. First developed in 1991, the SORH program is a federal-state matching-fund partnership. Offices of Rural Health work as clearinghouses of information on rural health services delivery issues. They also coordinate state-level rural health programs to avoid redundancies in state-level action, provide technical assistance to public and private healthcare providers, and promote the recruitment and retention of physicians, nurses, and other healthcare professionals in rural settings.

State Offices of Rural Health also administer most CAH programs. Other responsibilities typically include loan-repayment programs, administration of public health conferences and other information-exchange efforts, grant writing assistance, and support for health clinics and emergency medical services in rural communities.

FCC Rural Health Outreach Programs

The Federal Communications Commission (FCC) maintains a Rural Health Care Program that provides funding to eligible health care providers for telecommunications and broadband services. The Program consists of four distinct programs: the Healthcare Connect Fund, the Telecommunications Program, the Internet Access Program, and the Rural Health Pilot Program.

The Healthcare Connect Fund is the most prominent of these programs. It fosters high-capacity broadband connectivity among rural health care providers, including the formation of state and regional broadband networks, by offering deep discounts on the purchase of broadband services and equipment. The Fund also includes a pilot program to explore ways to support broadband connectivity in skilled nursing facilities.

KEY TERMS

Acute care—Intensive but short-term treatment for a serious injury or illness.

Inpatient—A patient who is admitted to a hospital while undergoing medical treatment.

Outpatient—A patient who receives medical treatment without being admitted to a hospital.

Referrals—Sending a patient to another medical facility or specialist for further treatment.

Why this is important to the consumer

Rural healthcare outreach programs provide important financial assistance and educational resources to rural healthcare providers, enabling them to expand the quality and breadth of services they provide to rural Americans. Without these grants, educational campaigns, and special payment arrangements, the quality of health care available to people living in the more sparsely populated regions of the United States would be dramatically reduced.

Resources

BOOKS

Talley, Ronda C., Kathleen Chwalisz, and Kathleen C. Buckwalter, eds. *Rural Caregiving in the United States: Research, Practice, Policy*. New York: Springer, 2011.

PERIODICALS

Colias, Mike. "Rural Areas Still Not Wired for Digital Health Care: FCC Pilot Program Highlights the Need to Close the Broadband Gap." *Hospitals & Health Networks (H&HN)* 86, no. 9 (September 2012): 18.

Hanratty, Rebecca, et al. "Reaching individuals at risk for cardiovascular disease through community outreach in Colorado." *Preventive Medicine* 52.1 (2011): 84.

WEBSITES

Office of Rural Health Policy. "Rural Health." U.S. Department of Health and Human Services, Health Resources and Services Administration. www.hrsa.gov/ruralhealth/index.html (accessed August 25, 2013)

Rural Assistance Center. "Critical Access Hospitals." RAC Online, last reviewed September 25, 2012.http://www.raconline.org/topics/critical-access-hospitals/ (accessed August 25, 2013).

ORGANIZATIONS

National Rural Health Association, 4501 College Blvd., No. 225, Leawood, KS 66211-1921, (816) 756-3140, Fax: (816) 756-3144, mail@NRHArural.org, http://www.ruralhealthweb.org.

Office of Rural Health Policy, 5600 Fishers Lane, Rockville, MD 20857, (888) 275-4772, ask@hrsa.gov, http://www.hrsa.gov.

Rural Assistance Center, School of Medicine and Health Sciences Room 4520, 501 North Columbia Road Stop 9037, Grand Forks, ND 58202-9037, (800) 270-1898, Fax: (800) 270-1913, info@raconline.org, http://www.raconline.org.

Kevin Hillstrom

S

SBC *see* **Summary of Benefits and Coverage (SBC)**

▋School-based health care

Definition

For more than a century, schools have been important venues for the administration of health care. School nurses have long been a feature in public and private schools, there to assist if students fall ill and need to go home. But school-based health care is more than just giving out cough drops. Today, school-based health care aims to provide students with all the health care they need, at the logical place: the school where they come every day. Yet, fewer than half of public schools have a full-time nurse on staff.

Description

The history of health professionals in schools dates to the 1890s, when physicians went into schools in Boston and New York City to examine children and determine who might be carrying potentially contagious diseases. School health services spread throughout the first decade of the 1900s but ran into opposition from the American Medical Association in 1910. However, school continued to be an important source of health education and care for children, especially those who had little or no access to health care otherwise. From the 1920s through the 1950s, schools played an important role in making sure that children received necessary immunizations and basic screenings, such as for vision problems, as well as care for minor injuries.

By the 1960s, the face of school-based health care began changing. The federal government mandated that schools provide healt hcare for students with disabilities. New types of health care providers became available, including nurse practitioners, who are registered nurses who have received advanced training and are qualified to treat certain conditions independent of a physician.

The 1970s and 1980s saw the development of **school-based health centers** (SBHCs). Their growth was encouraged by the Robert Wood Johnson Foundation, which funds the Center for Health and Health Care in Schools.

The health care services provided through schools vary. Many schools may have the traditional form of a nurse or **nurse practitioner** with an office at the school. The nurse or NP delivers emergency care in the case of accident, injury, or allergic reaction. The nurse assesses student health status and identifies hearing and vision problems that can affect students' ability to learn. School nurses also provide health counseling and education, including the simple, but effective, infection-control measures of hand-washing and sneezing into the sleeve that help prevent the spread of germs.

Purpose

School-based health care plays a vital role in keeping students healthy, and studies have shown healthy students learn better. In addition, many students come to school with health conditions that must be monitored and taken care of during the course of the school day. For example, approximately 13% are on prescription medication, 10% have asthma, and 5% have food allergies. Among older students, the concerns include illicit drug use (reported by 47% of high school seniors) and sexual activity (reported by 65% of high school seniors).

School nurses are on the front lines of public health, and a good nurse can spot trends that are cause for concern. In New York City, a school nurse named Mary Pappas was alarmed at the number of

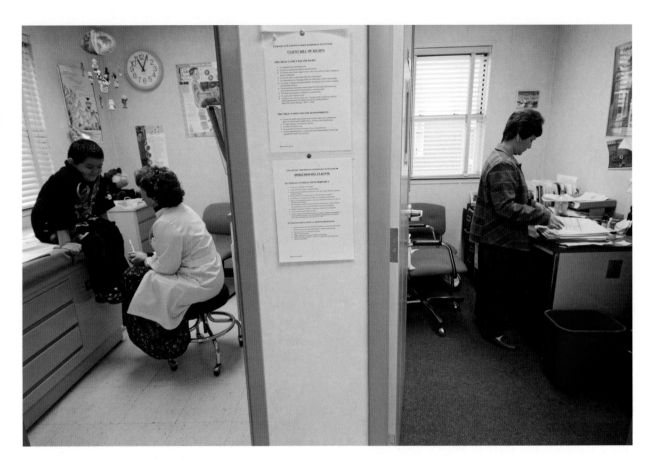

Fewer than half of public schools have a full-time nurse on staff. *(© RGB Ventures LLC dba SuperStock / Alamy)*

sick students she was seeing at her high school, and alerted the city health department; her action identified the entrance of the H1N1 flu virus into New York.

Challenges

The number of school nurses varies from state to state. The professional organization for school nurses, the National Association for School Nurses, and Healthy People 2010, a health-improvement initiative led by a number of federal agencies, recommends a nurse-to-student ratio of 1 to 750. According to the NASN, in 2010 Michigan had the largest number of school nurses, with 4,411, while Vermont had the fewest, with 396. More than 70,000 registered nurses work as school nurses, some independently and some in SBHCs.

According to the School-Based Health Alliance, as of 2011, nearly 2000 SBHCs were serving students at schools in the United States. Approximately 54% of SBHCs are located in urban areas, 28% in rural areas, and 18% in suburban areas. Most are located in traditional public schools/Title 1 schools.

The grade-level breakdown of the school populations served by SBHCs is as follows:

• Kindergarten through 5: 13.4%

• Kindergarten through 8: 8%

• Kindergarten through 12: 14.9%

• 6 through 8: 10.3%

• 6 through 12: 4.6%

• 9 though 12: 29.8%

• Other: 19%

However, as school districts have been under pressure to cut costs, school health care resources, especially school nurses, have been facing funding challenges. School-based health centers may be more resistant to this pressure, as they often receive financial support from their sponsors (often hospitals or medical centers in the area the SBHC serves), from nonprofit foundations, or from state government.

Despite all the clear benefits of having school nurses and health care professionals, fewer than half of public schools have a full-time nurse on staff. School-based health care is not federally mandated, nor is it required by all states, and nurses may find they are asked to cover several schools in an area, while office staff or teachers cover the days when the nurse is not present. Because teachers and office staff do not have medical training, they cannot tell when a student needs to be dismissed for health reasons. Citing a study published in *The Journal of School Nursing,* Carol Mithers notes that "only 5% of kids coming sick or injured to the health office were sent home when evaluated by a school nurse, while untrained staff sent home 18%. Indeed, when a nurse position was cut at the Davis-Emerson Middle School, in Tuscaloosa, Alabama, the attendance rate declined—instead of students with problems getting help and going back to class, they were going home, showing up late, or just not coming to school at all."

Disaster can strike when an untrained person attempts to fill the nurse's role. There have been several cases in which students have died because they did not receive their medication from office staff as they should have, received inappropriate dosages, or did not receive emergency treatment as quickly as possible.

The benefits of school-based health care are many, and in some cases, the ability of a child to reach a qualified health professional can make the difference between life and death.

Resources

WEBSITES

Mithers, Carol. *Are School Nurses Disappearing?* http://www.cnn.com/2011/HEALTH/04/04/school.nurse.shortage.parenting/index.html (September 20, 2013).

ORGANIZATIONS

National Association of School Nurses, 1100 Wayne Ave., Suite 925, Silver Spring, MD 20910, (240) 821-1130, https://www.nasn.org/Home.
School-Based Health Alliance, 1010 Vermont Ave. NW, Washington, DC 20005, (202) 638-5872, http://www.sbh4all.org.

Fran Hodgkins

School-based health centers

Definition

School-based health centers (SBHCs) provide health services to students from kindergarten through high school. They can provide primary care to

The School-Based Health Alliance was founded in 1995 and is the national voice for school-based health centers (SBHCs). *(School-based Health Alliance)*

students who do not otherwise have primary care physicians, or work in coordination with the student's primary care provider, as well as emergency care, and vision, hearing and dental services.

Description

American schools have been providing health care services since the 1890s, when physicians in New York City and Boston screened students in those cities' schools for contagious disease in order to prevent outbreaks. Schools often provide vision and hearing screenings and immunizations.

SBHCs are an expansion of these services. They evolved during the 1970s and 1980s, and now, nearly 2000 SBHCs are providing care to students in the United States. Approximately 54% of SBHCs are located in urban areas, 28% in rural areas, and 18% in suburban areas.

Most SBHCs are located in traditional public schools/Title 1 schools. The grade-level breakdown of the school populations served by SBHCs is as follows:

- Kindergarten through 5: 13.4%
- Kindergarten through 8: 8%
- Kindergarten through 12: 14.9%
- Grade 6 through 8: 10.3%
- Grade 6 through 12: 4.6%
- Grade 9 though 12: 29.8%
- Other: 19 %

By providing care at a place where children already are, an SBHC removes logistical and transportation barriers that students and families might otherwise face. In addition, schools can help students and their families apply for free or low-cost health insurance (such as **Medicare** or the **Children's Health Insurance Program**).

SBHCs do not bill children or families for the care they provide. When parents enroll their children in the center (enrollment in the center by providing a

School based health centers (SBHCs) provide health services to students from kindergarten through high school who do not have primary care physicians, or they work in coordination with the student's primary care provider; SBHCs also offer emergency care, and vision, hearing, and dental services. *(Denver Post via Getty Images)*

parental consent form is essential for the SBHC to provide treatment), they provide information about their insurance coverage (if any). The providers submit claims to the insurance companies or to Medicare for the services provided. SBHCs may also be financially supported by local or state health departments, through grants from charitable foundations, or by sponsoring facilities, usually medical centers, hospitals, or health care networks.

Purpose

SBHCs deliver a wide range of services to students, including medical care, dental services, vision services, mental health care, nutrition services, and **case management** services.

Staffing of an SBHC depends on the services provided. There are three basic staffing models that most SBHCs use. In the primary care/mental health model, a **nurse practitioner** (NP) or physician assistant (PA) (under the supervision of a physician) provides health services while a **psychologist** or licensed clinical **social worker** (LCSW) provides mental health care. This model is used by approximately 40% of SBHCs. The primary care model, which includes 25% of SBHCs, includes only an NP or PA, also under a physician's supervision. The third model, which is used by 35% of centers, provides basic health care, mental health care, and additional services provided by professionals such as nutritionists and case managers.

The services SBHCs provide include:

- comprehensive health assessments (97% of SBHCs),
- acute illness treatment of acute illness (96%),
- prescriptions (96%),
- vision and hearing screenings (92%),
- physical examinations for sports participation (92%),
- nutrition counseling (91%), and
- anticipatory guidance (90%).

In high schools, SBHCs may provide reproductive health services, though the provision and extent of the services varies among school districts; 57% of SBHCs are prohibited by school district policy from dispensing contraception, while 10% are blocked from doing so by state law and 13% by health center policy. Although they may not be able to dispense contraception, approximately 68% of SBHCs 68% of SBHCs provide screening and treatment of sexually transmitted infections and 70% provide counseling about birth control methods.

In New York City, for example, high school students can obtain pregnancy tests, PAP smears, screening and treatment for sexually transmitted diseases, counseling and access to contraception, and referrals ad follow up for conditions requiring further evaluation and treatment, such as abnormal PAP smears.

SBHCs can also provide health care services to school administration and staff.

A local hospital or medical center may sponsor the SBHC. A sponsoring facility is actively involved in the SBHC's administration and operation, and students who need referrals for treatment beyond the scope of the SBHC can be sent to the sponsoring facility. In New York City, where the New York State Department of Health oversees the operation of all the SBHCs, health center sponsors include the Lutheran Medical Center, Long Island Jewish Medical Center, Mt. Sinai Hospital, and the Queens Hospital Network.

Benefits

According to a study by the **Centers for Disease Control and Prevention**, SBHCs improved school performance, and a New York City study found that students attending schools that had SBHCs were more satisfied with their learning environments than were those whose schools did not have them.

Resources

WEBSITES

American Academy of Pediatrics. *Policy Statement on School Based Health Centers and Pediatrics* http://pediatrics.aappublications.org/content/129/2/387.full (September 18, 2013).

New York City Department of Education. *What Is a School-Based Health Center?* http://schools.nyc.gov/Offices/Health/SBHC/SBHC.htm (September 18, 2013).

ORGANIZATIONS

School-Based Health Alliance, 1010 Vermont Ave. NW, Washington, DC 20005, (202) 638-5872, http://www.sbh4all.org.

Fran Hodgkins

SHIP *see* State Health Insurance Assistance Program (SHIP)

SHOP *see* Small Business Health Options Program (SHOP)

Shortage of Nurses

Description

The United States, and most of the world, has been experiencing a shortage of qualified health care professionals. This shortage has been most severe in the profession of nursing. Although the economic downturn that began in 2007 had the effect of alleviating the shortage by inducing nurses who had left the labor force to return, while other nurses delayed retirement or otherwise remained, employed. The United States Bureau of Labor Statistics has estimated a need for 711,000 new nurses in the interval from 2010 to 2020, but this figure appears to cover only newly created positions. If the estimate is to include replacements for nurses approaching retirement age, the United States will have to train over one million nurses to meet anticipated needs. This challenge is exacerbated by an acute shortage of faculty members in colleges of nursing.

Background

Since World War II, the United States has faced a series of shortages of professional nurses, but in the past, it was possible to alleviate these shortages by training additional nurses. The current and projected shortage is more severe than those of the past. In a 2011 press release, the American Nurses Association wrote, "Converging new forces, including an increasingly complex and technological health care landscape, more sophisticated treatment regimens, expanding numbers of elderly, the explosion in outpatient and chronic care, an aging nurse workforce and coming wave of RN retirements, plus shortages of nursing faculty all have heightened the demands on the health system's capacity to provide quality, sufficient, and accessible care."

In 2010, the Bureau of Labor Statistics estimated that nursing is profession with the fastest growth in the United States, growing from 2,737,400 registered nurses in 2010 to 3,449,300 in 2020. While this growth will be needed to cope for the expanding role of nursing and an aging population, there will also be a need to cope with a declining workforce as nurses themselves age and retire from the workforce.

History

The first reported nursing shortage in the past century was around 1936. During the early years of the Great Depression, there were too few paying jobs, and anyone who could draw a salary was happy to find work. As the economy recovered, nurses began to withdraw from the work force, and hospitals began to report difficulty recruiting qualified nurses. This was followed by World War II, when nursing was a critical-need occupation, both on the home front and overseas. This may be considered as either the start of a chronic shortage or a series of interconnected shortages that have lasted into the present day.

According to Dr. Jean Whelan RN of the University of Pennsylvania School of Nursing, "Each nurse shortage is unique, a function of the particular social, economic, technological, and cultural context in which it occurs." Each shortage has been addressed appropriately, and for a time has been alleviated, but was very shortly followed by another shortage. The initial shortage, 1936 and after, was primarily a shortage of nurses in acute care hospitals. Two factors may be at work here. With the partial economic recovery, women retired from the work force since it was still considered inappropriate for married women to work outside the home. Working conditions may also have been poor. Dr. Whelan reports, "Unaccustomed to dealing with nurse shortages, hospital administrators reacted slowly to the situation. Some blamed nurses themselves for creating the shortage by failing to live up to the ideals of their profession and refusing to work."

The war, which spread Americans over much of the world and caused tremendous need for all health professions, was its own source of nurse shortages. By the end of World War II, 77,000 nurses had been admitted to the armed forces, causing an acute shortage of nurses on the home front. The number of returning injured and disabled soldiers extended the need for nurses both in traditional roles and long-term care. It was during this period that the Licensed Practical Nurse program, which had been started in the 1930s, became more formalized. This was the first of several efforts to deal with the nursing shortage by reassigning some tasks to persons with less training than was required of Registered Nurses.

After the war, the nursing shortage persisted. Dr. Whelan cites a Department of Labor study that reported low salaries, lack of pensions, poor working conditions, and limited opportunities for promotion. The shortage was exacerbated by federal funding for hospital construction without efforts to deal with staffing problems. However, **Medicare** and **Medicaid** increased the size of the patient populations, and hospitals were either better able, or simply forced, to offer a better salary structure to nurses. While this produced a transient increase in the number of students pursuing nursing careers, other social changes held back the growth of the nursing workforce. To compensate, nurses were increasingly assigned to supervise paraprofessionals rather than perform direct patient care.

In the 1960s, additional factors added to the staffing problem. The United States was still at war, now in Vietnam, but two other factors contributed to the shortage. While hospital-based training programs were still accepted for Registered Nurse status, there was increasing demand for nurses with four-year academic degrees. In addition, social changes made an increasing number of career options available to women. Nursing had been a female-dominated profession and, along with teaching, among the few occupations fully open to women. Although full gender equality was not achieved, a growing number of women, who in earlier years would have been expected to enter nursing or teaching, were able enter medicine, law, and dentistry, as well as business and finance.

The economic downturn that began in 2007 produced a pause in the healthcare staffing shortage, since the depressed economy and drop in value of retirement savings caused many professions to postpone retirement or return to work after leaving the labor force. *Hospitals & Health Networks* magazine published the following: "Nursing is one staffing area in which some hospitals went from famine to feast. 'When you look at the current economic situation, a lot of older nurses are staying in their positions,' says Cheryl Peterson, R.N., senior policy fellow for the American Nurses Association. 'As a result, we are hearing that new graduates are finding it difficult to get jobs.' . . . But be warned: This is the calm before the storm. A larger, more challenging shortage across multiple disciplines is on the horizon. Experts predict a shortage of about 260,000 registered nurses and 150,000 physicians by 2025 and 38,000 pharmacists by 2030."

In recent years, the overall staffing problem has become even more complex. The aging population has increased the need for all health professionals. Nurses have been enlisted to provide primary care and alleviate the shortage of physicians. In addition, nurses have been sought after for patient education, case review, sales positions, and other areas where a solid background in health and treatment are required. This expansion of functions has further increased the need for qualified nurses, while increased sophistication of basic care has increased the educational demands. The Bureau of Labor Statistics continues to list an associate's degree (two-year) as the entry-level degree, and these requirements may usually be met through a two- or three-year hospital diploma program; the bachelor of science in nursing (four years) is increasingly demanded for professional advancement. In many areas of practice, advanced degrees, master's or doctorate, are now routinely expected. Specialization has also created shortages when nurses are needed in specific clinical areas.

Published estimates of need

There have been many estimates of the need for additional nurses, but they are usually confounded by the impact of the **Patient Protection and Affordable Care Act** and the state-by-state response to the expansion of Medicaid. As of the time of writing, thirteen states have rejected the Medicaid expansions that were part of the Affordable Care Act. These decisions, on a state-by-state basis, will alter the size of the projected patient populations and change the projected need for additional nurses.

According to the United States Bureau of Labor Statistics, "Employment of registered nurses is expected to grow 26 percent from 2010 to 2020, faster than the average for all occupations. Growth will occur primarily because of technological advancements; an increased emphasis on preventative care; and the large, aging baby-boomer population who will demand more healthcare services as they live longer and more active lives." This review calls for the addition of 711,900 nurses to the work force; it does not analyze the need to replace nurses who will retire during this period of time.

A KPMG survey in 2011 indicated that hospitals experience a turnover rate of approximately 14%. Wanted Analytics reported that employers and staffing agencies posted over 121,000 new job ads for registered nurses in May, an increase of 46% from May 2010.

In 2010, the *Journal of Medicine* published a report entitled "The Future of Nursing: Leading Change, Advancing Health." This extensive study dealt primarily with the role of nurses, in the future, in areas of specialized care and primary care. Because the authors were focused on expanding the role of nurses they wrote about the need to expand resources for nurse education. They reported that only 50% of nurses in the current work force held baccalaureate degrees, and that the goal should be 80%. They further called for doubling the number of nurses with doctoral degrees. In contrast, Canada, other than

Quebec, has established a mandatory BSN degree (four years) as entry level for the profession.

Significantly, although the economic downturn, which began in 2007, led to a great increase in applications to nursing schools, since nursing was perceived as a reliable source of steady employment, the American Association of Colleges of Nursing reported, "U.S. nursing schools turned away 75,587 qualified applicants from baccalaureate and graduate nursing programs in 2011 due to an insufficient number of faculty, clinical sites, classroom space, clinical preceptors, and budget constraints. Almost two-thirds of the nursing schools responding to the survey pointed to faculty shortages as a reason for not accepting all qualified applicants into entry-level baccalaureate programs." The association had reported an estimated 7.6% faculty vacancy rate, with most of the open positions calling for a doctoral degree. They listed 1,181 faculty vacancies and estimated that an additional 103 positions would be needed in order to expand student enrollment.

Approaches to the problem

Use of paraprofessionals and others to reduce work load

A number of methods have been developed to deal with the shortage. These depend on the position of those trying to cope with the problem. Hospitals and other employers may focus on recruitment, while government agencies and professional organizations may look towards offering inducements for people to enter the profession of nursing, or shift tasks to paraprofessionals in order to save time for registered nurses.

The job description of a registered nurse is extensive. The Bureau of Labor Statistics describes the job as follows: "Nurses, also called registered nurses or RNs, take care of sick and injured people. They give people medicine. They treat wounds. And they give emotional support to patients and their families. Nurses ask patients about their symptoms and keep detailed records. They watch for signs that people are sick. Then, nurses help doctors examine and treat patients. Some nurses help to give tests to find out why people are sick. Some also do lab work to get test results. Nurses also teach people how to take care of themselves and their families. Some nurses teach people about diet and exercise and how to follow doctors' instructions. Some nurses run clinics and immunization centers. Nurses can focus on treating one type of patient, such as babies or children. They can also focus on one type of problem. Some focus on helping doctors during surgery. Others work in emergency rooms or intensive care units. Many nurses work in doctors' offices. They help with medical tests, give medicines, and dress wounds. Some also do lab and office work. Home health nurses go to people's homes to help them. Flight nurses fly in helicopters to get to sick people in emergencies. Some nurses have special training and can do more advanced work. Nurse practitioners can prescribe medicine. Nurse midwives can help women give birth."

In contrast to the extensive job description for registered nurse, the licensed practical nurse is described as follows: "Licensed practical and licensed vocational nurses (known as LPNs or LVNs, depending on the state in which they work) provide basic nursing care. They work under the direction of registered nurses and doctors."

Yet another occupation in this group would be the nursing assistants, although various titles are used, including nursing care attendants, nursing aides, and nursing attendants. The category does not include home health aides, orderlies, personal care aides, or psychiatric aides, who all have separate job descriptions. The role of the nursing assistant is to provide basic patient care under direction of nursing staff. These people perform duties such as feeding, bathing, dressing, grooming, or moving patients, or changing linens. Here, too, the Bureau of Labor Statistics anticipates faster growth than for other occupations, with a 20% increase in need between 2010 and 2020.

The position of medication technician is not a recognized occupation but has been developed at some hospitals in an attempt to reduce the work load of nurses. It was estimated that RNs spend as much as 20% of their time administering and charting medication. The Ohio State University Hospitals developed a program whereby technicians administer and chart drugs given by mouth or applied to the skin. Nurses are still responsible for administration of injectable drugs.

Finally, phlebotomists may draw blood for laboratory tests, while in some areas pharmacists may administer injectable vaccines.

Recruitment overseas

The nursing shortage is international in scope, and so hospitals and agencies attempt to recruit nurses from other nations. This opportunity is particularly attractive when the work site is in a tourist destination such as London, Rome, or New York. International travel has been one of the attractions of military nursing. Other inducements may be high salaries or working in an area with attractive recreation, such as beaches or ski resorts. There are some programs that move nurses from one location to another so they can visit many different places.

Recruitment, domestic

The first step in recruitment is to offer a competitive benefits package. This commonly covers salary, retirement benefits, and educational allowances. If possible, staff should be able to meet all continuing education requirements through in-service programs, although opportunities to attend meetings and conventions should be provided.

Because many young nurses may have families, flexible scheduling and on-site child care may be major selling points.

According to the Hospitals & Health Networks recommendations, the interview process should focus on attitude rather than skills. People who fit in with the organization are more likely to stay. Peer interviews, which are interviews by current employees at the same level as the prospective employee, may help identify those people who will become valued, long-term members of the organization.

Other methods of recruitment have also been used, including signing and referral bonuses. Home care nurses may be offered a company car.

Government programs

A number of government programs have been developed to provide educational loans and/or scholarships for study of the health professions, with a particular emphasis on nursing. These are administered through the Health Resources and Services Administration, which is a division of the Department of Health and Human Services.

• NURSE Corps loan repayment program (formerly the Nursing Education Loan Repayment Program): Registered nurses and advanced practice registered nurses, such as nurse practitioners, working in a critical shortage facility can receive 60 percent of their total qualifying nursing education loan balance for two years of service. Full-time nursing faculty working at accredited, public or private, non-profit schools of nursing are also eligible. For an optional third year of service, participants may receive an additional 25 percent of their original total qualifying nursing education loan balance.

• Faculty Loan Repayment Program: Degree-trained health professionals from disadvantaged backgrounds serving on the faculty at an accredited health professions college or university can receive

$40,000, plus a tax benefit, for two years of service preparing the clinicians of the future.

- NURSE Corps Scholarship Program: Students enrolled or accepted for enrollment in accredited RN or graduate nursing training programs located in the U.S. can receive tuition, fees, other educational costs and a living stipend in exchange for a minimum two-year service after graduation at a health care facility with a critical shortage of nurses. The NURSE Corps Scholarship Program was formerly called the Nursing Scholarship Program
- Nursing Student Loans: Need-based, competitive program. Must pursue diploma, associate, baccalaureate, or graduate degree in nursing and apply for aid to participating school.

The uniformed services offer extensive programs of scholarships and loan repayments for nursing students and nurses. These financial programs are available in both active duty and reserve assignments. The amount of aid depends on specialty and length of service commitment.

The Affordable Care Act provides for increased personnel needs by including some funds for nurse training. One section of the act, Investment In Nurse Managed Clinics, is expected to have trained 900 nurses to manage outpatient clinics by the time the ACA is fully implemented. Another part of the act, the **Prevention and Public Health Fund**, was prepared to train an additional 600 nurse practitioners and nurse midwives by 2015.

Why this is important to the consumer

A number of studies have documented the importance of adequate nursing staffing to patient well-being, including its effect on both morbidity and mortality:

- A 2002 study, published in the Journal of the American Medical Association, tried to find an association between levels of nurse staffing and patient death. It reported: "In our sample of 168 Pennsylvania hospitals in which the mean patient-to-nurse ratio ranged from 4:1 to 8:1, 4535 of the 232 342 surgical patients with the clinical characteristics we selected died within 30 days of being admitted. Our results imply that had the patient-to-nurse ratio across all Pennsylvania hospitals been 4:1, possibly 4000 of these patients may have died, and had it been 8:1, more than 5000 of them may have died. While this difference of 1000 deaths in Pennsylvania hospitals across the 2 staffing scenarios is approximate, it represents a conservative estimate of preventable deaths attributable to nurse staffing in the state."

- A 2013 study conducted at the Cincinnati Children's Hospital found that when nurses are responsible for more than four patients, there is a greater chance that the child will have to be readmitted to the hospital from two to four weeks after discharge. This likelihood increases by 11% for each additional patient. For children admitted for surgery, the chance of readmission between two and four weeks after discharge jumped 48% when the nursing work load was increased.

- A 2010 study from Orlando, Florida, reported: "Findings from this review demonstrate an association of nurse staffing in the intensive care unit with patient outcomes and are consistent with findings in studies of the general acute care population."

Resources

BOOKS

Cohen, S.D., D. Sherropd. *Surviving the Nursing Shortage: Strategies for Recruitment and Retention*. Opus Communications, 2003.

Feldman, H. (ed). *The Nursing Shortage: Strategies for Recruitment and Retention in Clinical Practice and Education*. Springer Publishing, 2003.

Satterly, F. *Where Have All the Nurses Gone?* Prometheus Books, 2004.

Schaffner J., P. Ludwig-Beymer. *Rx For The Nursing Shortage: a guidebook*. Health Administration Press, 2003.

PERIODICALS

Aiken, Linda H., et al. "Hospital use of agency-employed supplemental nurses and patient mortality and failure to rescue." *Health Services Research* (June 2013): 931.

Ilingworth, A., K.F. Arabnda, S.M. De Goeas, et al. "Changing the way that I am: Students' experience of educational preparation for advanced nursing roles in the community." *Nurse Education in Practice* 13, no. 5 (2013): 338–343.

Kowalski, Karren, and Brian M. Kelley. "What's the ROI for resolving the nursing faculty shortage?" *Nursing Economics* (March-April 2013): 70.

Mbemba, Gisele, et al. "Interventions for supporting nurse retention in rural and remote areas: an umbrella review." *Human Resources for Health* 11 (2013): 44.

Peters, Kath, and Debra Jackson. "New graduate nursing unemployment: a threat to the future health care workforce." *Contemporary Nurse* 44, no. 2 (2013): 130.

WEBSITES

"Nursing Shortage." NursingWorld. http://www.nursingworld.org/MainMenuCategories/ThePracticeofProfeser 24, 2013).

"Nursing Shortage Resources." American Association of Colleges of Nursing. http://www.aacn.nche.edu/media-relations/nursing-shortage (accessed September 24, 2013).

"Nursing Workforce, Background Brief." KaiserEDU.org, Health Policy Education from the Henry J. Kaiser Family Foundation. July 2012. http://www.kaiseredu.org/Issue-Modules/Nursing-Workforce/Background-Brief.aspx (accessed September 24, 2013).

ORGANIZATIONS

The American Association of Colleges of Nursing, One Dupont Circle, NW Suite 530, Washington, DC, US 20036, (202) 463-6930, Fax: (202) 785-8320, info@aacn.nche.edu, http://www.aacn.nche.edu/.

American Nurses Association, 8515 Georgia Avenue Suite 400, Silver Spring, Maryland, US 20910-3492, 1-800-274-4ANA (4262) , Check website for email directory, http://www.nursingworld.org/default.aspx.

Canadian Nurses Association, 50 Driveway, Ottawa, CanadaOntario K2P 1E2, 613-237-2133, 1-800-361-8404, Fax: 613-237-3520, See website for email directory, http://www.cna-aiic.ca.

Samuel D. Uretsky, Pharm.D.

Shortage of primary care physicians

Definition

A **primary care physician** (PCP) is a medical doctor (MD) or osteopathic doctor (DO) who provides the first contact for an individual with a new health concern and who provides continuing care for patients with ongoing medical conditions. Primary care physicians are also called "general practitioners" or "family physicians." The number of PCPs graduating from medical schools has not kept up with demand, resulting in shortages, especially in rural areas and the inner city.

Description

Primary care physicians are doctors who have graduated from medical school and received postgraduate training in family medicine, internal medicine, or pediatrics. They normally are the first physician an individual with an undiagnosed medical problem sees. One exception is when the patient goes to the emergency room. Here the first doctor a patient meets provides acute care to treat the immediate medical problem but, unlike a PCP, does not provide continuing care.

Ideally, a patient will develop a long-term relationship with a PCP. The PCP will:

• see the patient for regular checkups

• diagnose new diseases or disorders as they occur

• treat common illnesses (e.g., bronchitis, urinary tract infections, common childhood illnesses)

• refer the patient to specialist physicians as needed

• manage and monitor common chronic illnesses (e.g., hypertension, type 2 diabetes)

• order basic tests (e.g., blood tests, urine tests, x rays) necessary for diagnosis or monitoring.

The shortage problem

The shortage of PCPs in the United States has three components: the absolute number of PCPs, their uneven distribution, and an aging population that is living longer with chronic diseases.

Inadequate numbers

In 1950, 50% of physicians in the United States were primary care physicians. By 2007, only 30% of physicians were in a primary care practice. There are several reasons for this decline.

• Higher earnings in medical specialties such as ophthalmology, neurology, and surgery attract recent medical school graduates.

• More women are graduating from medical school and choose specialties such as dermatology or emergency medicine with more regular hours or that allow them to work part-time.

• The older generation of PCPs is retiring in large numbers and is not being replaced.

• PCPs often feel undervalued when compared to specialists, making the field less attractive.

A 2013 report in the journal *Academic Medicine* found that only 25.2% of new physicians went into primary care. The American Association of Medical Colleges estimated that by 2020, the United States will have a deficit of 45,000 PCPs.

Uneven distribution of PCPs

The problem of access to primary care is worsened by the uneven distribution of PCPs. As of 2013, about 20% of Americans live in either rural or inner-city locations that have a health professional shortage. The same 2013 *Academic Medicine* report found that only 4.8% of new physicians chose to practice in rural areas. When PCPs do choose to practice in an underserved area, they often find that they are overwhelmed and frequently on call with no relief physician available. They work unusually long hours and see large numbers of patients, resulting in work-related stress and family disruption.

Aging population

Americans are living longer and are living with more chronic diseases such as diabetes, hypertension, chronic obstructive pulmonary disease (COPD) and renal (kidney) disease. Currently, 87% of Americans between the ages of 65 and 79 have at least one chronic condition. The NEHI estimates that the number of Americans age 65 and older will increase to over 20% of the population by 2050. In addition, with implementation of the Affordable Care Act beginning in 2013, 32 million younger Americans will become insured, thus increasing the demand for primary care. The number of individuals eligible for **Medicaid** will also increase.

Why this is important to the consumer

Direct impact on the consumer

The shortage of primary care physicians directly affects those seeking health care. PCP practices become closed to new patients when they reach capacity and are unable to hire additional PCPs, making finding a doctor more difficult or inconvenient. An NEHI assessment of primary care in 2010 found that 46% of family medicine practices and 56% of internal medicine practices were not accepting new patients. The problem is likely to worsen.

Seeing a PCP will take longer. The NEHI study found that in 2009, the average wait time for a new patient to see a PCP was 44 days in internal medicine. Even established patients are likely to experience increased wait time for PCP services. In addition, time spent with the physician during the visit may decrease, as doctors come under pressure to see as many patients as possible.

Indirect impacts on the consumer

One result of long wait times to see a PCP is likely to be an increase in visits to the emergency room by patients who feel they cannot wait days or weeks to be seen. These visits are expensive, driving up the cost of health insurance and using resources intended for patients whose medical condition constitutes a true medical emergency. Alternatively, patients faced with long delays may give up trying to see a doctor and let their condition go undiagnosed or untreated.

Another indirect impact is that patients may be more likely to see a **nurse practitioner** or **physician assistant** instead of a PCP. The quality of patient health outcomes when treated by a nurse practitioner or physician assistant is unclear. Some studies have found that health outcomes were about equal, but

---

KEY TERMS

Chronic obstructive pulmonary disease (COPD)— Lung diseases, such as emphysema and chronic bronchitis, in which airflow is obstructed, causing labored breathing and impairing gas exchange.

Hypertension—Persistently high blood pressure.

Type 2 diabetes—formerly called "adult-onset diabetes." In this form of diabetes, either the pancreas does not make enough insulin, or cells become insulin resistant and do not use insulin efficiently.

---

patient satisfaction was higher when treated by nurse practitioners, primarily because nurse practitioners spent more time with the patient than physicians did. However, these studies were limited to select groups of patients, and the results cannot be generalized to the entire population of patients seeking primary care. More research needs to be done on the effectiveness of using nonphysician health care professionals to provide primary care in specific situations. Various physician groups have lobbied strongly against an expansion of the role of nonphysician health care professionals in treating patients.

Possible solutions

The following changes have been suggested as ways to reduce the impact of the PCP shortage in the coming years.

- Increase the number of residencies in family medicine.
- Increase reimbursement for services provided by PCPs to decrease the differential in earning power between specialists and PCPs.
- Offer incentives to PCPs to practice in underserved areas.
- Train physicians to lead teams of nonphysician healthcare professionals to deliver more efficient care.
- Offer primary care in nontraditional settings such as retain clinics, workplaces, and homes.
- Effectively use health information technology and electronic health records to reduce duplication of testing and unnecessary services.
- Move to a system that rewards preventive care instead of basing payment on treatment of illness.
- Offer alternatives to emergency room treatment during non-office hours.

Resources

PERIODICALS

Associated Press Writers. "Newly Insured to Deepen Primary Care Doctor Gap." *The Times and Democrat.* July 16, 2013 http://thetandd.com/news/topnews/ newly-insured-to-deepen-primary-care-doctor-gap/ article_824e0062-ed91-11e2-883e-0019bb2963f4.html (accessed July 16, 2013).

Chen, Candice, et al. "Toward Graduate Medical Education (GME) Accountability: Measuring the Outcomes of GME Institutions." *Academic Medicine* June 7, 2013. http://journals.lww.com/academicmedicine/Abstract/ publishahead/Toward_Graduate_Medical_Education__ GME_.99378.aspx (accessed July 16, 2013).

Glenn, Brandon. "Is the unequal distribution of PCPs worse than the shortage?" *Medical Economics* (10 July 2013): 68.

Samuels, Jennifer. "Primary problem: how locum tenens can solve the shortage of primary care physicians." *Locum Life* (March 2010): 12.

WEBSITES

Association of American Medical Colleges. "Physician Shortages to Worsen Without Increases in Resident Training." https://www.aamc.org/download/286592/ data (accessed July 16, 2013).

New England Healthcare Institute (NEHI). "Remaking Primary Care: A Framework for the Future." January 20, 2010. http://www.nehi.net/publications/45/remaking_ primary_care_a_framework_for_the_future (accessed July 16, 2013).

ORGANIZATIONS

American Academy of Family Physicians, P.O. Box 11210, Shawnee Mission, KS 66207, (913) 906-6000, (800) 274-2237, Fax: (913) 906-6075, http://familydoctor.org.

New England Healthcare Institute (NEHI), One Broadway, 15th Floor, Cambridge, MA 02142, (617) 225-0857, Fax: (617) 225-9025, info@nehi.net, http://www. nehi.net.

Tish Davidson, AM

Skilled nursing facility *see* **Nursing home**

Small Business Health Options Program (SHOP)

Definition

The Small Business Health Options Program (SHOP) is a provision of the **Patient Protection and Affordable Care Act** of 2010 (ACA) that is designed to help small businesses find and purchase health insurance for their employees. Accessible via **Healthcare. gov**, the SHOP Marketplace is available to employers with 50 or fewer full-time-equivalent employees (FTEs) beginning in 2014.

Description

In accordance with the Patient Protection and Affordable Care Act of 2010 (also known as the Affordable Care Act or "Obamacare"), Healthcare.gov was designed to simplify the process in which consumers explore and compare health plans, with the objective of increasing the adoptability and affordability of health insurance coverage in the United States. The SHOP Exchange, or SHOP Marketplace, is a section of the website that provides small business owners with a central point of access to compare the price, coverage, and quality of healthcare plans for their employees. Launched on October 1, 2013, SHOP will begin providing coverage to companies with 50 or fewer FTEs in 2014; in 2016, the program will open up to employers with up to 100 FTEs.

Enrolling in SHOP

SHOP offers small employers a self-service portal from which to compare quality health insurance plans and determine coverage options that are right for their business. Business owners may also use a licensed insurance agent or broker to help navigate plan options, compare features, or apply for insurance at no additional cost. In addition, starting in 2014, small employers will be able to pick a specific benefit level and allow their employers the freedom to select their own plan at that level.

To participate in SHOP, businesses that meet the company size requirements must commit to providing health insurance coverage to all employees working 30 or more hours a week. In addition, most states require that a minimum of 70 percent of employees enroll in the offered plan at some point during the year in question; employers who do not meet the minimum participation numbers can enroll at the SHOP Marketplace from November 15 to December 15 to earn an exception.

Beginning in 2014, companies with less than 25 FTEs may qualify for a tax credit to help offset the cost of contributing toward employee premiums. The Small Business Health Care Tax Credit requires that companies pay at least 50 percent of employee premium costs, provided the average FTE salary at the company is less than $50,000 and the insurance plan was purchased through the SHOP Marketplace. The tax credit is worth up to 50 percent of employer premium contributions and is highest for smaller companies with lower average yearly salaries.

KEY TERMS

Full-time-equivalent employee (FTE)—Under the ACA, an employee who works an average of 30 hours a week, or two half-time employees.

Patient Protection and Affordable Care Act (ACA)—Legislation signed into law in 2010 as part of a large-scale initiative to increase the availability, value, and affordability of health insurance in the United States.

Premium—Fees paid to an insurance company in exchange for coverage under a specific insurance plan.

SHOP provides small business owners with the flexibility to choose plans that fit their employees' coverage needs and budgets. The SHOP Marketplace offers four different levels of healthcare coverage, with each level influencing how much employees will pay for out-of-pocket expenses:

• Bronze: Covers 60% of the total average costs of care

• Silver: Covers 70% of the total average costs of care

• Gold: Covers 80% of the total average costs of care

• Platinum: Covers 90% of the total average costs of care

Why this is important to the consumer

In July 2012, the Congressional Budget Office (CBO) estimated that 55 million or 1 in 5 Americans under the age of 65 were uninsured. Without the ACA, the CBO estimates that the uninsured rate would rise from 20.4 percent in 2012 to 21.1 percent in 2022; conversely, the uninsured rate is now expected to be halved with more than 30 million eligible to receive private or public coverage.

According to the Small Business Administration, small businesses pay on average 18 percent more for health insurance than larger businesses due to administrative costs. By offering small business owners the opportunity to pool their risk, SHOP makes it possible for small companies to provide higher-quality health plans for their employees at a lower cost.

In September 2013, the Obama administration announced that certain functions of the SHOP Marketplace would not be online with the general Health Insurance Marketplace launch on October 1, 2013 but instead would be rolled out later in the year. In the interim, small business owners were asked to mail or fax their enrollment information in order to join the SHOP exchange.

Resources

BOOKS

Obama, Barack and the 111th Congress. *The Patient Protection and Affordable Care Act*. Dallas, TX: Primedia eLaunch Publishing, 2010.

PERIODICALS

Aaron, Henry J. and Kevin W. Lucia. "Only the Beginning: What's Next at the Health Insurance Exchanges?" *New England Journal of Medicine* 369, no. 13 (September 26, 2013): 1185–87.

WEBSITES

Centers for Medicare and Medicaid Services. "Key Facts about the Small Business Health Options Program (SHOP) Marketplace." CMS.gov. http://marketplace.cms.gov/getofficialresources/publications-and-articles/key-facts-about-shop.pdf (accessed October 20, 2013).

deMause, Neil. "What Health Care Reform Means for Your Business." Money.cnn.com. http://money.cnn.com/2010/03/22/smallbusiness/small_business_health_rexform (accessed October 20, 2013).

Klein, Ezra. "11 Facts about the Affordable Care Act." washingtonpost.com. http://www.washingtonpost.com/blogs/wonkblog/wp/2012/06/24/11-facts-about-the-affordable-care-act (accessed October 20, 2013).

ORGANIZATIONS

Centers for Medicare and Medicaid Services, 7500 Security Blvd., Baltimore, MD 21244, (410) 786-0727, (877) 267-2323, http://www.cms.gov.

U.S. Department of Health and Human Services, 200 Independence Ave. SW., Washington, DC 20201, (877) 696-6775, http://www.hhs.gov.

Stephanie Dionne

SNAP *see* **Supplemental Nutrition Assistance Program (SNAP)**

Social Media and Health Care

Definition

What Are Social Media?

"Social media" is a broad term that can be used to include any and all technology for sharing information. Facebook, Twitter, and Pinterest are currently among the most common forms of social media in the United States, but other options include Tumblr, Digg, Delicious, and StumbleUpon. Also, blogs and email fall under the broad category of social media.

Description

Why are social media and health care important to the consumer?

One of the key issues related to social media and health care is privacy. Currently, no definitive rules exist for how patients and physicians may use social media to communicate with each other about health issues. Several major medical organizations have recognized the role of social media in daily life and communication, and they have developed guidelines for their physician members on the appropriate use of social media.

When Not to Share

Savvy consumers should hesitate before sharing personal health information in a social media setting, such as Facebook or Twitter, if they want to keep the information private. Sharing information about a health condition on social media sites could result in unwanted attention from companies who mine these sites for information.

When to Share

Many people value their social media networks highly, and want to share all the details as a way to get more support. In addition, social media can be a useful educational tool and support system for patients with the same condition. Online forums exist for nearly every medical condition and situation, including chronic conditions such as diabetes or heart disease. There are sites for cancer survivors, parents of children with serious medical problems, and patients preparing for or recovering from joint replacements. There are also websites, online communities, and other social media outlets for almost all health-related topics, such as pregnancy, allergies, sports injuries, and cosmetic surgery.

Communicating with Doctors

Some doctors are willing to have email dialogues with patients, but others are not, because of concerns that they cannot guarantee the confidentiality of patients' personal medical information sent electronically. But it depends on the doctor, and on the information, so consumers who want to communicate with their doctors via social media should ask. Some doctors' offices use email for sending prescription information, making or confirming appointments, and sending out information about events at the practice (e.g., changes in hours, inclement weather policies, and general information about conditions such as the flu).

Managing Health Care with Social Media

Data from more and more studies suggest that social media can be a simple, useful tool to help consumers manage their health. Specific consumer applications of social media include smartphone "apps" that remind individuals to take their medications, or settings that provide regular inspirational messages and tips for individuals who are trying to lose weight or quit smoking. Smartphone apps also exist to help patients with chronic conditions such as diabetes or heart disease. The apps help track their data on blood sugar, cholesterol, and blood pressure. Consumers can share this information via social media with their doctors' offices, in some cases, and they can share with members of their own social networks to show their progress. Social media also can be used to track workouts for anyone ranging from a previously sedentary beginning walker to a weekend warrior, or a serious competitor.

Government Resources

The **Centers for Disease Control and Prevention**, a branch of the federal government under the U.S. **Department of Health and Human Services**, has embraced the role of social media in consumer health. The CDC has a unique section on its website with a collection of information and social media tools designed to provide information to consumers and help improve public health. These tools include:

- Games. For example, the Solve the Outbreak app lets users play the role of Disease Detective and teaches them about how diseases spread.

- Statistics. The CDC makes its Vital Signs data available via its Facebook page and Twitter feed, and has developed a widget that can be added to any website.

- Updates. Need the latest information about this year's flu activity? The CDC has the information via social media that consumers can check online or on a smartphone.

Facebook and Health Care

Given the popularity of Facebook among much of the U.S. population, the CDC has developed Facebook pages designed to provide accessible information to consumers about a range of health care topics. Some of the CDC's Facebook profiles include Act Against AIDS (to educate consumers about how to reduce the spread of AIDS), Travelers' Health (with posts about staying safe and healthy while traveling), and Million Hearts (a national initiative to help prevent heart attacks and strokes).

Resources

WEBSITES

"CDC—Social Media." August 19, 2013. http://www.cdc.gov/socialmedia/ (accessed November 25, 2013).

"CDC—Social Media Tools for Consumers and Partners." April 10, 2013. http://www.cdc.gov/SocialMedia/Tools/ (accessed November 25, 2013).

"Get 'In the Know' on Social Media: HHS.gov/Digital Strategy." March 7, 2013. http://www.hhs.gov/digitalstrategy/blog/2013/03/get-in-the-know-social-media.html (accessed November 25, 2013).

"Social Media Improves Chronic Disease Care." InformationWeek. March 7, 2013. http://www.information week.com/healthcare/patient-tools/social-media-improves-chronic-disease-care/d/d-id/1110560? (accessed November 25, 2013).

Heide Splete

Social worker

Definition

A social worker helps people to optimize their functioning within their specific social environment. A social worker may also work to improve social systems. Clinical social workers can provide mental health services.

Description

The term "social work" is extremely broad and encompasses a wide variety of practice locations, clients, and activities. The common theme, however, is the application of social theory to help individual clients address problems in their lives, to improve the

The term "social work" is extremely broad and encompasses a wide variety of practice locations, clients, and activities, but the common aim is the application of social theory to help individuals address problems in their lives. *(Boston Globe via Getty Images)*

lot of vulnerable populations, to connect individuals with the resources they need to thrive, and to examine social problems in an effort to remedy them for the good of the community. There are about 650,500 social workers in the United States.

Education, licensure, and skills

The entry-level degree for social work is a Bachelor's degree in the field. A Master's of Social Work is required for some positions. To provide clinical mental health care and therapy, a Master's degree and licensure are required; licensure is granted by individual states and generally requires that candidates

- complete 3,000 hours of supervised clinical counseling within two years of receiving their degree
- pass either a national or state licensing exam, usually consisting of both written and oral sections
- pursue continuing education credits
- adhere to practice standards and ethical guidelines delineated by individual states

Licensed clinical social workers may provide therapy to individuals of all ages, groups, married couples, or families.

Social workers need a good fundamental background in human growth and development, normal and abnormal psychology, behavior change theory, interviewing techniques, addictions, counseling theories, public policy, and cultural issues. To stay current in the field, social workers need to develop literacy in reading and critically analyzing ongoing research in the field. Social workers must possess excellent communication skills and an understanding of different cultures. Clinical social workers will need some understanding of neurology and psychiatry, so that it is clear when clients require referral to other practitioners who can evaluate a client for psychiatric or neurological illness and potentially prescribe medication. Social workers who will be involved in education need to have public speaking skills, as well as an ability to translate more complex concepts into language easily understood by laypeople. Social workers who work in research will need specific skills pertinent to the type of investigations they will be conducting, as well as a good understanding of research methods and design.

Places of employment

Social workers may work in private practice, healthcare facilities such as hospitals or nursing homes, mental health clinics, schools or colleges, public social service offices, or employee assistance programs.

As of 2011, the breakdown of employment areas for social workers was as follows:

- Individual and Family services: 21%
- State government, other than schools or hospitals: 21%
- Local government, other than schools or hospitals: 19%
- Schools, elementary and secondary: 12%
- Health care: 9%

Tasks of a social workers

Social workers start by assessing a client, and collaborating to delineate appropriate goals. Common issues that social workers work on with clients include:

- Relationship challenges, including marriage problems or difficulties with family systems
- Domestic violence and child abuse
- Placement of children removed from family homes
- Evaluating hospitalized patients for appropriate post-discharge disposition
- Assisting clients with life transitions, including divorce, unemployment, and illness
- Connecting clients with community resources to assist them with crises
- Helping patients with new medical diagnoses obtain necessary medications and durable medical goods
- Helping people living in poverty connect with community resources that can help them provide for their families
- Working with homeless clients to try to find housing and assistance
- Helping clients fill out paperwork to allow them to receive public assistance or disability

Clinical social workers also start by assessing a client, and collaborating to delineate appropriate goals. Common issues that clinical social workers work on with clients include:

- Relationship challenges, including marriage problems or difficulties with family systems
- Gender and/or sexuality issues
- Anger management
- Phobias
- Eating disorders
- Trauma history
- Employment difficulties and career planning
- Behavioral challenges
- Addictions

- Mood disorders
- Anxiety and obsessive-compulsive disorder
- Personality disorders
- Schizophrenia

Therapy sessions then focus on the client's issues, feelings, behaviors, and goals. The licensed clinical social worker helps the client understand the source of his or her issues and supports the client to help them make positive behavioral changes leading to improved emotional health.

Why this is important to the consumer

Social workers are involved with some of the toughest problems within our society—domestic violence, child abuse, poverty, to name only a few. All of these issues undermine the fabric of our communities, so any help proffered helps the whole community. In the United States:

- About 46.5 million Americans are subsisting at an income level lower than the poverty line.
- About 700,000 Americans are homeless on any given night of the year.
- 25% of women experience domestic violence at some point in their lives.
- More than three million child abuse reports are filed yearly, pertaining to more than 6 million children, and five children die every day due to injuries from child abuse.
- About 400,5400 children are receiving care outside of their homes on any given day—in relatives' homes, children's homes, group homes, or foster homes.
- About half of all marriages end in divorce.
- The unemployment rate in the United States has exceeded 7% during every month in 2013.

Licensed clinical social workers play a crucial role in the treatment of mental health and addictions in the United States. These are widespread problems, with serious consequences for the lives of the sufferers and their families, their friends, and their coworkers. Each year in the United States

- About 26.2% of American adults have a diagnosable mental disorder; this is more than 57 million people.
- Of those American adults who have some diagnosable mental disorder, about 45% have two more coexisting mental condition.
- Around 10% of Americans suffer from a mood disorder.

KEY TERMS

Behavioral therapy—Uses strategies to reinforce positive, and extinguish negative, behaviors.

Cognitive therapy—Cognitive therapy seeks to change negative thought patterns, thereby improving symptoms of mood and anxiety disorders, and/or improving on negative behaviors that are leading to dysfunction.

Interpersonal therapy—Interpersonal therapy works on an individual's communication and social skills, allowing him or her to improve the dysfunctional relationship patterns that may be contributing to emotional distress.

Supportive therapy—Uses a variety of modalities to support a client's emotional and mental health.

- Around 18% of Americans suffer from a mood disorder.
- About 7.7 million Americans have post-traumatic stress disorder.
- About 8 million Americans have eating disorders.
- About 8.9 of the American population have used illicit drugs within the prior month.
- About 15 million people abuse alcohol.

Resources

BOOKS

EZ Occupational Outlook Handbook, 2nd ed. St. Paul, MN: JIST Publishing, 2011.

U.S. Department of Labor. *Occupational Outlook Handbook*. St. Paul, MN: JIST Publishing, 2013.

Wischnitzer, Saul. *Top 100 Health-Care Careers*. St. Paul, MN: JIST Publishing, 2011.

ORGANIZATIONS

ExploreHealthCareers.org, American Dental Education Association, 1400 K Street, NW, Suite 1100, Washington, DC 20005, (202) 289-7201, cmsa@cmsa.org, http://explorehealthcareers.org/en/home/.

National Association of Social Workers, 750 First Street NE, Suite 700, Washington, DC 20002, (202) 408-8600, http://www.socialworkers.org/.

School Social Work Association of America, P.O. Box 1086, Sumner, WA 98390, http://www.sswaa.org/.

U.S. Department of Labor, Frances Perkins Building, 200 Constitution Ave., NW, Washington, DC 20210, (866) 487-2365, http://www.dol.gov/.

Rosalyn Carson-DeWitt, MD

Special Supplemental Nutrition Program for Women, Infants, and Children (WIC)

Definition

The Special Supplemental Nutrition Program for Women, Infants, and Children (commonly known as WIC) is a federal program administered by the USDA Food & Nutrition Services that began as a pilot program in 1972. The WIC program provides grants to states to enable them to deliver supplemental nutritious foods, and nutrition education and counseling to low-income pregnant, breastfeeding women for up to six weeks after birth or pregnancy and to non-breastfeeding postpartum women for up to six months after the birth of an infant or after pregnancy ends.

WIC also provides screening and referrals to other health, welfare, and social services, and to expectant and new mothers, and serves infants and children up to age five who are considered to be at nutritional risk—those who already have poor nutritional status as well as infants and children who are at high risk of food and nutritional problems.

In 2013 throughout the United States, 90 state agencies administered the WIC program, providing supplemental food through an estimated 47,000 authorized retailers and nearly 2,000 local agencies, including 34 Indian Tribal Organizations, delivered services at 10,000 clinic sites. WIC programs also operated in the District of Columbia and five territories—Northern Mariana, American Samoa, Guam, Puerto Rico, and the Virgin Islands.

Purpose

The stated mission of WIC is to "safeguard the health of low-income women, infants, and children up to age 5 who are at nutrition risk by providing nutritious foods to supplement diets, information on healthy eating, and referrals to health care."

A pregnant woman uses WIC coupons to purchase produce from a farmers market cooperative. *(The Washington Post/Getty Images)*

WIC is a short-term program intended to improve the health and diets of expectant mothers, infants, and young children. Participants are generally eligible for one or more periods, such as during pregnancy, postpartum, and while breastfeeding. Most participants receive WIC benefits for 6 months to one year, at which time they must reapply to the program.

Eligibility

Pregnant women, women who have given birth, infants, and children up to age five are eligible for the WIC program if their family income is at or below 185% of the U.S. Poverty Income Guidelines. Although most states use the maximum guidelines, states may set lower income-limit standards. Applicants also may be considered automatically income-eligible based on participation in programs such as **Supplemental Nutrition Assistance Program** (**SNAP**, formerly know as the Food Stamp Program), **Medicaid**, Temporary Assistance for Needy Families (TANF, formerly known as AFDC, Aid to Families with Dependent Children), or other state-administered programs.

In addition, the woman or child's physician or a health professional at a WIC clinic must certify that the woman and/or child is at nutritional risk, which means that they have health or dietary problems that may be addressed by improved nutrition.

Nutritional Risk

A variety of behavioral, cultural, nutritional, and health conditions can place people at high risk of poor nutrition status. Examples of health risks that are considered high priorities in terms of their impact on nutritional risk are anemia, underweight, very young maternal age, a history of pregnancy-related complications or poor outcomes of pregnancy. Along with the well-known risks of inadequate food consumption and poor diet, homelessness, and migrancy (the condition of moving from one area or region to another, generally to seek farm-related work), other risk factors that make people eligible for participation in the WIC program include passive smoking (involuntarily inhaling smoke from others' cigarettes, cigars, or pipes, and low levels of maternal education. Young caregivers, those who have suffered battering, children of mentally retarded parents, and those who have endured child abuse and neglect also may be at increased nutritional risk.

Screening for nutritional risk is provided free of charge by the WIC program and is performed by a health professional—a physician, **nutritionist**, or nurse—and is based on federal guidelines. However, the states and local WIC agencies have the ability to define their own criteria for nutritional risk.

WIC Program Sites

WIC programs and services are offered at a wide range of sites, including county health departments, hospitals, mobile clinics (vans), community centers, schools, public housing sites, migrant health centers and camps, and Indian Health Service facilities. Most state WIC programs give program participants vouchers that they can use to purchase food from authorized food stores. A wide range of state and local organizations cooperate to deliver the food and health care benefits, and 47,000 merchants throughout the United States accept WIC vouchers.

WIC Program Food Benefits

The overwhelming majority of WIC State agencies give participants monthly checks or vouchers or an electronic benefit card to help them purchase specific foods to supplement their diets with specific nutrients. The use of electronic benefit cards is increasing, and all WIC State agencies are required to implement WIC electronic benefit transfer (EBT) statewide by October 1, 2020. Several state agencies still dispense WIC foods from warehouses or deliver food to participants' homes.

WIC distributes infant cereal, iron-fortified adult cereal, vitamin C-rich fruit or vegetable juice, eggs, milk, cheese, peanut butter, dried and canned beans/peas, canned fish, soy-based beverages, tofu, fruits and vegetables, baby foods, whole-wheat bread, and other whole-grain products. The food packages have a wide range of options, which enables state agencies to offer WIC participants choice and variety as well as the flexibility to prepare culturally appropriate food packages. For example, tortillas, brown rice, soy-based beverages, canned salmon, and a variety of fruits and vegetables allow state agencies to meet the needs of ethnically diverse participants.

The contents of food packages have changed over time in response to updated nutritional guidelines. For example, in 2009 New York was the first state to revise WIC food packages, adding fruits, vegetables, and whole grains and replacing whole milk with low-fat or nonfat milk for children ages 2 to 4.

The content of the food packages varies for different categories of participants. WIC acknowledges and promotes breastfeeding as the optimal source of nutrition for infants. The food packages for breastfeeding infants and their mothers offer incentives for mothers to fully breastfeed (using no formula or only very small amounts of formula feeding) and to continue breastfeeding. Food packages for fully breastfeeding mothers contain greater amounts of foods, including a higher dollar value for fruits and vegetables. Infants that are solely breastfeeding are given baby food meats in addition to greater amounts of baby food fruits and vegetables. Less infant formula is provided to partially breastfeeding infants so that they may receive the benefits of breast milk. A minimal amount of infant formula is provided to partially breastfeeding infants in the first month after birth in order to help mothers build and maintain their milk production.

WIC provides iron-fortified infant formula for mothers unable or choosing not to not fully breastfeed. When prescribed by a physician, WIC also provides special infant formulas and medical foods for infants with specific medical conditions.

Program Results

WIC has proven effective in improving the health of expectant and new mothers and their infants. Research confirms that WIC participation is associated with longer pregnancies (with fewer premature births), higher birth weights, and lower infant mortality. WIC program participants were more likely to receive prenatal care earlier and continue to receive it throughout their pregnancies and were more likely to breastfeed their infants.

The WIC program also has had a favorable effect on children's health. Research has found it more effective than SNAP or cash benefits at improving preschoolers' intake of key nutrients. The **Centers for Disease Control and Prevention (CDC)** credit the program with reducing iron deficiency anemia in young children, and children participating in WIC consume more iron, vitamin C, thiamin, niacin, and vitamin B6, without an increase in food energy intake (calories), which means that they are consuming more nutrient-dense foods as opposed to empty calories.

Children participating in WIC have higher rates of immunization and improved cognitive development as evidenced by better vocabulary test scores and significantly improved number recognition and memory. WIC participation also has been found to improve children's growth rates and increase the likelihood of their having a regular source or provider of medical care.

The program reduces health care costs—WIC program participants also had lower Medicaid costs than did pregnant women and babies who had not participated.

KEY TERMS

Immunization—The creation of immunity, or protection against a specific disease or disease-causing agent, usually by vaccination.

Infant mortality—The rate of infant deaths during the first year of life. The infant mortality rate is expressed as the number of infant deaths per 1,000 live births in a specific geographic area.

Iron deficiency anemia—Without an adequate supply of iron, the body is unable to make enough red blood cells or makes red blood cells that are too small.

Medicaid—A program funded by the federal and state governments that helps to pay for medical care for persons unable to afford such care.

Migrancy—Movement from one place of residence to another that is often associated with seeking work.

Passive smoking—Involuntary inhalation of smoke from other people's cigarettes, cigars, or pipes. Often termed "second-hand smoke," passive smoking poses health risks, especially for children.

Postpartum—The period shortly after childbirth.

Resources

BOOKS

Baydar, N. et al. *The WIC Infant Feeding Practices Study*, Final Report. Alexandria, VA: USDA Office of Analysis and Evaluation Food and Consumer Service, 1997.

Committee on Scientific Evaluation of WIC Nutrition Risk Criteria, Institute of Medicine *WIC Nutrition Risk Criteria: A Scientific Assessment (1996)*. Washington, D.C.: National Academy of Sciences, 1966.

Richardson, J., Porter, D.V., and Yavis Jones, J. *Child Nutrition and WIC Programs: Background and Funding*. Hauppauge NY: Nova Science Publishers, 2003.

PERIODICALS

Centers for Disease Control and Prevention (CDC). "Eligibility and Enrollment in the Special Supplemental Nutrition Program for Women, Infants, and Children (WIC)—27 states and New York City, 2007-2008." *Morbidity and Mortality Weekly Report (MMWR)* 62 (March 15, 2013): 189–193.

Chiasson, M.A., et al. "Changing WIC changes what children eat." *Obesity* 21 (July 2013): 1423–1429.

Guerrero A.D. et al., "A WIC-Based Curriculum to Enhance Parent Communication with Healthcare Providers." *Journal of Community Health* (June 13, 2013).

Hedberg, I. "Barriers to Breastfeeding in the WIC Population." *American Journal of Maternal Child Nursing* 38 (July–August 2013): 244–249.

Martin K.S. et al. "Formative Research to Examine Collaboration Between Special Supplemental Nutrition Program for Woman, Infants, and Children and Head Start Programs." *Maternal and Child Health Journal* (February 2013).

Odoms-Young, A.M. et al, "Evaluating the initial impact of the revised Special Supplemental Nutrition Program for Women, Infants, and Children (WIC) food packages on dietary intake and home food availability in African-American and Hispanic families." *Public Health Nutrition* (April 2, 2013): 1–11.

Zenk, S.N. et al., "Fruit and vegetable availability and selection: federal food package revisions, 2009." *American Journal of Preventive Medicine* 43 (October 2012): 423–428.

WEBSITES

U.S.D.A. Food & Nutrition Service. About WIC. http://www.fns.usda.gov/wic/aboutwic/ (accessed August 23, 2013).

U.S.D.A. Food & Nutrition Service. Who Gets WIC and How to Apply. http://www.fns.usda.gov/wic/howto apply/whogetswicandhowtoapply.htm (accessed August 23, 2013).

U.S.D.A. Food & Nutrition Service. Benefits & Service: WIC Food Packages. http://www.fns.usda.gov/wic/benefitsandservices/foodpkg.HTM (accessed August 23, 2013).

ORGANIZATIONS

U.S.D.A. Food and Nutrition Service, 3101 Park Center Drive, Alexandria, VA 22302, acip@cdc.gov

Barbara Wexler, MPH

The Stark Law

Definition

The Stark Law—also referred to as the "Physician Self-Referral Law"—is federal legislation authored by Congressman Pete Stark that was passed by the U.S. Congress in 1993. It was enacted after a number of studies in the 1980s suggested that physicians who own interests in ancillary service organizations (e.g., outside laboratories or imaging centers) tend to make more referrals to those organizations (and thus enrich themselves). The law limits referrals for medical services for **Medicare** and **Medicaid** patients if the referring physician—or member of his or her family—has a financial interest in the entity providing the services. The law excludes certain entities such as publically owned organizations and some joint ventures, but the law is complex and exclusions must be worked out carefully with lawyers. The Stark law is commonly referred to as a "strict liability" law because it can be violated without any intention to do so.

In addition to limiting the fees charged to Medicare and Medicaid, the law was designed to promote fair competition among service providers and keep costs down. Critics of the law have said that over-referral is not as common as is widely believed, and that physician-owned services reduce costs by offering services at lower rates than hospitals. This is particularly the case in rural areas, where quality medical care is often not readily available. Critics have also argued that the restrictions imposed by the Law may not allow for the best care to be provided; in order to avoid the appearance of self-interest, physicians may have to refer to less competent providers.

Why this is important to the consumer

Even though the Stark Law has not completely eliminated improper practice, its strong deterrents to fraud and abuse have been effective. The deterrents include requirements for physicians to return fees for improper services, fines, civil penalties, and the denial of future opportunities for physicians to participate in federal or state healthcare programs.

Resources

WEBSITES

"Stark Law—Information, Regulations, Legal Solutions." http://starklaw.org/default.htm (accessed October 15, 2013).

"Stark Law—Limitation on certain physician referrals." Qui Tam Whistleblower's Guide to the False Claims Act. http://quitamguide.org/stark-law-limitation-on-certain-physician-referrals (accessed October 15, 2013).

"The Stark Law Rules of the Road: An overview of the Stark Law to help interested physicians acquire an introductory knowledge of this intricate law." American Medical Association. 2011. http://www.ama-assn.org/resources/doc/psa/stark-law/stark-law.pdf (accessed October 15, 2013).

Joel C. Kahane, PhD

State Health Insurance Assistance Program (SHIP)

Definition

The State Health Insurance Assistance Program (SHIP) is a nationwide program that offers free counseling and assistance to **Medicare** beneficiaries, their families, and their caregivers.

Description

In an effort to help Medicare patients make better, more informed decisions about their benefits and healthcare, the Omnibus Budget Reconciliation Act of 1990 established the SHIP program to provide grants for states that create free Medicare advisory services. The primary objective of SHIP is to provide Medicare beneficiaries with easy-to-read, accurate, and unbiased information about their healthcare coverage so they can better understand their rights and protections under Medicare.

Formerly known as the Information, Counseling and Assistance (ICA) Grants Program, SHIP grants help to support a broad range of state-based programs that provide personalized counseling on topics related to Medicare, such as **Medigap, Medicare Advantage** plans, Medicare Savings Programs, **Medicaid**, and **long-term care insurance**. A key focus of SHIP is helping Medicare patients understand and obtain prescription drug coverage, a provision of the Medicare Prescription Drug Improvement and Modernization Act that was enacted in 2003.

SHIP counselors are specialists trained in Medicare and Medicaid law and regulations as well as other related health topics. Since they are not connected in any way to insurance companies, SHIP counselors can maintain a high level of objectivity and confidentiality. They are also trained in counseling techniques so that they may best help serve Medicare beneficiaries, many of whom are senior and/or disabled and have a great deal of difficulty understanding and navigating government healthcare policies and programs.

Why this is important to the consumer

As of 2013, all fifty American states and a number of U.S. territories were participating in SHIP. At the state level, SHIPs are responsible to recruit staff and volunteers to support more than 1,300 sponsoring agencies across the country, including social services agencies, geriatric care providers, senior housing programs, and hospitals. The result is a nationwide team of over 12,000 SHIP counselors who provide the option of one-on-one assistance to more than 45 million Medicare beneficiaries and their families.

Consumers can locate SHIP services in their area by visiting www.shiptalk.org and selecting their respective state. Available SHIP services may include but are not limited to:

• Identifying resources for prescription drug assistance
• Explaining Medicare health plan options

> **KEY TERMS**
>
> **Geriatric care**—A medical specialty that focuses on providing healthcare to individuals of advancing age.
>
> **Medicaid**—The largest source of healthcare-related funding for people with low income and/or disabilities in the United States.
>
> **Medicare**—A national health insurance program that guarantees health insurance to Americans aged 65 or older and some younger disabled individuals.
>
> **Medigap**—Private supplemental insurance plans that are available to Medicare beneficiaries to help cover out-of-pocket expenses.

• Navigating doctor and hospital bills
• Clarifying Medicare and/or Medicaid eligibility, enrollment, coverage, claims, and appeals
• Reviewing supplemental insurance needs
• Identifying potential Medicare fraud and/or abuse

Resources

BOOKS

U.S. Department of Health and Human Services. *Medicare & You 2013: The Official U.S. Government Handbook*. Seattle, WA: CreateSpace Independent Publishing, 2013.

WEBSITES

National Association of States United for Aging and Disabilities. "State Health Insurance Assistance Programs." NASUAD.org. http://www.nasuad.org/ship/ship.html (accessed October 20, 2013).

Seniors Resource Guide. "Find your State's State Health Insurance Assistance Program (SHIP)." seniorsresourceguide.com. http://www.seniorsresourceguide.com/directories/National/SHIP (accessed October 20, 2013).

State of New Jersey Department of Human Services. "State Health Insurance Assistance Program (SHIP)." state.nj.us. http://www.state.nj.us/humanservices/doas/services/ship/index.html (accessed October 20, 2013).

ORGANIZATIONS

Centers for Medicare and Medicaid Services, 7500 Security Blvd., Baltimore, MD 21244, (410) 786-0727, (877) 267-2323, http://www.cms.gov.

National Association of States United for Aging and Disabilities, 1201 15th St. NW, Ste. 350, Washington, DC 20005, (202) 898-2578, Fax: (202) 898-2583, info@ nasuad.org, http://www.nasuad.org.

Stephanie Dionne

Storefront clinic

Definition

A storefront clinic (also called a "retail health clinic") is a walk-in clinic located within a larger retail store, such as a supermarket, pharmacy, or "big box" discount store.

Description

Storefront clinics provide walk-in care for uncomplicated illnesses, such as strep throat, urinary tract infections, the flu, ear infections, or sinusitis. Storefront clinics also offer some immunizations, such as flu shots and shingles vaccines. Many clinics only treat individuals who do not have chronic illnesses, such as asthma, high blood pressure, or diabetes, while others are willing to help monitor chronic problems. Some storefront clinics offer sports or school physicals.

Most storefront clinics are staffed by mid-level care providers, such as nurse practitioners or physician assistants; the majority do not have a physician on-site, although a physician may be available by telephone. While simple labs can be obtained (such as rapid strep or flu tests), there are no on-site x-rays available, and procedures such as setting a fracture or stitching up a laceration are not performed. If a situation is deemed too complex or too urgent for the staff of the clinic, the patient is referred back to his or her primary care provider, or on to an urgent care or emergency department; about 2% of storefront clinic visits end in the patient being sent elsewhere for care.

Storefront clinics have increased rapidly in number (1,423 exist in 2013, and there are projected to be as many as 3,200 by the beginning of 2015). They have also skyrocketed in popularity. In 2007, there were 1.48 million visits to these types of clinics. In 2009, there were 5.97 million such visits. In 2012, more than 10 million storefront clinic visits occurred.

Why this is important to the consumer

Consumers explain that they favor these storefront clinics because there is no need for an appointment, they typically have extended evening and weekend hours (studies show that almost half of

Many storefront clinics are located within larger retail stores such as supermarkets and pharmacies. *(Spencer Platt/Getty Images)*

KEY TERMS

Acute—Having a rapid or sudden onset, and often lasting for a short period.

Chronic—Occurring over a long period of time; persistent, recurrent.

Nurse practitioner—An advanced practice nurse whose practice scope includes diagnosis and treatment, in some cases outside of the direct supervision of a physician.

Physician assistant—A healthcare provider whose practice scope includes diagnosis and treatment, which must be provided under the direct supervision of a physician.

storefront clinic visits occur during times when traditional doctor's offices are usually closed), and the storefront clinics usually offer a clear price list. Many clinic visits are covered entirely or in part by insurance, although individuals should verify whether their insurance company considers a given clinic to be in- or out-of-network. Although patients can take their prescriptions anywhere to be filled, many appreciate the one-stop-shopping aspect of filling their prescriptions at the store within which the clinic is located.

Drawbacks of obtaining care at a storefront clinic include the loss of continuity of care, the inability of the clinic to access past medical records from other care providers, a disconnect with an individual's primary care provider, decreased emphasis on preventive care (as compared to the mission of most primary care providers), and the possible overuse of antibiotics.

The United States has been facing a severe **shortage of primary care physicians** for some time now. Projections state that 2015 will see a shortage of 62,900 physicians, compared to the number necessary for the nation's population, and that 2020 will see that shortage reach 90,000 physicians. At the same time, the **Patient Protection and Affordable Care Act** will provide medical coverage to 3 million more Americans, thus further stressing the healthcare system. Storefront clinics, with their focus on affordable medical care provided by mid-level practitioners, are thought to be one answer to the healthcare shortages.

Resources

BOOKS

Kovner Anthony R. et al. *Health Care Delivery in the United States*, 10th ed. New York: Springer Publishing Company, 2011

Schulte, Margaret F.*Health Care Delivery in the U.S.A.: An Introduction*, 2nd ed. New York: Productivity Press, 2012

Sultz, Harry A. et al. *Health Care USA: Understanding Its Organization and Delivery*, 7th ed. Sudbury, MA: Jonas & Bartlett Learning, 2010

WEBSITES

National Caregivers Library. Types of Care Facilities [accessed September 22, 2013]. http://www.caregivers library.org/caregivers-resources/grp-care-facilities/types-of-care-facilities-article.aspx

USA.gov. Choosing a Health Care Facility. 2013. [accessed September 22, 2013]. http://www.usa.gov/topics/health/caregivers/health-care-facility.shtml/

ORGANIZATIONS

American Hospital Association, 155 N. Wacker Dr., Chicago, IL 60606, (312) 422-3000, http://www.aha.org/.

Convenient Care Association, 260 South Broad Street, Suite 1800, Philadelphia, PA 19102, (215) 731-7140, http://www.ccaclinics.org/.

United States Department of Labor, 200 Constitution Ave. NW, Washington, DC 20210, (800) 321-6742, https://www.osha.gov/.

Urgent Care Association of America, 387 Shuman Blvd., Suite 235W, Naperville, IL 60563 , (877) 698-2262, http://www.ucaoa.org/.

Rosalyn Carson-DeWitt, MD

Substance abuse and addiction treatment plans

Definition

Substance abuse, beginning with recreational use of drugs and alcohol and leading to addiction, is a complex problem both for the individual and society. The National Institute on Drug Abuse has reported, "23.2 million persons (9.4 percent of the U.S. population) aged 12 or older needed treatment for an illicit drug or alcohol use problem in 2007. Of these individuals, 2.4 million (10.4 percent of those who needed treatment) received treatment at a specialty facility (i.e., hospital, drug or alcohol rehabilitation, or mental health center). Thus, 20.8 million persons (8.4 percent of the population aged 12 or older) needed treatment for an illicit drug or alcohol use problem but did not receive it."

The Substance Abuse and Mental Health Services Administration's (SAMHSA) National Drug and Alcohol Treatment Service has a list of drugs that are subject to abuse or may cause adverse health consequences when used recreationally, and may in specific cases lead to addiction. Note that alcohol is not included in this list, although alcohol abuse and addiction also require appropriate treatment.

- Anabolic steroids
- Cigarettes and other tobacco products
- Club drugs—a group of rapid-acting sedative/hypnotics not chemically related
- Cocaine
- Hallucinogens—not chemically related
- Heroin—an opioid narcotic similar to other drugs on this list
- Inhalants—a variety of commercial products, not always medicinal, which may have psychoactive effects when inhaled.
- Khat—a stimulant substance with no medicinal use.
- Marijuana—may have useful medicinal properties, and its status appears to be under debate at this time.
- MDMA—3,4-methylenedioxy-methamphetamine, a synthetic substance which has both stimulant and hallucinogenic properties.
- Methamphetamine—a stimulant with medicinal properties, it is related to amphetamine, dextroamphetamine, and other drugs.
- Prescription and over-the-counter medications—this is a catch-all term but refers to abuse of narcotic analgesics that are available by prescriptions, as well as over-the-counter decongestants that are chemically related to the amphetamine group. Dextromethophan, an over-the-counter cough suppressant, has also been subject to abuse.
- Stimulant medications (e.g., methylphenidate and amphetamines) are often prescribed to treat individuals diagnosed with attention-deficit hyperactivity disorder (ADHD). These are of the same chemical family as the previously listed methamphetamine and decongestant drugs.

Description

Well-controlled studies have demonstrated that treatment can help people overcome even serious addiction problems, however, there are a number of principles that must be followed.

1. It is important for the patient to recognize that addiction is a complex problem that affects both their brain function and behavior. Unless they understand the effects that addiction is having on their lives, treatment is unlikely to be successful.
2. No single treatment is appropriate for all patients. Some patients may fail with one particular course of treatment but succeed with a different modality.
3. Effective treatment should consider all the needs of the patient, not simply the drug abuse. Patients may be successfully detoxified but revert to drug abuse unless the problems that made them turn to drugs are adequately resolved.
4. Patients must remain in treatment for an adequate period of time. In some cases, this may require a lifelong commitment to participating in programs.
5. Counseling, either individual or group, should be part of any drug abuse treatment.
6. Medications are a valuable part of treatment when combined with counseling. Medications may have different properties. Some may help treat the underlying problems that led to drug abuse, others may provide a form of aversion therapy, while still others may reduce the craving for abuse drugs.
7. Treatment plans must be routinely reviewed and revised as necessary.
8. Because many people with drug abuse problems have other mental disorders, a full psychiatric and/or psychological evaluation should be part of any treatment plan. When an underlying disorder is found, it must be treated appropriately.
9. The patient must understand that detoxification is only the first step in a comprehensive program.
10. Treatment does not have to be voluntary to be effective.
11. Drug use during treatment must be routinely monitored, commonly by blood-level tests. Lapses during treatment are common.
12. The patient should be evaluated for medical conditions that may be coincidental or secondary to drug abuse. For example, patients who take drugs intravenously may be subject to HIV (AIDS) and hepatitis, and tuberculosis may also be a hazard. Counseling should include discussion of behaviors to avoid infectious diseases.

Principles of Treatment

In 2005, Volkow and Li of the National Institute on Drug Abuse and the National Institute on Alcohol Abuse and Alcoholism published a report in the journal Pharmacologu & Therapeutics, which stated, "Addiction is now recognized as a chronic brain disease that involves complex interactions between repeated exposure to drugs, biological (i.e., genetic and developmental), and environmental (i.e., drug availability, social, and economic variables) factors. Its treatment, therefore, requires, in general, not only a long-term intervention but also a multipronged approach that addresses the psychiatric, medical, legal, and social consequences of addiction. Also, because addiction usually starts in adolescence or early adulthood and is frequently comorbid with mental illness, we need to expand our treatment interventions in this age group both for substance abuse and psychiatric disorders." However, it has been estimated that only 10% of people with substance abuse problems receive treatment, and many fail due to use of unproven therapies.

Use of medications

Disulfiram

Disulfiram, commonly known as Antabuse, is a longstanding treatment for alcohol abuse and alcoholism. It acts by altering the metabolism of alcohol and leads to the accumulation of acetaldehyde, which causes unpleasant reactions, including flushing, nausea, and palpitations. Obviously, compliance can be a problem, since patients are more likely to discontinue taking disulfiram than to discontinue using alcohol, but in highly motivated patients the drug has been useful.

Substitutes

Replacement drugs may be used as an intermediate step, to provide the patient with a drug that is similar to the abuse drug but which is more socially acceptable and may be easier to control and/or withdraw from. One typical example is nicotine, available in patch, lozenge, and inhalation for smoking reduction. Although nicotine is the addictive substance in tobacco, many of the health hazards are related to the tars in tobacco smoke. Nicotine patches and lozenges have a long duration of action, which reduces the frequent craving for nicotine, which occurs when the substance is rapidly absorbed through inhalation.

Varenicline is a synthetic substance that occupies the nicotine receptor sites in the brain and may also reduce the urge for nicotine.

Methadone, a long-acting opioid, may serve a similar function for patients with addiction to opioids. The drug is taken by mouth and so does not have the rapid onset of intravenous narcotics. Methadone has a long duration of action so that patients may be able to maintain a daily routine, including holding a job.

Antagonists

Buprenorphine is a partial narcotics agonist. While it may produce some of the effects of narcotics, the effects, euphoria and respiratory depression, are milder than those of full narcotics such as methadone,

and even with increasing doses, buprenorphine reaches a plateau and does not provide the same level of response as true narcotics agonists. It is routinely supplied in combination with the antagonist naloxone in order to prevent the tablets from being dissolved and administered intravenously. This is because naloxone is far better absorbed intravenously than sublingually. As such, naloxone given intravenously will block absorption of buprenorphine, but when given sublingually, the bupreorphine will have its full effect of providing a mild narcotic euphoria.

While substitutes belong to the same class of drugs as the addictive substance, antagonists are substances that bind to the same receptor site but lack the effects of the addictive drug. Thus, they block the effects of the addictive drug. In some cases, they may serve as antidotes to the addictive substance, Naloxone, an opioid antagonist, is added to bupreorphone, an opioid, to prevent the combination tablets from being dissolved and administered intravenously. Taken orally, the patient gets the effects of the buprenorphine, which are much the same as those of methadone.

Naltrexone is an opioid receptor antagonist that would fall under the category of "substitutes" because, like varencicline, it occupies the receptor sites in the brain normally occupied by narcotic analgesics; however, this drug has shown a number of related uses, including ultra-rapid detoxification, in which the patient is anesthetized and given a dose of naltrexone. The naltrexone replaces the narcotics, while the anesthesia keeps the patient unaware of the withdrawal syndrome. Maintenance treatment with naltrexone prevents the opioid from producing a pleasurable response, which, in time, reduces the craving.

Acamprosate

Acamprosate, sold under the brand name Campral, is used in combination with therapy to treat alcoholism. The mechanism of action is unknown.

Therapy

Although drugs have been shown to be useful in treating drug and alcohol abuse, they are ineffective in producing a true cure. This is because they do not treat the underlying considerations that made the patient turn to drugs or alcohol. As noted above, no single treatment is effective in all cases; any treatment plan must take into consideration the particular needs of each patient. Treatment facilities must be readily available, and the patient must stay in therapy for an adequate amount of time in order to obtain lasting results. According to the National Institute on Drug and Alcohol Abuse: "Research indicates that most addicted individuals need at least 3 months in treatment to significantly reduce or stop their drug use and that the best outcomes occur with longer durations of treatment. Recovery from drug addiction is a long-term process and frequently requires multiple episodes of treatment. As with other chronic illnesses, relapses to drug abuse can occur and should signal a need for treatment to be reinstated or adjusted. Because individuals often leave treatment prematurely, programs should include strategies to engage and keep patients in treatment."

Behavioral therapies are the most common form of drug treatment and include individual therapy, family therapy, or group therapy. While they must be tailored to the specific needs of the patient, they must provide support and motivation for change. This may include providing rewards for abstinence, such as provision of alternative rewards, as well as work on building interpersonal skills and relationships. In addition to formal therapy, peer group meetings both during and following treatment can provide useful support.

Outpatient therapies of this type are quite cost-effective and, even allowing for the need to repeat therapy, have a good record of success. In contrast, residential therapy, in which the patient remains at a treatment center for 30 days, is rarely effective and may be inordinately expensive.

Why this is important to the consumer

Substance abuse is both a serious problem for patients and their families and a tremendous social expense. According to a September 9, 2013, report by Jake Bernstein of ProPublica: "Outpatient addiction treatment for the poor has become a mainstay of the social safety net, costing the federal, state and local governments $6.7 billion in 2009, the most recent figure available. The money pays for an estimated 1.5 million admissions a year, nearly three-fourths of them to outpatient programs like NYSN's, according to a study by the National Center on Addiction and Substance Abuse at Columbia University." These costs are in addition to the estimated $80 billion per year that is spent on imprisonment of low-level drug offenders.

The Columbia University program notes that, based on the number of people affected, treatment for drug addiction and availability of treatment is seriously underfunded. The Columbia group reports that in 2010, $28 billion was spent on addiction treatment, although 40 million people have a drug or

alcoholism problem. In contrast, $44 billion was spent to treat diabetes, which affects 26 million people, and $87 billion to treat cancer, which affects 19 million people.

Resources

BOOKS

Henningfield P. (ed). *Addiction Treatment: Science and Policy for the Twenty-First Century*. Johns Hopkins University Ptress, Baltimore: 2007.

McFarland Bentson H., Dennis McCarty, and Anne E. Kovas (eds.). *Medicaid & Treatment for People with Substance Abuse Problems*. Nova Science Publishers: 2011.

PERIODICALS

Miller, Michael, and Ken Roy. "Parity and the medicalization of addiction treatment." *Journal of Psychoactive Drugs* 42, no. 2 (2010): 115.

Molfenter, Todd, et al. "The readiness of addiction treatment agencies for health care reform." *Substance Abuse Treatment, Prevention, and Policy* 7 (2012): 16.

Roy, A. Kenison, III, and Michael M. Miller. "The medicalization of addiction treatment professionals." *Journal of Psychoactive Drugs* 44, no. 2 (2012): 107.

Tovino, Stacey A. "A proposal for comprehensive and specific essential mental health and substance use disorder benefits." *American Journal of Law & Medicine* (Summer–Fall 2012): 471.

WEBSITES

Beck, Deborah. "Can't Get Treatment Through Your Health Insurance Plan?" HBO. http://www.hbo.com/addiction/treatment/362_not_covered_by_insurance.html (accesed September 24, 2013).

"Principles of Drug Addiction Treatment: A Research-Based Guide, 3rd edition." National Institute on Drug Abuse. December 2012. http://www.drugabuse.gov/publications/principles-drug-addiction-treatment (accesed September 24, 2013).

ORGANIZATIONS

Narcotics Anonymous, PO Box 9999, Van Nuys, CA, US 91409, (818) 773-9999, Fax: (818) 700-0700, fsmail@na.org, http://www.na.org.

National Insitute on Drug Abuse, 6001 Executive Boulevard, Bethesda, MD, US 20892-9561, (301) 443-1124, Contact form on website, http://www.drugabuse.gov.

Substance Abuse and Mental Health Services Administration, 1 Choke Cherry Road, Rockville,, MD, US 20857, (248) 699-8524, (877) SAMHSA-7, http://www.samhsa.gov/.

Samuel D. Uretsky, MD/Pharm.D.

Substance abuse and dependence

Approximately 22.1 million people* were classified as having a substance dependence or abuse disorder in 2010.

Dependence on specific drugs included:

Alcohol	17.0 million**
Marijuana	4.5 million
Pain relievers	1.9 million
Cocaine	1.0 million
Tranquilizers	521,000
Hallucinogens	397,000
Heroin	359,000
Stimulants	357,000
Sedatives	162,000
Inhalants	161,000

*Aged 12 and older
**Users may have abused more than one substance, so the number of users of each substance may be higher than the total estimated number of people with a substance abuse disorder.

SOURCE: Substance Abuse and Mental Health Services Administration, Office of Applied Studies, *Results from the 2010 National Survey on Drug Use and Health: Summary of National Findings* (September 2011).

(Table by PreMediaGlobal. Reproduced by permission of Gale, a part of Cengage Learning.)

Substance abuse clinic

Definition

A substance abuse clinic is a facility that provides treatment for people who are addicted to alcohol and/or other drugs. Substance abuse clinics may be in- or outpatient, or longer-term residential.

Description

Substance abuse clinics treat people with physical and psychological addictions to substances such as alcohol, cocaine, or prescription narcotics. Many individuals are considered poly-drug users, meaning that they are addicted to more than one substance. Physical addiction refers to the body's biological response to continued use of an addictive substance. Over time, the body requires that substance in order to function normally. When that substance is taken away, there may be severe, uncomfortable, painful, and even life-threatening effects. Psychological addiction refers to an individual's compulsive seeking of the drug, in response to strong cravings. Both of these two arms of addiction must be addressed to treat substance abuse effectively.

The goal of a substance abuse clinic is to help break the individual's addiction and to return that individual to his or her optimal level of functioning. Many people who suffer from substance abuse have fractured their relationships, destroyed their work life, and thrown themselves into financial ruin. They may be suffering physical illness from the effects of substance abuse. Effective substance abuse treatment must

- Prevent the dangerous toxic effects of withdrawing from an addictive substance
- Treat the physical discomfort associated with withdrawal
- Treat the emotional and psychological discomfort associated with withdrawal
- Uncover the psychological dynamics that may lead to and/or support continued drug use
- Assist with occupational rehabilitation
- Assist with rehabilitation of injured relationships

Treatment modalities in a substance abuse clinic include

- Medications: Both to treat the physiological effects of withdrawal, and to prevent the use of drugs or alcohol.
- Therapy: Can be individual or group. Helps deconstruct the environmental and emotional triggers to drug and alcohol use, and learn strategies to avoid

A man enters a community-based substance abuse clinic. *(© Jeff Greenberg / Alamy)*

falling back into use. Works on interpersonal dynamics to improve relationships damaged by substance abuse. Provides support and positive reinforcement as individuals work to rebuild their lives without substances. May involve family members in therapy.

Substance abuse clinics are usually staffed by a team of individuals, including a physician trained in addiction medicine or addiction psychiatry, psychologists, social workers, chemical dependency counselors, and nurses.

Why this is important to the consumer

Recent statistics suggest that there are 23.5 million people in need of treatment for substance abuse in the United States, yet only 11% of these individuals received that treatment in the last year. About 41% received treatment for alcohol abuse, 20% for their use of heroin or other opiates, and 17% for marijuana use. The government estimates an annual cost of more than $600 billion dollars associated with substance abuse, in the form of crime, decreased work productivity, and medical care.

Resources

BOOKS

Kovner Anthony R. et al. *Health Care Delivery in the United States* 10th ed. New York: Springer Publishing Company, 2011.

Schulte,Margaret F.*Health Care Delivery in the U.S.A.: An Introduction* 2nd ed. New York: Productivity Press, 2012.

Sultz, Harry A. et al. *Health Care USA: Understanding Its Organization and Delivery* 7th ed. Sudbury, MA: Jones & Bartlett Learning, 2010.

WEBSITES

National Caregivers Library. Types of Care Facilities [accessed September 22, 2013]. http://www.caregivers library.org/caregivers-resources/grp-care-facilities/ types-of-care-facilities-article.aspx.

USA.gov. Choosing a Health Care Facility. 2013 [accessed September 22, 2013]. http://www.usa.gov/topics/ health/caregivers/health-care-facility.shtml/.

ORGANIZATIONS

American Board of Addiction Medicine, 4601 North Park Avenue, Upper Arcade, Suite 101, Chevy Chase, MD 20815, (301) 656-3378, http://www.abam.net/about/ faqs/faqs-14/.

KEY TERMS

Addiction—Compulsive use of a substance despite negative outcomes. Tied to physiological and psychological cravings for the substance, as well as symptoms of withdrawal when the substance is not used.

Dependence—A state of physiological need for a substance. Abstinence results in unpleasant and even dangerous side effects.

Rehabilitation—The process necessary in order to return to normal functioning.

Withdrawal—A syndrome of physiological changes and symptoms that occur when an addicted substance abuser abstains from the substance.

National Institute on Drug Abuse, Office of Science Policy and Communications, Public Information and Liaison Branch, 6001 Executive Boulevard, Room 5213, MSC 9561., Bethesda, MD 20892, (301) 443-1124, (888) 478- 7653, http://www.drugabuse.gov/.

The Substance Abuse and Mental Health Services Administration, 1 Choke Cherry Road, 1 Choke Cherry Road, MD 20857, (877) 786-4787, http://www.samhsa.gov/.

United States Department of Labor, 200 Constitution Ave. NW, Washington, DC 20210, (800) 321-6742, https://www.osha.gov/.

Rosalyn Carson-DeWitt, MD

∎ Summary of Benefits and Coverage (SBC)

Definition

Under the **Patient Protection and Affordable Care Act** (ACA) of 2010, health insurers and group health plans must provide Americans who have private insurance with clear, consistent, and comparable information concerning their health care benefits and coverage. Consumers have two sources of information to help them understand and evaluate their health care choices. These sources include:

- An easy-to-understand summary of benefits and coverage (SBC)
- A uniform glossary of terms commonly used in health insurance coverage

Why this is important to the consumer

A summary of benefits and coverage document helps consumers better understand the coverage that they have as well as allow them to easily compare different coverage options.

Description

A provision of the ACA required that the United States **Department of Health and Human Services (HHS)** develop standards for use by health insurance issuers and group health plans that offer group or individual coverage to compile and provide a document that contains an accurate summary of benefits and explanation of coverage to plan participants. Willful failure to provide this information results in a $1,000 fine per enrollee for each failure. If a health plan or issuer makes any material modification to the terms of the plan or coverage that is different from what is in the most recent SBC, the plan or issuer must notify the enrollees of the modification at least 60 days in advance. Draft standards were developed by March 23, 2011, and the final rule was published in the *Federal Register* on February 14, 2012. Group health plans and insurance issuers were required to start implementing the requirements beginning September 23, 2012, depending on timing of open enrollment periods for group health plans.

Summary of benefits and coverage

Under ACA, insurance companies and group health plans must provide consumers with a concise standardized document that explains in clear language the benefits and coverage provided by specific plans. Consumers receive the summary when shopping for coverage, enrolling in coverage, at the beginning of each new plan year or upon renewal, during special enrollments, upon material modification during a plan year, and within seven business days of requesting a copy from their health insurance issuer or group health plan. An example of a summary of benefits and coverage can be downloaded at https://www.cms.gov/CCIIO/Resources/Files/Downloads/sbc-sample.pdf. More detailed information on specific plans is also available in the policy or plan documents for each plan developed by insurance companies and group health plans.

The standards used to guide the development of an SBC include:

- Appearance—An SBC must be presented in a uniform format, may not be longer than four double-sided pages, and may not include print smaller than the 12-point size.

KEY TERMS

Material Modification—Changes in coverage, which can include increases or decreases in benefits; coverage of previously excluded benefits; reduced cost-sharing; reductions in covered services or benefits; increases in premiums; increases in out-of-pocket amounts; adverse changes in an HMO service area; and any new requirements for receipt of benefits, such as new pre-certification requirements.

Minimum Essential Coverage—The type of coverage an individual needs to have to meet the individual responsibility requirement under the ACA. This includes individual market policies; job-based coverage; Medicare; Medicaid; Children's Health Insurance Program (CHIP); the health care program serving Uniformed Service members, retirees, and their families worldwide (TRICARE); and certain other coverages.

Minimum value statement—A statement that the insurance covers or does not cover at least 60% of the total cost of care.

Grandfathered plan—A health care plan that was in existence on March 23, 2010 and has stayed basically the same. A plan can enroll people after that date and still maintain its grandfathered status because that designation is determined by the date the plan was created, not when a participant joined it. Health plans must disclose if they are grandfathered in all materials describing plan benefits and offer contact information. In addition, all health plans, grandfathered or not, must: 1) end lifetime limits on coverage, 2) end arbitrary cancellations of health coverage, 3) cover adult children up to age 26, 4) provide an SBC, and 5) hold insurance companies accountable to spend premiums on health care and not on administrative costs and bonuses. However, grandfathered plans do not have to: 1) cover preventive care for free, 2) guarantee the participant's right to appeal, 3) protect the participant's choice of doctors and access to emergency care, and 4) be held accountable through Rate Review for excessive premium increases.

• Language—An SBC must be presented in a culturally and linguistically appropriate manner and must use terminology understandable by the average plan enrollee. Plans and issuers must offer and disclose the availability of language assistance for non-English speakers. The availability of SBCs in non-English languages is based on the number of people in a county who speak the same non-English language; if that number is or exceeds 10 percent of the county's population, then SBCs in that language must be made available. A list of counties meeting or exceeding the 10 percent threshold for the Spanish, Chinese, Tagalog, and Navajo languages (as determined by 2007–2011 American Community Survey [ACS] data published by the U.S. Census Bureau) can be downloaded at http://www.cms.gov/CCIIO/Resources/Fact-Sheets-and-FAQs/Downloads/2013-clas-data.pdf. The 2013 list presently on the web site will be updated annually.

• Form—An SBC must always be available in paper form, but it can be provided in electronic form as well.

• Content—At a minimum, an SBC must include:

1. Uniform definitions of standard insurance and medical terms

2. Description of coverage, including cost sharing

3. Exceptions, reductions, and limitations on coverage

4. Renewability and continuation of coverage provisions

5. Coverage examples

6. If the coverage begins after January 1, 2014, a statement of whether the plan or coverage provides minimum essential coverage and a minimum value statement

7. Statement that the outline is only a summary and that the coverage document itself should be used to understand controlling contractual provisions

8. Contact number for questions and for obtaining a copy of the plan document or policy

9. If applicable, contact information for obtaining a list of network providers

10. If applicable, information on prescription drug coverage

11. If applicable, an internet address and contact number for obtaining the uniform glossary, and

12. If applicable, a disclosure that paper copies are available

If a plan's benefits cannot be reasonably described within the SBC standard requirements and templates, the plan or issuer must still provide the information on the plan's terms while adhering as closely as possible to the instructions and templates for a standard SBC. A grandfathered plan, that is, one that was in existence on March 23, 2010 and has stayed basically the same, must also provide an SBC.

For health coverage that is provided outside the United States, rather than providing an SBC, a plan or issuer can provide an internet address or similar contact information for obtaining information about coverage or benefits. For coverage within the United States, the plan or issuer must still provide an SBC.

The summary of benefits and coverage also includes a comparison tool referred to as *coverage examples*. The coverage examples illustrate how a health insurance policy or plan covers two common health benefits scenarios: Type 2 diabetes care (routine maintenance of a well-controlled condition) and childbirth (normal delivery). Insurance issuers and plan administrators simulate claims processing for each scenario so consumers can understand the coverage they will get for their premium dollars.

Uniform glossary

Another resource for consumers to help them understand the terminology and jargon used in the summary of benefits and coverage documents is the Uniform Glossary of Terms. Insurance companies and group health plans will be required to provide upon request the glossary for their plans. An example of a Glossary can be downloaded at https://www.cms.gov/CCIIO/Resources/Files/Downloads/uniform-glossary-final.pdf. This sample glossary contains many commonly used terms but is not a full list. These glossary terms and definitions are intended to be educational and may be different from the terms and definitions in specific plans. Some of these terms also might not have exactly the same meaning when used in actual policies and plans.

Resources

BOOKS

Jones, Denecia A. *The Simple Reader's Guide to Understanding the Affordable Care Act (ACA) Health Care Reform.* Bloomington, IN: Abbot Press, 2013.

Selker, Harry P. and June S. Wasser. *The Affordable Care Act as a National Experiment: Health Policy Innovations and Lessons.* Springer: 2014.

WEBSITES

"Other Resources." The Center for Consumer Information & Insurance Oversight, Centers for Medicare & Medicaid Services. http://www.cms.gov/cciio/Resources/forms-reports-and-other-resources/index.html#sbcug (accessed October 4, 2013).

"Summary of Benefits and Coverage—How Does the Health Care Law Protect Me?" Healthcare.gov. https://www.healthcare.gov/how-does-the-health-care-law-protect-me-/#part = 4 (accessed October 4, 2013).

"Summary of Benefits and Coverage and Uniform Glossary, Affordable Care Act." U.S. Department of Labor, Employee Benefits Security Administration. http://www.dol.gov/ebsa/healthreform/#summaryofbenefits (accessed October 4, 2013).

"Summary of Benefits and Coverage and Uniform Glossary, Final Rule." *Federal Register* 77, no. 30 (February 14, 2012). https://www.federalregister.gov/articles/2012/02/14/2012-3228/summary-of-benefits-and-coverage-and-uniform-glossary (accessed October 4, 2013).

Judith L. Sims, M.S.

Supplemental insurance

Definition

Supplemental insurance is an extra or additional policy that consumers can purchase to help pay for medical services and expenses due to accident, disability, critical illness, or hospitalization that regular health insurance plans might not cover. Examples of the costs that supplemental insurance plans might cover include out-of-pocket medical expenses (such as deductibles, copayments, and coinsurance), lost wages due to certain medical conditions, travel and lodging costs for medical treatments, and basic living expenses during an illness or injury.

Description

As the cost of providing health insurance benefits to employees increased steadily through the 1990s and 2000s, many private employers moved toward consumer-driven insurance plans. Under these plans, employers offered only high-deductible health insurance policies that protected employees from catastrophic medical expenses. Employees were responsible for paying routine, non-catastrophic health care costs directly, outside of employer-provided insurance. Many consumers found that these everyday medical expenses and out-of-pocket costs added up quickly and placed a strain on their financial resources.

Insurance companies responded to this trend by offering supplemental insurance policies directly to consumers to help them pay for non-covered health-care expenses. Supplemental insurance is available from many sources, including private insurers like Aflac, MetLife, and Colonial Life as well as consumer

Percentage of noninstitutionalized Medicare enrollees age 65 and over with supplemental health insurance, by type of insurance, 1991–2005

| Year | Types of supplemental insurance | | | | | |
	Private (employer or union sponsored)	Private (Medigap)*	HMO	Medicaid	Other public	No supplement
			Percent			
1991	40.7	44.8	6.3	8.9	4.0	11.3
1992	41.0	45.0	5.9	9.0	5.3	10.4
1993	40.8	45.3	7.7	9.4	5.8	9.7
1994	40.3	45.2	9.1	9.9	5.5	9.3
1995	39.1	44.3	10.9	10.1	5.0	9.1
1996	37.8	38.6	13.8	9.5	4.8	9.4
1997	37.6	35.8	16.6	9.4	4.7	9.2
1998	37.0	33.9	18.6	9.6	4.8	8.9
1999	35.8	33.2	20.5	9.7	5.1	9.0
2000	35.9	33.5	20.4	9.9	4.9	9.7
2001	36.0	34.5	18.0	10.6	5.4	10.1
2002	36.1	37.5	15.5	10.7	5.5	12.3
2003	36.1	34.3	14.8	11.6	5.7	11.8
2004	36.6	33.7	15.6	11.3	5.2	12.6
2005	36.1	34.6	15.5	11.8	5.6	12.0

Note: *Includes persons with private supplement of unknown sponsorship.

SOURCE: Centers for Medicare and Medicaid Services, Medicare Current Beneficiary Survey

(Illustration by GGS Information Services. Cengage Learning, Gale)

groups like the **American Association of Retired Persons (AARP)**. It generally has a lower monthly premium than primary health insurance policies.

Supplemental insurance is also known as "voluntary insurance," because consumers purchase it on a voluntary basis to provide extra protection on top of their major medical policies. In addition, it is sometimes called "defined benefit insurance," because it pays specific dollar benefits for various types of covered medical expenses. Unlike regular health insurance benefits, which are paid to hospitals and doctors, supplemental insurance generally pays cash benefits directly to beneficiaries to use at their discretion.

Types of Supplemental Insurance Policies

One of the most common types of supplemental insurance is Medigap, which is a product offered by private insurance companies to people enrolled in the federal **Medicare** program. Medicare Part A (hospital insurance) and Part B (medical insurance) cover many health-related services and medical supplies for Americans over age 65 and younger people with disabilities. Medicare coverage does involve out-of-pocket expenses, however, and it does not cover vision or dental care, most long-term care, or any medical services rendered outside of the United States. Medigap policies are available to cover the "gaps" that are not covered by Medicare, including copayments, coinsurance, and deductibles. First Medicare pays its share of the Medicare-approved amounts for covered healthcare costs, and then the Medigap policy pays its share.

Another common type of supplemental insurance provides coverage for critical illnesses or specific diseases, such as cancer. This type of policy usually provides consumers with a cash benefit that they can use to pay costs related to their illness that are not covered by their regular health insurance policy. Such costs may include experimental treatments, out-of-network specialists, travel and lodging for treatments, child care, and living expenses.

An accidental death and dismemberment policy is a type of supplemental insurance that pays a lump-sum cash benefit to the named beneficiary of someone who dies or is severely injured in an accident. An accident health insurance policy covers medical costs resulting from an accident that may not be covered by regular insurance, such as home healthcare services. Finally, hospital confinement or indemnity insurance provides a cash benefit to patients who are hospitalized for long periods of time as a result of a serious illness or injury. Patients can use this money to pay for non-covered medical services or cover basic living expenses during their hospitalization.

KEY TERMS

Consumer-driven health insurance—A high-deductible policy that mainly covers catastrophic medical costs.

Medigap—Private insurance policies that pay health-related expenses not covered under the federal Medicare program.

Out-of-pocket costs—Healthcare expenses not covered under regular insurance policies, including deductibles and copayments.

Why this is important to the consumer

Supplemental insurance offers consumers an extra layer of protection against unexpected medical costs, beyond what traditional health insurance policies or the federal Medicare program may provide. Supplemental insurance policies tend to be affordable and easy to understand, and they often pay cash benefits that policyholders can use at their own discretion. Policies are available that can ease the financial burden of routine medical care by covering deductibles, copayments, and coinsurance. Other supplemental policies reduce the financial impact of lost wages for consumers who experience a serious accident or illness or require long-term hospitalization.

Despite the advantages of supplemental insurance, industry analysts emphasize that consumers should view these policies as an addition to—rather than a replacement for—traditional health insurance. Major medical policies provide broad coverage for a range of health care needs, from preventive services to catastrophic illnesses. Supplemental insurance policies, on the other hand, tend to focus on specific situations or costs that are not otherwise covered. The two types of insurance are intended to work together in combination to increase the level of protection available to consumers.

Insurance experts recommend that consumers only purchase supplemental insurance if they fully understand what the policy covers, what restrictions or conditions are attached to it, what coverage they already have under Medicare or private health insurance, how much the supplemental policy will cost, how much the premium rates might increase in the future, and whether their personal risk is great enough to justify the expense. Consumers who understand the costs and benefits associated with supplemental insurance are more likely to find an affordable policy that

eases the burden of rising out-of-pocket medical costs and protects against financial hardship.

Resources

BOOKS

Yang, Yan. *Medicare Supplemental Insurance.* Saarbrucken, Germany: VDM Publishing, 2009.

PERIODICALS

Fuscaldo, Donna. "Do You Need Supplemental Health-Care Insurance?" FoxBusiness.com, July 9, 2013. http://www.foxbusiness.com/personal-finance/2013/07/09/do-need-supplemental-health-care-insurance/ (accessed September 10, 2013).

WEBSITES

AARP. "Overview of Medicare Supplemental Insurance." AARP.org, May 2010. http://www.aarp.org/health/medicare-insurance/info-10-2008/overview_medicare_supplemental_insurance.html (accessed September 10, 2013).

Centers for Medicare and Medicaid Services. "Choosing a Medigap Policy: A Guide to Health Insurance for People with Medicare." Medicare.Gov, 2013. http://www.medicare.gov/pubs/pdf/02110.pdf (accessed September 10, 2013).

Zuna, Michael. "Why Voluntary Insurance Matters." TheIHCC.com, 2013. http://www.theihcc.com/en/communities/supplemental_health/why-voluntary-insurance-matters_hjuk4f78.html?s=XPf4nTtUOE BaAQa0r (accessed September 10, 2013).

ORGANIZATIONS

America's Health Insurance Plans (AHIP), 601 Pennsylvania Ave. NW, South Bldg., Suite 500, Washington, DC 20004, (202) 778-3200, Fax: (202) 331-7487, ahip@ahip.org, http://www.ahip.org.

Laurie Collier Hillstrom

▌Supplemental Nutrition Assistance Program (SNAP)

Definition

The Supplemental Nutrition Assistance Program (SNAP), which was known as the federal Food Stamp Program until October 2008, is one of the largest nutrition assistance programs for low-income households in the United States. It was launched nationwide in 1974 and is a federal program that is administered by the United States Department of Agriculture (USDA), Food and Nutrition Service (FNS).

Historically, SNAP has been the largest program in the U.S. hunger safety net, however, its importance has

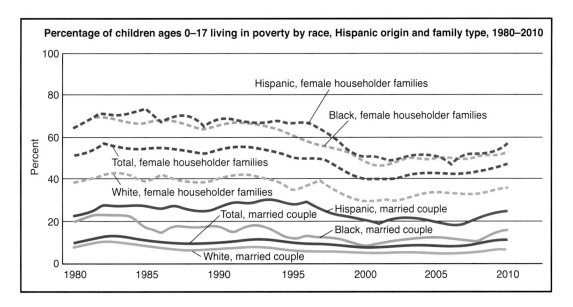

Percentage of children ages 0–17 living in poverty by race, Hispanic origin and family type, 1980–2010

(Illustration by Electronic Illustrators Group. © 2013 Cengage Learning.)

intensified in recent years as the program experienced record-high levels of participation. In fiscal year 2012, the program provided benefits to more than 46 million Americans—about one in seven people—every month.

SNAP is reassessed and reauthorized by Congress every five years as part of the Farm Bill. However, the most recent extension—through September 2013—was as part of the American Taxpayer Relief Act.

Purpose

SNAP helps to reduce hunger among low-income individuals and families and aims to improve the health of low-income people nationwide. The program is intended to reduce food insecurity, which is a measure of the extent to which a household has limited access to food due to lack of money or other resources.

Eligibility

Eligibility for SNAP considers a number of factors, including household income, the number of people in the household, and other financial resources, such as Social Security and unemployment benefits and Supplemental Security Income (SSI) benefits.

For example, using the standard of 130% of the federal poverty level, a family of four living in the 48 states, Guam, or the Virgin Islands, with a gross monthly income of $2,552 or less, was eligible for SNAP benefits in 2013–2014. This family would be eligible for a maximum SNAP benefit of $632 per month.

The USDA Food & Nutrition Service website has an online prescreening tool that is designed to help people determine whether they are eligible to receive SNAP benefits. By entering information including earnings, rent or mortgage, utility bills, child support, day care expenses, medical bills (for persons age 60 or older, or persons with disabilities), child support payments or SSI, social security, or **VA** payments, people can find out whether to apply for benefits at their local SNAP office. The online tool also can roughly estimate the dollar amount of the SNAP benefit an individual or household may receive.

Using SNAP Benefits

In accordance with the Food and Nutrition Act of 2008, SNAP benefits may be used to purchase foods for the household, such as meat, fish, poultry, dairy products, fruit and vegetables, bread and cereal, bottled water, baby food, and infant formula as well as seeds and plants that will produce food for the household to eat. In some areas, SNAP benefits may be used to purchase restaurant meals for persons who are homeless or disabled or for older adults.

SNAP benefits may not be used to purchase beer, wine, liquor, cigarettes, or tobacco or nonfood items, such as pet foods, soaps, paper products, and household supplies. Similarly, SNAP benefits may not be used to buy vitamins and medicines, cosmetics, grooming items, food that will be eaten in the store, or hot foods.

Although Congress has occasionally considered limiting or excluding some foods with low nutritional value (such as soft drinks, candy, and cookies) from SNAP benefits, it has never moved to do so, largely because it would be administratively difficult and costly to implement these exclusions. As a result, SNAP benefits may be used to purchase these items as well as cakes, other baked goods, ice cream, and energy drinks with nutrition facts labels. (Energy drinks with supplements are excluded.)

Because the Food & Nutrition Service is concerned about SNAP clients' health and nutritional status, it sponsors and produces programs to promote consumption of healthy foods. For example, the Healthy Incentives Pilot (HIP) program, which ran from November 2011 through December 2012 in Hampden County, Massachusetts, offered participating households a financial incentive—30 cents for every SNAP dollar spent, up to $60 per month—to purchase fruits and vegetables. As a result of this pilot program, participants increased their consumption 25% more than did persons in a control group that did not participate in the program. About 60% of the increase was due to increased consumption of vegetables, and the remaining 40% was attributable to increased consumption of fruits.

Other pilot programs aimed at increasing SNAP recipients' consumption of healthy foods are a project in Minnesota that gives SNAP households $5 coupons to purchase fresh fruits and vegetables, and a project in Michigan that make locally sourced produce available in corner grocery stores in metropolitan Detroit. Another initiative aimed at improving SNAP clients' diets is the Food & Nutrition Service effort to increase the number of farmers' markets that accept SNAP benefits.

Electronic Benefit Transfer

The overwhelming majority of SNAP programs give participants electronic benefit cards to help them purchase foods. Electronic Benefit Transfer (EBT) is an electronic system that enables a recipient to authorize transfer of their government benefits from a federal account to a retailer account to pay for products received. EBT is used in all 50 States, the District of Columbia, Puerto Rico, the Virgin Islands, and Guam. To use EBT systems, food stamp recipients apply for benefits by filling out a form at their local food stamp office. Once eligibility and the level of benefits are determined, an account is established in the participant's name, and benefits are deposited electronically in the account each month. A plastic card, which looks like a credit card, is issued, and the

---

recipient chooses a personal identification number (PIN) to enable secure access to the account. Recipients may change their PIN number at any time.

EBT overcomes many of the problems associated with the older, paper food stamp system. By eliminating paper coupons that may be lost, sold, or stolen, EBT may help cut back on food stamp fraud. Because EBT creates an electronic record of each SNAP transaction, it is easier to identify instances where food benefits are used inappropriately—exchanged for cash, drugs, or other illegal goods.

By July 2004, all 50 States, the District of Columbia, the Virgin Islands, and Guam operated EBT systems to issue SNAP benefits. The federal government supplies EBT equipment free of charge to SNAP retailers.

Program Results

Measuring the impact of SNAP on food insecurity using household survey data is challenging because households that participate in SNAP are different in many ways from households that do not participate in SNAP. For example, households that are more food-needy and have lower levels of food security are more likely to participate in SNAP. As a result, differences in food insecurity between SNAP participants and nonparticipants may be greater than the impact the program may have on participants' feelings of food insecurity.

A SNAP Food Security (SNAPFS) telephone survey conducted for the Food and Nutrition Service between October 2011 and September 2012 looked at the effect of SNAP participation on food security and food spending in 9,811 households in 30 states.

Among the study results was the finding that six months of participation in SNAP reduced household food insecurity by nearly 5%, and longer participation reduced the percentage of households experiencing food insecurity by nearly 11%. Participating in SNAP for six months was associated with a 8.6% decrease in households with children in which children were food insecure, and six months later the percentage of households with children in which children were food insecure decreased 10%.

Resources

BOOKS

Government Accountability Office. *Supplemental Nutrition Assistance Program: Improved Oversight of State Eligibility Expansions Needed*. CreateSpace Independent Publishing Platform, 2013.

Ramsey, Leonard, and Gillian Cummings, eds. *Supplemental Nutrition Assistance Program (Snap): A Primer and Profile*. Nova Science Pub Inc, 2013.

Richardson, J., Porter, D.V., and Yavis Jones, J. *Child Nutrition and WIC Programs: Background and Funding*. Hauppauge NY: Nova Science Publishers, 2003.

PERIODICALS

Basu S, Seligman H, and Bhattacharya J. "Nutritional Policy Changes in the Supplemental Nutrition Assistance Program: A Microsimulation and Cost-Effectiveness Analysis." *Medical Decision Making* (June 28, 2013).

Gundersen, C., "Food insecurity is an ongoing national concern." *Advances In Nutrition* 4 (January 1, 2013): 36–41.

Gustafson A, et al. "Neighbourhood and consumer food environment is associated with dietary intake among Supplemental Nutrition Assistance Program (SNAP) participants in Fayette County, Kentucky." *Public Health Nutrition* 18 (July 2013): 1229–1237.

Hood C, Martinez-Donate A, Meinen, A.,"Promoting healthy food consumption: a review of state-level policies to improve access to fruits and vegetables." *WMJ* 111 (December 2012): 283–288.

Mabli, J. et al. "Measuring the Effect of Supplemental Nutrition Assistance Program (SNAP) Participation on Food Security" *Nutrition Assistance Program Report* (August 2013].

McGuire, S., "IOM (Institute of Medicine) and NRC (National Research Council). 2013. Supplemental Nutrition Assistance Program: Examining the Evidence to Define Benefit Adequacy. Washington, D.C.: The National Academies Press, 2013" *Advances In Nutrition* 4 (July 1, 2013): 477–478.

Richards M.R., Sindelar, J.L., "Rewarding healthy food choices in SNAP: behavioral economic applications." *Milbank Quarterly* 91 (June 2013):395–412.

WEBSITES

U.S.D.A. Food & Nutrition Service. Supplemental Nutrition Assistance Program (SNAP). http://http://http://www.fns.usda.gov/snap/ (accessed August 28, 2013).

U.S.D.A. Food & Nutrition Service. Healthy Incentives Pilot (HIP) Interim Report—Summary. http://www.fns.usda.gov/ora/menu/Published/SNAP/FILES/ProgramDesign/HIP_Interim_Summary.pdf (accessed August 28, 2013).

ORGANIZATIONS

U.S.D.A. Food and Nutrition Service, 3101 Park Center Drive, Alexandria, VA 22302, acip@cdc.gov

Barbara Wexler, MPH.

Surgeon general

Definition

The office of the surgeon general of the United States is part of the U.S. **Department of Health and Human Services**. The post of surgeon general originated in the U.S. Marine Hospital Service, established by Congress in 1798 to provide health care to members of the merchant marine. When the service was restructured in 1870, a medical officer was named supervising surgeon, and this position became that of the surgeon general. Until 1968, the surgeon general directed the Public Health Service and reported to the Secretary of Health, Education, and

Surgeon General Regina Benjamin. *(Charley Gallay)*

Welfare. Today, the surgeon general reports to the Assistant Secretary for Health and Human Services. The surgeon general is the head of the U.S. Public Health Service Commissioned Corps, which includes thousands of full-time employees working to respond to public health issues and to promote scientific approaches to the advancement of public health.

Duties

The duties of the surgeon general include conducting research, issuing reports, and focusing public attention on health issues. Topics taken up by surgeons general have included tobacco use, healthy eating, increased physical activity, support for breastfeeding, and the importance of knowing your family's health history.

Why this is important to the consumer?

The surgeon general is often called "America's doctor." He or she is appointed by the president and is charged with improving public health, which means not only increasing awareness of public health problems, but also providing action plans to improve the health of all Americans. The surgeon general serves as the face of public health for the American people, and the reports and initiatives he or she produces tend to have a significant impact upon public health policies and understanding. For example:

Smoking

One of the most well-known surgeons general was C. Everett Koop, who served from 1982–1989. Although earlier surgeons general reports had addressed the health problems associated with smoking, Dr. Koop aggressively warned of the dangers of smoking and secondhand smoke, and his 1986 report on the subject is considered a significant step in the American public health campaign against smoking. More recently, a 2010 report issued by Surgeon General Regina Benjamin, *How Tobacco Smoke Causes Disease: The Biology and Behavioral Basis for Smoking-Attributable Disease,* provides basic information for consumers about the range of health problems associated with smoking, including heart disease, and includes resources to help smokers stop smoking.

Walking

Dr. Regina Benjamin, who served as surgeon general from 2009 to 2013, issued several reports emphasizing the role of a healthy lifestyle in the prevention of sickness and disease. In 2013, she introduced the Surgeon General's Every Body Walk! initiative to promote regular walking as an easy, inexpensive way for all Americans to improve their long-term health and fitness.

Breastfeeding

Data show that breastfeeding is not only the best source of nutrition for babies, it also has health benefits for the mothers who practice it. *The Surgeon General's Call to Action to Support Breastfeeding,* issued in 2011, reflects the government's recognition of the value of breastfeeding for public health. The report calls for employers to be supportive of breastfeeding women by allowing them the time and privacy to feed their babies or pump breast milk during the workday, and it calls on doctors and other health professionals to emphasize the importance of breastfeeding for mother and child health.

Family Health History

Family history is an important screening tool that can help identify and prevent a range of health problems, but many people are unfamiliar with the health history of even their immediate family members. To that end, a recent initiative from the office of the surgeon general, *My Family Health Portrait,* is an online tool that lets consumers enter information about their family health history in an organized form, which they can then save, print, and share with their doctors.

Prevention

The surgeon general is the leader of the National Prevention Council, created by the **Patient Protection and Affordable Care Act**. The council includes leadership from a range of government agencies with the common goal of improving the health and well-being of Americans. The council issues annual reports to the president outlining the nation's progress in meeting public health goals.

In addition, the surgeon general publishes "The Surgeon General's Perspectives" in the journal *Public Health Reports,* the official publication of the U.S. Public Health Service. Recent topics addressed in these reports include "Dietary Guidelines for Americans," "Improving Health by Improving Health Literacy," "Oral Health: The Silent Epidemic," "Bone Health: Preventing Osteoporosis," and "Preventing Tobacco Use Among Adolescents and Young Adults."

Resources

WEBSITES

The National Library of Medicine. Reports of the Surgeon General. http://profiles.nlm.nih.gov/ps/retrieve/Narrative/NN/p-nid/58 (accessed August 15, 2013).

U.S. Department of Health and Human Services. The Office of the Surgeon General. http://www.surgeongeneral.gov/index.html (accessed August 15, 2013).

Heidi Splete

Surgical Risk Assessment

Definition

Surgical risk assessment refers to the balance of the risks versus the benefits of having any surgical procedure. Before scheduling surgery, it is important to balance the benefits of the surgery with the potential risk of complications or side effects. Some common complications include infection at the site of a surgical incision or elsewhere, too much bleeding, or accidental injury during the procedure. Other risks include side effects from anesthesia, whether it is general anesthetic that puts you to sleep or local anesthetic that numbs a particular area of the body.

Why is surgical risk assessment important to the consumer?

Even relatively simple surgeries carry risks, and it is important to review them. The **Agency for Healthcare Research and Quality (AHRQ)**, part of the U.S. **Department of Health and Human Services**, is among many organizations working to develop protocols that reduce the risks associated with surgery. The **AHRQ** website also provides a useful list of questions for consumers to ask the doctor before surgery is scheduled. Their questions include:

- Why do you need surgery? Understanding how the surgery will benefit you and improve your health or medical condition helps with surgical assessment.

- Are there alternatives to surgery? Part of surgical risk assessment is understanding the alternatives. Other nonsurgical options, such as exercises, dietary changes, or medications, could be as helpful as surgery, without the risks associated with anesthesia and surgical infections.

Types of Risks Associated with Surgery

Risks and side effects associated with surgery range from relatively minor to life-threatening. Some of the minor problems include skin reactions near the site of a needle injection, or nausea related to anesthesia. More complicated risks include infections at the site of surgery, excessive bleeding that requires a transfusion, and blood clots that can lead to strokes.

Factors that Impact Surgical Risk

The amount of risk associated with surgery varies by procedure. Surgeries with the highest degree of risk include bone and joint operations, such as hip replacement or repair, heart or lung surgery, and prostate gland removal. In addition, a patient's health characteristics affect risk. An overall healthy person is at less risk for surgical complications than someone with other health problems. Some chronic problems that can increase your risk for surgical complications include poorly controlled diabetes, a recent heart attack, problems with your lungs, kidneys, or liver, or a weak immune system.

Safety During Surgery

In many cases, the benefits of surgery far outweigh the risks. The American College of Surgeons (ACS) has a special division, the Nora Institute for Patient Safety, to educate consumers as well as doctors about the latest information on keeping patients as safe. The Nora Institute section of the ACS website includes detailed, consumer-friendly information about surgical safety, and the Patient Resources section has other consumer information, such as how patients can prepare for surgery and reduce their risk for surgical complications.

Surgical risks

Although specific surgeries carry their own risks, some risks are inherent with all types of surgery. Possible risks include:

- Excess bleeding
- Reactions to anesthesia or other drugs
- Problems due to comorbid conditions (e.g., diabetes, obesity)
- Damage to other organs or blood vessels
- Postoperative infection
- Pain
- Deep vein thrombosis (blood clot)

SOURCE: American Cancer Society, "What are the Risks and Side Effects of Surgery?" Available online at: http://www.cancer.org/treatment/treatmentsandsideeffects/treatmenttypes/surgery/surgery-risks-and-side-effects.

(Table by PreMediaGlobal. Reproduced by permission of Gale, a part of Cengage Learning.)

Patients can do their part to help reduce the risks and maximize the benefits of any surgery, major or minor. Some suggestions from the American College of Surgeons include:

- Follow instructions. Doctors provide a list of instructions prior to surgery, which may include orders to not eat or drink anything after midnight the night before a procedure. Such rules make a difference; food or water in your stomach can contribute to anesthesia-related side effects such as nausea or vomiting.

- Tell all. Make sure your doctor knows about any medications you are taking prior to surgery. Even over-the-counter medications such as cold medication or aspirin can affect how your body will respond to anesthesia and to the surgery, and you can reduce your risk for complications if doctors know about your medication and can adjust accordingly.

- Quit smoking. Believe it or not, multiple studies have shown that smoking significantly increases the risk of almost any surgery. Why? Smoking affects the circulation, so smokers are at increased risk for potentially life-threatening blood clots.

- Ask questions. Be sure to ask your doctor if you do not understand something about the preparation for your surgery. It is better to ask in advance and help reduce the risk of side effects or complications.

Consider Cost

Cost can be a factor in surgical risk assessment, depending on the severity of the medical condition the surgery will treat. Other factors include the pain or disability associated with not having the surgery, versus the cost of the procedure and any post-surgical expenses, such as rehabilitation with a physical therapist. Consumers should talk to their insurance providers as well as the hospital billing department to get a sense of costs as part of a surgical risk assessment.

Resources

WEBSITES

Nora Institute for Surgical Patient Safety. American College of Surgeons. http://www.surgicalpatientsafety.facs.org/ (accessed November 26, 2013).

"Patient Safety—Surgical Risks Overview." The American Society for Aesthetic Plastic Surgery (ASAPS). http://www.surgery.org/consumers/patient-safety/surgical-risks-overview (accessed November 26, 2013).

"Proactive Risk Assessment of Surgical Site Infection in Ambulatory Surgery Centers." Agency for Healthcare Research & Quality (AHRQ). April 2013. http://www.ahrq.gov/research/findings/final-reports/stpra/index.html (accessed November 26, 2013).

"Smoking and surgery." MedlinePlus Medical Encyclopedia. August 17, 2012. http://www.nlm.nih.gov/medlineplus/ency/patientinstructions/000437.htm (accessed November 26, 2013).

"Surgery." Merck Manual Home Edition. February 2009. http://www.merckmanuals.com/home/special_subjects/surgery/surgery.htm (accessed November 26, 2013).

"What to Ask Before Surgery." Agency for Healthcare Research & Quality (AHRQ). January 2008. http://www.ahrq.gov/news/columns/navigating-the-health-care-system/011608.html (accessed November 26, 2013).

Heidi Splete

Telehealth

Definition

Telehealth is defined by the federal Health Resources and Services Administration (HRSA) as "the use of electronic information and telecommunications technologies to support long-distance clinical health care, patient and professional health-related education, public health, and health administration." It is not a separate medical specialty but rather described as the application of information technology (IT) to all fields of health care.

Some organizations, like the American Telemedicine Association (ATA), use the terms *telehealth* and *telemedicine* interchangeably: "telemedicine is the use of medical information exchanged from one site to another via electronic communications to improve a patient's clinical health status. Telemedicine includes a growing variety of applications and services using two-way video, e-mail, smart phones, wireless tools, and other forms of telecommunications technology." Other institutions, like HRSA, prefer to restrict *telemedicine* to the provision of clinical services via telecommunication and use *telehealth* as a broader term that includes such nonclinical health-related activities as continuing medical education (CME), telementoring among health care professionals, and hospital administration. An **Institute of Medicine** (IOM) workshop held on telehealth in late 2012 noted that the terminology related to it is not yet standardized.

Description

Telemedicine and telehealth have been in use in the United States and Canada since the 1970s. Originally limited to voice-only contact between patient and health care provider over the telephone, telehealth now makes use of an array of twenty-first-century communications technology, including videoconferencing, the Internet, wireless, and satellite media. As of 2013, there are over 200 telehealth networks in the United States linking 3,500 service sites. Over 50% of all hospitals in the United States use some form of telemedicine, and about a million heart patients currently make use of remote cardiac monitors.

The federal government in the United States is also actively involved in the development of telehealth, particularly for remote or underserved populations. The Office for the Advancement of Telehealth (OAT), which is part of HRSA's Office of Rural Health Policy (ORHP), has an annual budget of $11.6 million. Another federal telehealth program is conducted by the Department of Defense. Called the National Center for Telehealth and Technology, or "T2," it was established in 2008 to provide mental health services (sometimes called "elemental health") via videoconferencing and mobile video calling to veterans diagnosed with post-traumatic stress disorder (PTSD) or traumatic brain injuries (TBIs).

Modes of telehealth

Telehealth can be conducted by a range of telecommunications devices, from standard telephones and desktop computers to mobile smartphones, tablet computers, and videoconferencing equipment. There are two basic modes, known as "real-time" and "store-and-forward" telehealth, respectively. Real-time telehealth, also known as "synchronous telehealth," allows instantaneous long-distance interaction between a patient and health care provider or between two health care professionals. Videoconferencing is a common form of real-time telehealth. It can be used to perform physical examinations at a distance with the help of peripheral devices attached to the videoconferencing equipment, as well as to conduct psychotherapy, continuing medical education for health professionals, and telementoring. The site where the patient (or health professional receiving training) is located is called the "originating site"; it may be the patient's home, a hospital, a rural health care clinic, or

Telehealth uses an array of communications technology, including videoconferencing, the Internet, wireless, and satellite media. More than half of all hospitals in the United States use some form of telemedicine. *(Denver Post via Getty Images)*

other federally qualified health center. The site where the medical professional is providing the care or instruction is called the "distant site" or the "hub site."

Store-and-forward telehealth, also called "asynchronous telehealth," utilizes communications technology to record images as well as audio and video transmissions; these data can be stored on the client computer and then transmitted (forwarded) at a later time to another clinic or laboratory for purposes of diagnosis or analysis. Store-and-forward telehealth is increasingly used in such specialties as dermatology, radiology, and pathology, in which diagnosis is made in large part on the basis of images, and which do not require an immediate evaluation and reply.

A newer mode of telehealth is m-health (also spelled mHealth), or mobile health. M-health involves the use of cell phones, tablet computers, and other mobile devices. M-health can be used for either real-time or store-and-forward telehealth. M-health is a promising form of health care delivery in developing countries because of its usefulness in tracking diseases and collecting patient data as well as improving patient

access to health care in remote areas in these countries. As of 2013, there are over 20,000 healthcare-related applications (apps) available for mobile devices.

Uses of telehealth

There are four major uses of telehealth as of 2013. The first is direct access to primary care and referral to specialists. Primary care telehealth may involve either real-time videoconferencing or store-and-forward transmission of images, vital signs, and other patient data to a specialist. As noted earlier, videoconferencing technology allows for the use of digital stethoscopes, patient examination cameras, and other diagnostic equipment at the distant site. The Veterans Administration video, under Resources below, includes a demonstration of the use of diagnostic equipment at a specialist's distant site.

Remote patient monitoring is an increasingly important use of telehealth. It is especially useful in the care of homebound patients, particularly those who live in remote areas or those with such chronic diseases as congestive heart failure (CHF), asthma, diabetes, depression, or emphysema. A central monitoring system is placed in the patient's home to record information from sensors or specialized blood pressure or blood glucose level monitors, and transmit it to a remote diagnostic testing facility (RDTF) for interpretation and analysis. Remote patient monitoring can use either real-time or store-and-forward technology.

Personal access to medical and health information is important to many consumers. With the advent of **electronic health records (EHRs)** and online patient information portals provided by primary care physicians, patients can log on from computers or mobile devices and obtain their personal health information and records. They can also request prescription refills from their physician, who in turn can transmit a script via e-mail to the patient's pharmacy.

Medical education, remote training, and consultation is the fourth major use of telehealth. Videoconferencing allows a consultant at a distant site to confer with a number of primary care providers at different originating sites, to demonstrate a procedure or technique, or to present a special education lecture or seminar to practitioners in remote locations.

Why this is important to the consumer

Telehealth is important to consumers for a number of reasons. Perhaps the most important is its ongoing evolution as well as expansion. As new mobile as well as stationary telecommunications capabilities are developed, more and more consumers will be able to access more and more types of health care via telehealth, and to communicate with their providers as well as obtain online information about diseases, conditions, and treatments. Given the increasing speed of changes in this field, consumers should keep themselves informed about the latest communication devices and other developments in telehealth.

Access and convenience

Improved access to health care is a major factor in consumer interest in telehealth. For many people, the thought of being able to have routine wellness checkups or psychotherapy without having to drive to the doctor's office is appealing for the savings in time as well as gasoline. Access to health care via telehealth also improves patient compliance with therapy; patients who can keep appointments via videoconferencing are more likely to participate fully in their treatment than those who may live in remote areas or are housebound and have difficulty getting to the doctor's office. In addition, the technology involved in telehealth allows patients to record their appointments (sometimes called "e-visits") and play them back later if desired.

As noted above, telehealth also allows patients greater access to specialist care through referrals from the **primary care physician**. This ease of referral allows for faster diagnosis of potential problems before they become major health emergencies.

Patients interested in learning more about telehealth in their local area should begin by asking their primary care physician or a nearby hospital about the availability of telehealth services. Some primary care providers already have set up home monitoring systems or other services. There are also private companies that sell basic telehealth services, such as online health monitoring apps or 24/7 access to a physician.

Cost savings

Telehealth has been shown to reduce health care costs in terms of travel time, more effective use of brick-and-mortar facilities, more efficient deployment of hospital staff and equipment, better monitoring of chronic diseases, fewer and shorter hospital stays, and fewer emergency room admissions. Telehealth has proven particularly useful in the treatment and rehabilitation of stroke patients and in intensive care unit (ICU) monitoring and care.

Quality of care

A number of studies have shown that the quality of health care in many fields delivered by telehealth is as good as that provided during face-to-face meetings between physician and patient. In some fields, particularly ICU care and psychiatry, telemedicine delivers better care, with improved outcomes and a higher degree of patient satisfaction.

Concerns

On the other hand, telehealth is still a "work in progress" in many ways. One concern frequently expressed by consumers is privacy. The possibility that personal health information could be accessed, intercepted, or even altered by unauthorized persons is worrisome to many consumers. As of 2013, the **Health Insurance Portability and Accountability Act** (HIPAA) requires all telehealth networks in the United States to meet high security and privacy standards, including the use of data encryption during transmission and when the system is at rest. Best practices in telehealth include the full deletion of data from the system once a session is complete.

Other consumers are concerned about the loss of a sense of presence between physician and patient. Even the best video equipment or voice transmission cannot fully substitute for face-to-face meetings or consultations, and some consumers value this personal contact highly.

Connectivity is another important consumer concern as of 2013. The technological infrastructure needed to support telehealth equipment is not evenly distributed across the United States, and some consumers live in remote areas where access to affordable broadband is limited. Related to the issue of connectivity is reluctance on the part of some health care providers as well as patients to adopt the technology necessary to use telehealth. Some of this resistance to change is psychological, but some is also related to generational differences. Within the patient population, most adults have either grown up with computers and mobile devices or learned to use them in the 1970s and 1980s, and feel comfortable with them. There remains, however, a sizable number of elderly persons who are not accustomed to using e-mail and similar electronic means of communication, or who experience home health monitoring equipment as obtrusive or an invasion of their privacy.

The remaining major concern about telehealth is the complex and uneven schedules of reimbursement for telehealth services. **Medicare** covers the cost of some telehealth services, such as teleradiology or pathology, simply under the heading of physician services. People who are beneficiaries in **Medicare Advantage** plans have complete flexibility in using telehealth, but only as long as their provider offers the service. Medicare also covers physician services delivered via videoconferencing for beneficiaries living in rural areas; however, Medicare's definition of "rural," is complicated and often contradictory. According to a speaker at the 2012 IOM workshop mentioned earlier, Medicare's reimbursement rates remain low out of fear that physicians will abuse the system or that consumers will overutilize telehealth services and increase costs.

With regard to private insurance, 19 states as of 2013 require insurance companies to cover telehealth services at the same rate as face-to-face visits. Some other insurers cover at least some telehealth services, and still others are considering expanding their coverage of telehealth. Consumers with private health insurance should check with their benefits manager to find out whether their policy covers telehealth, and if so, what specific services are covered.

KEY TERMS

Distant site—The site where the telehealth physician or other health care provider is located. It is also known as the "hub site."

M-health—A term used for the practice of telehealth by mobile devices. It is also spelled mHealth.

Originating site—The site where the patient receiving telehealth care is located.

Real-time telehealth—Telehealth in which a telecommunications link (e.g., telephone, videoconferencing equipment, e-mail) allows for immediate communication. It is also called synchronous telehealth.

Store-and-forward telehealth—Telehealth in which images, video, or other patient data are captured and stored on a computer (or mobile device) and then transmitted (forwarded) at a later time to a specialist at another location for a diagnosis. Store-and-forward is also called "asynchronous telehealth."

Telemedicine—The use of electronic communication and information technologies to provide or support clinical care at a distance. It may include case management and psychological counseling.

Telemental health—The practice of psychiatry or psychotherapy via videoconferencing or similar communications technology.

Telementoring—The use of audio, video, and other telecommunications and electronic information processing technologies to provide individual guidance or direction among health care professionals.

Telemonitoring—The use of communications technologies and electronic information processing to monitor the vital signs or general health status of a patient from a distance.

Resources

BOOKS

Charness, Neil, George Demiris, and Elizabeth Krupinski. *Designing Telehealth for an Aging Population: A Human Factors Perspective*. Boca Raton, FL: Taylor and Francis, 2012.

Kumar, Sajeesh, and Helen Snooks, eds. *Telenursing*. New York: Springer, 2011.

L'Abate, Luciano, and David A. Kaiser, eds. *Handbook of Technology in Psychology, Psychiatry and Neurology: Theory, Research, and Practice*. Hauppauge, NY: Nova Science Publishers, 2011.

Smith, Anthony C., Nigel R. Armfield, and Robert H. Eikelboom, eds. *Global Telehealth 2012: Delivering Quality Healthcare Anywhere through Telehealth.* Washington, DC: IOS Press, 2012

PERIODICALS

Collins, B.T. "Telepathology in Cytopathology: Challenges and Opportunities." *Acta Cytologica* 57 (March 2013): 221–232.

Hanson, G.J. et al. "Emerging Technologies to Support Independent Living of Older Adults at Risk." *Care Management Journals* 14 (January 2013): 58–64.

Hilty, D.M. et al. "The Effectiveness of Telemental Health: A 2013 Review." *Telemedicine Journal and E-Health* 19 (June 2013): 444–454.

Kitsiou, S. "Systematic Reviews and Meta-analyses of Home Telemonitoring Interventions for Patients with Chronic Diseases: A Critical Assessment of Their Methodological Quality." *Journal of Medical Internet Research* 15 (July 23, 2013): e150.

Kumar, S., et al. "Tele-ICU: Efficacy and Cost-effectiveness of Remotely Managing Critical Care." *Perspectives in Health Information Management* 10 (April 1, 2013): 1f.

Logan, A.G. "Transforming Hypertension Management Using Mobile Health Technology for Telemonitoring and Self-Care Support." *Canadian Journal of Cardiology* 29 (May 2013): 579–585.

Odibo, I.N. et al. "Telemedicine in Obstetrics." *Clinical Obstetrics and Gynecology* 56 (December 2013): 422–433.

Weaver, D.T. "Telemedicine for Retinopathy of Prematurity." *Current Opinion in Ophthalmology* 24 (September 2013): 425–431.

WEBSITES

American Telemedicine Association (ATA). "Telemedicine Frequently Asked Questions (FAQs)." http://www.americantelemed.org/learn/what-is-telemedicine/faqs (accessed September 15, 2013).

American Telemedicine Association (ATA). "What Is Telemedicine?" http://www.americantelemed.org/learn/what-is-telemedicine (accessed September 15, 2013).

Health Resources and Services Administration (HRSA). "What Are the Reimbursement Issues for Telehealth?" http://www.hrsa.gov/healthit/toolbox/RuralHealthIT toolbox/Telehealth/whatarethereimbursement.html (accessed September 14, 2013).

Health Resources and Services Administration (HRSA). "What Is Telehealth?" http://www.hrsa.gov/healthit/toolbox/RuralHealthITtoolbox/Telehealth/whatistelehealth.html (accessed September 14, 2013).

Institute of Medicine (IOM) Workshop Summary, November 20, 2012. "The Role of Telehealth in an Evolving Health Care Environment." [free online version]http://www.nap.edu/openbook.php?record_id=13466&page=R1 (accessed September 14, 2013).

Mayo Clinic. "Telehealth: When Health Care Meets Cyberspace." http://www.mayoclinic.com/health/telehealth/MY01693 (accessed September 14, 2013).

Veterans Administration. "VA Telehealth: Real-Time Access to Care." This is a 9-minute video that illustrates the basic technology and the various clinical applications of telehealth. http://www.youtube.com/watch?v=JJvmsMZoBzw (accessed September 14, 2013).

ORGANIZATIONS

American Telemedicine Association (ATA), 1100 Connecticut Ave, NW, Suite 540, Washington, DC, United States 20036, (202) 223-3333, Fax: (202) 223-2787, info@americantelemed.org, http://www.americantelemed.org/.

Health Resources and Services Administration (HRSA), Office of Rural Health Policy (ORHP), 5600 Fishers Lane, Rockville, MD, United States 20857, (888) ASK-HRSA (275-4772), ask@hrsa.gov, http://www.hrsa.gov/ruralhealth/about/index.html.

Institute of Medicine of the National Academies, 500 Fifth St., NW, Washington, DC, United States 20001, (202) 334-2352, Fax: (202) 334-1412, iomwww@nas.edu, http://www.iom.edu/.

National Center for Telehealth and Technology (T2), 9933C West Hayes Street, Joint Base Lewis-McChord, WA, United States 98431, (253) 968-1914, Fax: (253) 968-4192, AskUs@t2health.org, https://www.t2health.org/.

Rebecca J. Frey, Ph.D.

▌Traditional Chinese medicine

Definition

Traditional Chinese medicine (TCM) is a complete alternative system of medicine that has been practiced in China and other countries bordering on China. Its origins can be traced back to about 3,000 B.C., although its major writings, such as the *Yellow Emperor's Inner Classic* (*Huangdi Neijing*) were composed around A.D. 111. TCM, as it is practiced in contemporary China, is an updated version of traditional remedies and treatments often used in combination with Western medicine.

In the late 1940s, the Chinese Communist Party recognized that there was a shortage of health care in rural areas and encouraged the revival of TCM on the grounds that its treatments were relatively inexpensive and readily accepted by the farmers. Interventions that were found to be ineffective were rejected, and the remainder brought closer to Western evidence-based medicine. The basic worldview underlying TCM remains, however, and it is very different from that of Western scientific medicine.

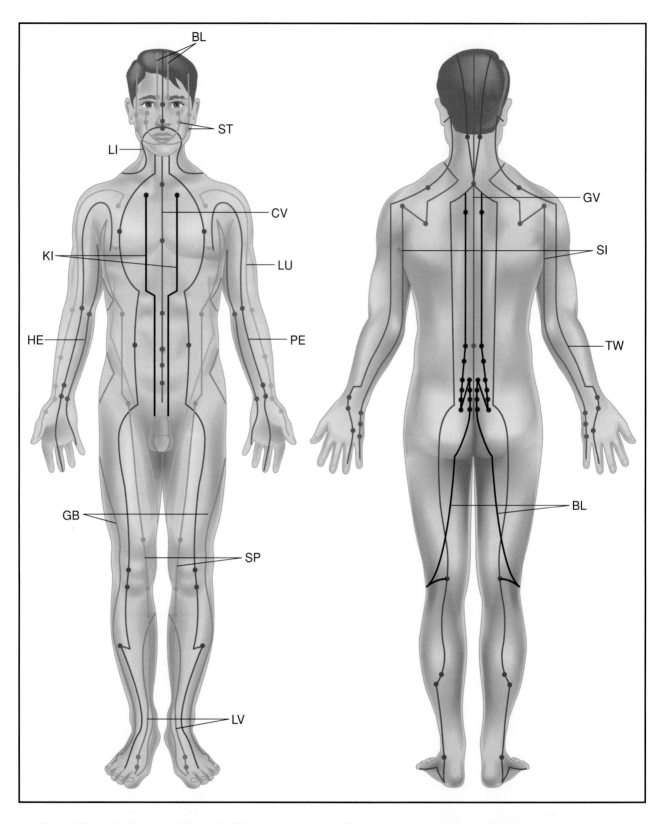

Traditional Chinese medicine teachings state that channels of energy flow throughout the body, and that disease is caused by too much or too little flow of energy along these channels. Points along the channels, called meridians, are manipulated in acupuncture. In the illustration, points are shown on the bladder (BL), conception vessel (CV), gallbladder (GB), governing vessel (GV), heart (HE), kidney (KI), large intestine (LI), liver (LV), lung (LU), pericardium (PE), small intestine (SI), spleen (SP), and stomach (ST), and triple warmer (TW) meridians. *(Illustration by Electronic Illustrators Group. Reproduced by permission of Gale, a part of Cengage Learning.)*

Description

Traditional Chinese medicine differs from Western medicine in that it is holistic, regarding body, mind, and soul as a unified whole to be kept in harmony within itself and with the surrounding natural environment. Although Westerners often associate TCM with herbal medicines, it incorporates four other practices: acupuncture, physical exercise (qigong), a specialized form of massage called *tui na*, and dietary therapy. TCM is thus a way of life and not just a single isolated practice. This holistic approach and combination of therapies is relatively unfamiliar to Westerners, who are more accustomed to picking and choosing among a variety of conventional and alternative practices rather than following an alternative system like TCM in its entirety. A survey done in the late 1980s of almost 600 consumers of Chinese medicine in the United States found that the vast majority "behave[d] as astute consumers within a plural health care system" rather than as converts to a complete non-Western approach to health care.

The natural world

To understand TCM, it is helpful to begin with an outline of the Chinese approach to the natural world before turning to the place of the human being within it. TCM regards human beings as microcosms, or miniature reflections, of the wider universe. Thus, human health consists of a proper balance of the various forces and elements in the universe, and illness represents an imbalance of these natural forces and functions. Disease is thus identified as a pattern of an underlying imbalance rather than a condition with a single cause (e.g., infection, traumatic injury, genetic mutation), and diagnosis is directed toward differentiating among various symptom complexes.

Traditional Chinese medicine has been strongly influenced by Taoism (also spelled Daoism), a philosophy or religion that is best translated as a "way" or "path"; it is less formal and structured than the three major Western religions, and is noted for its emphasis on simplicity of life, compassion for all creatures, and moderation in all things. Some of the Taoist beliefs that helped to shape TCM include:

• Yin and yang. The duality of yin and yang is an ancient Chinese concept that goes back at least as far as 1,100 B.C.. Yin and yang are two opposite, but complementary, aspects of reality that can be found in natural phenomena and the human body. For example, the moon, water, cold weather, the lower half of the body, and femaleness represent the yin principle, while the sun, fire, warm weather, the upper half of the body, and maleness represent yang. The yin/yang distinction extends to body functions and disease conditions, in that the patient's combination of symptoms can be understood as a deficiency or overabundance of yin or yang.

• The five elements. Also called the "five phases," this belief holds that all natural phenomena as well as physical objects can be reduced to five elements or elemental qualities represented by wood, fire, earth, metal, and water. Each element is identified with a point of the compass, color, weather condition, sense organ, internal organ, and season of the year. For example, wood is associated with the east, the color turquoise, the eye, the liver and gallbladder, and spring. Similarly, fire is associated with the south, the color red, the tongue, the heart and small intestine, and early summer. The other three elements have similar associations. The five elements theory also maintains that each element interacts with or counteracts the others in predictable ways that can be used to diagnose symptom patterns in the human body.

The human body

The primary focus of TCM is the overall functioning of the human body rather than disorders or diseases of specific anatomical organs, as in Western medicine. It is important to note that when a TCM practitioner uses the term "Heart," for example, he or she is referring to blood flow and temperature regulation rather than the organ itself. Similarly, "Stomach" and "Small Intestine" refer to the processes of nutrition and digestion in TCM. Most writers on the subject of TCM capitalize the names of internal organs in order to distinguish between the meaning of these body parts in TCM and their usage in Western medicine; this convention will be used in the remainder of this entry. Other important features of TCM's understanding of the human body include:

• Qi. Qi (also spelled chi) is, according to TCM, a vital force or life energy that animates the human body and is essential to all its functions. Qi is partly inherited from one's parents and partly derived from food and drink (digestion) and air (respiration). A practitioner of TCM will evaluate the condition of a person's qi as part of diagnosis. For example, a person who is tired, short of breath, weak, slow to speak, complaining of digestive problems, and sweating profusely will be diagnosed as deficient in qi.

• Zang-fu organs. The zang-fu organs in TCM are a set of internal entities identified more as bodily functions than as the anatomical organs whose names they bear. The five zang organs (Heart, Liver, Kidney, Spleen, and Lung) are associated with yin, while the six fu organs (Small Intestine, Large Intestine, Gallbladder, Urinary Bladder, Stomach, and San Jiao [usually translated as "Triple Burner"]) are associated with yang. The zang organs function to produce and store qi, blood, and other bodily fluids, essentially regulating digestion, respiration, and mental health, while the fu organs digest food and dispose of bodily wastes. The five zang-fu pairs are also linked to the five elements and to the system of meridians, or energy channels.

• Meridians. The meridians, also known as "channels," are a system of conduits that convey qi from the zang-fu organs to the muscles, skin, and exterior of the body. TCM identifies twelve "regular" and eight "extraordinary" meridians. Acupuncture therapy is based on the belief that needling or stimulation of traditional acupoints along a meridian can redirect the flow of qi to correct blockages or imbalances in its distribution in the body.

• Eight guiding principles. The eight guiding principles are four pairs of opposites that TCM practitioners use to identify patterns of disharmony or energy imbalances in the body. They are: cold/heat (identifies the energy level of the body); interior/exterior (identifies location of the disorder); deficiency/excess (roughly corresponds to the Western distinction between a chronic condition and an acute illness); and yin/yang.

Diagnosis

To diagnose a patient's condition, a TCM practitioner will first conduct an interview much like a Western physician, asking about the patient's presenting complaint. The TCM practitioner, however, will also inquire about such matters as the patient's sleep habits, favorite foods, dreams or nightmares, recent stresses, and appetite. The practitioner will also note the quality of the patient's voice as well as his or her external appearance.

There are three diagnostic techniques in TCM that are not standard in Western medicine. The first is smell. The TCM practitioner will smell the patient's breath as a clue to diagnosis in the belief that each of the five elements affects the odor of human breath in a characteristic way. The second technique is examining the patient's tongue in detail for its size, shape, color, texture, and coating (if any). Each part of the tongue is associated with one of the zang-fu organs, so its condition provides further information about the patient's condition.

The third diagnostic technique in TCM is pulse-taking. Both Western physicians and TCM practitioners take the pulse at the radial artery that runs along the inside of the wrist. TCM practitioners, however, take twelve pulses, not just one. They take six pulses on each wrist, three shallow and three deep, at specific points along the radial artery, and note the rhythm and volume as well as the frequency of the pulse. Each pulse location is associated with one of the zang-fu organs.

The diagnosis is given in terms of the eight guiding principles; for example, the practitioner might say that the patient has an interior heat condition with yang excess. Therapy is chosen according to the pattern rather than the disease entity thus two patients with the same disease (in Western terms) might receive different treatments if their patterns (including their environments) are different. For example, a middle-aged man living in Denver who develops a cold in early spring would be given a different TCM treatment from that given to a young adult woman living in Philadelphia who develops a cold in late fall. The two patients differ in age, sex, geographical location, and the time of year their symptoms appear.

Treatment

Traditional Chinese medicine utilizes five major forms of therapy:

• Herbal medicine. Chinese herbal medicines differ from Western herbal preparations in being compounds of many different plant (and animal) ingredients; some contain as many as 18 different plants. TCM medicines are compounded for the individual patient. The practitioner takes into account the zang-fu organ involved, the condition of the patient's qi, the pattern of the illness, and the energetic quality of each herb—which can be described not only as heating or cooling, but as moistening, relaxing, or energizing. The herbal remedy may be brewed as a tea or formulated as a tonic, powder, or capsule.

• Acupuncture. Acupuncture is the TCM treatment most familiar in the West, being practiced by some mainstream physicians (M.D.s) as well as practitioners of TCM. It is also the therapy most likely to be used in isolation from the other forms of TCM treatment. According to the National Center for Complementary and Alternative Medicine (NCCAM), over 3 million people in the United States receive acupuncture treatments each year. About a third of those receiving acupuncture at TCM clinics also take herbal medicines at the clinics. Acupuncture consists of the insertion of thin sterile needles at various points called acupoints in the skin over the meridians in order to stimulate or redirect the flow of qi. Acupuncture is often accompanied by moxibustion, a treatment in which the practitioner holds a cylinder of burning mugwort (moxa) on or near the skin. The heat is thought to stimulate the flow of qi.

- Massage and cupping. TCM is noted for an intense form of massage called tui na, which can be translated as push-pull. The masseur vigorously grasps, kneads, and rolls the patient's skin and muscles over selected acupoints to relax the tissues as well as stimulate the flow of qi. Tui na is also believed to encourage the body to release waste products. Unlike Western massage, tui na does not use oils or lotions to lubricate the skin. Cupping is a practice that involves heating the inside of a glass cup with a lighted match, blowing out the match, and immediately placing the heated cup on the patient's back. As the air inside the cup cools, it creates a partial vacuum that provides a kind of reverse-pressure massage.

- Dietary therapy. The belief that a person's qi is affected by diet underlies the use of food as medicine in TCM. Like herbs, foods are associated with the eight guiding principles and the zang-fu organs. Thus, foods are chosen for their warming or cooling, moistening or drying properties rather than for their protein, fat, or carbohydrate content as in Western nutritional theory.

- Physical exercise. Qigong is a form of exercise that incorporates meditation and conscious intent along with movement, posture, and breathing to cleanse or purify the qi in the body. A typical qigong practice consists of rhythmic breathing, slow and stylized movements, and a visualization of qi moving through the body.

Western readers will notice that surgery is not included on the list; the reason is that physicians in ancient China did not attempt surgery as a treatment for disease, because of their theories about the nature of the universe and the place of humans within it. Contemporary Chinese medical students are trained in surgery and Western medicine but may also study TCM if they wish.

Why this is important to the consumer

If acupuncture is included, traditional Chinese medicine is one of the most popular forms of alternative medicine in the United States.

Chinese medicine in the United States

Although many people associate TCM with the upsurge of interest in Eastern religions and belief systems that characterized the New Age movement of the late 1960s, TCM has actually been practiced in the United States since the eighteenth century, when French practitioners trained in TCM in Europe came to North America. In the nineteenth century, Chinese immigrants coming to the West Coast to work as laborers on the Transcontinental Railroad brought TCM with them. It was the normalization of diplomatic relations between China and the United States in the early 1970s that helped to popularize TCM across the United States, in particular the practice of acupuncture. As of 2013, there are an estimated 35,000 licensed practitioners of TCM in the United States.

Practitioner education and licensure

The practice of acupuncture and TCM is strictly regulated in all but six of the 50 states. (The exceptions are Alabama, Kansas, North Dakota, South Dakota, Oklahoma, and Wyoming.) Most people seeking licensure at the state level complete coursework in one of the 78 schools of Oriental medicine and acupuncture currently accredited by the Accreditation Commission for Acupuncture and Oriental Medicine (ACAOM). Most of these schools require a minimum of two, preferably three, years of college-level study as a prerequisite for admission.

Following completion of their course of study, candidates may take examinations for one of four credentials administered by the National Certification Commission for Acupuncture and Oriental Medicine (NCCAOM). These credentials are: the diploma in Oriental medicine (Dipl. O.M.); the diploma in acupuncture (Dipl. Ac.); the diploma in Chinese herbology (Dipl. C.H.); and the diploma in Asian Bodywork Therapy (Dipl. A.B.T.). NCCAOM examinations are lengthy and rigorous, and are accepted as prerequisites for licensure by the 44 states that regulate practitioners of TCM.

TCM and acupuncture are covered by some health insurance plans in the United States but not by **Medicare** or **Medicaid** as of 2013. Consumers interested in TCM as an alternative medical system should contact their health care plan to find out whether it will cover TCM treatments. They should also ask any practitioner of TCM about his or her credentials and licensing. If their state does not regulate TCM, they can contact the NCCAOM for a list of certified practitioners in their area.

Risks

There are some risks in using TCM as a form of treatment. Although acupuncture is generally considered safe when performed by a licensed practitioner

KEY TERMS

Holistic—In medicine, an approach that takes all dimensions of a human being into account, the psychosocial and spiritual as well as the physical. Traditional Chinese medicine has a holistic understanding of the human body and its place in the universe.

Meridians—In TCM, a system of twenty channels or energy pathways for the flow of qi throughout the body.

Moxibustion—The use of a burning cigar-shaped cylinder of mugwort to heat the skin over an acupoint in order to stimulate the flow of qi. Moxibustion is usually used together with acupuncture.

Qi—A vital force or energy that animates the human body. In TCM theory, it is partially inherited from a person's parents and partly derived from food, drink, and proper breathing.

Tui na—A form of massage practiced in TCM characterized by vigorous gripping and rolling of the soft tissues. Its name means "push-pull" in Chinese.

Zang-fu organs—A group of eleven internal entities associated in traditional Chinese medicine with the five elements, the meridians, the flow of qi in the body, and the overall harmony of the human body with nature. Although the names of the zang-fu organs are familiar to Westerners, they are usually capitalized to indicate that they refer to the internal functions of the body rather than to the anatomical organs in the strict sense.

with sterile needles, most of the other interventions used in TCM have not been thoroughly studied for effectiveness in clinical trials in the United States; of the 346 trials of TCM registered with the NIH as of September 2013, only 53 are being conducted in North America. Some TCM treatments, such as tui na massage, may not be suitable for people with osteoporosis or who have had recent surgery.

The greatest risk to consumers from TCM is the use of premixed herbal treatments made outside the United States. Although classical TCM practice is based on formulating herbal remedies for the individual patient, there are also Chinese patent medicines on the market. The **Food and Drug Administration** (FDA) has banned certain herbal products imported from China on the grounds that they were contaminated by lead and other dangerous substances. In 2011, the agency alerted health food stores and other

consumers to the fact that some Chinese medicines were found to contain prescription drugs, including diazepam (Valium), the male hormone testosterone, acetaminophen (Tylenol), prednisolone (Medrol), hydrochlorothiazide (a diuretic or water pill), and indomethacin (Indocin), an anti-inflammatory drug. More importantly, the FDA banned an herb known as ephedra (ma huang in Chinese) in 2004. The herb was popular as a dietary supplement and appetite suppressant but was found to cause side effects ranging from dizziness and a racing heartbeat to seizures, heart attacks, stroke, and even death.

Resources

BOOKS

Crawford, Gregory. *Medical Library Association Guide to Finding Out about Complementary and Alternative Medicine: The Best Print and Electronic Resources.* New York: Neal-Schuman Publishers, 2010.

Yuqun, Liao. *Traditional Chinese Medicine.* New York: Cambridge University Press, 2011.

Wu, Emily S. *Traditional Chinese Medicine in the United States.* Lanham, MD: Lexington Books, 2013.

PERIODICALS

Gu, Q., et al. "Drug Discovery Inspired by Mother Nature: Seeking Natural Biochemotypes and the Natural Assembly Rules of the Biochemome." *Journal of Pharmacy and Pharmaceutical Sciences* 16 (February 2013): 331–341.

He, X.R., et al. "Acupuncture and Moxibustion for Cancer-related Fatigue: A Systematic Review and Meta-analysis." *Asian Pacific Journal of Cancer Prevention* 14 (May 2013): 3067–3074.

Kong, H., and E. Hsieh. "The Social Meanings of Traditional Chinese Medicine: Elderly Chinese Immigrants' Health Practice in the United States." *Journal of Immigrant and Minority Health* 14 (October 2012): 841–849.

Shin, h.K., et al. "Adverse Events Attributed to Traditional Korean Medical Practices: 1999–2010." *Bulletin of the World Health Organization* 91 (August 1, 2013): 569–575.

Wang, J. "Treatment of Food Anaphylaxis with Traditional Chinese Herbal Remedies: From Mouse Model to Human Clinical Trials." *Current Opinion in Allergy and Clinical Immunology* 13 (August 2013): 386–391.

Woolf, A.D., et al. "The Severity of Toxic Reactions to Ephedra: Comparisons to Other Botanical Products and National Trends from 1993–2002." *Clinical Toxicology* 43 (May 2005): 347–355. This is an older article but a useful summary of the poisoning cases that led to the FDA's banning of ephedra in 2004.

WEBSITES

Food and Drug Administration (FDA). "Import Alert 66-10: Chinese Herbal Medicines." http://www.access data.fda.gov/cms_ia/importalert_173.html (accessed August 29, 2013).

National Center for Complementary and Alternative Medicine (NCCAM). "Traditional Chinese Medicine: An Introduction." http://nccam.nih.gov/health/what iscam/chinesemed.htm (accessed August 27, 2013).

National Certification Commission for Acupuncture and Oriental Medicine (NCCAOM). "Fact Sheet: Examinations and Certification Process." http://www.nccaom. org/about/nccaom-national-standards (accessed August 28, 2013).

Traditional Chinese Medicine Basics. "Introduction to Traditional Chinese Medicine." http://tcmbasics.com/ introduction.htm (accessed August 29, 2013).

University of California Television (UCTV). "Complementary/Alternative Medicine: Traditional Chinese." This is an hour-long video about TCM. http://www.youtube. com/watch?v=9EkwukyMV9o (accessed August 28, 2013).

ORGANIZATIONS

Accreditation Commission for Acupuncture and Oriental Medicine (ACAOM), 8941 Aztec Drive, Eden Prairie, MN, United States 55347, (952) 212-2434, Fax: (301) 313-0912, coordinator@acaom.org, http:// www.acaom.org/.

American College of Traditional Chinese Medicine , 455 Arkansas Street, San Francisco, CA, United States 94107, (415) 282-7600, Fax: (415) 282-0856, http:// www.actcm.edu/.

Food and Drug Administration (FDA), 10903 New Hampshire Avenue, Silver Spring, MD, United States 20993, (888) INFO-FDA (463-6332), http://www.fda.gov/ AboutFDA/ContactFDA/default.htm, http:// www.fda.gov/.

National Center for Complementary and Alternative Medicine (NCCAM), 9000 Rockville Pike, Bethesda, MD, United States 20892, (888) 644-6226, http://nccam. nih.gov/tools/contact.htm, http://nccam.nih.gov/.

National Certification Commission for Acupuncture and Oriental Medicine (NCCAOM), 76 South Laura Street, Suite 1290, Jacksonville, FL, United States 32202, (904) 598-1005, Fax: (904) 598-5001, http://www. nccaom.org/.

Rebecca J. Frey, Ph.D.

▌Travel Health Insurance Plans

Definition

Travel health insurance plans are plans specifically designed to provide medical insurance when traveling. Some United States health insurance plans provide coverage when policyholders are traveling abroad, but others do not. Whether anyone needs travel insurance for any given trip depends on many factors, including the nature of the trip (staying in youth hostels, a five-star hotel, a tent) and the destination.

Why is travel health insurance important to the consumer?

Illness or injury while traveling overseas can result in a huge financial burden without insurance. The **Centers for Disease Control and Prevention** describes three types of travel insurance: travel insurance, travel health insurance, and medical evacuation insurance. All three types can be purchased before traveling. Consumers should check to find out whether some basic level of travel or accident insurance may be required, before traveling to certain areas.

Travel guru Rick Steves notes that travel insurance plans and policies can vary widely, and it is important to read the fine print. He mentions that age is one of the key factors in the price of a policy. For older adults, a comprehensive travel insurance policy might be more cost-effective than a travel health insurance policy only.

Comprehensive Travel Insurance

Travel insurance plans are designed to protect consumers from the financial losses of lost baggage or cancellation of travel plans. According to the Centers for Disease Control and Prevention, consumers who have purchased travel insurance are less likely to proceed with travel plans if they get sick. Some travel insurance plans cover medical expenses overseas, as well as baggage insurance and trip cancellation insurance.

Travel Health Insurance

To help protect against the high cost of medical care overseas, consumers can purchase short-term supplemental travel health care policies that are for health care expenses only. Some travel health insurance includes medical evacuation coverage (if the traveler must be transported elsewhere for medical care), but medical evaluation coverage also may be purchased separately. Of note to **Medicare** participants: Medicare does not cover medical costs outside the United States, except in special circumstances.

Medical Evacuation Insurance

When selecting medical evacuation insurance, consumers should be sure that the policy includes arrangements with hospitals to guarantee payments. The policy should also allow for emergency medical transport to health care facilities equal to those available in the United States, or allow for transport to medical facilities in the U.S., if necessary.

Adventure Travel Health Insurance

Going skydiving, bungee jumping, or skiing? Check with your insurer. These activities might be too dangerous to be covered by regular travel health insurance. Adventure travelers should seek out specific companies that offer travel health insurance for these types of trips, such as the International Medical Group (IMG Global). These types of plans also can be good choices for traveling students, or for participants in missionary groups or other non-profit charity organizations to potentially dangerous areas.

For Traveling Students

Students who are participating in study-abroad programs might want to consider a form of travel health insurance. Such plans for students are available through various travel organizations, such as the American Automobile Association (AAA). Similarly, academic faculty members who are going on sabbaticals or accompanying student groups for extended study-abroad periods might consider types of travel health insurance.

Government Resources

The U.S. Department of State maintains a website with information for travelers that includes country-specific travel information, alerts, and warnings. This information includes health and safety issues that might impact the decision whether or not to purchase travel health insurance.

Consumer Strategies

The following steps are recommended for consumers whether or not they choose to purchase some form of travel health insurance:

- Review domestic health insurance to see what overseas medical services might be covered.
- Identify health care services in the areas to be visited; carry this information in a convenient place while traveling.
- Bring copies of all domestic health insurance cards, and some blank insurance claim forms.
- Keep copies of bills and receipts for any medical treatment received while traveling overseas.

The **CDC** especially recommends some type of travel health insurance for overseas travelers with chronic medical conditions, such as heart disease. The CDC travel health insurance website recommends that, regardless of their travel health insurance plan, these individuals should carry a letter from their doctor explaining their condition, and a list of necessary medications, written in the local language of the country they are visiting, in case medical care is needed in a local hospital.

Resources

WEBSITES

Centers for Medicare and Medicaid Services. http://www.cms.gov/Center/Special-Topic/People-With-Medicare-and-Medicaid-Center.html (accessed September 12, 2013).

Centers for Medicare and Medicaid Services. https://www.medicare.gov/claims-and-appeals/index.html (accessed September 12, 2013).

Centers for Medicare and Medicaid Servces. http://www.cms.gov/About-CMS/Agency-Information/History/index.html (accessed September 12, 2013).

Centers for Medicare and Medicaid Services. http://www.cms.gov/Medicare/Medicare-General-Information/MedicareGenInfo/index.html (accessed September 12, 2013).

Medicaid. http://www.medicaid.gov/ (accessed September 12, 2013).

Medicaid. http://www.medicaid.gov/CHIP/CHIP-Program-Information.html (accessed September 12, 2013).

Medicaid. http://medicaid.gov/Medicaid-CHIP-Program-Information/By-Topics/Benefits/Medicaid-Benefits.html (accessed September 12, 2013).

Heidi Splete

▮ TRICARE

Definition

TRICARE is the health care program for approximately 9.6 million active-duty service members, National Guard and Reserve members, retirees, their families, survivors, and certain former spouse. Benefits vary according to the sponsor's military status. TRICARE covers most inpatient and outpatient care that is medically necessary and considered proven. However, there are special rules or limits on certain types of care, while other types of care are excluded in all cases. While the list of exclusions is quite long, it covers most forms of cosmetic and alternative treatments.

Description

TRICARE is a federally funded health program, the successor to the Civilian Health and Medical Program of the Uniformed Services (CHAMPUS). The two basic categories of eligibility are sponsors, which includes active duty service members, retired service members, and National Guard/Reserve members, and family members, dependent spouses and children who are registered in the Defense Enrollment Elighibility Reporting System (DEERS). Other eligible beneficiaries include Medal of Honor recipients and their family members, surviving family members and former spouses. The eligibility of reservists and National Guard members varies with service, and whether or not activated, and if activated for a period of 30 days or less.

There are a number of options for TRICARE coverage, depending on the sponsor's military status, and whether the sponsor and/or family are stationed in the United States or overseas. TRICARE gets its name based on the three levels of coverage—TRICARE Prime, Standard, and Extra. In addition, there are variations. TRICARE Prime remote is coverage available to active-duty personnel and their families who are stationed at some distance, usually 50 miles or 1 hour's drive time from a military hospital or clinic.

Although the TRICARE web site lists 15 options, there are essentially three coverage options with the variations based on military status and location.

All TRICARE plans have a maximum out-of-pocket expense, also known as the "Catastrophic Cap," of $1,000/year for active duty, national guard, and reserve families and $3,000.year for retirees.

• TRICARE Standard and Extra—a fee-for-service plan available to all non-active-duty beneficiaries anywhere in the United States. Enrollment is not required. Members may obtain care from any TRICARE authorized provider but may have to pay for services at the time they are provided, and file for reimbursement. There is an annual deductible, which depends on the rank of the sponsor, but it is quite low. For enlisted personnel with as rank of E-4 or below (corporal or petty officer 3rd class), the family deductible is $100 per year. All those of higher rank have a deductible of $300. Under some circumstances, the annual deductible may be waived. Tricare Standard beneficiaries can use the Tricare Extra option by consulting a civilian health care provider from the regional contractor's network. There is no fee for use of the Tricare Extra benefit other than the coinsurance.

• TRICARE Prime is a managed care option which offers expanded services compared to TRICARE standard. The vision plan is expanded over the most basic services, and preventive treatments are also covered. Enrollment is required, but free for active-duty personnel and their dependents. Active-duty personnel are automatically enrolled in TRICARE. Prime Retirees must pay an enrollment fee, but there is normally no charge for an outpatient visit. The TRICARE web site describes TRICARE Prime as "... offering the most affordable and comprehensive coverage."

• US Family Health Plan is an option abvailable under TRICARE Prime. Care is provided through a network of not-for-profit providers, but all care comes through these providers and members do not access military hospitals or other TRICARE-authorized providers. The benefits include discounts for eyeglasses, hearing aids, and dental care, subject to regional availability. Enrollment is required and includes a one-year commitment to receive all care from the plan. Retirees are eligible but must pay an annual enrollment fee.

Services provided

The list of covered services is extensive and covers virtually all services which might be considered medically necessary. Fees for services vary with the plan. In addition to the medical services, TRICARE provides vision, drug, and dental coverage.

1. Vision: benefits for vision vary with the plan, however all eye diseases are covered under the medical benefits. Annual eye examinations are covered for all active duty personnel and enrollees with diabetes. For others, an eye exam is covered once every two years. Eyeglasses and/or contact lenses are provided only for a limited number of conditions:

   • Infantile glaucoma

   • Corneal or scleral lenses for treatment of keratoconus.

   • Scleral lenses to retain moisture when normal tear production is absent or is inadequate

   • Corneal or scleral lenses to reduce corneal irregularities other than astigmatism

   • Intraocular lenses, contact lenses, or eyeglasses for loss of human lens function resulting from intra-ocular surgery, ocular injury, or congenital absence

   • "Pinhole" glasses prescribed for use after surgery for a detached retina

2. Dental: active duty personnel are covered automatically by the military dental program. Family members may be covered by a supplementary program, which is managed under contract by MetLife. Coverage includes:

Astigmatism—A visual problem in which changes in the curvature of parts of the eye, most often the cornea, prevent light from focusing properly and causes blurred vision.

Corneal—Pertaining to the cornea, which is the transparent membrane at the front of the eye.

Infantile glaucoma—Gaucoma—an eye condition in which the pressure inside the eye is abnormally high and may damage the optic nerve. The infantile form, also called childhood, pediatric, or congenital glaucoma, is seen in babies and young children, and is commonly diagnosed in the first year of life.

Keratoconus—Degenerative condition of the eye in which the cornea thins and changes to a conical shape rather than a gradual curve

"Pinhole" glasses—Glasses with a number of small holes in each lens. This allows only a single beam of light to enter through each hole and may help produce clearer vision.

Root planing (dental)—Removing the causes of inflammation from the teeth. Plaque, the common cause of inflammation, is a resilient bacterial residue which adheres to the teeth. It can combine with calcium and form a hard deposit. Scaling and root planing remove plaque with physical scraping, or ultrasonic instruments.

Scaling (dental)—Similar to root planing.

Scleral—Pertaining to the sclera, the white of the eye.

- Diagnostic and preventive services (exams, cleanings, fluorides, sealants, and X-rays)
- Basic restorative services (fillings, including tooth-colored fillings on back teeth).
- Endodontics (root canals)
- Periodontics (gum surgery)
- Oral surgery (tooth extractions)
- Prosthodontics (crowns, dentures)
- Orthodontics (braces)
- Additional services include scaling and root planing for diabetics, and additional cleaning during pregnancy

3. Prescription services: managed by Express Scripts and subject to a specific TRICARE formulary. The formulary is developed by US Department of Defense Pharmacy and Therapeutics Committee, depending on how the prescription is written—formulary or not formulary, brand or generic—and where the prescription is filled, there may be a copay. Prescriptions filled at a military hospital pharmacy have no out-of-pocket costs. When a military pharmacy is not available, a mail-in-option will normally be the least expensive. TRICARE also has a network of 57,000 participating pharmacies, which will honor the TRICARE prescription plan just as any other prescription insurance. One final option is to fill the prescription at a non-network pharmacy and apply for reimbursement, however, this may be subject to co-pays and deductibles.

4. Live well—these are a group of programs designed to help members maintain a healthy lifestyle. They include alcohol awareness, smoking-cessation programs, and a crisis hotline for emotional emergencies.

Benefits and services for retirees and/or personnel injured while on active duty may be coordinated between TRICARE and the Veteran's Administration. Participants over the age of **Medicare** eligibility will be routinely assigned to Medicare for primary health coverage with TRICARE as secondary coverage. TRICARE participants who have Medicare part A, hospital coverage must also have Medicare part B (physician coverage) in order to remain TRICARE eligible except when the sponsor is on active duty, or the family is enrolled in the US Family Health Plan, or other exceptions as specified. Persons enrolled in Medicare parts A and B qualify for TRICARE For Life.

Quality of Care

A number of studies have compared the quality of care seen with TRICARE to care financed through civilian insurance or care for the uninsured. In one study of cancer care, the quality of follow-up care was found to be consistent with patterns in the geographic region where treatment was provided. A study by Harvard University reported few differences in decision to treat, or quality of care in upper arm surgery for patients, regardless of how their surgery was financed. TRICARE was one of the financing options considered.

Why this is important to the consumer

TRICARE serves an estimates 9.6 million beneficiaries around the world. This includes approximately 2 million people enrolled in the TRICARE For Life program. Aside from the absolute number of people covered by this health insurance program, it is worth noting that the beneficiaries are all active-duty military personnel, military retirees, and their beneficiaries. An effective military force requires well trained and experienced personnel, and benefits, including commissary privileges, secure retirement, and quality health coverage, serve as inducements for people to select the armed forces as a career.

Resources

BOOKS

Powers, Rod. *Veterans Benefits for Dummies*. For Dummies, 2009.

Tricare Operations and Patient Administration Functions. U.S. Air Force, 2012.

PERIODICALS

Buckler, Aileen G. "The Military Health System and TRI-CARE: breastfeeding promotion." *Breastfeeding Medicine* 6 no. 5 (2011): 295.

Camp, William J. "Health care options for former military spouses: Tricare and the Continued Health Care Benefit Program (CHCBP)." *Family Law Quarterly* (Summer 2009): 227.

Kime, P. "Tricare charging more for Medicare-covered services." *Army Times* (August 27, 2013).

Philpott, P. "VA outpatient costs to rise for some retirees using Tricare for Life." *Stars and Stripes* (August 22, 2013).

WEBSITES

Humana Military. http://www.humana-military.com (accessed September 24, 2013).

TRICARE Prime and TRICARE Prime Remote Handbook: Your guide to program benefits. Department of Defense. November 2012. http://www.tricare.mil/~/media/Files/TRICARE/Publications/Handbooks/TP_TPR_HBK.ashx (accessed September 24, 2013).

TRICARE. http://www.tricare.mil (accessed September 24, 2013).

TRICARE Reserve Select. MyArmyBenefits. http://myarmy benefits.us.army.mil/Home/Benefit_Library/Federal_Benefits_Page/TRICARE_Reserve_Select.html (accessed September 24, 2013).

ORGANIZATIONS

TRICARE Management Activity, 7700 Arlington Boulevard, Suite 5101, Falls Church, Va, US 22042-5101, 1-877-874-2273, http://www.tricare.mil.

Samuel D. Uretsky, PharmD

United States Public Health Service

Definition

The United States Public Health Service (USPHS) is the primary division of the **Department of Health and Human Services (HHS)** of the federal government. It is the government's major health agency and is charged in the twenty-first century with promoting health and preventing disease in areas of special need around the world as well as in the United States. The responsibilities of the USPHS have expanded from its original mission to care for the health of American seamen to cover not only disease prevention and control but also biomedical research; regulation of food, drugs, and medical devices; disaster prevention and response; medical care for Native Americans and other underserved populations; improving the quality and availability of mental health care for drug-dependent persons and others; and reducing people's exposure to toxic chemicals and other environmental hazards. In addition to the eight federal agencies within its domain, the USPHS carries out its work through the Public Health Service Commissioned Corps, which will be described more fully below.

Description

Overall structure of the Public Health Service

As of 2013, the USPHS (hereafter referred to simply as the Public Health Service or PHS) is headed by the **Surgeon General**, who in turn reports to the Assistant Secretary for Health (ASH) within **HHS**. The Office of the Surgeon General (OSG) is responsible for managing the day-to-day operations of the PHS Commissioned Corps (PHSCC). Depending on whether the current ASH is a member of the Commissioned Corps, the Surgeon General is either the senior or the second-highest-ranking officer of the PHSCC,

and holds the naval rank of a vice admiral (three stars). The naval ranking reflects the historical connection between the Public Health Service and the United States Navy.

The eight federal agencies (sometimes called "operating divisions") within the Public Health Service currently report directly to the Secretary of the Department of Health and Human Services. As of 2013, they are:

- Agency for Healthcare Research and Quality (AHRQ)
- Agency for Toxic Substances and Disease Registry (ATSDR)
- Centers for Disease Control and Prevention (CDC)
- Food and Drug Administration (FDA)
- Health Resources and Services Administration (HRSA)
- Indian Health Service (IHS)
- National Institutes of Health (NIH)
- Substance Abuse and Mental Health Services Administration (SAMHSA)Most of these agencies are described in detail in other entries in this encyclopedia.

Background

The development of the Public Health Service over the two centuries and more of its history reflects the evolution of the medical field of public health as well as the expansion and increasing complexity of the federal government. The PHS began in 1798, when President John Adams signed an act passed by Congress "for the relief of sick and disabled seamen." As the new republic depended on its ships for trade as well as defense, the health of its merchant seamen was an important concern. The 1798 act established a Marine Hospital Fund administered by the Treasury Department. Marine hospitals were established along the Great Lakes as well as the Atlantic and Pacific coasts, and offered treatment to men in the Navy and the Coast Guard as well as the merchant marine.

The marine hospital system remained relatively unchanged until the Civil War, when both Union and Confederate forces made use of the hospitals' facilities. After the war, the loose network of hospitals was centralized in 1870 to form the Marine Hospital Service. In 1871, John Maynard Woodworth (1837–1879) was appointed the first Supervising Surgeon of the new service; his title was later changed to Surgeon General. A surgeon who had served as the medical director of W.T. Sherman's Army of the Tennessee, Woodworth wanted the physicians in his new service to be organized on a military model with uniforms and ranks. He also insisted that they pass rigorous examinations for admission to the service, and that they be a mobile force that could be assigned to different locations as needed, rather than attached to a fixed location. This combination of selectivity and mobility still characterizes the PHS Commissioned Corps. It was after Woodworth's death that legislation was passed in 1889 to formally identify the new uniformed service as the Commissioned Corps.

There were three developments in the last three decades of the nineteenth century that changed the Marine Hospital Service into a public health agency in the modern sense. The first was an outbreak of yellow fever in New Orleans that led to the passage of the National Quarantine Act of 1878, transferring medical quarantines for contagious diseases from state to federal control. The second was an immigration act passed in 1891 that tasked the Commissioned Corps with the medical examination (and detainment if needed) of incoming immigrants to prevent the spread of infectious diseases. The third was the service's establishment of a bacteriological laboratory on Staten Island in 1887. Moved to Washington, D.C., in 1891, the Hygienic Laboratory, as it was then called, grew into what is now the **National Institutes of Health** (NIH).

With its expansion into the fields of epidemiology, disease prevention, and biological research, the name of the Marine Hospital Service was changed in 1902 to the Public Health and Marine Hospital Service, and shortened further to the Public Health Service (PHS) in 1912. The passage of the Biologics Control Act of 1902 gave the service regulatory control over vaccines, serums, and similar products. In 1928, the PHS began a cooperative venture with the Bureau of Indian Affairs to improve health care on Native American reservations, which eventually led to the creation of the Indian Health Service in the 1950s.

The PHS underwent a number of restructurings as the federal government itself was reorganized during the New Deal and World War II. In 1939, the PHS was removed from the Treasury Department and assigned to what was then called the Federal Security Agency. In 1944, the PHS was formally restructured by the Public Health Service Act into an entity with four subdivisions: the Office of the Surgeon General, the National Institute of Health, the Bureau of Medical Services, and the Bureau of State Services. One of the PHS's activities during the war, malaria control and prevention, was so successful that it was given permanent form in 1946 as the Communicable Diseases Center, or CDC. The original CDC grew over the years into the present **Centers for Disease Control and Prevention (CDC)**.

The Federal Security Agency was renamed the Department of Health, Education, and Welfare (HEW), and given Cabinet status in 1953. This change did not affect the PHS at first. In 1968, however, the leadership structure of the PHS was radically revised. Prior to that time, it had always been led by an officer from the ranks of the Commissioned Corps, namely the Surgeon General. Responsibility for directing the corps was transferred from the Surgeon General to the Assistant Secretary for Health, a political appointee. In addition, the heads of bureaus or agencies within the PHS were increasingly drawn from outside the Commissioned Corps. When HEW's name was changed in 1980 to the Department of Health and Human Services, the eight agencies within the PHS at that time began to report directly to the Secretary of HHS rather than to the Assistant Secretary for Health.

The PHS Commissioned Corps

The formation and early years of the PHS Commissioned Corps has already been outlined within the description of the Public Health Service. Originally open only to physicians, the Commissioned Corps was opened in the 1930s and 1940s to nurses, engineers, dentists, and research scientists as well as physicians. As of 2013, the corps also includes veterinarians, dietitians, pharmacists, behavioral health specialists, environmental health specialists, and clinical and rehabilitation therapists.

The PHS Commissioned Corps is one of the seven uniformed services of the United States, the others being the five branches of the armed forces (Army, Navy, Air Force, Marines, and Coast Guard) and the National Oceanic and Atmospheric Administration (NOAA) Commissioned Corps. The PHS Commissioned Corps consists of commissioned officers only;

it has no enlisted personnel or warrant officers. Although members of the corps wear the same uniforms as officers of the U.S. Navy (with PHS insignia), they are classified as noncombatants unless militarized during wartime or assigned to one of the service branches of the armed forces. There are about 6,700 persons serving in the Commissioned Corps as of 2013.

At present the Public Health Service Commissioned Corps has the following responsibilities:

• Help with the provision of basic health care services to Native Americans, Alaska Natives, other underserved groups, and other special-needs populations.

• Prevent and control contagious diseases; identify disease transmission hazards; and promote health education and healthy lifestyles.

• Improve the quality of mental health services and substance abuse treatment where needed.

• Conduct biomedical, psychiatric, and health services research; publish relevant findings; and communicate the results to the general public as well as to other researchers in the field.

• Ensure the safety of drugs, medical devices, foods, and cosmetics.

• Work with counterparts in other nations to find solutions to global health problems.

Officers in the Commissioned Corps may be assigned to various branches of the armed forces or to such other federal agencies as the Department of Defense, Department of Homeland Security, Department of the Interior, the State Department, and even the Central Intelligence Agency. Officers are also expected to be available for deployment to other federal, state, and local agencies when a natural disaster, act of terrorism, or other health emergency overwhelms the available resources at the location of the disaster. Recent deployments of the corps included Hurricane Andrew in 1994, the Oklahoma City bombing in 1995, the attack on the World Trade Center on 9/11, Hurricane Katrina in 2005, and Hurricane Sandy in 2012. The corps currently has a tiered system of response teams for such emergencies, with Tier 1 teams prepared to respond within 12 hours, Tier 2 teams within 36 hours, and Tier 3 teams within 72 hours. Tier 2 teams include such specialized groups as an applied public health team and a mental health team.

Why this is important to the consumer

Given the current structure of the U.S. Public Health Service, consumers are most likely to encounter

the work of the PHS either through one of its eight federal agencies or through the presence of Commissioned Corps officers at the site of a local emergency. One reason why the PHS is little known to the general public is that so much of its work is now distributed through the channels of different government agencies at the state as well as federal levels. Nevertheless, the PHS Commissioned Corps is seeking to expand its programs to keep pace with the growing need for health promotion and disease prevention as well as direct health care in special-needs areas in and beyond the United States.

Since 1972, the PHS has offered students in the health professions scholarships in exchange for a commitment to serve in the **National Health Service Corps** (NHSC) after graduation. Consumers who are interested in entering a health care profession and concerned about the rising cost of the necessary education may wish to consider applying for an NHSC scholarship. Contact information for the NHSC is provided under Organizations below.

Resources

BOOKS

DeJong, David H. *Plagues, Politics, and Policy: A Chronicle of the Indian Health Service, 1955–2008*. Lanham, MD: Lexington Books, 2011.

Mullan, Fitzhugh. *Plagues and Politics: The Story of the United States Public Health Service*. New York: Basic Books, 1989. This is the most recent general history of the USPHS.

PERIODICALS

Flowers, L. et al. "U.S. Public Health Service Commissioned Corps Pharmacists: Making a Difference in Advancing the Nation's Health." *Journal of the American Pharmacists Association* 49 (May-June 2009): 446–452.

Galson, S.K. "USPHS Commissioned Corps: A Global Emergency Preparedness and Response Asset." *Public Health Reports* 124 (September-October 2009): 622–623.

Hill, K. et al. "U.S. Public Health Service Commissioned Corps Pharmacist Promoting and Advancing

Pharmaceutical Services Abroad." *Military Medicine* 176 (September 2011): 974–975.

Knebel, A.R. et al. "Ground Zero Recollections of U.S. Public Health Service Nurses Deployed to New York City in September 2001." *Nursing Clinics of North America* 45 (June 2010): 137–152.

Oakley, F. et al. "Occupational Therapists' Role on U.S. Army and U.S. Public Health Service Commissioned Corps Disaster Mental Health Response Teams." *American Journal of Occupational Therapy* 62 (May-June 2008): 361–364.

Taylor, M.M. et al. "Mobilizing Mobile Medical Units for Hurricane Relief: The United States Public Health Service and Broward County Health Department Response to Hurricane Wilma, Broward County, Florida." *Journal of Public Health Management and Practice* 13 (September-October 2007): 447–452.

WEBSITES

Commissioned Officers Association of the USPHS Inc. (COA). "Public Health History." http://www.coausphs. org/phhistory.cfm (accessed September 17, 2013).

National Library of Medicine (NLM). "Images from the History of the Public Health Service." http://www. nlm.nih.gov/exhibition/phs_history/contents.html (accessed September 16, 3013).

Public Health Service Commissioned Officers Foundation for the Advancement of Public Health. "U.S. Public Health Service: Little Known But Important." http:// www.youtube.com/watch?v=lYGLqn0KdCo (accessed September 16, 2013).

U.S. Public Health Service Commissioned Corps. "Overview: FAQs." http://www.usphs.gov/questions answers/overview.aspx (accessed September 16, 2013).

ORGANIZATIONS

Commissioned Officers Association of the USPHS Inc. (COA), 8201 Corporate Drive, Suite 200, Landover, MD, United States 20785,   (301) 731-9080, (866) 366-9593, Fax: (301) 731-9084, http://www.coausphs. org/index.cfm.

National Health Service Corps (NHSC), [no other contact information], (800) 221-9393, gethelp@hrsa.gov, http://nhsc.hrsa.gov/.

Office of the Surgeon General, Tower Building, Plaza Level 1, Room 100, 1101 Wootton Parkway, Rockville, MD, United States 20852, (240) 276-8853, Fax: (240) 453-6141, http://www.surgeongeneral.gov/.

U.S. Department of Health and Human Services (HHS), 200 Independence Avenue, S.W., Washington, DC, United States 20201, (877) 696-6775, http://wcdapps.hhs.gov/ HHSFeedback/, http://www.hhs.gov/.

U.S. Public Health Service Commissioned Corps, (800) 279-1605, http://ccmis.usphs.gov/ccmis/contact_usphs. aspx, http://www.usphs.gov/.

Rebecca J. Frey, Ph.D.

Universal bed concept

Definition

The universal bed concept, also sometimes referred to in the healthcare industry as the "acuity-adaptable care model," is based on the idea of keeping a patient in a single room throughout his or her hospitalization, from admission to discharge. Under a universal bed or acuity-adaptable unit (AAU) system, all necessary tests, procedures, and monitoring activities are carried out in the patient's room rather than via transfers to other parts of the hospital. To meet this goal, universal rooms are designed so that they have the necessary space and infrastructure to accommodate critical care equipment, family visitations, and in-room staff stations.

This patient care model is designed to reduce medical errors and alleviate patient stress associated with transfers to multiple hospital departments for various medical purposes—what some critics have dubbed the "conveyor belt" approach to medical care—and to give patients higher levels of comfort and privacy during their hospital stay.

The universal bed approach to patient care has been lauded for improving patient health outcomes, strengthening the relationship between patient and nursing staff, and making family visitation events a more pleasant experience for patients and loved ones alike. Elimination of patient transfers has also been cited as a path to increased operational efficiency, which can, in turn, reduce overall operating expenses. However, hospitals and healthcare experts have also identified potential pitfalls associated with the universal bed concept, including difficulties in maintaining important nursing competencies, heightened rates of nursing staff turnover, and increased operating expenses.

Description

Interest in the universal bed concept for healthcare delivery grew throughout the 1990s and 2000s, when hospital administrators, healthcare professionals health researchers, patient advocates, and architects all sought to develop a model of care that would promote a positive healing environment and tangibly improve health outcomes. The result was a caregiving model that pivots on bringing medical services to the patient rather than taking the patient to the medical services.

Hallmarks of the most successful universal bed models of care include the following:

- Room designs that fully accommodate the medical needs of the most critically ill patients as well as those with lower acuity levels.
- Nursing staff who use cross-functional training and a flexible work environment to execute a wide range of both critical-care and telemetry-related tasks.
- Floor/unit designs that maintain appropriate levels of security while still reducing patient exposure to traffic flow and staff operations that can compromise their comfort and privacy.
- Significant reductions in inter-unit patient transfers, which are associated with heightened risk of medical errors and higher levels of patient dissatisfaction, and require the involvement of numerous hospital staff members.
- Room layouts that provide dedicated space for extended family visitation without impeding the ability of nurses and other staff to fulfill their duties. Hospitals with universal bed units typically offer expansive visiting hours and often feature sleeping accommodations for family members wishing to stay with the patient overnight.
- Room configurations that emphasize patient safety and ease of use. For example, universal bed concepts usually situate bathrooms so that the risk of a patient falling while trying to reach the bathroom—the single greatest culprit in patient falls during hospitalization—is minimized.
- Patients usually arrive in universal bed units from emergency rooms or surgical-medical departments where they have been treated for serious medical issues. These patients range from those undergoing standard "recovery" care and monitoring prior to discharge to those who are in critical condition and require life support technology.

The universal bed concept has been hailed as a forward-looking, efficient, and patient-oriented approach to hospital care. Advocates also say that it is an economically viable caregiving model, especially for hospitals with intensive care units (ICUs) that are heavily utilized by the surrounding community. Savings can be realized through the reduction of negative events associated with patient transfers, including increased incidence of medication errors, medical complications, and delays in treatment.

Concerns about Universal Beds

Despite the many purported benefits and increased prevalence of universal rooms, these units have their detractors as well. Some hospital facilities that experimented with universal bed concepts have even retreated from that mode of care and returned to the traditional patient-transfer model of treatment. These reversals do not generally center around patient quality-of-care issues; rather, they tend to be due to the operational challenges that the model places on the hospital and its staff members.

Nurses who have worked in universal bed systems freely acknowledge that the caregiving model enables them to establish a stronger rapport with patients, and they emphasize that witnessing a patient's progress from sickness or post-operative recovery to the point where he or she is discharged can be enormously satisfying on both professional and personal levels. However, some nurses have indicated that the universal room model necessitates a degree of cross-training proficiency that can be difficult to attain and maintain, and that it increases their overall workload. Adequate training of nursing staff can be a particular challenge for community hospitals, where ICU admissions may not be high enough for nursing staff to maintain all the skills required of ICU nurses. In addition, some nurses simply prefer to specialize in certain types of care and attend to certain types of patients. These nurses are unenthusiastic about providing care to patients at all levels of acuity. These factors have resulted in high levels of nurse turnover and problems with understaffing at some hospitals that have turned to the universal bed model.

Universal bed models are also expensive on a per-unit basis. Initial construction costs are high, as AAUs require extensive electrical wiring, plumbing, and other infrastructure. In addition, universal rooms are typically outfitted with an extensive array of sophisticated medical equipment, from basic telemetry tools to IV pumps, ventilators, and other vital critical care equipment. Some hospitals have learned that the cost of maintaining these rooms can be prohibitive when only a fraction of this high-tech equipment is regularly used.

Why this is important to the consumer

Whereas the universal bed concept has received mixed reviews from nursing professionals (some of whom object to the heightened workplace demands that the model places on them) and hospital administrators (who worry about the long-term financial viability of such systems), the model is widely recognized as beneficial for patients. It offers a more holistic approach to patient care, creates a more tranquil environment for healing, and gives patients the opportunity to engage in extensive and meaningful contact with family members throughout the recovery process. Studies confirm that hospitals with universal bed systems of care enjoy higher levels of patient satisfaction

KEY TERMS

Acuity—Severity of an illness, disease, or injury.

Acuity-Adaptable Unit (AAU)—Often understood as a synonym for universal bed models, this term is also sometimes used to designate patient rooms that feature all the necessary infrastructure for future conversion into universal rooms.

Critical care—Intensive care.

Holistic—Emphasis on treatment of the whole person rather than just isolated bodily systems and functions.

Telemetry—Measuring, monitoring, collection, and transmission of medical data on patients.

than hospitals that rely on multiple patient transfers to meet healthcare needs.

Resources

BOOKS

Hamilton, Kirk, and Mardelle McCuskey Shepley. *Design for Critical Care: An Evidence-Based Approach.* Burlington, MA: Architectural Press, 2010.

PERIODICALS

Brown, Katherine Kay. "The Universal Bed Care Delivery Model: Facility Design and Operations Combine to Impact the Patient Experience." *Patient Safety and Quality Healthcare* (March/April 2007). http://www.psqh.com/marapr07/caredelivery.html

Evans, Jennie, Debajyoti Pati, and Tom Harvey. "Rethinking Acuity Adaptability." *Healthcare Design* 8, no. 4 (April 2008): 22.

Zimring, Craig, and Hyun-Bo Seo. "Making Acuity-Adaptable Units Work: Lessons from the Field." *Health Environments Research and Design Journal* 5, no. 3 (2012): 115-28.

WEBSITES

Healthcare Design staff. "Rooms and Workspaces." HealthcareDesignMagazine.com http://www.healthcaredesignmagazine.com/category/interior-design/rooms-and-workspaces (accessed September 6, 2013).

ORGANIZATIONS

American Hospital Association, 155 N. Wacker Dr., Chicago, IL 60606, (312) 422-3000, (800) 424-4301, http://www.aha.org.

American Society for Healthcare Engineering, 155 N. Wacker Dr., Ste. 400, Chicago, IL 60606, (312) 422-3800, Fax: (312) 422-4571, ashe@aha.org, http://www.ashe.org.

Kevin Hillstrom

Value-based purchasing *see* **Hospital Value-Based Purchasing (HVBP)**

Veterans Administration (VA) System

History

The Veterans Health Administration is one of three branches of the U.S. Department of Veterans Affairs, or VA. The establishment of the VA dates back to the earliest settlement of British pilgrims in America. According to the VA website, the Pilgrims passed a law supporting benefits for wounded soldiers. The post–Civil War era saw the establishment of soldiers' homes at the state level, where veterans of not only the Civil War, but other wars of the period, including the Spanish-American War, were cared for. The tradition of caring for veterans has persisted and evolved, and the Veterans Health Administration is now part of the U.S. Department of Veterans Affairs. The current VA was established in 1930 as part of a government effort to consolidate veterans' affairs.

Structure

The VA includes the Veterans' Health Administration, Veterans Benefits Administration, and National Cemetery Administration. The Veterans Health Administration focuses on meeting the health care needs of all veterans. This care is provided through a combination of VA medical centers, outpatient clinics, and ambulatory care clinics located throughout the United States. The Veterans Health Administration serves more than 8 million veterans in the U.S. each year.

Why is the VA important to the consumer?

The VA provides a variety of important benefits to veterans and the dependents of veterans, including spouses and children. The surviving spouses, children, and parents of deceased veterans also are eligible for benefits. The services provided by the VA to these individuals include not only medical treatment, but also disability, education and training, vocational rehabilitation and employment services, and burial benefits. Any member of the uniformed services, including current and former reservists and members of the National Guard, are eligible for health and other benefits through the VA. The passage of the Affordable Care Act did not affect veterans' benefits or out-of-pocket costs.

Health benefits summary

The health benefits available to veterans through the Veterans Health Administration range from prescription refills and regular doctor visits, to support for managing post-traumatic stress disorder and other health issues unique to military service personnel, such as exposure to radiation, chemicals (including airborne hazardous materials), and excessive noise. Veterans Health Administration benefits also include surgical procedures and hospital care.

Mental Health/PTSD

Post-traumatic stress disorder and related mental health issues are, unfortunately, not uncommon among veterans and active members of the military. But the Veterans Health Administration offers information not only for patients, but also for clinicians about how to help military personnel and veterans manage these conditions, often with a combination of behavioral and medical therapies.

Public Health

The Veterans Health Administration's general health services for veterans and their dependents

Total number of U.S. veterans age 65 and over who are enrolled in or receiving health care from the Veterans Health Administration, 1990–2006

Year	VA enrollees	VA patients	Total
		Number in millions	
1990	n/a	0.9	7.9
1991	n/a	0.9	8.3
1992	n/a	1.0	8.7
1993	n/a	1.0	9.0
1994	n/a	1.0	9.2
1995	n/a	1.1	9.4
1996	n/a	1.1	9.7
1997	n/a	1.1	9.8
1998	n/a	1.3	9.9
1999	1.9	1.4	10.0
2000	2.2	1.6	10.0
2001	2.8	1.9	9.9
2002	3.2	2.2	9.8
2003	3.3	2.3	9.7
2004	3.4	2.4	9.5
2005	3.5	2.4	9.3
2006	3.5	2.4	9.2

n/a = designates data not available. Department of Veterans Affairs enrollees are veterans who have signed up to receive health care from the Veterans Health Administration. VA patients are veterans who have received care each year through VHA.

SOURCE: Department of Veterans Affairs, Veteran Population 2004 Version 1.0; Fiscal 2006 Year-end Office of the Assistant Deputy Under Secretary for Health for Policy and Planning Enrollment file linked with August 2007 VHA Vital Status data (including data from VHA, VA, Medicare, and SSA)

(Illustration by GGS Information Services. Cengage Learning, Gale)

include routine vaccinations, medical visits, preventive tests, and hospital services when necessary. The Veterans Health Administration website also provides consumer-friendly information about diseases and conditions, including the flu, HIV/AIDS, and hepatitis C, along with resources for health and wellness, such as support for quitting smoking, infection prevention, and health information specifically for women.

Military-Specific Health Issues

The Veterans Health Administration offers health services to veterans that address the unique health concerns associated with military service, and they provide information not only for veterans, but also for the civilian doctors who are likely to treat them. For example, the VA website includes a section aimed at doctors that educates them about some of the symptoms particular to individuals who served in the Persian Gulf War in 1990 and 1991, including environmental exposures, infectious diseases, and mental/social concerns specific to this population of veterans.

Research

In addition to caring for veterans and their families, the Veterans Health Administration's goals include conducting research to improve the health of current and future veterans by identifying new problems in recent veterans (such as issues related to specific types of environmental exposures) and responding to their health concerns. The VA provides information for veterans about volunteering to participate in research studies. Past data from Veterans Health Administration research have included the development of improved prosthetic limbs, treatments for conditions including Alzheimer's disease and osteoporosis, and the creation of new devices, including the cardiac pacemaker and the nicotine patch.

Online Resources: My HealtheVet

Health care for veterans has adapted to the digital age with the development of My HealtheVet, the online **personal health record** system designed specifically for the Veterans Health Administration. The program is designed to allow participants to enter their health care data and coordinate care online. The system offers three account types: basic, advanced, and premium. With the basic account, participants can track personal health and insurance information, and set fitness goals. The advanced account is only available for veterans or VA patients, but allows users to access some of the health information in their veterans or Department of Defense records. The premium account (which requires additional validation of identity) allows users to view more of their personal health information within the VA health care system, including test results, medication history, appointments, and clinical notes.

Resources

WEBSITES

"Diagnosis & Treatment of Gulf War Veterans' Illnesses." United States Department of Veterans Affairs. http://www.publichealth.va.gov/exposures/gulfwar/treating_diagnosing.asp (accessed August 26, 2013).

"History—VA History." United States Department of Veterans Affairs. http://www.va.gov/about_va/vahistory.asp (accessed August 26, 2013).

"My HealtheVet—The Gateway to Veteran Health and Wellness." United States Department of Veterans Affairs https://www.myhealth.va.gov/index.html (accessed August 26, 2013).

"Veterans Health Administration." United States Department of Veterans Affairs. http://www.va.gov/health/ (accessed August 26, 2013).

"War Related Illness and Injury Study Center (WRIISC)." United States Department of Veterans' Affairs. http://www.warrelatedillness.va.gov/ (accessed August 26, 2013).

Heidi Splete

Veterans Integrated Service Networks (VISN)

Definition

The U.S. government coordinates the provision of healthcare services to American military veterans through a system of 21 regional networks called Veterans Integrated Service Networks (VISN). As the operational arm of the Veterans Health Administration (VHA), these networks are responsible for budgeting, planning, and management of services at medical centers, outpatient clinics, nursing homes, and other healthcare facilities for veterans in their respective geographical regions.

Description

The U.S. Department of Veterans Affairs (**VA**) is the agency that administers federal benefits and services to the nation's military veterans and their families. These benefits and services include financial assistance, education and training, burial benefits, and health care. The VHA is the agency within the VA that is dedicated to providing health care to veterans. The VHA operates the largest integrated healthcare system in the United States, providing services to more than eight million veterans at 1,700 facilities across the country each year. The VHA provides primary care, specialized care, and rehabilitative and social services to military veterans. It also provides education and training to health professionals and conducts medical research.

In 1995, the VHA underwent a major reorganization at the urging of Dr. Kenneth Kizer, former Undersecretary of Health for the VA. Kizer presented a report to Congress entitled *Vision for Change: A Plan to Restructure the Veterans Health Administration*. The implementation of this plan resulted in the creation of 22 Veterans Integrated Service Networks. (Two networks were later combined to bring the total number to 21.) The new, decentralized VISN structure was intended to improve service to patients by eliminating layers of bureaucracy, increasing efficiency, and aligning resources with local needs. The VHA headquarters reduced its staff and shifted its focus toward supporting the regional VISNs. Each VISN was charged with handling budget, planning, management, and oversight decisions for the VA medical facilities located within its geographical boundaries.

The original VISN boundaries were established on the basis of patient referral patterns at VA medical facilities and the number of enrolled veterans in the system. Many of the networks cover multiple states, such as the VA Northwest Network (VISN 20), which encompasses Alaska, Idaho, Oregon, and Washington. A few networks cover only part of a state, such as the VA Heart of Texas Healthcare Network (VISN 17). An interactive map showing the geographic distribution of the Veterans Integrated Service Networks is available on the VA website at http://www2.va.gov/directory/guide/division.asp?dnum = 1.

Each VISN provides healthcare services to veterans through several different types of facilities, including VA Healthcare Systems, VA Medical Centers, Vet Centers, community-based outpatient clinics, and nursing homes. The Veterans In Partnership Healthcare Network (VISN 11), for instance, is comprised of seven VA Medical Centers that contain more than 1,800 beds for acute medical, surgical, and psychiatric care. The network also includes 29 community-based outpatient clinics that are run by civilian medical practitioners in partnership with the VA. Finally, VISN 11 features 12 Vet Centers, which offer postwar adjustment, counseling, and outreach services for veterans and their families.

For many years, the reorganization of the VHA into 21 regional VISNs led to significant improvements in key performance measures, including those related to patient care. By 2012, however, the VISN structure had come under criticism from some lawmakers. U.S. Senator Richard Burr, ranking member of the Senate Committee on Veterans Affairs, argued that the VISN geographic boundaries should be redefined to reflect significant shifts in veteran demographics. He also claimed that staffing levels at the 21 VISN headquarters had increased to the point that they lost their focus on budget, management, and oversight. To address these problems, Burr introduced the VISN Reorganization Act of 2012, which was intended to streamline VISN operations. The proposed legislation would combine the 21 regional networks into 12 larger networks, redefine their geographical boundaries, and reduce staffing levels at VISN headquarters. According to Burr, it would also realign the system toward the goal of delivering health care to the nation's veterans safely,

KEY TERMS

U.S. Department of Veterans Affairs (VA)—The agency that administers federal benefits and services to American military veterans and their families.

Vet Center—A VA medical facility that offers post-war adjustment, counseling, and outreach services for veterans and their families.

Veterans Health Administration (VHA)—An agency within the Veterans Administration that is dedicated to providing health care to veterans.

effectively, and efficiently. Although the original bill died in committee, Burr reintroduced it in 2013.

Why this is important to the consumer

Veterans Integrated Service Networks are important to U.S. military service members, veterans, and their families because they coordinate the delivery of health care to this population. Each of the 21 VISNs maintains a website with a comprehensive listing of all of the VA medical facilities that are available to serve the needs of veterans who live in that region. The coordination of healthcare delivery within the networks helps ensure that veterans receive the treatment they need, even if it requires care at several different types of facilities.

Resources

WEBSITES

Senator Richard Burr. "VISN Reorganization Act of 2012." Burr.Senate.Gov. http://www.burr.senate.gov/public/_files/VISNAct.pdf (accessed August 21, 2013).

U.S. Government Printing Office. "S. 3084 (112th): VISN Reorganization Act of 2012." GovTrack.US. http://www.govtrack.us/congress/bills/112/s3084/text (accessed August 21, 2013).

U.S. Senate Committee on Veterans Affairs. "Burr Reorganization Bill Would Put Veterans' Health Care First." Veterans.Senate.Gov. http://www.veterans.senate.gov/rankingmember/ranking-press-releases. cfm?action = release.display&release_id = cd6 1b011-97 ab-4f85-a7a5-246777921cfb (accessed August 21, 2013).

Veterans Health Administration. "Administrative History Project: Executive Summary of VHA." ClintonLibrary.Gov. http://www.clintonlibrary.gov/assets/storage/Research%20-%20Digital%20Library/Clinton AdminHistoryProject/101-111/Box%20108/1756368-administrative-history-project-veterans-health-administration-executive-summary.pdf (accessed August 21, 2013).

ORGANIZATIONS

U.S. Department of Veterans Affairs, 810 Vermont Ave. NW, Washington, DC 20420, (877) 222-8387, http://www.va.gov/.

Laurie Collier Hillstrom

Vital records registration systems

Definition

The Statistics Division of the Department of Economic and Social Affairs of the United Nations (UN) has defined a vital statistics system as "the total process of (a) collecting information by civil registration or enumeration on the frequency or occurrence of specified and defined vital events, as well as relevant characteristics of the events themselves and the person or persons concerned, and (b) compiling, processing, analyzing, evaluating, presenting, and disseminating these data in statistical form." The UN further defines a civil registration process that is used to collect vital statistics as "the continuous, permanent, compulsory recording of occurrence and characteristics of vital events." Vital events that are often tracked include live births, deaths, fetal deaths, adoptions, marriages, legal separations, divorces, and annulments. The process of collecting and evaluating vital statistics provides a means to help in the understanding of a population's health, influences on health, and health outcomes.

Description

Vital statistics are a critical component of a national health information system, allowing the monitoring of progress toward achieving important health goals. Registration of vital events and the development of rates and other quantitative measures from vital events data can provide government programs with essential data and information crucial for planning, policy-making and the evaluation of population-based programs such as the health status of a population, the protection of human and family rights, the well-being of children, and the allocation of health services. Without a registration system in place, such information becomes available only by conducting special studies or one-time surveys, or through other sampling approaches.

Examples of vital statistics that are often used to monitor achievement of health goals include:

- Teen births and birth rates;
- Prenatal care and birth weigh;t
- Risk factors for adverse pregnancy outcomes;
- Infant mortality rates;
- Leading causes of death;
- Life expectancy.

In the United States, the National Vital Statistics System is the data-sharing program used by the National Center for Health Statistics (NCHS) for collecting and disseminating the nation's vital statistics. Data are provided to the NCHS by the vital records registration systems operated by the various jurisdictions legally responsible for maintaining registries of vital events, including births, deaths, marriages, divorces, and fetal deaths. The legal authorities responsible in the U.S. for recording these vital events include the fifty states, two cities (Washington, D.C., and New York City), and five territories (Puerto Rico, the Virgin Islands, Guam, American Samoa, and the Commonwealth of the Northern Mariana Islands). These jurisdictions are also responsible for issuing copies of birth, marriage, divorce, and death certificates.

The NCHS has developed model procedures and standard forms that are recommended for use in the collection of vital statistic data in order to facilitate uniform registration of the events. In addition, the NCHS has developed procedures for collection, coding, editing and transmitting information based on multiple race and Hispanic original data. NSHS also provides training and instructional materials concerning procedures to the responsible legal authorities.

An automated mortality medical data system has been developed by NCHS to code and classify cause-of-death information from death certificates. The National Death Index (NDI) is the central computerized index of death record information compiled from state data. The NCHS, in collaboration with state offices, established the NDI as a resource to facilitate epidemiological follow-up studies and to allow researchers to verify death and cause of death for individuals.

Why this is important to the consumer

The jurisdictions responsible for maintaining registries of vital events are responsible for issuing copies of birth, marriage, divorce, and death certificates to the public. An official certificate of every birth, death, marriage, and divorce should be on file in the locality where the event occurred. The federal government does not maintain files or indexes of these records, but the records are filed permanently in a state vital statistics office or in a city, county, or other local office. An individual may

---

KEY TERMS

U.S. National Center for Health Statistics (NCHS)—The nation's principal health statistics agency that provides data to identify and address health issues. The NCHS compiles statistical information to help guide public health and health policy decisions. The NCHS collaborates with other public and private health partners, and employs a variety of data-collection mechanisms to obtain accurate information from multiple sources.

---

obtain a certified copy of any of the certificates by writing the vital statistics office in the state or area where the event occurred. Addresses and fees may be obtained from the **Centers for Disease Control and Prevention** (http://www.cdc.gov/nchs/w2w/guidelines.htm) for the state or area concerned.

The individual should provide the following information when requesting birth or death records:

- Full name of person whose record is requested;
- Sex;
- Parents' names, including maiden name of mother;
- Month, day, and year of birth or death;
- Place of birth or death (city or town, county, and state; and name of hospital if known);
- Purpose for which copy is needed;
- Relationship to person whose record is requested; and
- Daytime telephone number with area code.

The individual should provide the following information when requesting marriage records:

- Full names of bride and groom;
- Month, day, and year of marriage;
- Place of marriage (city or town, county, and state);
- Purpose for which copy is needed;
- Relationship to persons whose record is requested; and
- Daytime telephone number with area code.

The individual should provide the following information when requesting divorce or annulment records:

- Full names of husband and wife;
- Date of divorce or annulment;
- Place of divorce or annulment;
- Type of final decree;
- Purpose for which copy is needed;
- Relationship to persons whose record is requested; and
- Daytime telephone number with area code.

Resources

BOOKS

Department of Economic and Social Affairs, Statistics Division, United Nations. *Handbook on Civil Vital Registration and Statistics Systems: Computerization.* New York: United Nations Press, 1998.

Department of Economic and Social Affairs, Statistics Division, United Nations. *Handbook on Civil Vital Registration and Statistics Systems: Developing Information, Education and Communication.* New York: United Nations Press, 1998.

Department of Economic and Social Affairs, Statistics Division, United Nations. *Handbook on Civil Vital Registration and Statistics Systems: Management, Operation and Maintenance.* New York: United Nations Press, 1998.

Department of Economic and Social Affairs, Statistics Division, United Nations. *Handbook on Civil Vital Registration and Statistics Systems: Policies and Protocols for the Release and Archiving of Individual Records.* New York: United Nations Press, 1998.

Department of Economic and Social Affairs, Statistics Division, United Nations. *Handbook on Civil Vital Registration and Statistics Systems: Preparation of a Legal Framework.* New York: United Nations Press, 1998.

Hetzel, Alice M. *U.S. Vital Statistics Systems: Major Activities and Development 1950-95.* Hyattsville, MD: National Center for Health Statistics, Centers for Disease Control and Prevention, 1997.

Ryan, Mary Meghan (Editor). *Vital Statistics of The United States: Births, Life Expectancy, Deaths, and Selected Health Data.* Blue Ridge Summit, PA: Bernan Press, 2012.

WEBSITES

Where to Write for Vital Records. http://www.cdc.gov/nchs/w2w.htm.

ORGANIZATIONS

National Center for Health Statistics, Centers for Disease Control and Prevention, 1600 Clifton Road, Atlanta, GA 30333, Atlanta, GA 30333, (800) 232-4636, http://www.cdc.gov/nchs/index.htm.

Judith L. Sims, M.S.

Vulnerable populations and the U.S. health care system

Definition

Within the parameters of the American healthcare system, vulnerable populations are understood to be people living in the United States who are most likely to have difficulty obtaining quality health care. In some cases, economic barriers block vulnerable people from entrance into the nation's healthcare system altogether. In other cases, the vulnerability stems not from the absence of care, but from the poor quality of the care received. Studies of vulnerable populations also typically incorporate population groups that are more likely to have complex medical problems—many of which are exacerbated by limited access to preventive care, regular primary care, and other important elements of the nation's wider healthcare system.

Vulnerable populations are partly defined in racial terms. Most racial and ethnic minorities across the United States, including African Americans, Hispanics, American Indians, and Native Hawaiians, are less likely to enjoy regular access to quality health care. Social factors are another contributor. Individuals who are poor or comparatively uneducated, or who live in substandard housing, or reside in rural or inner-city communities are less likely to receive regular health care. Other groups often designated as vulnerable include low-income children, homeless people, the elderly, immigrants, people with chronic physical or mental illnesses, people who do not speak English, and people who do not have any form of private health insurance and do not qualify for **Medicare** or **Medicaid**. In many cases, these economic, social, and cultural vulnerability factors are closely intertwined and feed into one another.

Description

Vulnerable populations have always been a part of the healthcare landscape in the United States, and the last few decades have been no exception. From the 1990s through the first decade of the 21st century, in fact, the percentage of the U.S. population without adequate access to competent and regular healthcare services steadily rose. From 2003 to 2007 alone, the nonpartisan Center for Studying Health System Change estimated that the number of people in the United States who delayed or did not receive necessary medical care—including those covered by health insurance plans—jumped from 36 million to 57 million. This rising vulnerability rate was attributed to a wide range of factors, including a rise in the rate of various age-related chronic illnesses (due to the rising median age of the nation's population), growing inequities in income, and the increased difficulty of securing and keeping employer-provided health insurance coverage.

The consequences of this diminished access to basic healthcare services have been well-documented. They range from spiraling rates of comorbidity among Hispanic and African-American senior citizens to wide disparities in basic preventive dental care

In the United States, the cost of healthcare has been rising rapidly for decades, increasing more than an estimated $250 billion in 2012 alone, and many people can't afford it. *(Scott Olson/Getty Images)*

between low-income children and children from middle-class and upper-class households. Researchers agree that economically and educationally disadvantaged populations of any age are much more likely to face diminished access to quality and timely health care. These decisions to forsake or delay visits to the doctor are even common among lower-income families who have health insurance coverage, since many insurers have raised deductibles and co-payments in their health policies in recent years.

Analysts caution, however, that lifestyle choices, environmental factors, and race/ethnicity factors also contribute to disparities in health treatment outcomes in ways that scientists are still trying to understand. For example, researchers are conducting intensive studies in an effort to better understand why even college-educated black women register higher infant mortality rates than white women without a college education. Studies are also being undertaken to better understand how wider cultural and industry factors contribute to disparities in healthcare treatment outcomes between racial and ethnic groups. As the

Institute of Medicine reported in *Unequal Treatment: Confronting Racial and Ethnic Disparities in Health Care,* a seminal 2002 study on vulnerable healthcare populations, "racial and ethnic minorities tend to receive lower quality health care than non-minorities even when controlled for access-related factors such as insurance status and income. The sources of these disparities are complex; they are rooted in historic inequalities; perpetuated through stereotyping and biases in the healthcare system, health professionals, and patients; and aggravated by barriers such as language, geography, and cultural familiarity." The authors of the IOM report noted, for example, that up to 20% of Spanish-speaking Americans reported not seeking medical care because of language barriers.

Although healthcare experts acknowledge that U.S. healthcare vulnerabilities and disparities are driven by a vast array of factors that intersect in complex ways, they are in general agreement that health insurance coverage is the single most critical determinant of an individual's healthcare security. Expanding health insurance coverage, then, has been a primary

KEY TERMS

Comorbidity—Two or more coexisting but unrelated medical conditions.

Disparities—Inequalities in health status between different population groups.

Inequities—Unfair or unjust elements.

goal of healthcare experts, social scientists, policymakers, and consumer advocates seeking to achieve greater equity within the U.S. healthcare system.

The most ambitious and controversial effort to extend health insurance coverage to vulnerable populations in recent years is the **Patient Protection and Affordable Care Act** of 2010, sometimes known as "Obamacare" in recognition of President Barack Obama's pivotal role in getting the law passed. Critics of the Affordable Care Act have alleged that the law is deeply flawed and doomed to fail. Proponents, however, assert that it will rein in healthcare costs and integrate millions of vulnerable Americans into the U.S. healthcare system through expansions of state Medicaid programs, prohibitions against denial of coverage based on preexisting conditions, the establishment of individual and small group insurance exchanges, and a variety of other initiatives and programs.

Why this is important to the consumer

Many lawmakers, public officials, consumer advocates, and progressive organizations are acting on their belief that everyone in the United States should have access to quality health care, whatever their socioeconomic status, race, ethnicity, gender, age, geographic location, or personal health history. Proponents of this view hold that the continued presence of vulnerable populations constitutes one of the most glaring weaknesses of the U.S. healthcare system and diminishes the country's overall vitality. Supporters of the Affordable Care Act express hope that when the ACA is fully operational, it will provide millions of these vulnerable people with entrance into the healthcare system. However, health reform groups say that healthcare providers will also have to take additional measures to fully integrate vulnerable populations and

reduce disparities in quality of care and treatment outcomes. "[Vulnerable populations] … are likely to have special needs arising from their personal, social, and financial circumstances, any of which may negatively affect health and hamper efforts to obtain care," cautioned the Commonwealth Fund, a health policy think tank. "The health care systems where vulnerable populations seek treatment must be equipped to address these needs."

Resources

BOOKS

Aday, Lu Ann. *At Risk in America: The Health and Health Care Needs of Vulnerable Populations in the United States.* San Francisco: Jossey-Bass, 2001.

Shi, Leiyu, and Gregory D. Stevens. *Vulnerable Populations in the United States.* San Francisco: Jossey-Bass, 2010.

Smedley, Brian D., Adrienne Y. Stith, and Alan R. Nelson, eds. *Unequal Treatment: Confronting Racial and Ethnic Disparities in Health Care.* Washington, D.C.: Institute of Medicine, National Academies Press, 2002.

PERIODICALS

Schor, Edward L., et al. "Ensuring Equity: A Post-Reform Framework to Achieve High Performance Health Care for Vulnerable Populations." The Commonwealth Fund, October 7, 2011. http://www.commonwealth fund.org/Publications/Fund-Reports/2011/Oct/ Ensuring-Equity.aspx

WEBSITES

Centers for Disease Control and Prevention staff. "Populations." CDC.gov. http://www.cdc.gov/minority health/populations.html (accessed September 9, 2013).

Commonwealth Fund staff. "Vulnerable Populations." CommonwealthFund.org. http://www.common wealthfund.org/Topics/Vulnerable-Populations.aspx (accessed September 9, 2013).

ORGANIZATIONS

Center for Studying Health System Change, 1100 1st St. NE, 12th Fl., Washington, DC 20002-4221, (202) 484-5261, Fax: (202) 863-1763, hscinfo@hschange.org, http:// www.hschange.com.

Commonwealth Fund, One East 75th St., New York, NY 10021, (212) 606-3800, Fax: (212) 606-3500, http:// www.commonwealthfund.org.

Health Policy Center at the Urban Institute, 2100 M St. NW, Washington, DC 20037, (202) 833-7200, http:// www.urban.org.

Kevin Hillstrom

W

Walk-in ambulatory clinic

Definition

A walk-in ambulatory clinic is a no-appointment-necessary medical clinic, usually for the care of relatively uncomplicated acute problems.

Description

Walk-in ambulatory clinics may be freestanding, located in retail stores (often called "storefront" or "retail clinics"), or they may be associated with hospitals or healthcare systems.

Storefront or retail clinics are generally staffed by mid-level care providers, such as nurse practitioners or physician assistants, and have only limited capacity to do simple blood work or other testing (e.g., strep tests and flu screens). These clinics are designed to take care of minor acute health problems, such as bladder or ear infections, strep throat, and rashes. Storefront or retail clinics clinics may offer some immunizations and may be

Consumers like walk-in ambulatory clinics because they don't require an appointment, typically have extended evening and weekend hours, and usually offer a clear price list. *(Alamy)*

willing to help monitor chronic conditions such as high cholesterol or high blood pressure.

On the other hand, clinics that are associated with healthcare systems are frequently staffed by physicians as well as **nurse practitioners** and/or **physician assistants.** These health system-associated clinics often have the capacity to do more extensive laboratory work (e.g., blood and urine tests), as well as imaging (x-rays and CT scans). In some cases, this is because they have access to the resources of the healthcare system or hospital under whose auspices they are run. In addition to treating the minor, acute conditions that can be treated at storefront clinics, health system-associated clinics may be able to treat more complex, chronic conditions (such as diabetes or high blood pressure), stitch lacerations, treat uncomplicated fractures, and even provide IV fluids to treat dehydration.

Smaller, storefront clinics usually have to send patients to other medical facilities if the care they need is deemed too complex or too urgent for the staff of the clinic. About 2% of **storefront clinic** visits result in the patient being referred back to his or her primary care provider, or on to an urgent care or emergency department for further treatment. Clinics that are associated with hospitals may have the advantage of another tier of medical services available on-site to which more complicated patients can be transferred.

Why this is important to the consumer

Consumers explain that they favor these walk-in ambulatory clinics because there is no need for an appointment, they typically have extended evening and weekend hours (studies show that almost half of walk-in clinic visits occur during times when traditional doctor's offices are usually closed), and the walk-in clinics usually offer a clear price list. Many clinic visits are covered entirely or in part by insurance, although individuals should verify whether their insurance company considers a given clinic to be in- or out-of-network.

Drawbacks of obtaining care at a walk-in ambulatory clinic include the loss of continuity of care, the inability of the clinic to access past medical records from other care providers, a disconnect with an individual's primary care provider, and a decreased emphasis on preventive care (as compared to the mission of most primary care providers).

Research into these relatively new healthcare options have shown that about 17% of all patient

---

KEY TERMS

Acute—Having a rapid or sudden onset, and often lasting for a short period.

Chronic—Occurring over a long period of time; persistent, recurrent.

Nurse practitioner—An advanced practice nurse whose practice scope includes diagnosis and treatment, in some cases outside of the direct supervision of a physician.

Physician assistant—A healthcare provider whose practice scope includes diagnosis and treatment, which must be provided under the direct supervision of a physician

---

visits to hospital emergency departments are actually appropriate for much cheaper options, such as walk-in ambulatory or urgent-care clinics. Shifting care to these venues would save about $4.4 billion per year.

The United States has been facing a severe **shortage of primary care physicians** for some time now. Projections state that 2015 will see a shortage of 62,900 physicians, compared to the number necessary for the nation's population, and 2020 will see that shortage reach 90,000 physicians. At the same time, the **Patient Protection and Affordable Care Act** will provide medical coverage to 3 million more Americans, thus further stressing the healthcare system. Storefront clinics, with their focus on affordable medical care provided by mid-level practitioners, are thought to be one answer to the healthcare shortages.

Resources

BOOKS

Kovner Anthony R. et al. *Health Care Delivery in the United States* 10th ed. New York: Springer Publishing Company, 2011

Schulte,Margaret F.*Health Care Delivery in the U.S.A.: An Introduction* 2nd ed. New York: Productivity Press, 2012

Sultz, Harry A. et al. *Health Care USA: Understanding Its Organization and Delivery* 7th ed. Sudbury, MA: Jones & Bartlett Learning, 2010

WEBSITES

National Caregivers Library. Types of Care Facilities [accessed September 22, 2013]. http://www.caregivers library.org/caregivers-resources/grp-care-facilities/ types-of-care-facilities-article.aspx

USA.gov. Choosing a Health Care Facility. 2013 [accessed September 22, 2013]. http://www.usa.gov/topics/ health/caregivers/health-care-facility.shtml/

ORGANIZATIONS

American Hospital Association, 155 N. Wacker Dr., Chicago, IL 60606, (312) 422-3000, http://www. aha.org/.

Convenient Care Association, 260 South Broad Street, Suite 1800, Philadelphia, PA 19102, (215) 731-7140, http:// www.ccaclinics.org/ .

United States Department of Labor, 200 Constitution Ave. NW, Washington, DC 20210, (800) 321-6742, https:// www.osha.gov/.

Urgent Care Association of America, 387 Shuman Blvd., Suite 235W, Naperville, IL 60563 , (877) 698-2262, http://www.ucaoa.org/.

Rosalyn Carson-DeWitt, MD

WIC *see* **Special Supplemental Nutrition Program for Women, Infants, and Children (WIC)**

Workplace safety

Definition

Workplace safety refers to all those policies, practices, rules, and regulations designed to protect workers from physical, chemical, biological, and other hazards associated with their jobs and the physical locations in which they work. It also includes efforts by employers, unions, and workers themselves to maintain the highest level of good health possible for employees, their families, and the general community. Workplace safety is also often referred to as "occupational safety and health."

Description

Employees in virtually every occupation face some type of hazard to their physical or mental well-being. Construction workers are at risk for falls or injuries from falling objects. Workers in refineries are exposed to chemical fumes and are at risk for fires and explosions. Farm workers handle fertilizers and

One of the purposes of workplace safety programs is to develop programs and other systems to protect workers from possible hazards. *(©Corepics VOF/Shutterstock.com)*

pesticides that may cause respiratory issues and other problems. Office workers may have to deal with boredom, frustration, stress, or other emotional issues. The purposes of workplace safety programs are to identify possible hazards faced by workers in their specific place of employment, to develop programs and other systems to protect workers from those hazards, and to provide an environment that will maximize the physical and mental health of employees.

Machines are a major source of injury in a variety of occupations because of their moving parts. An employee can easily become entangled in gears, sprockets, or rotating shafts, causing loss of a finger, hand, arm, or other body part. Presses and other machines that crush objects can also trap an employee's hand or arm. Objects with knife-like or other sharp edges can also sever body parts. Leaks or breaks in hoses, pipes, liquid reservoirs, or other devices that contain fluids may increase the likelihood of slips and falls that result in broken bones, sprains, or strains.

Inhalation of dust and powders can cause a number of chronic respiratory problems, such as:

• asbestosis
• byssinosis (also known as "brown lung disease")
• pneumoconiosis (also known as "coal worker's pneumoconiosis" or "black lung disease"
• silicosis
• chronic beryllium disease
• chronic pleural disease
• mesothelioma
• hypersensitivy pneumonitis
• occupational lung cancer

Respiratory diseases such as these are a particular hazard in resource recovery occupations, such as coal and metal mining, where naturally occurring materials are broken apart, and small particles, dust, and powders released in the process are inhaled by workers. Once those particles are inhaled, they can become lodged in the lungs, where they accumulate, blocking air passages and causing inflammation of tissues that may result in chronic respiratory disorders, such asbestosis (caused by particles of the mineral asbestos), silicosis (caused by small particles of silicon dioxide, or sand), and chronic beryllium disease (caused by small particles of beryllium metal or its ore).

Other possible hazards present in the workplace include:

• heat from hot machinery, escaping steam, furnaces, molten materials, and other sources that may cause severe burns, heat stroke, exhaustion, cramps, dehydration, dizziness, or other effects, or that scorch clothing or fog safety glasses
• cold, which can produce numbness, frostbite, hypothermia, or other effects that incapacitate a person or reduce work efficiency and effectiveness
• electric shock, which can cause burns, falls, incapacitation, or even death
• chemical exposure to a range of materials, including acids and bases, heavy metals, poisonous compounds, solvents, and flammable and explosive materials, all of which can cause internal distress if swallowed, burns and scarring if in contact with the skin, and respiratory distress if inhaled, any of which can be fatal in the most extreme cases
• fumes and gases that may range from annoying to life threatening, such oxides of nitrogen, sulfur dioxide, and carbon monoxide
• noise, the effects of which can range from the annoying to physical damage, as when exposure to very loud sounds causes damage to the eardrum resulting in permanent hearing loss
• high-intensity light or other forms of electromagnetic radiation, such as ultraviolet or infrared radiation, x-rays, or gamma radiation, all of which can damage the eyes, skin, or other parts of the body
• exposure to illegal and unhealthy practices of fellow workers, including smoking, drinking, substance abuse, and careless work behaviors that pose a risk not only to the person doing such behaviors, but also to co-workers in the surrounding environment
• biological agents, including viruses, bacteria, fungi, parasites, and other pathogens that can cause a host of infections
• psychological and social factors, such as stress, violence, burnout, bullying, harassment, and repetitive stress injuries, such as carpal tunnel syndrome

An additional safety hazard in many occupations is posed by confined spaces. A confined space is a region with one or only a few openings that is not designed for long-term occupancy by employees, with poor ventilation and possibly contaminated air. Examples of confined spaces are storage tanks, compartments of ships, process vessels, pits, silos, vats, degreasing tanks, reaction vessels, boilers, ventilation and exhaust ducts, sewers, tunnels, underground utility vaults, and pipelines. Employees are often required to enter confined spaces for the purpose of service or cleaning such areas and face the risk of becoming trapped inside them. According to the U.S. Bureau of Labor Statistics (BLS), an average of about 92 people in the United States die each year after becoming trapped in a confined space.

Demographics

State, national, and international government and labor organizations collect and maintain extensive databases on the number, causes, and circumstances of workplace injuries and deaths. In the United States, the relevant agency for these data is the U.S. Department of Labor of the Bureau of Labor Statistics. The number of workplace fatalities in the United States has decreased slowly over the past two decades from a high of 6,632 in 1995 to a low of 4,383 in 2012. The most common cause of fatal incidents are transportation events, such as on-road vehicle accidents (24% of deaths), followed by other transportation incidents (17%), falls, slips, and trips (17%), and death due to contact with an object or equipment (16%). Violence and other injuries by persons or animals accounted for 17% of deaths, with homicides accounting for 11 of that 17%, exposure to harmful substances or environments accounted for 7% of deaths, and fires and explosions accounted for the last 3% of fatalities.

The construction industry had the highest total number of fatalities in 2012, 775, however at 9.5 deaths per 100,000 full-time equivalent workers it did not have the highest rate of fatalities. The agriculture, forestry, fishing and hunting industry had the highest per capita fatality rate, with a total of 21.1 deaths per 100,000 full-time equivalent workers, followed by mining and related industries (15.6 per 100,000) and transportation and warehousing (13.3 per 100,000).

History

Prior to the twentieth century, workplace safety was a matter of little or no concern to governmental agencies or the public. Certain jobs, such as those in mining and manufacturing, were simply regarded as hazardous, and workers just accepted the risk involved in going to work each day in such jobs. The fatality rate among U.S. coal miners in the last decade of the nineteenth century, for example, was in excess of 325 per 100,000 workers. The death rate among railroad workers at the time was somewhat less than that, about 267 deaths per 100,000 workers. Public attitudes began to change during the early part of the twentieth century with the rise of the progressive movement in the United States. For the first time, social reformers began to demand that business and industry accept some measure of responsibility for providing their workers with safe working conditions. One of the first steps in this area by the U.S. government was the creation of the Bureau of Mines in 1910 following a series of disastrous mine accidents resulting in hundreds of deaths and injuries. In the same year, New York adopted the first workmen's compensation law,

a law allowing employees to sue employers for damages resulting from accidents that occurred in the workplace. Within a decade, largely through the efforts of the new workers unions that were being formed across the country, 44 other states had adopted similar legislation.

Alice Hamilton (1869-1970) was a pioneer in correcting the medical problems caused by industrialization, awakening the country in the early twentieth century to the dangers of industrial poisons and hazardous working conditions. Through her efforts, toxic substances in the lead, mining, painting, pottery, and rayon industries were exposed and legislation was passed to protect workers. She was also a champion of worker's compensation laws and was instrumental in bringing about this type of legislation in the state of Illinois. A medical doctor and researcher, she was the first woman of faculty status at Harvard University and was a consultant on governmental commissions, both domestic and foreign.

In 1971, the U.S. Congress established the first federal agency with specific responsibility for overseeing the safety and health of U.S. workers, the Occupational Safety and Health Administration (OSHA) in the Department of Labor. Under provisions of its original enabling legislation, the **Occupational Safety and Health Act** of 1970, as well as numerous later bills, OSHA is responsible for overseeing a large variety of potential safety hazards and risks as well as a number of occupations and industries. A short list of some of the topics with which OSHA deals includes agricultural operations, the airline industry, anthrax, arsenic, asbestos, biofuels, beryllium, biological agents, cadmium, combustible dust, compressed gas and equipment, demolition, diacetyl, ELF radiation, ergonomics, green jobs, hantavirus, heat illness, isocyanates, logging, meat packing, microwave radiation, nursing homes, oil and gas well drilling, the plastic industry, popcorn, Portland cement, reproductive hazards, sawmills, scaffolding, tularemia, and violence in the workplace.

Costs to society of workplace accidents

The deaths and injuries resulting from workplace accidents are only two measures of their cost to society. Every death and injury is also related to a number of financial and economic costs, both to the injured person and her or his family, as well as to the employer and to society as a whole. A number of economists have attempted to estimate the total cost in dollars to the United States as a result of workplace injuries and deaths, with results that range widely across the board. A 2012 estimate, for example, placed that cost at more than $250 billion. Other estimates range from about $50 billion upwards. These costs include the obvious direct costs associated with an injury: visits to an emergency department, physician fees, other medical bills, medications, and costs of rehabilitation. However, they also include more indirect costs such as administrative costs in dealing with the injury, increases in insurance premiums, costs of hiring a substitute for the injured worker, effects on employee morale, loss of products and services, delays in filling orders, potential governmental penalties, and attorney fees associated with possible claims. By some estimates, these indirect costs can amount to as much as four times the direct costs of the injury itself.

Prevention

Government, business, and individual employees generally agree that the financial and personal costs of workplace injuries and death are so great that programs of injury prevention are well worth the time and effort they take to implement. A number of businesses have adopted accident prevention programs on their own, and others have done so because of federal, state, and local regulatory requirements. An injury prevention program has a number of primary elements, including:

• Acceptance of management responsibility: The first step in any injury prevention program is an acceptance by a company that it has a responsibility to reduce injuries in its workplace. One concrete expression of this responsibility is the provision of all safety technology available and appropriate for the industry, such as safeguards on machinery, adequate rest times, sufficient safety equipment (safety glasses and gloves, for example), and adequate first aid facilities and equipment.

• Communication with employees: Businesses need to make employees aware of safety issues within the workplace and, preferably, to involve them in the injury-prevention program. For this reason, most businesses today now have safety committees that consist of both managers and employees, to carry out company policies on injury-prevention efforts.

• Hazard assessment and control: One essential step in any injury-prevention program involves a review of the workplace to identify potential risks and hazards to employees and then to develop specific mechanisms for reducing them.

• Accident investigation: Even under the best of circumstances, accidents will occur. A good injury prevention program will include, therefore, a specific mechanism for investigating the conditions and circumstances surrounding accidents in the workplace

to determine what changes are needed to reduce future risks from the same hazard.

• Safety and health recording systems: In some industries, it may be necessary to keep ongoing records of employee exposure to certain types of hazards, such as levels of radiation or exposures to harmful chemicals. These records ensure that employees are not exposed to levels of hazards greater than those recommended by regulatory agencies.

• Safety and health training: Management and unions can work together to provide classes and other training sessions to make employees more aware of the hazards present in the workplace, the steps needed to avoid accidents, and the proper ways to use safety equipment provided by the company.

Why this is important to the consumer

Workplace safety is important to all consumers who work, or who have family or loved ones who work. This is true both for individuals who work in industries that are easily identifiable as higher-risk, such as mining or logging, and those in lower-risk professions such as administrative or retail jobs. Workplace safety regulations cover not just those highly visible hazards such as large machinery and heavy tools, but also more mundane but real hazards such as the risk of slipping and falling on wet floors and repetitive stress injuries from performing the same task repeatedly. Workplace safety standards benefit all consumers by reducing the risk of workplace injuries and fatalities, allowing all consumers to be healthier, happier, and more secure while at work.

Resources

BOOKS

American Industrial Hygiene Association; American National Standards Institute. *Occupational Health and Safety Management Systems.* Falls Church, VA: American Industrial Hygiene Association, 2012.

English, Paul F. *Safety Performance in a Lean Environment: A Guide to Building Safety into a Process.* Boca Raton, FL: CRC Press, 2012.

Reese, Charles D. *Accident Incident Prevention Techniques.* Boca Raton, FL: Taylor & Francis, 2012.

PERIODICALS

Kongsvik, T., J. Fenstad, and C. Wendelborg. "Between a Rock and a Hard Place: Accident and Near-miss Reporting on Offshore Service Vessels." *Safety Science* 50 no. 9 (2012): 1839–46.

Lortie, M. "Analysis of the Circumstances of Accidents and Impact of Transformations on the Accidents in a Beverage Delivery Company." *Safety Science* 50 no. 9 (2012): 1792–1800.

"Protecting staff in the workplace." *Occupational Health* 1 (November 2013).

Saleh, J.H., and C.C. Pendley. "From Learning from Accidents to Teaching about Accident Causation and Prevention: Multidisciplinary Education and Safety Literacy for All Engineering Students." *Reliability Engineering and System Safety* 99 (2012): 105–13.

Smith, E.L. "How Are Nurses at Risk?" *Work* 41 (2012): 1911–9.

WEBSITES

"Industry Injury and Illness Data." U.S. Bureau of Labor Statistics. November 7, 2013. http://www.bls.gov/iif/oshsum.htm (accessed December 11, 2013).

"Workers." Occupational Safety and Health Administration. United States Department of Labor. https://www.osha.gov/workers.html (accessed December 11, 2013).

"Workplace safety." Legal Information Institute. Cornell University Law School. http://www.law.cornell.edu/wex/workplace_safety (accessed December 11, 2013).

"Workplace Safety and Health." Centers for Disease Control and Prevention. November 30, 2011. http://www.cdc.gov/workplace/ (accessed December 11, 2013).

"Workplace Safety & Health." United States Small Business Administration. http://www.sba.gov/content/workplace-safety-health (accessed December 11, 2013).

ORGANIZATIONS

U.S. Department of Labor. Occupational Safety & Health Administration (OSHA), 200 Constitution Ave., Washington, DC 20210, (800) 321-6742, http://www.osha.gov/.

David E. Newton, Ed.D.
Tish Davidson, AM

World Health Organization (WHO)

Definition

The World Health Organization (WHO) is the directing and coordinating agency for health within the United Nations (UN).

Description

The WHO is responsible for establishing **health policies** for the UN, providing leadership on health issues worldwide, setting the international health research agenda, monitoring and assessing health trends throughout the world, and providing assistance to individual countries and regions where that may be necessary.

During conferences on the drafting of the United Nations charter after the end of World War II, specific mention was made of the important role of health in the future activities of any international organization created by the charter. By July 22, 1946, all 61 original members of the United Nations had signed a charter for such an organization, which came to be known as the World Health Organization. The WHO officially came into existence when its constitution came into force on April 7, 1948, a day that was proclaimed, and continues to be celebrated annually, as World Health Day.

In total, 194 nations are members of the WHO, with two associate members (Puerto Rico and Tokelau). The organization is run by the World Health Assembly, which meets annually and appoints a Director General and sets general policy for the agency. This policy is carried out by an Executive Board consisting of 34 members, each with technical expertise in some area of health. The WHO operates regional offices in six parts of the world: Africa, the Americas, Europe, the Eastern Mediterranean, Southeast Asia, and the Western Pacific, and in 147 individual countries. The organization's annual budget amounts to nearly $4 billion, about a quarter of which comes from contributions from member countries and the rest from donations from other entities. The largest donor to the WHO has traditionally been the United States, followed by Japan, the United Kingdom, Germany, and France.

The WHO has a six-point agenda that is not disease specific. It also has specific targets and goals for diseases, regions, and other health-related issues that it addresses. The general agenda includes:

• Promoting development. The WHO aims to improve health development by helping to ensure that life-saving

The World Health Organization headquarters in Geneva, Switzerland. (*©Martin Good/Shutterstock.com*)

and health-improving services are not restricted for unfair or unjust reasons, and by increasing access to health care for low-income and disadvantaged individuals.

• Fostering health security. The WHO promotes action that will help reduce the occurrence and spread of epidemics, including improving the way antibiotics are used and food is handled.

• Strengthening health systems. The WHO supports the improvement of health systems, especially in developing countries, to ensure that they have adequate staff, facilities, and funding to reach the populations that need them.

• Harnessing research, information and evidence. The WHO emphasizes the collection of data and research to generate evidence-based recommendation and standards, and encourages adherence to those standards.

• Enhancing partnerships. The WHO works with many organizations across the world, including governmental, private, and non-profit organizations to

reach the goals of the WHO and enhance health for all people.

• Improving performance. The WHO also focuses on improving its own operations, including making improvements to staff well-being, budget oversight, and results-based management approaches.

The WHO also has a very ambitious set of goals for specific diseases, risk-factors, and areas. It has developed a number of specific programs for carrying out these goals and objectives. Some of the organization's current programs and areas of work include the African Programme for Onchocerciasis, avian influenza, child growth standards, Global Alliance against Chronic Respiratory Diseases, humanitarian health action, Initiative for Vaccine Research, Intergovernmental Forum on Chemical Safety, malaria, medical devices, Partners for Parasite Control, Polio Eradication Initiative, sexual and reproductive health, Tobacco Free Initiative, and the United Nations Road Safety Collaboration. An especially important function of the agency is the collection, analysis, and distribution of data on global health

KEY TERMS

Disparity—Inequality or lack of similarity; may be associated with differences in care or treatment.

Malaria—Disease caused by the presence of sporozoan parasites of the genus Plasmodium in the red blood cells, transmitted by the bite of anopheline mosquitoes, and characterized by severe and recurring attacks of chills and fever).

Parasite—An organism that lives in or with another organism, called the host, in parasitism, a type of association characterized by the parasite obtaining benefits from the host, such as food, and the host being injured as a result.

issues. These statistical reports are available on the WHO website.

Why this is important to the consumer

The World Health Organization is the leading international organization working to improve the health and well-being of all individuals everywhere on earth. It seeks to reduce **health disparities** and improve access to healthcare for everyone, especially individuals in very low-income countries or regions. All consumers have benefited directly or indirectly from WHO programs, agencies, or research. The WHO was an integral part of efforts to stop the avian influenza epidemic, has reduced the incidence of malaria and other tropical diseases, and is working to stop the spread of HIV/AIDS around the world. The WHO also collects data on health-related topics, tracks the spread of diseases, and issues guidelines that are the basis for health recommendations and treatment all over the world.

Resources

BOOKS

Chorev, Nitsan. *The World Health Organization between North and South*. Ithaca, NY: Cornell University Press, 2012.

Lee, Kelley and Fang, Jennifer. *Historical dictionary of the World Health Organization*, 2nd Ed. Lanham, MD: Scarecrow Press, 2013.

Markle, William and Fisher, Melanie, eds. *Understanding Global Health*, 2nd Ed. New York: McGraw-Hill, 2013.

PERIODICALS

Banerji, Debabar. "The World Health Organization and Public Health Research and Practice in Tuberculosis in India." *International Journal of Health Services* 42 no. 2 (2012): 341–57.

Chorev, Nitsan. "Restructuring Neoliberalism at the World Health Organization." *Review of International Political Economy* 3 (2012): 1–40.

Sinimole, K. R. "Evaluation of the Efficiency of National Health Systems of the Members of World Health Organization." *Leadership in Health Services* 25 no. 2 (2012): 139–50

WEBSITES

Leveraging the World Health Organization's Core Strengths. Global Health Policy Center. http://csis.org/files/publication/110502_Reeves_LeveragingWHO_Web.pdf (accessed December 2, 2013).

World Health Organization. New York Times Topics. http://topics.nytimes.com/topics/reference/time stopics/organizations/w/world_health_organization/index.html (accessed December 2, 2013).

ORGANIZATIONS

World Health Organization (WHO), Avenue Appia 20, 1211 Geneva 27, Switzerland, 4122 791 21 11, Fax: 4122 791 31 11, http://www.who.int/about/contact_form/en/index.html, http://www.who.int/en/.

David E. Newton, EdD
Tish Davidson, AM

GLOSSARY

ABHYANGA. A type of gentle oil message used by Ayurveda practitioners to calm the mind as well as relax the body. The sesame or coconut oils that are used are scented with herbs to provide a form of aromatherapy as well as ease the movement of the therapist's hands over the patient's skin.

ABSTRACT. A summary of a journal article.

ABUSE. In a medical or health context, it is the improper or excessive use of any substance that is usually prescribed for medicinal purposes.

ACA. A common abbreviation for the Affordable Care Act, the full name of which is the Patient Protection and Affordable Care Act. The legislation is also informally referred to as "Obamacare," after President Barack Obama.

ACCOUNTABILITY. The process that health care providers and delivery systems use to provide efficient, quality care and fulfill the expectations of health care consumers and other stakeholders. Accountability also entails the communication of these processes to all stakeholders.

ACCREDITATION. The process of evaluating and certifying the quality of healthcare organizations against official standards.

ACTIVITIES OF DAILY LIVING (ADLs). A term used in healthcare to refer to daily self-care activities such as bathing and showering, bowel and bladder management, toilet and personal hygiene, feeding and eating, and mobility.

ACUITY. The severity of an illness, disease, or injury. Also, the keenness of one's sense perceptions.

ACUITY-ADAPTABLE UNIT (AAU). Often understood as a synonym for universal bed models, this term is also sometimes used to designate patient rooms that feature all the necessary infrastructure for future conversion into universal rooms.

ACUTE. Having a rapid or sudden onset, and often lasting for a short period.

ACUTE CARE. Intensive but relatively short-term medical treatment for medical emergencies (such as severe injury or illness) or post-operative recovery.

ADAPTATION. Altering a tool so that an individual with an injury or disability is better able to use it and function independently or with minimal assistance.

ADDICTION. Compulsive use of a substance despite negative outcomes. Tied to physiological and psychological cravings for the substance, as well as symptoms of withdrawal when the substance is not used.

ADDICTION MEDICINE. The specialized branch of medicine that deals with the diagnosis and treatment of alcohol and substance addictions.

ADDICTION SPECIALIST. A physician who is certified either in addiction medicine or addiction psychiatry in addition to either board certification in a medical specialty or board certification in psychiatry.

ADDICTIVE. Causing a strong, harmful need to ingest or otherwise elevate blood levels of a substance.

ADJUSTMENT. Changes to a standard fee. Changes may be made because of managed care agreements or other discounts.

ADVANCE DIRECTIVES. A set of signed, witnessed documents that lay out an individual's preferences regarding health care, including a living will, durable power of attorney for healthcare, and (if desired) a do-not-resuscitate order.

ADVERSE EVENT. Any unpleasant or undesirable outcome or experience associated with the use of a drug or medical device.

AFFORDABLE CARE ACT (ACA). The Patient Protection and Affordable Care Act (PPACA; informally known as "Obamacare"); signed into law by President Barack Obama in March of 2010. The act overhauled the U.S. healthcare system, including major changes to private health insurance plans and to Medicaid.

AGING POPULATION. The increase in the proportion of the nation's population over the traditional retirement age.

AGING SCHEDULE. In a medical billing context, a list of overdue medical accounts calculated from the date of the original bill to the current date.

AIR EMBOLISM. An obstruction in the circulatory system caused by an air bubble accidentally created as a result of surgery or other medical treatment.

ALCOHOLISM. A medical and psychological condition in which excessive and compulsive alcohol ingestion leads to addiction and the impairment of the activities and abilities of normal life.

ALGORITHM. A series of steps that are followed in order to solve a mathematical problem or to complete a computer process.

ALLERGEN. A substance that causes an allergic reaction.

ALLERGY. An overreaction by the body's immune system to substance that is usually nonthreatening to most people.

ALLOPATHIC MEDICINE. A term for scientific or evidence-based medicine that was coined by Samuel Hahnemann (1755–1843) to differentiate standard medical care from the brand of medicine he created and practiced, which he called homeopathic medicine.

ALPHAFETOPROTEIN (AFP). A substance present in the blood of pregnant women. Levels higher or lower than normal usually signal the need for more tests.

ALTERNATIVE MEDICINE. A system of healing that rejects the primacy of standard, evidence-based medicine and advocates the use of dietary supplements and therapies such as herbs, vitamins, minerals, massage, and cleansing diets. Alternative medicine includes homeopathy, traditional Chinese medicine, Ayurvedic medicine, and many more-recent fad treatments.

ALZHEIMER'S DISEASE. Progressive dementia characterized by worsening memory and other cognitive impairment.

AMA. In Ayurveda, a toxin that collects in the body as a result of incomplete digestion and then enters the bloodstream to disrupt normal metabolism and other bodily processes.

AMBULATORY. Able to move, not bedridden; referring to a surgical procedure performed on an outpatient basis, where the patient is able to leave after the procedure is complete.

AMERICAN RECOVERY AND REINVESTMENT ACT (ARRA). An economic stimulus package enacted by the U.S. government in 2009 in response to a period of global economic decline; its primary objectives were to improve the U.S. job market by investing heavily in infrastructure, education, health, and renewable energy.

ANGIOPLASTY. A surgical procedure intended to widen or remove an obstruction from an artery.

ANOINTING OF THE SICK. A ritual practiced in the Roman Catholic, Anglican (Episcopalian), Lutheran, and Eastern Orthodox churches, in which the priest or pastor recites a series of prayers with the sick person and anoints the person with oil. The ritual is intended to comfort the sick person and help him or her cope with the illness as well as aid his or her recovery. Anointing of the sick should not be confused with faith healing.

ANTIBODIES. Proteins produced by the body's immune system in reaction to the presence of antigens, foreign substances or organisms such as bacteria or viruses. Antibodies mark the invaders, making it easier for other components of the immune system to find and disable them.

ANTIGEN. Any foreign substance, usually a protein, that stimulates the body's immune system to produce antibodies.

APGAR TEST. A wellness assessment used to measure how well a neonate (new born) is doing immediately after birth. Babies get two points each for color, heartbeat, respiration, muscle tone and grimace, or response to stimuli. Named for pediatric anesthesiologist Virginia Apgar.

APH (ANTEPARTUM HEMORRHAGE). Bleeding before the birth.

ARTHRITIS. A general term for the inflammation of a joint or a condition characterized by joint inflammation.

ASSERTIVE COMMUNITY TREATMENT (ACT). A service-delivery model for providing comprehensive, highly individualized, locally based treatment directly to patients with serious, persistent mental illnesses.

ASTIGMATISM. A visual problem in which changes in the curvature of parts of the eye, most often the cornea, prevent light from focusing properly and causes blurred vision.

AT-RISK POPULATION. A group that shares a characteristic that makes its members more susceptible to a particular adverse event.

AUTISM. A syndrome characterized by a lack of responsiveness to other people or outside stimuli, often in conjunction with a severe impairment of verbal and non-verbal communication skills.

AUTOMATED EXTERNAL DEFIBRILLATOR (AED). A portable electronic device that has the ability to diagnose and treat several cardiac abnormalities, with only minimal training on the part of the user.

AYURVEDIC MEDICINE. A 5,000-year old system of holistic medicine developed on the Indian subcontinent. Ayurvedic medicine is based on the idea that illness results from a personal imbalance or lack of physical, spiritual, social, or mental harmony. Ayurvedic treatments include diet, exercises, herbal treatments, meditation, massage, breathing techniques, and exposure to sunlight.

B

BACTERIA. Single-celled life forms, many of which can cause diseases and infections.

BASAL METABOLIC RATE (BMR). The lowest rate of body metabolism (rate of energy use) that can sustain life, measured after a full night's sleep in a laboratory under optimal conditions of quiet, rest, and relaxation.

BASELINE FUNCTIONING. A term used in medicine to describe the initial set of measurements taken of a patient's vital functions in order to have a basis for comparison with later observations.

BATTERY. Any improper, nonconsensual, or violent contact with another person.

BEHAVIORAL THERAPY. Uses various strategies to reinforce positive behaviors and control and minimize negative ones.

BENEFICIARIES. Persons determined by the Social Security Administration to be eligible for Medicare benefits.

BEST PRACTICES. Actions that are based on the best evidence available from the relevant literature and clinical experience. New knowledge informs best practices.

BETA BLOCKER. Class of drugs that treats high blood pressure, glaucoma, migraines, and other health conditions.

BIOLOGICS. Medical products created by a biological process rather than being chemically synthesized. They include vaccines, tissues and tissue products, gene therapy products, blood and blood products, or allergenic substances.

BOUNCE BACK. Preventable readmission of a patient to a hospital.

BRAXTON-HICKS. Light, usually painless uterine contractions. Sometimes called "false labor." Women can experience these throughout pregnancy often note that they increase in the last weeks before birth.

BUPRENORPHINE. A semi-synthetic opioid that can be used to treat narcotic addiction as well as relieve pain. Addiction specialists must undergo specialized training in order to treat opioid-addicted patients with buprenorphine on an outpatient basis.

C

CAHPS SURVEY. A 32-question survey for patients to rate their experience at a health care facility. The acronym stands for Consumer Assessment of Healthcare Providers and Systems, and the survey is administered by the Agency for Healthcare Research and Quality (AHRQ).

CAPITATED. Of, relating to, participating in, or being a health-care system in which a medical provider is given a set fee per patient (for example, as in an HMO) regardless of treatment required. The fixed fee itself is called capitation.

CARDIAC IMPLANTABLE ELECTRONIC DEVICES (CIEDs). Heart pacemakers and other permanently implanted devices designed to improve a patient's cardiac functions.

CARDIOPULMONARY RESUSCITATION (CPR). An emergency procedure, often employed after cardiac arrest, in which cardiac massage, artificial respiration, and drugs are used to maintain the circulation of oxygenated blood to the brain

CASE MANAGEMENT. Assessment, planning, coordination, management, and evaluation of medical services to meet the comprehensive health needs of patients and their families.

CASUISTRY. A method of moral and ethical reasoning in which the issue at hand is argued to be analogous to a previous case that is considered settled or resolved.

CATEGORICAL IMPERATIVE. The concept, described by philosopher Immanuel Kant (1724–1804), that morality and ethics are universally ("categorically") binding ("imperitive") upon all rational individuals.

CATEGORICALLY NEEDY. Groups of people who qualify for the basic mandatory Medicaid benefits; also, groups that state Medicaid programs are either required to cover or have the option of covering.

CENTER FOR MEDICARE & MEDICAID INNOVATION. A group associated with the Centers for Medicare and Medicaid Services that supports the development and testing of innovative health care payment and service delivery models.

CENTERS FOR DISEASE CONTROL AND PREVENTION (CDC). The federal agency responsible for identifying the origin and patterns of disease with the goal of reducing the occurrence of disease.

CENTERS FOR MEDICARE AND MEDICAID SERVICES (CMS). The federal agency within the United States Department of Health and Human Services (HHS) that administers the Medicare program and works in partnership with state governments to administer Medicaid, the State Children's Health Insurance Program (SCHIP), and health insurance portability standards. CMS has other responsibilities, including the administrative simplification standards from the Health Insurance Portability and Accountability Act (HIPAA) of 1996, quality standards in long-term care facilities through its survey and certification process, and clinical laboratory quality standards under the Clinical Laboratory Improvement Amendments. Previously known as the Health Care Financing Administration (HCFA).

CERTIFIED NURSE MIDWIFE. An advanced practice nurse with specialized education and training in midwifery. Certified nurse midwives care for women and/or newborns before, during, and after birth and provide well-woman health care.

CHARISMATIC. In contemporary Christianity, a belief in the renewal of supernatural gifts and powers among all believers, not just ordained clergy. One of these charisms (gifts) is the gift of healing.

CHILDREN'S HEALTH INSURANCE PROGRAM (CHIP). Children's Medicaid; a federal program administered by the states that provides low-cost or free health insurance to children from families with incomes that have traditionally been too high to qualify for Medicaid and too low to afford private health insurance coverage.

CHIROPRACTIC. A form of manipulative therapy that emphasizes the adjustment and realignment of joints and muscles. Chiropractic is most often used as an alternative treatment for low back pain.

CHOLERA. A bacterial infection of the small intestine. The disease is spread by drinking water or eating seafood or other foods that have been contaminated with the feces of infected people. It occurs in parts of Asia, Africa, Latin America, India, and the Middle East. Symptoms include watery diarrhea and exhaustion; the disease is often fatal to young children and the elderly.

CHRONIC. Occurring over a long period of time; persistent, recurrent.

CHRONIC CARE. Treatment of ongoing diseases, such as high blood pressure or diabetes.

CHRONIC DISEASE. A condition lasting a long time.

CHRONIC DISEASE MANAGEMENT. Coordinated programs of patient education, service delivery, and payment systems that focus on supporting patients' efforts and building the capacity of patients and families to manage disease effectively.

CHRONIC OBSTRUCTIVE PULMONARY DISEASE (COPD). Lung diseases, such as emphysema and chronic bronchitis, in which airflow is obstructed, causing labored breathing and impairing gas exchange.

CHRONIC RENAL FAILURE. Kidney disease that results in the loss of kidney function, which is to remove waste and excess water from the body.

CLAIM. Medical bill.

CLINICAL CARE. Pertaining to hospital patients or hospital care.

CLINICAL PRACTICE GUIDELINES. Recommendations developed by experts intended to optimize patient care; the recommendations are informed by a systematic review of evidence and provide ratings of both the quality of evidence and the strength of the recommendations.

CO-PAYMENT (OR CO-PAY). The amount that an insured individual pays out-of-pocket for healthcare services.

COBRA. The Consolidated Omnibus Budget Reconciliation Act (COBRA; 1986) health benefit provisions that enables people to buy individual insurance coverage from their previous employer-based plan for a limited time period.

COGNITIVE. Relating to the act of the mental processes of perception, judgment, reasoning, and memory.

COGNITIVE THERAPY. Cognitive therapy seeks to change negative thought patterns, thereby improving symptoms of mood and anxiety disorders, and/or improving on negative behaviors that are leading to dysfunction.

COINSURANCE. The amount a patient may be required to pay for services after any plan deductibles are paid. In Original Medicare, this is a percentage (such as 20 percent) of the Medicare approved amount.

COMMUNICABLE. Capable of being transmitted. A communicable disease can be spread by contact with a person with the disease.

COMMUNITY HEALTH CENTER. Nonprofit, community-directed centers that provide primary care to all people in communities with high needs because residents have low incomes or high infant mortality rates, or because there are too few physicians available.

COMMUNITY MENTAL HEALTH CENTER. A facility that provides core services as described in the Public Health Service Act, including outpatient services, 24-hour emergency care, day treatment, or other partial hospitalization services, psychosocial rehabilitation services, and screening for patients being considered for admission to state mental health facilities.

COMMUNITY MENTAL HEALTH CLINIC (CMHC). A community-based provider of limited or comprehensive mental health services; usually at least partially publicly funded.

COMMUNITY-BASED CARE. Also called community-based health care, it involves and empowers local communities and individuals in promoting and achieving better health and preventing disease.

COMMUNITY-BASED HEALTH CENTER. A provider of health services located in an underserved area that is open to all residents and tailored to fit their needs.

COMORBIDITY. Two or more coexisting but unrelated medical conditions.

COMPLEMENTARY MEDICINE. Nonconventional therapy that is used in conjunction with mainstream treatment.

CONFIDENTIALITY. The protection and maintenance of strict privacy and secrecy in relationships between professionals and their patients or clients.

CONFLICT OF INTEREST. A set of circumstances creating a risk that a professional judgment or action regarding a primary interest will be unduly influenced by a secondary interest, most often financial gain.

CONSULTATION. Evaluation by an expert or specialist.

CONSUMER OPERATED AND ORIENTED PLANS (CO-OPs). Independent, nonprofit, member-owned, and member-operated health insurance companies established under the PPACA.

CONSUMER-DRIVEN HEALTH INSURANCE. A high-deductible policy that mainly covers catastrophic medical costs.

CONSUMER-MEDIATED EXCHANGE. A form of health information exchange (HIE) that provides patients with secure online access to their medical records and other health information.

CONTINUITY. Consistency or coordination of details.

CONTINUITY OF CARE. Uninterrupted health care delivery in which the same practitioner sees the patient from the initial contact through the stages of illness and recovery.

CONTINUOUS QUALITY IMPROVEMENT (CQI). An approach to quality assurance that emphasizes the organization and systems, focuses on processes rather than the individuals, recognizes all stakeholders, and acknowledges the need for objective data to analyze and improve processes.

CONTRAINDICATION. A factor that makes administration of a particular drug or treatment inadvisable.

CONTROLLED SUBSTANCES ACT (CSA). A law passed by Congress in 1970 to regulate the manufacture, distribution, and possession of narcotics and certain other drugs. Drugs are divided into five schedules (categories) according to their potential for abuse, potential for addiction, and accepted medical use(s). The classification of drugs is administered jointly by the Department of Justice and the Food and Drug Administration (FDA).

CORNEAL. Pertaining to the cornea, which is the transparent membrane at the front of the eye.

CORONER. An officer who holds inquests regarding violent, sudden, or unexplained deaths. Coroners in the United States may be elected officials who are finders of fact or they may be physicians. In the latter case, they are usually called medical examiners. The name is derived from "crown," because coroners in medieval England were minor officials of the Crown.

COST SHARING. An effort by insurance companies to make consumers cover part of the cost of their own health care by requiring deductibles and copayments.

COST-BENEFIT ANALYSIS. An analysis that compares the financial costs with the benefits of two or more health care treatments or programs.

COWPOX. A mild disease in cows that is caused by a poxvirus.

CRITICAL CARE. Intensive care.

CT SCAN. The abbreviated term for "computed or computerized axial tomography." The test may involve injecting a radioactive contrast dye into the body. Computers are used to scan for radiation and create cross-sectional images of internal organs.

CULTURAL CLIMATE. The political and social environment of an institution or a society.

CULTURE. Culture refers to the shared ideas, values, and meanings that people who are members of society share.

D

DAVENING. The English form of a Yiddish word for the act of prayer. In contemporary American Judaism, davening refers to the recitation of the prescribed prayers in the Jewish liturgy. Also spelled "davvening."

DEDUCTIBLE. The amount that an insured person is required to pay on each claim or over the course of a year.

DEEP VEIN THROMBOSIS (DVT). The formation of a blood clot in a vein deep in the body. DVT is most common in the leg veins. Clots can break off and circulate through the body blocking vital arteries and causing death.

DEPARTMENT OF HEALTH AND HUMAN SERVICES (DHHS). The U.S. government's principal agency charged with protecting the health of all Americans and providing essential human services, especially for vulnerable populations. DHHS is responsible for nearly 25% of all federal expenditures and administers more grant funding than all other federal agencies combined.

DEPENDENCE. A state of physiological need for a substance. Abstinence results in unpleasant and even dangerous side effects.

DESIGNER DRUG. An informal term for psychoactive drugs that were discovered by experimenting with existing drugs or through research to develop new drugs.

DEVELOPMENTAL SCHEDULES. A type of assessment instrument designed to identify developmental delays by comparing a child's behavior to the typical behavior of a child of the same age, usually normed in months or half years.

DIABETES. A disease in which insufficient insulin is made by the body (type 1 diabetes) to metabolize sugars, or the cells of the body do not respond adequately to insulin circulating in the blood (type 2 diabetes).

DIABETIC KETOACIDOSIS. A serious, life-threatening complication of diabetes in which patients with insulin deficiencies burn fatty acids, creating excess acidic chemicals in the body.

DIAGNOSIS. The decision a physician reaches regarding the cause of a patient's symptoms by evaluating the pattern and severity of the symptoms compared to other known cases.

DIAGNOSTIC RELATED GROUPS (DRGS). Diagnosis categories that are used when doing physician or hospital billing. Each diagnosis is placed into the appropriate category.

DIALYSIS. An artificial method of cleansing the blood when the kidneys have failed and are unable to do so.

DILATION. Opening, specifically in birthing of the cervix. Cervical dilation happens in the first stage of labor and is measured in centimeters, with 10 cm considered "complete" and ready for a woman to begin the second stage of labor (pushing and birth).

DIPHTHERIA. A serious infectious disease that produces a toxin (poison) and an inflammation in the membrane lining of the throat, nose, trachea, and other tissues.

DIRECT PRIMARY CARE (DPC). Health care delivery in which primary care is offered by the physician directly to the consumer without the involvement of an insurance company. DPC is sometimes used as a synonym for concierge medicine.

DISCHARGE PLANNERS. A health care professional who haelps hospital patients and their families to transition from the hospital to another level of care such as rehabilitation in a skilled nursing facility, home health care in the patient's home, or long-term care in another facility.

DISCIPLINE. In health care, a specific area of preparation or training, for example, social work, nursing, or nutrition.

DISEASE. Any threat to the human body from an organism living within the human body.

DISPARITY. Inequality or lack of similarity; in a healthcare context, it refers to differences in care or access to care because of race, ethnicity, socioeconomic status, or other factors.

DISTANT SITE. The site where the telehealth physician or other health care provider is located. It is also known as the "hub site."

DOCUMENTATION. The process of recording information in the medical chart, or the materials in a medical chart.

DOSHA. One of three principles or energies that govern the structure and functioning of the human body. An imbalance among the doshas is held to be one of the root causes of physical or mental illness in Ayurveda.

DOULA. A doula is someone who undergoes special training in order to support women during childbirth and into the postpartum period.

DRESSING STICK. A long rod with a hook attached to the end that a patient uses in place of the hands. Typically a dressing rod would be used to pull on a pair of pants or socks.

DRUG ADMINISTRATION. The various ways that a medication may enter the body. Among other avenues, it can include orally, rectally, intravenously, and intradermally (through the skin).

DRUG INTERACTIONS. Side effects that come about when more than one drug is administered at the same time; this can cause one or more of the medications to be more potent or less potent than usual, or it can cause side effects that one or more of the medications would not otherwise produce.

DUAL DIAGNOSIS. A term used to describe a patient diagnosed with a mental illness and a comorbid substance abuse disorder. Some specialists prefer the term "co-occurring disorder" (COD).

DUAL ELIGIBLES. Low-income elderly and those with physical or mental disabilities who are eligible for both Medicaid and Medicare.

DURABLE POWER OF ATTORNEY FOR HEALTHCARE. A document in which an individual names another party to be responsible for making medical decisions on his or her behalf.

E

EARLY AND PERIODIC SCREENING, DIAGNOSIS, AND TREATMENT (EPSDT). Children's services that Medicaid programs are required to cover.

ECLECTIC MEDICINE. A form of medicine that emerged in the United States in the nineteenth century and essentially combined herbal remedies with physical therapy.

ECOLOGICAL. Related to the conditions in the environment that contribute to beneficial interaction among all life in that environment.

EDEMA. Swelling or fluid retention, usually in the ankles, fingers, or feet.

EFFICACY. The effectiveness of a drug in treating a disease or condition.

ELECTIVE. Referring to a surgical procedure that is a matter of choice; an elective operation may be beneficial to the patient but is not urgently needed.

ELECTRONIC BENEFIT TRANSFER (EBT). An electronic system that enables a recipient to authorize transfer of their government benefits from a federal account to a retailer account to pay for products received.

ELECTRONIC HEALTH RECORD (EHR). Digital documentation of an individual's medical history such as demographic data, test results, medication lists, drug allergies, etc.

ELECTRONIC PRESCRIBING. Digital authorization and transmission of a patient prescription by a healthcare provider directly to a pharmacy.

EMBOLUS. The medical term for any solid, liquid, or gaseous mass that can travel through the bloodstream and block a blood vessel.

EMERGENCY MANAGEMENT. An overall term for organization and management procedures for critical events that includes response to, and recovery from, emergencies as well as emergency preparedness.

EMERGENCY MEDICAL TECHNICIAN (EMT). A healthcare provider of emergency medical services. EMTs are ambulance clinicians, trained to respond quickly to emergency situations regarding medical issues, trauma injuries and accident scenes. A national exam is required for certification following mandated in-class hours and patient-contact requirements. In the United States, EMTs' activities in the field are governed by state regulations, local regulations, and the policies of their Emergency Medical Services (EMS) organization. The development of these policies are overseen by a physician medical director, often with the advice of a medical advisory committee.

EMERGENCY MEDICAL TREATMENT AND LABOR ACT (EMTALA). A 1986 law that requires hospitals to provide emergency medical treatment to patients regardless of their citizenship, legal status, or ability to pay.

ENCEPHALITIS. Inflammation of the brain, usually caused by a virus. The inflammation may interfere with normal brain function and may cause seizures, sleepiness, confusion, personality changes, weakness in one or more parts of the body, and even coma.

END-STAGE RENAL DISEASE (ESRD). A disease where the kidneys are no longer able to work at a level needed for day-to-day life. The most common causes of ESRD in the United States are diabetes and high blood pressure. A person with ESRD will usually get health care coverage through Original Medicare, although in certain situations, the patient may be able to join a Medicare Advantage Plan, which might include a Medicare Special Needs Plan.

ENVIRONMENTAL HEALTH. A part of public health that specifically focuses on how the natural and built environment may affect human health.

EPIDEMIC. The condition of a disease increasing over a widespread area.

EPIDEMIOLOGY. A branch of medicine that focuses on the distribution, spread, and control of diseases.

EPISIOTOMY. A surgical incision made to enlarge the perineal area for delivery, to avoid tearing of the tissues, especially with a large neonate or during a difficult birth. Many women request the avoidance of a routine episiotomy. To avoid performing an episiotomy, certified nurse midwives may stretch the perineum with perineal massage.

ESSENTIAL HEALTH BENEFITS (EHB). Minimum services that must be provided by health insurance plans under the PPACA.

ETHICS. Principles of conduct that help individuals and groups decide courses of action.

EVIDENCE-BASED PRACTICE. The process by which health care providers incorporate the best research or evidence into clinical practice in combination with clinical expertise and within the context of patient values.

EXCHANGES. American Health Benefit Exchanges; state systems through which individuals can compare and purchase health insurance under the Patient Protection and Affordable Care Act (PPACA).

EXCLUSION. the practice of not allowing a physician to participate in the Medicaid or Medicare programs.

EXPERT WITNESS. A person called to appear in court in order to explain certain facts or points of information relevant to the case that lie outside the general knowledge of most nonspecialists.

F

FAITH HEALING. Healing that is alleged to take place through supernatural, miraculous means, often immediately. Faith healing is associated primarily with Pentecostal and charismatic Christians in the United States but is also practiced by some Roman Catholics.

FECES. The solid waste that is left after food is digested. Feces form in the intestines and pass out of the body through the anus. Also called stool.

FEDERAL POVERTY LEVEL (FPL). The U.S. government's definition of poverty for families of a given size, adjusted annually for inflation and used as the reference point for determining eligibility for Medicaid and health insurance subsidies under the Patient Protection and Affordable Care Act (PPACA).

FEDERALLY QUALIFIED HEALTH CENTERS (FQHCs). Community-based organizations that provide comprehensive primary care and preventive care, including health, oral, and mental health/substance abuse services to persons of all ages, regardless of their ability to pay, or health insurance status. They are a critical component of the health care safety net.

FEE SPLITTING. Accepting payment for referring patients to another physician.

FEE-FOR-SERVICE. A healthcare payment model in which individual services such as office visits, tests, or medical procedures are paid for separately and typically at time of service.

FEE-FOR-VALUE. A health insurance model designed to reduce over-utilization of services and improve quality of healthcare

FELLOW. An M.D. who has completed a residency and is undergoing further training in a particular medical subspecialty.

FETUS. A developing human being inside the womb, generally understood as the stage beginning three months after conception until birth.

FIRST RESPONDER. A generic term for the first medically trained responder to arrive at the scene of an emergency. First responders include police officers, firefighters, emergency medical technicians, and paramedics.

FITNESS. Being physically healthy and capable of carrying out appropriate physical activities with a minimum of fatigue.

FOOD AND DRUG ADMINISTRATION (FDA). A federal organization under the U.S. Federal Drug and Cosmetic Act (FD&C Act) that has the power to oversee the safety of drugs, foods, cosmetics, and medical devices.

FOOD INSECURITY. The circumstance of limited access to food, or anxiety about food sufficiency or a shortage of food in the home. Food insecurity may result from reduced quantity quality, variety, or desirability of food.

FORENSIC. Referring to legal or courtroom matters.

FORMULARY. A pre-approved list of prescription drugs that is covered under a healthcare plan.

FREE RADICAL. a molecule with an unpaired electron that has a strong tendency to react with other molecules in DNA (genetic material), proteins, and lipids (fats), resulting in damage to cells. Free radicals are neutralized by antioxidants.

FULL-TIME-EQUIVALENT EMPLOYEE (FTE). Under the ACA, an employee who works an average of 30 hours a week, or two half-time employees.

FUNCTIONAL RESERVE. The degree to which a vital organ can tolerate a workload higher than its usual level.

G

GENERAL PRACTITIONER. Personal physicians who are responsible for providing comprehensive and continuing care to a patient, regardless of age, sex, or medical condition.

GENERIC DRUG. A generically branded drug that is comparable to a name brand in formulation, strength, quality, and intended use, but is often considerably less expensive.

GERIATRIC. Related to the elderly.

GERIATRIC CARE. A medical specialty that focuses on providing healthcare to individuals of advancing age.

GERIATRIC GIANTS. A list of four major impairments that affect older adults: immobility, instability, incontinence, and impaired intellect. The phrase was introduced by Bernard Isaacs, a British physician.

GERIATRICIAN. A physician who specializes in the health care of the elderly. Geriatrics is considered a subspecialty of internal medicine and family practice.

GERONTOLOGY. A multidisciplinary field of academic research that investigates the process of human aging, including the psychological, intellectual, and social aspects of aging as well as the physical.

GLOBALIZATION. The increasing integration of the world's economies, cultures, and politics, with particular emphasis on the free flow of capital and trade and the use of cheaper foreign labor.

GRANDFATHERED PLAN. A health care plan that was in existence on March 23, 2010 and has stayed basically the same. A plan can enroll people after that date and still maintain its grandfathered status because that designation is determined by the date the plan was created, not when a participant joined it. Health plans must disclose if they are grandfathered in all materials describing plan benefits and offer contact information. In addition, all health plans, grandfathered or not, must: 1) end lifetime limits on coverage, 2) end arbitrary cancellations of health coverage, 3) cover adult children up to age 26, 4) provide an SBC, and 5) hold insurance companies accountable to spend premiums on health care and not on administrative costs and bonuses. However, grandfathered plans do not have to: 1) cover preventive care for free, 2) guarantee the participant's right to appeal, 3) protect the participant's choice of doctors and access to emergency care, and 4) be held accountable through Rate Review for excessive premium increases.

GRIEF COUNSELING. A form of psychotherapy designed to help people cope with emotional responses to extraordinarily stressful events in their lives, such as the death of a loved one or long-term unemployment.

GROSS DOMESTIC PRODUCT (GDP). The total value of goods and services produced within a country during a specified period.

GUARANTEED ISSUE. A requirement for insurance companies to offer health insurance plans to eligible applicants, regardless of their health status.

H

H1N1 (SWINE FLU). A disease which was originally found in pigs and can be passed from animal to human or human to human. Symptoms of H1N1 include fever, cough, chills, fatigue, headache, and body aches.

HALLUCINOGEN. A substance that acts on the central nervous system in a way that alters perception.

HARD SCIENCES. A general term for the sciences that apply mathematical models in their work and obtain a high degree of objectivity and accuracy, such as physics, chemistry, and pure mathematics. They are also known as the "exact sciences."

HAZARD. In the context of emergency preparedness, a general term for any agent, whether biological, chemical, mechanical, or other, that is likely to cause harm to humans or the environment in the absence of protective measures.

HAZARD ASSESSMENT. An attempt to survey an environment to determine which hazards are present in that environment.

HBAC. Home Birth After Cesarean.

HCAHPS INITIATIVE. The Hospital Consumer Assessment of Healthcare Providers and Systems (HCAHPS) initiative is an attempt to provide a standardized survey instrument and data-dcollection methodology for measuring patients' perspectives on hospital care.

HEALTH COMMUNICATION. The study and use of communication tools to instruct, inform, and influence individual and community decisions affecting health and wellness.

HEALTH INFORMATION ORGANIZATION (HIO). An entity that provides the infrastructure and governance required to support and secure HIE at the local or state level.

HEALTH INSURANCE. Funding for healthcare services. Participants pay monthly fees, "premiums," in the eventuality of requiring these services.

HEALTH INSURANCE EXCHANGE. A shopping area for health insurance. These exchanges are set up by states as part of the Affordable Care Act.

HEALTH INSURANCE PORTABILITY AND ACCOUNTABILITYACT (HIPAA). Enacted in 1996, HIPAA is made up of two main parts (titles). Title I protects the health insurance coverage of workers when they change or lose their jobs. Title II requires the establishment of a national standard for electronic healthcare transactions.

HEALTH LITERACY. How well people can obtain and understand information about their health and health services so that they can make health care decisions.

HEALTH MAINTENANCE ORGANIZATION (HMO). A comprehensive private insurance plan that provides a primary care physician who controls referrals to specialists and other services within the HMO's network.

HEALTH MAINTENANCE ORGANIZATION POINT OF SERVICE PLAN (HMOPOS). A less common variation on an HMO plan that may allow the patient to receive services out-of-network for a higher cost.

HEALTH MARKETING. A multidisciplinary method of communicating health information using traditional marketing, science, and social marketing with the goals of disease prevention, health promotion, and health protection.

HEALTH PROFESSIONAL SHORTAGE AREA (HPSA). A federally designated area in which residents lack adequate access to primary health care providers and services.

HEALTH RESOURCES AND SERVICES ADMINISTRATION (HRSA). The primary federal agency within the Department of Health and Human Services (DHHS) that acts to improve access to health care services for vulnerable individuals and populations.

HEALTHCARE. The collective term for all processes related to treating and preventing injury and disease.

HEALTHCARE DISPARITY. An inequality in health status due to decreased access to timely, quality healthcare; often brought on by issues of culture, gender, race, or socioeconomic status, and also impacted by behavioral factors.

HEARTBURN. A burning sensation in the chest that can sometimes also be felt in the neck, throat, and face. It is the primary symptom of gastroesophageal reflux disease (GERD).

HERBAL EXTRACT. A preparation made by soaking a plant in a liquid, such as alcohol, to extract one or more of its ingredients. Extracts may be taken in liquid form or dried and used as a powder.

HERBAL MEDICINE. A plant or any part of a plant used for medicinal or therapeutic purposes.

HEROIC MEDICINE. An approach to medicine that emphasized aggressive and potentially harmful treatments of disease. The term was invented by Benjamin Rush (1745–1813), one of the signers of the Declaration of Independence as well as a physician. Heroic medicine was practiced in the United States from the 1790s through the end of the Civil War.

HIPPOCRATIC OATH. The ethical pledge attributed to Hippocrates that is used as a standard for care by physicians worldwide.

HOLISTIC. In medicine, an approach that takes all dimensions of a human being into account, the psychosocial and spiritual as well as the physical.

HOME MODIFICATION. Altering the physical environment of the home to remove hazards and provide an environment that is more functional for the individual. Examples of home modification include installing grab bars and no-slip foot mats in the bathroom to prevent falls.

HOMEOPATHY. A system of alternative medicine invented by Samuel Hahnemann in Germany in the late eighteenth century. It operates on the principle that "like heals like," which means that a disease can be cured by treating it with substances that cause the disease. The quantities of these sunstances follow another homeopathic law, the Law of Infinitesimals, which states that the *lower* a dose of curative, the more effective it is. To make a homeopathic remedy, the curative is diluted many times, often until only a tiny amount remains in a huge amount of the diluting liquid. Homeopathy is considered pseudoscience by the vast majority of medical doctors and scientists.

HOSPICE. A term that refers both to institutions that provide palliative care for the terminally ill, and to the philosophy of care that guides these institutions.

HOSPITAL INPATIENT QUALITY REPORTING (IQR) PROGRAM. Federally mandated initiative that monitors the healthcare performance of hospitals in order to help patients make more informed healthcare decisions.

HOUSE STAFF. The collective term for the residents of a hospital, who traditionally spent most of their time "in house," that is, in the hospital.

HYDROTHERAPY. The use of water to relieve pain and treat various diseases. Hydrotherapy may involve drinking the water, bathing in it, or having water at various temperatures applied under pressure to the body.

HYGIENE. an awareness of the presence of micro-organisms that can lead to disease, and the practices resulting from this awareness.

HYPEROSMOLARITY. Abnormal increase in the movement of bodily fluids through the walls of cells.

HYPERSENSITIVITY. The condition where the physical body over-reacts to food as source of nutrition, resulting in an allergy or intolerance.

HYPERTENSION. Persistently high blood pressure.

HYPOGLYCEMIC COMA. A type of diabetic coma caused by a severe imbalance in blood sugar.

I

IATROGENIC. Illness or other adverse health impact resulting from medical treatment.

IMMUNE SYSTEM. The body's defenses against foreign substances such as bacteria and virsus that disease and infection.

IMMUNIZATION. Administering a vaccine that stimulates the body's immune system to create antibodies to fight a specific disease (immunity) without causing symptoms of the disease.

IMPAIRMENT. A condition of incompetence to practice medicine resulting from a physical injury or disease, psychiatric disorder, or substance abuse.

INCIDENCE. The rate of development of a disease in a given population over time.

INDEMNITY INSURANCE. Plans that reimburse health care providers based on a fee schedule or usual, customary, and reasonable charges.

INDIAN HEALTH SERVICE. The agency of the Department of Health and Human Services that is responsible for providing federal health services to American Indians and Alaska Natives.

INDICATION. In medicine, a reason for prescribing a drug or medical device, or for ordering a specific test.

INDIGENOUS PEOPLES OF AUSTRALIA. Descendants of the original inhabitants of the Australian continent and nearby islands, representing several hundred regional groups.

INEQUITIES. Unfair or unjust elements.

INFANT MORTALITY. The rate of infant deaths during the first year of life. The infant mortality rate is expressed as the number of infant deaths per 1,000 live births in a specific geographic area.

INFANTILE GLAUCOMA. Gaucoma—an eye condition in which the pressure inside the eye is abnormally high and may damage the optic nerve. The infantile form, also called childhood, pediatric, or congenital glaucoma, is seen in babies and young children, and is commonly diagnosed in the first year of life.

INFECTIOUS DISEASE. Any disease caused by invasion by a pathogen which subsequently grows and multiplies in the body.

INFLAMMATION. Pain, redness, swelling, and heat that usually develop in response to injury or illness.

INFLUENZA. A disease caused by viruses that infect the respiratory tract.

INFORMATION TECHNOLOGY. The term that refers to computers and related technology, such as the hardware, software, networking, and the Internet that are used to produce, store, and transmit digital or electronic information and communication.

INFORMED DECISION. A decision that has been made in consultation with a physician without being subjected to coercion and with a full understanding and appreciation of the risks, benefits, and alternatives.

INNATE INTELLIGENCE. A phrase coined by D.D. Palmer to describe the body's internal ability to maintain its health and heal its own disorders when the spine is in proper alignment.

INPATIENT. A patient who is admitted to a hospital for care that requires at least an overnight stay.

INPATIENT PROSPECTIVE PAYMENT SYSTEM. Medicare payment system for acute inpatient hospital services that sets reimbursement rates according to diagnosis groupings.

INSURANCE COPAYMENT. The fee that a person insured by an insurance company pays at the time of receiving health services

INSURANCE PREMIUM. The fee that a person covered by an insurance company pays in advance of requiring health services.

INTEGRATIVE MEDICINE (IM). A holistic approach to health care that incorporates complementary and alternative (CAM) treatments within conventional medicine. IM is used primarily to treat chronic complains and lifestyle issues rather than acute emergencies or traumatic injuries.

INTERDISCIPLINARY. Consisting of several interacting disciplines that work together to care for the patient.

INTERPERSONAL THERAPY. Interpersonal therapy works on an individual's communication and social skills, allowing him or her to improve the dysfunctional relationship patterns that may be contributing to emotional distress.

INTERVENTION-STYLE PROGRAM. A program designed to change the behavior and perspective of the target audience.

INTOLERANCE. The physical body's inability to digest certain type of foods, such as milk or wheat, usually because of absence of a digestive enzyme.

IRON DEFICIENCY ANEMIA. Without an adequate supply of iron, the body is unable to make enough red blood cells or makes red blood cells that are too small.

J

JOINT COMMISSION. The accrediting organization that evaluates virtually all U.S. healthcare facilities and programs. Accreditation is maintained with on-site surveys every three years; laboratories are surveyed every two years.

K

KERATOCONUS. Degenerative condition of the eye in which the cornea thins and changes to a conical shape rather than a gradual curve

KICKBACK. An unethical practice of accepting money or other reward paid by a business for referrals.

L

LACTATION. The production or secretion of milk by the mammary glands.

LAWFULLY PRESENT. Immigrants and other non-citizens of the United States who are lawfully residing in the country according to the terms under which they were officially admitted.

LAYING ON OF HANDS. A religious ritual in which an ordained person (in most situations) or lay leader places his or her hands on the head of another in order to impart a blessing or other spiritual gift. The Hebrew and Christian Scriptures contain references to the laying on of hands in many circumstances, ranging from healing to bestowing a personal blessing to the transfer of spiritual authority in ordination.

LEGAL ADVOCATE. a person who has been duly authorized by law to advocate and to make decisions for another person.

LIABILITY. Financial obligation or debt. Also, the state or condition of being legally responsible for an act or event.

LITURGICAL CHURCHES. Christian bodies that use a highly structured form of worship characterized by a standard order of events, formal rather than improvised prayers, elaborate vestments for the clergy, and the use of art and music to add beauty to worship. The major liturgical churches in North America are (in alphabetical order) the Anglican (Episcopalian), Eastern Orthodox, Lutheran, and Roman Catholic.

LITURGY. In the broadest sense, a set pattern or order for public worship that is followed on a regular basis, with prescribed prayers, responses, scripture readings, and similar actions.

LIVING WILL. A document detailing which medical interventions an individual does or does not want.

LOBOTOMY. A surgical procedure in which portions of the frontal lobe of the brain are cut in an effort to relieve symptoms of mental illness. Rarely used in modern medicine.

LONG-TERM CARE. Services and support that people need for a long period of time. Long-term care includes assistance with regular activities of daily living, such as dressing, eating, bathing, and using the toilet.

M

M-HEALTH. A term used for the practice of tele-health by mobile devices. It is also spelled mHealth.

MAGNETIC HEALING. A nineteenth-century form of alternative medicine based on the notion that humans possess a vital force called "animal magnetism" that a healer can use to treat disease. Magnetic healing is a form of vitalism. The founder of chiropractic began his career as a magnetic healer.

MALARIA. Disease caused by the presence of sporozoan parasites of the genus Plasmodium in the red blood cells, transmitted by the bite of anopheline mosquitoes, and characterized by severe and recurring attacks of chills and fever).

MALNUTRITION. A condition resulting when a person's diet does not provide adequate nutrients for growth and maintenance or if they are unable to fully utilize the food they eat, due to illness.

MALPRACTICE. according to medical law, the condition of a physician's actions or recommendations leading to the injury of the patient.

MANAGED CARE. A type of health plan with a network of providers and pre-arranged fee schedule. Examples include a health maintenance organization (HMO) or preferred provider organization (PPO).

MANAGED CARE ORGANIZATION (MCO). A healthcare provider that offers health plans designed to control the cost and quality of care by coordinating medical and other health-related services.

MANDATORY FUNDING. Government funding that is essentially automatic, and thus bypasses the congressional appropriations process. Social Security and Medicare are examples of federal programs supported with mandatory funding provisions.

MASTER PATIENT INDEX. A database housed in the transaction hub that stores patient demographic information and medication history. Patient information sent by a prescriber to the transaction hub is verified against the master patient index before being sent to a pharmacy benefit manager for further processing.

MATERIAL MODIFICATION. Changes in coverage, which can include increases or decreases in benefits; coverage of previously excluded benefits; reduced cost-sharing; reductions in covered services or benefits; increases in premiums; increases in out-of-pocket amounts; adverse changes in an HMO service area; and any new requirements for receipt of benefits, such as new pre-certification requirements.

MEANINGFUL USE. Specific eligibility requirements regarding the adoption and use of EHRs that must be satisfied in order for a healthcare provider to earn incentive payments under the HITECH Act.

MEASLES. An acute and highly contagious viral disease marked by distinct red spots followed by a rash that occurs primarily in children.

MEDICAID. The largest source of healthcare-related funding for people with low income and/or disabilities in the United States. The program is administered by individual states and is being greatly expanded under the Patient Protection and Affordable Care Act (PPACA).

MEDICAL HOME. The medical home is a patient-centered care concept that attempts to meet patients where they are and better coordinate their care.

MEDICAL MALPRACTICE. Intentional abandonment of duty or failure to exercise medical skill on the part of a physician rendering services that results in loss, injury, or damage.

MEDICAL RESIDENT. An individual who has received an M.D. and is undergoing further training in a medical specialty.

MEDICAL SAVINGS ACCOUNT (MSA) PLAN. A less common type of health plan that combines a high deductible health plan with a bank account. Medicare deposits a certain amount of money per year, which is used to pay for Medicare Part A and Medicare Part B expenses, and when the Plan deductible is met, the Plan pays for any further Medicare-covered services. MSAs do not offer Medicare Part D prescription drug coverage.

MEDICAL TOURISM. The act of traveling to a foreign country specifically to obtain medical care at a lower cost than is available in one's home country.

MEDICAL TOURISM PROVIDER. A group or organization that acts as an intermediary between the prospective patient and the foreign physician, hospital, or clinic. Such providers are also known as "medical concierge services."

MEDICALLY NEEDY. Defined as people with high medical expenses whose incomes are above the eligibility limits for Medicaid, but whom states have the option of covering.

MEDICARE. A federal system of health insurance in the United States for people over the age of 65 years and some people under the age of 65 years who suffer from a disability.

MEDICARE ADVANTAGE PLANS. Also called Medicare Part C; private managed-care plans that include all Medicare Part A and Part B benefits and usually some additional benefits.

MEDICARE LEVY. A surcharge of 1.5 percent of taxable income that is paid by most taxpayers in Australia to help fund a universal healthcare program.

MEDICARE PART A. Original Medicare; hospitalization insurance that is provided for free to most Americans aged 65 and older.

MEDICARE PART B. Health insurance that pays for some services not covered by Medicare Part A and that requires recipients to pay a monthly premium.

MEDICARE PART D. Medicare prescription drug coverage; an optional, subsidized outpatient prescription drug benefit provided through a private insurer.

MEDICARE SUPPLEMENTAL INSURANCE (MEDIGAP). An insurance policy sold by private companies that can help pay some of the health care costs that original Medicare (Medicare Part A) does not cover, such as copayments, coinsurance, and deductibles. Some Medigap policies also offer coverage for services that original Medicare does not cover, such as medical care when the patient travels outside the United States. When a patient has original Medicare and buys a Medigap policy, Medicare will pay its share of the Medicare-approved amount for covered health care costs, and then the Medigap policy pays its share.

MENINGITIS. Inflammation of tissues that surround the brain and spinal cord.

MENTAL HEALTH PARITY AND ADDICTION EQUITY ACT OF 2008 (MHPAEA, OR THE FEDERAL PARITY LAW). Law that requires group health plans and insurers that offer mental health and substance use disorder benefits to provide coverage that is comparable to coverage for general medical and surgical care.

MERIDIANS. In TCM, a system of twenty channels or energy pathways for the flow of qi throughout the body.

MICRONUTRIENTS. Essential vitamins and minerals required by the body throughout the lifecycle in minuscule amounts.

MICROORGANISMS. Organisms too small to be seen without a microscope, such as viruses or bacteria.

MIGRANCY. Movement from one place of residence to another that is often associated with seeking work.

MINERALS. Inorganic (non-living) elements that are essential to the nutrition of humans, animals, and plants. Examples: zinc, copper, iron.

MINIMAL RISK. any risk that is equivalent to what one could reasonably expect in the context of an ordinary condition or situation.

MINIMUM ESSENTIAL COVERAGE. The type of coverage an individual needs to have to meet the individual responsibility requirement under the Patient Protection and Affordable Care Act (PPACA). This includes individual market policies; job-based coverage; Medicare; Medicaid; Children's Health Insurance Program (CHIP); the health care program serving Uniformed Service members, retirees, and their families worldwide (TRICARE); and certain other coverages.

MINIMUM VALUE STATEMENT. A statement that the insurance covers or does not cover at least 60% of the total cost of care.

MIRACLE. In traditional theology, a miracle represents God's intervention into the natural order for the purpose of bringing about that which could not otherwise occur. In a medical context, a miracle would be an unexplainable and otherwise impossible act of healing.

MITIGATION. A general term for attempts to prevent disasters or reduce their impact.

MIXER CHIROPRACTOR. A chiropractor who combines traditional chiropractic techniques with other forms of treatment, both mainstream and alternative, and is open to the evidence-based approach of mainstream medicine.

MOTIVATIONAL INTERVIEWING. Client-centered technique of helping bring about behavioral change by understanding psychological or dynamic impediments, thus helping the client overcome such obstacles.

MOXIBUSTION. The use of a burning cigar-shaped cylinder of mugwort to heat the skin over an acupoint in order to stimulate the flow of qi. Moxibustion is usually used together with acupuncture.

MRI. The abbreviated term for Magnetic Resonance Imaging. MRI uses a large circular magnet and radio waves to generate signals from atoms in the body. These signals are used to construct images of internal structures.

MUMPS. An acute and highly contagious viral illness that usually occurs in childhood.

N

NARCOTIC. A drug, whether natural or synthetic, chemically related to opium, which reduces pain. Narcotic drugs typically cause sedation and may cause changes in mood and/or behavior.

NATIONAL ACADEMIES. A group of four non-profit organizations that provide policy advice to the U.S. government; includes the National Academy of Science, National Academy of Engineering, Institute of Medicine, and National Research Council.

NATURALIZED. Foreign-born individual who obtains full, officially recognized citizenship in another country.

NATUROPATHY. An alternative system of healing that maintains that humans have an innate vital force that can be fostered by noninvasive treatments, encouragement of natural healing, and minimal use of surgery and drugs. Naturopathy uses primarily homeopathy, herbal medicine, diet modification, and hydrotherapy and rejects most conventional drugs as toxic.

NEGLIGENCE. Failure to perform one's professional duties according to an accepted standard of care.

NONKETOTIC HYPEROSMOLAR COMA. A type of diabetic coma in which the patient's body tries to release excess blood glucose through the urinary tract.

NOSODE. A homeopathic remedy made from pus or diseased tissue, and used by some homeopaths as a substitute for conventional vaccines.

NURSE PRACTITIONER. An advanced practice nurse who is trained to provide primary health care. Nurse practitioners perform many of the functions previously assumed by physicians.

NUTRIENTS. Substances obtained from food and used in the body to provide energy and structural materials and to regulate growth, maintenance, and repair of the body's tissue.

NUTRITION. Providing substances that are necessary for health and growth.

O

OBESE. Weighing considerably more than is recommended for a given height. In terms of body mass index, or BMI, obesity is defined as a BMI greater than or equal to 30. Obesity is a serious threat to one's health.

OBJECTIVE. Not biased by personal opinion

OBSERVATIONAL STUDY. A form of research that involves tracking results without trying to influence them.

OCCUPATIONAL THERAPY. Therapy aimed at recovering the ability to independently attend to the activities of daily living, such as dressing, eating, bathing, and toiling, as well as more complex activities such as shopping, cooking, cleaning, and doing laundry.

OFFICE OF INSPECTOR GENERAL. the branch of the Department of Health and Human Services responsible for detecting and preventing fraud and abuse.

OFFICE OF PERSONNEL MANAGEMENT. The federal agency responsible for administrating human resources policies and regulations.

OPIOID. A drug that is chemically related to opium. Opioids may be natural (e.g., morphine, codeine) or synthetic (e.g., dextromethorphan, propoxyphen).

ORGAN TRAFFICKING. The illegal trade in organs for transplantation, often involving the kidnapping, coercion, or deception of people for the purpose of organ removal and exploitation.

ORGANIZATION FOR ECONOMIC CO-OPERATION AND DEVELOPMENT (OECD). An international organization that promotes policies to improve the economic and social wellbeing of individuals and populations around the world.

ORIGINATING SITE. The site where the patient receiving telehealth care is located.

OSTEOPATHIC MANIPULATIVE TREATMENT (OMT). A distinctive feature of osteopathic medical practice that involves hands-on manipulation of muscles and joints to allow the lymphatic system and other parts of the body to function unhindered. OMT may be used as a primary treatment for musculoskeletal disorders and an adjunctive treatment for other conditions.

OUT-OF-POCKET COSTS. Healthcare expenses not covered under regular insurance policies, including deductibles and copayments.

OUTCOMES. Results or consequences of care or treatment.

OUTPATIENT. A patient who receives medical treatment without being admitted to a hospital.

OVERWEIGHT. Weighing more than is recommended for a given height. In terms of body mass index, or BMI, obesity is defined as a BMI between 25.0 and 29.9.

P

PALLIATIVE CARE. Medical care centered around the relief of symptomatology, but not the preservation or prolongation of life.

PANCHAKARMA. A five-stage cleansing program used in Ayurveda to clear the body of toxins. The five stages are induced vomiting, administration of laxatives, administration of an enema, cleansing of the nasal cavity, and bloodletting.

PANDEMIC. An epidemic of infectious disease that spreads over several continents or worldwide.

PARASITE. An organism that lives in or with another organism, called the host, in parasitism, a type of association characterized by the parasite obtaining benefits from the host, such as food, and the host being injured as a result.

PASSIVE SMOKING. Involuntary inhalation of smoke from other people's cigarettes, cigars, or pipes. Often termed "second-hand smoke," passive smoking poses health risks, especially for children.

PATHOGEN. Anything that produces a disease. Bacteria and viruses are pathogens.

PATHOLOGIST. A scientist who studies the threats that microorganism may present.

PATIENT PROTECTION AND AFFORDABLE CARE ACT (ACA). Legislation signed into law in 2010 as part of a large-scale initiative to increase the availability, value, and affordability of health insurance in the United States. Also referred to as the Affordable Care Act and, informally, as Obamacare, for President Barack Obama who championed healthcare reform and signed the act into law.

PATIENT-CENTERED CARE. A healthcare approach in which medical providers partner with patients and patients' families to offer education, support, and care that respects patients' needs and wishes.

PATIENT-CENTERED MEDICAL HOME. The patient-centered medical home is a patient-centered care concept that attempts to meet patients where they are, and better coordinate their care.

PAY-FOR-SERVICE. The health insurance model that pays doctors and medical technicians for each service provided to the insured.

PAYOR. One who pays a medical claim. A third party payor is an entity other than the patient, such as the insurance company.

PERCUTANEOUS. Through the skin.

PERFORMANCE-BASED OBJECTIVE. An objective that is measured by some type of action and defined by the results of that action.

PERINEUM. The area encompassing the anus and the vagina.

PERJURY. The making of verifiably false statements under oath in a court of law.

PERSONALIZED MEDICINE. The use of genetic information and other new discoveries to customize medical diagnosis and treatment for the individual patient. Integrative medicine is considered one approach to personalized medicine.

PHARMACEUTICALS. Chemicals manufactured for use as medication.

PHARMACODYNAMICS. The science of how drugs enter and travel through the body; the ways in which drugs affect the body.

PHARMACOKINETICS. The science of how a drug behaves in an organism, including its absorption, distribution, concentration in tissues, and metabolism by the organism.

PHARMACOLOGY. The science of drugs, their uses, their effects on the body, and how the body metabolizes them.

PHARMACOPOEIA. A reference book containing descriptions of drugs, chemicals, and medicinal preparations, especially one issued by the authority of a medical society or government agency.

PHARMACY BENEFIT MANAGER (PBM). A third-party administrator that processes pharmacy claims and performs other functions related to the management of drug prescription programs.

PHYSIATRIST. A physician who has specialized training in physical medicine and rehabilitation.

PHYSICAL THERAPY. Therapy aimed at recovering or improving gross motor skills, such as mobility, balance, and muscle strength.

PHYSICIAN ASSISTANT. A health care professional licensed to practice medicine under the supervision of a physician. Like nurse practitioners, physician assistants perform many of the functions previously assumed by physicians.

PINHOLE GLASSES. Glasses with a number of small holes in each lens. This allows only a single beam of light to enter through each hole and may help produce clearer vision.

PLACEBO. An inactive substance used as a control in medical research.

PLACEBO EFFECT. A term used to describe a patient's response to a treatment that is affected by the patient's expectations of positive (or negative) results.

PLAIN LANGUAGE. A way to communicate to an audience so that people understand the meaning the first time they hear or read it.

POLYPHARMACY. The use of five or more prescription medications on a regular basis, which includes about 40% of adults over 65. The term is sometimes used to refer to the use of unnecessary medications.

POPULATION HEALTH QUALITY MEASURES. Indicators used to assess groups of persons identified by geographic location, organizational affiliation, or other characteristics to assess public health programs, community influences on health, or population-level health characteristics.

POST-ACUTE CARE. Medical services that aid a patient's post-hospitalization recovery from illness, surgical procedure, or management of a chronic medical condition.

POST-TRAUMATIC STRESS DISORDER (PTSD). A psychological response to a highly stressful event; typically characterized by depression, anxiety, flashbacks, nightmares, and avoidance of reminders of the traumatic experience.

POSTMARKETING SURVEILLANCE. The practice of monitoring the safety of a drug or treatment after it is made available to the public.

POSTPARTUM. The period shortly after childbirth.

POTABLE. Safe to drink.

POTENTIZATION. The process of preparing a homeopathic remedy by a repeated process of dilution and succussion.

PRAGMATISM. A philosophical position that regards practical results, rather than abstract principles or theories, as the essential criterion of moral value.

PRAKRITI. The Sanskrit word for a person's unique constitution, including psychological as well as physical health. The prakriti is thought to be unchanged over the course of the person's life.

PRE-ECLAMPSIA. Dangerously high blood pressure occurring during pregnancy.

PREFERRED PROVIDER ORGANIZATION (PPO) PLAN. A type of health insurance plan offered by a private insurance company. In a PPO Plan, the patient pays less when using doctors, hospitals, and other health care providers that belong to the plan's network (preferred providers); the costs are higher when the patient uses doctors, hospitals, and providers outside of the network. The patient does not need to select a primary care physician and does not need referrals to see other providers in the network.

PREMIUM. The amount paid by a beneficiary for insurance coverage, usually on a monthly basis.

PRESCRIBER. A qualified healthcare provider who is authorized to access an electronic prescribing system to review patient information and generate prescriptions that are electronically transmitted to a patient's pharmacy.

PRESCRIPTION. The doctor's written authorization for a patient to buy and use a drug that is regulated by law, with recommendations for its safe and effective use.

PRESCRIPTION DRUG "DONUT HOLE." The coverage gap in Medicare Part D that requires participants to pay all of their annual prescription drug costs that fall between approximately $3,000 and $5,000 annually.

PRESSURE ULCER. Open wounds and lesions that form when skin covering bony parts of the body is subjected to prolonged pressure; also known as bedsores.

PREVALENCE. The rate describing the characteristics of a given population at a specific moment in time.

PREVENTIVE CARE. Medical care focused on preventing the onset of illness.

PRIMARY CARE. Medical care offered by a physician, physician assistant, nurse practitioner, or other health care provider who is the patient's first contact with the health care system before the patient is referred to a specialist.

PRIMARY CARE PHYSICIANS. Medical doctors, including general practitioners, internists, pediatricians, family practitioners, and obstetrician-gynecologists who diagnose and treat a variety of health-related problems and refer patients to specialists as needed.

PRIMARY HEALTH CARE. A level of health care that is necessary for an individual to maintain good health that normally involves preventive education and treatment and early diagnosis and treatment of possible health and medical problems.

PRIVATE FEE-FOR-SERVICE (PFFS) PLAN. A type of Medicare Advantage Plan in which you may go to any Medicare-approved doctor or hospital that accepts both Medicare and the plan's payment terms and conditions. The insurance plan, rather than the

Medicare Program, decides how much it will pay and what the patients pays for the services received. The patient may pay more or less for Medicare-covered benefits and may have extra benefits that the Original Medicare Plan does not cover. The PFFS Plans are the most flexible, but a doctor or hospital can make patient-by-patient or visit-by-visit decisions of whether to accept the PFFS Plan Member.

PROCESS. The steps, actions, or operations used to bring about the desired outcome.

PROCESS ADDICTION. An umbrella term used to refer to a group of impulse control disorders or mood-altering behaviors that resemble substance addictions in their effects on people's lives. Process addictions, which are also known as "behavioral addictions" or "nonsubstance-related addictions," include compulsive spending, sex addiction, Internet addiction, exercise addiction, pornography addiction, self-cutting, and video game addiction.

PRODUCT LOYALTY. The business goal of having customers associate a brand name with effectiveness and other positive attributes.

PROGNOSIS. The medical term for predicting the likely outcome of a patient's present health condition.

PROSPECTIVE PAYMENT SYSTEM (PPS). A method of making medical payments based on a standard developed through the analysis of previous payments for particular types of services.

PROTEASE INHIBITORS. Drugs prescribed to treat severe viral infections such as AIDS or hepatitis C.

PROTECTED HEALTH INFORMATION (PHI). Information that is protected by law that relates to an individual's past, present, or future physical or mental health, as well as conditions, treatments, services, and payments that can be traced to an identifiable individual.

PROTOCOL. A formal plan that details how a clinical trial will be conducted.

PROVIDER. Health team professional or entity (hospital) that offers care.

PSEUDOSCIENCE. A belief or practice that claims to be scientific but cannot be tested by any known scientific method and lacks supporting evidence or credibility.

PSYCHIATRIC BOARDING. The practice of holding mentally ill patients in emergency department corridors and waiting areas, because of the lack of hospital beds or other facilities.

PULMONARY EMBOLISM. An obstruction in one of the arteries of the lung that prevents oxygen-carrying blood from returning to the heart. The obstruction usually is a blood clot that has migrated from another part of the body. Pulmonary embolism is often a life-threatening complication of deep vein thrombosis or surgery.

Q

QI. In Traditional Chinese medicine (TCM), the vital force or energy that animates the human body. In TCM theory, it is partially inherited from a person's parents and partly derived from food, drink, and proper breathing.

QUALITATIVE DATA. Research findings, collected and analyzed in a reliable manner, that emphasize unique characteristics rather than a comparison to a typical case or prototype.

QUALITY IMPROVEMENT ORGANIZATION. A group of practicing physicians and other health care experts paid by the federal government to check and improve the care given to people with Medicare.

QUARANTINE. The separation of persons or animals who have been exposed to a communicable disease for a period of time to see whether they fall ill. The English word comes from the Italian word for "forty," the number of days that ships and their passengers were quarantined in port during the fourteenth century to prevent the spread of bubonic plague.

QUICKENING. The first movements of the baby that you can feel.

R

RABIES. A rare but serious disease caused by a virus carried in saliva. It is transmitted when an infected animal bites a person.

REAL-TIME TELEHEALTH. Telehealth in which a telecommunications link (e.g., telephone, videoconferencing equipment, e-mail) allows for immediate communication. It is also called synchronous telehealth.

RECOMMENDED DIETARY ALLOWANCE (RDA). The amount of an essential nutrient, as a vitamin or mineral, that has been established by the Food and Nutrition Board of the National Academy of Sciences as adequate to meet the average daily nutritional needs of most healthy persons according to age group and sex.

REFERENCE DAILY INTAKES (RDI). Food labeling values for protein, vitamins and minerals based on population-adjusted means of the RDA.

REFERRALS. Sending a patient to another medical facility or specialist for further treatment.

REFORM CHIROPRACTOR. A chiropractor who rejects the Palmers' vitalistic theories in favor of a scientific approach to treatment, and who does not use other alternative therapies in his or her practice.

REGULATORY ORGANIZATION. Organization designed to maintain or control quality in health care, such as The Joint Commission (TJC) formerly the Joint Commission on Accreditation of Healthcare Organizations (JCAHO), Department of Health (DOH), or the Food and Drug Administration (FDA).

REHABILITATION. The process necessary in order to return to normal functioning.

REIKI. A spiritual practice that developed in Japan in the 1920s that is considered a form of energy therapy. Reiki practitioners believe that they can convey healing energy to others through stylized hand positions that can be placed on or near the patient.

REIMBURSEMENT. Repayment for the outlay of money for medical expenses, usually by a health insurance company, or by the government (Medicare or Medicaid).

RELIABILITY. The quality of a test or measurement instrument to produce consistent results under comparable conditions.

REPERTORY. In homeopathy, a reference book containing detailed lists of symptoms with appropriate homeopathic remedies.

REPETITIVE STRESS INJURY. An injury that occurs as a result of repeating some physical action over and over again many times in sequence.

RESPITE CARE. Temporary care of a patient to provide caregivers with a period of physical, mental, and emotional rest.

RESPONDEAT SUPERIOR. The legal principle that holds an employer responsible for the actions of employees performed in the course of employment.

RETAINER. A fee paid in advance to a doctor, lawyer, or other professional to secure his or her services when needed.

RISK. The probability that exposure to a hazard will have a negative consequence. There are mathematical equations and computer programs that can be used to calculate risk in specific situations.

ROOT PLANING (DENTAL). Removing the causes of inflammation from the teeth. Plaque, the common cause of inflammation, is a resilient bacterial residue which adheres to the teeth. It can combine with calcium and form a hard deposit. Scaling and root planing remove plaque with physical scraping, or ultrasonic instruments.

RUBELLA. A contagious viral disease that is milder than typical measles but is damaging to the fetus when it occurs early in pregnancy. Also called German measles.

S

SALICYLATES. Anti-inflammatory compounds found in aspirin and many other common prescription and over-the-counter medications, as well as some herbal medicines such as black cohosh. These agents are used as blood thinners as well as painkillers, and high doses may increase the risk of abnormal bleeding.

SAMHSA. The Substance Abuse and Mental Health Services Administration, the agency within the Department of Health and Human Services responsible for initiatives related to public mental health.

SANITATION. The various systems and processes imposed on a community to reduce threats from disease.

SCALING (DENTAL). Similar to root planing.

SCHIZOPHRENIA. A severe mental illness characterized by hallucinations, paranoia, and bizarre thoughts and behavior.

SCLERAL. Pertaining to the sclera, the white of the eye.

SCREENING. Testing an individual for the presence of a condition for which he or she may have a statistically increased risk of developing, although no signs or symptoms.

SECONDARY CARE. Health care provided by specialist physicians and other health care providers (e.g., physical therapists, respiratory therapists) who do not usually have the initial contact with patients. Secondary care also includes acute care provided in hospital emergency departments.

SEIZURE. A sudden attack, spasm, or convulsion.

SELF-REFERRAL. An unethical practice of a professional (such as a physician) deceptively referring customers to a business owned in some way by the professional.

SENSITIVITY. The quality of a test or instrument to reduce the occurrence of false negatives.

SEQUESTRATION. A fiscal policy process in which across-the-board budget cuts are made to most departments and agencies.

SEROTONIN SYNDROME. A potentially life-threatening syndrome resulting from an excess of the brain chemical serotonin. Symptoms include diarrhea, tremors, muscle stiffness, confusion, and an extreme decrease in body temperature.

SHAMAN. A person who is regarded as having special spiritual powers or access to the spirit world, and serves as a mediator between the spirit world and other members of the tribe. Although the term was originally used to describe the indigenous healers of Siberia, it is now widely applied to healers in other indigenous societies, including Native American tribes.

SHELTER IN PLACE. A phrase used to describe remaining indoors in a safe location during an emergency rather than evacuating the area.

SIDE EFFECT. An unwanted effect of a drug, separate from its intended effect.

SMALL BUSINESS HEALTH OPTIONS PROGRAM; SHOP. State systems under the PPACA through which small businesses can compare and purchase health insurance for their employees.

SMALLPOX. A highly contagious viral disease characterized by fever and weakness and skin eruption with pustules that form scabs that slough off leaving scars.

SOCIAL SECURITY DISABILITY INSURANCE (SSDI). A federal program that pays benefits and provides Medicare to disabled workers under age 65.

SOCIAL WORKER. An individual with a bachelor's degree or master's degree that has educated them about social systems and how to provide assistance to individuals with needs within these realms.

SOCIO-ECONOMIC STATUS. The level of empowerment that a family or community has, based on the educational level, average income, and access to policy-makers of its members.

SPECIAL NEEDS PLAN (SNP). A Medicare Advantage Plan with coverage designed especially for Medicare beneficiaries with certain chronic conditions (like diabetes) or some other specific need. Usually, only people with certain conditions or needs are allowed into a SNP.

SPECIFICITY. The quality of a test or instrument to reduce the occurrence of false positives.

SPEECH THERAPY. Therapy aimed at improving an individual's ability to speak and/or understand speech. Speech therapy also assists individuals who have difficulty swallowing and are therefore at risk of aspiration and lung injury while eating or drinking.

SPONSOR. An entity (such as a drug company, university health center, or government agency) that conducts a clinical trial.

STAKEHOLDER. An individual or organization with an interest in or concern for some specific topic or problem.

STATE CHILDREN'S HEALTH INSURANCE PROGRAM; SCHIP; CHIP. A state-administered health insurance program for lower- and middle-income children who are without private health insurance and whose family incomes are above the Medicaid eligibility limits.

STATINS. Drugs that are commonly prescribed to lower excessively high cholesterol levels.

STIGMA. A physical feature or characteristic behavior that detracts from a person's reputation; a mark of reproach or social disapproval. The English word comes from the Greek word for a brand or tattoo used in ancient Greece to mark criminals.

STORE-AND-FORWARD TELEHEALTH. Telehealth in which images, video, or other patient data are captured and stored on a computer (or mobile device) and then transmitted (forwarded) at a later time to a specialist at another location for a diagnosis. Store-and-forward is also called "asynchronous telehealth."

STRAIGHT CHIROPRACTOR. A chiropractor who accepts the Palmers' theories about the nature of the human body and its innate intelligence, and rejects mainstream medicine.

SUBACUTE. A condition that is less severe than acute and is between acute and chronic. Subacute care is a level of care needed by patients who do not require hospital acute care, but who requires more intensive skilled nursing care than is provided to the majority of patients in a skilled nursing facility.

SUBJECTIVE. Influenced by personal opinion or experience.

SUBLUXATION. A term used in chiropractic to refer to a dysfunctional segment of the vertebral column in the spine. It is important to note that the chiropractic definition of subluxation is not the same as the standard medical definition, which identifies a subluxation as a significant displacement or partial dislocation of a bone or joint that is visible on an x-ray. In chiropractic, however, a segment of the spine that is not functioning properly is referred to as a subluxation whether or not it is dislocated and whether or not it has an abnormality that appears on an x-ray image.

SUBSECTION D HOSPITAL. General, acute care, short-term hospital that accepts Medicare patients.

SUBSIDIES. Financial assistance granted by the government to help individuals or families that meet minimum eligibility requirements afford comprehensive insurance coverage.

SUBSTANCE. In this context, any chemical, whether or not it is recognized as a drug, which is taken for the purpose of altering mood and/or perception.

SUCCUSSION. A step in the preparation of a homeopathic remedy that involves vigorously shaking the liquid in which the remedial substance is dissolved.

SUMMARY OF BENEFITS AND COVERAGE (SBC). A standard form that health insurance companies and plans must use under the PPACA to explain their plans and allow for easy comparisons of plans.

SUPPLEMENTAL SECURITY INCOME (SSI). A federal program that provides cash assistance to low-income blind, disabled, and elderly people; in most states, people receiving SSI benefits are eligible for Medicaid.

SUPPORTIVE THERAPY. Uses a variety of modalities to support a client's emotional and mental health.

SURGICENTER. Another term for ambulatory surgical center.

SWEDANA (ALSO SPELLED SVEDANA). An Ayurvedic steam treatment intended to produce sweating and the release of toxins through the opened skin pores.

SWING BED. A swing bed can be used for inpatient acute care or skilled nursing facility care. There is no time limit on length of patient stay for swing beds.

SYMBIOTIC. Living together in a mutually beneficial manner, such as the way some microbes find nourishment by assisting digestion in humans.

T

TELEMEDICINE. The use of electronic communication and information technologies to provide or support clinical care at a distance. It may include case management and psychological counseling.

TELEMENTAL HEALTH. The practice of psychiatry or psychotherapy via videoconferencing or similar communications technology.

TELEMENTORING. The use of audio, video, and other telecommunications and electronic information processing technologies to provide individual guidance or direction among health care professionals.

TELEMETRY. Measuring, monitoring, collection, and transmission of medical data on patients.

TELEMONITORING. The use of communications technologies and electronic information processing to monitor the vital signs or general health status of a patient from a distance.

TERMINAL ILLNESS. A medical term that describes a disease that cannot be cured or adequately treated and that is reasonably expected to result in the death of the patient within a short period of time. It usually refers to progressive diseases such as cancer or advanced heart disease and not trauma.

THIRD-PARTY ADMINISTRATOR. An organization that processes insurance claims for insurance companies.

THROMBOSIS. Formation of a clot within a blood vessel.

TORT. A wrongful act against another person or property that results in harm. Torts are considered civil cases and are settled by common law (court decisions) rather than by statutory law.

TOTAL QUALITY MANAGEMENT (TQM). TQM is the integration of an ongoing, dynamic organizational approach involving management, teamwork, defined processes, systems thinking, and change to create an environment that supports and promotes quality improvement.

TOXICOLOGY. A branch of science that focuses on the effects of chemicals and poisons on the body.

TRADITIONAL CHINESE MEDICINE (TCM). The system of folk medicine from mainland China. It is based on maintaining a balance in vital energy, or *qi* (pronounced "chee"), that controls emotional, spiritual, and physical well-being. Diseases and disorders result from imbalances in qi (the life force), and treatments such as massage, exercise, acupuncture, and nutritional and herbal therapy are designed to restore balance and harmony to the body.

TRANSACTION HUB. A centralized system that electronically connects prescribers, pharmacy benefit managers, and pharmacies in order to establish patient prescription eligibility as well as identify any potential adverse drug interactions.

TRAVEL MEDICINE. A medical specialty that focuses on preventing injuries, medical emergencies, and the spread of infectious diseases among international travelers. It should not be confused with medical tourism.

TREATMENT. the recommended procedure to alleviate symptoms and to eliminate their expected cause.

TRIAGE. A method for determining the priority of patient treatment during a disaster or mass casualty event according to the severity of the injuries.

TRICARE. A health care program for active-duty and retired uniformed services members and their families.

TUBERCULOSIS. An infectious disease that usually affects the lungs, but may also affect other parts of the body. Symptoms include fever, weight loss, and coughing up blood.

TUI NA. A form of massage practiced in TCM characterized by vigorous gripping and rolling of the soft tissues. Its name means "push-pull" in Chinese.

TYPE 2 DIABETES. formerly called "adult-onset diabetes." In this form of diabetes, either the pancreas does not make enough insulin, or cells become insulin resistant and do not use insulin efficiently.

TYPHOID FEVER. An infectious disease caused by a type of bacterium. People with this disease have a lingering fever and feel depressed and exhausted. Diarrhea and rose-colored spots on the chest and abdomen are other symptoms. The disease is spread through poor sanitation.

U

U.S. DEPARTMENT OF VETERANS AFFAIRS (VA). The agency that administers federal benefits and services to American military veterans and their families.

U.S. NATIONAL CENTER FOR HEALTH STATISTICS (NCHS). The nation's principal health statistics agency that provides data to identify and address health issues. The NCHS compiles statistical information to help guide public health and health policy decisions. The NCHS collaborates with other public and private health partners, and employs a variety of data-collection mechanisms to obtain accurate information from multiple sources.

UNCOMPENSATED CARE. The total of bad debt and charity care that the hospital provides. Typically, this means the hospital provides some care to patients who do not or cannot pay their bills, and other care to patients who apply for charity.

UNDERNUTRITION. An insufficient intake and/or inadequate absorption of energy, protein, or micronutrients that, in turn, leads to nutritional deficiency.

UNDERSERVED POPULATION. A group of individuals who receive fewer services than would generally be considered necessary for a normal lifestyle.

UNIFORM RESOURCE LOCATOR (URL). A URL is a unique Internet address, usually including an address protocol (http), a domain name (www.domain.com) and other letters, numbers, and symbols that identify a specific web page or website.

UTILITARIANISM. An ethical position based on the premise that usefulness is the best measure of moral worth, and that ethical decisions should promote the good of the largest number of persons.

UTILIZATION REVIEW. The process of comparing requests for medical services to guidelines or criteria that are deemed appropriate for such services, and making a recommendation based on that comparison.

V

VALIDITY. Measurement validity refers to whether a test is measuring what it claims to.

VASCULAR. Related to blood vessels.

VBAC. Vaginal Birth After Cesarean.

VECTOR. In epidemiology, any person, animal, or microorganism that transmits a disease agent into another organism.

VET CENTER. A VA medical facility that offers postwar adjustment, counseling, and outreach services for veterans and their families.

VETERANS HEALTH ADMINISTRATION (VHA). An agency within the Veterans Administration that is dedicated to providing health care to veterans.

VIRUS. A tiny, disease-causing particle that can reproduce only in living cells.

VITALISM. A term used to describe a set of beliefs that bodily functions in humans (and other animals) are governed by a vital force or energy that is distinct from all chemical or physical substances or processes and cannot be explained in material terms.

VITAMIN. A nutrient that the body needs in small amounts to remain healthy but that the body cannot manufacture for itself and must acquire through diet.

W

WELLNESS. An approach to healthcare that emphasizes maintaining good health rather than merely addressing illness.

WHOOPING COUGH. An infectious disease, also called pertussis, especially of children that is caused by a bacterium and is marked by a convulsive, spasmodic cough, sometimes followed by a shrill intake of breath.

WIKI. A wiki is a Web site on which the content is provided by users of, or visitors to, the site.

WITHDRAWAL. A syndrome of physiological changes and symptoms that occur when an addicted substance abuser abstains from the substance.

Y

YELLOW FEVER. An infectious disease caused by a virus. The disease, which is spread by mosquitoes, is most common in Central and South America and Central Africa. Symptoms include high fever, jaundice (yellow eyes and skin) and dark-colored vomit, a sign of internal bleeding. Yellow fever can be fatal.

Z

ZANG-FU ORGANS. A group of eleven internal entities associated in traditional Chinese medicine with the five elements, the meridians, the flow of qi in the body, and the overall harmony of the human body with nature. Although the names of the zang-fu organs are familiar to Westerners, they are usually capitalized to indicate that they refer to the internal functions of the body rather than to the anatomical organs in the strict sense.

ORGANIZATIONS

The following is an alphabetical compilation of relevant organizations listed in the *Resources* sections of the main body entries. Although the list is comprehensive, it is by no means exhaustive. It is a starting point for gathering further information. The physical, email, and web addresses listed here were provided by the associations; Gale, Cengage Learning is not responsible for the accuracy of the addresses or the contents of the websites.

A

AARP
601 E Street, NW
Washington, DC 20049
Phone: (202) 434-3525
Toll free: (888) OUR-AARP (687-2277)
E-mail: member@aarp.org
Web site: http://www.aarp.org

Academy of Nutrition and Dietetics
120 South Riverside Plaza, Suite 2000
Chicago, IL 60606
Phone: (312) 899-0040
E-mail: foundation@eatright.org
Web site: http://www.eatright.org/

Accreditation Association for Ambulatory Health Care (AAAHC)
5250 Old Orchard Rd., Ste. 200
Skokie, IL 60077
Phone: (847) 853-6060
Fax: (847) 853-9028
E-mail: info@aaahc.org
Web site: http://www.aaahc.org

Accreditation Commission for Acupuncture and Oriental Medicine (ACAOM)
8941 Aztec Drive
Eden Prairie, MN 55347
Phone: (952) 212-2434
Fax: (301) 313-0912
E-mail: coordinator@acaom.org
Web site: http://www.acaom.org/

Accreditation Commission for Homeopathic Education in North America (ACHENA)
19400 Turkey Road
Rockville, VA 23146

Phone: (518) 477-1416
E-mail: info@achena.org
Web site: http://www.achena.org/

Acute Long Term Hospital Association (ALTHA)
1667 K Street, NW, Suite 1050
Washington, DC 20006
Phone: (202) 266-9800
Web site: http://www.altha.org

Administration for Community Living—Eldercare Locator
Administration for Community Living
Washington, DC 20201
Toll free: (800) 677-1116
Fax: (202) 357-3555
E-mail: eldercarelocator@n4a.org
Web site: http://eldercare.gov

Administration on Aging
One Massachusetts Avenue, NW
Washington, DC 20001
Phone: (202) 619-0724
Web site: http://www.aoa.gov/

Administration on Community Living
One Massachusetts Avenue NW
Washington, DC 20001
Phone: (202) 619-0724
Fax: (202) 357-3555
E-mail: aclinfo@acl.hhs.gov
Web site: http://acl.gov

Aerobic and Fitness Association of America
15250 Ventura Blvd., Suite 200
Sherman Oaks, CA 91403
Phone: (877) 968-7263
Web site: http://www.afaa.com/

Agency for Healthcare Research and Quality, (AHRQ)
540 Gaither Road, Suite 2000
Rockville, MD 20850

Phone: (301) 427-1104
Web site: http://www.ahrq.gov

Alliance for Healthy Cities
Kanda-surugadai 2-1-19-1112, Chiyoda-ku
Tokyo, 101-0062
Japan
Phone: +813 5577 6780
Fax: +813 5577 6780
E-mail: alliance.ith@tmd.ac.jp
Web site: http://www.alliance-healthycities.com/

Ambulatory Surgery Center Association (ASCA)
1012 Cameron St.
Alexandria, VA 22314-2427
Phone: (703) 836-8808
Fax: (703) 549-0976
E-mail: asc@ascassociation.org
Web site: http://www.ascassociation.org

America's Health Insurance Plans
601 Pennsylvania Avenue, NW, South Building, Suite 500
Washington, DC 20004
Phone: (202) 778-3200
Fax: (202) 331-7487
E-mail: ahip@ahip.org
Web site: http://www.ahip.org

American Academy of Addiction Psychiatry (AAAP)
400 Massasoit Ave., Suite 307, 2nd Floor
East Providence, RI 02914
Phone: (401) 524-3076
Fax: (401) 272-0922
E-mail: information@aaap.org
Web site: http://www.aaap.org/

American Academy of Exercise
4851 Paramount Drive
San Diego, CA 92123
Phone: (888) 825-3636
Web site: http://www.acefitness.org/

American Academy of Family Physicians (AAFP)
P.O. Box 11210
Shawnee Mission, KS 66207-1210
Phone: (913) 906-6000
Toll free: (800) 274-2237
Fax: (913) 906-6075
E-mail: contactcenter@aafp.org
Web site: http://www.aafp.org/home.html

American Academy of Family Practice
P.O. Box 11210
Shawnee Mission, KS 66207
Phone: (913) 906-6000
Web site: http://www.aafp.org/home.html

American Academy of Hospice and Palliative Medicine (AAHPM)
8735 West Higgins Road, Suite 300
Chicago, IL 60631
Phone: (847) 375-4712
Fax: (847) 375-6475
E-mail: info@aahpm.org
Web site: http://www.aahpm.org/

American Academy of Husband-Coached Childbirth
Box 5224
Sherman Oaks, CA 91413-5224
Phone: (818) 788-6662
Toll free: (800) 4-A-BIRTH
Web site: www.bradleybirth.com

American Academy of Pediatrics
141 Northwest Point Boulevard
Elk Grove Village, IL 60007-1098
Phone: (847) 434-4000
Toll free: (800) 433-9016
Fax: (847) 434-8000
E-mail: http://www2.aap.org/guestbook/
    contactus-form.cfm
Web site: http://www.aap.org

American Academy of Physician Assistants
2318 Mill Road, Suite 1300
Alexandria, VA 22314
Phone: (703) 836-2272
Fax: (703) 684-1924
E-mail: aapa@aapa.org
Web site: www.aapa.org

American Academy of Private Physicians (AAPP)
P.O. Box 5129
Glen Allen, VA 23058-5129
Phone: (877) 746-7301
E-mail: http://aapp.org/contact/contact.php
Web site: http://www.aapp.org/

American Aging Association
750 17th St. NW, Suite 1100
Washington, DC 20006
Phone: (202) 293-2856 ext.150
Fax: (202) 955-8394
E-mail: Contact@AmericanAgingAssociation.org
Web site: http://www.americanagingassociation.org

American Association for Accreditation of Ambulatory Surgery Facilities (ALAS)
PO Box 9500, Washington St. 2F
Gurnee, IL 60031
Toll free: (888) 545-5222
Fax: (847) 775-1985
E-mail: reception@aaaasf.org
Web site: http://www.aaaasf.org

American Association for Geriatric Psychiatry (AAGP)
7910 Woodmont Ave, Suite 1050
Bethesda, MD 20814-3004
Phone: (301) 654-7850
Fax: (301) 654-4137
Web site: http://www.aagponline.org/

American Association for Long-Term Care Insurance
3835 E. Thousand Oaks Blvd. Suite 336
Westlake Village, CA 91362
Phone: (818) 597-3227
Fax: (818) 597-3206
Web site: http://www.aaltci.org/

American Association of Colleges of Nursing
One Dupont Circle, NW Suite 530
Washington, DC 20036
Phone: (202) 463-6930
Fax: (202) 785-8320
E-mail: info@aacn.nche.edu
Web site: http://www.aacn.nche.edu/

American Association of Colleges of Osteopathic Medicine (AACOM)
5550 Friendship Boulevard, Suite 310
Chevy Chase, MD 20815-7231
Phone: (301) 968-4100
Fax: (301) 968-4101
Web site: http://www.aacom.org/Pages/default.aspx

American Association of Naturopathic Physicians (AANP)
818 18th Street, NW, Suite 250
Washington, DC 20006
Phone: (202) 237-8150
Toll free: (866) 538-2267
Fax: (202) 237-8152
E-mail: member.services@naturopathic.org
Web site: http://www.naturopathic.org/index.asp

American Association of Nurse Practitioners
P.O. Box 12846
Austin, TX 78711
Phone: (512) 442-4262
Fax: (512) 442-6469
E-mail: admin@aanp.org
Web site: www.aanp.org

American Bar Association (ABA)
321 North Clark Street
Chicago, IL 60654
Phone: (312) 988-5000
Toll free: (800) 285-2221
Web site: http://www.americanbar.org

American Board of Addiction Medicine (ABAM)
4601 North Park Avenue, Upper Arcade, Suite 101
Chevy Chase, MD 20815-4520
Phone: (301) 656-3378
Fax: (301) 656-3815
E-mail: email@abam.net
Web site: http://abam.net/

American Board of Family Medicine
1648 McGrathiana Parkway Suite 550
Lexington, KY 40511
Phone: (859) 269-5626
Toll free: (888) 335-7509
E-mail: help@theabfm.org
Web site: https://www.theabfm.org

American Board of Preventive Medicine
111 West Jackson Boulevard, Suite 1110
Chicago, IL 60604
Phone: (312) 939-ABPM [2276]
Fax: (312) 939-2218
E-mail: abpm@theabpm.org
Web site: https://www.theabpm.org

American Board of Psychiatry and Neurology
2150 E Lake Cook Rd., Ste. 900
Buffalo Grove, IL 60089
Phone: (847) 229-6500
Fax: (847) 229-6600
E-mail: questions@abpn.com
Web site: http://www.abpn.com

American Chiropractic Association (ACA)
1701 Clarendon Boulevard
Arlington, VA 22209
Phone: (703) 276-8800
Fax: (703) 243-2593
Web site: http://www.acatoday.org/index.cfm

American Chronic Pain Association
P.O. Box 850
Rocklin, CA 95677
Toll free: (800) 533-3231
Fax: (916) 632-3208
E-mail: ACPA@theacpa.org
Web site: http://theacpa.org

American College of Allergy, Asthma & Immunology
85 West Algonquin Road, Suite 550
Arlington Heights, IL 60005
Phone: 847-427-1200
Toll free: 800-282-6632
E-mail: mail@acaai.org
Web site: http://www.acaai.org

American College of Clinical Pharmacology (ACCP)
416 Hungerford Dr., Suite 300
Rockville, MD 20850
Phone: (240) 399-9070
Fax: (240) 399-9071
Web site: http://www.accp1.org/

American College of Healthcare Executives
One North Franklin Street, Suite 1700
Chicago, IL 60606-3529
Phone: (312) 424-2800
Fax: (312) 424-0023
E-mail: contact@ache.org
Web site: http://www.ache.org

American College of Hospital Administrators
1321 Duke St, Suite 400
Alexandria, VA 22314
Phone: (202) 536-5120
Fax: (866) 874-1585
Web site: http://www.achca.org

American College of Legal Medicine
Two Woodfield Lake, 1100 E. Woodfield Road, Suite 350
Schaumburg, IL 60173
Toll free: (800) 969-0283
Web site: www.aclm.org

American College of Nurse-Midwives
8403 Colesville Rd, Ste 1550
Silver Spring, MD 20910-6374
Phone: (240) 485-1800
E-mail: www.midwife.org
Web site: http://www.midwife.org

American College of Occupational and Environmental Medicine (ACOEM)
25 Northwest Point Blvd. Suite 700
Elk Grove Village, IL 60007
Phone: (847)818-1800
Fax: (847) 818-9266
E-mail: memberinfo@acoem.org
Web site: http://www.acoem.org

American College of Physicians (ACP)
190 N. Independence Mall West
Philadelphia, PA 19106-1572
Phone: (215) 351-2400
Toll free: (800) 523-1546
E-mail: http://www.acponline.org/cgi-bin/feedback
Web site: http://www.acponline.org

American College of Traditional Chinese Medicine
455 Arkansas Street
San Francisco, CA 94107
Phone: (415) 282-7600
Fax: (415) 282-0856
Web site: http://www.actcm.edu/

American Council on Science and Health
1995 Broadway, Ste. 202
New York, NY 10023-5882
Phone: (212) 362-7044
Toll free: (866) 905-2694
Fax: (212) 362-4919
E-mail: acsh@acsh.org
Web site: http://www.acsh.org

American Counseling Association
5999 Stevenson Ave.
Alexandria, VA 22304
Phone: (800) 347-6647
Web site: http://www.counseling.org/

American Dental Association (ADA)
211 East Chicago Ave.
Chicago, IL 60611-2678
Phone: (312) 440-2500
Web site: http://www.ada.org/

American Geriatrics Society (AGS)
40 Fulton St., 18th floor.
New York, NY 10038
Phone: (212) 308-1414
Fax: (212) 832-8646
E-mail: info.amger@americangeriatrics.org
Web site: http://www.americangeriatrics.org

American Health Care Association
1201 L Street, N.W.
Washington, DC 20005
Phone: (202) 4444
Fax: (202) 842-3860
Web site: www.ahcancal.org

American Health Information Management Association (AHIMA)
233 N. Michigan Avenue, 21st Floor
Chicago, IL 60601-5809

Phone: (312) 233-1100
Toll free: (800) 335-5535
Fax: (312) 233-1500
E-mail: myphrinfo@ahima.org
Web site: http://www.ahima.org

American Health Lawyers Association
1620 Eye St. NW, 6th Fl.
Washington, DC 20006-4010
Phone: (202) 833-1100
Fax: (202) 833-1105
E-mail: MbrDept@healthlawyers.org
Web site: http://www.healthlawyers.org

American Health Quality Association
1776 I Street, NW, 9th Floor
Washington, DC 20006
Phone: (202) 331-5790
E-mail: info@ahqa.org
Web site: http://www.ahqa.org

American Hospital Association
155 N. Wacker Dr.
Chicago, IL 60606
Phone: (312) 422-3000
Toll free: (800) 424-4301
Web site: http://www.aha.org

American Medical Association
330 N. Wabash Avenue
Chicago, IL 60611-58851
Phone: 312-464-4430
Toll free: 800-621-8335
E-mail: mss@ama-assn.org
Web site: http://www.ama-assn.org

American Medical College of Homeopathy (AMCH)
1951 W. Camelback Rd., Suite 300
Phoenix, AZ 85015
Phone: (602) 347-7950
Fax: (602) 864-2949
E-mail: info@amcofh.org
Web site: http://amcofh.org/

American Medical Informatics Association
4720 Montgomery Lane, Suite 500
Bethesda, MD 20814
Phone: (301) 657-1291
Fax: (301) 657-1296
Web site: http://www.amia.org

American Midwifery Certification Board
849 International Drive, Suite 120
Linthicum, MD 21090
Toll free: (866) 366-9632
E-mail: www.amcbmidwife.org
Web site: http://www.amcbmidwife.org

American Nurses Association
8515 Georgia Ave, Suite 400
Silver Spring, MD 20910
Toll free: (800) 274-4ANA (4262)
Fax: (301) 628-5001

E-mail: http://nursingworld.org/FunctionalMenuCategories/
ContactUs
Web site: http://www.ana.org

American Nurses Credentialing Center
8515 Georgia Ave, Suite 400
Silver Spring, MD 20910
Phone: (800) 284-2378
Web site: http://www.nursecredentialing.org/default.aspx/

American Occupational Therapy Association Inc.
4720 Montgomery Lane. Ste. 200
Bethesda, MD 20814
Phone: (301) 652-6611
Toll free: (800) SAY-AOTA (729-2682)
TTY:(800) 377-8555
Fax: (301) 652-7711
Web site: http://www1.aota.org

American Osteopathic Association (AOA)
142 E. Ontario St.
Chicago, IL 60611
Phone: (312) 202-8000
Toll free: (800) 621-1773
Fax: (312) 202-8200
E-mail: info@osteopathic.org
Web site: http://www.osteopathic.org/Pages/default.aspx

American Osteopathic Board of Family Physicians
330 E. Algonquin Road, Suite 6
Arlington Heights, IL 60005
Phone: (847) 640-8477
Toll free: (800) 390-5801
E-mail: aobfp@aobfp.org
Web site: http://www.aobfp.org

**American Osteopathic College of Occupational and
Preventive Medicine (AOCOPM)**
PO Box 3043
Tulsa, OK 74101
Toll free: (800) 558-8686
E-mail: AOBPM@osteopathic.org
Web site: http://www.aocopm.org

American Pharmacists Association
2215 Constitution Avenue NW
Washington, DC 20037
Phone: (202) 628-4410
Web site: http://www.pharmacist.com/

American Psychiatric Association
1000 Wilson Blvd., Ste. 1825
Arlington, VA 22209-3901
Phone: (703) 907-7300
E-mail: apa@psych.org
Web site: http://www.psych.org

American Psychological Association
750 1st Street NE
Washington, DC 20002-4242
Phone: (202) 336-5500
TTY: (202) 336-6123
Toll free: (800) 374-2721
Web site: http://www.apa.org

American Public Health Association (APHA)
800 I Street, NW
Washington, DC 20001
Phone: (202) 777-APHA (777-2742)
Fax: (202) 777-2534
E-mail: comments@apha.org
Web site: http://www.apha.org

American Red Cross
2025 E Street
Washington, DC 20006
Phone: (202) 303-4498
Toll free: (800) RED-CROSS (733-2767)
Web site: http://www.redcross.org/

**American Society for Clinical Pharmacology and
Therapeutics**
528 N. Washington St
Alexandria, VA 22314
Phone: (703) 836-6981
E-mail: info@ascpt.org
Web site: http://www.ascpt.org/

American Society for Healthcare Engineering
155 N. Wacker Dr., Ste. 400
Chicago, IL 60606
Phone: (312) 422-3800
Fax: (312) 422-4571
E-mail: ashe@aha.org
Web site: http://www.ashe.org

American Society for Nutrition
9650 Rockville Pike
Bethesda, MD 20814
Phone: (301) 634-7050
E-mail: info@nutrition.org
Web site: http://www.nutrition.org

**American Society for Pharmacology and Experimental
Therapeutics (ASPET)**
9650 Rockville Pike
Bethesda, MD 20814-3995
Phone: (301) 634-7060
Fax: (301) 634-7061
Web site: http://www.aspet.org/

American Society of Addiction Medicine (ASAM)
4601 North Park Avenue, Upper Arcade, Suite 101
Chevy Chase, MD 20815-4520
Phone: (301) 656-3920
Fax: (301) 656-3815
E-mail: email@asam.org
Web site: http://www.asam.org/

American Society of Plastic Surgeons (ASPS)
444 E. Algonquin Rd.
Arlington Heights, IL 60005
Phone: (847) 228-9900
Web site: http://www.plasticsurgery.org/

American Stroke Association
7272 Greenville Ave.
Dallas, TX 20001

Phone: (888) 478- 7653
Web site: http://www.strokeassociation.org/STROKEORG//

American Telemedicine Association (ATA)
1100 Connecticut Ave, NW, Suite 540
Washington, DC 20036
Phone: (202) 223-3333
Fax: (202) 223-2787
E-mail: info@americantelemed.org
Web site: http://www.americantelemed.org/

Assisted Living Federation of America
1650 King St. Suite 602
Alexandria, VA 22314
Phone: (703) 894-1805
Fax: (703) 894-1831
E-mail: info@ALFA.org
Web site: www.alfa.org

Association for Healthcare Documentation Integrity
4230 Kiernan Ave., Ste. 170
Modesto, CA 95356
Phone: (209) 527-9620
Toll free: (800) 982-2182
Fax: (209) 527-9633
E-mail: ahdi@ahdionline.org
Web site: http://www.ahdionline.org

Association for Medical Education and Research in Substance Abuse (AMERSA)
P.O. Box 20160
Cranston, RI 02920
Phone: (401) 243-8460
Fax: (877) 418-8769
Web site: http://www.amersa.org/index.asp

Association of Academic Physiatrists
7250 Parkway Drive, Suite 130.
Hanover, MD 21076
Phone: (410) 712-7120
Web site: http://www.physiatry.org//

Association of American Medical Colleges
2450 N Street, NW
Washington, DC 20037
Phone: (202) 828-0400
Fax: (202) 828-1125
Web site: www.aamc.org

Association of State and Territorial Health Officials
2231 Crystal Dr., Suite 450
Arlington, VA 22202
Phone: (202) 371-9090
Fax: (571) 527-3189
Web site: http://www.astho.org/

Ayurvedic Institute
11311 Menaul Blvd. NE
Albuquerque, NM 87112
Phone: (505) 291-9698
Fax: (505) 294-7572
Web site: http://www.ayurveda.com/index.html

B

Bastyr University
14500 Juanita Drive N.E.
Kenmore, WA 98028-4966
Phone: (425) 602-3000
Fax: (425) 823-6222
E-mail: http://www.bastyr.edu/about/contact-info-department
Web site: http://www.bastyr.edu/

Brain Injury Association of America
1608 Spring Hill Rd., Suite 110
Vienna, VA 22182
Phone: (703) 761-0750
Web site: http://www.biausa.org/

Bravewell Collaborative
2300 8th Street
Encinitas, CA 92024
Phone: (760) 815-0238
E-mail: info@bravewell.org
Web site: http://www.bravewell.org/

C

Canadian Nurses Association
50 Driveway
Ottawa, K2P 1E2
Ontario Canada
Phone: (613) 237-2133
Toll free: 1-800-361-8404
Fax: (613) 237-3520
E-mail: http://www.cna-aiic.ca/en/contact-us
Web site: http://www.cna-aiic.ca

Case Management Society of America
6301 Ranch Drive
Little Rock, AR 72223
Phone: (501) 221-9068
E-mail: cmsa@cmsa.org
Web site: http://www.cmsa.org/

CDC's Office of Minority Health and Health Equity (OMHHE)
Mail Stop K-77, 4770 Buford Highway
Atlanta, GA 30341
Phone: (770) 488-8343
Toll free: (800) CDC-INFO (232-4636) (CDC)
E-mail: OMHHE@cdc.gov
Web site: http://www.cdc.gov/minorityhealth

Center for Food Safety and Applied Nutrition (CFSAN), U.S. Food and Drug Administration
5100 Paint Branch Pkwy
College Park, MD 20740
Toll free: (888) SAFEFOOD (723-3366)
Phone: (312) 899-0040
E-mail: consumer@fda.gov
Web site: http://www.fda.gov/Food/default.htm

Center for Managing Chronic Disease
1415 Washington Heights
Ann Arbor, MI 48109
Phone: (734) 763-1457
Web site: http://cmcd.sph.umich.edu/

Center for Medicare Advocacy
P.O. Box 350
Willimantic, CT 06226
Phone: (860) 456-7790
Fax: (860) 456-2614
Web site: http://www.medicareadvocacy.org

Center for Studying Health System Change
1100 1st St. NE, 12th Fl.
Washington, DC 20002-4221
Phone: (202) 484-5261
Fax: (202) 863-1763
E-mail: hscinfo@hschange.org
Web site: http://www.hschange.com

Center on Medical Record Rights and Privacy
Health Policy Institute, Georgetown University,
Box 57144
Washington, DC 20057-1485
Phone: (202) 687-0880
Fax: (202) 687-3110
Web site: http://hpi.georgetown.edu/privacy

Center to Advance Palliative Care (CAPC)
1255 Fifth Avenue, Suite C-2
New York, NY 10029
Phone: (212) 201-2670
E-mail: capc@mssm.edu
Web site: http://www.capc.org/

Centers for Disease Control and Prevention (CDC)
1600 Clifton Road
Atlanta, GA 30333
Phone: (404) 639-3534
Toll free: (800) CDC-INFO (800-232-4636)
TTY:(888) 232-6348
E-mail: inquiry@cdc.gov
Web site: http://www.cdc.gov

Centers for Medicare & Medicaid Services
7500 Security Boulevard
Baltimore, MD 21244
Phone: (410) 786-3000
Toll free: (877) 267-2323
TTY:(410) 786-0727
TTY:(866) 226-1819
Web site: www.cms.gov

Chemical Safety and Hazard Investigation Board (CSB)
2175 K Street NW
Washington, DC 20037
Phone: (202) 261-7600
E-mail: http://www.csb.gov/service/contact.aspx
Web site: http://www.csb.gov

Child Welfare Information Gateway
1250 Maryland Avenue, SW, eighth floor
Washington, DC 20024
Toll free: (800) 394-3366
E-mail: info@childwelfare.gov
Web site: https://www.childwelfare.gov

Clinical Nutrition Certification Board (CNCB)
115280 Addison Road, Suite 130
Addison, TX 75001
Phone: (972)250-2829
E-mail: ddc@clinicalnutrion.com
Web site: http://www.cncb.org

Commission for Case Manager Certification
15000 Commerce Parkway, Suite C
Mount Laurel, NJ 08054
Phone: (856) 380-6836
Web site: http://ccmcertification.org/

Commission on Accreditation for Health Informatics and Information Management Education
233 N. Michigan Ave., 21st Floor
Chicago, IL 60601-5809
Phone: (312) 233-1100
Fax: (312) 233-1948
Web site: www.cahiim.org

Commission on the Accreditation of Healthcare Management Education
1700 Rockville Pike, Ste. 400
Rockville, MD 20852
Phone: (301) 998-6101
E-mail: info@cahme.org
Web site: https://www.cahme.org

Commissioned Officers Association of the U.S. Public Health Service (COA)
8201 Corporate Drive, Suite 200
Landover, MD 20785
Phone: (301) 731-9080
Toll free: (866) 366-9593
Fax: (301) 731-9084
E-mail: http://www.coausphs.org/contactus.cfm
Web site: http://www.coausphs.org/index.cfm

Commonwealth Fund
One E. 75th St.
New York, NY 10021
Phone: (212) 606-3800
Fax: (212) 606-3500
E-mail: info@cmwf.org
Web site: http://www.commonwealthfund.org

Community Action Partnership
1140 Connecticut Ave, NW, Suite 1210
Washington, DC 20036
Phone: (202) 595-0660
Fax: (202) 265-5048
E-mail: dharlow@communityactionpartnership.com
Web site: www.communityactionpartnership.com

Organizations

Consortium of Academic Health Centers for Integrative Medicine (CAHCIM)
D513 Mayo, Mail Code 505, 420 Delaware Street SE
Minneapolis, MN 55455
Phone: (612) 624-9166
Fax: (612) 626-5280
E-mail: cahcim@umn.edu
Web site: http://www.imconsortium.org/home.html

Consumer Federation of America
1620 I St. NW, Suite 200
Washington, DC 20006
Phone: (202) 387-6121
E-mail: cfa@consumerfed.org
Web site: http://www.consumerfed.org

Convenient Care Association
260 South Broad Street, Suite 1800
Philadelphia, PA 19102
Phone: (215) 731-7140
Web site: http://www.ccaclinics.org/

Council on Chiropractic Education (CCE)
8049 N. 85th Way
Scottsdale, AZ 85258-4321
Phone: (480) 443-8877
Toll free: (888) 443-3506
Fax: (480) 483-7333
E-mail: cce@cce-usa.org
Web site: http://www.cce-usa.org/

Council on Naturopathic Medical Education (CNME)
P.O. Box 178
Great Barrington, MA 01230
Phone: (413) 528-8877
E-mail: http://www.cnme.org/contact.html
Web site: http://www.cnme.org/

D

Department of Human Services (Australia)
Reply Paid 7800
Canberra, ACT 2610
Australia
Phone: 132 011
Fax: 1300 786 102
E-mail: medicare@humanservices.gov.au
Web site: http://www.humanservices.gov.au

Direct Primary Care Coalition
[no other contact information]
E-mail: info@dpcare.org
Web site: http://www.dpcare.org/

Directors of Health Promotion and Education
1015 18th Street NW, Suite 300
Washington, DC 20036
Phone: (202) 659-2230
Web site: http://www.dhpe.org

E

Electronic Privacy Information Center (EPIC)
1718 Connecticut Ave. NW, Ste. 200
Washington, DC 20009
Phone: (202) 483-1140
Fax: (202) 483-1248
Web site: http://epic.org

Environmental Protection Agency (EPA)
Ariel Rios Building, 1200 Pennsylvania Avenue, N.W.
Washington, DC 20460
Phone: (202) 272-0167
Web site: http://www.epa.gov

Essential Health Benefits Coalition
1341 G Street, NW Suite 1100
Washington, DC 20005
Phone: (202) 585-0258
E-mail: joe.wagner@ketchum.com
Web site: http://ehbcoalition.org

Evidence Based Practice Resource Area (EBPRA), Oncology Nursing Society
125 Enterprise Drive
Pittsburgh, PA 15275
Phone: (866) 257-4667
Web site: http://www.ons.org

F

Families USA
1201 New York Avenue NW, Suite 1100
Washington, DC 20005
Phone: (202) 628-3030
Fax: (202) 347=2417
E-mail: info@familiesusa.org
Web site: http://www.familiesusa.org

Federal Emergency Management Agency (FEMA)
500 C Street SW
Washington, DC 20472
Phone: (202) 646-2500
E-mail: http://www.fema.gov/contact-us
Web site: http://www.fema.gov

Food and Drug Administration (FDA)
10903 New Hampshire Avenue
Silver Spring, MD 20993
Toll free: (888) INFO-FDA (463-6332)
E-mail: http://www.fda.gov/AboutFDA/ContactFDA/default.htm
Web site: http://www.fda.gov/

H

Harold P. Freeman Patient Navigation Institute
55 Exchange Place, Suite 405
New York, NY 08054
Phone: (646) 380-4060
Web site: http://www.hpfreemanpni.org/

Health Canada
Address Locator 0900C2
Ottawa, Ontario K1A 0K9
Canada
Phone: (613) 957-2991
Toll free: (866) 225-0709
Fax: (613) 941-5366
E-mail: info@hc-sc.gc.ca
Web site: http://www.hc-sc.gc.ca

Health Care Cost Institute
1310 G Street NW, Suite 720
Washington, DC 20005
Phone: (202) 803-5200
Web site: http://www.healthcostinstitute.org

Health Policy Center at the Urban Institute
2100 M St. NW
Washington, DC 20037
Phone: (202) 833-7200
Web site: http://www.urban.org

Health Resources and Services Administration
5600 Fishers Ln.
Rockville, MD 20857
Toll free: (888) 275-4772
E-mail: ask@hrsa.gov
Web site: http://www.hrsa.gov

Health Resources and Services Administration (HRSA),
   Office of Rural Health Policy (ORHP)
5600 Fishers Lane
Rockville, MD 20857
Toll free: (888) ASK-HRSA (275-4772)
E-mail: ask@hrsa.gov
Web site: http://www.hrsa.gov/ruralhealth/about/index.html

Healthcare Facilities Accreditation Program
142 E. Ontario Street
Chicago, IL 60611
Phone: (312) 202-8258
Web site: http://www.hfap.org/

Healthcare Information and Management Systems Society
33 West Monroe Street, Suite 1700
Chicago, IL 60604-5616
Phone: (312) 664-4467
Fax: (312) 664-6143
E-mail: himss@himss.org
Web site: www.himss.org

HealthCare Tourism International, Inc.
809B Cuesta Drive, Suite 141
Mountain View, CA 94040
Phone: (310) 928-3611
E-mail: health@healthcaretrip.org
Web site: http://www.healthcaretrip.org

Henry J. Kaiser Family Foundation
2400 Sand Hill Rd.
Menlo Park, CA 94025
Phone: (650) 854-9400
Fax: (650) 854-4800
E-mail: http://kff.org/contact-us/
Web site: http://www.kff.org

HSC Business Services Organisation Headquarters
2 Franklin Street
BelfastNorthern Ireland
BT2 8DQ
Phone: 44 028 (9032) 4431
E-mail: Admin.Office@hscni.net
Web site: http://www.hscbusiness.hscni.net

I

Improving Chronic Illness Care
1730 Minor Avenue, Suite 1600
Seattle, WA 98101
Phone: (206) 287-2903
Fax: (206) 287-2138
Web site: http://www.improvingchroniccare.org

Institute for Health Policy Solutions
1444 "Eye" St., N.W., Suite 900
Washington, DC 20005
Phone: (202) 789-1491
E-mail: pshrestha@ihps.org
Web site: http://www.ihps.org/

Institute for Healthcare Improvement (IHI)
20 University Road, 7th Floor
Cambridge, MA 02138
Phone: (617) 301-4800
Toll free: (866) 787-0831
Fax: (617) 301-4848
E-mail: info@ihi.org
Web site: http://www.ihi.org

Institute for Patient-and Family-Centered Care
6917 Arlington Road, Suite 309
Bethesda, MD 20814
Phone: (301) 652-0281
E-mail: institute@ipfcc.org
Web site: www.ipfcc.org

Institute for Quality and Efficiency in Health Care
Im Mediapark 8 (KölnTurm)
Cologne Germany 50670
Phone: +49 (0)221-35685-0
Fax: +49 (0)221-35685-1
Web site: http://www.iqwig.de

Institute of Medicine of the National Academies
500 Fifth St., NW
Washington, DC 20001
Phone: (202) 334-2352
Fax: (202) 334-1412
E-mail: iomwww@nas.edu
Web site: http://www.iom.edu/

Institute of Medicine, Board of Global Health
500 Fifth St. NW
Washington, DC 20001
Phone: (202) 334-2352
Toll free: (888) 624-8373
E-mail: iomwww@nas.edu
Web site: http://www.iom.edu/Global/Topics/Global-
   Health.aspx

Institute of Traditional Medicine (ITM)
553 Queen St. West, 2nd Floor
Toronto, ON M5V 2B6
Canada
Phone: (416) 537-0928
E-mail: info@itmworld.org
Web site: http://www.itmworld.org/home

International Association for Impact Assessment
1330 23rd St. S., Ste. C
Fargo, ND 58103
Phone: (701) 297-7908
Web site: http://www.iaia.org

**International Association for Medical Assistance
    to Travelers (IAMAT)**
1623 Military Rd., #279
Niagara Falls, NY 14304-1745
Phone: (716) 754-4883
E-mail: http://www.iamat.org/contact.cfm
Web site: http://www.iamat.org/index.cfm

International Childbirth Education Association
1500 Sunday Drive, Suite 102
Raleigh, NC 27607
Phone: (919) 863-9487
Toll free: (800) 624-4934
Fax: (919) 787-4916
E-mail: info@icea.org
Web site: www.icea.org

International Committee of the Red Cross
19 Avenue de la paix CH
1202 Geneva Switzerland
Phone: +41 22 734 60 01
Fax: +41 22 733 20 57
Web site: http://www.icrc.org

International Labour Organization
4 route des Morillons
Geneva 22, CH-1211
Switzerland
Phone: 41 22 799 6111
Fax: 41 22 798 8685
E-mail: ilo@ilo.org
Web site: http://www.ilo.org

International Partnership for Innovative Healthcare Delivery
324 Blackwell Street, Suite 960, Washington Building
Durham, NC 27701
Web site: http://www.ipihd.org

International Society for Quality in Health Care
Joyce House, 8-11 Lombard St. East
Dublin, 2
Ireland
Phone: 353 (0) 1 6706750
Web site: http://www.isqua.org

J

Job Accommodation Network
P.O. Box 6080
Morgantown, WV 26506-6080

Toll free: (800) 526-7234
Web site: http://askjan.org

Johns Hopkins University Center for Communication Programs
111 Market Place, Ste. 310
Baltimore, MD 21202
Phone: (410) 659-6300
Fax: (410) 659-6266
E-mail: info@jhuccp.org
Web site: http://www.jhuccp.org

Joint Commission
One Renaissance Blvd.
Oakbrook Terrace, IL 60181
Phone: (630) 792-5800
Fax: (630) 792-5005
Web site: http://www.jointcommission.org

Joint Commission International (JCI)
1515 West 22nd Street, Suite 1300W
Oak Brook, IL 60523
Phone: (630) 792-5800
Phone: (630) 268-4800 (accreditation)
Web site: http://www.jointcommissioninternational.org/

K

Kaiser Family Foundation
2400 Sand Hill Road
Menlo Park, CA 94025
Phone: (650) 854-9400
Fax: (650) 854-4800
Web site: http://www.kff.org

Kaiser Family Foundation, KaiserEDU.org
2400 Sand Hill Road
Menlo Park, CA 94025
Phone: (650) 854-9400
Fax: (650) 854-4800
Web site: www.kaiseredu.org

Kirksville College of Osteopathic Medicine (KCOM)
800 W. Jefferson St.
Kirksville, MO 63501
Phone: (660) 626-2121
Toll free: (866) 626-2878
E-mail: admissions@atsu.edu
Web site: http://www.atsu.edu/kcom/

L

Lamaze International
2025 M Street NW, Suite 800
Washington, DC 20036
Phone: (202) 367-1128
Toll free: (800) 368-4404
Fax: (202) 367-2128
Web site: www.lamaze.org

Leapfrog Group
1660 L Street NW, Suite 308
Washington, DC 20036

Phone: (202) 292-6713
Fax: (202) 292-6813
E-mail: info@leapfroggroup.org
Web site: http://www.leapfroggroup.org

M

Medical Group Management Association
104 Inverness Terrace E.
Englewood, CO 80112-5306
Phone: (303) 799-1111
Toll free: (877) 275-6462
E-mail: infocenter@mgma.org
Web site: http://www.mgma.com

Medical Library Association
65 East Wacker Place, Suite 1900
Chicago, IL 60601-7246
Phone: (312) 419-9094
E-mail: info@mlahq.org
Web site: www.mlanet.org

Medicare Rights Center
520 Eighth Avenue, North Wing, 3rd Floor
New York, NY 10018
Phone: (212) 869-3850
Toll free: (800) 333-4114
Fax: (212) 869-3532
E-mail: info@medicarerights.org
Web site: http://www.medicarerights.org

MedWatch
5600 Fishers Lane
Rockville, MD 20857
Toll free: (800) FDA-1088 (to report adverse events by
    telephone)
Fax: (800) 332-0178
Web site: http://www.fda.gov/Safety/MedWatch/
    default.htm

Mental Health America
2000 North Beauregard Street, 6th Floor
Alexandria, VA 22311
Phone: (703) 683-7733
Toll free: (800) 969-6642
Fax: (703) 684-5968
Web site: http://www.mentalhealthamerica.net

Midwife Alliance of North America
1500 Sunday Drive, Suite 102
Raleigh, NC 27607
Toll free: (888) 923-MANA(6262)
E-mail: info@mana.org
Web site: http://www.mana.org

N

Narcotics Anonymous
P.O. Box 9999
Van Nuys, CA 91409

Phone: (818) 773-9999
Fax: (818) 700-0700
E-mail: fsmail@na.org
Web site: http://www.na.org

National Academies
500 Fifth St., NW
Washington, DC 20001
Phone: (202) 334-2000
Fax: (202) 334-2229
Web site: http://www.nationalacademies.org/index.html

National Academies Press (NAP)
500 Fifth Street NW, Keck 360
Washington, DC 20001
Toll free: (800) 624-6242
E-mail: Customer_Service@nap.edu
Web site: http://nap.edu/

National Academy of Sports Medicine
1750 E. Northrop Blvd., Suite 200
Chandler, AZ 85286
Phone: (602) 383-1200
Web site: http://www.nasm.org/

National Adult Day Services Association
1421 E. Broad Street, Suite 425
Fuquay Varina, NC 27526
Toll free: (877) 745-1440
Fax: (919) 825-3945
E-mail: NADSA@NADSA.org
Web site: http://nadsa.org

National Advisory Council on the National Health Service Corps
5600 Fishers Lane, Parklawn Building, Room #13-92
Rockville, MD 20857
E-mail: KHuffman@hrsa.gov
Web site: http://nhsc.hrsa.gov/corpsexperience/aboutus/
    nationaladvisorycouncil/

National Alliance on Mental Illness
3803 N. Fairfax Drive, Suite 100
Arlington, VA 22203
Phone: (703) 524-7600
Toll free: (800) 950-6264
Fax: (703) 524-9094
Web site: http://www.nami.org/

National Association for Healthcare Quality
4700 West Lake Avenue
Glenview, IL 60025
Phone: (847) 375-4720
Toll free: (800) 966-9392
Fax: (847) 375-6320
Web site: http://www.nahq.org

National Association for Homecare and Hospice
228 Seventh Street, SE
Washington, DC 20003
Phone: (202) 547-7424
Web site: http://www.nahc.org/

National Association of Boards of Pharmacy
1600 Feehanville Dr
Mount Prospect, IL 60056

Phone: (847) 391-4406
Web site: http://www.nabp.net/boards-of-pharmacy/

National Association of Certified Professional Midwives
243 Banning Road
Putney, VT 05346
E-mail: admin@nacpm.org
Web site: http://www.nacpm.org

National Association of Community Health Centers
7501 Wisconsin Ave., Suite 1100W
Bethesda, MD 20814
Phone: (301) 347-0400
Web site: http://www.nachc.com

National Association of County & City Health Officials (NACCHO)
1100 17th Street, NW, Seventh Floor
Washington, DC 20036
Phone: (202) 783-5550
Fax: (202) 783-1583
E-mail: info@naccho.org
Web site: http://www.naccho.org

National Association of Insurance Commissioners
1100 Walnut Street, Suite 1500
Kansas City, MO 64106-2197
Phone: (816) 842-3600
Web site: www.naic.org/

National Association of School Nurses
1100 Wayne Ave., Suite 925
Silver Spring, MD 20910
Phone: (240) 821-1130
Web site: https://www.nasn.org/Home

National Association of Social Workers
750 First Street NE, Suite 700
Washington, DC 20002
Phone: (202) 408-8600
Web site: http://www.socialworkers.org/

National Association of States United for Aging and Disabilities
1201 15th St. NW, Ste. 350
Washington, DC 20005
Phone: (202) 898-2578
Fax: (202) 898-2583
E-mail: info@nasuad.org
Web site: http://www.nasuad.org

National Ayurvedic Medical Association (NAMA)
620 Cabrillo Avenue
Santa Cruz, CA 95065
Phone: (612) 345-7082
Toll free: (800) 669-8914
Fax: (612) 605-1989
E-mail: info@ayurvedaNAMA.org
Web site: http://www.ayurvedanama.org/?

National Board for Certified Counselors
P.O. Box 77699
Greensboro, NC 27417

Phone: (336) 547-0607
E-mail: nbcc@nbcc.org
Web site: http://www.nbcc.org//

National Board of Medical Examiners
3750 Market Street
Philadelphia, PA 19104
Phone: (215) 590-9500
Web site: http://www.nbme.org

National Cancer Institute (NCI)
BG 9609 MSC 9760, 9609 Medical Center Drive
Bethesda, MD 20892-9760
Fax: (800) 4-CANCER (422-6237)
E-mail: http://www.cancer.gov/global/contact/email-us
Web site: http://www.cancer.gov/

National Care Planning Council (NCPC)
P.O. BOX 1118
Centerville, UT 84014
Phone: (801) 298-8676
Toll free: (800) 989-8137
Fax: (801) 295-3776
E-mail: info@longtermcarelink.net
Web site: http://www.longtermcarelink.net

National Center for Assisted Living
1201 L Street, N.W.
Washington, DC 20005
Phone: (202) 842-4444
Fax: (202) 842-3860
Web site: http://www.ahcancal.org

National Center for Biotechnology Information
8600 Rockville Pike, Building 38A
Bethesda, MD 20894
Phone: (301) 496-2475
Web site: http://www.ncbi.nlm.nih.gov

National Center for Complementary and Alternative Medicine (NCCAM)
9000 Rockville Pike
Bethesda, MD 20892
Phone: (248) 699-8524
Toll free: (888) 644-6226
E-mail: http://nccam.nih.gov/tools/contact.htm
Web site: http://nccam.nih.gov/

National Center for Health Statistics, Centers for Disease Control and Prevention
1600 Clifton Road, Atlanta, GA 30333
Atlanta, GA 30333
Toll free: (800) 232-4636
Web site: http://www.cdc.gov/nchs/index.htm

National Center for Homeopathy (NCH)
1760 Old Meadow Road, Suite 500
McLean, VA 22102
Phone: (703) 506-7667
Fax: (703) 506-3266
E-mail: info@nationalcenterforhomeopathy.org
Web site: http://nationalcenterforhomeopathy.org/

National Center for Jewish Healing (NCJH)
135 West 50th St.
New York, NY 10020

Phone: (212) 582-9100
Toll free: (888) 523-2769
E-mail: admin@jbfcs.org
Web site: http://www.jbfcs.org/programs-services/jewish-community-services-2/national-center-jewish-healing/

National Center for Telehealth and Technology (T2)
9933C West Hayes Street
Joint Base Lewis-McChord, WA 98431
Phone: (253) 968-1914
Fax: (253) 968-4192
E-mail: AskUs@t2health.org
Web site: https://www.t2health.org/

National Certification Commission for Acupuncture and Oriental Medicine (NCCAOM)
76 South Laura Street, Suite 1290
Jacksonville, FL 32202
Phone: (904) 598-1005
Fax: (904) 598-5001
Web site: http://www.nccaom.org/

National College of Natural Medicine (NCNM)
049 S.W. Porter Street
Portland, OR 97201
Phone: (503) 552-1555
E-mail: reception@ncnm.edu
Web site: http://www.ncnm.edu/

National Commission on Certification of Physician Assistants
12000 Findley Road, Suite 100
Johns Creek, GA 30097
Phone: (678) 417-8100
Fax: (678) 417-8135
E-mail: nccpa@nccpa.net
Web site: www.nccpa.net

National Committee for Quality Assurance
1100 13th St., NW Suite 1000
Washington, DC 20006
Phone: (202) 992-3500
Fax: (202) 992-3599
E-mail: customersupport@ncqa.org
Web site: http://www.ncqa.org

National Consumers League
1701 K St. NW, Suite 1200
Washington, DC 20006
Phone: (202) 835-3323
Fax: (202) 835-0747
Web site: http://www.nclnet.org

National Council for Community Behavioral Healthcare
1701 K St. NW, Ste. 400
Washington, DC 20006
Phone: (202) 684-7457
E-mail: communications@thenationalcouncil.org
Web site: http://www.TheNationalCouncil.org

National Council of La Raza (NCLR)
1126 16th Street NW, Suite 600
Washington, DC 20036-4845
Phone: (202) 785-1670
Fax: (202) 776-1792

E-mail: comments@nclr.org
Web site: http://www.nclr.org

National eHealth Collaborative
1250 24th Street NW, Suite 300
Washington, DC 20037
Phone: (877) 835-6506
E-mail: info@nationalehealth.org
Web site: http://www.nationalehealth.org

National Federation of Professional Trainers
P.O. Box 4579
Lafayette, IN 47903
Phone: (800) 729-6378
Web site: http://www.afaa.com/

National Health Institutes Center to Reduce Cancer Health Disparities
9609 Medical Center Dr., MSC 9746, Sixth Floor, West Tower
Bethesda, MD 20892
Phone: (856) 380-6836
E-mail: nci-crchd@mail.nih.gov
Web site: http://crchd.cancer.gov/pnp/what-are.html

National Health Service Corps (NHSC)
Toll free: (800) 221-9393
E-mail: gethelp@hrsa.gov
Web site: http://nhsc.hrsa.gov/

National Hospice and Palliative Care Organization (NHPCO)
1731 King Street, Suite 100
Alexandria, Virginia 22314
Phone: (703) 837-1500
Toll free: (800) 658-8898
Toll free: (800) 646-6460
Fax: (703) 837-1233
E-mail: nhpco_info@nhpco.org
Web site: http://www.nhpco.org

National Immigration Law Center
3435 Wilshire Blvd, Ste 2850
Los Angeles, CA 90010
Phone: (213) 639-3900
Fax: (213) 639-3911
Web site: http://www.nilc.org

National Institute of Ayurveda (NIA)
Jorawar Singh Gate, Amer Road
Jaipur, RajasthanIndia
302002
Phone: 91 141 2635816
Fax: 91 141 2635709
E-mail: nia-rj@nic.in
Web site: http://www.nia.nic.in/

National Institute of Environmental Health Sciences (NIEHS)
P.O. Box 12233, MD K3-16
Research Triangle Park, NC 27709-2233
Phone: (919) 541-3345
Web site: http://www.niehs.nih.gov

National Institute of Mental Health
6001 Executive Blvd.
Bethesda, MD 20892-9663
Phone: (301) 443-4513
Toll free: (866) 615-6464
E-mail: nimhinfo@nih.gov
Web site: http://www.nimh.nih.gov

National Institute on Aging (NIA)
Building 31, Room 5C27, 31 Center Drive, MSC 2292
Bethesda, MD 20892
Phone: (301) 496-1752
TTY: (800) 222-4225
Toll free: (800) 222-2225
E-mail: niaic@nia.nih.gov
Web site: http://www.nia.nih.gov/

National Institute on Drug Abuse (NIDA)
6001 Executive Boulevard, Room 5213, MSC 9561
Bethesda, MD 20892-9561
Phone: (301) 443-1124
Toll free: (888) 478- 7653
E-mail: http://www.drugabuse.gov/about-nida/contact-nida
Web site: http://www.drugabuse.gov/

National Institute on Minority Health and Health Disparities
6707 Democracy Boulevard, Suite 800
Bethesda, MD 20892-5465
Phone: (301) 402-1366
Web site: http://www.nimhd.nih.gov/default.html

National Institutes of Health (NIH)
9000 Rockville Pike
Bethesda, MD 20892
Phone: (301) 496-4000
TTY: (301) 402-9612
E-mail: NIHinfo@od.nih.gov
Web site: http://www.nih.gov

National Network of Libraries of Medicine, National Library of Medicine
8600 Rockville Pike, Bldg. 38, Room B1-E03
Bethesda, MD 20894
Toll free: (800) 338-7657
Web site: http://nnlm.gov

National Prevention Information Network, Centers for Disease Control and Prevention
PO Box 6003
Rockville, MD 20849-6003
Toll free: (800) 232-4636
E-mail: info@cdcnpin.org
Web site: http://www.cdcnpin.org

National Quality Forum
1030 15th Street NW, Ste 800
Washington, DC 20005
Phone: (202) 783-1300
Fax: (202) 783-3434
E-mail: info@qualityforum.org
Web site: http://www.qualityforum.org

National Rural Health Association
4501 College Blvd., No. 225
Leawood, KS 66211-1921

Phone: (816) 756-3140
Fax: (816) 756-3144
E-mail: mail@NRHArural.org
Web site: http://www.ruralhealthweb.org

National Spinal Cord Injury Association
75-20 Astoria Blvd.
Jackson Heights, NY 11370
Phone: (718) 803-3782
Web site: http://www.spinalcord.org/

National Vaccine Information Center
407 Church Street, Suite H
Vienna, VA 22180
Phone: (703) 938-0342
Fax: (703) 938-5768
E-mail: ContactNVIC@gmail.com
Web site: http://www.nvic.org

National Vaccine Injury Compensation Program
Parklawn Building, Room 11C-26
5600 Fishers Lane
Rockville, MD 20857
Toll free: (800) 338-2382
Web site: http://www.hrsa.gov/vaccinecompensation/
index.html

New England Healthcare Institute (NEHI)
One Broadway, 15th Floor
Cambridge, MA 02142
Phone: (617) 225-0857
Fax: (617) 225-9025
E-mail: info@nehi.net
Web site: http://www.nehi.net

NHS England
P.O. Box 16738
RedditchUnited Kingdom
B97 9PT
Phone: 44 0300 311 22 33
E-mail: england.contactus@nhs.net
Web site: http://www.england.nhs.uk

NHS Scotland Patient/Customer Relations Department
NHS 24, Caledonia House, Cardonald Park
GlasgowUnited Kingdom
G51 4EB
Phone: 44(0800) 377 7330
E-mail: ask@spso.org.uk
Web site: http://www.nhs24.com/

NHS Wales
Web site: http://www.wales.nhs.uk

North American Registry of Midwives
5257 Rosestone Dr.
Lilburn, GA 30047
Toll free: (888) 842-4784
E-mail: info@narm.org
Web site: http://narm.org

North American Society of Homeopaths (NASH)
P.O. Box 450039
Sunrise, FL 33345-0039

Phone: (206) 720-7000
Fax: (208) 248-1942
E-mail: nashinfo@homeopathy.org
Web site: http://www.homeopathy.org/

O

Office of Cancer Complementary and Alternative Medicine (OCCAM)
9609 Medical Center Dr., Room 5-W-136
Rockville, MD 20850
Phone: (240) 276-6595
Fax: (240) 276-7888
E-mail: ncioccam1-r@mail.nih.gov
Web site: http://cam.cancer.gov/

Office of Disability, Aging, and Long-Term Care Policy (HHS)
200 Independence Avenue, S.W.
Washington, DC 20201
Phone: 202-690-6443
Toll free: 877-696-6775
E-mail: Peter.Kemper@hhs.gov
Web site: http://aspe.hhs.gov/office_specific/daltcp.cfm

Office of Inspector General, U.S. Department of Health and Human Services
330 Independence Avenue, SW
Washington, DC 20201
Phone: (202) 619-0335
Toll free: 1-800-447-8477
E-mail: Public.Affairs@oig.hhs.gov
Web site: https://oig.hhs.gov

Office of Rural Health Policy
5600 Fishers Lane
Rockville, MD 20857
Toll free: (888) 275-4772
E-mail: ask@hrsa.gov
Web site: http://www.hrsa.gov

Office of the National Coordinator for Health Information Technology
200 Independence Ave. SW, Ste. 729-D
Washington, DC 20201
Phone: (202) 690-7151
Fax: (202) 690-6079
E-mail: onc.request@hhs.gov
Web site: http://www.healthit.gov

Office of the Surgeon General
Tower Building, Plaza Level 1, Room 100, 1101 Wootton Parkway
Rockville, MD 20852
Phone: (240) 276-8853
Fax: (240) 453-6141
Web site: http://www.surgeongeneral.gov/

Office on Women's Health, U.S. Department of Health and Human Services
200 Independence Ave., SW, Room 712E
Washington, DC 20201

Phone: (202) 690-7650
Toll free: (800) 994-9662
Fax: (202) 205-2631
Web site: http://www.womenshealth.gov

Oregon Health Study
5211 NE Glisan St.
Portland, OR 97213
Toll free: (877) 215-0686
E-mail: info@oregonhealthstudy.org
Web site: http://oregonhealthstudy.org

Organisation for Economic Co-operation and Development
2, rue André Pascal
75775 Paris Cedex 16
France
Phone: +33 1 45 24 82 00
Fax: +33 1 45 24 85 00
Web site: http://www.oecd.org

P

Palmer College of Chiropractic
1000 Brady Street
Davenport, IA 52803
Phone: (563) 884-5000
Toll free: (800) 722-2586
Web site: http://www.palmer.edu/

Patient Navigation in Cancer Care
E-mail: patientnavigation@paladinhealthcom.com
Web site: http://www.patientnavigation.com/content/default.aspx/

Patient Navigator Training Collaborative
Anschutz Medical Campus, 13001 E. 17th Place
Aurora, CO 80045
Phone: (303) 724-5846
E-mail: admin@patientnavigatortraining.org
Web site: http://www.patientnavigatortraining.org

Patient-Centered Primary Care Collaborative
601 Thirteenth Street, NW, Suite 430 North
Washington, DC 20005
Phone: (202) 2081
Fax: (202) 2082
Web site: http://www.pcpcc.org

Patients Beyond Borders
P.O. Box 17057
Chapel Hill, NC 27516
Phone: (919) 924-0636
Web site: http://www.patientsbeyondborders.com/

Pharmaceutical Research and Manufacturers of America
950 F Street NW, Suite 300
Washington, DC 20004
Phone: (202) 835-3400
Fax: (202) 835-3414
E-mail: newsroom@phrma.org
Web site: www.PhRMA.org

Privacy Rights Clearinghouse
3108 Fifth Ave., Ste. A
San Diego, CA 92103

Phone: (619) 298-3396
Web site: https://www.privacyrights.org

Public Citizen's Commercial Alert
1600 20th Street NW
Washington, DC 20009
Phone: (202) 588-7751
Web site: http://www.commercialalert.org

Q

Qliance
2101 Fourth Avenue, Suite 600
Seattle, WA 98121
Phone: (877) 754-2623
Fax: (206) 381-3035
E-mail: info@qliance.com
Web site: http://qliance.com/

R

Rural Assistance Center
School of Medicine and Health Sciences, Room 4520, 501
North Columbia Road Stop 9037
Grand Forks, ND 58202-9037
Toll free: (800) 270-1898
Fax: (800) 270-1913
E-mail: info@raconline.org
Web site: http://www.raconline.org

S

School Social Work Association of America
P.O. Box 1086
Sumner, WA 98390
Web site: http://www.sswaa.org/

School-Based Health Alliance
1010 Vermont Ave. NW
Washington, DC 20005
Phone: (202) 638-5872
Web site: http://www.sbh4all.org

Society for General Internal Medicine
1500 King Street, Suite 303
Alexandria, VA 22314
Phone: (202) 887-5150
Web site: http://www.sgim.org/

Society for Public Health Education (SOPHE)
10 G St., N.W., Suite 605
Washington, DC 20002
Phone: (202) 408-9804
E-mail: info@sophe.org
Web site: www.sophe.org

Substance Abuse and Mental Health Services Administration (SAMHSA)
1 Choke Cherry Road
Rockville, MD 20857
Phone: (240) 276-2130
Toll free: (877) 726-4727
E-mail: samhsa.media@ees.hhs.gov
Web site: http://www.samhsa.gov

T

TRICARE Management Activity
7700 Arlington Boulevard, Suite 5101
Falls Church, VA 22042-5101
Phone: 1-877-874-2273
Web site: http://www.tricare.mil

U

U.S. Bureau of Labor Statistics
Postal Square Building, 2 Massachusetts Ave., NE
Washington, DC 20212
Phone: (202) 691-5200
Web site: http://www.bls.gov

U.S. Department of Health and Human Services (HHS)
200 Independence Avenue, S.W.
Washington, DC 20201
Toll free: (877) 696-6775
E-mail: http://wcdapps.hhs.gov/HHSFeedback/
Web site: http://www.hhs.gov/

U.S. Department of Health and Human Services, Office of Disease Prevention and Health Promotion
1101 Wootton Parkway, Suite LL100
Rockville, MD 20852
Phone: (240) 453-8280
Web site: http://odphp.osophs.dhhs.gov

U.S. Department of Justice, Civil Rights Division, Disability Rights Section
950 Pennsylvania Ave. NW
Washington, DC 20530
Phone: (202) 307-0663
Web site: http://ada.gov

U.S. Department of Labor
Frances Perkins Building, 200 Constitution Ave., NW
Washington, DC 20210
Phone: (866) 487-2365
Web site: http://www.dol.gov/

U.S. Department of Labor, Occupational Safety & Health Administration
200 Constitution Avenue
Washington, DC 20210
Toll free: (800) 321-OSHA (6742)
TTY: (877) 889-5627
Web site: http://www.osha.gov/

U.S. Department of Veterans Affairs
810 Vermont Ave. NW
Washington, DC 20420
Toll free: (877) 222-8387
Web site: http://www.va.gov/

U.S. Environmental Protection Agency (EPA)
Ariel Rios Building, 1200 Pennsylvania Avenue, N.W.
Washington, DC 20460
Phone: (202) 272-0167
TTY: (202) 272-0165
Web site: http://www.epa.gov

U.S. Food and Drug Administration
10903 New Hampshire Ave.
Silver Spring, MD 20993
Phone: (301) 796-3400
Toll free: (888) 463-6332
E-mail: http://www.fda.gov/AboutFDA/ContactFDA/
default.htm
Web site: http://www.fda.gov

U.S. National Library of Medicine
8600 Rockville Pike
Bethesda, MD 20894
Web site: http://www.nlm.nih.gov/

U.S. Office of Personnel Management, Federal Employees Health Benefits Program
Room 3424, 1900 E Street, NW
Washington, DC 20415-0001
Phone: 202-606-1800
Toll free: 800-582-3337
E-mail: fehb@opm.gov
Web site: http://www.opm.gov/healthcare-insurance

U.S. Preventive Services Task Force
540 Gaither Road
Rockville, MD 20850
Phone: (301) 427-1584
Web site: http://www.uspreventiveservicestaskforce.org

U.S. Public Health Service Commissioned Corps
Toll free: (800) 279-1605
E-mail: http://ccmis.usphs.gov/ccmis/contact_usphs.aspx
Web site: http://www.usphs.gov/

U.S.D.A. Food and Nutrition Service
3101 Park Center Drive
Alexandria, VA 22302
E-mail: acip@cdc.gov

University of Arizona Center for Integrative Medicine
P.O. Box 245153
Tucson, AZ 85724-5153
Phone: (520) 626-6489
E-mail: http://integrativemedicine.arizona.edu/contact_us.
html (clinic)
Web site: http://integrativemedicine.arizona.edu/index.html

University of Maryland School of Medicine Center for Integrative Medicine
Kernan Hospital, 2200 Kernan Drive, 2nd Floor
[for clinical care]
Baltimore, MD 21207
Phone: (410) 448-6361
Fax: (410) 448-1873
E-mail: clinic@compmed.umm.edu
Web site: http://www.compmed.umm.edu/default.asp

Urgent Care Association of America
387 Shuman Blvd., Suite 235W
Naperville, IL 60563
Phone: (877) 698-2262
Web site: http://www.ucaoa.org/

USA.gov
U.S. General Services Administration, Office of Citizen Services and Innovative Technologies. 1800 F Street, NW
Washington, DC 20405
Toll free: (800) FED-INFO (333-4636)
Web site: www.usa.gov

V

Vaccine Adverse Event Reporting System (VAERS)
P.O. Box 1100
Rockville, MD 20849-1100
Toll free: (800) 822-7967
Fax: (877) 721-0366
E-mail: info@vaers.org
Web site: http://vaers.hhs.gov/index

Visiting Nurses Association
601 Thirteenth Street, NW, Suite 610N
Washington, DC 20005
Phone: (202) 384-1420
Web site: http://vnaa.org/

W

World Health Organization (WHO)
Avenue Appia 20
1211 Geneva 27Switzerland
Phone: 4122 791 21 11
Fax: 4122 791 31 11
E-mail: http://www.who.int/about/contact_form/en/
index.html
Web site: http://www.who.int/en/

World Health Organization (WHO; Regional Office for the Americas)
525 23rd St. NW
Washington, DC 20037
Phone: (202) 974-3000
Fax: (202) 974-3663
Web site: http://www.paho.org/hq/index.php?lang=en

STATE HEALTH INSURANCE EXCHANGES

Under the Patient Protection and Affordable Care Act, each state was given the option to either establish its own health insurance exchange—an online marketplace of health insurance plans—or direct its citizens to the national exchange called HealthCare.gov. Below is a list of the states that have their own exchanges; it shows the name of the state, the name of the website, and the site's URL.

The following states do not have their own health insurance exchanges and will use the official national website https://www.healthcare.gov/: Alabama, Alaska, Arizona, Delaware, Florida, Georgia, Illinois, Indiana, Iowa, Kansas, Louisiana, Maine, Michigan, Mississippi, Missouri, Montana, Nebraska, New Hampshire, New Jersey, North Carolina, North Dakota, Ohio, Oklahoma, Pennsylvania, South Carolina, South Dakota, Tennessee, Texas, Virginia, West Virginia, Wisconsin, and Wyoming.

Arkansas

HealthCare.gov
Website: http://ahc.arkansas.gov/

Individuals and small businesses in Arkansas use the national exchange, HealthCare.gov; more information specific to the state is available from the Arkansas official health care website, Arkansas Health Connector Division.

California

Covered California
Website: https://www.coveredca.com/

Colorado

Connect for Health Colorado
Website: http://connectforhealthco.com/

Connecticut

AccessHealthCT
Website: https://www.accesshealthct.com/AHCT/
    LandingPageCTHIX

District of Columbia

DC Health Link
Website: https://dchealthlink.com/

Hawaii

Hawaii Health Connector
Website: http://www.hawaiihealthconnector.com/

Idaho

Your Health Idaho
Website: http://www.yourhealthidaho.org/

Kentucky

kynect—Kentucky's Healthcare Connection
Website: https://kyenroll.ky.gov/

Maryland

Maryland Health Connection
Website: http://marylandhealthconnection.gov/

Massachusetts

Massachusetts Health Connector
Website: https://www.mahealthconnector.org/

Minnesota

MNsure
Website: http://www.mnsure.org/

Nevada

Nevada Health Link
Website: https://www.nevadahealthlink.com/

New Mexico

BeWellNM—New Mexico Health Insurance Exchange
Website: http://bewellnm.com/

New York

New York State of Health—Health Plan Marketplace for Individual and Small Business Health Insurance
Website: https://nystateofhealth.ny.gov/

Oregon

Cover Oregon
Website: https://www.coveroregon.com/

Rhode Island

HealthSource RI
Website: http://www.healthsourceri.com/

Utah

HealthCare.gov / Avenue H
Website: http://www.avenueh.com/

Individuals use the official national website, HealthCare.gov. Small businesses and their employees use Avenue H—Utah's Health Insurance Marketplace.

Vermont

Vermont Health Connect
Website: https://portal.healthconnect.vermont.gov/

Washington

Washington Healthplanfinder
Website: https://www.wahealthplanfinder.org/

STATE HEALTH AGENCIES

ALABAMA

Alabama Department of Public Health
The RSA Tower, 201 Monroe St.
Montgomery, AL 36104
Phone: (334) 206-5300
Toll free: (800) 252-1818
Website: http://www.adph.org/

ALL Kids—Children's Health Insurance Program
Alabama Department of Public Health, PO Box 304839
Montgomery, AL 36130-4839
Phone: (334) 206-5568
Toll free: (888) 373-5437
Fax: (334) 206-3783
Website: http://www.adph.org/allkids/

State Health Insurance Assistance Program (SHIP)
RSA Tower, Ste. 350, 201 Monroe St.
Montgomery, AL 36130
Phone: (334) 242-5743
Toll free: (800) 243-5463
Website: http://www.alabamaageline.gov/

ALASKA

Alaska Department of Health and Social Services
350 Main St., Rm. 404
Juneau, AK 99811-0601
Phone: (907) 465-3030
Website: http://dhss.alaska.gov/Pages/default.aspx

Denali KidCare
Frontier Bldg., 1st Fl., 3601 C St.
Anchorage, AK 99503
Phone: (907) 269-6529
Toll free: (888) 318-8890
Fax: (855) 769-0986
E-mail: denali.kid.care@alaska.gov
Website: http://dhss.alaska.gov/dhcs/Pages/
    DenaliKidCare/default.aspx

Medicare Information Office—SHIP
Seniors and Disabilities Services, 350 Main St., Rm. 404
Juneau, AK 99811
Phone: (907) 269-3680
TTY: (907) 269-3691
Website: http://dhss.alaska.gov/dsds/Pages/medicare/
    default.aspx

AMERICAN SAMOA

Department of Public Health
A.P. Lutali Executive Office Bldg.
Pago Pago, AS 96799
Phone: (684) 633-4606
Fax: (684) 633-5379
Website: http://americansamoa.gov/index.php/2012-04-25-
    19-44-32/2012-04-25-19-52-04/departments/public-
    health

American Samoa Children's Health Insurance Program
American Samoa Medicaid Program, Medicaid Office,
    PO Box 998383
Pago Pago, AS 96799
Phone: (684) 633-4818
Website: http://americansamoa.gov/index.php/2012-04-25-19-
    44-32/2012-04-28-01-30-33/offices/2012-04-30-18-49-47

ARIZONA

Arizona Department of Health Services
150 N 18th Ave.
Phoenix, AZ 85007
Phone: (602) 542-1025
Fax: (602) 542-0883
Website: http://www.azdhs.gov/

Arizona KidsCare
801 E Jefferson, MD 7500
Phoenix, AZ 85034
Phone: (602) 417-5437
Toll free: (800) 962-6690
Fax: (602) 257-7016
Website: http://www.azahcccs.gov/applicants/categories/
    KidsCare.aspx

Arizona State Health Insurance Assistance Program (SHIP)
1789 W Jefferson St. (Site Code 950A)
Phoenix, AZ 85007
Phone: (602) 542-4446
Toll free: (800) 432-4040
Website: https://www.azdes.gov/daas/ship/

ARKANSAS

Arkansas Department of Health
4815 W Markham St.
Little Rock, AR 72205

Phone: (501) 661-2000
Toll free: (800) 462-0599
Website: http://www.healthy.arkansas.gov/Pages/
default.aspx

ARKids First
Main St. & E St.
Little Rock, AR 72201
Toll free: (888) 474-8275
Website: http://www.arkidsfirst.com/home.htm/

Senior Health Insurance Information Program (SHIIP)
1200 W Third St.
Little Rock, AR 72201-1904
Phone: (501) 371-2782
Toll free: (800) 224-6330
Fax: (501)371-2781
Website: http://www.insurance.arkansas.gov/shiip.htm

CALIFORNIA

California Department of Health Care Services
California Health and Human Services,
1600 Ninth St., Rm. 460
Sacramento, CA 95814
Phone: (916) 445-4171
Website: http://www.dhcs.ca.gov/Pages/default.aspx

HealthyFamilies—CHIP
PO Box 138005
Sacramento, CA 95813-9984
Toll free: (866) 848-9166
Website: http://www.healthyfamilies.ca.gov/Home/
default.aspx

**California Health Insurance Counseling & Advocacy Program
(HICAP)—SHIP**
1300 National Dr., Ste. 200
Sacramento, CA 95834-1992
Toll free: (866) 848-9166
Fax: (866) 848-4977
E-mail: HealthyFamilies@MAXIMUS.com
Website: https://www.aging.ca.gov/hicap/

COLORADO

Colorado Department of Public Health and Environment
4300 Cherry Creek Dr. S
Denver, CO 80246-1530
Phone: (303) 692-2000
TTY: (303) 691-7700
Toll free: (800) 886-7689
Website: http://www.colorado.gov/cs/Satellite/CDPHE-
Main/CBON/1251583470000

Colorado Child Health Plan Plus (CHP +)
PO Box 929
Denver, CO 80201-0929

Toll free: (800) 359-1991
Fax: (303) 893-1780
Website: http://www.cchp.org/

Senior Health Insurance Assistance Program (SHIP)
1560 Broadway, Ste. 110
Denver, CO 80202
Phone: (720) 321-8850
TTY: (303) 894-7880
Toll free: (888) 696-7213
Toll free: (866) 665-9668 (Spanish)
Website: http://cdn.colorado.gov/cs/Satellite/DORA-
HealthIns/CBON/DORA/1251645703837

CONNECTICUT

Department of Public Health
410 Capitol Ave., PO Box 340308
Hartford, CT 06134
Phone: (860) 509-8000
Website: http://www.ct.gov/dph/site/default.asp

HUSKY Plan—CHIP
25 Sigourney St.
Hartford, CT 06106-5033
Toll free: (877) 284-8759
Website: http://www.huskyhealth.com/hh/site/default.asp

CHOICES—SHIP
Aging Services Division, 25 Sigourney St., 10th Fl.
Hartford, CT 06106
Phone: (860) 424-5274
Toll free: (800) 994-9422
Website: http://www.ct.gov/agingservices/site/default.asp

DELAWARE

Delaware Health and Social Services
1901 N Du Pont Hwy., Main Bldg.
New Castle, DE 19720
Phone: (302) 255-9040
Toll free: (800) 372-2022
Fax: (302) 255-4429
Website: http://dhss.delaware.gov/dhss/

Delaware Healthy Children Program
1901 N Du Pont Hwy., Lewis Bldg.
New Castle, DE 19720
Toll free: (800) 372-2022
Website: http://dhss.delaware.gov/dhss/dmma/dhcp.html/

ELDERinfo (SHIP)
1901 N Du Pont Hwy., Lewis Bldg.
New Castle, DE 19720
Phone: (302) 674-7364
Toll free: (800) 336-9500
Website: http://www.delawareinsurance.gov/services/
elderinfo.shtml

DISTRICT OF COLUMBIA

Department of Health
899 N Capitol St. NE
Washington, DC 20002
Phone: (202) 442-5955
TTY: 711
Toll free: (888) 557-1116
Fax: (202) 442-4795
E-mail: doh@dc.gov
Website: http://doh.dc.gov/

DC Healthy Families—CHIP
6856 Eastern Ave. NW, Ste. 206
Washington, DC 20012
Phone: (202) 639-4030
TTY: (202) 639-4041
Toll free: (800) 620-7802
Website: https://www.dchealthyfamilies.com/Member/
    MemberHome.aspx

Health Insurance Counseling Project (HICP)—SHIP
500 K St., NE
Washington, DC 20002
Phone: (202) 724-5622
TTY: (202) 724-8925
Fax: (202) 724-4979
E-mail: dcoa@dc.gov
Website: http://dcoa.dc.gov/

FLORIDA

Florida Department of Health
2585 Merchants Row Blvd.
Tallahassee, FL 32399
Phone: (850) 414-2000
TTY: (850) 414-2001
Website: http://www.medicare.gov/contacts/search-
    results.aspx?cacheKill = 593

Florida KidCare
PO Box 980
Tallahassee, FL 32302
TTY: (877) 316-8748
Toll free: (888) 540-5437
Website: http://www.floridahealth.gov/AlternateSites/
    KidCare/

Serving Health Insurance Needs of Elders (SHINE)—SHIP
4040 Esplanade Way, Ste. 270
Tallahassee, FL 32399-7000
TTY: (850) 955-8771
Toll free: (800) 963-5337
Website: http://www.floridashine.org/

GEORGIA

Georgia Department of Community Health
2 Peachtree St. NW
Atlanta, GA 30303

Phone: (404) 656-4507
Website: http://dch.georgia.gov/

PeachCare for Kids
PO Box 2583
Atlanta, GA 30301-2583
Toll free: (877) 427-3224
Website: https://www.peachcare.org/

GeorgiaCares—SHIP
2 Peachtree St. NW, 33rd Fl.
Atlanta, GA 30303
TTY: (404) 657-1929
Toll free: (866) 552-4464
Website: http://www.mygeorgiacares.org/

GUAM

Department of Public Health and Social Services
123 Chalan Kareta
Mangilao, GU 96913-6304
Phone: (671) 735-7305/7297
Fax: (671) 734-2066
Website: http://www.dphss.guam.gov/

**Guam Department of Health Care Financing, Children's
    Health Insurance Program**
123 Chalan Kareta
Mangilao, GU 96913-6304
Phone: (671) 735-7102
Toll free: (877) 548-7669
Website: http://www.dphss.guam.gov/content/bureau-
    health-care-financing-administration

**Guam Medicare Assistance Program (GUAM MAP), State
    Health Insurance Assistance Program (SHIP)**
123 Chalan Kareta
Mangilao, GU 96913-6304
Phone: (671) 735-7421
TTY: (671) 735-7415
Website: http://www.dphss.guam.gov/content/state-health-
    insurance-assistance-program-ship

HAWAII

Hawaii Department of Health
1250 Punchbowl St.
Honolulu, HI 96813
Phone: (808) 586-4400
Website: http://health.hawaii.gov/

Children's Health Insurance Program
Department of Human Services of Hawaii,
1250 Punchbowl St.
Honolulu, HI 96813
Phone: (808) 692-7364
Website: http://www.med-quest.us/index.html/

**Sage PLUS Program. State Health Insurance Assistance
    Program (SHIP)**
1250 Punchbowl St.

Honolulu, HI 96813
Phone: (808) 586-7299
TTY: (866) 810-4379
Website: http://health.hawaii.gov/eoa/home/sage-plus/

IDAHO

Idaho Department of Health and Welfare
PO Box 83720
Boise, ID 83720-0036
Phone: (208) 334-5500
Toll free: (800) 926-2588
Website: http://healthandwelfare.idaho.gov/

Idaho Children's Health Insurance Program
211 Idaho CareLine, PO Box 83720
Boise, ID 83720-0026
Toll free: (800) 926-2588
Website: http://www.211.idaho.gov/

Senior Health Insurance Benefits Advisors (SHIBA), State Health Insurance Assistance Program (SHIP)
700 W State St.
Boise, ID 83720-0043
Toll free: (800) 247-4422
Website: http://www.doi.idaho.gov/shiba/shibahealth.aspx

ILLINOIS

Illinois Department of Human Services
100 S Grand Ave. E
Springfield, IL 62762
Phone: (217) 782-4977
TTY: (800) 447-6404
Toll free: (866) 843-6154
Website: http://www.dhs.state.il.us/page.aspx?

Illinois KidCare
100 S Grand Ave. E
Springfield, IL 62762
TTY: (877) 204-1012
Toll free: (866) 255-1012
Website: http://www.allkidscovered.com/

Senior Health Insurance Program (SHIP)
One Natural Resources Way, Ste. 100
Springfield, IL 62702-1271
Phone: (217) 785-9021
TTY: (217) 524-4872
Toll free: (800) 548-9034
Website: http://www.state.il.us/aging/SHIP/

INDIANA

Indiana State Department of Health
2 N Meridian St.
Indianapolis, IN 46204
Phone: (317) 233-1325
Website: http://www.in.gov/isdh/

Hoosier Healthwise—CHIP
Indiana Government Center S, 402 W Washington St., Rm. W160A
Indianapolis, IN 46204-2725
Toll free: (800) 889-9949
Toll free: (888) 855-3838 (Spanish)
E-mail: hoosierhealthwise@maximus.com
Website: http://member.indianamedicaid.com/programs–
    benefits/medicaid-programs/hoosier-healthwise.aspx

State Health Insurance Assistance Program (SHIP)
714 W 53rd St.
Anderson, IN 46013
Phone: (765) 608-2318
Toll free: (800) 452-4800
Website: http://www.in.gov/idoi/2495.htm

IOWA

Iowa Department of Public Health
321 E 12th St.
Des Moines, IA 50319-0075
Phone: (515) 281-7689
Phone: (515) 281-7230 (Spanish)
Toll free: (866) 227-9878
Website: http://www.idph.state.ia.us/

hawk-i—Children's Health Insurance Program
PO Box 71336
Des Moines, IA 50325-9958
TTY: (515) 457-8051
Toll free: (800) 257-8563
Website: http://www.hawk-i.org/

Senior Health Insurance Information Program (SHIIP)
601 Locust St., 4th Fl.
Des Moines, IA 50309-3738
Phone: (515) 281-5705
TTY: (800) 735-2942
Toll free: (800) 351-4664
Website: http://www.therightcalliowa.gov/

KANSAS

Kansas Department of Health and Environment
Curtis State Office Bldg., 1000 SW Jackson
Topeka, KS 66612
Phone: (785) 296-4986
Toll free: (800) 432-3535
Website: http://www.kdheks.gov/

HealthWave Program—CHIP
Kansas Department of Health and Environment, Curtis State Office Bldg., 1000 SW Jackson
Topeka, KS 66612
Toll free: (800) 792-4884
Website: http://www.ksresourceguide.org/healthwave.htm

Senior Health Insurance Counseling for Kansas (SHICK)
New England Bldg., 503 S Kansas Ave.
Topeka, KS 66603-3404

Toll free: (800) 860-5260
Website: http://www.kdads.ks.gov/SHICK/shick_
   index.html/

KENTUCKY

Kentucky Cabinet for Health Services
Office of the Secretary, 275 E Main St.
Frankfort, KY 40621
Phone: (502) 564-3970
Website: http://chfs.ky.gov/

Kentucky Children Health Insurance Program
PO Box 55270
Lexington, KY 4055-5270
TTY: (877) 524-4719
Toll free: (877) 524-4718
Toll free: Spanish: (800) 662-5397
Website: http://kidshealth.ky.gov/en/

State Health Insurance Assistance Program (SHIP)
275 E Main St.
Frankfort, KY 40621
Phone: (502) 564-6930
Toll free: (877) 293-7447
Website: http://www.chfs.ky.gov/dail/ship.htm

LOUISIANA

Department of Health and Hospitals
PO Box 629
Baton Rouge, LA 70821-0629
Phone: (225) 342-9500
Fax: (225) 342-5568
E-mail: dhhwebinfo@la.gov
Website: http://www.dhh.louisiana.gov/

LaCHIP
Department of Health and Hospitals, PO Box 629
Baton Rouge, LA 70821-0629
Toll free: (877) 252-2447
Website: http://www.dhh.louisiana.gov/index.cfm/faq/
   category/18

Senior Health Insurance Information Program (SHIIP)
1702 N Third St.
Baton Rouge, LA 70802
Phone: (225) 342-5301
Toll free: (800) 259-5300
Website: http://www.ldi.la.gov/SHIIP/

MAINE

Department of Health and Human Services
221 State St.
Augusta, ME 04333-0040
Phone: (207) 287-3707
TTY: Maine relay 711
Fax: (207)287-3005
Website: http://www.state.me.us/dhhs/

Maine Care -CHIP
Department of Health and Human Services, 221 State St.
Augusta, ME 04333
Phone: (207) 287-2674
Toll free: (800) 965-7476
Website: http://www.maine.gov/dhhs/mainecare.shtml

Maine State Health Insurance Assistance Program (SHIP)
11 State House Station, 32 Blossom Ln.
Augusta, ME 04333
Phone: (207) 287-9200
TTY: Maine relay 711
Toll free: (800) 262-2232
Fax: (207) 287-9229
Website: http://www.maine.gov/dhhs/oads/aging/
   community/ship.shtml

MARYLAND

Maryland Department of Health and Mental Hygiene
201 W Preston St.
Baltimore, MD 21201
Phone: (410) 767-6500
Toll free: (877) 463-3464
E-mail: dhmh.healthmd@maryland.gov
Website: http://dhmh.maryland.gov/SitePages/Home.aspx

Maryland Children's Health Insurance Program
201 W Preston St.
Baltimore, MD 21201
Phone: (410) 649-0512
Toll free: (800) 456-8900
Website: https://mmcp.dhmh.maryland.gov/chp/SitePages/
   Home.aspx

Senior Health Insurance Assistance Program (SHIP)
301 W Preston St., Ste. 1007
Baltimore, MD 21201
Phone: (410) 767-1100
Toll free: (800) 243-3425
Website: http://www.aging.maryland.gov/

MASSACHUSETTS

Massachusetts Department of Public Health
250 Washington St.
Boston, MA 02108
Phone: (617) 624-6000
TTY: (617) 624-6001
Toll free: (866) 627-7968
Website: http://www.mass.gov/eohhs/gov/departments/dph/

Massachusetts Children's Health Insurance Program
Executive Office of Elder Affairs—SHIP, One Ashburton
   Pl., 5th Fl.
Boston, MA 02108
TTY: (800) 497-4648
Toll free: (877) 841-2900
Website: http://www.insurekidsnow.gov/state/mass/

Executive Office of Elder Affairs—SHIP
One Ashburton Pl., 5th Fl.
Boston, MA 02108
Phone: (617) 727-7750
TTY: (800) 8720166
Toll free: (800) 243-4636
Fax: (617) 727-9368
Website: http://www.mass.gov/elders/healthcare/shine/
    serving-the-health-information-needs-of-elders.html

MICHIGAN

Michigan Department Community Health
Capitol View Bldg., 201 Townsend St.
Lansing, MI 48913
Phone: (517) 373-3740
Website: http://www.michigan.gov/mdch

MIChild
Capitol View Bldg., 201 Townsend St.
Lansing, MI 48913
Toll free: (888) 263-5897
Website: http://michigan.gov/mdch/0,1607,7-132-
    2943_4845_4931- - -,00.html

MMAP, Inc.—SHIP
Michigan Office of Services to the Aging, PO Box 30676
Lansing, MI 48909-8176
Phone: (517) 373-8230
Toll free: (800) 803-7174
Fax: (517) 373-4092
Website: http://mmapinc.org/

MINNESOTA

Minnesota Department of Health
PO Box 64975
St. Paul, MM 55164-0975
Phone: (651) 201-5000
Toll free: (888) 345-0823
Website: http://www.health.state.mn.us/

MinnesotaCare—CHIP
PO Box 64838
St. Paul, MM 55164-0838
Phone: (651) 297-3862
TTY: (800) 627-3529
Toll free: (800) 657-3672
Website: http://www.dhs.state.mn.us/main/
    idcplg?IdcService = GET_DYNAMIC_CONVERSION
    &dDocName = id_006255&Revision
    SelectionMethod = LatestReleased

**Minnesota State Health Insurance Assistance Program/
    Senior LinkAge Line**
Support Services Center, 2079 Ellis Ave.
Saint Paul, MM 55114
Toll free: (800) 333-2433
Website: http://www.minnesotahelp.info/Public/default.
    aspx?se = senior

MISSISSIPPI

Mississippi Department of Health
570 E Woodrow Wilson Dr.
Jackson, MS 39216
Phone: (601) 576-7400
Toll free: (866) 458-4948
Website: http://www.msdh.state.ms.us/

Mississippi Health Benefits Program
Sillers Bldg., Ste. 100, 50 High St.
Jackson, MS 39201-1399
Phone: (601) 576-4111
Toll free: (800) 421-2408
Website: https://www.medicaid.ms.gov/Chip.aspx

**MS State Health Insurance Assistance
    Program (SHIP)**
750 N State St.
Jackson, MS 39202
Phone: (601) 359-4366
Toll free: (800) 948-3090
Website: http://www.mdhs.state.ms.us/aas_ship.html/

MISSOURI

Missouri Department of Health & Senior Services
912 Wildwood, PO Box 570
Jefferson City, MO 65102
Phone: (573) 751-6400
Fax: 573-751-6010
E-mail: info@health.mo.gov
Website: http://health.mo.gov/index.php

MO HealthNet Division—CHIP
615 Howerton Ct., PO Box 6500
Jefferson City, MO 65102-6500
Phone: (573) 751-3221
Toll free: (888) 275-5908
Website: http://dss.mo.gov/mhd/index.htm

**CLAIM—State health Insurance Assistance
    Program (SHIP)**
301 W High St., Rm. 530
Jefferson City, MO 65102
Phone: (573) 817-8320
Toll free: (800) 390-3330
Website: http://www.missouriclaim.org/welcome

MONTANA

Department of Public Health and Human Services
SRS Bldg., 111 N Sanders St.
Helena, MT 59601
Phone: (406) 444-5622
Website: http://www.dphhs.mt.gov/

Montana Children's Health Insurance Plan
Healthy Montana Kids, PO Box 202951
Helena, MT 59620-2951
Phone: (406) 444-6971
Toll free: (877) 543-7669
Website: http://www.dphhs.mt.gov/hmk/

Montana State Health Insurance Assistance Program (SHIP)
2030 11th Ave.
Helena, MT 59601
Toll free: (800) 551-3191
Website: http://www.dphhs.mt.gov/sltc/services/aging/
    SHIP/ship.shtml

NEBRASKA

Nebraska Department of Health and Human Services
301 Centennial Mall S
Lincoln, NE 68509
Phone: (402) 471-3121
Website: http://dhhs.ne.gov/Pages/default.aspx

Nebraska Kids Connection—CHIP
301 Centennial Mall S
Lincoln, NE 68509
Phone: (402) 471-6035
Toll free: (877) 632-5437
Website: http://dhhs.ne.gov/medicaid/Pages/
    med_kidsconxfaq.aspx

**Nebraska Senior Health Insurance Information
    Program (SHIIP)**
NE Department of Insurance, 941 O St., PO Box 82089
Lincoln, NE 68501-2089
Phone: (402) 471-2841
Toll free: (800) 234-7119
Website: http://www.doi.nebraska.gov/shiip/

NEVADA

Nevada Department of Health and Human Services
4126 Technology Way, Rm. 100
Carson City, NV 89706-2009
Phone: (775) 687-4000
Fax: (775) 687-4010
Website: http://dhhs.nv.gov/

Nevada Check Up—CHIP
Division of Health Care Financing and Policy, 1100 E
    William St., Ste. 101
Carson City, NV 89701
Phone: (775) 684-3777
Toll free: (877) 543-7669
Website: http://www.nevadacheckup.nv.gov/

State Health Insurance Assistance Program (SHIP)
3416 Goni Rd., Ste. D-132
Carson City, NV 89706

Phone: (702) 486-3478
Toll free: (800) 307-4444
Website: http://nevadaadrc.com/services-and-programs/
    medicare/ship

NEW HAMPSHIRE

New Hampshire Department of Health and Human Services
129 Pleasant St.
Concord, NH 03301-3852
Phone: (603) 271-9000
Toll free: (800) 852-3345
Website: http://www.dhhs.state.nh.us/

Children's Medicaid
129 Pleasant St.
Concord, NH 03301-3852
Phone: (603) 271-9750
Toll free: (877) 464-2447
Website: http://www.dhhs.nh.gov/dfa/medical/
    children.htm

**NH SHIP—ServiceLink Aging and Disability
    Resource Center**
67 Water St., Ste. 105
Laconia, NH 03246
Toll free: (866) 634-9412
Website: http://www.nh.gov/servicelink/

NEW JERSEY

State of New Jersey Department of Health
PO Box 360
Trenton, NJ 08650-0360
Phone: (609) 292-7837
Toll free: (800) 367-6543
Website: http://www.state.nj.us/health/index.shtml

NJ Family Care—CHIP
PO Box 8367
Trenton, NJ 08650-9802
Toll free: (800) 701-0710
Website: http://www.njfamilycare.org/default.aspx

State Health Insurance Assistance Program (SHIP)
Division of Aging Services, 12b Quakerbridge Plz.,
    PO Box 715
Mercerville, NJ 07625-0715
Phone: (877) 222-3737
Toll free: (800) 792-8820
Website: http://www.state.nj.us/humanservices/doas/
    services/ship/index.html/

NEW MEXICO

New Mexico Department of Health
1190 S St. Francis Dr.
Santa Fe, NM 87502

Phone: (505) 827-2613
Phone: (505) 476-3656 (Spanish)
Fax: (505) 827-2530
Website: http://www.health.state.nm.us/

New Mexikids/SCHIP
2009 S Pacheco St.
Santa Fe, NM 87505
Toll free: (888) 997-2583
E-mail: INMInfo.HSD@state.nm.us
Website: http://www.insurenewmexico.state.nm.us/
    NewMexiKidsandTeens.htm

**Benefits Counseling Program—State Health Insurance
    Assistance Program (SHIP)**
2550 Cerrillos Rd.
Santa Fe, NM 87505
Phone: (505) 476-4846
Toll free: (800) 432-2080
Website: http://www.nmaging.state.nm.us/
    State_Health_Insurance_Assistance_Program.aspx

NEW YORK

New York State Department of Health
Corning Tower, Empire State Plz.
Albany, NY 12237
Toll free: (866) 881-2809
Website: http://www.health.ny.gov/

New York Child Health Plus
New York State Department of Health, Corning Tower,
    Empire State Plz.
Albany, NY 12237
TTY: (877) 898-5849
Toll free: (800) 698-4543
Website: http://www.health.ny.gov/health_care/child_
    health_plus/index.htm

**Health Insurance Information Counseling and Assistance
    Program (HIICAP)—SHIP**
New York State Office for the Aging, 2 Empire State Plz.
Albany, NY 12223-1251
Phone: (800) 342-9871
Toll free: (800) 701-0501
Website: http://www.aging.ny.gov/HealthBenefits/
    Index.cfm

NORTH CAROLINA

North Carolina Department of Health and Human Services
2001 Mail Service Center
Raleigh, NC 27699-2001
Phone: (919) 855-4800
Toll free: (800) 622-7030
Website: http://www.ncdhhs.gov/

North Carolina Health Choice for Children
NC Division of Medical Assistance,
2501 Mail Service Center
Raleigh, NC 27699-2501
Phone: (919) 855-4100
Toll free: (800) 662-7030
Website: http://www.ncdhhs.gov/dma/healthchoice/
    index.htm

Seniors' Health Insurance Information Program (SHIIP)
11 S Boylan Ave.
Raleigh, NC 27603
Phone: (919) 807-6900
Toll free: (800) 443-9354
Website: http://www.ncdoi.com/SHIIP/Default.aspx

NORTH DAKOTA

North Dakota Department of Health
600 E Boulevard Ave.
Bismarck, ND 58505-0200
Phone: (701) 328-2372
Fax: (701) 328-4727
Website: http://www.ndhealth.gov/

Heatlhy Steps—CHIP
Department of Human Services, 600 E Boulevard Ave.,
Dept. 325
Bismarck, ND 58505-0250
Phone: (701) 328-4019
Toll free: (800) 755-2604
Website: http://www.nd.gov/dhs/services/medicalserv/chip/

Senior Health Insurance Counseling (SHIC)
600 E Boulevard Ave.
Bismark, ND 58505-2320
Phone: (701) 328-2440
TTY: (800) 366-6888
Toll free: (800) 247-0560
E-mail: ndshic@nd.gov
Website: http://www.nd.gov/ndins/shic/

NORTHERN MARIANAS

Department of Public Health
PO Box 500409CK
Saipan, MP 96950
Phone: (670) 234-8950
Website: http://www.dphsaipan.com/

OHIO

Ohio Department of Health
246 N High St.
Columbus, OH 43215
Phone: (614) 466-3543
Website: http://www.odh.ohio.gov/

Healthy Start—CHIP
50 W Town St., Ste. 400
Columbus, OH 43215
Phone: (614) 466-2100
Toll free: (800) 324-8680
Website: http://medicaid.ohio.gov/FOROHIOANS/
Programs/ChildrenFamiliesandWomen.aspx

Ohio Senior Health Insurance Information Program (OSHIIP)
50 W Town St., 3rd Fl., Ste. 300
Columbus, OH 43215
Toll free: (800) 686-1578
Website: http://www.insurance.ohio.gov/Consumer/Pages/
ConsumerTab2.aspx

OKLAHOMA

Oklahoma State Department of Health
1000 NE 10th
Oklahoma City, OK 73117
Phone: (405) 271-5600
Toll free: (800) 522-0203
Website: http://www.ok.gov/health/

SoonerCare—CHIP
2401 NW 23rd St., Ste. 1A
Oklahoma City, OK 73107
Phone: (405) 522-7300
Toll free: (800) 987-7767
Website: http://www.okhca.org/

SHIP—Senior Health Insurance Counseling Program
Oklahoma Medicare Assistance Program (MAP),
5 Corporate Plz., 3625 NW 56th St., Ste. 100
Oklahoma City, OK 73112
Phone: (405) 521-6628
Toll free: (800) 763-2828
Website: http://www.ok.gov/oid/Consumers/
Information_for_Seniors/SHIP.html/

OREGON

Oregon Department of Human Services
500 Summer St. NE
Salem, OR 97301
Phone: (503) 945-5944
TTY: (503) 945-6214
Website: http://www.oregon.gov/DHS/Pages/index.aspx

Oregon Health Plan—CHIP
Division of Medical Assistance Programs, Administrative
Office, 500 Summer St. NE
Salem, OR 97301-1079

Phone: (503) 945-5772
Toll free: (877) 314-5678
Toll free: (800) 273-0557 (Spanish)
Website: http://www.oregon.gov/OHA/OPHP/kids
connect/Pages/index.aspx

Senior Health Insurance Benefits Assistance (SHIBA)
350 Winter St. NE, Ste. 330, PO Box 14480
Salem, OR 97309-0405
Phone: (503) 947-7979
TTY: (800) 735-2900
Toll free: (800) 722-4134
Fax: (503) 947-7092
Website: http://www.oregon.gov/DCBS/SHIBA/Pages/
index.aspx

PENNSYLVANIA

Pennsylvania Department of Health
Health and Welfare Bldg., 8th Fl. W, 625 Forster St.
Harrisburg, PA 17120
Toll free: (877) 724-3258
Website: http://www.portal.health.state.pa.us/portal/
server.pt/community/department_of_health_home/
17457

Pennsylvania's Children's Health Insurance Program
1326 Strawberry Sq.
Harrisburg, PA 17120
Toll free: (800) 986-5437
Fax: (717) 705-1643
Website: http://www.chipcoverspakids.com/

APPRISE—SHIP
Department of Aging, 555 Walnut St., 5th Fl.
Harrisburg, PA 17101-1919
Toll free: (800) 783-7067
Website: http://www.portal.state.pa.us/portal/
server.pt?open = 514&objID = 616587&mode = 2

PUERTO RICO

Administration of Medical Services (Health Department
PO Box 2129
San Juan, PR 00919-2129
Phone: (787) 777-3535
Fax: (877) 725-4300
Website: http://www.oppte.pr.gov/

State Health Insurance Assistance Program (SHIP)
Avenida Ponce de León Parada 16 Edificio 1064 tercer piso,
Santurce (altos del edificio de Marshalls)
San Juan, PR 00919-1179
Phone: (787) 721-6121
Toll free: (877) 725-4300
Website: http://www.oppte.pr.gov/

RHODE ISLAND

Rhode Island Department of Health
3 Capitol Hill
Providence, RI 02908
Phone: (401) 462-5300
Toll free: (800) 942-7434
Website: http://www.health.ri.gov/

RIte Care—CHIP
Louis Pasteur Bldg., Ste. 57, 600 New London Ave.
Cranston, RI 02920
Phone: (401) 462-5300
TTY: (401) 462-3363
Website: http://www.dhs.ri.gov/

Senior Health Insurance Program (SHIP)
74 West Rd.
Cranston, RI 02920
Phone: (401) 462-0510
TTY: (401) 462-0740
Website: http://www.dea.ri.gov/

SOUTH CAROLINA

**South Carolina Department of Health and
Environmental Control**
2600 Bull St.
Columbia, SC 29201
Phone: (803) 898-3432
Toll free: (888) 549-0820
Website: https://www.scdhec.gov/

Healthy Connection—CHIP
PO Box 8206
Columbia, SC 29202-8206
Toll free: (888) 549-0820
E-mail: info@scdhhs.gov
Website: https://www.scdhhs.gov/

**(I-CARE) Insurance Counseling Assistance and
Referrals for Elders**
1301 Gervais St., Ste. 350
Columbia, SC 29201
Phone: (803) 734-9900
Toll free: (800) 868-9095
Website: http://aging.sc.gov/seniors/medicare/Pages/
default.aspx

SOUTH DAKOTA

South Dakota Department of HealthRobert Hayes Bldg.
600 E Capitol Ave.
Pierre, SD 57501-2536
Phone: (605) 773-3361
Toll free: (800) 738-2301 (SD only)
Fax: 605-773-5683
Website: http://doh.sd.gov/

South Dakota Children's Health Insurance Program
South Dakota Department of Social Services,
700 Governors Dr.
Pierre, SD 57501
Phone: (605) 773-4678
Toll free: (800) 305-3064
Website: http://dss.sd.gov/medicalservices/chip/index.asp

Senior Health Information & Insurance Education (SHIINE)
Division of Adult Services and Aging, South Dakota Department of Social Services, 700 Governors Dr.
Pierre, SD 57501
Toll free: (800) 536-8197
Website: http://www.shiine.net/

TENNESSEE

Tennessee Department of Health
Andrew Johnson Tower, 710 James Robertson Pkwy.
Nashville, TN 37243
Phone: (615) 741-3111
E-mail: tn.health@tn.gov
Website: http://health.state.tn.us/

TennCare
310 Great Circle Rd.
Nashville, TN 37243
Toll free: (866) 311-4287
Website: http://www.state.tn.us/tenncare/

TN SHIP
Tennessee Commission on Aging and Disability
502 Diaderick St., 9th Fl.
Nashville, TN 37243-0860
Phone: (615) 741-2056
TTY: (615) 532-3893
Toll free: (877) 801-0044
Website: http://www.tn.gov/comaging/ship.html/

TEXAS

Department of State Health Services
1100 W 49th St.
Austin, TX 78756
Phone: (512) 458-7111
Toll free: (888) 963-7111
Website: http://www.dshs.state.tx.us/

TexCare Partnership
Brown-Heatly Bldg., 4900 N Lamar Blvd.
Austin, TX 78751-2316
Toll free: (800) 647-6558
Website: http://www.chipmedicaid.org/

**Health Information Counseling and Advocacy Program
(HICAP)—SHIP**
701 W 51st St.
Austin, TX 78751
Toll free: (800) 252-9240
Website: http://www.dads.state.tx.us/

UTAH

Utah Department of Health
PO Box 141010
Salt Lake City, UT 84114-1010
Phone: (801) 538-6155
Toll free: (800) 662-9651
Website: http://www.health.utah.gov/

Utah Children's Health Insurance Program
PO Box 143107
Salt Lake City, UT 83113-3107
Toll free: (877) 543-7669
Toll free: (866) 435-7414
E-mail: chip@utah.gov
Website: http://health.utah.gov/chip/

Senior Health Insurance Information Program (SHIP)
195 N 1950 W
Salt Lake City, UT 84116
Phone: (801) 538-3910
Toll free: (800) 541-7735
Website: http://daas.utah.gov/senior-services/

VERMONT

Vermont Department of Health
108 Cherry St.
Burlington, VT 05402
Phone: 802-863-7200
TTY: 711
Toll free: (800) 464-4343
Fax: 802-865-7754
Website: http://www.healthvermont.gov/

Green Mountain Care: Dr. Dynasaur—CHIP
312 Hurricane Ln., Ste. 201
Williston, VT 05495
Toll free: (800) 250-8427
Website: http://www.greenmountaincare.org/vermont-
    health-insurance-plans/dr-dynasaur

Vermont State Health Insurance Assistance Program (SHIP)
481 Summer St., Ste. 101
St. Johnsbury, VT 05819
Toll free: (800) 642-5119
Website: http://www.medicarehelpvt.net/

VIRGIN ISLANDS

U.S. Virgin Islands Department of Health
St. Croix Office, Charles Harwood Complex, 3500 Est.
  Richmond
Christiansted, VI 00820
Phone: (340) 773-1311
Website: http://www.healthvi.org/

U.S. Virgin Islands Department of Health
St. Thomas/St. John Office, 1303 Hospital Ground, Ste.10

Charlotte Amalie St. Thomas, VI 00802
Phone: (340) 774-9000
Website: http://www.healthvi.org/

**Virgin Islands Bureau of Health Insurance and Medical
    Assistance—CHIP**
St. Croix Office, Charles Harwood Complex, 3500 Est.
Richmond
Christiansted, VI 00820
Phone: (340) 773-1311
Website: http://www.healthvi.org/contact/index.html/

**Virgin Islands Bureau of Health Insurance and Medical
    Assistance—CHIP**
St. Thomas/St. John Office, 1303 Hospital Ground, Ste.10
Charlotte Amalie St. Thomas, VI 00802
Phone: (340) 774-9000
Website: http://www.healthvi.org/contact/index.html/

**Virgin Islands State Health Insurance Assistance
    Program (VISHIP)**
Schneider Regional Medical Center,
9048 Sugar Estate, 1st Fl.
St. Thomas, VI 00802
Phone: (340) 714-4354
Fax: (340) 774-2636
Website: http://ltg.gov.vi/vi-ship-medicare.html/

**Virgin Islands State Health Insurance Assistance Program
    (VISHIP)**
Gov. Juan F. Luis Hospital & Medical Center, 4007 Estate
Diamond, 1st Fl.
St. Croix, VI 00820
Phone: (340) 772-7368
Fax: (340) 772-9120
Website: http://ltg.gov.vi/vi-ship-medicare.html/

VIRGINIA

Virginia Department of Health
109 Governor St., PO Box 2448
Richmond, VA 23218-2448
Phone: (804) 864-7001
Website: http://www.vdh.state.va.us/

Family Access to Medical Security Insurance Plan
PO Box 1820
Richmond, VA 23218-1820
Toll free: (866) 873-2647
Website: http://www.famis.org/

**Virginia Insurance Counseling and Assistance Program
    (VICAP)—SHIP**
1610 Forest Ave., Ste. 100
Henrico, VA 23229
Phone: (804) 662-9333
Toll free: (800) 552-3402
Website: http://www.vda.virginia.gov/

▌WASHINGTON

Washington State Department of Health
PO Box 47890
Olympia, WA 98504-7890
Phone: (360) 236-4501
Toll free: (800) 525-0127
Website: http://www.doh.wa.gov/

Apple Health for Kids—CHIP
626 8th Ave. SE
Olympia, WA 98501
Toll free: (877) 543-7669
Website: http://www.hca.wa.gov/applehealth/Pages/
default.aspx

Statewide Health Insurance Benefits Advisors (SHIBA)
Insurance 5000 Bldg., 5000 Capitol Blvd. SE
Tumwater, WA 98501
TTY: (360) 586-0241
Toll free: (800) 562-6900
Website: http://www.insurance.wa.gov/about-oic/what-
we-do/advocate-for-consumers/shiba/

▌WEST VIRGINIA

West Virginia Department of Health & Human Resources
One Davis Sq., Ste. 100 E
Charleston, WV 25301
Phone: (304) 558-0684
Toll free: (888) 483-0797
Fax: (304) 558-1130
Website: http://www.wvdhhr.org/

West Virginia Children's Health Insurance Program
1900 Kanawha Blvd. E
Charleston, WV 25305
Phone: (304) 558-2732
Toll free: (877) 982-2447
Website: http://www.chip.wv.gov/Pages/default.aspx

West Virginia State Health Insurance Assistance Program (WV SHIP)
1900 Kanawha Blvd. E
Charleston, WV 25305
Phone: (304) 558-3317
Toll free: (877) 987-4463
Fax: (304) 558-0004
Website: http://www.wvship.org/

▌WISCONSIN

Wisconsin Department of Health Services
1 W Wilson St.
Madison, WI 53703
Phone: (608) 266-1865
TTY: (888) 701-1251
Toll free: (800) 362-3002
E-mail: DHSwebmaster@wisconsin.gov
Website: http://www.dhs.wisconsin.gov/

Badger Care -CHIP
Department of Health Services, 1 W Wilson St.
Madison, WI 53703
Toll free: (800) 362-3002
Website: http://www.dhs.wisconsin.gov/badgercareplus/

Wisconsin State Insurance Assistance Program (SHIP)
Department of Health Services, 1 W Wilson St.
Madison, WI 53703
Phone: (608) 267-3201
TTY: (888) 701-1251
Toll free: (800) 242-1060
Toll free: (888) 701-1255 (Spanish)
Website: http://www.dhs.wisconsin.gov/aging/EBS/
ship.htm

▌WYOMING

Wyoming Department of Health
401 Hathaway Bldg.
Cheyenne, WY 82002
Phone: (307) 777-7656
Toll free: (866) 571-0944
Fax: (307) 777-7439
Website: http://www.health.wyo.gov/default.aspx

Wyoming Kid Care
6101 Yellowstone Rd., Ste. 210
Cheyenne, WY 82002
Phone: (855) 294-2127
Toll free: (888) 996-8786
Fax: (307) 777-7085
Website: http://www.health.wyo.gov/healthcarefin/chip/
index.html/

Wyoming State Health Insurance Information Program (WSHIIP)
106 W Adams Ave.
Riverton, WY 82501
Phone: (307) 856-6880
Toll free: (800) 856-4398
Website: http://www.wyomingseniors.com/

TOP U.S. HEALTH INSURANCE COMPANIES

The following is a list of some of the top health insurance companies in the United States. The physical, email, and web addresses listed here were provided by the companes; Gale, Cengage Learning is not responsible for the accuracy of the addresses or the contents of the websites.

UnitedHealth Group Inc.
PO Box 1459
Minneapolis, MN 55440-1459
Phone: (952) 936-1300
Fax: (952)936-1819
Toll free: (800) 328-5979
E-mail: info@unitedhealthgroup.com
Website: http://www.unitedhealthgroup.com

UnitedHealth Group Inc. is diversified health and wellness company providing health care services in the United States. UnitedHealth Group's companies include UnitedHealthcare, Ovations and AmeriChoice; OptumHealth; Ingenix; and prescription solutions. United Healthcare offers a comprehensive array of consumer-oriented health benefit plans and services for large national employers, public sector employers, mid-sized employers, small businesses and individuals nationwide. Ovations provides health and well-being services for those 50 and older, addressing needs for preventive and acute health care services, as well as for services dealing with chronic disease and other issues for older individuals, and AmeriChoice provides health insurance coverage to eligible Medicaid beneficiaries in exchange for a fixed monthly premium per member. The OptumHealth segment serves approximately 60 million individuals with its diversified offering of health, financial and ancillary benefit services and products that assist consumers in navigating the health care system and accessing services, support their emotional health, provide ancillary insurance benefits and facilitate the financing of health care services through account-based programs. The Ingenix segment offers products and services sold through a direct sales force focused on specific customers and market segments across the pharmaceutical, biotechnology, employer, government, hospital, physician, payer and property, and casualty insurance market segments. The prescription solutions segment offers a comprehensive suite of integrated pharmacy benefit management services, delivering drug benefits through a network of retail pharmacies and two mail service facilities. It is a public company traded on the New York Stock Exchange under the symbol UNH.

KEY INFORMATION:

- Total Revenue: $1,106,180,000
- Employees: 133,000
- Sales Per Employee: $8,317
- Year Founded: 1977

OFFICERS:

- William W. McGuire—Chief Executive Officer
- Mike Mikan—Chief Financial Officer, Executive Vice President
- Anthony Welters—Executive Vice President, Marketing
- Rod Hamilton—Chief Information Officer
- Lori Sweere—Executive Vice President, Human Resources
- Marianne D. Short—Executive Vice President
- Matthew Ladegaard—Director
- Joetta Fontaine—Manager
- G. Mike Mikan—Chief Financial Officer, Executive Vice President
- Stephen J. Hemsley—Chief Executive Officer, President
- David S. Wichmann—Chief Financial Officer, Executive Vice President
- Dr. Reed V. Tuckson, M.D.—Executive Vice President
- John S. Penshorn—Senior Vice President
- Gail K. Boudreaux—Executive Vice President
- William A. Munsell—Executive Vice President
- Don Nathan—Senior Vice President, Corporate Communications
- Eric S. Rangan—Executive Vice President, Accounting
- Larry C. Renfro—Executive Vice President
- Simon Stevens—Executive Vice President
- Mitchell Zamoff—Executive Vice President
- Christopher J. Walsh—Executive Vice President
- Rodger A. Lawson—Director
- William Ballard, Jr—Director
- Richard Burke—Director
- Robert Darretta—Director
- Douglas Leatherdale—Director
- Glenn Renwick—Director
- Kenneth Shine—Director
- Gail Wilensky—Director
- Rich Baer—Head of Legal Department
- Jeannine M. Rivet—Executive Vice President
- Michele J. Hooper—Director
- William Mcguire—President
- Aubrey Miller—Chairman of the Board
- George Micken—Chief Financial Officer
- John Mach—Officer
- Bob Lyons—Executive Officer
- Eric S. Rangen—Senior Vice President

HISTORICAL REVENUE (TOTAL REVENUE):

- $1,106,180,000 (2012)
- $67,889,000,000 (2011)
- $63,063,000,000 (2010)
- $80,415,000,000 (2009)
- $55,815,000,000 (2008)

- $50,899,000,000 (2007)
- $48,320,000,000 (2006)
- $41,288,000,000 (2005)
- $27,862,000,000 (2004)
- $17,668,000,000 (2003)
- $14,187,000,000 (2002)
- $12,486,000,000 (2001)
- $11,053,000,000 (2000)
- $10,273,000,000 (1999)
- $9,675,000,000 (1998)
- $11,794,000,000 (1997)
- $10,073,800,000 (1996)
- $5,670,900,000 (1995)
- $3,768,800,000 (1994)
- $2,527,300,000 (1993)
- $1,759,900,000 (1992)
- $847,100,000 (1991)
- $605,500,000 (1990)

WellPoint Inc.

120 Monument Cir.
Indianapolis, IN 46204
Phone: (317) 532-6000
Fax: (317) 488-6028
E-mail: investor.relations@wellpoint.com
Website: http://www.wellpoint.com

WellPoint Inc. was formed in 2004, when WellPoint Health Networks Inc. and Anthem Inc. merged. WellPoint is a publicly traded company on the NYSE. The health benefits company is an independent licensee of the Blue Cross and Blue Shield Association in California, Colorado, Connecticut, Georgia, Indiana, Kentucky, Maine, Missouri, Nevada, New Hampshire, New York, Ohio, Virginia and Wisconsin. In a majority of these areas the company does business as Anthem Blue Cross, Anthem Blue Cross Blue Shield or Empire Blue Cross Blue Shield and UniCare. The company is licensed to conduct insurance operations in all 50 states. WellPoint offers network-based managed care plans to the large and small employer, individual, Medicaid and senior markets. Managed care plans include preferred provider organizations (PPOs), health maintenance organizations (HMOs), point-of-service plans (POS plans), traditional indemnity plans and other hybrid plans, including consumer-driven health plans (CDHPs), hospital-only and limited-benefit products. The company also provides an array of specialty and other products and services, including life and disability insurance benefits, pharmacy benefit management (PBM), specialty pharmacy, dental, vision, behavioral health benefit services, radiology benefit management, analytics-driven personal health care guidance, long-term care insurance and flexible spending accounts.

KEY INFORMATION:

- Total Revenue: $61,711,700,000
- Employees: 43,500
- Sales Per Employee: $1,418,660
- Year Founded: 2004

OFFICERS:

- Dijuana Lewis—Chief Executive Officer, President
- Wayne S. DeVeydt—Chief Financial Officer, Executive Vice President
- Kate Quinn—Chief Marketing Officer
- Andrew J. Lang—Chief Information Officer, Senior Vice President
- Randy L. Brown—Chief Human Resources Officer, Executive Vice President
- Elizabeth Tallett—Director
- John Short—Director
- Brad M. Fluegel—Executive Vice President
- Cynthia S. Miller—Executive Vice President
- Susan B. Bayh—Executive Vice President, Director
- Lenox D. Baker—Director
- Julie A. Hill—Director
- Warren Y. Jobe—Director
- Ramiro G. Peru—Director
- William J. Ryan—Director
- George A. Schaefer, Jr.—Director
- Lance Chrisman—Director
- Linda Jimenez—Vice President
- Jackie M. Ward—Chairman of the Board
- Dr. Samuel R. Nussbaum—Executive Vice President
- John Cannon—Executive Vice President
- Ken Goulet—Executive Vice President
- Brian A. Sassi—Executive Vice President
- Lori Beer—Executive Vice President
- Harlan Levine—Executive Vice President
- Dr. Lisa Latts—Vice President
- Raja Rajamannar—Executive Vice President
- Gloria McCarthy—Executive Vice President
- Lenox D. Baker—Director
- Susan B. Bayh—Director
- Sheila P. Burke—Director
- Robert L. Dixon, Jr.—Director

HISTORICAL REVENUE (TOTAL REVENUE):

- $61,711,700,000 (2012)
- $52,018,800,000 (2011)
- $50,166,900,000 (2010)
- $52,125,400,000 (2009)
- $48,403,200,000 (2008)
- $52,060,000,000 (2007)
- $51,574,000,000 (2006)
- $51,574,900,000 (2005)
- $39,738,400,000 (2004)
- $13,438,600,000 (2003)
- $12,439,300,000 (2002)
- $6,276,600,000 (2001)
- $5,708,500,000 (2000)
- $4,816,200,000 (1999)
- $4,359,200,000 (1998)
- $5,241,700,000 (1997)

Kaiser Foundation Health Plan Inc.

1 Kaiser Plz.
Oakland, CA 94612-3610
Phone: (510) 271-5800
Fax: (510)271-6493
Website: http://www.kaiserpermanente.org

Kaiser Foundation Health Plan, Inc., operates one of the largest nonprofit health plans in the United States. The company is a subsidiary business of Kaiser Permanente; the parent company comprises Kaiser Foundation Health Plan, Inc., Kaiser Foundation Hospitals, and the Permanente Medical Groups. Serving about 8.2 million members in nine states and Washington, D.C., the Oakland, California-based organization underwrites the Permanente Medical Groups, whose 14,000 physicians furnish medical care to Kaiser Permanente subscribers. Kaiser Permanente follows an integrated care model and provides an array of services to its members: it organizes and coordinates or provides its subscribers' health care (including preventive medicine), and it also provides other medical and pharmacy services through its network of Kaiser Foundation Hospitals and their subsidiaries.

KEY INFORMATION

- Total Assets: $29,692,000,000
- Employees: 167,300
- Sales Per Employee: $177,478
- Year Founded: 1945

OFFICERS:

- George C. Halvorson—Chairman of the Board, Chief Executive Officer, President
- Robert E. Briggs—Chief Financial Officer, Senior Vice President
- Dresdene Flynn-White—Director of Human Resources
- Richard G. Barnaby—Chief Operating Officer, President
- Tom Wylie—Vice President of Administration
- William Caswell—Vice President of Marketing

HISTORICAL REVENUE (TOTAL ASSETS):

- $29,692,000,000 (2009)
- $28,355,000,000 (2008)
- $28,355,000,000 (2007)
- $28,355,000,000 (2005)
- $28,355,000,000 (2003)
- $19,700,000,000 (2001)
- $14,500,000,000 (1997)
- $11,729,000,000 (1995)
- $10,762,000,000 (1994)
- $9,762,000,000 (1993)
- $8,145,000,000 (1992)
- $7,110,000,000 (1991)
- $5,965,000,000 (1990)

Aetna Inc.
151 Farmington Ave.
Hartford, CT 06156
Phone: (860) 273-0123
Fax: (860) 275-2677
Toll free: (800) 872-3862
E-mail: https://member.aetna.com/MemberPublic/
featureRouter/forms?page=contactPublicForm
Website: http://www.aetna.com

The predecessor of Aetna Inc., Aetna Insurance Company, was founded in 1850. The company operates as a diversified health care benefits company, offering a range of health insurance products and related services, including medical, pharmacy, dental, behavioral health, group life and disability plans, and medical management capabilities and health care management services for Medicaid plans. It markets its products to employer groups, individuals, college students, part-time and hourly workers, health plans, governmental units, government-sponsored plans, labor groups and expatriates. The business is operated in three segments: Health Care, Group Insurance and Large Case Pensions. The company's Health Care products consist of medical, pharmacy benefits management, dental and vision plans offered on both an insured basis and an employer-funded basis. The Group Insurance products consist principally of life insurance, offered on an insured basis; disability insurance, offered on both an insured and employer-funded basis and long-term care insurance products, which were offered primarily on an Insured basis. The long-term care insurance products are in the process of being transferred to other carriers. The company operates in the United States with a nationwide provider network of participating health care providers.

KEY INFORMATION

- Sales: $1,537,600,000
- Employees: 33,300
- Sales Per Employee: $46,174
- Year Founded: 1853

OFFICERS:

- Mark T. Bertolini—Chairman of the Board, Chief Executive Officer, President
- Joseph M. Zubretsky—Chief Financial Officer, Executive Vice President
- Meg Mccarthy—Chief Information Officer
- Denice Parker—Director, Human Resources
- Hunt Tim—Director, Data Processing
- Vin Urbanowicz—Manager
- Gregory Galdau—Director, Research and Development
- Louise Murphy—Director, Research and Development
- Bill Sullivan—Director, Engineering
- Matthew Strelecky—Manager
- Katharine Zirolli—Accountant
- Rachel Ouellette—Analyst
- Mike Rogers—Analyst
- Alison Rogers-Mccoy—Vice President, Human Resources
- Fran Raifstanger—Director, Personnel
- Robert M. Mead—Senior Vice President, Marketing
- Meg McCarthy—Vice President, Operations
- Elease E. Wright—Senior Vice President, Human Resources
- William J. Casazza—General Counsel
- Lonny Reisman, M.D.—Officer
- Jeff D. Emerson—Officer
- Patricia A. Farrell—Senior Vice President
- Richard J. Leonard—Chief Technical Officer
- Katherine Fry—Chairman of the Board
- Kristi A. Matus—Executive Vice President
- Frank McCauley—Executive Vice President

HISTORICAL REVENUE (SALES):

- $1,537,600,000 (2011)
- $1,537,600,000 (2010)
- $38,550,400,000 (2009)
- $35,852,500,000 (2008)
- $50,724,700,000 (2007)
- $47,626,400,000 (2006)
- $44,365,000,000 (2005)
- $42,113,700,000 (2004)
- $11,240,000,000 (2003)
- $11,520,000,000 (2002)
- $13,468,600,000 (2000)
- $1,640,000,000 (1997)
- $1,667,100,000 (1995)
- $1,463,900,000 (1994)
- $1,343,700,000 (1993)
- $981,100,000 (1992)
- $758,200,000 (1991)
- $613,500,000 (1990)

Humana Inc.

500 W Main St.
Louisville, KY 40202
Phone: (502) 580-1000
Fax: (502)580-3639
Toll free: (800) 486-2620
E-mail: Corporateprocurement@humana.com
Website: http://www.humana.com

Humana Inc. offers various health and supplemental benefit plans, managing its business with three reportable segments: Retail, Employer Group, and Health and Well-Being Services. The Retail segment consists of government and commercial fully-insured medical and specialty health insurance benefits, including dental, vision, and other supplemental health and financial protection products, marketed directly to individuals. The Employer Group segment also consists of government and commercial fully-insured benefits, including dental, vision, and other supplemental health and financial protection products, as well as administrative services only products marketed to employer groups. The Health and Well-Being Services segment includes services to health plan members as well as to third parties that promote health and wellness, including primary care, pharmacy, integrated wellness, and home care services. The company markets its products through various channels, including television, radio, Internet, telemarketing, and direct mailings. Founded in 1961, the company's stock is traded as HUM on the NYSE.

KEY INFORMATION:

- Total Revenue: $9,557,000,000
- Employees: 40,000
- Sales Per Employee: $238,925
- Year Founded: 1964

OFFICERS:

- Michael B. McCallister—Chairman of the Board, Chief Executive Officer
- James H. Bloem—Chief Financial Officer, Senior Vice President, Treasurer
- Raja Rajamannar—Chief Marketing Officer, Senior Vice President
- Brian P. LeClaire—Chief Information Officer, Senior Vice President
- Bonita C. Hathcock—Chief Human Resources Officer, Senior Vice President
- James E. Murray—Chief Operating Officer, Executive Vice President
- Thomas J. Liston—Senior Vice President, Production
- Heidi S. Margulis—Senior Vice President
- Bruce J. Goodman—Chief Information Officer, Senior Vice President
- Steven E. McCulley—Controller, Vice President
- Paul B. Kusserow—Chief Strategy Officer, Senior Vice President
- Christopher M. Todoroff—Senior Vice President
- Bruce D. Broussard—President
- Regina Nethery—Vice President, Investor Relations
- Brian LeClaire—Chief Information Officer, Senior Vice President
- Kurt J. Hilzinger—Director
- Frank A. D'Amelio—Director
- W. Roy Dunbar—Director
- David A. Jones, Jr.—Director
- William J. McDonald—Director
- William E. Mitchell—Director
- David B. Nash—Director
- James J. O'Brien—Director
- Marissa T. Peterson—Director
- Roy A. Beveridge—Chief Human Resources Officer, Senior Vice President, Executive Officer

HISTORICAL REVENUE (TOTAL REVENUE):

- $9,557,000,000 (2012)
- $17,708,000,000 (2011)
- $16,103,300,000 (2010)
- $14,153,500,000 (2009)
- $13,041,800,000 (2008)
- $12,879,000,000 (2007)
- $10,127,500,000 (2006)
- $6,869,600,000 (2005)
- $5,657,600,000 (2004)
- $5,293,300,000 (2003)
- $4,879,900,000 (2002)
- $4,681,600,000 (2001)
- $4,597,500,000 (2000)
- $4,951,500,000 (1999)
- $5,495,600,000 (1998)
- $5,418,000,000 (1997)
- $3,153,000,000 (1996)
- $2,878,000,000 (1995)
- $1,957,000,000 (1994)
- $1,731,000,000 (1993)

Health Care Service Corp.

300 E Randolph St.
Chicago, IL 60601
Phone: (312) 653-6000
Fax: (312)540-0544

Toll free: (800) 654-7385
E-mail: Greg_Thompson@hcsc.net
Website: http://www.hcsc.com

Health Care Service Corporation is a health benefits company that boasts customer ownership. It focuses on health and wellness and provides health and life insurance products and related services. Health Care Service Corporation offers coverage under affiliates such as Blue Shield of Illinois, Blue Cross and Blue Shield of New Mexico, Blue Cross and Blue Shield of Texas, among others. The company claims to be one of the fastest growing in the U.S.

KEY INFORMATION:

- Total Assets: $110,179,000,000
- Employees: 16,000
- Sales Per Employee: $6,886,188
- Year Founded: 1936

OFFICERS:

- Patricia A. Hemingway Hall—Chief Executive Officer, President
- Kenneth S. Avner—Chief Financial Officer, Senior Vice President
- Brian Hedberg—Chief Information Officer, Senior Vice President
- Nazneen Razi—Chief Human Resources Officer, Senior Vice President
- Martin Foster—Executive Vice President, President
- Colleen F. Reitan—Chief Operating Officer, Executive Vice President

HISTORICAL REVENUE (TOTAL REVENUE):

- $110,179,000,000 (2011)
- $1,740,000,000 (2005)
- $1,740,000,000 (2004)
- $1,740,000,000 (2003)
- $1,740,000,000 (2001)
- $1,740,000,000 (1999)
- $1,740,000,000 (1997)
- $1,452,100,000 (1994)
- $1,313,800,000 (1993)
- $1,110,500,000 (1992)
- $959,500,000 (1991)
- $796,000,000 (1990)

Coventry Health Care Inc.

6705 Rockledge Dr., Ste. 700
Bethesda, MD 20817
Phone: (301) 581-0600
Fax: (301) 493-0742
E-mail: Investor-Relations@cvty.com
Website: http://www.coventryhealthcare.com

Coventry Health Care Inc. was incorporated under the laws of the State of Delaware in December 1997 although its roots can be traced back to 1986 through its predecessor, Coventry Corp. The company operates health plans, insurance companies, network rental and workers' compensation services companies. It functions in three divisions: commercial business, individual consumer and government and specialty business. Its commercial business division provides products such as health maintenance organization, preferred provider organization and point of service products to employer groups of all sizes. The company's individual consumer and government division provides health benefits to members of Medicare and Medicaid programs. Its specialty business division provides workers' compensation managed care services and offers provider network rental services through a national PPO network to third party administrators and insurance carriers. Additionally, this division includes the company's mental-behavioral health and dental benefits businesses. The company operates health plans that serve 23 markets, primarily in the mid-Atlantic, midwest and southeast U.S. In 2008, the company acquired Mental Health Network Institutional Services Inc. and majority interest in Group Dental Services. It operates health plans under the names Altius Health Plans, Carelink Health Plans, Coventry Health Care, Coventry Health and Life, Group Health Plan, HealthAmerica, HealthAssurance, HealthCare USA, OmniCare, PersonalCare, Southern Health, Vista and WellPath. Coventry was acquired by Aetna Inc. in 2012.

KEY INFORMATION:

- Total Assets: $8,813,500,000
- Employees: 14,400
- Sales Per Employee: $612,049
- Year Founded: 1986

OFFICERS:

- Allen F. Wise—Chairman of the Board, Chief Executive Officer
- Randy Giles—Chief Financial Officer, Executive Vice President
- Maria Fitzpatrick—Chief Information Officer, Senior Vice President
- Patrisha L. Davis—Chief Human Resources Officer, Senior Vice President
- Joel Ackerman—Director
- L. Dale Crandall—Director
- Lawrence N. Kugelman—Director
- Daniel N. Mendelson—Director
- Rodman W. Moorhead, III—Director
- Michael Stocker—Director
- Joseph R. Swedish—Director
- Elizabeth E. Tallett—Director
- Timothy T. Weglicki—Director
- Drew Asher—Senior Vice President, Finance
- John J. Ruhlmann—Senior Vice President
- Thomas C. Zielinski—Executive Vice President
- Kevin Conlin—Executive Vice President
- Harvey C. DeMovick, Jr.—Executive Vice President
- Michael D. Bahr—Executive Vice President
- Timothy E. Nolan—Executive Vice President
- James E. McGarry—Senior Vice President

HISTORICAL REVENUE (TOTAL REVENUE):

- $8,813,500,000 (2011)
- $8,495,000,000 (2010)
- $8,166,500,000 (2009)

- $7,727,400,000 (2008)
- $7,158,800,000 (2007)
- $5,665,100,000 (2006)
- $4,895,200,000 (2005)
- $2,340,600,000 (2004)
- $1,981,700,000 (2003)
- $1,643,400,000 (2002)
- $1,451,300,000 (2001)
- $1,239,000,000 (2000)
- $1,081,600,000 (1999)
- $2,110,400,000 (1998)

Highmark, Inc.

120 5th Ave.
Pittsburgh, PA 15222-3000
Phone: (412) 544-7000
Fax: (412)544-8368
Website: http://www.highmark.com

Highmark Inc. is a hospital plan and professional health service plan, offering a wide range of insurance coverage for medical, dental, long term care service policies and more options. Highmark was founded when Pennsylvania Blue Shield and Blue Cross of Western Pennsylvania were consolidated to form Highmark. Blue Shield is now Highmark Blue Shield and Blue Cross is now Highmark Blue Cross Blue Shield. The vision that Highmark has for its company is to help provide all member of every community it serves with access to affordable, quality health care. Highmark is an independent licensee of the Blue Cross and Blue Shield Association. This is a private company so stocks are not publicly available for Highmark, Inc.

KEY INFORMATION:

- Total Assets: $13,351,000,000
- Employees: 19,500
- Sales Per Employee: $684,667
- Year Founded: 1996

OFFICERS:

- Dr. Kenneth R. Melani—Chief Executive Officer, President
- Nanette P. DeTurk—Chief Financial Officer, Executive Vice President, Treasurer
- Thomas Kerr—Chief Marketing Officer, Executive Vice President
- Matthew V. T. Ray—Chief Information Officer, Executive Vice President
- William Winkenwerder—Chief Human Resources Officer, Executive Vice President, Chief Strategy
- Officer, Chief Executive Officer, President
- Glen T. Meakem—Director
- Gregory B. Jordan—Director
- J. Robert Baum—Chairman of the Board
- Melissa Anderson—Executive Vice President
- R. Yvonne Campos—Director
- Ray H. Carson—Executive Vice President
- David L. Holmberg—Executive Vice President

- Thomas R. Donahue—Director
- Victor A. Roque—Director

HISTORICAL REVENUE (TOTAL ASSETS):

- $13,351,000,000 (2011)
- $14,036,000,000 (2010)
- $13,694,200,000 (2009)
- $7,767,000,000 (2008)
- $7,767,000,000 (2007)
- $7,767,000,000 (2006)
- $7,767,000,000 (2004)
- $7,767,000,000 (2002)
- $4,744,000,000 (2001)
- $4,830,200,000 (2000)
- $8,190,000,000 (1999)
- $750,000,000 (1998)

Independence Blue Cross

1901 Market St.
Philadelphia, PA 19103-1400
Phone: (215) 241-2400
Fax: (215)241-0403
Toll free: (800) 555-1514
Website: http://www.ibx.com

Insurance: Underwriter of health insurance and preferred provider and health maintenance organization.

KEY INFORMATION:

- Total Assets: $3,605,000,000
- Employees: 6,000
- Sales Per Employee: $600,833
- Year Founded: 1938

OFFICERS:

- Chris Butler—Chief Operating Officer, Executive Vice President
- John G. Foos—Chief Financial Officer
- William F. Haggett—Chief Marketing Officer
- Chris Butler—Chief Operating Officer, Executive Vice President
- Virginia Barakat—Vice President, Human Resources
- Joseph A. Frick—Chief Executive Officer, President
- Carolyn W. Luther—Senior Vice President, Information Systems
- Christopher Cashman—Senior Vice President, Corporate Communications
- John A. Daddis—Senior Vice President, Operations
- Robert J. Fascia—Senior Vice President
- Richard J. Neeson—Senior Vice President
- Paul A. Tufano—Senior Vice President
- Daniel C. Lyons—Senior Vice President
- Robert A. McKeown—Senior Vice President
- Robert H. Young—Chairman of the Board
- Robert W. Sorrell—Vice Chairman of the Board
- Linda Taylor—Director, Marketing

HISTORICAL REVENUE (TOTAL ASSETS):

- $3,605,000,000 (2010)
- $3,605,000,000 (2009)
- $5,708,000,000 (2007)
- $6,008,000,000 (2005)
- $3,605,300,000 (2003)
- $3,274,000,000 (2002)
- $2,128,000,000 (2001)
- $2,127,600,000 (1999)
- $13,558,000,000 (1998)
- $11,621,000,000 (1997)
- $938,500,000 (1993)
- $940,700,000 (1992)
- $895,600,000 (1991)
- $884,300,000 (1990)

Blue Shield of California

50 Beale Street
San Francisco, CA 94105-1808
Phone: (415) 229-5000
Toll free: (800) 393-6130
Website: https://www.blueshieldca.com

KEY INFORMATION:

- Annual Revenue: $10.5 billion
- Employees: 5,000
- Year Founded: 1939

OFFICERS:

- Paul Markovich—President and Chief Executive Officer
- Juan Davila—Executive Vice President, Health Care Quality and Affordability
- Rob Geyer—Senior Vice President, Customer Quality
- Kirsten Gorsuch—Senior Vice President, External Affairs
- John Hedberg—Senior Vice President, Consumer and Small Business Market
- Jeff Hermosillo—Senior Vice President, Enterprise Sales and Service
- Seth A. Jacobs, Esq.—Senior Vice President, General Counsel and Corporate Secretary
- Michael Mathias—Senior Vice President and Chief Information Officer
- Michael Murray—Senior Vice President and Chief Financial Officer
- Mary O'Hara—Senior Vice President and Chief Human Resources Officer
- Marcus Thygeson, M.D.—Senior Vice President, Chief Health Officer
- Janet Widmann—Executive Vice President, Markets

HISTORICAL ASSETS (TOTAL ASSETS):

- $6,052,000,000 (2012)
- $5,679,000,000 (2011)
- $5,329,000,000 (2010)

CIGNA Corp.

900 Cottage Grove Rd.
Bloomfield, CT 06002
Phone: (860) 226-6000
Fax: (860)226-6741
Toll free: (800) 244-6224
E-mail: info@cigna.com
Website: http://www.cigna.com

CIGNA Corp. provides health care and related benefits in the United States and internationally. It operates in five segments: Health Care, Disability and Life, International, Run-off Reinsurance and Other Operations. The Health Care segment offers insured and self-funded medical, dental, behavioral health, vision and prescription drug benefit plans; health advocacy programs; other products and services that provide individuals with health care benefit programs; and disability and life insurance products, as well as operating retail pharmacies. The Disability and Life segment provides various insurance products and related services, including group long-term and short-term disability insurance, as well as case management and related services to workers' compensation insurers and employers; group life insurance products comprising group term life and group universal life; and personal accident insurance consisting of accidental death and dismemberment and travel accident insurance to employers. This segment also offers specialty insurance services that consist primarily of disability and life, accident and medical insurance to professional associations, financial institutions and participant organizations. The International segment offers life, accident and supplemental health insurance products, as well as international health care products and services. The Run-off Reinsurance segment manages its run-off reinsurance coverage for risks written by other insurance companies under life and annuity, accident and health policies. The Other Operations segment offers corporate-owned life insurance, which consists of permanent insurance contracts sold to corporations to provide coverage on the lives of certain employees. CIGNA distributes its products and services through consultants, independent brokers, agents and direct sales personnel as well as the Internet.

KEY INFORMATION:

- Total Assets: $51,047,000,000
- Employees: 31,400
- Sales Per Employee: $1,625,701
- Year Founded: 1981

OFFICERS:

- David M. Cordani—Chief Executive Officer, President
- Ralph J. Nicoletti—Chief Financial Officer, Executive Vice President
- Mark Boxer—Chief Information Officer, Executive Vice President
- John M. Murabito—Executive Vice President, Human Resources
- Nicole S. Jones—General Counsel
- Jeffrey Kang—Officer
- Maggie FitzPatrick—Director, Corporate Communications, Manager
- William Atwell—President
- Matt Manders—President

- Herb Fritch—President
- David Guilmette—President
- Shawn Morris—President
- Tom McCarthy—Vice President, Finance
- Susan Gaca—Officer
- Alan Muney—Officer
- Eric J. Foss—Director
- Ike Harris—Director
- Jane Henney—Director
- Roman Martinez, IV—Director
- John M. Partridge—Director
- James E. Rogers—Director
- Joseph P. Sullivan—Director
- Nicole Jones—Executive Vice President
- Ralph Nicoletti—Chief Financial Officer
- Annmarie Hagan—Chief Financial Officer, Executive Vice President
- Michael D. Woeller—Executive Vice President, Chief Information Officer
- Carol Ann Petren—General Counsel
- Eric C. Wiseman—Director
- Donna F. Zarcone—Director
- William D. Zollars—Director
- Joan Kennedy—Vice President
- Alan M. Muney—Officer

HISTORICAL REVENUE (TOTAL REVENUE):

- $51,047,000,000 (2011)
- $13,000,000 (2010)
- $13,000,000 (2009)
- $13,000,000 (2008)
- $40,065,000,000 (2007)
- $42,399,000,000 (2006)
- $44,863,000,000 (2005)
- $81,059,000,000 (2004)
- $90,953,000,000 (2003)
- $88,950,000,000 (2002)
- $91,589,000,000 (2001)
- $95,088,000,000 (2000)
- $95,333,000,000 (1999)
- $114,612,000,000 (1998)
- $108,199,000,000 (1997)
- $95,903,000,000 (1995)
- $86,102,000,000 (1994)
- $84,975,000,000 (1993)
- $69,827,000,000 (1992)
- $66,737,000,000 (1991)
- $63,691,000,000 (1990)

Blue Cross and Blue Shield of Michigan Inc.
PO Box 44407
Detroit, MI 48244
Phone: (313) 225-9000
Fax: (313)225-6239
Toll free: (877) 469-2583
E-mail: contact@bcbsm.com
Website: http://www.bcbsm.com

Insurance: Underwriter of health insurance, preferred provider and health maintenance organization.

KEY INFORMATION:

- Total Assets: $2,197,000,000
- Employees: 7,500
- Sales Per Employee: $292,933
- Year Founded: 1939

OFFICERS:

- Daniel Loepp—Chief Executive Officer
- Mark R. Bartlett—Chief Financial Officer
- Kevin Seitz—Executive Vice President
- Kenneth Dallafior—Senior Vice President
- Thomas Simmer—Senior Vice President

HISTORICAL REVENUE (TOTAL REVENUE):

- $2,197,000,000 (2011)
- $2,197,000,000 (2010)
- $2,197,000,000 (2009)
- $2,503,000,000 (2008)
- $2,343,000,000 (2007)
- $2,343,000,000 (2006)
- $2,343,000,000 (2005)
- $2,343,000,000 (2004)
- $2,343,000,000 (2003)
- $2,527,000,000 (2002)
- $2,585,000,000 (2000)
- $2,585,000,000 (1998)
- $2,914,500,000 (1997)
- $1,962,000,000 (1996)
- $1,903,000,000 (1994)
- $2,626,100,000 (1993)
- $2,488,600,000 (1992)
- $2,153,000,000 (1991)
- $1,927,000,000 (1990)

Health Net Inc.
21650 Oxnard St.
Woodland Hills, CA 91367
Phone: (818) 676-6000
Fax: (818)676-8591
Toll free: (800) 291-6911
E-mail: Investor.Relations@healthnet.com
Website: http://www.health.net

Founded in 1985, Health Net, Inc. is a publicly traded managed care organization that delivers managed health care services through health plans and government-sponsored managed care plans. Its mission is to help people be healthy, secure and comfortable. The company provides health benefits to approximately 6 million individuals across the country through group, individual, Medicare (including the Medicare prescription drug benefit commonly referred to as "Part D"), Medicaid, Department of Defense, including TRICARE, and Veterans Affairs programs. Health Net's behavioral health services subsidiary, Managed Health Network, Inc., provides behavioral health, substance abuse and employee assistance programs to approximately 5.4 million individuals, including Health Net's own health plan members. The company's subsidiaries also offer managed health care products related to prescription drugs, and offer managed health care product coordination for multi-region employers and administrative services for medical groups and self-funded benefits programs. On November 19, 2010, the Centers for Medicare and Medicaid Services suspended Health Net immediately because the insurer improperly administered the Medicare drug benefit in contracts for its national prescription drug plan and local Medicare Advantage prescription drug plans. The suspension required Health Net to cease the marketing and enrollment of new members of all Health Net Medicare Advantage Prescription Drug and stand-alone Prescription Drug Plan contracts, effective November 20, 2010. The sanctions relate to compliance with certain Part D requirements. The suspension did not affect existing Health Net Medicare enrollees.

KEY INFORMATION:

- Total Assets: $3,607,700,000
- Employees: 7,351
- Sales Per Employee: $490,777
- Year Founded: 1985

OFFICERS:

- Jay M. Gellert—Chief Executive Officer
- Jonathan Rollins—Treasurer
- Jonathan Rollins—Vice President
- James E. Woys—Chief Operating Officer
- Patricia T. Clarey—Senior Vice President
- Karin D. Mayhew—Senior Vice President
- Linda V. Tiano—President
- Steven J. Sell—President
- Steven D. Tough—President
- Angelee F. Bouchard—General Counsel
- Chris Ellertson—President
- Scott R. Kelly—Officer
- Bret A. Morris—President
- Marie Montgomery—Controller, Senior Vice President
- Joseph C. Capezza—Chief Financial Officer, Executive Vice President
- Juanell Hefner—Senior Vice President
- Roger F. Greaves—Director
- Mary Anne Citrino—Director
- Theodore F. Craver, Jr.—Director
- Vicki B. Escarra—Director
- Gale S. Fitzgerald—Director
- Patrick Foley—Director
- Bruce G. Willison—Director
- Frederick C. Yeager—Director

HISTORICAL REVENUE (TOTAL ASSETS):

- $3,607,700,000 (2011)
- $4,131,700,000 (2010)
- $4,282,700,000 (2009)
- $4,816,400,000 (2008)
- $4,933,000,000 (2007)
- $4,297,000,000 (2006)
- $3,940,700,000 (2005)
- $3,641,900,000 (2004)
- $3,549,200,000 (2003)
- $3,460,700,000 (2002)
- $3,566,800,000 (2001)
- $3,670,100,000 (2000)
- $3,696,500,000 (1999)
- $3,863,300,000 (1998)
- $4,076,300,000 (1997)
- $3,204,100,000 (1996)
- $1,213,700,000 (1995)
- $894,400,000 (1994)
- $606,500,000 (1993)

Horizon Healthcare Services Inc.

PO Box 820
Newark, NJ 07101-0820
Phone: (973) 466-4000
Fax: (973)466-7550
Toll free: (800) 355-2583
E-mail: horizon_helpdesk@horizonblue.com
Website: http://www.bcbsnj.com

Horizon Healthcare Services Inc. was founded in 1932. It is a not-for-profit organization that sells insurance. Plans offered include Horizon HMO, Horizon Point of Service, Horizon Preferred Provider Organization, Horizon Direct Access Open Access, Horizon Medical Savings Account and Traditional Indemnity Plans. Customers with mental health and substance abuse treatment needs get help from Magellan Behavioral Health through Horizon Blue Cross Blue Shield New Jersey. Magellan provides 24-hour service to those customers. The administrator of the Horizon Blue Cross Blue Shield dental plans is Horizon Healthcare Dental Services. Horizon Casualty Services handles workers' compensation and auto injury management services. Horizon Healthcare is the only provider of Blue Cross Blue Shield plans in the state of New Jersey, and its coverage area is all of North, Central and South New Jersey. There are affiliates of Horizon Healthcare Services Inc. that don't offer Blue Cross Blue Shield plans. Rayant Insurance Company of New York and Rayant Insurance Agency, Inc. are both affiliates of Horizon.

KEY INFORMATION:

- Total Assets: $4,652,700,000
- Employees: 5,200
- Sales Per Employee: $894,750
- Year Founded: 1932

OFFICERS:

- Robert A. Marino—Chief Executive Officer, President, Chairman
- Robert Pures—Chief Financial Officer, Senior Vice President
- Douglas E. Blackwell—Chief Information Officer, Senior Vice President
- Lawrence B. Altman—Vice President of Marketing
- Christopher M. Lepre—Vice President of Sales

- Margaret Coons—Vice President of Human Resources
- Patrick Geraghty—Senior Vice President
- Carol Banks—Vice President
- Donna Celestini—Vice President
- Jackie Jennifer—Vice President
- John J. Lynch—Vice President
- Dr. Richard Popiel—Director of Research
- Robert E. Meehan—Vice President
- Vincent J. Giblin—Chairman of the Board
- Kenneth A. Brause—Vice President
- John W. Campbell—Head of Legal Department
- David R. Huber—Senior Vice President, Administration
- William J. Marino—Chief Executive Officer, President
- Christy W. Bell—Senior Vice President
- Charles C. Emery,, Jr.—Chief Information Officer, Senior Vice President
- Mark Barnard—Senior Vice President

HISTORICAL REVENUE (TOTAL ASSETS):

- $4,652,700,000 (2011)
- $4,474,500,000 (2010)
- $3,345,000,000 (2009)
- $3,023,000,000 (2007)
- $3,023,000,000 (2006)
- $2,766,000,000 (2005)
- $2,765,700,000 (2004)
- $2,571,600,000 (2003)
- $2,237,900,000 (2002)
- $1,425,400,000 (2001)
- $1,243,600,000 (2000)
- $1,238,500,000 (1999)
- $99,000,000 (1998)
- $992,500,000 (1997)
- $992,500,000 (1994)
- $992,500,000 (1993)
- $916,300,000 (1992)
- $897,100,000 (1991)
- $933,700,000 (1990)

Regence Group
PO Box 1071
Portland, OR 97207
Phone: (503) 225-5221
Fax: (503)225-5274
Toll free: (800) 452-7278
E-mail: wa_info@regence.com
Website: http://www.regence.com

Insurance: Health maintenance and preferred provider organization and underwriter of health and life insurance. Finance: Holding company.

KEY INFORMATION:

- Total Assets: $4,968,000,000
- Employees: 6,543
- Sales Per Employee: $759,285
- Year Founded: 1940

OFFICERS:

- Mark B. Ganz—President
- Vince Price—Chief Financial Officer
- Cheron Vail—Chief Information Officer
- Mohan Nair—Executive Vice President
- Steve Hooker—Chief Financial Officer, Senior Vice President
- Bill Barr—Executive Vice President
- David Clark—Senior Vice President
- JoAnn Long—Senior Vice President
- Peggy Maguire—Vice President

HISTORICAL REVENUE (TOTAL ASSETS):

- $4,968,000,000 (2010)
- $4,968,000,000 (2009)
- $4,968,000,000 (2007)
- $4,556,000,000 (2005)
- $4,556,000,000 (2004)
- $4,176,000,000 (2002)
- $4,100,000,000 (2001)
- $783,000,000 (2000)
- $2,049,000,000 (1998)
- $2,048,800,000 (1997)

Carefirst of Maryland Inc.
10455 Mill Run Cir.
Owings Mills, MD 21117-4208
Phone: (410) 581-3000
Fax: (410)998-5576
Toll free: (800) 321-3497
Website: http://www.member.carefirst.com

Insurance: Underwriter of health insurance and preferred provider organization serving southern Delaware, Maryland, Washington DC, and northern Virginia.

KEY INFORMATION:

- Total Assets: $4,500,000,000
- Employees: 6,000
- Sales Per Employee: $750,000
- Year Founded: 1984

OFFICERS:

- Louise Hamil—Director
- Lasandra Teixeira—Director, Finance and Administration
- Mike Felber—Director, Marketing
- Eric Strausman—Director, Management Information Systems
- Jackie Slayer—Director, Human Resources
- Joanna Cannon—Manager, Marketing
- Debby Lloyd—Director, Corporate Communications
- Elizabeth Hammond—Director
- Margo Mcintyre—Director
- Mark Scrimshire—Director

- James Bailey—Manager
- Patricia Davis—Manager
- Sherin Hawkins—Manager
- Gwendolyn Skillern—Vice President
- Maria Tildon—Vice President
- Steve Wiggins—Vice President
- Stephanie Heckart—Director
- John Hamper—Manager
- Maryanne Ustead—Manager
- Brian Porter—Manager
- Denise Ambrose—Analyst
- Robert George—Analyst
- Chester Burrell—Chief Executive Officer, President
- Michael Merson—Chairman of the Board
- Gregory Devou—Chief Marketing Officer, Executive Vice President
- Jason Littlefield—Manager
- Eric Baugh—President
- Joseph Petraila—Secretary
- Ann Gallant—Vice President
- Ed Mallon—Vice President
- Mike Mcshain—Vice President
- Kevin O'neil—Vice President
- Glenn Rothman—Vice President

HISTORICAL REVENUE (TOTAL REVENUE):

- $4,500,000,000 (2007)
- $4,500,000,000 (2005)
- $4,500,000,000 (2004)
- $4,500,000,000 (2003)
- $4,500,000,000 (2002)
- $4,500,000,000 (2000)
- $4,500,000,000 (1999)
- $3,900,000,000 (1998)
- $916,700,000 (1996)
- $340,000,000 (1995)
- $343,100,000 (1993)
- $410,000,000 (1992)
- $761,300,000 (1991)
- $783,000,000 (1990)

WellCare Health Plans Inc.

PO Box 31372
Tampa, FL 33631-3372
Phone: (813) 290-6200
Fax: (813)262-2802
Toll free: (866) 530-9491
E-mail: investorrelations@wellcare.com
Website: http://www.wellcare.com

WellCare Health Plans Inc. provides managed care services targeted exclusively to government-sponsored health care programs, focused on Medicaid and Medicare (which encompass the company's two business segments), including prescription drug plans and health plans for families, children and the aged, blind and disabled. The plans include those for beneficiaries of Temporary Assistance for Needy Families programs; Supplemental Security Income programs; and ABD programs and state-based programs, such as Children's Health Insurance Programs and Family Health Plus programs for qualifying families who are not eligible for Medicaid. The company operates these health plans in multiple states. The company is traded publicly on the New York Stock Exchange under the symbol WCG.

KEY INFORMATION:

- Sales: $2,488,100,000
- Employees: 3,990
- Sales Per Employee: $623,584
- Year Founded: 1985

OFFICERS:

- Alec R. Cunningham—Chief Executive Officer, Director
- Thomas L. Tran—Chief Financial Officer, Senior Vice President
- Lawrence D. Anderson—Chief Human Resources Officer, Vice President
- Jesse Thomas—President
- Walter W. Cooper—Chief Administration Officer
- Marc Russo—President
- Ann Wehr—Officer
- Daniel R. Paquin—President
- Lisa G. Iglesias—Senior Vice President
- Charles G. Berg—Chairman of the Board
- Carol Burt—Director
- David J. Gallitano—Director
- D. Robert Graham—Director
- Kevin F. Hickey—Director
- Christian P. Michalik—Director
- Glenn D. Steele—Director
- William L. Trubeck—Director
- Paul E. Weaver—Director
- Rex M. Adams—Chief Operating Officer, Senior Vice President
- Jonathan P. Rich—Senior Vice President
- Timothy S. Susanin—Senior Vice President
- Scott D. Law—Senior Vice President
- Blair W. Todt—Senior Vice President
- Christina C. Cooper—President

HISTORICAL REVENUE (SALES):

- $2,488,100,000 (2012)
- $2,488,100,000 (2011)
- $2,247,300,000 (2010)
- $2,118,400,000 (2009)
- $2,203,500,000 (2008)
- $2,082,000,000 (2007)
- $1,664,000,000 (2006)
- $896,000,000 (2005)
- $803,000,000 (2004)
- $497,100,000 (2003)

EmblemHealth Inc.

55 Water St.
New York, NY 10041
Phone: (646) 447-5000
Fax: (646)447-3011
Toll free: (877) 411-3625
Website: http://www.emblemhealth.com

EmblemHealth Inc., through subsidiaries Group Health Inc. (GHI) and Health Insurance Plan of New York (HIP), is the largest health insurer based in New York, serving more than 3.4 million members. There are more than 106,000 participating providers in 150,000 locations throughout New York, New Jersey, and Connecticut. Formed as a holding company for GHI and HIP, both not-for-profit organizations, EmblemHealth offers a full range of medical, hospital, dental, mental health, vision, and prescription drug plans.

KEY INFORMATION:

- Sales: $8,610,000,000
- Employees: 5,400
- Sales Per Employee: $1,594,444
- Year Founded: 2006

OFFICERS:

- Richard Berman—Director
- Michael Fullwood—Chief Financial Officer, Executive Vice President
- Frank Branchini—Chief Operating Officer, President
- Thomas A. Nemeth—Senior Vice President, Human Resources
- Anthony Watson—Chairman of the Board, Chief Executive Officer
- Michael Wise—President
- Nicholas P. Kambolis—General Counsel

HISTORICAL REVENUE (TOTAL REVENUE):

- $8,610,000,000 (2008)

Unum Group
1 Fountain Sq.
Chattanooga, TN 37402
Phone: (423) 294-1011
Toll free: (800) 887-2180
E-mail: investorrelations@unum.com
Website: http://www.unum.com

Unum Group provides disability insurance products in the U.S. and the U.K. It also provides a portfolio of other insurance products and related services. The company has three major business segments: Unum US, Unum UK and Colonial Life. The Unum US segment includes group long-term and short-term disability insurance, group life and accidental death and dismemberment products, and supplemental and voluntary lines of business issued primarily by Unum America, Provident and Paul Revere Life. The Unum UK segment includes group long-term disability insurance, group life products, and individual disability products issued by Unum Limited and sold primarily in the U.K. through field sales personnel and independent brokers. The Colonial Life segment includes insurance for accident, sickness, and disability; life products; and cancer and critical illness products issued primarily by Colonial Life and Accident Insurance Company and marketed to employees at the workplace through an agency sales force and brokers. The company was previously known as Unum Provident Corporation, and acquired its current name in 2007.

KEY INFORMATION:

- Operating Revenue: $2,658,200,000
- Employees: 9,400
- Sales Per Employee: $282,787
- Year Founded: 1848

OFFICERS:

- Susan Ring—Chief Executive Officer
- Richard P. McKenney—Chief Financial Officer, Executive Vice President
- Joseph R. Foley—Chief Marketing Officer, Senior Vice President
- Kate Miller—Senior Vice President, Chief Information Officer
- Diane Garofalo—Senior Vice President, Human Resources
- Theodore Bunting—Director
- Wendy Walker—Director
- E. Michael Caulfield—Director
- William J. Ryan—Chairman of the Board
- Timothy F. Keaney—Director
- Thomas R. Watjen—Chief Executive Officer, President, Director
- Kevin P. McCarthy—Chief Operating Officer, Executive Vice President
- E. Michael Caulfield—Director
- Pamela H. Godwin—Director
- Ronald E. Goldsberry—Director
- Kevin T. Kabat—Director
- Thomas Kinser—Director
- Gloria C. Larson—Director
- A.S. MacMillan, Jr.—Director
- Edward J. Muhl—Director
- Michael J. Passarella—Director

HISTORICAL REVENUE (OPERATING REVENUE):

- $2,658,200,000 (2012)
- $60,179,000,000 (2011)
- $57,307,700,000 (2010)
- $54,477,000,000 (2009)
- $49,417,400,000 (2008)
- $52,432,700,000 (2007)
- $52,823,300,000 (2006)
- $51,866,800,000 (2005)
- $50,832,300,000 (2004)
- $49,718,300,000 (2003)
- $45,259,500,000 (2002)
- $42,442,700,000 (2001)
- $40,363,900,000 (2000)
- $38,447,500,000 (1999)

Universal American Corp.
6 International Dr.
Rye Brook, NY 10573-1068
Phone: (914) 934-5200
Fax: (914)934-0700
Toll free: (800) 975-8089
E-mail: info@universalamerican.com
Website: http://www.universalamerican.com

Universal American Corporation was incorporated on August 31, 1981 in New York and on December 3, 2007, the company began trading on the New York Stock Exchange (UAM). Universal American's insurance subsidiaries are authorized to sell health insurance, life insurance and annuities in all 50 states, the District of Columbia, Puerto Rico and some U.S. territories. The company's Senior Managed Care-Medicare Advantage segment reflects the company's Medicare Advantage HMO, PFFS and PPO businesses. Their plans provide all basic Medicare covered benefits with reduced member cost-sharing as well as additional supplemental benefits, including a defined prescription drug benefit. Universal American offers the products TexanPlus, TexanFirst Health Plans, Today's Health, Today's Options and Today's Options PPO. Universal American's Medicare Part D segment includes PrescribaRxSM and Community CCRxSM products. The company's traditional insurance segment reflects its Medicare supplement, other senior, life and specialty health insurance and annuity products marketed through the company's Senior Solutions career agencies. Universal American's Senior Administrative Services segment provides outsourcing services to companies that support the senior market. The company's corporate segment reflects debt service, which is a portion of senior executive compensation and compliance with regulatory requirements resulting from its status as a public company.

KEY INFORMATION:

- Sales: $2,388,500,000
- Employees: 2,300
- Sales Per Employee: $1,038,478
- Year Founded: 1981

OFFICERS:

- Richard A. Barasch—Chairman of the Board, Chief Executive Officer
- Robert A. Waegelein—Chief Financial Officer, Co-President
- Robert M. Hayes—Senior Vice President
- Jason J. Israel—President
- Patrick J. McLaughlin—Director
- Richard Perry—Director
- Sally W. Crawford—Director
- Thomas A. Scully—Director
- Matthew W. Etheridge—Director
- Robert A. Spass—Director
- Mark K. Gormley—Director
- Sean M. Traynor—Director
- Mark M. Harmeling—Director
- Christopher E. Wolfe—Director
- David S. Katz—Director
- Robert F. Wright—Director
- Linda H. Lamel—Director
- Theodore M. Carpenter, Jr.—Chief Executive Officer, President
- John Wardle—President

HISTORICAL REVENUE (SALES):

- $2,388,500,000 (2012)
- $2,282,720,000 (2011)
- $3,501,780,000 (2010)
- $2,979,390,000 (2009)
- $2,835,920,000 (2008)
- $4,089,800,000 (2007)
- $2,585,000,000 (2006)
- $2,227,000,000 (2005)
- $2,017,100,000 (2004)
- $1,780,900,000 (2003)
- $1,401,700,000 (2002)
- $1,270,200,000 (2001)
- $1,189,900,000 (2000)
- $1,153,400,000 (1999)
- $283,300,000 (1998)
- $272,600,000 (1997)
- $242,200,000 (1996)
- $183,000,000 (1995)
- $164,900,000 (1994)
- $95,600,000 (1992)
- $87,000,000 (1991)
- $60,000,000 (1990)

Blue Cross and Blue Shield of North Carolina

PO Box 2291
Durham, NC 27702-2291
Phone: (919) 489-7431
Fax: (919)765-7818
Toll free: (800) 250-3630
Website: http://www.bcbsnc.com

Blue Cross Blue Shield of North Carolina was founded in 1933. The not-for-profit health insurance company offers health care products, services and information to more than 3.7 million people in North Carolina. The company offers several types of insurance plans, including PPO, HMO, Indemnity and BlueCard products, for individuals, families, small businesses (1 to 50 employees), medium businesses (51 to 99 employees), and large businesses (100+ employees). Blue Cross Blue Shield of North Carolina also offers Medicaid plans and dental insurance plans. The company's health provider network includes 92% of medical doctors and 99% of hospitals in North Carolina.

KEY INFORMATION:

- Total Assets: $29,036,000,000
- Employees: 4,600
- Sales Per Employee: $6,312,174
- Year Founded: 1933

OFFICERS:

- J. Bradley Wilson—Chief Executive Officer, President
- Daniel E. Glaser—Chief Financial Officer
- Alan Hughes—Chief Information Officer, Senior Vice President
- Fara M. Palumbo—Chief Human Resources Officer, Senior Vice President
- Gerald Petkau—Chief Financial Officer, Senior Vice President

- John T. Roos—Senior Vice President, Marketing and Sales
- Robert Greczyn—Chief Executive Officer, President

HISTORICAL REVENUE (TOTAL REVENUE):

- $29,036,000,000 (2011)
- $29,036,000,000 (2010)
- $29,036,000,000 (2009)
- $30,930,000,000 (2008)
- $28,405,000,000 (2007)
- $23,355,000,000 (2006)

- $23,355,000,000 (2005)
- $22,724,000,000 (2004)
- $18,937,000,000 (2003)
- $890,000,000 (2000)
- $890,000,000 (1998)
- $889,700,000 (1997)
- $771,200,000 (1994)
- $771,200,000 (1993)
- $667,900,000 (1992)
- $562,900,000 (1991)

FEDERAL HEALTH INFORMATION CENTERS
AND CLEARINGHOUSES

The following is a list of federal health information centers and clearinghouses that provide free public information and resources. Many offer toll-free numbers and websites. Their services include distributing publications, providing referrals, and answering questions.

The list is arranged alphabetically by keyword, which appears in the organization or agency's title in uppercase letters (for example, "AGING" in the first entry below).

Most phone numbers can be reached Monday through Friday during normal business hours (eastern time), except on Federal holidays or when otherwise noted.

This directory is compiled every year by the National Health Information Center, which is a service of the Office of Disease Prevention and Health Promotion (ODPHP), Office of Public Health and Science, U.S. Department of Health and Human Services.

[Source: 2013 Federal Health Information Centers and Clearinghouses, National Health Information Center, Office of Disease Prevention and Health Promotion, U.S. Department of Health and Human Services, Washington, DC.]

A

National AGING Information and Referral Support Center, National Association of State Units on Aging
1201 15th Street NW, Suite 350
Washington, DC 20005
Phone: (202) 898-2578
Fax: (202) 898-2583
E-mail: info@nasua.org
Website: http://www.nasuad.org/I_R/ir_index.html

The National Aging Information and Referral Support Center is designed to enhance the capacity of aging information and referral/assistance (I&R/A) systems to provide the information, counseling, decision supports, and advocacy needed to secure services and benefits for an ever-growing and increasingly diverse population of older persons and caregivers. Major funding for the center is provided by the U.S. Administration on Aging. The center provides a full range of assistance at the state and local levels on I&R/A systems design and management, quality improvements in I&R/A service delivery, and professionalism and training of the aging I&R/A workforce. Hours of operation: 9:00 a.m.–5:00 p.m., Monday–Friday (eastern time, except Federal holidays).

National Institute on AGING Information Center
P.O. Box 8057
Gaithersburg, MD 20898-8057
Toll free: (800) 222-2225
Phone: (301) 496-1752
TTY: (800) 222-4225
Fax: (301) 589-3014

E-mail: niaic@nih.mail.gov
Website: http://www.nia.nih.gov

The National Institute on Aging Information Center provides publications on health topics of interest to older adults, doctors, nurses, social activities directors, health educators, and the public. Hours of operation: 8:30 a.m.–5:00 p.m., Monday–Friday (eastern time, except Federal holidays).

ALZHEIMER'S DISEASE Education and Referral Center, National Institute on Aging
P.O. Box 8250
Silver Spring, MD 20907-8250
Toll free: (800) 438-4380
Fax: (301) 495-3334
Website: http://www.nia.nih.gov/alzheimers

The Alzheimer's Disease Education and Referral (ADEAR) Center provides information about Alzheimer's disease and related disorders to health professionals, patients and their families, and the public. Most of the publications are provided at no charge as a service of the National Institute on Aging, one of the Federal Government's National Institutes of Health. Hours of operation: 8:30 a.m.–5:00 p.m., Monday–Friday (eastern time, except Federal holidays).

ASPE Library, Office of the Assistant Secretary for Planning and Evaluation, U.S. Department of Health and Human Services
Hubert H. Humphrey Building, Room 443-F, 200 Independence Avenue, SW
Washington, DC 20201
Phone: (202) 690-6445
E-mail: pic@hhs.gov
Website: http://aspe.hhs.gov/library

The ASPE library is a centralized repository of evaluations, short-term evaluative research reports and program inspections/audits relevant to the department's operations, programs, and policies. Final reports and executive summaries are available for review at the facility, some may be purchased from the National Technical Information Service. Others are linked as full-text documents to abstract records in the Evaluation Database. In addition, the HHS Evaluation Database is accessible through the ASPE Web site, http://aspe.hhs.gov. The database includes more than 9,000 project descriptions of both in-process and completed studies. Hours of operation: 8:30 a.m.–4:30 p.m., Monday–Friday (eastern time, except Federal holidays).

National Institute of ARTHRITIS and MUSCULOSKELETAL and SKIN DISEASES Information Clearinghouse, NIAMS/National Institutes of Health

1 AMS Circle
Bethesda, MD 20892-3675
Toll free: (877) 22-NIAMS (226-4267)
Phone: (301) 495-4484
TTY: (301) 565-2966
Fax: (301) 718-6366
E-mail: niamsinfo@mail.nih.gov
Website: http://www.niams.nih.gov

The National Institute of Arthritis and Musculoskeletal and Skin Diseases (NIAMS) Information Clearinghouse serves the public, patients, and health professionals by providing information about bones, joints, muscles, and skin, locating other information sources, creating health information materials, and participating in a national federal database on health information. Hours of operation: 8:30 a.m.–5:00 p.m., Monday–Friday (eastern time, except Federal holidays).

AbleData (ASSISTIVE DEVICES, REHABILITATION)

8630 Fenton Street, Suite 930
Silver Spring, MD 20910
Toll free: (800) 227-0216
TTY: (301) 608-8912
Fax: (301) 608-8958
E-mail: abledata@macrointernational.com
Website: http://www.abledata.com/abledata.cfm

AbleData is an internationally recognized resource for objective information on assistive technology and rehabilitation equipment, serving the Nation's disability, rehabilitation, and senior communities. Offering the most comprehensive listing of assistive products available, AbleData provides information on more than 40,000 assistive products, 5,000 manufacturers and distributors, and 3,000 disability-related organizations as well as abstracts of over 11,000 books and articles relating to assistive technology. AbleData provides detailed descriptions of each product's functions and features, price information (when available), and contact information for the manufacturer and distributors. The AbleData website, www.abledata.com offers freee, 24/7 access to all of AbleData's information resources. AbleData staff are available to respond to public inquiries about assistive technology by telephone via a toll-free number as well as by

email, fax, text telephone, and regular mail. Staff are available 8:30 a.m.–5:30 p.m., Monday–Friday (eastern time) except Federal holidays. AbleData is funded by the National Institute on Disablity and Rehabilitation Research, U.S. Department of Education.

National AUDIOVISUAL Center, National Technical Information Service, U.S. Department of Commerce

5301 Shawnee Road
Alexandria, VA 22312
Toll free: (800) 553-NTIS (553-6847)
Phone: (703) 605-6000
Fax: (703) 605-6900
E-mail: info@ntis.gov
Website: http://www.ntis.gov/products/nac.aspx

The National Audiovisual Center is a unique centralized resource for federally developed training and education materials. Its collection contains more than 9,000 audiovisual and media productions. The range of subject areas includes training in occupational safety and health, fire services, law enforcement, and foreign languages. Information and educational materials include areas such as history, health, agriculture, and natural resources. Hours of operation: 8:00 a.m.–6:00 p.m., Monday–Friday (eastern time, except Federal holidays).

B

National Library Service for the BLIND and PHYSICALLY HANDICAPPED, Library of Congress, Reference Section

1291 Taylor Street NW
Washington, DC 20542-0001
Phone: (202) 707-5100
TTY: (202) 707-0744
Fax: (202) 707-0712
E-mail: nls@loc.gov
Website: http://www.loc.gov/nls

The National Library Service for the Blind and Physically Handicapped administers a national library service that provides braille and recorded books and magazines on free loan to eligible residents of the United States or American citizens living abroad who cannot read or use standard printed materials because of permanent or temporary visual or physical disabilities. Hours of operation: 8:00 a.m.–4:30 p.m., Monday–Friday (eastern time, except Federal holidays).

C

CANCER Information Service, Office of Communications and Education, National Cancer Institute

6116 Executive Boulevard, Suite 300
Bethesda, MD 20892-8322

Toll free: (800) 4-CANCER (422-6237)
Toll free: (877) 44U-QUIT (448-7848) (Smoking Cessation)
E-mail: cancergovstaff@mail.nih.gov
Website: http://www.cancer.gov

The Cancer Information Service (CIS) provides information about cancer and cancer-related resources to patients, the public, and health professionals. Inquiries are handled by trained information specialists and Spanish-speaking staff members are available. CIS distributes free publications from the National Cancer Institute. Hours of operation: Phone— 8:00 a.m.–8:00 p.m., and Live Help/Chat—8:00 a.m.–11:00 p.m., Monday–Friday (eastern time, except Federal holidays).

National CHILD CARE INFORMATION and TECHNICAL ASSISTANCE Center, Administration for Children and Families
9300 Lee Highway
Fairfax, VA 22031
Toll free: (800) 616-2242
Fax: (800) 716-2242
E-mail: info@nccic.org
Website: http://nccic.acf.hhs.gov

The National Child Care Information and Technical Assistance Center (NCCIC), a service of the Child Care Bureau, is a national clearinghouse and technical assistance center that provides comprehensive child care information resources and technical assistance services to Child Care and Development Fund administrators and other key stakeholders. NCCIC also provides question and answer services, the NCCIC Online Library and Web site, technical assistance and training to states, conference and meeting support, and publications. Hours of operation: 8:30 a.m.–5:30 p.m., Monday–Friday (eastern time, except Federal holidays).

Eunice Kennedy Shriver National Institute of CHILD HEALTH and HUMAN DEVELOPMENT Information Resource Center
P.O. Box 3006
Rockville, MD 20847
Toll free: (800) 370-2943
TTY: (888) 320-6942
Fax: (866) 760-5947
Toll free: (800) 505-2742 ("Safe to Sleep" Campaign)
E-mail: nichdinformationresourcecenter@mail.nih.gov
Website: http://www.nichd.nih.gov

The Eunice Kennedy Shriver National Institute of Child Health and Human Development (NICHD) Information Resource Center provides information on health issues related to NICHD research. NICHD supports and conducts research on health topics related to children, adults, families, and communities. NICHD has primary responsibility for conducting and supporting basic, clinical, and translational research in the biomedical, behavioral, and social sciences related to child and maternal health, in medical rehabilitation, and in the reproductive sciences. NICHD also sponsors health education programs including: "Back to Sleep," designed to educate families and caregivers about reducing the risk of sudden infant death syndrome (SIDS); "Milk Matters," designed to educate children, parents, and health care providers about the importance of calcium for strong bones and lifelong health; and "Media-

Smart Youth: Eat, Think, and Be Active!" designed to teach 11- to 13-year-olds about media and how it impacts decisions on nutrition and physical activity. NICHD also leads a consortium of Federal agencies in leading the National Children's Study, which will examine environmental effects on child health and development. The NICHD Information Resource Center offers trained information specialists who have access to information and referral services on topics related to the mission of NICHD. The information specialists provide information in both English and Spanish. Hours of operation: 8:30 a.m.–4:00 p.m., Monday–Friday (eastern time, except Federal holidays).

CHILD WELFARE Information Gateway, Children's Bureau, Administration for Children and Families
1250 Maryland Avenue SW, 8th Floor
Washington, DC 20024
Toll free: (800) 394-3366
Phone: (703) 225-2331
Fax: (703) 225-2357
E-mail: info@childwelfare.gov
Website: http://www.childwelfare.gov

The Child Welfare Information Gateway provides access to information and resources to help protect children and strengthen families. The Child Welfare Information Gateway promotes the safety, permanency, and well-being of children and families by connecting child welfare, adoption and related professionals, as well as concerned citizens to timely, essential information. A service of the Children's Bureau, Administration for Children and Families, U.S. Department of Health and Human Services, they also provide access to print and electronic publications, Web sites, and online databases covering a wide range of topics from prevention to permanency, including child welfare, child abuse and neglect, adoption, search and reunion, and more. Hours of operation: 8:30 a.m.–5:00 p.m., Monday–Friday (eastern time, except Federal holidays).

Federal CITIZEN INFORMATION Center
Pueblo, CO 81009
Toll free: (800) 333-4636 (FED-INFO)
Website: http://www.pueblo.gsa.gov

The Federal Citizen Information Center (FCIC) has been a trusted one-stop source for answers to questions about consumer problems and government services for more than 35 years. The quarterly Consumer Information Catalog lists more than 200 free or low-cost Federal publications on a variety of topics. The Consumer Action Handbook is a 160-page guide designed to help citizens find the best and most direct source for assistance with their consumer problems and questions. FCIC on the web (USA.gov, Kids.gov, Pueblo.gsa. gov, Consumer Action.gov, GobiernoUSA.gov and Consumidor.gov) features these publications and many more that visitors can view, print, or download for free. It also features consumer news and tips and updates from various Federal agencies. FCIC's National Contact Center has specially trained staff who can answer questions in English and Spanish about all aspects of the Federal Government or direct callers to an appropriate contact. Hours of operation: 8:00 a.m.–8:00 p.m., Monday–Friday (eastern time, except Federal holidays). Recorded information on popular topics is available around the clock.

National Center for COMPLEMENTARY and ALTERNATIVE MEDICINE Information Clearinghouse

P.O. Box 7923
Gaithersburg, MD 20898-7923
Toll free: (888) 644-6226
Phone: (301) 519-3153 (International callers)
TTY: (866) 464-3615
Fax: (866) 464-3616
E-mail: info@nccam.nih.gov
Website: http://nccam.nih.gov

The National Center for Complementary and Alternative Medicine (NCCAM) Information Clearinghouse operates a toll-free telephone service. Information specialists search NCCAM databases for scientific information on complementary medicine practices therapies or conditions and can answer inquiries in English and Spanish. The Fax-on-Demand service, with factsheets and other information, is also available through the toll-free number. NCCAM services and materials are provided at no cost. The clearinghouse does not provide medical referrals, medical advice, or recommendations for specific complementary medicine practices therapies. Hours of operation: 8:30 a.m.–5:00 p.m., Monday–Friday (eastern time, except Federal holidays).

National CRIMINAL JUSTICE Reference Service

P.O. Box 6000
Rockville, MD 20849-6000
Toll free: (800) 851-3420
Phone: (301) 519-5500 (International Callers)
TTY: (877) 712-9279
TTY: (301) 947-8374
Fax: (301) 519-5212
Website: http://www.ncjrs.org

The National Criminal Justice Reference Service (NCJRS) was established in 1972 as a centralized information service for criminal justice practitioners and researchers. NCJRS provides reference services; distributes publications of the U.S. Department of Justice, Office of Justice Programs; acquires publications for its collection; and provides other services, such as document loan and information dissemination, via the Internet. A computerized database includes abstracts of all materials in the NCJRS collection. (The database is available on CD-ROM and on DIALOG.) Health issues covered by NCJRS include violence prevention; mental illness and crime; victimization; human development and criminal behavior; family violence and child abuse; health care fraud; substance abuse and treatment; and correctional health care, including AIDS and tuberculosis. Hours of operation: 10:00 a.m.–6:00 p.m., Monday–Friday (eastern time, except Federal holidays).

D

National Consortium on DEAF-BLINDNESS, Teaching Research Institute, Western Oregon University

345 North Monmouth Avenue
Monmouth, OR 97361

Toll free: (800) 438-9376
TTY: (800) 854-7013
Fax: (503) 838-8150
E-mail: info@nationaldb.org
Website: http://www.nationaldb.org

DB-LINK at the National Consortium on Deaf-Blindness (NCDB) provides information related to children and youth who are deaf-blind. Parents, service providers, administrators, and others who need information are invited to contact DB-LINK for information. NCDB is a collaborative effort of the Helen Keller National Center, Perkins School for the Blind, and the Teaching Research Institute of Western Oregon University. NCDB is the sponsor of the publication Deaf-Blind Perspectives. Hours of operation: 9:00 a.m.–5:00 p.m., Monday–Friday (eastern time, except Federal holidays); voicemail 24 hours a day.

National Institute on DEAFNESS and Other COMMUNICATION DISORDERS Information Clearinghouse

1 Communication Avenue
Bethesda, MD 20892-3456
Toll free: (800) 241-1044
TTY: (800) 241-1055
Fax: (301) 770-8977
E-mail: nidcdinfo@nidcd.nih.gov
Website: http://www.nidcd.nih.gov

The National Institute on Deafness and Other Communication Disorders (NIDCD) Information Clearinghouse collects and disseminates information on hearing, balance, smell, taste, voice, speech, and language for health professionals, patients, people in industry, and the public. NIDCD maintains a database of references to brochures, books, articles, factsheets, organizations, and educational materials, called the NIDCD Health Information Index. It also develops publications, including directories, factsheets, brochures, information packets, and newsletters. Hours of operation: 8:30 a.m.–5:00 p.m., Monday–Friday (eastern time, except Federal holidays).

National DIABETES Information Clearinghouse

1 Information Way
Bethesda, MD 20892-3560
Toll free: (800) 860-8747
TTY: (866) 569-1162
Fax: (703) 738-4929
E-mail: ndic@info.niddk.nih.gov
Website: http://diabetes.niddk.nih.gov

The National Diabetes Information Clearinghouse (NDIC) is an information and referral service of the National Institute of Diabetes and Digestive and Kidney Diseases, one of the National Institutes of Health. The clearinghouse responds to written, telephone, and e-mail inquiries; develops and distributes publications about diabetes; and provides referrals to diabetes organizations, including support groups. NDIC has developed valuable tools and resources for consumers and health professional, which can be accessed at http://www.diabetes.niddk.nih.gov/resources. Hours of operation: 8:30 a.m.–5:00 p.m., Monday–Friday (eastern time, except Federal holidays).

National DIGESTIVE DISEASES Information Clearinghouse
2 Information Way
Bethesda, MD 20892-3570
Toll free: (800) 891-5389
TTY: (866) 569-1162
Fax: (703) 738-4929
E-mail: nddic@info.niddk.nih.gov
Website: http://digestive.niddk.nih.gov

The National Digestive Diseases Information Clearinghouse (NDDIC) is an information and referral service of the National Institute of Diabetes and Digestive and Kidney Diseases, one of the National Institutes of Health. A central information resource on the prevention and management of digestive diseases, the clearinghouse responds to written inquiries, develops and distributes publications about digestive diseases, and provides referrals to digestive disease organizations, including support groups. NDDIC has developed valuable tools and resources for consumers and health professionals which can be accessed at http://www.digestive.niddk.nih.gov/resources. Hours of operation: 8:30 a.m.–5:00 p.m., Monday–Friday (eastern time, except Federal holidays).

National Dissemination Center for Children with DISABILITIES
1825 Connecticut Avenue NW, Suite 700
Washington, DC 20009-5722
Toll free: (800) 695-0285
Phone: (202) 884-8200 (also TTY)
Fax: (202) 884-8441
E-mail: nichcy@fhi360.org
Website: http://nichcy.org

The National Dissemination Center for Children with Disabilities (formerly the National Information Center for Children and Youth with Disabilities) is funded by the U.S. Department of Education, Office of Special Education Programs. The center serves as a central source of information on: disabilities in children and youth; programs and services for infants, children, and youth with disabilities; IDEA, the Nation's special education law; and research-based information on effective educational practices. All information and services are provided free of charge. Hours of operation: 9:00 a.m.–5:00 p.m., Monday–Friday (eastern time, except Federal holidays).

Clearinghouse on DISABILITY Information, Office of Special Education and Rehabilitative Services, U.S. Department of Education
550 12th Street SW, Room 5133
Washington, DC 20202-2550
Phone: (202) 245-7307
TTY: (202) 205-5637
Fax: (202) 245-7636
Website: http://www.ed.gov/about/offices/list/osers

The clearinghouse provides information to people with disabilities, or anyone requesting information, by doing research and providing documents in response to inquiries. Information provided includes areas of Federal funding for disability-related programs. Clearinghouse staff is trained to refer requests to other sources of disability-related information, if necessary.

Information provided may be useful to individuals with disabilities, their families, schools and universities, teachers and school administrators, and organizations that have persons with disabilities as clients. Hours of operation: 8:30 a.m.–5:00 p.m., Monday–Friday (eastern time, except Federal holidays).

National Center for the Dissemination of DISABILITY Research, SEDL
4700 Mueller Boulevard
Austin, TX 78723-3081
Toll free: (800) 266-1832
Phone: (512) 476-6861
Fax: (512) 476-2286
E-mail: ncddr@sedl.org
Website: http://www.sedl.org
Website: http://www.ncddr.org

Funded by the National Institute on Disability and Rehabilitation Research (NIDRR), the National Center for the Dissemination of Disability Research (NCDDR) responds to NIDRR's concern for increasing the effective use of NIDRR-sponsored research results in shaping new technologies, improving service delivery, and expanding decision-making options for people with disabilities and their families. NCDDR leverages resources through collaborative working relationships with experts in standards of evidence and systematic reviews, NIDRR-funded researchers, and agencies engaged in disseminating disability research results. Hours of operation: 8:00 a.m.–5:00 p.m., Monday–Friday (Central time, except Federal holidays).

Safe DRINKING WATER Hotline, Office of Ground Water and Drinking Water, U.S. Environmental Protection Agency
Ariel Rios Building, 4606M, 1200 Pennsylvania Avenue NW
Washington, DC 20460
Toll free: (800) 426-4791
Phone: (703) 412-3330 (Local and International Calls)
Website: http://water.epa.gov/drink/hotline/index.cfm

The EPA Safe Drinking Water Hotline is a service of the Office of Ground Water and Drinking Water. It provides the general public, regulators, medical and water professionals, academia, and media, with information about drinking water and ground water programs authorized under the Safe Drinking Water Act. The hotline responds to factual questions in the following program areas: local drinking water quality; drinking water standards; public drinking water systems; source water protection; large-capacity residential septic systems; commercial and industrial septic systems; injection wells; and drainage wells. Hours of operation: 10:00 a.m.–4:00 p.m., Monday–Friday (eastern time, except Federal holidays).

National Institute on DRUG ABUSE Virtual Information Center, Office of Science policy and Communications, Natinoal Institute on Drug Abuse
6001 Executive Boulevard, Room 5213
Bethesda, MD 20892-9561
Phone: (301) 443-1124
Phone: (240) 221-4007 (en Español)
Phone: (877) 643-2644 (Publication Orders)
E-mail: information@nida.nih.gov

Website: http://www.nida.nih.gov
Website: http://teens.drugabuse.gov (NIDA for Teens)
Website: http//easyread.drugabuse.gov (NIDA Easy-to-Read Drug Facts)

The National Institute on Drug Abuse Virtual Information Center (NIDA VIC) responds to inquiries sent to the Institute (via information@nida.nih.gov or the NIDA and NIDA for Teens Web sites) by the public, medical and health professionals, educators, researchers, people in the substance abuse field, and the media. Information is provided on the common drugs of abuse and a variety of topics related to drug abuse and addiction. The NIDA Research Dissemination Center (NIDA RDC) distributes publications for NIDA. To order free print copies of publication within the United States, call the NIDA RDC at (877) 643-2644, send them a fax at (240) 645-0227, or e-mail them at drugpubs@nida.nih.gov. E-mail or fax NIDA RDC for information on international shipping. Hours of operation: 8:30 a.m.– 5:00 p.m., Monday–Friday (eastern time, except Federal holidays).

DRUG POLICY Information Clearinghouse, Office of National Drug Control Policy
P.O. Box 6000
Rockville, MD 20849-6000
Toll free: (800) 666-3332
Fax: (301) 519-5212
Website: http://www.whitehousedrugpolicy.gov/about/clearingh.html

The clearinghouse supports the White House Office of National Drug Control Policy, National Criminal Justice Reference Service. Staffed by subject matter specialists, the clearinghouse serves as a resource for statistics, research data, and referrals useful for developing and implementing drug policy. It disseminates publications; writes and produces documents on drug-related topics; coordinates with Federal, state, and local agencies to identify data resources; and maintains a reading room offering a broad range of policy-related materials. Hours of operation: 10:00 a.m.–6:00 p.m., Monday–Friday (eastern time, except Federal holidays).

E

EDUCATION Resources Information Center, ERIC Program, c/o Computer Sciences Corporation
655 15th Street NW, Suite 500
Washington, DC 20005
Toll free: (800) 538-3742
Website: http://www.eric.ed.gov

The Education Resources Information Center (ERIC) is a digital library of education-related resources, sponsored by the Institute of Education Sciences of the U.S. Department of Education. ERIC's mission is to provide a comprehensive, easy-to-use, searchable, Internet-based bibliographic and full-text database of education research and information that also meets the requirements of the Education Sciences Reform Act of 2002. A fundamental goal for ERIC's future

is to increase the availability and quality of research and information for educators, researchers, and the general public. Hours of operation: 8:00 a.m.–8:00 p.m., Monday–Friday (eastern time, except Federal holidays).

National Center on ELDER ABUSE, c/o University of California-Irvine, Program in Geriatric Medicine
200 Building, Route 81, 101 The City Drive South
Orange, CA 92868-3201
Phone: (855) 500-3537
Fax: (714) 456-7933
E-mail: ncea-info@aoa.hhs.gov
Website: http://www.ncea.aoa.gov

The National Center on Elder Abuse is a national resource for elder rights, law enforcement and legal professionals, public policy leaders, researchers, and the public. The center's mission is to promote understanding, knowledge sharing, and action on elder abuse, neglect, and exploitation. Hours of operation: 9:00 a.m.–4:00 p.m., Monday–Friday (eastern time, except Federal holidays).

ELDERCARE Locator, Administration on Aging, U.S. Department of Health and Human Services
Toll free: (800) 677-1116
Phone: (301) 419-3900 (International callers)
E-mail: eldercarelocator@spherix.com
Website: http://www.eldercare.gov/Eldercare.NET/Public/Index.aspx

The Eldercare Locator, a toll-free, operator-assisted service funded by the U.S. Administration on Aging, helps older adults and their caregivers find local services for seniors. The service links family members and the public to the information and referral (I&R) services of their state and area agencies on aging. These I&R programs can help you identify appropriate services in the area where you or your family members reside. Internet users can access the directory of information and referral/assistance service centers through a Web site maintained by the Center for Communication and Consumer Services in the U.S. Administration on Aging. The site is currently being expanded to include factsheets on aging services and programs. Hours of operation: 9:00 a.m.–8:00 p.m., Monday–Friday (eastern time, except Federal holidays); voicemail 24 hours a day.

National ENDOCRINE and METABOLIC DISEASES Information Service
6 Information Way
Bethesda, MD 20892-3569
Toll free: (888) 828-0904
TTY: (866) 569-1162
Fax: (703) 738-4929
E-mail: endoandmeta@info.niddk.nih.gov
Website: http://www.endocrine.niddk.nih.gov

The National Endocrine and Metabolic Diseases Information Service (NEMDIS) is a service of the National Institute of Diabetes and Digestive and Kidney Diseases (NIDDK). The NIDDK is part of the National Institutes of Health of the U.S. Department of Health and Human Services. The NEMDIS answers inquiries, develops and distributes publications, and works closely with professional and patient organizations and Government agencies to coordinate resources about endocrine and metabolic diseases. NEMDIS' resources for consumers and health professionals can be accessed at http://www.endocrine. niddk.nih.gov/resources Hours of operation: 8:30 a.m.–5:00 p.m., Monday–Friday (eastern time, except Federal holidays).

ENVIRONMENTAL Protection Agency, National Library Network, MC 3404T

1200 Pennsylvania Avenue NW
Washington, DC 20460-0001
Phone: (202) 566-0566
E-mail: epalibrarynetwork@epa.gov
Website: http://www.epa.gov/libraries

The libraries offer general information about the agency and refer inquiries to the appropriate regional or program office. The public may visit and use the libraries collections onsite, but materials do not circulate to non-EPA staff. The libraries do not distribute agency publications. The EPA National Library Network is composed of libraries and repositories located in the Agency's Headquarters, Regional and Field Offices, Research Centers, and specialized laboratories, as well as Web-based access to electronic collections. Information about the EPA National Library Network, including a listing of libraries, may be accessed at http://www.epa.gov/libraries/libraries.htm. The combined network collections contain information about the environment and related scientific, technical, management, and policy information. The EPA Online Library System is the Network's online catalog of library holdings and is available at http://www.epa.gov/libraries/ols.htm. The public can request EPA library materials, including journals, books, and EPA documents, via interlibrary loan from their local library. The National Environmental Publications Internet Site, http://www.epa.gov/nepis, the Agency's gateway for EPA publications, provides free access to more than 31,000 electronic EPA documents and more than 7,000 hard-copy EPA documents. Hours of operation: Public—8:30 a.m.–4:30 p.m., Monday–Friday; EPA Staff—8:30 a.m.–4:30 p.m., Monday–Friday (eastern time, except Federal holidays).

F

National Clearinghouse on FAMILIES & YOUTH

P.O. Box 13505
Silver Spring, MD 20911-3505
Phone: (301) 608-8098
Fax: (301) 608-8721
Website: http://ncfy.acf.hhs.gov

The clearinghouse links those interested in youth issues with the resources they need to better serve young people, families, and communities. It offers materials for distribution at conferences. The Web site includes a searchable literature database and information on funding sources. Hours of operation: 9:00 a.m.–5:00 p.m., Monday–Friday (eastern time, except Federal holidays).

FOOD and NUTRITION Information Center, Agricultural Research Service, USDA, National Agricultural Library

10301 Baltimore Avenue, Room 108
Beltsville, MD 20705-2351
Fax: (301) 504-6409
E-mail: fnic@ars.usda.gov
Website: http://fnic.nal.usda.gov

The Food and Nutrition Information Center (FNIC) is one of several information centers located at the National Agricultural Library, part of the U.S. Department of Agriculture's Agricultural Research Service. FNIC provides information on food, human nutrition, and food safety. Resource lists, databases, and many other food and nutrition-related links are available on the FNIC Web site. FNIC collection includes books, manuals, journal articles, and audiovisual materials. Eligible patrons may borrow directly; others may borrow through interlibrary loan. Hours of operation: 8:30 a.m.–4:30 p.m., Monday–Friday (eastern time, except Federal holidays).

Center for FOOD SAFETY and Applied Nutrition Outreach and Information Center, U.S. Food and Drug Administration

5100 Paint Branch Parkway (HFS-009)
College Park, MD 20740-3835
Toll free: (888) 723-3366
E-mail: consumer@fda.gov
Website: http://www.cfsan.fda.gov/

The goal of the Center for Food Safety and Applied Nutrition's (CFSAN) Communications and Coordination Branch (CCB) is to enhance CFSAN's ability to provide and respond to the public's desire/demand for more useful, timely, and accurate information regarding its regulated products. CCB was also established to enhance the Food and Drug Administration's ability to provide accurate and meaningful information to the public about food safety. In addition to providing food safety information, CCB provides assistance with other CFSAN issues including nutrition, dietary supplements, food labeling, cosmetics, food additives, and food biotechnology. Hours of operation: 10:00 a.m.–4:00 p.m., Monday–Friday (central time). Consumer recorded information available 24 hours a day, 7 days a week.

G

GENETIC and RARE DISEASES Information Center

P.O. Box 8126
Gaithersburg, MD 20898-8126
Toll free: (888) 205-2311
Phone: (301) 251-4925 (International Callers)
TTY: (888) 205-3223
Fax: (301) 251-4911
E-mail: gardinfo@nih.gov
Website: http://rarediseases.info.nih.gov/GARD

The National Human Genome Research Institute (NHGRI) and the Office of Rare Diseases Research (ORDR) created the Genetic and Rare Diseases Information Center to help people find useful information, in English or Spanish, about genetic and rare diseases. You can write to GARD anytime via e-mail, letter, or fax. Bilingual Information Specialists are available to respond to inquiries in Spanish. All information requests are completely confidential. Hours of operation: 12:00 p.m–6:00 p.m., Monday–Friday (eastern Time, except Federal holidays).

National GUIDELINE Clearinghouse, Center for Outcomes and Evidence, Agency for Healthcare Research and Quality

540 Gaither Road, 6th Floor
Rockville, MD 20850
Phone: (301) 427-1600
E-mail: info@guideline.gov
Website: http://www.guideline.gov

The National Guideline Clearinghouse (NGC) is a public resource for evidence-based clinical practice guidelines. NGC is an initiative of the Agency for Healthcare Research and Quality (AHRQ), U.S. Department of Health and Human Services. NGC was originally created by AHRQ in partnership with the American Medical Association and the American Association of Health Plans (now America's Health Insurance Plans [AHIP]). Hours of operation: 8:00 a.m.–5:00 p.m., Monday–Friday (eastern time, except Federal holidays).

H

National HEALTH Information Center

P.O. Box 1133
Washington, DC 20013-1133
Toll free: (800) 336-4797
Phone: (301) 565-4167
Fax: (301) 984-4256
E-mail: info@nhic.org
Website: http://www.health.gov/nhic

The National Health Information Center (NHIC) helps the public and health professionals locate health information through identification of health information resources, an information and referral system, and publications. NHIC uses a database containing descriptions of health-related organizations to refer inquirers to the most appropriate resources. NHIC does not diagnose medical conditions or give medical advice. NHIC prepares publications and directories on health promotion and disease prevention topics. Hours of operation: 9:00 a.m.–5:30 p.m., Monday–Friday (eastern time, except Federal holidays).

HEALTH RESOURCES and SERVICES Administration Information Center

P.O. Box 2910
Merrifield, VA 22118
Toll free: (888) ASK-HRSA (275-4772)
TTY: (877) 4TY-HRSA (489-4772)
Phone: (703) 442-9051
Fax: (703) 821-2098
E-mail: ask@hrsa.gov
Website: http://www.hrsa.gov

The Health Resources and Services Administration (HRSA) Information Center provides publications, resources, and referrals on health care services for medically underserved individuals and populations. Trained information specialists answer questions, refer callers to subject-specific information resources, and provide HRSA publications. Spanish-speaking information specialists are available. Hours of operation: 8:30 a.m.–5:00 p.m., Monday–Friday (eastern time, except Federal holidays).

National Information Center on HEALTH SERVICES RESEARCH and Health Care Technology, National Library of Medicine

Building 38A, Room 4S-410, 8600 Rockville Pike, MSC 3833
Bethesda, MD 20894
Phone: (301) 496-0176
Fax: (301) 402-3193
E-mail: nichsr@nlm.nih.gov
Website: http://www.nlm.nih.gov/nichsr

The 1993 NIH Revitalization Act created a National Information Center on Health Services Research and Health Care Technology at the National Library of Medicine. The center works closely with the Agency for Healthcare Research and Quality to improve the dissemination of the results of health services research, with special emphasis on the growing body of evidence reports and technology assessments, which provide organizations with comprehensive, science-based information on common, costly medical conditions and new health care technologies. Hours of operation: 8:30 a.m.–5:00 p.m., Monday–Friday (eastern time, except Federal holidays).

National HEART, LUNG, and BLOOD Institute Health Information Center

P.O. Box 30105
Bethesda, MD 20824-0105
Phone: (301) 592-8573
TTY: (240) 629-3255
Fax: (301) 592-8563
E-mail: nhlbinfo@nhlbi.nih.gov
Website: http://www.nhlbi.nih.gov

The National Heart, Lung, and Blood Institute (NHLBI) provides leadership for a national program in diseases of the heart, blood vessels, lungs, and blood; blood resources; and sleep disorders. The NHLBI plans and directs research in development and evaluation of interventions and devices related to prevention, treatment, and rehabilitation of patients suffering from such diseases and disorders. For health professionals and the public, the NHLBI conducts educational activities, including development and dissemination of materials in the above areas, with an emphasis on prevention. Hours of operation: 8:30 a.m.–5:00 p.m., Monday–Friday (eastern time, except Federal holidays).

National HEMATOLOGIC DISEASES Information Service

7 Information Way
Bethesda, MD 208923571
Toll free: (888) 828-0877
TTY: (866) 569-1162
Fax: (703) 738-4929

E-mail: hematologic@info.niddk.nih.gov
Website: http://www.hematologic.niddk.nih.gov

The National Hematologic Diseases Information Service (NHDIS) is a service of the National Institute of Diabetes and Digestive and Kidney Diseases (NIDDK). The NIDDK is part of the National Institutes of Health of the U.S. Department of Health and Human Services. The NHDIS provides information about hematologic diseases to people with hematologic diseases and to their families, health care professionals, and the public. The NHDIS answers inquiries, develops and distributes publications, and works closely with professional and patient organizations and Government agencies to coordinate resources about hematologic diseases. Hours of operation: 8:30 a.m.–5:00 p.m., Monday–Friday (eastern time, except Federal holidays).

SAMHSA's HOMELESSNESS Resource Center,
c/o Center for Social Innovation
200 Reservoir Street, Suite 202
Needham, MA 02494
Phone: (617) 467-6014
Fax: (617) 467-6015
E-mail: generalinquiry@center4si.com
Website: http://www.homeless.samhsa.gov

SAMHSA's Homelessness Resource Center (HRC), seeks to improve the daily lives of people affected by homelessness and who have mental health, substance use problems and trauma histories. HRC does this through training and technical assistance, online learning opportunities, and publications for Homeless Service Providers. HRC also maintains an extensive knowledge database of studies, papers, and reports related to homelessness. Hours of operation: 9:00 a.m.–5:00 p.m., Monday–Friday (eastern time, except Federal holidays).

HUD USER (HOUSING and Urban Development)
P.O. Box 23268
Washington, DC 20026-3268
Toll free: (800) 245-2691
Phone: (202) 708-3178
TTY: (800) 927-7589
Fax: (202) 708-9981
E-mail: helpdesk@huduser.org
Website: http://www.huduser.org

HUD USER disseminates publications for the U.S. Department of Housing and Urban Development's Office of Policy Development and Research. HUD USER offers database searches on housing research and provides reports on housing safety, housing for elderly and handicapped persons, and lead-based paint. Hours of operation: 8:00 a.m.–5:15 p.m., Monday–Friday (eastern time, except Federal holidays).

I

National INJURY Information Clearinghouse, U.S.
Consumer Product Safety Commission
4330 East West Highway, Room 820

Bethesda, MD 20814
Phone: (301) 504-7921
Fax: (301) 504-0025
Website: http://www.cpsc.gov/about/clrnghse.html

Sponsored by the U.S. Consumer Product Safety Commission (CPSC), the clearinghouse collects and disseminates information on the causes and prevention of death, injury, and illness associated with consumer products. It compiles data obtained from accident reports, consumer complaints, death certificates, news clips, and the National Electronic Injury Surveillance System operated by the CPSC. Publications include statistical analyses of data and hazard and accident patterns. Hours of operation: 8:00 a.m.–4:30 p.m., Monday–Friday (eastern time, except Federal holidays).

K

National KIDNEY and UROLOGIC Diseases Information
Clearinghouse
3 Information Way
Bethesda, MD 20892-3580
Toll free: (800) 891-5390
TTY: (866) 569-1162
Fax: (703) 738-4929
E-mail: nkudic@info.niddk.nih.gov
Website: http://www.kidney.niddk.nih.gov/

The National Kidney and Urologic Diseases Information Clearinghouse (NKUDIC) is an information and referral service of the National Institute of Diabetes and Digestive and Kidney Diseases, one of the National Institutes of Health. The clearinghouse responds to written inquiries, e-mail, and telephone requests, develops and distributes publications about kidney and urologic diseases, and provides referrals to kidney and urologic disease organizations, including support groups. NKUDIC maintains a database of patient and professional education materials from which literature searches are generated. Hours of operation: 8:30 a.m.–5:00 p.m., Monday–Friday (eastern time, except Federal holidays).

L

National LEAD Information Center

422 South Clinton Avenue
Rochester, NY 14620
Toll free: (800) 424-LEAD (424-5323)
Fax: (585) 232-3111
Website: http://www.epa.gov/lead/pubs/nlic.htm

The National Lead Information Center (NLIC) is sponsored by the Environmental Protection Agency. NLIC provides information on lead poisoning and children, lead-based paint, a list of local and state contacts who can help, and other lead-related questions. Hours of operation: 8:00 a.m.–6:00 p.m., Monday–Friday (eastern time, except Federal holidays).

M

MATERNAL and CHILD HEALTH Information Resource Center
1200 18th Street NW, Suite 700
Washington, DC 20036
Phone: (202) 842-2000
Fax: (202) 728-9469
E-mail: mchirc@altarum.org
Website: http://www.mchb.hrsa.gov/mchirc

The Maternal and Child Health Information Resource Center (MCHIRC) is dedicated to the goal of helping MCH practitioners on the Federal, state, and local levels improve their capacity to gather, analyze, and use data for planning and policymaking. MCHIRC is funded by the Health Resources and Services Administration, Maternal and Child Health Bureau's Office of Data and Information Management. Hours of operation: 8:30 a.m.–5:00 p.m., Monday–Friday (eastern time, except Federal holidays).

MATERNAL and CHILD HEALTH Library, National Center for Education in Maternal and Child Health, Georgetown University
P.O. Box 571272
Washington, DC 20057-1272
Phone: (202) 784-9770
Fax: (202) 784-9777
E-mail: mchlibrary@ncemch.org
Website: http://www.mchlibrary.info

The Maternal and Child Health (MCH) Library at Georgetown University provides the MCH community with accurate and timely information on a broad range of topics. Materials include the weekly newsletter MCH Alert, resource guides, full text publications, databases, and links to quality MCH sites. The MCH Library is funded under a cooperative agreement with the Maternal and Child Health Bureau, Health Resources and Services Administration, U.S. Department of Health and Human Services. Hours of operation: 8:30 a.m.–5:00 p.m., Monday–Friday (eastern time, except Federal holidays).

National MATERNAL and CHILD ORAL HEALTH Resource Center, Georgetown University
Box 571272
Washington, DC 20057-1272
Phone: (202) 784-9771
Fax: (202) 784-9777
E-mail: ohrcinfo@georgetown.edu
Website: http://www.mchoralhealth.org

The purpose of the National Maternal and Child Oral Health Resource Center (OHRC) is to respond to the needs of states and communities in addressing current and emerging public oral health issues. OHRC supports health professionals, program administrators, educators, policymakers, and others with the goal of improving oral health services for infants, children, adolescents, and their families. ORHC collaborates with Federal, state, and local agencies; national and state organizations and associations; and foundations, to gather, develop, and share quality and valued information and materials. Hours of operation: 8:30 a.m.–5:00 p.m., Monday–Friday (eastern time, except Federal holidays).

Office of MINORITY HEALTH Resource Center, Office of Minority Health
P.O. Box 37337
Washington, DC 20013-7337
Toll free: (800) 444-6472
Phone: (301) 251-1797
TTY: (301) 251-1432
Fax: (301) 251-2160
E-mail: info@minorityhealth.hhs.gov
Website: http://minorityhealth.hhs.gov

The center responds to information requests from health professionals and consumers on minority health issues and locates sources of technical assistance. It provides referrals to relevant organizations and distributes materials. Spanish-speaking operators are available. Hours of operation: 9:00 a.m.–5:00 p.m., Monday–Friday (eastern time, except Federal holidays).

O

National Institute for OCCUPATIONAL SAFETY and Health Information Inquiry Service
4676 Columbia Parkway, C-19
Cincinnati, OH 45226-1998
Toll free: (800) CDC-INFO (232-4636)
Phone: (513) 533-8328
TTY: (888) 232-6348
Fax: (513) 533-8347
E-mail: cdcinfo@cdc-gov
Website: http://www.cdc.gov/niosh

The National Institute for Occupational Safety and Health (NIOSH) Information Inquiry Service is a toll-free technical information service that provides convenient public access to NIOSH and its information resources. The service is available to anyone in the continental United States, Alaska, Hawaii, Puerto Rico, or the Virgin Islands. Hours of operation: 9:00 a.m.–4:00 p.m., Monday–Friday (eastern time, except Federal holidays).

National ORAL HEALTH Information Clearinghouse, National Institute of Dental and Craniofacial Research
1 NOHIC Way
Bethesda, MD 20892-3500
Phone: (866) 232-4528
Fax: (301) 480-4098
E-mail: nidcrinfo@mail.nih.gov
Website: http://www.nidcr.nih.gov/

The National Oral Health Information Clearinghouse (NOHIC) focuses on general oral health as well as the information needs of special care patients, including people with generic or systemic disorders that compromise oral health, whose medical treatments cause oral problems, or whose mental or physical disabilities complicate oral hygiene or treatment. NOHIC develops and distributes information and educational materials on general oral health and special care topics and provides information services with trained staff to respond to specific interests and questions. Hours of operation: 8:30 a.m.–5:00 p.m., Monday–Friday (eastern time, except Federal holidays); voicemail available after hours.

NIH OSTEOPOROSIS and Related BONE DISEASES—National Resource Center

2 AMS Circle
Bethesda, MD 20892-3676
Toll free: (800) 624-BONE (624-2663)
Phone: (202) 223-0344
TTY: (202) 466-4315
Fax: (202) 293-2356
E-mail: nihboneinfo@mail.nih.gov
Website: http://www.niams.nih.gov/Health_Info/Bone/
    default.asp

The National Institutes of Health (NIH) Osteoporosis and Related Bone Diseases National Resource Center (NRC), a part of the U.S. Department of Health and Human Services, provides patients, health professionals, and the public with an important link to resources and information on metabolic bone diseases including osteoporosis, Paget's disease of the bones, and osteogenesis imperfecta. The NRC is dedicated to increasing the awareness, knowledge, and understanding of physicians, health professionals, patients, underserved and at-risk populations (such as Hispanic and Asian women, adolescents, and men), and the general public about the prevention, early detection, and treatment of osteoporosis and related bone diseases. The NRC is supported by the National Institute of Arthritis and Musculoskeletal and Skin Diseases with contributions from the National Institute on Aging, Eunice Kennedy Shriver National Institute of Child Health and Human Development, National Institute of Dental and Craniofacial Research, National Institute of Diabetes and Digestive and Kidney Diseases, NIH Office of Research on Women's Health and HHS Office on Women's Health. Hours of operation: 8:30 a.m.–5:00 p.m., Monday–Friday (eastern time, except Federal holidays).

P

National PESTICIDE Information Center, Oregon State University

310 Weniger Hall
Corvallis, OR 97331-6502
Toll free: (800) 858-7378
Fax: (541) 737-0761
E-mail: npicupdates@ace.orst.edu
Website: http://npic.orst.edu

The National Pesticide Information Center (NPIC) provides objective, science-based information about a wide variety of pesticide-related topics, including pesticide product information, information on the recognition and management of pesticide poisonings, toxicology, and environmental chemistry. Highly trained specialists can also provide referrals for the following: laboratory analyses, investigation of pesticide incidents, emergency treatment information, safety information, health and environmental effects, and clean-up and disposal procedures. NPIC is a toll-free telephone service available to anyone in the United States, Puerto Rico, and the Virgin Islands, including the general public, the hearing impaired, and medical, veterinary, and other health care professionals. Spanish-speaking specialists are available to assist with pesticide questions and provide services in more than 170 different languages including Mandarin, French, and German. Pesticide information is also available by visiting their new user-friendly Web site at http://npic.orst.edu. Both their full-color English and Spanish brochures are available online. Other research materials are available on request. NPIC is a cooperative effort between Oregon State University and the U.S. Environmental Protection Agency. Hours of operation: 7:30 a.m.–3:30 p.m., daily, Monday–Friday (Pacific time, except Federal holidays); voicemail available after hours.

Office of POPULATION AFFAIRS Clearinghouse, Office of Population Affairs, Office of the Assistant Secretary for Health, U.S. Department of Health and Human Services

P.O. Box 30686
Bethesda, MD 20824-0686
Phone: (866) 640-7827
Fax: (866) 592-3299
E-mail: info@opaclearinghouse.org
Website: http://www.opaclearinghouse.org

The Office of Population Affairs (OPA) Clearinghouse collects, develops, and distributes information on family planning, adoption, reproductive health care, and sexually transmitted diseases, including HIV and AIDS. The OPA Clearinghouse also maintains a database of the Title X Family Planning Clinics located through out the United States. Hours of operation: 9:00 a.m.–5:00 p.m., Monday–Friday (eastern time, except Federal holidays), voicemail available after hours.

CDC National PREVENTION Information Network

P.O. Box 6003
Rockville, MD 20849-6003
E-mail: info@cdcnpin.org
Website: http://www.cdcnpin.org

The CDC National Prevention Information Network (NPIN) is the United States reference, referral, and distribution service for information on HIV/AIDS, sexually transmitted diseases (STDs), and tuberculosis (TB). NPIN produces, collects, catalogs, processes, stocks, and disseminates materials and information on HIV/AIDS, STDs, and TB to organizations and people working in those disease fields in international, national, state, and local settings. All NPIN services are designed to facilitate sharing of information and resources on education and prevention services, published materials, research findings, and trends among users.

National QUALITY MEASURES Clearinghouse, Center for Outcomes and Evidence, Agency for Healthcare Research and Quality

540 Gaither Road, 6th Floor
Rockville, MD 20850
Phone: (301) 427-1600
E-mail: info@qualitymeasures.ahrq.gov
Website: http://www.qualitymeasures.ahrq.gov

The National Quality Measures Clearinghouse (NQMC) is a public resource for evidence-based quality measures and measure sets. NQMC is an initiative of the Agency for Healthcare Research and Quality, U.S. Department of Health and Human Services. The NQMC database and Web site provide information on specific evidence-based healthcare measures and measure sets. Hours of operation: 8:00 a.m.–5:00 p.m., Monday–Friday (eastern time, except Federal holidays).

R

National REHABILITATION INFORMATION Center

8400 Corporate Drive, Suite 500
Landover, MD 20785
Toll free: (800) 346-2742
Phone: (301) 459-5900
TTY: (301) 459-5984
Fax: (301) 459-4263
E-mail: naricinfo@heitechservices.com
Website: http://www.naric.com

The National Rehabilitation Information Center (NARIC) is a library and information center on disability and rehabilitation. Funded by the National Institute on Disability and Rehabilitation Research, NARIC collects and disseminates the results of federally funded research projects. The collection, which also includes books, journal articles, and audiovisuals, grows at a rate of about 300 documents per month. Information or referral free; $5.00 USD minimum for documents. Hours of operation: 9:00 a.m.–5:00 p.m., Monday–Friday (eastern time, except Federal holidays).

RURAL ASSISTANCE Center, University of North Dakota, Center for Rural Health

School of Medicine & Health Sciences, Room 4520, 501 North Columbia Road, Stop 9037
Grand Forks, ND 58202-9037
Toll free: (800) 270-1898
Fax: (800) 270-1913
E-mail: info@raconline.org
Website: http://www.raconline.org

The Rural Assistance Center (RAC) serves as a rural health and human services information portal which helps rural communities and other rural stakeholders access the full range of available programs, funding, and research that can enable them to provide quality health and human services to rural residents. Services provided include RAC's Web site, electronic mailing lists, and customized assistance. Hours of operation: 8:00 a.m.–5:00 p.m., Monday–Friday (central time, except Federal holidays).

RURAL INFORMATION Center, National Agricultural Library, U.S. Department of Agriculture

10301 Baltimore Avenue, Room 115
Beltsville, MD 20705-2351
Toll free: (800) 633-7701
Phone: (301) 504-5273
Fax: (301) 504-5181
Website: http://ric.nal.usda.gov

The Rural Information Center provides information and funding sources to tribal, local, state, and Federal Government officials; community organizations; rural electric and telephone cooperatives; libraries; businesses; and rural citizens working to maintain the vitality of America's rural areas. Hours of operation: 8:30 a.m.–4:30 p.m., Monday–Friday (eastern time, except Federal holidays).

S

National Center on SLEEP DISORDERS Research, National Heart, Lung, and Blood Institute, National Institutes of Health

6701 Rockledge Drive, Suite 10042
Bethesda, MD 20892
Phone: (301) 435-0199
Fax: (301) 480-3451
Website: http://www.nhlbi.nih.gov/sleep

The National Center on Sleep Disorders Research (NCSDR) promotes basic, clinical, and applied research on sleep and sleep disorders by strengthening existing sleep research programs, training new investigators, and creating new programs to address important gaps and identify opportunities in sleep and sleep disorders. NCSDR sponsors workshops and conferences, and develops written and Web-based resources to educate health care professionals and the general public about sleep disorders, sleep-related research findings, and sleep-related public health. Hours of operation: 8:30 a.m.–5:00 p.m., Monday–Friday (eastern time, except Federal holidays).

Office on SMOKING and Health, National Center for Chronic Disease Prevention and Health Promotion, Centers for Disease Control and Prevention

4770 Buford Highway NE, Mail Stop K-50, Publications
Atlanta, GA 30341-3717
Toll free: (800) 232-4636
E-mail: tobaccoinfo@cdc.gov
Website: http://www.cdc.gov/tobacco

The Office on Smoking and Health develops and distributes the annual Surgeon General's Report on Smoking and

Health, coordinates a national public information and education program on tobacco use and health, and coordinates tobacco education and research efforts within the Department of Health and Human Services and throughout both Federal and State governments. The office provides information on smoking cessation, secondhand smoke, professional/technical information, and publications. Hours of operation: 8:00 a.m.–4:00 p.m., Monday–Friday (eastern time, except Federal holidays).

SUBSTANCE ABUSE and MENTAL HEALTH SERVICES Administration
P.O. Box 2345
Rockville, MD 20847-2345
Toll free: (877) SAMHSA-7 (726-4727)
TTY: (800) 487-4889
Phone: (240) 221-4036
Fax: (240) 221-4292
E-mail: samhsainfo@samhsa.hhs.gov
Website: http://store.samhsa.gov

SAMHSA's mission is to disseminate information and products to promote the adoption of effective prevention, intervention, and treatment policies, programs, and practices; provide access to scientific research on substance abuse and mental health issues; and serve as a first point of contact for individuals seeking information on the prevention and treatment of mental and substance use disorders.

National SUID/SIDS Resource Center, Georgetown University
2115 Wisconsin Avenue NW, Suite 601
Washington, DC 20057-1272
Toll free: (866) 866-7437
Phone: (202) 687-7466
Fax: (202) 784-9777
E-mail: info@sidscenter.org
Website: http://www.sidscenter.org

The National SUID/SIDS Resource Center serves as a central source of information on sudden infant death and on promoting healthy outcomes for infants from the prenatal period through the first year of life and beyond. The Resource Center provides a toll-free information line and e-mail service to answer requests for information or publications; maintains an accessible Web site with continuously updated information, resources, and links to programs and services; identifies informational and educational needs within the Maternal and Child Health (MCH) and sudden infant death communities; develops print and Web-based materials for professionals and the public; dedicates one issue per month of the MCH Alert electronic newsletter to highlighting current infant mortality topics; maintains comprehensive searchable databases of information; connects people with programs and services through direct referrals; promotes awareness and enhances knowledge through outreach activities; and works closely with the Maternal and Child Health Bureau and its consortium partners, parents-professional organizations, and government agencies. Hours of operation: 8:30 a.m.–5:00 p.m., Monday–Friday (eastern time, except Federal holidays).

T

National TECHNICAL INFORMATION Service, U.S. Department of Commerce
5301 Shawnee Road
Alexandria, VA 22312
Toll free: (800) 553-6847
Phone: (703) 605-6000
TTY: (703) 487-4639
Fax: (703) 605-6900
E-mail: info@ntis.gov
Website: http://www.ntis.gov

The National Technical Information Service (NTIS) is the Federal Government's central source for the sale of scientific, technical, engineering, and related business information produced by or for the U.S. Government and complementary material from international sources. NTIS also offers thousands of multimedia, training, and educational programs produced by Federal agencies. Approximately 3 million products are available from NTIS in a variety of formats: electronic download, online access, computer products, multimedia, microfiche, and paper. Hours of operation: 8:00 a.m.–6:00 p.m., Monday–Friday (eastern time, except Federal holidays); TDD 8:30 a.m.–5:00 p.m., Monday–Friday (eastern time, except Federal holidays).

W

WEIGHT-CONTROL Information Network, National Institute of Diabetes and Digestive and Kidney Diseases
1 WIN Way
Bethesda, MD 20892-3665
Toll free: (877) 946-4627
Phone: (202) 828-1025
Fax: (202) 828-1028
E-mail: win@info.niddk.nih.gov
Website: http://win.niddk.nih.gov

The Weight-Control Information Network (WIN) was established by the National Institutes of Health's, National Institute of Diabetes and Digestive and Kidney Diseases in June 1994. WIN is a national source of information on weight control, obesity, and weight-related nutritional disorders for health professionals and the public. WIN responds to both written and telephone requests for information and referrals, and provides a variety of written materials on obesity, weight control, and nutritional disorders. Hours of operation: 8:30 a.m.–5:00 p.m., Monday–Friday (eastern time, except Federal holidays).

WOMENSHEALTH.GOV, Office on Women's Health
200 Independence Avenue SW, Room 728F
Washington, DC 20201

Toll free: (800) 994-9662
TTY: (888) 220-5446
Fax: (202) 260-6537
Website: http://www.womenshealth.gov
Website: http://www.girlshealth.gov

Womenshealth.gov is the most reliable and current information resource on women's health today. They offer free women's health information on more than 800 topics through their call center and Web site. By phone (in English and Spanish) or via our Web site you can find: original health information on special topics like pregnancy, breastfeeding, body image, HIV/AIDS, girls health, heart health, menopause and hormone therapy, mental health,

quitting smoking, and violence against women; original health information and resources for special populations (minority women, women with disabilities, girls, men, and Spanish speakers); thousands of health publications; statistics on women's health; daily news on women's health; and more. Womenshealth.gov also sponsors the National Breastfeeding Helpline! Trained breastfeeding peer counselors can give support and encouragement and help with basic breastfeeding questions and concerns by phone at 1-800-994-9662 or by visiting: http://www.womenshealth.gov/breastfeeding. Womenshealth.gov is a service of the Office on Women's Health, U.S. Department of Health and Human Services. Hours of operation: 9:00 a.m.–6:00 p.m., Monday–Friday (eastern time, except Federal holidays).

TOLL-FREE NUMBERS FOR HEALTH INFORMATION

The following is a list of toll-free numbers that provide health-related information, education, and support. They do not diagnose or recommend treatment for any disease. Some of the toll-free numbers use recorded messages. Others offer personalized counseling and referrals. Most toll-free numbers provide educational materials. (Some organizations may charge handling fees.) Most toll-free numbers can be reached 24 hours a day, 7 days a week unless otherwise noted.

This directory is organized alphabetically by subject, and the entries fall into one of three general categories:
- Crisis Intervention. Organizations that provide crisis assistance.
- Rare Disorders. Organizations that provide information about diseases and disorders that affect less than 1 percent of the population.
- Professional Organizations. Organizations that offer information about health professions (such as nursing or counseling) or health topics (such as blindness or lymphoma).

This directory is compiled every year by the National Health Information Center, which is a service of the Office of Disease Prevention and Health Promotion (ODPHP), Office of Public Health and Science, U.S. Department of Health and Human Services. Note: Not all information listed here is endorsed by the U.S. Department of Health and Human Services.

[Source: 2013 Toll-Free Numbers for Health Information, National Health Information Center, Office of Disease Prevention and Health Promotion, U.S. Department of Health and Human Services, Washington, DC.]

ADOPTION

AdoptUSKids
Toll free: (888) 200-4005

Bethany Christian Services
Toll free: (800) 238-4269 (Crisis Hotline)

Child Welfare Information Gateway
Toll free: (800) 394-3366

National Adoption Center
Toll free: (800) TO-ADOPT (862-3678)

AGING

American Health Assistance Foundation
Toll free: (800) 437-2423
9:00 a.m.–5:00 p.m., Monday–Friday (Eastern time)

Caring Connections (A program of the National Hospice and Palliative Care Organization)
Toll free: (800) 658-8898 (Helpline)
9:00 a.m.–5:00 p.m., Monday–Friday (Eastern time)

Eldercare Locator
Toll free: (800) 677-1116
9:00 a.m.–8:00 p.m., Monday–Friday, except Federal holidays (Eastern time)

National Institute on Aging Information Center
Toll free: (800) 222-2225
TTY: (800) 222-4225
8:30 a.m.–5:00 p.m., Monday–Friday, except Federal holidays (Eastern time)

AIDS/HIV

AIDSinfo
Toll free: (800) 448-0440
TTY: (888) 480-3739
12:00 p.m.–5:00 p.m., Monday–Friday (Eastern time)

CDC INFO
Toll free: (800) CDC-INFO (232-4636) (English/Spanish)
TTY: (888) 232-6348

CDC National Prevention Information Network
Toll free: (800) 458-5231 (English/Spanish)
TTY: (800) 243-7012
Fax: (888) 282-7681
9:00 a.m.–8:00 p.m., Monday–Friday (Eastern time)

Project Inform HIV/AIDS Treatment Hotline
Toll free: (800) 822-7422
10:00 a.m.–4:00 p.m., Monday–Friday (Pacific time)

ALCOHOL ABUSE (See also Drug Abuse)

AdCARE Hospital Helpline
Toll free: (800) 252-6465

Al-Anon Family Group Headquarters
Toll free: (888) 4AL-ANON (425-2666)
8:00 a.m.–6:00 p.m., Monday–Friday (Eastern time)

Alcohol and Drug Helpline
Toll free: (800) 821-4357
24 hours a day, 7 days a week, 365 days a year

Calix Society
Toll free: (800) 398-0524
9:00 a.m.–4:00 p.m., Monday–Friday (Central time)

National Council on Alcoholism and Drug Dependence, Inc.
Toll free: (800) NCA-CALL (622-2255)

National Institute on Drug Abuse Research Dissemination Center
Toll free: (877) NIDA-NIH (643-2644)

Substance Abuse and Mental Health Services Administration
Toll free: (877) 767-4727

ALLERGY/ASTHMA
(See also LUNG DISEASE/ ASTHMA/ALLERGY)

Asthma and Allergy Foundation of America
Toll free: (800) 7-ASTHMA (727-8462)
9:00 a.m.–5:00 p.m., Monday–Friday (Eastern time)

Food Allergy and Anaphylaxis Network
Toll free: (800) 929-4040
9:00 a.m.–5:00 p.m., Monday–Friday (Eastern time)

National Jewish Medical and Research Center
Toll free: (800) 222-5864 (LUNG LINE)
8:30 a.m.–4:30 p.m., Monday–Friday (Central time)

ALZHEIMER'S DISEASE
(See also AGING)

Alzheimer's Association Helpline
Toll free: (800) 272-3900
Toll free: (866) 403-3073 (TDD)
9:00 a.m.–5:00 p.m., Monday–Friday (Eastern time)

Alzheimer's Disease Education and Referral Center
Toll free: (800) 438-4380
8:30 a.m.–5:00 p.m., Monday–Friday, except Federal holidays (Eastern time)

ARTHRITIS

Arthritis Foundation
Toll free: (800) 283-7800

Arthritis National Research Foundation
Toll free: (800) 588-2873
8:00 a.m.–4:00 p.m., Monday–Friday (Pacific time)

National Institute of Arthritis and Musculoskeletal and Skin Diseases Information Clearinghouse
Toll free: (877) 226-4267
8:30 a.m.–5:00 p.m., Monday–Friday, except Federal holidays (Eastern time)

AUDIOVISUALS, See LIBRARY SERVICES

AUTISM, See CHILD DEVELOPMENT/PARENTING

AUTOIMMUNE DISEASES

American Autoimmune Related Diseases Association, Inc.
Toll free: (800) 598-4668

National Institute of Arthritis and Musculoskeletal and Skin Diseases Information Clearinghouse
Toll free: (877) 226-4267
8:30 a.m.–5:00 p.m., Monday–Friday, except Federal holidays (Eastern time)

BLINDNESS, See VISION

BONE DISEASE

National Osteoporosis Foundation
Toll free: (800) 231-4222
8:30 a.m.–5:00 p.m., Monday–Friday (Eastern time)

NIH Osteoporosis and Related Bone Diseases—National Resource Center
Toll free: (800) 624-2663
8:30 a.m.–5:00 p.m., Monday–Friday, except Federal holidays (Eastern time)

BONE MARROW
(See also CANCER)

Aplastic Anemia and MDS International Foundation, Inc.
Toll free: (800) 747-2820
8:30 a.m.–4:30 p.m., Monday–Friday (Eastern time)

National Bone Marrow Transplant Link
Toll free: (800) LINK-BMT (546-5268)
8:30 a.m.–4:30 p.m., Monday–Friday (Eastern time)

National Marrow Donor Program
Toll free: (800) MARROW-2 (627-7692)
8:00 a.m.–5:00 p.m., Monday–Friday (Central time)

▌BRAIN TUMORS

American Brain Tumor Association
Toll free: (800) 886-2282
8:30 a.m.–5:00 p.m., Monday–Friday (Central time)

Children's Brain Tumor Foundation
Toll free: (866) 228-HOPE (228-4673)
9:00 a.m.–5:00 p.m., Monday–Friday (Eastern time)

National Brain Tumor Society
Toll free: (800) 770-8287
Toll free: (800) 934-2873 (Patient Services)
9:00 a.m.–5:00 p.m., Monday–Friday (Pacific time)

▌CANCER

American Cancer Society
Toll free: (800) 227-2345 (Voice/TDD/TTY)

American Childhood Cancer Organization
Toll free: (855) 858-2226
9:00 a.m.–5:00 p.m., Monday–Friday (Eastern time)

American Institute for Cancer Research
Toll free: (800) 843-8114
8:30 a.m.–9:30 p.m., MondayThursday; 8:30 a.m.–6:00 p.m.,
   Friday (Eastern time)

Breast Cancer Network of Strength
Toll free: (800) 221-2141 (English)
Toll free: (800) 986-9505 (Spanish)

CancerCare, Inc.
Toll free: (800) 813-4673

Cancer Hope Network
Toll free: (800) 552-4366
8:00 a.m.–5:30 p.m., Monday–Friday (Eastern time)

Kidney Cancer Association
Toll free: (800) 850-9132
9:00 a.m.–5:00 p.m., Monday–Friday (Central time)

National Bone Marrow Transplant Link
Toll free: (800) LINK-BMT (546-5268)
8:30 a.m.–4:30 p.m., Monday–Friday (Eastern time)

National Cancer Institute's Cancer Information Service
Toll free: (800) 4-CANCER (422-6237)
TTY: (800) 332-8615
9:00 a.m.–4:30 p.m., Monday–Friday, except Federal holidays (Eastern time)

National Marrow Donor Program
Toll free: (800) MARROW-2 (627-7692)
8:00 a.m.–5:00 p.m., Monday–Friday (Central time)

Support for People with Oral and Head and Neck Cancer
Toll free: (800) 377-0928

Susan G. Komen for the Cure
Toll free: (877) 465-6636
9:00 a.m.–5:00 p.m., Monday–Friday (Central time)

Us TOO International Prostate Cancer Education and
   Support Network
Toll free: (800) 808-7866
9:00 a.m.–5:00 p.m., Monday–Friday (Central time)

Zero—The Project to End Prostate Cancer
Toll free: (888) 245-9455

▌CHEMICAL PRODUCTS/ PESTICIDES (See also HOUSING)

National Pesticide Information Center
Toll free: (800) 858-7378 (TDD capability)
6:30 a.m.–4:30 p.m., 7 days a week (Pacific time)

▌CHILD ABUSE/MISSING CHILDREN/CHILDREN'S MENTAL HEALTH

Child Find of America, Inc.
Toll free: (800) I-AM-LOST (426-5678)
Toll free: (800) A-WAY-OUT (292-9688) (Parental abduction)
9:00 a.m.–4:00 p.m., Monday–Friday (Eastern time)

Childhelp—National Child Abuse Hotline
Toll free: (800) 4-A-CHILD (422-4453)

Child Welfare Information Gateway
Toll free: (800) 394-3366
8:00 a.m.–5:30 p.m., Monday–Friday (Eastern time)

Covenant House Nineline
Toll free: (800) 999-9999

Girls & Boys Town National Hotline
Toll free: (800) 448-3000
Toll free: (800) 448-1833 (TDD)
Spanish-speaking operators are available.

National Center for Missing and Exploited Children
Toll free: (800) THE-LOST (843-5678)
TTY: (800) 826-7653

National Institute of Mental Health Resource Information Center
Toll free: (866) 615-6464
TTY: (866) 415-8051
8:30 a.m.–5:00 p.m., Monday–Friday, except Federal holidays (Eastern time)

National Runaway Switchboard
Toll free: (800) RUNAWAY (786-2929)
Toll free: (800) 621-0394 (TDD)
Has access to AT&T Language Line

▌ CHILD CARE

National Child Care Information and Technical Assistance Center
Toll free: (800) 616-2242
Fax: (800) 716-2242
TTY: (800) 516-2242
8:30 a.m.–5:30 p.m., Monday–Friday, except Federal holidays (Eastern time)

▌ CHILD DEVELOPMENT/ PARENTING

Eunice Kennedy Shriver National Institute of Child Health and Human Development Information Resource Center
Toll free: (800) 370-2943
TTY: (888) 320-6942
Fax: (866) 760-5947
8:30 a.m.–5:00 p.m., Monday–Friday, except Federal holidays (Eastern time)

Human Growth Foundation
Toll free: (800) 451-6434
9:00 a.m.–5:00 p.m., Monday–Friday (Eastern time)

MAGIC Foundation for Children's Growth
Toll free: (800) 362-4423
9:00 a.m.–4:00 p.m., Monday–Friday (Central time)

National Association for the Education of Young Children
Toll free: (800) 424-2460
9:00 a.m.–5:00 p.m., Monday–Friday (Eastern time)

National Lekotek Center
Toll free: (800) 366-7529
9:00 a.m.–5:00 p.m., Monday–Friday (Central time)

National Organization on Fetal Alcohol Syndrome
Toll free: (800) 66-NOFAS (666-6327)
9:00 a.m.–6:00 p.m., Monday–Friday (Eastern time)

Safe Sleep Campaign—Eunice Kennedy Shriver National Institute of Child Health and Human Development
Toll free: (800) 505-CRIB (505-2742)
8:30 a.m.–5:00 p.m., Monday–Friday, except Federal holidays (Eastern time)

Starlight Children's Foundation
Toll free: (800) 274-7827
8:00 a.m.–5:00 p.m., Monday–Friday (Pacific time)

Zero to Three: National Center for Infants, Toddlers and Families
Toll free: (800) 899-4301
9:00 a.m.–5:00 p.m., Monday–Friday (Eastern time)

▌ CHRONIC PAIN

American Chronic Pain Association
Toll free: (800) 533-3231

American Pain Foundation
Toll free: (888) 615-7246

▌ CLINICAL TRIALS

CenterWatch Clinical Trials Listing Service
Toll free: (866) 219-3440

National Institutes of Health Clinical Center
Toll free: (800) 411-1222 (Patient Recruitment)

▌ CRISIS INTERVENTION (All operate 24 hours/7 days a week)

A-WAY-OUT
Toll free: (800) 292-9688
Provides unique crisis mediation program for parents contemplating abduction of their children, or who have already abducted their children and want to use Child Find Volunteer Family Mediators to resolve their custody dispute.

Childhelp: National Child Abuse Hotline
Toll free: (800) 4-A-CHILD (422-4453)
Provides multilingual crisis intervention on child abuse and domestic violence issues. Gives referrals to local agencies offering counseling and other services related to child abuse, adult survivor issues, and domestic violence. Provides literature on child abuse in English and Spanish. Calls are anonymous, toll-free, and counselors are paid, degreed professionals.

Covenant House Nineline
Toll free: (800) 999-9999
Crisis line for youth, teens, and families. Locally based referrals throughout the United States. Help for youth and parents regarding drugs, abuse, homelessness, runaway children, and message relays.

Girls & Boys Town National Hotline
Toll free: (800) 448-3000
Toll free: (800) 448-1833 (TDD)
Provides short-term intervention and counseling and refers callers to local community resources. Counsels on parent-child conflicts, family issues, suicide, pregnancy, runaway youth, physical and sexual abuse, and other issues that impact children and families. Spanish-speaking operators are available.

National Center for Missing & Exploited Children
Toll free: (800) THE-LOST (843-5678)
TTY: (800) 826-7653
The National Center for Missing & Exploited Children's mission is to help prevent child abduction and sexual exploitation; help find missing children; and assist victims of child abduction and sexual exploitation, their families, and the professionals who serve them.

National Runaway Switchboard
Toll free: (800) RUNAWAY (786-2929)
Toll free: (800) 621-0394 (TDD)
Provides crisis intervention and travel assistance information to runaways. Gives referrals to shelters nationwide. Also relays messages to, or sets up conference calls with, parents at the request of the child. Has access to AT&T Language Line.

National Suicide Prevention Lifeline
Toll free: (800) 273-TALK (273-8255)
TTY: (800) 799-4TTY (799-4889)
Toll free: (888) 628-9454 (Spanish)
The National Suicide Prevention Lifeline is a 24-hour, toll-free suicide prevention service that routes calls from anywhere in the country to the nearest available certified crisis center where trained crisis counselors talk to callers and can link them to local services.

Rape, Abuse, and Incest National Network
Toll free: (800) 656-4673
Connects caller to the nearest counseling center that provides counseling for rape, abuse, and incest victims.

▌DENTAL/ORAL HEALTH

Academy of General Dentistry
Toll free: (888) 243-3368
Toll free: (877) 292-9327 (Referral Line)

American Association of Orthodontists
Toll free: (800) 424-2841

American Dental Association
Toll free: (800) 947-4746 (Catalog Sales and Service)
8:00 a.m.–5:00 p.m., Monday–Friday (Central time)

CDC Division of Oral Health—Centers for Disease Control and Prevention
Toll free: (800) 232-4636
TTY: (888) 232-6348

National Oral Health Information Clearinghouse— National Institute of Dental and Craniofacial Research
Toll free: (866) 232-4528
8:30 a.m.–5:00 p.m., Monday–Friday, except Federal holidays (Eastern time)

▌DIABETES/DIGESTIVE DISEASES

American Association of Diabetes Educators
Toll free: (800) 338-3633
8:00 a.m.–5:00 p.m., Monday–Friday (Central time)

American Diabetes Association
Toll free: (800) 342-2383
Toll free: (800) ADA-ORDER (232-6733) (Fax, Order Fulfillment)
8:30 a.m.–8:00 p.m., Monday–Friday (Eastern time)

Crohn's and Colitis Foundation of America, Inc.
Toll free: (800) 932-2423
9:00 a.m.–5:00 p.m., Monday–Friday (Eastern time)

Juvenile Diabetes Research Foundation International
Toll free: (800) 533-CURE (533-2873)
9:00 a.m.–5:00 p.m., Monday–Friday (Eastern time)

National Diabetes Information Clearinghouse
Toll free: (800) 860-8747
TTY: (866) 569-1162
8:30 a.m.–5:00 p.m., Monday–Friday (Eastern time)

National Digestive Diseases Information Clearinghouse
Toll free: (800) 891-5389
TTY: (866) 569-1162
8:30 a.m.–5:00 p.m., Monday–Friday (Eastern time)

▌DISABLING CONDITIONS/ DISABILITIES ACCESS

Americans with Disabilities Act Information Line
Toll free: (800) 514-0301
TTY: (800) 514-0383
9:30 a.m.–5:30 p.m., Monday–Wednesday and Friday; 12:30 p.m.–5:30 p.m., Thursday, except Federal holidays (Eastern time). Spanish-speaking operators are available.

Amputee Coalition of America
Toll free: (888) AMP-KNOW (267-5669)
TTY: (865) 525-4512
8:00 a.m.–5:00 p.m., Monday–Friday (Eastern time)

Children's Craniofacial Association
Toll free: (800) 535-3643
9:00 a.m.–5:00 p.m., Monday–Friday (Central time)

Cleft Palate Foundation
Toll free: (800) 242-5338

DBTAC: Mid-Atlantic Americans with Disabilities Act Center
Toll free: (800) 949-4232 (Voice/TTY)
8:30 a.m.–5:00 p.m., Monday–Friday, except Federal holidays (Eastern time)

Easter Seals
Toll free: (800) 221-6827
8:30 a.m.–5:00 p.m., Monday–Friday (Central time)

FACES: The National Craniofacial Association
Toll free: (800) 332-2373
9:00 a.m.–5:00 p.m., Monday–Friday (Eastern time)

Families of Spinal Muscular Atrophy
Toll free: (800) 886-1762
7:00 a.m.–3:00 p.m., Monday–Friday (Central time)

Job Accommodation Network
Toll free: (800) ADA-WORK (232-9675)
Toll free: (800) 526-7234
Toll free: (877) 781-9403 (TTY)
9:00 a.m.–6:00 p.m., Monday–Friday (Eastern time).
  Services available in English, Spanish, and French.

**National Center on Birth Defects and Developmental
  Disabilities, Centers for Disease Control
  and Prevention**
Toll free: (800) 232-4636
TTY: (800) 232-6348

National Dissemination Center for Children with Disabilities
Toll free: (800) 695-0285 (Voice/TTY)
9:00 a.m.–5:00 p.m., Monday–Friday, except Federal holidays (Eastern time)

National Rehabilitation Information Center
Toll free: (800) 346-2742
9:00 a.m.–5:00 p.m., Monday–Friday (Eastern time)

Scoliosis Association
Toll free: (800) 800-0669
1:00 p.m.5:30 p.m., Monday–Friday (Eastern time)

DRINKING WATER SAFETY

Safe Drinking Water Hotline
Toll free: (800) 426-4791 (English/Spanish)
8:30 a.m.–5:45 p.m., Monday–Thursday, 8:30 a.m.–4:45
  p.m., Friday.

DRUG ABUSE (See also ALCOHOL ABUSE and SUBSTANCE ABUSE

Drug-Free Workplace Helpline
Toll free: (800) 967-5752
9:00 a.m.–5:30 p.m., Monday–Friday (Eastern time)

Drug Help
Toll free: (800) 378-4435
9:00 a.m.–5:00 p.m., Monday–Friday (Eastern time)

**Housing and Urban Development Drug Information and
  Strategy Clearinghouse**
Toll free: (800) 955-2232
8:00 a.m.–8:00 p.m., Monday–Friday (Eastern time)

Pride Surveys
Toll free: (800) 279-6361
8:30 a.m.–4:00 p.m., Monday–Friday (Central time)

PRIDE Youth Programs
Toll free: (800) 668-9277
8:00 a.m.–5:00 p.m., Monday–Friday (Central time)

Substance Abuse and Mental Health Services Administration
Toll free: (877) 767-4727

DWARFISM

Human Growth Foundation
Toll free: (800) 451-6434
9:00 a.m.–5:00 p.m., Monday–Friday (Eastern time)

DYSLEXIA, See LEARNING DISORDERS

EATING DISORDERS

National Eating Disorders Association
Toll free: (800) 931-2237 (Helpline)

ENVIRONMENT

Asbestos Ombudsman Hotline
Toll free: (800) 368-5888
8:00 a.m.–4:30 p.m., Monday–Friday, except Federal holidays (Eastern time)

**Environmental Justice Information Line (U.S. Environmental
  Protection Agency)**
Toll free: (800) 962-6215 (English/Spanish)
8:00 a.m.–5:30 p.m., Monday–Friday (Eastern time)

ESSENTIAL TREMOR

International Essential Tremor Foundation
Toll free: (888) 387-3667
8:00 a.m.–4:30 p.m., Monday–Friday (Central time)

FIRE PREVENTION

National Fire Protection Association
Toll free: (800) 344-3555 (Customer Service)
9:00 a.m.–5:00 p.m., Monday–Friday (Eastern time)

FITNESS

Aerobics and Fitness Foundation of America
Toll free: (800) 968-7263 (Consumer Hotline)
Toll free: (800) 446-2322 (For Professionals)
6:30 a.m.–6:00 p.m., Monday–Friday (Pacific time)

American Council on Exercise
Toll free: (888) 825-3636
7:00 a.m.–5:00 p.m., Monday–Friday (Pacific time)

American Running Association
Toll free: (800) 776-2732
9:00 a.m.–5:00 p.m., Monday–Friday (Eastern time)

Shaping America's Youth
Toll free: (800) SAY-9221 (729-9221)

TOPS (Taking Off Pounds Sensibly) Club, Inc.
Toll free: (800) 932-8677
8:00 a.m.–4:30 p.m., Monday–Friday (Central time)

Weight Control Information Network—National Institute of Diabetes and Digestive and Kidney Diseases
Toll free: (877) 946-4627
8:30 a.m.–5:00 p.m., Monday–Friday, except Federal holidays (Eastern time)

YMCA of the USA
Toll free: (800) 872-9622
8:00 a.m.–5:00 p.m., Monday–Friday
(Central time)

FOOD SAFETY

Center for Food Safety and Applied Nutrition, FDA
Toll free: (888) SAFEFOOD (723-3366)
10:00 a.m.–4:00 p.m., Monday–Friday, except Federal holidays (Eastern time)

U.S. Department of Agriculture Meat and Poultry Hotline
Toll free: (888) MPHotline (674-6854)
TTY: (800) 256-7072
10:00 a.m.–4:00 p.m., Monday–Friday; 8:00 a.m.–2:00 p.m. on Thanksgiving (Eastern time)

U.S. Fish & Wildlife Service
Toll free: (800) 344-WILD (344-9453)
8:00 a.m.–8:00 p.m., Monday–Friday, except Federal holidays (Eastern time)

GAY, LESBIAN, BISEXUAL, TRANSGENDER HEALTH

Gay, Lesbian, Bisexual, and Transgender Helpline
Toll free: (888) 340-4528
6:00 p.m.–11:00 p.m., 7 days a week (Eastern time)

Gay, Lesbian, Bisexual, and Transgender National Hotline
Toll free: (888) 843-4564
4:00 p.m.–12:00 a.m., Monday–Friday; 12:00 p.m.–5:00 p.m., Saturday (Eastern time)

Lambda Legal Defense and Education Fund
Toll free: (866) 542-8336 (Help Desk)
9:00 a.m.–5:00 p.m., Monday–Friday
(Eastern time)

National Center for Lesbian Rights
Toll free: (800) 528-6257 (Youth Legal Information Line)
9:00 a.m.–5:00 p.m., Monday–Friday
(Pacific time)

Peer Listening Line
Toll free: (800) 399-7337
5:30 p.m.–10:00 p.m., 7 days a week
(Eastern time)

Trevor Helpline
Toll free: (866) 4-U-TREVOR (488-7386)

GENERAL HEALTH

Agency for Healthcare Research and Quality Clearinghouse
Toll free: (800) 358-9295
8:30 a.m.–5:00 p.m., Monday–Friday, except Federal holidays (Eastern time)

American Academy of Family Physicians
Toll free: (800) 274-2237

American Chiropractic Association
Toll free: (800) 986-4636
8:30 a.m.–5:30 p.m., Monday–Friday
(Eastern time)

American Osteopathic Association
Toll free: (800) 621-1773
8:00 a.m.–5:00 p.m., Monday–Friday
(Central time)

American Podiatric Medical Association, Inc.
Toll free: (800) ASK-APMA (275-2762)

Angel Flight Mid-Atlantic
Toll free: (800) 296-3797
9:00 a.m.–5:00 p.m., Monday–Friday
(Eastern time)

Health Resources and Services Administration Information Center
Toll free: (888) ASK-HRSA (275-4772)
TTY: (877) 4TY-HRSA (489-4772) (TTY/TDD)
8:30 a.m.–5:00 p.m., Monday–Friday
(Eastern time)

MedicAlert Foundation
Toll free: (888) 633-4298

National Center for Chronic Disease Prevention and Health Promotion—Centers for Disease Control and Prevention
Toll free: (800) 232-4636
TTY: (888) 232-6348

National Center for Complementary and Alternative Medicine Clearinghouse
Toll free: (888) 644-6226
TTY: (866) 464-3615
Fax: (866) 464-3616
8:30 a.m.–5:00 p.m., Monday–Friday, except Federal holidays (Eastern time)

National Center for Health Statistics—Centers for Disease Control and Prevention
Toll free: (800) 232-4636

National Health Information Center
Toll free: (800) 336-4797
9:00 a.m.–5:30 p.m., Monday–Friday, except Federal holidays (Eastern time)

National Health Service Corps
Toll free: (800) 221-9393 Scholarships/Loan Repayment & Job Opportunities in Underserved Areas
TTY: (877) 897-9910
9:00 a.m.–5:30 p.m., Monday–Friday (Eastern time)

National Hispanic Family Health Helpline
Toll free: (866) SU-FAMILIA (783-2645)
9:00 a.m.–6:00 p.m., Monday–Friday (Eastern time)

National Injury Information Clearinghouse
Toll free: (800) 638-2772 (Consumer Hotline)
TTY: (800) 638-8270

National Patient Travel Helpline
Toll free: (800) 296-1217
9:00 a.m.–5:00 p.m., Monday–Friday (Eastern time)

U.S. Food and Drug Administration
Toll free: (800) 332-1088 (MedWatch)
Toll free: (888) 463-6332 (Consumer Inquiries)

Well Spouse Association
Toll free: (800) 838-0879
10:00 a.m.–3:00 p.m., Monday–Friday (Eastern time)

GENETIC DISEASES

Genetic Alliance
Toll free: (800) 336-4363
9:00 a.m.–5:30 p.m., Monday–Friday (Eastern time)

Genetic and Rare Diseases Information Center
Toll free: (888) 205-2311
TTY: (888) 205-3223
12:00 p.m.6:00 p.m., Monday–Friday, except Federal holidays (Eastern time)

March of Dimes
Toll free: (888) 663-4637
Toll free: (800) 925-1855 (Spanish)

National Hematologic Diseases Information Service
Toll free: (888) 828-0877
Toll free: (866) 569-1162 (TTY)

HEADACHE/HEAD INJURY

National Brain Injury Information Center
Toll free: (800) 444-6443
9:00 a.m.–5:00 p.m., Monday–Friday (Eastern time)

National Headache Foundation
Toll free: (888) 643-5552
9:00 a.m.–5:00 p.m., Monday–Friday (Central time)

HEALTHY WEIGHT/WEIGHT LOSS

Shaping America's Youth
Toll free: (800) SAY-9221 (729-9221)

TOPS (Taking Off Pounds Sensibly) Club, Inc.
Toll free: (800) 932-8677
8:00 a.m.–4:30 p.m., Monday–Friday (Central time)

Weight Control Information Network—National Institute of Diabetes and Digestive and Kidney Diseases
Toll free: (877) 946-4627
8:30 a.m.–5:00 p.m., Monday–Friday, except Federal holidays (Eastern time)

HEARING AND SPEECH

American Society for Deaf Children
Toll free: (800) 942-ASDC (942-2732)

American Speech-Language-Hearing Association
Toll free: (800) 638-8255
8:30 a.m.–5:00 p.m., Monday–Friday (Eastern time)

Dial A Hearing Screening Test (Occupational Hearing Services)
Toll free: (800) 222-3277 (Voice/TTY)
9:00 a.m.–4:00 p.m., Monday–Friday, except Federal holidays (Eastern time)

Hear Now
Toll free: (800) 3288602 (Voice/TDD)
8:00 a.m.–4:00 p.m., Monday–Friday (Mountain time)

International Hearing Society
Toll free: (800) 521-5247
8:00 a.m.–5:00 p.m., Monday–Friday (Eastern time)

National Consortium on Deaf-Blindness
Toll free: (800) 438-9376
TTY: (800) 854-7013
9:00 a.m.–4:00 p.m., Monday–Friday, except Federal holidays (Eastern time)

National Family Association for Deaf-Blind
Toll free: (800) 255-0411 (Voice/TTY)
8:45 a.m.–4:30 p.m., Monday–Friday (Eastern time)

National Institute on Deafness and Other Communication Disorders Information Clearinghouse
Toll free: (800) 241-1044
TTY: (800) 241-1055
8:30 a.m.–5:00 p.m., Monday–Friday, except Federal holidays (Eastern time)

Vestibular Disorders Association
Toll free: (800) 837-8428
8:00 a.m.–5:00 p.m., Monday–Friday (Pacific time)

HEART DISEASE

American Heart Association
Toll free: (800) 242-8721
24 hours a day, 7 days a week, 365 days a year

Heart Information Center
Toll free: (800) 292-2221 (English/Spanish)
8:00 a.m.–4:00 p.m., Monday–Friday (Central time)

HORMONAL DISORDERS

American Thyroid Association
Toll free: (800) 849-7643

Hormone Foundation
Toll free: (800) HORMONE (467-6663)
8:30 a.m.–5:00 p.m., Monday–Friday (Eastern time)

National Endocrine and Metabolic Diseases Information Service
Toll free: (888) 828-0904
Toll free: (866) 569-1162 (TTY)

HOSPITAL/HOSPICE CARE

Caring Connections (A program of the National Hospice and Palliative Care Organization)
Toll free: (800) 658-8898 Helpline
9:00 a.m.–5:00 p.m., Monday–Friday (Eastern time)

Children's Hospice International
Toll free: (800) 242-4453
9:00 a.m.–5:00 p.m., Monday–Friday (Eastern time)

Hill-Burton Medical Care Program
Toll free: (800) 638-0742
Toll free: (800) 492-0359 (Maryland)

National Association of Hospital Hospitality Houses, Inc.
Toll free: (800) 542-9730
9:00 a.m.–5:00 p.m., Monday–Friday (Eastern time)

Shriners Hospital for Children Referral Line
Toll free: (800) 237-5055
8:00 a.m.–5:00 p.m., Monday–Friday (Eastern time)

HOUSING (See also CHEMICAL PRODUCTS/ PESTICIDES and LEAD)

HUD USER
Toll free: (800) 245-2691
Toll free: (800) 927-7589 (TDD)
8:30 a.m.–5:15 p.m., Monday–Friday, except Federal holidays (Eastern time)

Public and Indian Housing Information and Resource Center
Toll free: (800) 955-2232
9:00 a.m.–5:00 p.m., Monday–Friday (Eastern time)

IMMUNIZATION

National Center for Immunization and Respiratory Diseases, Centers for Disease Control and Prevention
Toll free: (800) CDC-INFO (232-4636) (English/Spanish)
TTY: (800) 232-6348

IMPOTENCE

American Urological Association Foundation, Inc.
Toll free: (800) RING-AUA (746-4282)
8:30 a.m.–5:00 p.m., Monday–Friday (Eastern time)

INFECTIOUS DISEASES & INFLUENZA (FLU)

American Lung Association
Toll free: (800) 586-4872

Centers for Disease Control and Prevention
Toll free: (800) 232-4636
TTY: (800) 232-6348

National Institute of Allergy and Infectious Diseases
Toll free: (866) 284-4107
Toll free: (800) 877-8339 (TDD)

INSURANCE/MEDICARE/ MEDICAID

Centers for Medicare & Medicaid Services
Toll free: (877) 267-2323 (Headquarters)
Toll free: (800) 633-4227 (Medicare Service Center)
TTY: (866) 226-1819 (Headquarters)
TTY: (877) 486-2048 (Medicare Service Center)

DHHS Office of Inspector General
Toll free: (800) 447-8477 (Hotline)
8:00 a.m.–5:30 p.m., Monday–Friday (Eastern time)

Insure Kids Now Hotline—Health Resources and Services Administration
Toll free: (877) 543-7669
8:00 a.m.–5:00 p.m., Monday–Friday (Eastern time)

Pension Benefit Guaranty Corporation
Toll free: (800) 400-PBGC (400-7242)
8:00 a.m.–5:00 p.m., Monday–Friday (Eastern time)

Social Security Administration
Toll free: (800) 772-1213
TTY: (800) 325-0778
7:00 a.m.–7:00 p.m., Monday–Friday (Eastern time)

▌JUSTICE

National Criminal Justice Reference Service
Toll free: (800) 851-3420
TTY: (877) 712-9279
10:00 a.m.–6:00 p.m., Monday–Friday (Eastern time)

▌KIDNEY DISEASE, See UROLOGICAL DISORDERS

▌LEAD (See also HOUSING)

National Lead Information Center
Toll free: (800) 424-5323
8:00 a.m.–6:00 p.m., Monday–Friday, except Federal holidays (Eastern time)

▌LEARNING DISORDERS

Children and Adults with Attention Deficit/Hyperactivity Disorders
Toll free: (800) 233-4050 (English/Spanish)
9:00 a.m.–5:00 p.m., Monday–Friday (Eastern time)

International Dyslexia Association
Toll free: (800) ABCD123 (222-3123)

▌LIBRARY SERVICES

Captioned Media Program, National Association for the Deaf
Toll free: (800) 237-6213
TTY: (800) 237-6819
Fax: (800) 538-5636
8:30 a.m.–5:00 p.m., Monday–Friday (Eastern time)

Learning Ally
Toll free: (800) 221-4792
8:30 a.m.–4:45 p.m., Monday–Friday (Eastern time)

National Library of Medicine—National Institutes of Health
Toll free: (888) 346-3656
Toll free: (800) 735-2258 (TDD)
8:30 a.m.–5:00 p.m., Monday–Friday; 8:30 a.m.–2:00 p.m., Saturday, except Federal holidays (Eastern time)

National Library Service for the Blind and Physically Handicapped
Toll free: (800) 424-8567
8:00 a.m.–4:30 p.m., Monday–Friday, except Federal holidays (Eastern time)

▌LIVER DISEASES

American Liver Foundation
Toll free: (800) GO-LIVER (465-4837)
8:00 a.m.–4:00 p.m., Monday–Friday (Central time)

Hepatitis Foundation International
Toll free: (800) 891-0707
9:00 a.m.–5:00 p.m., Monday–Friday (Eastern time)

▌LUNG DISEASE/ASTHMA/ ALLERGY

American Lung Association
Toll free: (800) LUNG-USA (586-4872)
7:00 a.m.–9:00 p.m., Monday–Friday (Central time)

Asthma and Allergy Foundation of America
Toll free: (800) 7-ASTHMA (727-8462)
9:00 a.m.–5:00 p.m., Monday–Friday (Eastern time)

National Jewish Medical and Research Center
Toll free: (800) 222-5864 (LUNG LINE)
8:30 a.m.–4:30 p.m., Monday–Friday (Central time)

▌MATERNAL AND CHILD HEALTH

Eunice Kennedy Shriver National Institute of Child Health and Human Development Information Resource Center
Toll free: (800) 370-2943
8:30 a.m.–5:00 p.m., Monday–Friday, except Federal holidays (Eastern time)

La Leche League International
Toll free: (800) La Leche (525-3243)
9:00 a.m.–5:00 p.m., Monday–Friday (Central time)

National Prenatal Helpline
Toll free: (800) 311-2229
Toll free: (800) 504-7081 (Spanish)
9:00 a.m.–6:00 p.m., Monday–Friday (Eastern time)

National Life Center/Pregnancy Hotline
Toll free: (800) 848-5683

Zero to Three: National Center for Infants, Toddlers and Families
Toll free: (800) 899-4301
9:00 a.m.–5:00 p.m., Monday–Friday (Eastern time)

MEDICARE/MEDICAID, See INSURANCE/MEDICARE/MEDICAID

MENTAL HEALTH (See also CHILD ABUSE/MISSING CHILDREN/CHILDREN'S MENTAL HEALTH)

The ARC of the United States
Toll free: (800) 433-5255
8:00 a.m.–5:00 p.m., Monday–Friday (Eastern time)

Mental Health America Resource Center
Toll free: (800) 969-6642
TTY: (800) 433-5959
9:00 a.m.–5:00 p.m., Monday–Friday (Eastern time)

National Alliance on Mental Illness
Toll free: (800) 950-6264 Helpline
10:00 a.m.–6:00 p.m., Monday–Friday (Eastern time)

National Council on Problem Gambling
Toll free: (800) 522-4700
9:30 a.m.–5:30 p.m., Monday–Friday (Eastern time)

National Gaucher Foundation
Toll free: (800) 504-3189
9:00 a.m.–5:00 p.m., Monday–Friday (Eastern time)

National Institute of Mental Health Resource Information Center
Toll free: (866) 615-6464
TTY: (866) 415-8051
8:30 a.m.–5:00 p.m., Monday–Friday, except Federal holidays (Eastern time)

Substance Abuse and Mental Health Services Administration
Toll free: (877) 767-4727
8:00 a.m.–12:00 a.m., Monday–Friday, except Federal holidays (Eastern time)

MINORITY HEALTH

National Hispanic Family Health Helpline
Toll free: (800) 311-2229
Toll free: (866) SU-FAMILIA (783-2645)
9:00 a.m.–6:00 p.m., Monday–Friday (Eastern time)

National Prenatal Helpline
Toll free: (800) 311-2229
Toll free: (800) 504-7081 (Spanish)
9:00 a.m.–6:00 p.m., Monday–Friday (Eastern time)

Office of Minority Health Resource Center
Toll free: (800) 444-6472
9:00 a.m.–5:00 p.m., Monday–Friday, except Federal holidays (Eastern time)

NUTRITION

American Institute for Cancer Research
Toll free: (800) 843-8114
8:30 a.m.–9:30 p.m., Monday–Thursday; 8:30 a.m.–6:00 p.m., Friday (Eastern time)

Center for Food Safety and Applied Nutrition—U.S. Food and Drug Administration
Toll free: (888) 723-3366 (Seafood line)

National Dairy Council
Toll free: (800) 426-8271
Fax: (800) 974-6455
8:00 a.m.–5:00 p.m., Monday–Friday (Central time)

Shaping America's Youth
Toll free: (800) SAY-9221 (729-9221)

ORGAN DONATION (See also VISION and UROLOGICAL DISORDERS)

Living Bank
Toll free: (800) 528-2971
7:30 a.m.–4:30 p.m., Monday–Friday (Central time)

National Marrow Donor Program
Toll free: (800) MARROW-2 (627-7692)
8:00 a.m.–5:00 p.m., Monday–Friday (Central time)

United Network for Organ Sharing
Toll free: (888) TXINFO1 (894-6361)
8:00 a.m.–6:00 p.m., Monday–Friday (Eastern time)

PAIN

American Chronic Pain Association
Toll free: (800) 533-3231

American Pain Foundation
Toll free: (888) 615-7246

PARALYSIS AND SPINAL CORD INJURY (See also STROKE)

Christopher and Dana Reeve Foundation
Toll free: (800) 225-0292
9:00 a.m.–5:00 p.m., Monday–Friday (Eastern time)

National Rehabilitation Information Center
Toll free: (800) 346-2742
9:00 a.m.–5:00 p.m., Monday–Friday (Eastern time)

National Spinal Cord Injury Association
Toll free: (800) 962-9629
8:30 a.m.–5:30 p.m., Monday–Friday (Eastern time)

Paralyzed Veterans of America
Toll free: (800) 424-8200
TTY: (800) 795-4327
9:00 a.m.–5:00 p.m., Monday–Friday (Eastern time)

PARKINSON'S DISEASE

American Parkinson's Disease Association
Toll free: (800) 223-2732
8:30 a.m.–4:30 p.m., Monday–Friday (Eastern time)

National Parkinson Foundation, Inc.
Toll free: (800) 473-4636
9:00 a.m.–5:00 p.m., Monday–Friday (Eastern time)

Parkinson's Disease Foundation
Toll free: (800) 457-6676
9:00 a.m.–5:00 p.m., Monday–Friday (Eastern time)

PESTICIDES, See CHEMICAL PRODUCTS/PESTICIDES

POISON CONTROL

Poison Help Hotline
Toll free: (800) 222-1222

PRACTITIONER REPORTING

Institute for Safe Medication Practices
Toll free: (800) 324-5723

PREGNANCY/MISCARRIAGE

Bradley Method of Natural Childbirth
Toll free: (800) 422-4784
9:00 a.m.–5:00 p.m., Monday–Friday (Pacific time)

DES Action USA
Toll free: (800) DES-9288 (337-9288)
9:00 a.m.–3:00 p.m., Monday–Friday (Pacific time)

International Childbirth Education Association
Toll free: (800) 624-4934 (Book Center orders)
8:30 a.m.–4:00 p.m., Monday–Friday (Central time)

Lamaze International
Toll free: (800) 368-4404
9:00 a.m.–5:00 p.m., Monday–Friday (Eastern time)

Liberty Godparent Home
Toll free: (800) 542-4453

National Abortion Federation
Toll free: (800) 772-9100
8:00 a.m.–9:00 p.m., Monday–Friday; 9:00 a.m.–5:00 p.m.,
    SaturdaySunday (Eastern time)

National Prenatal Helpline
Toll free: (800) 311-2229
Toll free: (800) 504-7081 (Spanish)
9:00 a.m.–6:00 p.m., Monday–Friday (Eastern time)

PROFESSIONALS

AboutFace
Toll free: (800) 665-3223

Academy of General Dentistry
Toll free: (888) 243-3368
Toll free: (877) 292-9327 (Referral Line)

Academy of Laser Dentistry
Toll free: (877) 527-3776

American Academy of Cosmetic Dentistry
Toll free: (800) 543-9220

American Academy of Family Physicians
Toll free: (800) 274-2237

American Academy of Oral and Maxillofacial Pathology
Toll free: (888) 552-2667

**American Alliance for Health, Physical Education,
    Recreation and Dance**
Toll free: (800) 213-7193
8:00 a.m.–4:30 p.m., Monday–Friday (Eastern time)

American Association of Critical Care Nurses
Toll free: (800) 899-2226
7:30 a.m.–4:30 p.m., Monday–Friday (Pacific time)

American Association of Endodontists
Toll free: (800) 872-3636

American Academy of Oral and Maxillofacial Surgeons
Toll free: (800) 822-6637

American Association of Women Dentists
Toll free: (800) 920-2293

American Chronic Pain Association
Toll free: (800) 533-3231

American Council for the Blind
Toll free: (800) 424-8666
9:00 a.m.–5:00 p.m., Monday–Friday (Eastern time)

American Counseling Association
Toll free: (800) 347-6647
8:00 a.m.–4:30 p.m., Monday–Friday (Eastern time)

American Dental Assistants Association
Toll free: (877) 874-3785

American Nurses Association
Toll free: (800) 274-4ANA (274-4262)
9:00 a.m.–5:00 p.m., Monday–Friday (Eastern time)

American Orthodontic Society
Toll free: (800) 448-1600

AmeriFace
Toll free: (888) 486-1209

Arthritis National Research Foundation
Toll free: (800) 588-2873
8:00 a.m.–4:00 p.m., Monday–Friday (Pacific time)

Association for Applied Psychophysiology and Biofeedback
Toll free: (800) 477-8892
8:00 a.m.–5:00 p.m., Monday–Friday (Mountain time)

Association of periOperative Registered Nurses
Toll free: (800) 755-2676
7:00 a.m.–4:30 p.m., Monday–Friday (Mountain time)

CDC National Prevention Information Network
Toll free: (800) 458-5231 (English/Spanish)
TTY: (800) 243-7012
Fax: (888) 282-7681
9:00 a.m.–8:00 p.m., Monday–Friday (Eastern time)

College of American Pathologists
Toll free: (800) 323-4040
8:00 a.m.–5:00 p.m., Monday–Friday (Central time)

DBTAC: Mid-Atlantic Americans with Disabilities Act Center
Toll free: (800) 949-4232 (Voice/TTY)
8:30 a.m.–5:00 p.m., Monday–Friday, except Federal holidays (Eastern time)

Dystonia Medical Research Foundation
Toll free: (800) 377-3978
8:00 a.m.–5:00 p.m., Monday–Friday (Central time)

Federal Emergency Management Agency
Toll free: (800) 621-FEMA (621-3362)
Toll free: (800) 462-7585 (TDD)
Fax: (800) 827-8112

Glaucoma Research Foundation
Toll free: (800) 826-6693
8:30 a.m.–5:00 p.m., Monday–Friday (Pacific time)

Immune Deficiency Foundation
Toll free: (800) 296-4433
9:00 a.m.–5:00 p.m., Monday–Friday (Eastern time)

Indian Health Service Division of Oral Health
Toll free: (800) 447-3368 (Dental Vacancies)

International Childbirth Education Association
Toll free: (800) 624-4934 (Book Center orders)
8:30 a.m.–4:00 p.m., Monday–Friday (Central time)

International Chiropractors Association
Toll free: (800) 423-4690
9:00 a.m.–5:30 p.m., Monday–Friday (Eastern time)

Leukemia & Lymphoma Society
Toll free: (800) 955-4572
9:00 a.m.–6:00 p.m., Monday–Friday (Eastern time)

Lighthouse International
Toll free: (800) 829-0500
9:00 a.m.–5:00 p.m., Monday–Friday (Eastern time)

Medical Institute for Sexual Health
Toll free: (800) 892-9484 (publication orders only)
8:15 a.m.–5:00 p.m., Monday–Friday (Central time)

National Child Care Information and Technical Assistance Center, ACF
Toll free: (800) 616-2242
TTY: (800) 516-2242
Fax: (800) 716-2242
8:30 a.m.–5:30 p.m., Monday–Friday, except Federal holidays (Eastern time)

National Clearinghouse of Rehabilitation Training Materials
Toll free: (866) 821-5355
8:00 a.m.–5:00 p.m., Monday–Friday (Mountain time)

National Institute for Occupational Safety and Health Information Inquiry Service
Toll free: (800) 232-4636
TTY: (888) 232-6348
9:00 a.m.–4:00 p.m., Monday–Friday, except Federal holidays (Eastern time)

National Jewish Medical and Research Center
Toll free: (800) 222-5864 (LUNG LINE)
8:30 a.m.–4:30 p.m., Monday–Friday (Central time)

National Resource Center on Domestic Violence
Toll free: (800) 537-2238
TTY: (800) 553-2508
8:00 a.m.–5:00 p.m., Monday–Friday (Eastern time)

National Technical Information Service
Toll free: (800) 553-6847
8:00 a.m.–6:00 p.m., Monday–Friday, except Federal holidays (Eastern time)

Prevent Child Abuse America
Toll free: (800) 244-5373

Research to Prevent Blindness
Toll free: (800) 621-0026
9:00 a.m.–5:00 p.m., Monday–Friday (Eastern time)

School Nutrition Association
Toll free: (800) 877-8822
8:30 a.m.–5:30 p.m., Monday–Friday (Eastern time)

RARE DISEASES/DISORDERS

(A rare disorder is defined as a disorder that affects less than 1 percent of the population at any given time.)

ALS Association (Amyotrophic Lateral Sclerosis, Lou Gehrig's Disease)
Toll free: (800) 782-4747
7:30 a.m.–4:00 p.m., Monday–Friday (Pacific time)

American Behcet's Disease Association
Toll free: (800) 723-4238

American Cleft Palate-Craniofacial Association/Cleft Palate Foundation
Toll free: (800) 242-5338 (Parent Hotline Only)
8:30 a.m.–5:30 p.m., Monday–Friday (Eastern time)

American Leprosy Missions (Hansen's Disease)
Toll free: (800) 543-3135
8:00 a.m.–5:00 p.m., Monday–Thursday; 8:00 a.m.–12:00 p.m., Friday (Eastern time)

American SIDS Institute
Toll free: (800) 232-7437
9:00 a.m.–5:00 p.m., Monday–Friday (Eastern time)

Batten Disease Support and Research Association
Toll free: (800) 448-4570
8:00 a.m.–5:00 p.m., Monday–Friday (Eastern time)

Charcot-Marie-Tooth Association
Toll free: (800) 606-2682
9:00 a.m.–5:00 p.m., Monday–Friday

Children's Tumor Foundation
Toll free: (800) 323-7938
9:00 a.m.–5:00 p.m., Monday–Friday (Eastern time)

Cooley's Anemia Foundation
Toll free: (800) 522-7222
9:00 a.m.–5:00 p.m., Monday–Friday (Eastern time)

Cornelia de Lange Syndrome Foundation, Inc.
Toll free: (800) 223-8355
Toll free: (800) 753-2357 (U.S.)
9:00 a.m.–5:00 p.m., Monday–Friday (Eastern time)

Cystic Fibrosis Foundation
Toll free: (800) 344-4823
8:00 a.m.–6:00 p.m., Monday–Friday (Eastern time)

Epilepsy Foundation of America
Toll free: (800) 332-1000
Toll free: (866) 748-8008 (Spanish)
Toll free: (800) 332-4050 (National Epilepsy Library)
Toll free: (866) 330-2718 (Publications)
9:00 a.m.–5:00 p.m., Monday–Friday (Eastern time)

Epilepsy Information Service
Toll free: (800) 642-0500 (voice mail after hours)
8:00 a.m.–5:00 p.m.

Fibromyalgia Network
Toll free: (800) 853-2929
9:00 a.m.–5:00 p.m., Monday–Thursday (Mountain time)

First Candle/SIDS Alliance
Toll free: (800) 221-7437

Genetic Alliance
Toll free: (800) 336-4363
9:00 a.m.–5:30 p.m., Monday–Friday (Eastern time)

Genetic and Rare Diseases Information Center
Toll free: (888) 205-2311
TTY: (888) 205-3223
12:00 p.m.–6:00 p.m., Monday–Friday, except Federal holidays (Eastern time)

Histiocytosis Association of America
Toll free: (800) 548-2758
9:00 a.m.–5:00 p.m., Monday–Friday (Eastern time)

Huntington's Disease Society of America, Inc.
Toll free: (800) 345-4372
9:00 a.m.–9:00 p.m., Monday–Friday (Eastern time)

International Rett Syndrome Association
Toll free: (800) 818-7388
9:00 a.m.–5:00 p.m., Monday–Friday (Eastern time)

Les Turner Amyotrophic Lateral Sclerosis Foundation, Ltd.
Toll free: (888) ALS-1107 (257-1107)
8:30 a.m.–4:30 p.m., Monday–Friday (Central time)

Lupus Foundation of America
Toll free: (800) 558-0121
Toll free: (800) 558-0231 (Spanish)
8:30 a.m.–5:00 p.m., Monday–Friday (Eastern time)

March of Dimes
Toll free: (888) 663-4637
Toll free: (800) 925-1855 (Spanish)

Multiple Sclerosis Association of America
Toll free: (800) 532-7667 (National Headquarters)
8:30 a.m.–8:00 p.m., Monday–Thursday; 8:30 a.m.–5:00 p.m., Friday (Eastern time)

Multiple Sclerosis Foundation
Toll free: (888) 673-6287
8:30 a.m.–7:00 p.m., Monday–Friday (Eastern time)

Muscular Dystrophy Association
Toll free: (800) 572-1717
9:00 a.m.–5:00 p.m., Monday–Friday (Mountain time)

Myasthenia Gravis Foundation
Toll free: (800) 541-5454
8:30 a.m.–5:00 p.m., Monday–Friday (Central time)

National Down Syndrome Congress
Toll free: (800) 232-6372
9:00 a.m.–5:30 p.m., Monday–Friday (Eastern time)

National Down Syndrome Society Hotline
Toll free: (800) 221-4602
9:00 a.m.–5:00 p.m., Monday–Friday (Eastern time)

National Fibromyalgia Partnership
Toll free: (866) 725-4404

National Fragile X Foundation
Toll free: (800) 688-8765
8:30 a.m.–5:00 p.m., Monday–Friday (Pacific time)

National Hansen's Disease Programs
Toll free: (800) 642-2477
8:00 a.m.–4:30 p.m., Monday–Friday (Central time)

National Hemophilia Foundation
Toll free: (800) 42-HANDI (424-2634)
9:00 a.m.–5:00 p.m., Monday–Friday (Eastern time);
    Summer: 9:00 a.m.–5:00 p.m., MondayThursday, 9:00
    a.m.–3:00 p.m., Friday (Eastern time)

**National Institute of Arthritis and Musculoskeletal and Skin
Diseases Information Clearinghouse**
Toll free: (877) 226-4267
8:30 a.m.–5:00 p.m., Monday–Friday, except Federal holi-
    days (Eastern time)

National Institute of Neurological Disorders and Stroke
Toll free: (800) 352-9424
8:30 a.m.–5:00 p.m., Monday–Friday, except Federal holi-
    days (Eastern time)

National Jewish Medical and Research Center
Toll free: (800) LUNG LINE (222-5864)
8:30 a.m.–4:30 p.m., Monday–Friday (Central time)

National Lymphedema Network
Toll free: (800) 541-3259
9:00 a.m.–5:00 p.m., Monday–Friday (Pacific time)

National Marfan Foundation
Toll free: (800) 8-MARFAN (862-7326)
9:00 a.m.–5:00 p.m., Monday–Friday (Eastern time)

National Multiple Sclerosis Society
Toll free: (800) 344-4867
9:00 a.m.–5:00 p.m., Monday–Friday (Eastern time)

National Organization for Albinism and Hypopigmentation
Toll free: (800) 473-2310
Fax: (800) 648-2310

National Organization for Rare Disorders
Toll free: (800) 999-6673
9:00 a.m.–5:00 p.m., Monday–Friday (Eastern time)

National Reye's Syndrome Foundation
Toll free: (800) 233-7393
8:00 a.m.–5:00 p.m., Monday–Friday (Eastern time)

National Spasmodic Torticollis Association
Toll free: (800) 487-8385
9:00 a.m.–5:00 p.m., Monday–Friday (Pacific time)

**National Sudden and Unexpected Infant/Child Death &
Pregnancy Loss Resource Center**
Toll free: (866) 866-7437
9:00 a.m.–5:00 p.m., Monday–Friday (Eastern time)

Neurofibromatosis, Inc.
Toll free: (800) 942-6825 (Hotline)

Osteogenesis Imperfecta Foundation, Inc.
Toll free: (800) 981-2663
8:30 a.m.–5:00 p.m., Monday–Friday (Eastern time)

Paget's Foundation
Toll free: (800) 237-2438
9:00 a.m.–5:00 p.m., Monday–Friday (Eastern time)

Prader-Willi Syndrome Association
Toll free: (800) 926-4797
9:00 a.m.–7:00 p.m., Monday–Friday (Eastern time)

Restless Legs Syndrome Foundation
Toll free: (877) 463-6757
8:00 a.m.–5:00 p.m., Monday–Friday (Central time)

Scleroderma Foundation
Toll free: (800) 722-4673 (Helpline)
8:30 a.m.–5:00 p.m., Monday–Friday (Eastern time)

Sickle Cell Disease Association of America, Inc.
Toll free: (800) 421-8453
8:30 a.m.–5:00 p.m., Monday–Friday, except Federal holi-
    days (Eastern time)

Sjögren's Syndrome Foundation, Inc.
Toll free: (800) 475-6473
9:00 a.m.–5:00 p.m., Monday–Friday (Eastern time)

Spina Bifida Association
Toll free: (800) 621-3141
9:00 a.m.–5:00 p.m., Monday–Friday (Eastern time)

Spondylitis Association of America
Toll free: (800) 777-8189
8:30 a.m.–5:00 p.m., Monday–Friday (Pacific time)

Sturge-Weber Foundation
Toll free: (800) 627-5482
8:00 a.m.–3:00 p.m., Monday–Friday (Eastern time)

**Support for People with Oral and Head and Neck
Cancer**
Toll free: (800) 372-0928

**Support Organization for Trisomy 18, 13 and Related
Disorders**
Toll free: (800) 716-SOFT (716-7638)

Tourette Syndrome Association, Inc.
Toll free: (888) 486-8738
9:00 a.m.–5:00 p.m., Monday–Friday (Eastern time)

Trigeminal Neuralgia Association
Toll free: (800) 923-3608

Tuberous Sclerosis Alliance
Toll free: (800) 225-6872
8:30 a.m.–5:00 p.m., Monday–Friday (Eastern time)

Turner Syndrome Society of the United States
Toll free: (800) 365-9944
8:30 a.m.–4:30 p.m., Monday–Friday (Central time)

United Cerebral Palsy Association
Toll free: (800) 872-5827
9:00 a.m.–5:00 p.m., Monday–Friday (Eastern time)

United Leukodystrophy Foundation
Toll free: (800) 728-5483
8:30 a.m.–8:00 p.m., 7 days a week (Central time)

Vasculitis Foundation
Toll free: (800) 277-9474
8:30 a.m.–5:00 p.m., Monday–Friday (Central time)

Wilson's Disease Association
Toll free: (866) 961-0533
9:00 a.m.–4:00 p.m., Monday–Friday (Eastern time)

REDUCED-COST HEALTH CARE SERVICES

Health Resources and Services Administration Information Center
Toll free: (888) 275-4772
TTY: (877) 489-4772

Hill-Burton Medical Care Program
Toll free: (800) 638-0742
Toll free: (800) 492-0359 (Maryland)

REHABILITATION (See also DISABLING CONDITIONS/ DISABILITIES ACCESS and PARALYSIS AND SPINAL CORD INJURY)

AbleData
Toll free: (800) 227-0216
8:30 a.m.–5:30 p.m., Monday–Friday, except Federal holidays (Eastern time)

Amputee Coalition of America—National Limb Loss Information Center
Toll free: (888) AMP-KNOW (267-5669)
8:00 a.m.–5:00 p.m., Monday–Friday (Eastern time)

National Institute for Rehabilitation Engineering
Toll free: (800) 736-2216
9:00 a.m.–5:00 p.m., Monday–Friday (Eastern time)

National Rehabilitation Information Center
Toll free: (800) 346-2742
9:00 a.m.–5:00 p.m., Monday–Friday (Eastern time)

Phoenix Society for Burn Survivors
Toll free: (800) 888-2876
9:00 a.m.–5:00 p.m., Monday–Friday (Eastern time)

SAFETY (See also CHEMICAL PRODUCTS/PESTICIDES)

National Institute for Occupational Safety and Health Information Inquiry Service
Toll free: (800) 356-4674
TTY: (888) 232-6348
9:00 a.m.–4:00 p.m., Monday–Friday, except Federal holidays (Eastern time)

National Program for Playground Safety
Toll free: (800) 554-PLAY (554-7529)
9:00 a.m.–4:00 p.m., Monday–Friday (Central time)

National Safety Council
Toll free: (800) 621-7615
Toll free: (800) 767-7236 (National Radon Hotline)
8:30 a.m.–4:45 p.m., Monday–Friday (Central time)

Safe Sitter
Toll free: (800) 255-4089
8:30 a.m.–4:30 p.m., Monday–Friday (Eastern time)

U.S. Consumer Product Safety Commission Hotline
Toll free: (800) 638-2772
TTY: (800) 638-8270
8:30 a.m.–5:00 p.m., Monday–Friday, except Federal holidays (Eastern time)

Vehicle Safety Hotline—National Highway Traffic Safety Administration
Toll free: (888) 327-4236
TTY: (800) 424-9153
8:30 a.m.–5:00 p.m., Monday–Friday (Eastern time)

SEXUAL EDUCATION

Medical Institute for Sexual Health
Toll free: (800) 892-9484 (publication orders only)
8:15 a.m.–5:00 p.m., Monday–Friday (Central time)

Planned Parenthood Federation of America, Inc.
Toll free: (800) 230-7526 (Recording)
Toll free: (800) 669-0156 (Order line)
9:00 a.m.–5:00 p.m., Monday–Friday (Eastern time)

SEXUALLY TRANSMITTED DISEASES (See also AIDS/HIV)

American Social Health Association
Toll free: (800) 227-8922
9:00 a.m.–6:00 p.m., Monday–Friday (Eastern time)

CDC INFO
Toll free: (800) CDC-INFO (232-4636) (English/Spanish)
TTY: (888) 232-6348

CDC National Prevention Information Network
Toll free: (800) 458-5231 (English/Spanish)
Fax: (888) 282-7681
9:00 a.m.–6:00 p.m., Monday–Friday (Eastern time)

SKIN DISEASE

Foundation for Ichthyosis and Related Skin Types, Inc.
Toll free: (800) 545-3286
9:00 a.m.–4:00 p.m., Monday–Friday (Eastern time)

National Institute of Arthritis and Musculoskeletal and Skin Diseases Information Clearinghouse
Toll free: (877) 226-4267
8:30 a.m.–5:00 p.m., Monday–Friday, except Federal holidays (Eastern time)

National Psoriasis Foundation
Toll free: (800) 723-9166
8:00 a.m.–5:00 p.m., Monday–Friday (Pacific time)

SMOKING/SMOKELESS TOBACCO

National Oral Health Information Clearinghouse
Toll free: (866) 232-4528

Smoking Quitline of the National Cancer Institute
Toll free: (877) 44U-QUIT (448-7848)
TTY: (800) 332-8615
9:00 a.m.–4:30 p.m., Monday–Friday, except Federal holidays (Eastern time)

Smoking, Tobacco and Health Information Line—Office on Smoking and Health, CDC
Toll free: (800) 232-4636 (Recording)
Toll free: (800) 784-8669 (QUIT NOW)
TTY: (888) 232-6348

SPINAL CORD INJURY, See PARALYSIS AND SPINAL CORD INJURY

STROKE (See also PARALYSIS AND SPINAL CORD INJURY)

American Heart Association Stroke Connection
Toll free: (888) 478-7653
24 hours a day, 7 days a week, 365 days a year

National Institute of Neurological Disorders and Stroke
Toll free: (800) 352-9424
8:30 a.m.–5:00 p.m., Monday–Friday, except Federal holidays (Eastern time)

National Stroke Association
Toll free: (800) STROKES (787-6537)
8:00 a.m.–4:30 p.m., MondayThursday, 8:00 a.m.–4:00 p.m., Friday (Eastern time)

STUTTERING

National Center for Stuttering
Toll free: (800) 221-2483
10:00 a.m.–5:00 p.m., Monday–Friday (Eastern time)

National Stuttering Association
Toll free: (800) We Stutter (937-8888)

Stuttering Foundation of America
Toll free: (800) 992-9392
9:00 a.m.–5:00 p.m., Monday–Friday (Eastern time)

SUBSTANCE ABUSE (See also ALCOHOL ABUSE and DRUG ABUSE)

National Inhalant Prevention Coalition
Toll free: (800) 269-4237 (Recording)
8:00 a.m.–6:00 p.m., Monday–Friday (Central time)

Substance Abuse and Mental Health Services Administration
Toll free: (877) 767-4727

SUICIDE PREVENTION HOTLINES

National Suicide Prevention Lifeline
Toll free: (800) 273-TALK (273-8255)
TTY: (800) 799-4TTY (779-4889)
Toll free: (888) 628-9454 (Spanish)
The National Suicide Prevention Lifeline is a 24-hour, toll-free suicide prevention service that routes calls from anywhere in the country to the nearest available certified crisis center where trained crisis counselors talk to callers and can link them to local services.

The Trevor Helpline
Toll free: (866) 4-U-TREVOR (488-7386)
The Trevor Helpline is a national toll-free suicide prevention hotline aimed at gay and questioning youth. It's open 24 hours a day, 7days a week, 365 days a year. Teens with nowhere to turn can call and talk confidentially to trained counselors and find local resources.

SURGERY/FACIAL PLASTIC SURGERY

American Society of Plastic Surgeons, Inc.
Toll free: (888) 475-2784 (Referral Service)

TRAUMA

American Trauma Society
Toll free: (800) 556-7890
8:30 a.m.–4:00 p.m., Monday–Friday (Eastern time)

UROLOGICAL DISORDERS

American Association of Kidney Patients
Toll free: (800) 749-2257
8:30 a.m.–4:30 p.m., Monday–Friday (Eastern time)

American Kidney Fund
Toll free: (800) 638-8299
9:00 a.m.–5:00 p.m., MondayThursday; 9:00 a.m.–2:00 p.m., Friday (Eastern time)

American Urological Association
Toll free: (866) RING-AUA (746-4282)
8:30 a.m.–5:00 p.m., Monday–Friday (Eastern time)

Health Care Services—National Kidney Foundation
Toll free: (800) 622-9010
8:30 a.m.–5:30 p.m., Monday–Friday (Eastern time)

National Association for Continence
Toll free: (800) 252-3337
9:00 a.m.–5:00 p.m., Monday–Friday (Eastern time)

National Kidney and Urologic Diseases Information Clearinghouse
Toll free: (800) 891-5390
Toll free: (866) 569-1162 (TTY)
8:30 a.m.–5:00 p.m., Monday–Friday (Eastern time)

PKD Foundation
Toll free: (800) 753-2873
8:00 a.m.–5:00 p.m., Monday–Friday (Central time)

Simon Foundation for Continence
Toll free: (800) 237-4666
9:00 a.m.–5:00 p.m., Monday–Friday (Central time)

VETERANS

National Veterans Services Fund, Inc.
Toll free: (800) 521-0198
9:00 a.m.–4:00 p.m., Monday–Friday (Eastern time)

Paralyzed Veterans of America
Toll free: (800) 424-8200
TTY: (800) 795-4327
9:00 a.m.–5:00 p.m., Monday–Friday (Eastern time)

U.S. Department of Veterans Affairs
Toll free: (800) 827-1000

Veterans Special Issue Helpline—Department of Veterans Affairs
Toll free: (800) 749-8387 (Agent Orange/Persian Gulf War)
8:00 a.m.–4:00 p.m., Monday–Friday (Central time)

VIOLENCE

National Domestic Violence Hotline
Toll free: (800) 799-SAFE (799-7233)
TTY: (800) 787-3224

National Organization for Victim Assistance
Toll free: (800) TRY-NOVA (879-6682)
9:00 a.m.–6:00 p.m., Monday–Friday (Eastern time)

Rape, Abuse, and Incest National Network
Toll free: (800) 656-4673

VISION (See also LIBRARY SERVICES)

American Council of the Blind
Toll free: (800) 424-8666
9:00 a.m.–5:00 p.m., Monday–Friday (Eastern time). 8:00 a.m.–4:00 p.m., Monday–Friday (Pacific time)

Braille Institute of America
Toll free: (800) BRAILLE (272-4553)
8:30 a.m.–5:00 p.m., Monday–Friday (Pacific time)

EyeCare America
Toll free: (800) 222-3937

Foundation Fighting Blindness
Toll free: (800) 683-5555
Toll free: (800) 683-5551 (TDD)
8:30 a.m.–5:00 p.m., Monday–Friday (Eastern time)

Glaucoma Research Foundation
Toll free: (800) 826-6693
8:30 a.m.–5:00 p.m., Monday–Friday (Pacific time)

Guide Dog Foundation for the Blind, Inc.
Toll free: (800) 548-4337
8:00 a.m.–5:00 p.m., Monday–Friday (Eastern time)

Guide Dogs for the Blind
Toll free: (800) 295-4050
8:00 a.m.–5:00 p.m., Monday–Friday (Pacific time)

Lighthouse International
Toll free: (800) 829-0500
9:00 a.m.–5:00 p.m., Monday–Friday (Eastern time)

Louisiana Center for the Blind
Toll free: (800) 234-4166
8:00 a.m.–5:00 p.m., Monday–Friday
 (Eastern time)

National Association for Parents of Children with Visual Impairments
Toll free: (800) 562-6265
9:00 a.m.–5:00 p.m., Monday–Friday (Eastern time)

National Consortium on Deaf-Blindness
Toll free: (800) 438-9376
TTY: (800) 854-7013
9:00 a.m.–4:00 p.m., Monday–Friday, except Federal
 holidays (Eastern time)

National Family Association for Deaf-Blind
Toll free: (800) 255-0411 (Voice/TTY)
8:45 a.m.–4:30 p.m., Monday–Friday (Eastern time)

Prevent Blindness America
Toll free: (800) 331-2020
8:30 a.m.–5:00 p.m., Monday–Friday (Central time)

Vision Council of America
Toll free: (800) 424-8422

WOMEN

Endometriosis Association
Toll free: (800) 992-3636 (Recording)

National Osteoporosis Foundation
Toll free: (800) 231-4222
8:30 a.m.–5:00 p.m., Monday–Friday
 (Eastern time)

Womenshealth.gov
Toll free: (800) 994-9662
Toll free: (888) 220-5446 (TDD)
9:00 a.m.–6:00 p.m., Monday–Friday, except Federal
 holidays (Eastern time)

Women's Sports Foundation
Toll free: (800) 227-3988
9:00 a.m.–5:00 p.m., 9:00 a.m.–4:45 p.m., Monday–Friday
 (Eastern time)

INDEX

The index is alphabetized using a word-by-word system. References to individual volumes are listed before colons; numbers following a colon refer to specific page numbers within that particular volume. **Boldface** references indicate main topical essays. Photographs and illustration references are highlighted with an italicized page number. Tables and figures are indicated with the page number followed by a lowercase, italicized t or f, respectively.

D

F

O

Y

Z

REFERENCE